NETWORKING QUALITY OF SERVICE AND WINDOWS® OPERATING SYSTEMS

Yoram Bernet

New Riders

Networking Quality of Service and Windows® Operating Systems

Yoram Bernet

International Standard Book Number: 1-57870-206-2

Library of Congress Catalog Card Number: 99-66363

05 04 03 02 01   7 6 5 4 3 2 1

Interpretation of the printing code: The rightmost double-digit number is the year of the book's printing; the rightmost single-digit number is the number of the book's printing. For example, the printing code 01-2 shows that the first printing of the book occurred in 2001.

Composed in Quark 4.0 and MCPdigital by New Riders Publishing

Printed in the United States of America

Trademarks

Warning and Disclaimer

PUBLISHER
David Dwyer

ASSOCIATE PUBLISHER
Al Valvano

EXECUTIVE EDITOR
Stephanie Wall

MANAGING EDITOR
Gina Brown

PRODUCT MARKETING MANAGER
Stephanie Layton

PUBLICITY MANAGER
Susan Petro

ACQUISITIONS EDITORS
Karen Wachs
Leah Williams

DEVELOPMENT EDITOR
Lisa M. Thibault

PROJECT EDITOR
Jake McFarland

COPY EDITOR
Krista Hansing

INDEXER
Christine Karpeles

MANUFACTURING COORDINATOR
Jim Conway
Chris Moos

BOOK DESIGNER
Louisa Klucznik

COVER DESIGNER
Aren Howell

PROOFREADER
Debbie Williams

COMPOSITION
Amy Parker

OVERVIEW

Introduction, 1

PART I

1 Introduction to Quality of Service, 7

2 The Quality/Efficiency Product, 31

PART II

3 Queuing Mechanisms, 61

4 Integrated Services, 101

5 RSVP, 131

6 Differentiated Services, 191

7 The Subnet Bandwidth Manager and 802 Networks, 251

8 QoS Over Layer 2 Media Other Than 802, 293

9 QoS Policy, 337

10 Putting the Pieces Together—End-to-End QoS, 409

PART III

11 The Microsoft QoS Components, 483

12 The GQoS API and the QoS Service Provider, 497

13 The Traffic Control API and Traffic Control Components, 545

14 The Microsoft Admission Control Service, 595

PART IV

A Troubleshooting and Demonstrating Windows 2000 QoS Functionality, 637

B References, 671

Index, 677

C ONTENTS

Introduction   *1*

PART I

1 *Introduction to Quality of Service*   *7*
   1.1 Defining Network QoS   *7*
     1.1.1   The Network   8
     1.1.2   Meeting Service Needs   9
   1.2 Network Resources   *10*
     1.2.1   Application Requirements   10
     1.2.2   Fundamental QoS Resources and Traffic-Handling
              Mechanisms   10
     1.2.3   Allocating QoS Resources in Network Devices   12
   1.3 Traffic-Handling Mechanisms   *14*
     1.3.1   802 user_priority   15
     1.3.2   Differentiated Services   16
     1.3.3   Integrated Services   18
     1.3.4   ATM, ISSLOW, and Others   19
     1.3.5   Per-Conversation versus Aggregate Traffic-Handling
              Mechanisms   20
   1.4 Provisioning and Configuration Mechanisms   *21*
     1.4.1   Provisioning versus Configuration   21
     1.4.2   Pushed versus Signaled Mechanisms   22
     1.4.3   Resource Reservation Protocol and the
              Subnet Bandwidth Manager   23
     1.4.4   Policy Mechanisms and Protocols   27
   1.5 Summary   *29*

2 *The Quality/Efficiency Product:*
  The Reason to QoS-Enable a Network   *31*
   2.1 Tradeoffs in the QoS-Enabled Network   *32*
     2.1.1   The Quality of a Service   33
     2.1.2   Efficiency   35
     2.1.3   The Quality/Efficiency Product   35
   2.2 Raising the QE Product of a Network   *36*
     2.2.1   Quality, Efficiency, and Overhead   37
   2.3 The Value of Different QoS Mechanisms in Raising the
     QE Product of a Network   *39*
     2.3.1   Overhead   39
     2.3.2   Tabulating the Impact of QoS Mechanisms
              on QE Product and Overhead   40

2.4   *Illustrative Examples*   43
   2.4.1   Push Provisioning and FIFO Traffic Handling   43
   2.4.2   Using Aggregate Traffic Handling to Raise
        the QE Product   43
   2.4.3   Supporting Higher-Quality Services in the LAN   45
   2.4.4   Supporting Higher-Quality Services in the WAN   46
   2.4.5   Raising the QE Product of the WAN Link
        by Using Signaling   48

2.5   *Sharing Network Resources: Multiple Resource Pools*   54
   2.5.1   Isolation Between Traffic Types Requiring Different
        Quality Service   54
   2.5.2   The Four Logical Networks   55

2.6   *Summary*   57

PART II

3 **Queuing Mechanisms**   61
  3.1   *Formation of Queues*   62
     3.1.1   Queuing and Forwarding   63
     3.1.2   Congestion   64

  3.2   *Taxonomy of Queuing Mechanisms*   66
     3.2.1   FIFO Queuing   66
     3.2.2   Work-Conserving Queuing   67
     3.2.3   Non-Work-Conserving Queuing   69
     3.2.4   Dropping Schemes and Congestion Avoidance   70

  3.3   *Evaluation of Queuing Schemes*   71
     3.3.1   Processing Cost   72
     3.3.2   Bandwidth and Latency Guarantees   72

  3.4   *Examples of Work-Conserving Queuing Schemes*   72
     3.4.1   Strict Priority Queuing   72
     3.4.2   Fair Queuing Algorithms   75

  3.5   *Examples of Non-Work-Conserving Queuing Schemes*   83
     3.5.1   Shaping Parameters and Buckets   84

  3.6   *Link Sharing and Class-Based Queuing*   90
     3.6.1   Sharing Hierarchy   91
     3.6.2   Class-Based Queuing   92

  3.7   *Examples of Dropping Schemes*   93
     3.7.1   Problems with Tail Dropping   93
     3.7.2   An Alternative to Tail Dropping:
         Random Early Detection   93

3.8   Application of Queuing Schemes   95
   3.8.1   Passive Configuration of Queuing Schemes   95
   3.8.2   Application Examples   96

3.9   Summary   99

4   Integrated Services   101

4.1   Overview of the IntServ Architecture   102
   4.1.1   Integrated Services in the Internet: RFC 1633   103
   4.1.2   Requirements Driving the IntServ Architecture
       and Their Implications   103
   4.1.3   The IntServ Service Model   104
   4.1.4   The Implementation Framework   107

4.2   The Services of the IntServ Model   114
   4.2.1   Application Types and Their Requirements   114
   4.2.2   The IntServ Services   118

4.3   Integrated Services Over Specific Link Layers   127

4.4   Summary   128

5   RSVP   131

5.1   The History of RSVP   131
   5.1.1   The Birth of RSVP   131
   5.1.2   The Rise and Fall of RSVP   133
   5.1.3   The Death Blow   135
   5.1.4   The Renaissance of RSVP   135

5.2   RSVP Concepts   136
   5.2.1   The Notion of a Reservation   136
   5.2.2   Soft-State Model   137
   5.2.3   Receiver Orientation   138
   5.2.4   IP Multicast   139
   5.2.5   RSVP Sessions   139

5.3   RSVP Messages and Basic Protocol Operation   140
   5.3.1   The Structure of RSVP Messages   140
   5.3.2   The Fundamental RSVP Messages: PATH and RESV   140
   5.3.3   The Reservation Cycle   147

5.4   Multicast Operation   149
   5.4.1   Merging Reservations   150
   5.4.2   Reservation Styles   156
   5.4.3   Receiver Heterogeneity and Reservation Styles   159

5.5   Policy and Security   159
   5.5.1   Admission Control Based on Policy   159
   5.5.2   Policy Objects   160

	5.5.3	Security	161
	5.5.4	Policy Errors	162
5.6		*Enhancements to RSVP*	*162*
	5.6.1	The SBM Protocol	163
	5.6.2	Aggregate RSVP Signaling	165
	5.6.3	RSVP over IP Tunnels	167
	5.6.4	RSVP for MPLS	171
	5.6.5	Refresh Reduction, Node Failure Detection, and Related Optimizations	175
	5.6.6	DCLASS and TCLASS Objects	178
	5.6.7	RSVP with IP Security	179
5.7		*Issues in the Application of RSVP*	*180*
	5.7.1	Admission Control Agents	180
	5.7.2	Signaling for Qualitative Applications	185
	5.7.3	RSVP Proxies	186
	5.7.4	Snooping	188
5.8		*Summary*	*188*
6		**Differentiated Services**	**191**
6.1		*The History and Background of Differentiated Services*	*191*
	6.1.1	Formation of the DiffServ Working Group and Its Charter	192
	6.1.2	DiffServ and RSVP/IntServ	192
	6.1.3	The Perspective of the DiffServ Provider	193
6.2		*Differentiated Service Architecture and Concepts*	*193*
	6.2.1	Per-Hop Behaviors and DiffServ Codepoints	194
	6.2.2	Services versus PHBs	195
	6.2.3	Traffic Conditioning, Service Level Specifications, and Service Level Agreements	196
6.3		*Standard Per-Hop Behaviors*	*197*
	6.3.1	The Expedited Forwarding PHB	197
	6.3.2	The Assured Forwarding PHB Group	199
	6.3.3	The Class Selector PHB Group	200
6.4		*Providing Services*	*201*
	6.4.1	Providers, Customers, and Network Boundaries	201
	6.4.2	Traffic Constraints and Quality of Offered Services	202
	6.4.3	Levels of Service Guarantees	203
	6.4.4	The Scope and Extent of a DiffServ Service	208
	6.4.5	Static versus Dynamic Service Level Specifications	210

6.5   *Traffic Conditioning*   *210*
   6.5.1   Traffic-Conditioning Components   212

6.6   *Using Traffic-Conditioning Blocks to Build
      Differentiated Services*   *217*
   6.6.1   TCB Supporting VLL Service at the DiffServ Ingress   217
   6.6.2   TCB Providing VLL Service with Marking
        and Shaping   221
   6.6.3   Ingress TCB Providing Olympic Services and
        BBE Service Using the AF PHB Group   223

6.7   *Provisioning the DiffServ Network*   *228*
   6.7.1   Boundary Provisioning versus Interior Provisioning   228
   6.7.2   Boundary Provisioning   230
   6.7.3   Interior Provisioning   231
   6.7.4   Static versus Dynamic Provisioning   235

6.8   *Policy in the DiffServ Network*   *235*
   6.8.1   Policy Components   235
   6.8.2   The Push Provisioning Model   236
   6.8.3   The Signaling Provisioning Model   237
   6.8.4   Provisioning Based on Real-Time Measurement   238

6.9   *DiffServ with RSVP*   *238*
   6.9.1   Admission Control   239
   6.9.2   Traffic Classification   241
   6.9.3   The DCLASS Object   243
   6.9.4   Mapping RSVP Signaled Services to DiffServ Services   243

6.10   *Issues in DiffServ*   *244*
   6.10.1   Customer Traffic Conditioning versus Provider
        Traffic Conditioning   244
   6.10.2   Mapping from DiffServ to Other QoS Mechanisms   247
   6.10.3   Multicast   248
   6.10.4   IPSec and DiffServ   249
   6.10.5   Tunneling and DiffServ   249

6.11   *Summary*   *249*

7   **The Subnet Bandwidth Manager and 802 Networks**   *251*

7.1   *user_priority*   *252*
   7.1.1   Comparison to Differentiated Services   253
   7.1.2   Providing Services Based on user_priority   254

7.2   *Using RSVP with 802 Networks—the SBM and SBM Protocol 262*
   7.2.1   The SBM as Admission Control Agent for
         802 Networks   263
   7.2.2   The SBM Protocol   273
   7.2.3   Admission Control at DSBMs and the
         TCLASS Object   284

7.3   *Supporting Heterogeneous Senders on 802 Subnets*   *286*
   7.3.1   Legacy 802 Subnets   287

7.4   *Summary*   *291*

8   QoS over Layer 2 Media Other Than 802   **293**

8.1   *ATM and QoS*   *294*
   8.1.1   Fundamental ATM Concepts   294
   8.1.2   Mapping IP to ATM   298
   8.1.3   Using ATM to Provide QoS   301
   8.1.4   IP over ATM and LAN Emulation   314

8.2   *Frame Relay and QoS*   *314*
   8.2.1   Overview of Frame Relay   314
   8.2.2   QoS in the Frame Relay Network   317
   8.2.3   Using Frame Relay to Provide QoS   320

8.3   *QoS on Low-Bit Rate Links*   *321*
   8.3.1   Supporting Different Qualities of Service   322
   8.3.2   Bandwidth Constraints and Admission Control   322
   8.3.3   Traffic Handling to Minimize Latency   325

8.4   *Summary*   *334*

9   QoS Policy   **337**

9.1   *Defining the Concept of Policy*   *337*
   9.1.1   Examples of QoS Policy Objectives   338
   9.1.2   Features of a Policy Management System   338
   9.1.3   Policy Taxonomy   339
   9.1.4   The Value of a Policy Management System   345

9.2   *Layers and Components of a Policy System*   *346*
   9.2.1   Policy Enforcement Point   347
   9.2.2   Policy Decision Point   349
   9.2.3   Policy Data Stores and Directories   356

9.3   *Applying Policies*   *362*
   9.3.1   The Format of Authored and Compiled Policies   363
   9.3.2   Applying Static Global Provisioning Policies   364
   9.3.3   Applying Semi-static Policies   370

9.3.4   Applying Dynamic Policies   378
9.3.5   Host Resident PEPs   400

9.4   *Administrative Domains and Bandwidth Brokers*   *402*
9.4.1   Domain Boundary Issues   402
9.4.2   Bandwidth Brokers as Admission Control Agents   403

9.5   *Summary*   *407*

10   *Putting the Pieces Together—End-to-End QoS*   *409*

10.1   *The Sample Network*   *410*
10.1.1   Overview of the Subnetworks of the
         Sample Network   411

10.2   *A-1 Corporation's Main Campus Network*   *413*
10.2.1   Building Networks   414
10.2.2   The ATM Backbone   425
10.2.3   The Interface to the Wide Area Network   440

10.3   *A-1 Corporation's Remote Networks*   *457*
10.3.1   Remote Campus D   457
10.3.2   Remote Campus A Through C Networks   460

10.4   *University Campus Network*   *461*
10.4.1   Building Networks   462
10.4.2   The University Backbone   463
10.4.3   Connecting the University Network to the
         Wide Area   464

10.5   *Provider Networks*   *465*
10.5.1   Traffic Handling in the Provider Networks   466
10.5.2   SLAs and Admission Control in the
         Provider Networks   467
10.5.3   Policy and Provisioning in the Provider Networks   472
10.5.4   Services Provided to Other Customer Networks   474

10.6   *The Cable Network*   *475*
10.6.1   Services and Traffic Handling Within the
         Cable Network   476
10.6.2   Admission Control Agents in the Cable Network   477
10.6.3   Nonsignaled QoS Within the Cable Network   478

10.7   *Summary*   *478*

PART III

11 *The Microsoft QoS Components*   *483*
   11.1 *Components Residing in the Host Operating System*   *483*
      11.1.1 User-Level Components   484
      11.1.2 Kernel-Level Components—The Traffic
              Control Providers   491
   11.2 *Policy Enforcement Components—the SBM*
      and the ACS   *493*
      11.2.1 Functionality Provided by the SBM and ACS   493
   11.3 *Summary*   *495*

12 *The GQoS API and the QoS Service Provider*   *497*
   12.1 *Overview of the GQoS API*   *497*
      12.1.1 Winsock Orientation   497
      12.1.2 Relation to RSVP and Traffic Control   500
   12.2 *Usage of the GQoS API*   *501*
      12.2.1 Creating a QoS Socket   502
      12.2.2 Using the QoS Socket   503
      12.2.3 QoS Status and Event Notification   507
      12.2.4 The QoS Parameters   508
   12.3 *Behavior of the QoS Service Provider*   *514*
      12.3.1 RSVP Signaling Behavior   514
      12.3.2 Information Provided to Applications by the
              QoS Service Provider   525
      12.3.3 Traffic Control Invocation   526
   12.4 *Application Considerations*   *530*
      12.4.1 Service Types   530
      12.4.2 Quantitative Applications   531
      12.4.3 Qualitative Applications   532
      12.4.4 Persistent versus Nonpersistent Applications   533
      12.4.5 The ShapeDiscard Mode   533
      12.4.6 Disabling Traffic Control   534
      12.4.7 Interpretation of Information from the QoS Service
              Provider   534
      12.4.8 Withholding Transmission   537
      12.4.9 The New Busy Signal   538
      12.4.10 Effecting Marking Under Application Control   539

12.5   *Enhancements Supporting Nonpersistent Applications*   *540*

12.5.1   Support for Nonpersistent Applications   540

12.6   *Functionality Supported on Different Platforms*   *541*

12.6.1   Windows 98   541

12.6.2   Windows 2000   542

12.7   *Summary*   *542*

13   ***The Traffic Control API and Traffic Control Components***   **545**

13.1   *Overview of Traffic Control Components and Their Functionality*   *545*

13.1.1   Traffic Control Consumers and Traffic Control Providers   546

13.1.2   The Traffic Control API and traffic.dll   551

13.1.3   Flows, Filters, and Classification   551

13.1.4   Traffic Scheduling   553

13.1.5   Marking   553

13.1.6   Signaling and Other Media-Specific Functionality   553

13.1.7   Native Traffic Control Providers   556

13.2   *The Traffic Control API*   *558*

13.2.1   Registering with Traffic Control   559

13.2.2   Selecting an Interface   559

13.2.3   Adding Flows and Filters   559

13.2.4   Setting and Querying Traffic Control Parameters   560

13.2.5   Remote Traffic Control   561

13.3   *The Structure and Behavior of the Packet Scheduler*   *562*

13.3.1   Instances of the Packet Scheduler   562

13.3.2   The Internal Structure of the Packet Scheduler   562

13.3.3   Parameters Affecting Scheduling Behavior   569

13.3.4   Derivation of Parameters Affecting Scheduling Behavior   570

13.3.5   Overall Scheduling Behavior   571

13.3.6   Marking Behavior   581

13.3.7   Controlling the Behavior of the Packet Scheduler from the Active Directory   583

13.4   *The Structure and Behavior of ATMARP*   *583*

13.4.1   ATMARP Interfaces   583

13.4.2   ATMARP Traffic Control Behavior   585

13.5   *Behavior of Two Traffic Control Consumers*   587
   13.5.1   The Interaction of the QoS Service Provider
     and Traffic Control   587
   13.5.2   TcMon   591

13.6   *Special Uses of Traffic Control*   592
   13.6.1   Limited Best-Effort Mode   592
   13.6.2   DiffServ Mode   592
   13.6.3   Automatic ISSLOW for RAS Dial-Up Servers 593

13.7   *Summary*   593

14   **The Microsoft Admission Control Service**   595

14.1   *The SBM and the ACS—Microsoft's QoS Policy*
   Infrastructure   596

14.2   *Microsoft's SBM*   600
   14.2.1   Fundamentals of the SBM Resource-Based
     Admission Control   600
   14.2.2   Issues Arising from the Switched Subnet Example 602

14.3   *Policy-Based Admission Control*   605
   14.3.1   The Hierarchical Nature of Active Directory
     QoS Policy Information   605
   14.3.2   Application-Based Policies   609

14.4   *Provisioning and Configuring ACS-Based QoS Policies*
   in an Enterprise Network   609
   14.4.1   The Role of Active Directory in ACS Management 610
   14.4.2   Enabling an ACS Instance   614
   14.4.3   Configuring SBM Parameters on an ACS Instance 616
   14.4.4   Configuring QoS Policies Based on User or
     Organizational Unit   621

14.5   *Deployment Scenarios and Considerations*   623
   14.5.1   802 Subnetwork Scenarios   623
   14.5.2   Extending the SBM-Based ACS Beyond 802
     Subnetworks   625
   14.5.3   ACS on RAS Servers   629

14.6   *ACS Extensibility*   629
   14.6.1   The Local Policy Module API   629
   14.6.2   Using the Microsoft LPM   631

14.7   *Security*   632

14.8   *Summary*   633

PART IV

A **Troubleshooting and Demonstrating Windows 2000 QoS Functionality** — 637

   A.1 QoS Troubleshooting Tools — 637
     tracert — 638
     wdsbm — 638
     RSVP Tracing — 638
     netmon — 639
     rsping — 641
     Network Device Management Consoles — 642
     TcMon — 643
     perfmon — 643
     qtcp — 643
     ACS Accounting Logs — 643
     readpol — 644
     Noise-Generation Tools — 644

   A.2 Review of Windows QoS and Host/Network Interaction — 645
     Types of Network Devices — 646

   A.3 Troubleshooting Methodology — 648
     Sketching the Network Topology — 649
     Verification of End-to-End Signaling Integrity — 649
     Verifying Traffic Control Functionality on the Sending Host — 657

   A.4 Demonstrating Windows 2000 Signaled QoS — 661
     Overview of the Demonstration Scenario — 662
     Operating the Demonstration — 663
     How It Works — 663
     Factors Delaying the Effects of Policy Changes — 664
     Variations on the Demonstration Scenario — 665
     Troubleshooting the Demonstration Scenario — 666

B **References** — 671

   Index — 677

About the Author

Yoram Bernet has led Microsoft in the formation of its QoS vision for the last four years, and has also played a leadership role in the Internet Engineering Task Force's QoS efforts. Currently an architect in Microsoft's Windows Networking Group, Yoram previously managed the Network QoS Development Group for Windows 2000. He has been an active participant and has authored several drafts in a number of IETF QoS-related working groups.

Before his involvement with QoS specifically, Yoram designed the network infrastructure for the Microsoft Interactive TV program. Prior to his move to Microsoft, he worked at Memorex/Telex briefly, and at AT&T and Bell Labs for nine years. At AT&T, Yoram developed graphics hardware and, later, communications software.

Yoram has a degree in biomedical engineering from Case Western Reserve University.

About the Technical Reviewers

These reviewers contributed their considerable hands-on expertise to the entire development process for *Networking Quality of Service and Windows Operating Systems*. As the book was being written, these dedicated professionals reviewed all the material for technical content, organization, and flow. Their feedback was critical to ensuring that *Networking Quality of Service and Windows Operating Systems* fits our reader's need for the highest quality technical information.

Joel Halpern is the Chief Technical Officer of Longitude Systems, Inc., a startup producing operational software for Internet service providers. He is an active member of the IETF and currently is co-chairing the Policy Framework working group. He has served as the Routing Area Director for the IETF.

Andrew Smith is a consultant on Internet topics and has worked in the networking industry for 13 years for companies including Ascom, Synoptics, and Bay Networks. He was the chief software architect at Extreme Networks for its first four years. Andrew has worked extensively on Internet and IEEE LAN standards, and has written and edited many RFCs and other standards in the areas of Quality of Service and network policy management. He is currently the co-chair of the IETF's Resource Allocation Policy working group. He holds a master of arts degree from Cambridge University.

Dedication

To Maya, who inspired me and who taught me about things that cannot be expressed with network diagrams and flowcharts, and that are far more important than things that can be expressed with network diagrams and flowcharts.

To my parents, who always affirmed that I could do anything I set my mind to.

Acknowledgments

There are so many people who helped to make this book happen. This could easily end up being the longest section of this book.

Thanks to the management at Microsoft for making it a great place to work, for encouraging creativity, and for recognizing the value in giving me the time to write this book. Thanks to Jawad Khaki specifically—our (the Windows Networking Group's) fearless leader.

Thanks to the diligent and devoted technical experts who reviewed my writing—Andrew Smith and Joel Halpern. It's tedious to review someone else's writing and easy to lose focus as the end of a chapter or the end of the book approaches. But Andrew and Joel hung in with tenacity. They let no detail slip by unscrutinized, challenging me where appropriate and offering valuable insight throughout. I have enjoyed and learned from my dialog with them—a dialog that takes the form of layers upon layers of revision marks and responses to them.

Thanks to Scott Bradner, who through his wisdom has guided much of the QoS work at the IETF and who graciously agreed to write the foreword for this book.

Thanks to the QoS team at Microsoft, who have contributed to this book by building and testing much of the technology on which this book is based and by reviewing and discussing with me much of the content of this book. Four years ago, I was asked to lead this team in the development of QoS features for Windows Operating Systems. QoS is a strange beast, it wasn't deployed then, it was an amorphous thing of the future— a moving target in constant flux. To tackle such a beast requires commitment and faith in the face of skepticism. It requires the ability to adapt to change with an open mind. It requires a great deal of patience. The QoS team members have exhibited all these traits. Ramesh Pabbati recently relieved me as the leader of the development group. He was there since day one and continues to carry the torch.

Additional developers who have worked in the QoS group over the years include Sanjay Kaniyar, Matthias Jourdain, Rajesh Sundaram, Shree Madhavapeddi, Aamer Hydrie, Jim Stewart, Charlie Wickham, Ofer Bar, Biao Wang, and Kam Lee. Microsoft's QoS components have been diligently tested by the QoS test group that has included Sachin Kukreja,

Eric Eilebrecht, Ali Turkoglu, Mahesh Keni, Lee Bandy, Steven Garka, Ari Pernick, Mark Wodrich, Thiru Bhat, Vikas Ramnani, Keshav Barker, Jay Srinivasan, and Hyunsang Lim.

The QoS team has had a number of program managers over the years, most notably Sharon Maffett, followed by Matt Nibler, Tony Hain, Peter Ford, Tim Moore, and David Eitelbach. Thanks to the current managers who tirelessly promote the QoS program—Narendra (Gibbs) Gidwani, Ron Cully, and Azfar Moazzam.

I also value input from discussions with our IT staff—including Jeffrey Wheeler, Alexander Levin, Bo King, and Eural Authement.

Thanks to my peers in the industry and at the IETF, who have been at times enthusiastic endorsers of my work and at times harsh critics, but whom I have learned so much from and all of whom have helped to bring QoS-enabled networks closer to reality. These include Raj Yavatkar of Intel, Fred Baker and Bruce Davie of Cisco, Scott Bradner of Harvard, John Wroclawski of MIT, Andrew Smith (formerly) of Extreme, Bob Braden of ISI, Lixia Zhang of UCLA, Don Hoffman of Teledesic, Steven Levi, Peter Ford, Bernard Aboba, and Larry Cleeton of Microsoft, Scott Hahn and David Durham of Intel, Hugh Mahon of Hewlett Packard, Shai Herzog of IP Highway, Eyal Felstaine (formerly) of Allot, Brian Carpenter of IBM, Kathie Nichols of Packet Design, Lou Berger of LabN, Rob Coulton of Redback Networks, and many, many others. Thanks also to Craig Schuman of Microsoft, who helped negotiate the finer details of the book contract.

And last, but certainly not least, I would like to thank the staff at New Riders—Linda Engelman, who somehow talked me into this project; Karen Wachs, who seems to keep it running; Lisa Thibault, who also seems to keep it running but with the added burden of putting up with me on an almost daily basis; Amy Parker, who generated several hundred illustrations for this book; and Jake McFarland, who managed the copy-editing.

Tell Us What You Think

As the reader of this book, you are the most important critic and commentator. We value your opinion and want to know what we're doing right, what we could do better, what areas you'd like to see us publish in, and any other words of wisdom you're willing to pass our way.

As an Executive Editor at New Riders Publishing, I welcome your comments. You can fax, email, or write me directly to let me know what you did or didn't like about this book—as well as what we can do to make our books stronger.

Please note that I cannot help you with technical problems related to the topic of this book, and that due to the high volume of mail I receive, I might not be able to reply to every message.

When you write, please be sure to include this book's title and author as well as your name and phone or fax number. I will carefully review your comments and share them with the author and editors who worked on the book.

Fax: 317-581-4663

Email: nrfeedback@newriders.com

Mail: Stephanie Wall
         Executive Editor
         New Riders Publishing
         201 West 103rd Street
         Indianapolis, IN 46290 USA

Foreword

From the very beginning, the Internet protocol (IP) has had some Quality of Service (QoS) hooks, but until recently they have gone almost entirely unused. Over the past few years, the Internet Engineering Task Force (IETF) has been developing a number of new QoS technologies including Integrated Services (IntServ), its associated Resource Reservations Protocol (RSVP) signaling protocol, the Subnet Bandwidth Manager (SBM), and Differentiated Services (DiffServ).

The development of these QoS technologies has not been easy. The basic architecture of IP networks, such as the Internet, does not lend itself to simple QoS techniques. Traditional networks, such as the telephone network and IBM's mainframe-centric SNA network, use a circuit-based technology and architecture. Separate logical circuits are set up for each phone call or application. The QoS characteristics of these logical circuits can be defined and generally guaranteed at setup time. IP networks are based instead on sending chunks of data known as datagrams from a sender to a receiver over a network that can have an arbitrarily complex topology. There is no requirement that succeeding packets will follow the same paths through the network. Because of this, it has been hard to develop technologies that can reliably deliver IP-QoS—it has taken a lot of work.

As co-director of the IETF Transport Area, I've watched and sometimes helped push along many of the IETF QoS developments. The work was done in a number of different IETF working groups, but a few names keep coming up on the working group mailing lists as authors of the working group documents and as speakers about the technology in non-IETF arenas. Yoram Bernet is one of those few names.

Now Yoram has put together a comprehensive book on these and other QoS technologies. (No wonder I've not been able to get quite the same high level of IETF input from him over the last few months as I'd become used to.) Unlike far too many book authors, Yoram writes from the knowledge of a major participant in the technology development rather than as a reader and summarizer of the resulting standards. This shows throughout this volume.

In addition to his involvement in the IETF, Yoram has been attending to his day job, which is to help get Microsoft products supporting new Internet standards such as the IETF QoS technologies. So he also writes from involvement rather than mere reading in the sections of this book that deal with Microsoft's QoS mechanisms.

I think this is a very useful book for anyone who wants to know how IP-QoS works—not just for fans of Windows—with added benefit for those readers who also want to know about Microsoft's specific implementations. I will be recommending this book to my students and others.

Scott Bradner—September 2000

INTRODUCTION

The astounding growth of computer networking in recent years has been characterized by the struggle of network managers to keep pace with the demand for network resources. As more and more users, running more and more applications, demand increased network bandwidth, network managers find themselves continually adding expensive capacity in an effort to satisfy the needs of their customers. And yet, networks remain congested. A new breed of aggressive applications that use networks to carry voice and video traffic compounds this struggle.

Some predict that soon there will be enough capacity for all and that congestion will disappear. Others are preparing for a future in which network capacity is always a valuable commodity, better managed than wasted. This book is about the mechanisms that are being introduced to enable network capacity to be effectively managed. These mechanisms are collectively referred to as *Quality of Service* (QoS) mechanisms, and the networks in which they are applied are referred to as *QoS-enabled networks*.

In the past decade, numerous mechanisms have evolved for providing QoS-enabled networks. These include such technologies as RSVP, ATM, Differentiated Services, 802 `user_` `priority`, and others. The ultimate goal of these mechanisms is to provide improved network "service" to the applications at the edges of the network. Despite this seemingly noble and straightforward goal, QoS mechanisms have been fraught with controversy and confusion. Intense media hype has touted first one, then another, as a panacea, to the exclusion of any other mechanism.

During the past couple of years, a new approach has emerged to QoS-enabling networks. This approach embraces a breadth of QoS mechanisms, recognizing the value that each brings to this complex problem. In a sense, this is the "grand unification" of QoS networking. This development promises to hasten the adoption of QoS-enabled networks, dramatically changing the nature of networking and enabling a new generation of applications. This book explains the myriad QoS technologies that play a role in the QoS-enabled network. It explains why a full-service, QoS-enabled network depends on the cooperation of the host operating system, and it describes Windows QoS mechanisms in detail.

Target Audience

This book is targeted at the following audiences:

- Network managers and network managers who are interested in understanding network QoS in general and in Windows QoS functionality specifically

- Developers of networked applications who are interested in using QoS mechanisms to improve the quality and manageability of their applications across the network

- Developers of network equipment (including routers, switches, and policy management systems) who are interested in learning how their equipment can best participate in the collaborative effort of supporting network QoS

- University students who are interested in advanced networking functionality

- Enterprise IT decision-makers who are interested in understanding how the various QoS mechanisms being touted interact with each other and the benefits that they offer to bring to an enterprise network

This book develops the subject matter in an orderly manner, with each section building on concepts presented in previous sections. However, it is not necessary to read it cover-to-cover. Readers may use it as a reference, reading only those chapters that are of particular interest.

Organization of This Book

The book is organized into three primary sections:

- "Introduction to QoS"

- "QoS Mechanisms"

- "Windows QoS Mechanisms"

It is recommended that all readers read at least Chapter 1, "Introduction to Quality of Service," and Chapter 2, "The Quality/Efficiency Product," which together form the "Introduction to QoS" section and establish terminology that is used throughout the remainder of the book.

Readers interested in a particular subset of QoS technology may then proceed directly to the corresponding chapters (Chapters 3–9) of the "QoS Mechanisms" section. Readers interested in the application of the various technologies to a general network should read the last chapter of this section (Chapter 10, "Putting the Pieces Together—End-to-End QoS").

Readers interested only in Windows QoS mechanisms should proceed directly from the

"Introduction to QoS" section to the "Windows QoS Mechanisms" section (Chapters 11–14).

The following section describes the contents of each chapter, by book section.

Introduction to QoS

Chapter 1, "Introduction to Quality of Service," defines network QoS and introduces taxonomy for general QoS mechanisms, including traffic-handling mechanisms as well as provisioning and configuration mechanisms. It includes a brief overview of specific mechanisms.

Chapter 2, "The Quality/Efficiency Product," provides the motivation for QoS-enabling a network. It describes the trade-offs that must be considered when QoS-enabling a network and introduces a key concept: the *quality/efficiency product* of a network. This chapter also explains how the various QoS technologies described in subsequent chapters can be used together to provide the desired quality/efficiency product in a variety of networks.

QoS Mechanisms

Chapter 3, "Queuing Mechanisms," describes the various queuing mechanisms that underlie any QoS traffic-handling technology.

Chapter 4, "Integrated Services," introduces *Integrated Services* (IntServ). The IntServ work of the IETF formed the backdrop against which much of the subsequent work on Internet QoS proceeded.

Chapter 5, "RSVP," discusses RSVP, the signaling protocol that is used to provide signaled QoS and is closely related to IntServ.

Chapter 6, "Differentiated Services," discusses Differentiated Services, which is generally used to provide QoS in large routed networks.

Chapter 7, "The Subnet Bandwidth Manager and 802 Networks," discusses Layer 2 QoS technologies, with a focus on 802 networks. It includes discussions of 802 user_priority and the Subnet Bandwidth Manager (SBM).

Chapter 8, "QoS over Layer 2 Media Other Than 802," discusses additional Layer 2 QoS technologies, including ATM, ISSLOW, and Frame Relay.

Chapter 9, "QoS Policy," discusses QoS policy mechanisms.

Chapter 10, "Putting the Pieces Together—End-to-End QoS," applies the QoS technologies discussed so far to a sample network.

Windows QoS Mechanisms

Chapter 11, "The Microsoft QoS Components," presents an overview of Windows QoS mechanisms.

Chapter 12, "The GQoS API and the QoS Service Provider," describes the Windows Generic QoS API and the functionality of the Windows QoS Service Provider.

Chapter 13, "The Traffic Control API and Traffic Control Components," describes the Windows Traffic Control API and introduces the notion of a traffic control provider and a traffic control consumer. It describes the functionality of the native Windows traffic control providers (including packet scheduling and marking) and shows how these can be used by traffic control consumers.

Chapter 14, "The Microsoft Admission Control Service," describes the Windows Admission Control Service (ACS) and the Subnet Bandwidth Manager (SBM), on which it is based. It discusses their interaction with Active Directory and explains how the combination of the ACS and Active Directory can be used to administer QoS policies.

Appendixes

Appendix A, "Troubleshooting and Demonstrating Windows 2000 QoS Functionality," describes how various tools may be used to analyze and troubleshoot networks that make use of Windows QoS mechanisms. It also describes a simple demonstration configuration that can be used to evaluate Windows QoS mechanisms.

Appendix B, "References," is a listing of references cited within the book.

WEB-Based Appendixes

In addition to the two appendixes included in the physical book, there are two WEB-based appendixes located at www.newriders.com.

Appendix C describes the qtcp tool in detail and illustrates some sample test measurements. qtcp is a tool that can be used to measure latency variations due to congestion.

Appendix D explains how vendors of network equipment can apply standard QoS mechanisms to enhance the manageability of network resources by leveraging Windows QoS functionality.

PART

I

Introduction to QoS

Chapter 1   Introduction to Quality of Service

Chapter 2   The Quality/Efficiency Product: The Reason to QoS-Enable a Network

Introduction to Quality of Service

There are many different interpretations regarding the definition of Quality of Service (QoS). To some, QoS may have little to do with anything that happens in a network. Some might believe QoS refers to the service offered by a CPU in rendering a video image on a locally attached disk. Others might have different misconceptions. For example, I recently visited a major bank to speak to them about our QoS work. I found myself presenting to the quality control group. They thought I would be speaking about quality control processes in an enterprise.

Before delving into the subject matter, it is important to define QoS from the perspective of this book and to establish a basic vocabulary for further discussion. This chapter first defines network QoS and then introduces a taxonomy that will be used throughout the book. It introduces the fundamental components of the QoS network: traffic handling mechanisms and the means to coordinate these mechanisms across multiple devices. It concludes with a discussion of policy components.

1.1 Defining Network QoS

Assume the following simplistic view of the host/network system: Applications run on hosts and exchange information with their peers. These applications send data by submitting it to the operating system to be carried across the network. After data has been submitted to the operating system for transmission, it becomes network *traffic*.

> **Note**
>
> Throughout this book, the term *host* refers to a source or sink of network traffic. As such, hosts are differentiated from switches, routers, and similar network devices that carry traffic but neither source nor sink traffic. The most common example of a host is a PC.

Network QoS is defined as

> The *capability to control traffic-handling mechanisms* in the network such that the network meets the service needs of certain applications and users *subject to network policies.*

Note that the emphasis is on the "capability to control traffic-handling mechanisms...subject to network policies." The network manager is thus the direct beneficiary of network QoS because QoS provides the tools necessary to effectively manage network resources. However, the network manager sells network services that are ultimately paid for by the end users of networked applications. Therefore, the manager can be expected to operate the network in a manner that maximizes its utility to the paying customers. As a result, end users benefit from improved services for their applications.

Although QoS could be defined passively—as the service quality experienced by traffic transiting the network—this book defines QoS more actively. Throughout this book, QoS refers to the set of mechanisms that can be brought to bear in controlling the service quality experienced by traffic transiting the network.

Providing network QoS relies on fundamental traffic-handling mechanisms and the capability to identify traffic and to associate it with the appropriate traffic-handling mechanism. Consider a very simple analogy from the life of a commuter: Route 520, which takes me from my house to Microsoft every day, is analogous to a network route. One of its traffic-handling mechanisms is a *high-occupancy vehicle* (HOV) lane. The HOV lane can be used subject to a policy. The policy states that carpooling traffic is entitled to use the HOV lane. The HOV lane benefits the authorities that manage traffic by optimizing the use of the roads. It also benefits commuters who carpool by reducing their commuting time. Note that drivers who use the HOV lane, as well as drivers who do not, experience QoS. The QoS experienced by those who use the HOV lane is, arguably, better than that experienced by those who do not.

1.1.1 The Network

For the purpose of the following discussion, a network consists of the following:

- The sending operating system's network stack

- All network components between sender and receiver

- The receiving operating system's network stack

The network stack in the host operating system is considered part of the network. As such, the host is an integral part of the QoS-enabled network, as illustrated in Figure 1.1.

Figure 1.1   The Network Includes Components of the Host Operating System

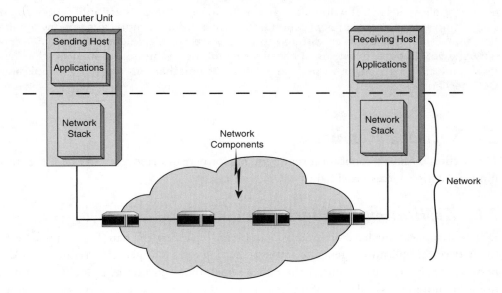

1.1.2 *Meeting Service Needs*

As previously mentioned, network QoS refers to meeting the service needs of *certain* applications and users. This conveys the notion of a network-based policy regarding applications and users. The goal of a QoS-enabled network is not necessarily to optimize service to each application and user individually. Rather, the goal is to maximize the utility of the network across all applications and users (thereby maximizing revenues generated in selling network services). To this end, network QoS provides mechanisms to control the allocation of resources among applications and users. The network manager then uses these mechanisms to distribute resources according to appropriate policies.

Of course, the individual needs of an application or user are an important consideration. Many applications require a minimum level of resources. If the minimum resources required cannot be provided to a certain instance of an application, it may be preferable to deny all resources to that application instance. The freed resources can then be put to better use serving a less-demanding application.

Note

Certain applications adapt (within limits) to network conditions. These applications can be said to implement a form of *application* QoS. Consider, for example, a telephony application that can switch between different quality voice encoders depending on measured network QoS. In other examples, applications might use various forms of application layer flow control. This discussion focuses on network QoS mechanisms rather than application QoS mechanisms.

1.2   Network Resources

This section discusses application requirements for network resources and describes the fundamental resources provided by the network.

1.2.1   Application Requirements

Different applications have different requirements regarding the handling of their traffic in the network. Applications generate traffic at varying rates and generally require that the network be able to carry traffic at the rate at which they generate it. In addition, applications are more or less tolerant of traffic delays in the network and of variation in traffic delay. Certain applications can tolerate some degree of traffic loss, whereas others cannot. These requirements are expressed using the following QoS-related parameters:

- **Bandwidth.** The rate at which an application's traffic must be carried by the network

- **Latency.** The delay that an application can tolerate in delivering a packet of data

- **Jitter.** The variation in latency

- **Loss.** The percentage of lost data

If infinite network resources are available, all application traffic can be carried at the required bandwidth, with zero latency, zero jitter, and zero loss. However, network resources are not infinite. As a result, there are parts of the network in which resources are unable to simultaneously satisfy the bandwidth, latency, jitter, and loss requirements of all applications and users in every part of the network. These are the application requirements that must be considered when using network QoS to allocate resources among applications and users.

1.2.2   Fundamental QoS Resources and Traffic-Handling Mechanisms

This section describes the fundamental network resources available to application traffic and the traffic-handling mechanisms that actually yield these resources.

Networks interconnect hosts using a variety of network devices, including host network adapters, routers, switches, and hubs. Each of these contains network *interfaces*. The interfaces interconnect the various devices via cables, fibers, or via wireless connections. Network devices generally use a combination of hardware and software to *forward* traffic from one interface to another.

Note

Hosts typically (but not necessarily) include only a single network interface that is used to forward traffic from applications to the network or from the network to applications.

Each interface can send and receive traffic at a finite rate. If the rate at which traffic is directed to an interface exceeds the rate at which the interface can forward the traffic onward, *congestion* occurs.

Note

Note that a time element must be considered when discussing congestion. Real network devices cannot be expected to instantaneously forward traffic. Thus, over arbitrary short periods of time, traffic is certain to arrive at a rate higher than that at which it can be forwarded. When measured over a finite period of time, however, the rate at which traffic leaves an uncongested interface should be equal to the rate at which it arrives. Latency-intolerant applications are sensitive to congestion measured on a timescale of milliseconds. On the other hand, less latency-sensitive applications can tolerate congestion measured on a timescale of seconds.

Network devices may handle congestion by *queuing* traffic in the device's memory until the congestion subsides. In other cases, network equipment may discard traffic to alleviate congestion. As a result, applications experience varying latency (as traffic backs up in queues, on interfaces) or traffic loss. Figure 1.2 illustrates the congestion that results when traffic is submitted at a rate of 15Mbps for transmission on a 10Mbps interface.

The capacity of interfaces to forward traffic and the memory available to store traffic in network devices (until it can be forwarded) are the fundamental resources required to provide QoS to application traffic flows. Mechanisms internal to network devices determine which traffic gets preferential access to these resources. These are the fundamental traffic-handling mechanisms that comprise a QoS-enabled network. The following section discusses these mechanisms.

Figure 1.2   Congestion and its Effects

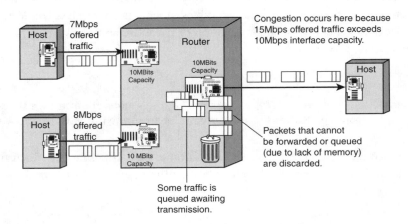

1.2.3 Allocating QoS Resources in Network Devices

Traditional network devices provide resources to network traffic on a first-come, first-serve basis. Devices that provide QoS support do so by intelligently allocating resources to certain traffic. Under congestion, for example, a network device might choose to queue traffic of applications that are more latency tolerant rather than traffic of applications that are less latency tolerant. As a result, traffic of applications that are less latency tolerant can be forwarded immediately to the next network device. In this example, interface capacity is a resource granted to the latency-intolerant traffic. Device memory is a resource that has been granted to the latency-tolerant traffic.

To allot resources preferentially to certain traffic, it is necessary to identify different traffic and to associate it with certain resources. This is typically achieved as follows: Traffic arriving at network devices is identified in each device and is separated into distinct *flows* via the process of *packet classification*. Traffic from each flow is directed to a corresponding queue. See the sidebar titled "Flows, Conversations, and Traffic Aggregates" for a description of a flow.

Flows, Conversations, and Traffic Aggregates

For the purpose of this discussion, a *flow* is a subset of all packets passing through a network device that has uniform QoS requirements.

Other uses of the term are also common. For example, all traffic carried between two points of a certain network domain, with a certain QoS, can be considered a flow, even though it transits multiple devices. In the remainder of this book, the term flow will be used to mean either of these definitions, except where otherwise noted. In all cases, a flow should be considered unidirectional.

A flow may consist of traffic from a single *conversation* or may *aggregate* traffic across multiple conversations (provided all are in the same direction).

In this book, the term *conversation* is used to include all traffic flowing in a single direction, from a specific instance of a specific application on one host to either of the following:

- A specific instance of the peer application on a peer host (unicast)
- Multiple instances of the peer application on multiple peer hosts (multicast)

In the case of IP traffic, the source/destination IP address, port, and protocol (also known as a 5-tuple) uniquely identify a conversation. Note that, while in general usage the term *conversation* implies the existence of traffic flowing in two directions, it is used in this book to refer only to traffic flowing in a single direction (regardless of the presence of return traffic).

A flow that includes traffic from multiple conversations is a *traffic aggregate*.

The queues are then *serviced* according to some *queue-servicing algorithm*. The queue-servicing algorithm determines the rate at which traffic from each queue is submitted to the network, and thereby determines the resources allotted to each queue and to the corresponding flows. Thus, to provide network QoS, it is necessary to provision or configure the following in network devices:

- Classification information by which devices separate traffic into flows
- Queues and queue-servicing algorithms that handle traffic from the separate flows

These are referred to jointly as *traffic-handling mechanisms*. Note that the term *traffic-handling mechanism* is used throughout this book. It is not used to refer to any specific approach to classification or to any specific queue-servicing algorithm. Rather, it is used to refer to various combinations of the two that are useful in the context of different network media or different types of network devices.

Figure 1.3 illustrates the concepts of classification, queues, and queue servicing.

These traffic-handling mechanisms must be provisioned or configured in a manner that provides useful end-to-end services across a network. As such, the various QoS technologies discussed fall into the category of a traffic-handling mechanism or a provisioning or configuration mechanism. The following sections describe QoS traffic-handling mechanisms and the associated provisioning and configuration mechanisms.

Figure 1.3   Classification, Queues, and Queue Servicing

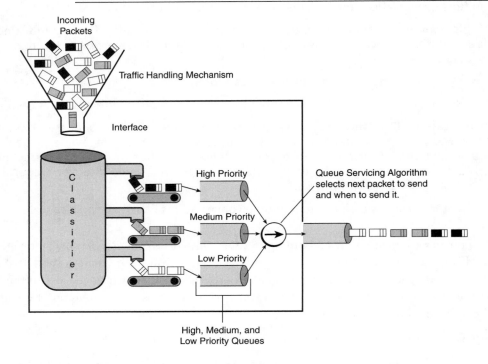

1.3 *Traffic-Handling Mechanisms*

This section briefly discusses a number of commonly used traffic-handling mechanisms. Note that underlying any traffic-handling mechanism is a set of queues and the schemes for servicing these queues. Chapter 3, "Queuing Mechanisms," discusses queuing schemes in detail. Examples of traffic-handling mechanisms include the following:

- 802 `user_priority`

- Differentiated Services (DiffServ) per-hop behaviors

- Mechanisms supporting Integrated Services (IntServ)

- ATM, ISSLOW, and others

Each of these traffic-handling mechanisms is appropriate for specific media or circumstances.

Traffic-handling mechanisms are closely related to services. As a result, the two are often confused. The word *services* refers to the overall behavior experienced by a traffic flow as a result of applying one or more traffic-handling mechanisms. Consider the following analogy: Package carriers offer services such as Next Day Delivery. To provide this service, they rely on package-handling mechanisms. These mechanisms may include planes, trains, and automobiles. Each package-handling mechanism has to be managed to ensure that the overall effect of the package-handling mechanism is Next Day Delivery.

Because services are so closely related to traffic-handling mechanisms, it is often difficult to tease them apart. The following sections describe some of the more common traffic-handling mechanisms (while recognizing the overlap between these and related services).

1.3.1 *802* user_priority

Most *local area networks* (LANs) are based on *IEEE 802* technology. These include Ethernet, token ring, FDDI, and other variations of shared media networks. Throughout this book, the term *802 user_priority* refers to a traffic-handling mechanism for supporting QoS in these networks.

The use of 802 user_priority has been standardized by the IEEE. The standard defines a field in the Layer 2 header of 802 packets, which carries one of eight priority values. Typically, hosts or routers sending traffic into a LAN mark each transmitted packet with the appropriate priority value. LAN devices, such as switches and bridges, are expected to treat the packets accordingly (by making use of underlying queuing mechanisms). The scope of the 802 user_priority mark is limited to the LAN and does not typically pass through Layer 3 devices.

Note that 802 user_priority does not define the specific behavior of the traffic-handling mechanism, nor does it define the services that can be expected as a result of its use. It defines only the format of the 802 user_priority field. It does suggest a default queuing scheme, which is strict priority service according to 802 user_priority value. (Chapter 3 defines strict priority service.)

Mechanisms that enable QoS in LANs may at first seem less interesting than their wide area network (WAN)-related counterparts. LAN resources tend to be less costly than WAN resources. Therefore, overprovisioning may be an attractive alternative to using QoS mechanisms in these networks. With the increasing usage of high-bandwidth multimedia applications on LANs, however, latencies introduced by LAN switches can become problematic. In addition, LANs comprise a large percentage of the networks in use on university campuses, corporate campuses, and in office complexes. As a result, technologies such as 802 user_priority are interesting.

1.3.2   Differentiated Services

Differentiated Services (DiffServ) is a Layer 3 traffic-handling mechanism. It is a specific case of a broader set of QoS technologies referred to as *class of service* mechanisms. The following paragraphs discuss it briefly. (Chapter 6, "Differentiated Services," addresses DiffServ in more detail.)

DiffServ defines a field, called the *DiffServ codepoint* (DSCP), in the Layer 3 header of IP packets.

> **Note**
>
> DiffServ applies only to the IP protocol. Because IP is the de facto standard Layer 3 (OSI network layer) protocol that has emerged for both the Internet and intranets, IP-centric approaches to QoS are common. Some of the Layer 2 technologies discussed in this book can be applied to network layer protocols other than IP. However, the focus remains largely on QoS for IP networks.

In typical applications of DiffServ, hosts or routers sending traffic into a DiffServ network mark each transmitted packet with the appropriate DSCP. Routers within the DiffServ network use the DSCP to classify packets and apply specific queuing or scheduling behavior (known as *per-hop behaviors* or PHBs) based on the results of the classification. Strictly speaking, DiffServ support is not limited to routers. Layer 2 devices such as switches and routers may also recognize DSCPs and support the corresponding PHBs.

1.3.2.1   Using DiffServ to Provide Services

The DiffServ working group of the IETF is standardizing DiffServ. Ironically, although the name of the working group implies work on services, the DiffServ working group's charter (at the time of this writing) specifically excludes work on services. The PHBs being standardized by the group are *local* behaviors applied at each forwarding node. These PHBs alone do not imply end-to-end services. By concatenating devices that support the same PHBs (and controlling the rate at which packets are admitted for any PHB), however, it is possible to use PHBs to construct an end-to-end service with certain useful characteristics. A concatenation of *expedited-forwarding* (EF) PHBs, along a prespecified route, with careful admission control, for example, can yield a service similar to leased-line service, which is suitable for interactive voice. Other concatenations of PHBs may yield a service suitable for video playback, and so forth. Service parameters are characterized at edges of the DiffServ network in the form of a *service level agreement* (SLA). SLAs specify the amount of customer traffic that can be accommodated at each service level and the QoS that the customer can expect to be applied to the traffic.

Note

Admission control is a concept discussed frequently throughout this book. In general, admission control is the process by which certain traffic is *admitted* to a network or to a particular service level within a network while other traffic is refused admission or rejected. Admission control may be explicit or implicit. In explicit admission control, an out-of-band signaling protocol is used to request admission (as in ATM UNI signaling). In implicit admission control, no out-of-band negotiation occurs. Instead, a network node just limits the amount of traffic that it admits, in the data plane, dropping or demoting service level for rejected traffic, without explicitly notifying the sender.

1.3.2.2 The Expedited-Forwarding, Assured-Forwarding, and Class Selector PHBs

One example of a PHB is the EF PHB. This behavior is defined to ensure that packets are transmitted from ingress to egress (at some limited rate) with very low latency. Other behaviors may specify that packets are to be given a certain preference relative to other packets, in terms of average throughput or in terms of drop preference, but with no particular emphasis on latency. The *assured-forwarding* (AF) PHB group is of this type. PHBs are implemented using various underlying queuing mechanisms. Although they are not supposed to specify these mechanisms, certain PHBs may be closely linked to specific implementations.

Note that the 6-bit DSCP field defined by DiffServ spans the fields formerly known as the *Type-of-Service* (TOS) field and the IP precedence field. These fields have been in limited use for many years to provide a form of DiffServ. In particular, network equipment has used the IP precedence field to identify important network control traffic and ensure that it is treated preferentially. As discussed in Chapter 6, the *class selector* PHB has been defined to ensure that DiffServ networks support senders using the traditional IP precedence markings.

Figure 1.3 illustrates the DiffServ concepts discussed in this section. Chapter 6 discusses these in detail.

Figure 1.4   Concepts in a DiffServ Network

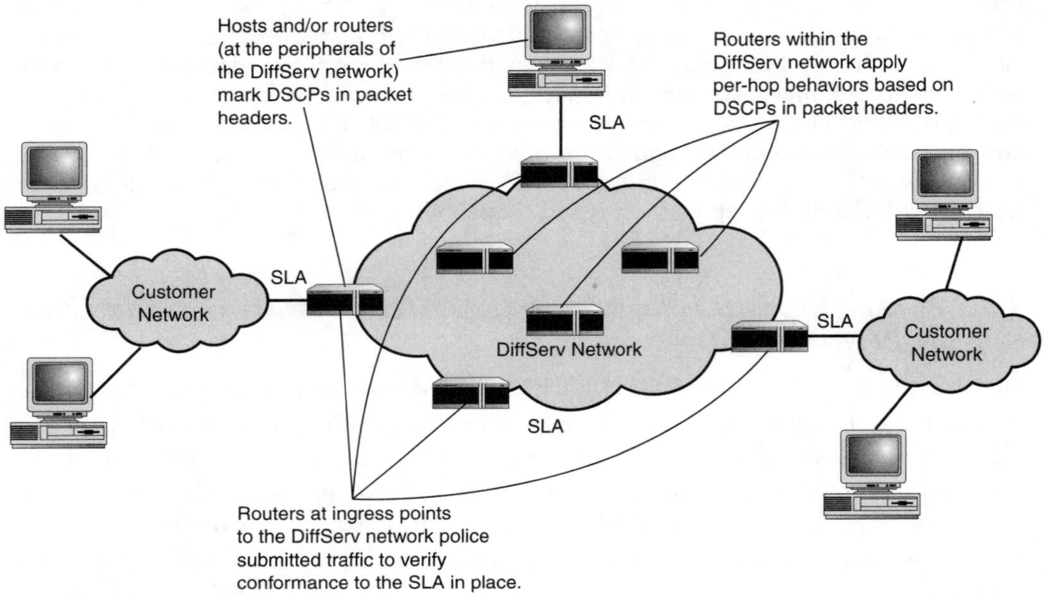

Hosts and/or routers
(at the peripherals of
the DiffServ network)
mark DSCPs in packet
headers.

Routers within the
DiffServ network apply
per-hop behaviors based on
DSCPs in packet headers.

SLA

Customer
Network

SLA

DiffServ Network

SLA

Customer
Network

SLA

Routers at ingress points
to the DiffServ network police
submitted traffic to verify
conformance to the SLA in place.

1.3.3   Integrated Services

Integrated Services (IntServ) is not actually a traffic-handling mechanism, but rather a framework for defining services. Nonetheless, it has come to be associated with certain traffic-handling expectations. It is discussed here in this context.

The IntServ working group of the IETF was formed in 1995 and was chartered with the definition of services to be provided by IP network elements. Its original focus was on services that enable the integration of voice, video, and data on the Internet. It assumes, but does not specify, a set of underlying traffic-handling mechanisms. Due to the focus on multimedia traffic, these traffic-handling mechanisms are expected to provide very quantifiable and measurable service characteristics. Note that IntServ documents do not necessarily assume per-conversation services or per-conversation traffic handling (as opposed to aggregate services and traffic handling). However, IntServ has evolved primarily in the context of RSVP per-conversation signaling. As a result, the predominant model of IntServ usage applies it on a per-conversation basis.

This contrasts starkly with the *aggregate* services and the underlying aggregate traffic-handling mechanisms provided by 802 user_priority and DiffServ. The concept of per-conversation versus aggregate traffic handling is expanded on later in this chapter.

At this time, two services are defined within the IntServ framework: the *Guaranteed Service*, and the *Controlled Load Service*. The Guaranteed Service promises to carry a certain traffic volume with a quantifiable, bounded latency. The Controlled Load Service agrees to carry a certain traffic volume with the "appearance" of a lightly loaded network. These are *quantifiable* services in the sense that they are defined to provide quantifiable QoS to a specific quantity of traffic. (As discussed in Chapter 6, certain DiffServ services, by comparison, may not be quantifiable.)

IntServ services are typically (but not necessarily) associated with the RSVP signaling protocol. (RSVP is discussed briefly in the section titled "Provisioning and Configuration Mechanisms" later in this chapter, and is discussed in depth in Chapter 4, "Integrated Services" and Chapter 5, "RSVP") Each of the IntServ services provides guidelines regarding *admission control*, which determines how much traffic can be admitted to an IntServ service class at a particular network device without compromising the quality of the service. IntServ services do not define the admission-control algorithms nor the underlying queuing algorithms to be used.

1.3.4   ATM, ISSLOW, and Others

802 user_priority is expected to be used broadly in 802 LANs. DiffServ is expected to be used in routed networks. Additional traffic-handling mechanisms are applicable to more specific link layers. These include, for example, ATM, ISSLOW (for slow WAN links), DOCSIS (for cable modems), P1394 mechanisms, wireless mechanisms, and others. Several of these are briefly reviewed in the following paragraphs.

Asynchronous Transfer Mode (ATM) is a link-layer technology that offers high-quality traffic handling and services. ATM fragments packets into fixed-size link-layer *cells*, which are then queued and serviced using queue-servicing algorithms appropriate for a particular ATM service. ATM traffic is separated into flows, which are referred to as *virtual circuits* (VCs). Each VC supports one of the numerous ATM services. These include *constant bit rate* (CBR), *variable bit rate* (VBR), *unknown bit rate* (UBR), and others. ATM actually goes beyond a strict traffic-handling mechanism in the sense that it includes a link-layer signaling protocol that can be used to set up and tear down ATM VCs.

Integrated Services Over Slow Links (ISSLOW) is defined by the *Integrated Services over Specific Link Layers* (ISSLL) working group of the IETF to tackle the following problem: Consider sending normal TCP/IP data traffic on slow modem links. A typical 1500-byte packet, when submitted for transmission on a 28.8Kbps modem link, occupies the link for about 400ms until it has been completely transmitted (preventing the transmission of any other packets on the same link). ISSLOW fragments IP packets at the link layer (using standard PPP multilink fragmentation) for transmission over slow links such that the fragments never occupy the link for longer than some threshold, thereby reducing the latency experienced by competing traffic.

1.3.5 Per-conversation versus Aggregate Traffic-Handling Mechanisms

An important general categorization of traffic-handling mechanisms is that of *per-conversation* mechanisms versus *aggregate* mechanisms. This categorization refers largely to the classification associated with the mechanism and can significantly effect the QoS experienced by traffic subjected to the mechanism. (See the sidebar earlier in this Chapter titled "Flows, Conversations, and Traffic Aggregates.")

Per-conversation traffic-handling mechanisms are mechanisms that handle each *conversation* as a separate flow. Traditionally (but not necessarily), IntServ services are expected to be supported by per-conversation traffic handling.

In aggregate traffic-handling mechanisms, a set of traffic from multiple conversations is classified to the same flow and is handled in aggregate. Aggregate classifiers generally look at some aggregate identifier in packet headers. DiffServ and 802 user_priority are examples of aggregate traffic-handling mechanisms at Layer 3 and at Layer 2, respectively. In both these mechanisms, packets corresponding to multiple conversations are marked with the same DSCP or 802 user_priority.

When traffic is handled on a per-conversation basis, resources are allotted on a per-conversation basis. From the application perspective, this means that the application's traffic is granted resources completely independent of the effects of traffic from other conversations in the network. Although this tends to enhance the quality of the service experienced by the application, it also imposes a burden on the network equipment. Network equipment is required to maintain independent state for each conversation and to apply independent processing for each conversation. In the core of large networks, in which it is possible to support millions of conversations simultaneously, per-conversation traffic handling may not prove practical.

When traffic is handled in aggregate, the state-maintenance and processing burdens on devices in the core of a large network are reduced significantly. On the other hand, the QoS perceived by an application's conversation is no longer independent of the effects of traffic from other conversations that have been aggregated into the same flow. As a result, the QoS perceived by the application tends to be somewhat compromised in aggregate traffic handling. Allocating excess resources to the aggregate traffic class can offset this effect. However, this approach tends to reduce the efficiency with which network resources are used.

1.4 Provisioning and Configuration Mechanisms

To effectively provide network QoS, it is necessary to effect the provisioning and configuration of the traffic-handling mechanisms described, consistently, across multiple network devices. Consider for example, Figure 1.5.

In this example, R1 assigns resources to protect flows A and B. R2 assigns resources to protect flows B and C. R1 does not protect flow C, and R2 does not protect flow A. As a result, users of flows A and C do not obtain the end-to-end service they require. Because the users of flows A and C are not experiencing the required service level, any resources assigned to these flows are wasted. Only the users of flow B are satisfied. When traffic-handling mechanisms are not configured consistently across multiple devices, resources are unnecessarily wasted.

Figure 1.5   The Importance of Coordinating Traffic-Handling Mechanisms

Provisioning and configuration mechanisms include the following:

- RSVP signaling and the Subnet Bandwidth Manager (SBM)

- Policy mechanisms and protocols

- Management tools and protocols

The following paragraphs introduce provisioning and configuration mechanisms. Chapter 9, "QoS Policy" addresses them in depth.

1.4.1 Provisioning versus Configuration

In this book, the term *provisioning* generally refers to more static and longer-term management tasks that affect traffic-handling mechanisms. These may include selection of network equipment, replacement of network equipment, interface additions or deletions, link-speed modifications, topology changes, capacity planning, and so forth. The term *configuration* generally refers to more dynamic and shorter-term direct management of traffic-handling mechanisms. Configuration includes direct modifications to traffic-handling parameters, such as modification of classification criteria used by traffic-handling mechanisms. Furthermore, provisioning tends to be applied to traffic aggregates, controlling resources at a coarser granularity than configuration. The distinction between provisioning and configuration is not clearly delineated and is used as a general guideline rather than as a strict categorization. The terms are often used interchangeably unless otherwise specified.

1.4.2   Pushed versus Signaled Mechanisms

It is important to note the distinction between *pushed* QoS configuration mechanisms and *signaled* QoS configuration mechanisms. Pushed mechanisms typically "push" configuration information from a management console down to network devices. Signaled mechanisms typically carry QoS requests (and implicit configuration requests) from one end of the network to the other, along the same path traversed by the traffic that requires QoS resources. Pushed configuration is typically applied by a network manager or a network management program. It is used to allocate resources in the managed network, to certain user groups and/or applications. Signaled configuration is typically initiated from applications on hosts. These inform affected devices along the traffic path regarding the nature of the application traffic and request admission of application traffic flows to certain preprovisioned service levels. Signaled configuration may also be used in an aggregate form, in which case it tends to be initiated by edge routers, and to request aggregate resources along the traffic path. Pushed mechanisms are generally more static than signaled mechanisms.

Figure 1.6 compares the two types of configuration mechanisms.

The two approaches are not mutually exclusive. Both are likely to be deployed in the same network and applied to different types of traffic to provide different service qualities. Also, note that signaled mechanisms claim resources dynamically, but within the constraints of preprovisioned limits.

Note

The term *signaling* can be applied to any protocol that exchanges information between any devices without regard to their location in the network topology. In this book, however, it is used in a more specific sense: Signaling refers to a protocol that traverses at least part of the traffic path, accumulating and disseminating (as it goes) information about the resources available in the traffic path.

Figure 1.6   Push versus Signaled Configuration Mechanisms

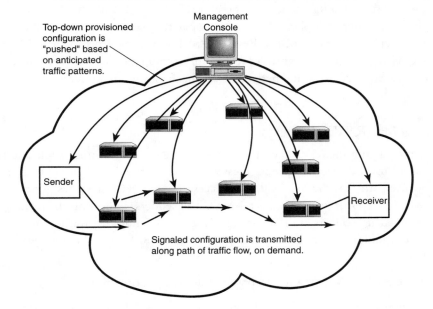

Management Console

Top-down provisioned configuration is "pushed" based on anticipated traffic patterns.

Sender

Receiver

Signaled configuration is transmitted along path of traffic flow, on demand.

1.4.3   Resource Reservation Protocol and the Subnet Bandwidth Manager

RSVP is a Layer 3 signaling protocol initially designed to reserve resources in a QoS-enabled network. In terms of the taxonomy introduced so far, it can abstractly be considered a signaled QoS configuration mechanism. It serves to coordinate the application of traffic-handling mechanisms in multiple devices to provide end-to-end QoS. In its originally intended usage, applications use RSVP to request end-to-end, per-conversation QoS from the network, and to indicate QoS requirements and capabilities to peer applications.

As currently defined, RSVP uses IntServ semantics with per-conversation classification criteria to convey per-conversation QoS requirements to the network. RSVP is not limited to per-conversation usage, however, nor to IntServ semantics. In fact, currently proposed extensions to RSVP enable it to be used to signal information regarding traffic aggregates. Other extensions enable it to be used to signal requirements for services beyond the traditional guaranteed and Controlled Load IntServ Services. This section introduces RSVP in its traditional per-conversation, IntServ form. (Chapter 5 discusses RSVP in detail. In that chpater, its applicability to aggregated traffic handling and to services that are not traditionally IntServ are also addressed.)

Because RSVP is a Layer 3 protocol, it is largely independent of the various underlying network media over which it operates. Furthermore, the IntServ parameters that it traditionally carries are media independent. Therefore, RSVP with IntServ can be considered an abstraction layer between applications (or host operating systems as agents of applications) and media-specific QoS mechanisms. Because RSVP is a Layer 3 protocol and IntServ expresses QoS requirements in abstract terms, the combination of the two can serve to unify the disparate media-specific network QoS mechanisms encountered along end-to-end traffic paths.

1.4.3.1 How RSVP Works

There are two significant RSVP messages: PATH and RESV. Transmitting applications send PATH messages toward receivers. These messages describe the data that will be transmitted and follow the path that the data will take. Receivers send RESV messages. These follow the path seeded by the PATH messages, back toward the senders, indicating the profile of traffic in which particular receivers are interested. In the case of multicast traffic flows, RESV messages from multiple receivers are "merged," making RSVP suitable for QoS for multicast traffic.

As initially defined, RSVP messages carry the following information:

- How the network can identify traffic on a conversation (classification information)

- The service type required from the network for the conversation's traffic (in IntServ terms)

- Quantitative parameters describing the traffic on the conversation (for example, data rate, which applies to quantitative services only)

- Policy information (identifying the user requesting resources for the traffic and the application to which it corresponds)

Classification information is conveyed using IP source and destination addresses and ports. In conventional IntServ usage of RSVP, an IntServ service type is specified and quantitative traffic parameters are expressed using a *token-bucket model*. In use of RSVP with other nonquantifiable services, there may be no quantitative parameters specified. Policy information is typically a secure means for identifying the user and the application requesting resources. Network managers use policy information to decide whether to allocate resources to a conversation.

PATH messages wind their way through all network devices en route from sender to receivers. RSVP-aware devices in the data path note the messages and establish state for the flow described by the message. (Other devices pass the messages through transparently.)

When a PATH message arrives at a receiver, the receiver responds with a RESV message (if the receiving application is interested in the traffic flow offered by the sender). The RESV message winds its way back toward the sender, following the path established by the incident PATH messages. As the RESV message progresses toward the sender, RSVP-aware devices verify that they have the resources necessary to meet the QoS requirements requested by the RESV message. If a device can accommodate the resource request, it installs classification state corresponding to the conversation and allocates resources for the conversation. The device then allows the RESV message to progress on up toward the sender. If a device cannot accommodate the resource request, the RESV message is rejected and a rejection is sent back to the receiver.

In addition, RSVP-aware devices in the data path may extract policy information from PATH messages and RESV messages for verification against network policies. Devices may reject resource requests based on the results of these policy checks by preventing the message from continuing on its path and by sending a rejection message.

When requests are not rejected for either resource-availability or policy reasons, the incident PATH message is carried from sender to receiver, and a RESV message is carried in return. In this case, a *reservation* is said to be installed. An installed reservation indicates that RSVP-aware devices in the traffic path have committed the requested resources to the corresponding flow and are prepared to allocate these resources to traffic belonging to the flow. This process, of approving or rejecting RSVP messages, is known as *explicit admission control* and is a key concept related to signaled QoS.

Chapter 5 discusses RSVP signaling in depth. Figure 1.7 illustrates the concepts described in this section.

Figure 1.7   Explicit Admission Control Using RSVP Signaling

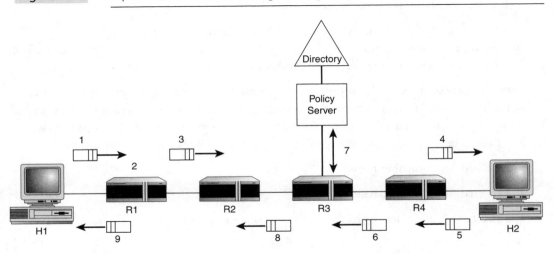

From the figure, note the following:

1. Transmitting host, H1, sends an RSVP PATH message describing transmitted traffic.
2. Router R1 installs 'PATH state'.
3. Router R1 forwards PATH message downstream, PATH state is installed in routers R2, R3 and R4.
4. Router R4 forwards PATH message to receiving host, H2.
5. H2 responds by sending RESV message upstream to request resources for traffic described in PATH message.
6. R4 verifies availability of requested resources and then forwards RESV message upstream.
7. R3 checks with policy server to verify that policy does not preclude allocation of requested resources.
8. Policy check approved, R3 forwards RESV message upstream where R2 and R1 verify availability of requested resources.
9. RESV message arrives at sender H1, indicating that a reservation is installed.

1.4.3.2   *Subnet Bandwidth Manager*

The *Subnet Bandwidth Manager* (SBM) is based on an enhancement to the RSVP protocol, which extends RSVP's utility to 802 networks, including traditional shared networks. In these networks, standard RSVP falls short. The traditional RSVP model assumes that devices whose resources will be impacted by the admission of a traffic flow can participate in the admission of the flow. This is true for Layer 3 networks in which RSVP messages pass through each Layer 3 device along the traffic path. If a device chooses to participate in RSVP signaling, it is ensured that it will be able to refuse admission to flows that would exceed the resources available in the device.

By contrast, in 802 networks resources may be committed in switches, hubs, and even "yellow wires," without these being able to participate in the process of admission control. As a result, resources within the Layer 2 network may be overcommitted.

The SBM protocol solves this problem by enabling Layer 2 devices to participate in RSVP admission control. In shared networks, a single device may volunteer to act as an admission-control agent on behalf of a group of devices (or wire segments) that cannot participate in RSVP signaling. In increasing order of suitability, the eligible devices are as follows:

- Attached SBM-capable hosts
- Attached SBM-capable routers
- SBM-capable switches, which comprise the shared network

These devices automatically run an election protocol that results in the most suitable device(s) being appointed *designated SBM* (DSBM). When eligible switches participate in the election, they subdivide the 802 network among themselves based on the Layer 2 network topology. Hosts and routers that send into the 802 network discover the closest DSBM and route RSVP messages through the device. Thus, the DSBM sees all messages that will affect resources in the 802 subnet and provides explicit admission control on behalf of the subnet.

1.4.4   Policy Mechanisms and Protocols

Network managers configure QoS mechanisms subject to certain policies. Policies determine which applications and users are entitled to varying amounts of resources in different parts of the network.

Policy components include the following:

- **A datastore.** The datastore contains the policy data itself, such as usernames, applications, and the network resources to which these are entitled.

- **Policy decision points (PDPs).** The PDPs translate network-wide higher-layer policies into specific configuration information to be pushed down to individual network devices. PDPs also inspect resource requests carried in RSVP messages and accept or reject them based on a comparison against policy data.

- **Policy enforcement points (PEPs).** The PEPs act on the decisions made by PDPs. These are typically (but not exclusively) network elements in the data path that either do or do not grant resources to arriving traffic.

- **Protocols between the datastore, PDPs, and PEPs.**

1.4.4.1   Policy Data Store—Directory Services

Policy mechanisms rely on a set of data describing how resources in various parts of the network can be allocated to traffic associated with specific users and applications. Policy *schemas* define the format of this information. Much of this information tends to be relatively static and (at least in part) needs to be distributed across the network; hence, directories tend to be suitable datastores.

1.4.4.2   Policy Decision Points and Policy Enforcement Points

Policy decision points (PDPs) interpret data stored in the schemas and control policy PEPs accordingly. PEPs are the switches and routers through which traffic passes. These devices have the ultimate control over which traffic is allocated resources. In the case of push-style provisioned QoS, the PDP pushes policy information to PEPs in the form of classification information (IP addresses and ports) and the resources to which classified packets are entitled.

In the case of signaling-configured QoS, RSVP messages transit through the network along the data path. When an RSVP message arrives at a PEP, the device extracts a *policy element* from the message, as well a description of the service type required, and the traffic profile. The policy element generally contains authenticated user and/or application identification. The router then passes the relevant information from the RSVP message to the PDP, for comparison of the resources requested against those allowable for the user and/or application (per-policy in the datastore). The PDP makes a decision regarding the admissibility of the resource request and returns an approval or denial to the PEP.

In certain cases, the PEP and the PDP can be colocated in the network device. In other cases, the PDP may be separated from the PEP in the form of a *policy server*. A single policy server may reside between the directory and multiple PEPs. Although many policy decisions can be made trivially by colocating the PDP and the PEP, certain advantages can be realized by the use of a separate policy server.

1.4.4.3   Use of Policy Protocols

When RSVP messages transit RSVP-aware network devices, they result in the configuration of traffic-handling mechanisms in PEPs, including classifiers and queuing mechanisms that provide IntServ or DiffServ services. In many cases, however, RSVP cannot be used to configure these mechanisms. Instead, more traditional push mechanisms must be used.

Push mechanisms include Command Line Interface (CLI) and protocols such as SNMP, Common Open Policy Service Protocol (COPS), and others. CLI is a set of vendor-specific person-machine commands, used initially to configure and monitor Cisco network equipment. Because of its popularity, a number of other network vendors provide CLI-like configuration interfaces to their equipment. SNMP has been in use for many years, primarily for the purpose of monitoring network device functionality from a central console. It can also be used to *set* or configure device functionality. COPS is a protocol that has been developed in recent years in the context of QoS. It was initially targeted as an RSVP-related policy protocol, but has recently been put to use as a DiffServ configuration protocol.

In the case of signaled QoS (as opposed to pushed QoS), detailed configuration information is generally carried to the PEP in the form of RSVP signaling messages. However, the PEP must outsource the decision (to the PDP) as to whether to honor the configuration request. COPS was initially developed to pass the relevant information contained in the RSVP message, from the PEP to the PDP, and to pass a policy decision in response. Obviously, when PEP and PDP are colocated, no such protocol is required.

A protocol is also required for communication between the PDP and the policy datastore. Because the datastore tends to take the form of a distributed directory, LDAP is commonly used for this purpose.

Figure 1.8 illustrates the policy concepts discussed in this section.

| **Figure 1.8** | Policy Components |

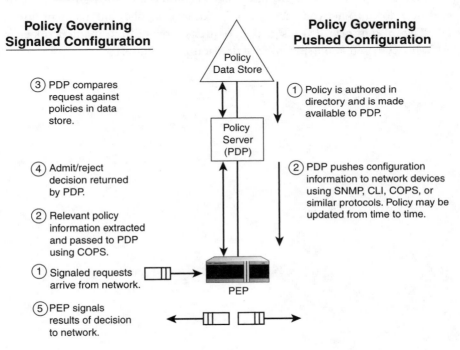

Policy Governing Signaled Configuration

③ PDP compares request against policies in data store.

④ Admit/reject decision returned by PDP.

② Relevant policy information extracted and passed to PDP using COPS.

① Signaled requests arrive from network.

⑤ PEP signals results of decision to network.

Policy Data Store

Policy Server (PDP)

PEP

Policy Governing Pushed Configuration

① Policy is authored in directory and is made available to PDP.

② PDP pushes configuration information to network devices using SNMP, CLI, COPS, or similar protocols. Policy may be updated from time to time.

1.5 *Summary*

Network QoS entails the capability to control traffic-handling mechanisms in the network to serve the requirements of applications and users in accordance with network policies. To provide network QoS, it is necessary to support traffic-handling mechanisms in the network and to provide the means to control these mechanisms.

Traffic-handling mechanisms can be applied on a per-conversation basis or across traffic from multiple conversations. IntServ services and the associated traffic-handling mechanisms are typically applied on a per-conversation basis. DiffServ and 802 user_priority are traffic-handling mechanisms typically applied on an aggregate basis.

Traffic-handling mechanisms are controlled by a combination of long-term provisioning and shorter-term configuration. In part, this control is exerted by pushing provisioning or configuration information from a management console to network equipment. In part it is exerted by using RSVP signaling, initiated by applications on end systems.

Policy servers apply policies based on information stored in a policy database or directory. To do so, these servers (also known as policy decision points, or PDPs) push configuration information down to network elements (also known as policy enforcement points, or PEPs). They also inspect RSVP signaling requests arriving from the network elements and return a policy-based admission control decision in response.

The Quality/Efficiency Product:
The Reason to QoS-Enable a Network

The previous chapter reviewed various QoS mechanisms. Subsequent chapters will discuss the use of these mechanisms to build a QoS-enabled network. The mechanisms described can offer significant benefits, but they are not cost-free. QoS mechanisms incur varying degrees of overhead both in terms of processing and memory in network elements and in terms of administration and management.

This chapter introduces the notion of the *quality/efficiency product*. This metric can be used to weigh the benefit of a particular QoS mechanism so that it can be compared to the cost of the mechanism. The net value that a QoS mechanism brings to a network then can be assessed in a relatively objective manner, avoiding much of the controversy and zeal that typically surrounds QoS mechanisms. Throughout this book, the concept of the quality/efficiency product will be used when evaluating various QoS mechanisms and their application.

The QoS Controversy

The tradeoffs between the benefits offered by QoS mechanisms and the overhead associated with these mechanisms is at the root of the controversy that has always surrounded the discussion of QoS mechanisms.

As it exists today, the Internet offers a simple best-effort service with very primitive QoS mechanisms. All packets generally are handled at the same service level and are forwarded in the order in which they are submitted to the network, with no assurances regarding available bandwidth or latency. QoS mechanisms in the Internet currently are limited to physical or logical reprovisioning (for example, adding links on specific routes or reconfiguring ATM VCs) or rerouting traffic around congested network regions.

continues

continued

The telephone network, on the other hand, makes use of heavyweight QoS mechanisms, including sophisticated per-conversation signaling (SS7) and per-conversation traffic handling (in which a 64Kbps channel is dedicated to each phone call). As a result, the telephone network is capable of offering very strict guarantees regarding available bandwidth and latency.

At one extreme, hardcore Internet traditionalists balk at the notion of bringing the overhead and complexity of any new QoS mechanisms to their simple best-effort Internet. At the other extreme are heretics who want to convert the Internet to a fully circuit-switched network (similar to the telephone network) by forcing per-conversation signaling and per-session traffic handling into every switch and router.

Early battles have been fought. ATM was adopted only to a limited degree and only in backbone networks, a far cry from the model of switched virtual circuits to every desktop that had been envisioned by ATM zealots. RSVP never even made it to the battlefield before being pulled back by the IETF's applicability statement (see Chapter 5, "RSVP" for further details on RSVP and the IETF applicability statement). Yet the Internet is currently falling short of its potential. Often it is unusable for mission-critical enterprise applications (which rely instead on private leased lines), and certainly is not suitable for most multimedia applications. Adopting some level of QoS functionality probably will enable the Internet to realize its full potential.

In addition to introducing the concept of the quality/efficiency product, this chapter briefly discusses the value of various combinations of QoS mechanisms in raising a network's quality/efficiency product. Some of the concepts discussed may be confusing at first, but these will become clearer throughout the book as each QoS mechanism is discussed in greater detail.

2.1 Tradeoffs in the QoS-Enabled Network

Recall the definition of *network QoS* from Chapter 1, "Introduction to Quality of Service":

> The capability to control traffic-handling mechanisms in the network such that the network meets the service needs of certain applications and users subject to network policies.

Chapter 1 also states that if network resources are infinite, the service needs of all applications can be met. Fortunately, it is possible to meet the service needs of important applications without infinite resources. However, in many cases, a great deal of resources may be required to do so. When QoS needs are met purely by adding resources to the network, the network is often *overprovisioned*. QoS mechanisms are valuable because they can make it possible to provide the QoS required by applications without overprovisioning the network. In other words, QoS mechanisms make it possible to simultaneously provide the required QoS and to operate the network more efficiently than would otherwise be possible.

> **Note**
>
> Note that QoS mechanisms do not *create* resources. They merely reallocate existing resources among different traffic flows. When certain traffic flows are allocated more resources, other traffic flows are allocated fewer resources. However, certain applications require additional resources for their traffic flows, while others operate satisfactorily with fewer resources.

This section defines the *quality* of a service and the *efficiency* of network resource usage. Subsequent sections explain how the required quality of a service drives the trade-off between efficiency of network resource usage and the use of QoS mechanisms with their associated costs.

2.1.1 *The Quality of a Service*

Different qualities of service are appropriate for different applications. The *quality* of a service refers to the level of commitment provided by the service and the integrity of that commitment.

> **Note**
>
> In this context, a *service* is intended to refer to the specific assurances that are provided to a set of network traffic regarding available capacity, delivery latency, and reliability of delivery. In other contexts, a service could be interpreted in broader terms to include such aspects as encryption, mean time between failure, and billing issues, among others.

The following are examples of services in order of decreasing quality:

- 100Kbps of traffic will be carried from point A to point B with zero packet loss. Each packet will be delivered from source to destination in less than 100 milliseconds.

- 1Mbps of traffic will be carried from point A to point B with the appearance of a lightly loaded network.

- 100Kbps of traffic will be carried from point A to point B; 95% of packets will be delivered in less than 5 seconds.

- 1Mbps of traffic will be carried from point A to point B in less time than it would be delivered without using this service.

- Traffic from point A will be delivered to its destination in less time than it would be delivered without using this service.

The first two services offer strictly quantifiable bounds on latency and packet loss. The third and fourth services offer somewhat less quantifiable service. The fifth service offers no quantifiable parameters at all. The first and second services correspond to the Integrated Services (IntServ) definition of Guaranteed and Controlled Load Service, respectively. (The relative quality of the second and third services described could be debated, depending on one's definition of a "lightly loaded network"). Finally, the fourth and fifth services are types of *better-than-best-effort* (BBE) service. The fourth service constrains the volume of traffic that will be serviced and the route along which it will be accommodated. The fifth service offers no constraints.

Generally, it is true that the stricter the constraints associated with a service, the higher the quality that can be offered. The value of the fifth service is hotly debated. I tend to refer to it as the "better-than-Joe" service because it seems to assure the customer only that no matter how bad the network appears to the customer, some poor soul is even worse-off. Nonetheless, I am sure that this is a marketable service. Often the terms *quantitative* and *qualitative* are used to refer to services such as Guaranteed and Controlled Load on the one hand, versus BBE services on the other hand. Other terms commonly used are *hard* services versus *soft* services.

It is fairly clear that the services listed offer progressively lesser levels of *commitment* (allowing for some ambiguity between the second and third services). Another aspect of the service that determines its quality is the *integrity* of the service. Conventional wired telephony services have high integrity in the sense that a call in progress generally does not diminish in quality after it has been granted, no matter how many other people in the neighborhood attempt to place calls.

A service quality is not necessarily related to the actual amount of resources committed, nor to the cost of the resources. In the previous example, the first service is of higher quality than the second service, even though it offers less network capacity. Furthermore, an appraisal of the quality of a service is not a judgment of its value to the end user, but rather a statement of its suitability to different applications. For example, a BBE service may be entirely satisfactory for a certain Web-surfing application, while a higher-quality service may be required to handle interactive voice traffic. It is reasonable to assume that, all else being equal, higher-quality services cost more than lower-quality services. Given this assumption, the high-quality service might be deemed excessive for the Web-surfing application. From a cost/performance perspective, the lower-quality service would be preferable to the end user.

2.1.2 *Efficiency*

In the context of this discussion, *efficiency* refers strictly to the amount of network capacity (in terms of bandwidth) required to provide a certain quality service. It does not refer to processing overhead, management burden, or any other potential inefficiencies that might be associated with providing network services. Efficiency is an important consideration because bandwidth is often expensive. Of course, in some situations bandwidth is inexpensive—in this case, efficiency is less of a concern.

2.1.3 *The Quality/Efficiency Product*

For any given network, the higher the Quality of Service required, the more bandwidth is required.

> **Note**
>
> Obviously, this is true only within certain limits. Above a certain bandwidth or network capacity, further bandwidth availability will not improve the QoS.

This is the essence of the quality/efficiency product. In a given network, with a given set of QoS mechanisms, the product of service quality and efficiency is fixed. If higher-quality service is required, the network must operate with higher capacity and, hence, less efficiently. If the network is operated more efficiently, the quality of services that can be offered is compromised. This can be expressed as follows:

Let Q be an abstract representation of the overall quality of services that can be offered by a given network with a given set of QoS mechanisms. Let E be an abstract representation of the overall efficiency with which resources are used in the same network. Then $Q \times E = C$, where C is some constant value.

This value characterizes the network from a QoS perspective and will be referred to in the remainder of this book as the *quality/efficiency* (QE) *product* of the network.

Figure 2.1 characterizes a specific network with a QE product of C. This is the *QE curve* of the network.

Figure 2.1   Quality/Efficiency Product for a Given Network

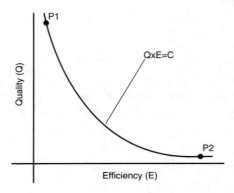

Networks may be operated at different points on their QE curve. For example, most LANs on the Microsoft campus are capable of offering reasonable quality for IP telephony sessions. This is because they tend to be overprovisioned. As such, the LAN operates at a point on the curve (P1) that corresponds to high quality but low efficiency. By contrast, most international WAN links are provisioned very efficiently (for cost reasons). Consequently, these offer poor quality with respect to IP telephony applications. The international WAN links are operated at a point on the QE curve (P2) that corresponds to high efficiency and low quality. In this example, the WAN and the LAN regions of the network are shown to be operating on the same QE curve. In general, different curves will correspond to the two networks.

2.2 Raising the QE Product of a Network

The utility of QoS mechanisms lies in their capability to raise the QE product of a network. This is illustrated in Figure 2.2.

By applying increasingly sophisticated QoS mechanisms, it is possible to incrementally raise the QE product of the network. By raising the QE product of a network, the network can provide improved QoS more efficiently. In many cases, this means that improved service can be offered *at a lower cost.*

Figure 2.2   Using QoS Mechanisms to Raise the QE Product of the Network

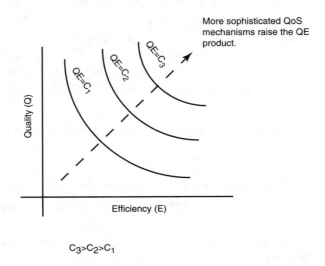

$C_3>C_2>C_1$

2.2.1   Quality, Efficiency, and Overhead

In designing a network, the network manager is faced with the following questions:

- Do I need to support high-quality services through my network?

- If so, can I afford to support these services by overprovisioning the network?

- If not, how much QoS mechanism am I willing to deploy in my network to provide the required QoS?

If the network manager wants to support high-quality services with respect to a certain set of applications, then the *quality* is fixed. Because $Q = C/E$, the manager must either reduce E or increase C until the required quality can be supported. In this case, the network manager is faced with the following options:

- Maintain the same QE curve, but shift the operating point of the network toward higher quality. This requires adding bandwidth with a resulting decrease in efficiency (reducing E).

- Apply QoS mechanisms to raise the QE curve of the network so that a higher quality can be provided without adding bandwidth (increasing C).

The first approach incurs the cost of increasing bandwidth. The second approach incurs the costs associated with the deployment of the QoS mechanisms selected. A variety of QoS mechanisms can improve the QE product to varying degrees with a corresponding savings in bandwidth and the associated cost. The marginal savings in bandwidth costs must be weighed against the marginal costs of deploying and managing the mechanism to determine just which mechanisms are worth deploying. In general, the more a specific QoS mechanism raises a network's QE product, the higher its complexity and, therefore, the higher its cost.

In the remainder of this book, various QoS mechanisms will be discussed in the context of their impact on the QE product, their complexity, and their cost.

2.2.1.1   It Is Not Always Necessary to Raise the QE Product

Often, there may be no need to raise the QE product. In certain cases, the network manager may not be interested in providing high-quality services. In other cases, bandwidth may be so inexpensive that the network manager can afford to overprovision and to operate the network inefficiently. This is often the case with LANs.

2.2.1.2   QoS Mechanisms Are Local, But Their Impact Is Global

The choice of which QoS mechanisms to apply to a network rests in the hands of the manager of each network. However, these days most networks are subnetworks of larger networks and, ultimately, of the Internet. Consequently, if a network manager decides not to support high-quality services through a subnetwork, that decision may compromise any application traffic traversing the subnetwork. QoS mechanisms may be applied on a local basis, but their impact is global.

2.2.1.3   QoS Mechanisms Do Not Create Bandwidth

As described previously, QoS mechanisms do not create bandwidth. No QoS mechanisms will make it possible for a 28.8Kbps modem link to support high-quality HDTV. In certain cases, the network manager will have no choice but to increase the bandwidth of the network to provide high-quality services. However, QoS mechanisms do increase the *efficiency* with which existing resources are used. Thus, in many cases, the existing bandwidth may be sufficient to offer the required service if it is used efficiently. In these cases, QoS mechanisms eliminate or at least defer the need to add bandwidth to the managed network.

2.2.1.4 *Quality Is Application-Specific*

When deciding whether to support high-quality services and how much overprovisioning is required, the network manager must consider the issue in the context of specific application requirements. For example, while the Microsoft LAN may be sufficiently overprovisioned to offer high-quality service for IP telephony, it may offer poor service quality for HDTV streams. A single physical network often can be partitioned into a number of logical networks, each offering different QE products, and each targeted at different application traffic. This concept will be discussed in the "Sharing Network Resources: Multiple Resource Pools" section of this chapter.

2.3   *The Value of Different QoS Mechanisms in Raising the QE Product of a Network*

The QoS mechanisms introduced in the previous chapter can be used in isolation or in various combinations to improve the QE product of a network to varying degrees. The following section ranks the various QoS mechanisms in terms of their impact on the QE product and discusses various combinations of these mechanisms.

2.3.1   *Overhead*

When considering the impact that a particular QoS mechanism has on the QE product of a network, it is important to also consider the cost of the mechanism in terms of deployment costs and management burden. The term *efficiency* was defined to specifically exclude these costs. Throughout the rest of this book, the term *overhead* will be used to discuss the various costs associated with specific QoS mechanisms. Overhead includes the following components, among others:

- Marginal hardware cost (processors, memory, and so on)

- Marginal software cost

- Management burden

- Increased likelihood of failure

As mentioned previously in this chapter, the value of a particular QoS mechanism should be based on weighing the improvement in the QE product against the increased overhead.

2.3.2 Tabulating the Impact of QoS Mechanisms on QE Product and Overhead

Figure 2.3 ranks the general QoS mechanisms described in the previous chapter and illustrates various combinations of them. Methods for combining the QoS mechanisms will be discussed throughout the book. In general, mechanisms and combinations of mechanisms in the lower-right corner of the table will offer a greater impact on QE product but also will incur increased overhead. Mechanisms and combinations of mechanisms in the upper-left corner will offer less impact on QE product but will incur less overhead.

Figure 2.3   Combinations of QoS Mechanisms and Their Impact on QE Product and Overhead

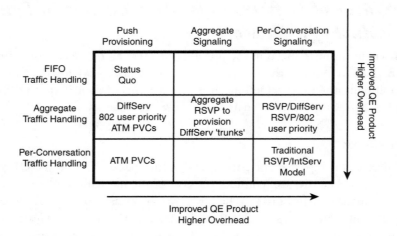

2.3.2.1 Traffic-Handling Mechanisms

The rows of Figure 2.3 correspond to various traffic-handling mechanisms. The topmost row corresponds to traditional FIFO queuing. The middle row corresponds to aggregate traffic-handling mechanisms such as DiffServ, 802 user_priority, and the use of ATM VCs to carry multiple conversation requiring similar QoS. The bottom row corresponds to per-conversation traffic handling, such as that implied by the original vision of per-conversation RSVP/IntServ or the use of per-conversation ATM VCs. Moving from top to bottom, these mechanisms offer greater impact on the QE product of a network, but they also incur the costs of increased overhead.

2.3.2.2 Provisioning and Configuration Mechanisms

As noted in the previous chapter, traffic-handling mechanisms must be configured and provisioned in a consistent manner. Thus, each traffic-handling mechanism can be combined with various provisioning and configuration mechanisms.

The columns in Figure 2.3 correspond to various provisioning and configuration mechanisms. The leftmost column corresponds to the lowest overhead approach to provisioning and configuration: simple push provisioning. The middle column corresponds to aggregate signaling, and the rightmost column corresponds to per-conversation signaling. Moving from left to right, these mechanisms offer greater impact on the QE product of a network, but they also incur the costs of increased overhead.

2.3.2.3 *Combinations of Traffic Handling and Provisioning and Configuration Mechanisms*

Various cells in Figure 2.3 represent combinations of the corresponding traffic-handling mechanism with the corresponding provisioning and configuration mechanism. For example, the top-left cell represents the status quo in which push provisioning is used with FIFO queuing. This approach provides no improvement in QE product, but it also incurs no overhead. The lower-right cell represents the other extreme: per-conversation signaling combined with per-conversation traffic handling. This is the original RSVP/IntServ model. It may offer significant improvement in QE product, but at a significant increase in overhead. Other cells represent various compromises between the two extremes. For example, the middle cell in the rightmost column represents the use of per-conversation signaling to gain admission to aggregate traffic-handling classes. The center cell represents the use of aggregate RSVP to establish DiffServ "trunks" that provide a certain service level between edges of a DiffServ network to an aggregation of conversations (aggregate RSVP is discussed in detail in Chapter 5).

The various cells represent only examples, and these examples are not exhaustive. Certain examples will be discussed in further depth throughout the book. Different combinations may be appropriate for different types of subnetworks. For example, in a routed network handling traffic of many different conversations, the combination of *aggregate* traffic handling with *per-conversation* signaling likely will offer a significantly better QE product than the status quo at a moderate increase in overhead. Beyond this, the marginal improvement in QE product offered by combining *per-conversation* traffic handling with *per-conversation* signaling is likely to be quite small relative to the marginal increase in overhead. Thus, the manager of a large routed network likely would find a 'sweet spot' in combining aggregate traffic handling with per-conversation signaling. Managers of other types of networks might prefer other combinations.

2.3.2.4 Continuous Nature of QoS Mechanisms and Density of Distribution

The table shown in Figure 2.3 illustrates how variations in traffic handling and signaling mechanisms can impact QE product and overhead. This table represents differing levels of traffic handling or provisioning and configuration mechanisms in discrete steps. In reality, however, these are not constrained to discrete steps. FIFO queuing represents no traffic handling, while per-conversation traffic handling represents a very fine granularity of traffic handling. Between these two extremes is a continuum of possibilities, representing different degrees of aggregation. The same is true for provisioning and configuration. At one extreme there is push provisioning only. At another extreme, there is per-conversation signaling. In between, a continuum of aggregate signaling possibilities exists.

Increasingly finer granularities of signaling and of traffic handling can offer an ever-increasing QE product. A third factor to consider is the *density of distribution* of the mechanism. When a mechanism is densely distributed, each device in the network topology applies the mechanism. When it is sparsely distributed, only certain key devices apply the mechanism. More dense distributions result in a higher QE product, but they also increase overhead. More sparse distributions result in a lower QE product but lower overhead.

Figure 2.4 illustrates the continuous nature of the three factors: traffic handling, provisioning, and configuration and density of distribution.

Figure 2.4   Traffic Handling, Provisioning, and Configuration and Density of Distribution Can Be Applied on a Continuum

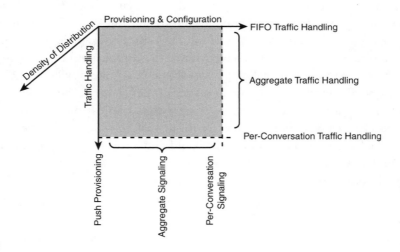

2.4   Illustrative Examples

This section presents a number of examples to illustrate the previously described concepts.

2.4.1   Push Provisioning and FIFO Traffic Handling

Most existing networks employ little (if any) QoS mechanism and provide a relatively low QE product. Consider a typical enterprise network (consisting of both LAN and WAN links) in which employees access internal Web sites. Users may be able to surf the Web fairly painlessly (assuming that the targeted Web servers are not a bottleneck). The extent of QoS mechanism present in these networks is that the network manager monitors the network usage level and from time to time (as the number of users on the network grows) adds capacity to (reprovisions) the network. It may take 1 second for a typical Web query to complete, or it may take 5 seconds, depending on the time of day and the activity level of other users on the network. The QoS is relatively low but is nonetheless satisfactory for the application.

This mode of operation corresponds to the top-left cell in the table in Figure 2.3. Traffic is handled using FIFO queuing, and the network occasionally is reprovisioned in a push manner. Instead of employing sophisticated QoS mechanisms to improve the QE product, the network manager increases quality as necessary by adding capacity (compromising efficiency). Because the service quality required by Web surfing is relatively low, relatively minor increases in capacity may be sufficient to meet the needs of the users. To the extent that service must be improved in the LAN (versus the WAN), efficiency may not be a concern at all.

Note

Network capacity may be increased by physically reprovisioning or by logically reprovisioning. An example of physical reprovisioning is replacing a 10Mbps interface card with a 100Mbps interface card. An example of logical reprovisioning is reconfiguring a 128Kbps ATM VC to a 256Kbps ATM VC. For the purpose of this discussion, both are considered to be forms of push provisioning.

2.4.2   Using Aggregate Traffic Handling to Raise the QE Product

While reprovisioning in the LAN may be reasonable, adding capacity to WAN links is typically quite expensive. If the network manager finds that he or she is continually adding capacity to WAN links to maintain the required quality of Web-surfing service, it may be appropriate to explore alternatives. If Web surfing is deemed mission-critical in the enterprise network, QoS mechanisms may be employed to improve the QE product of the

WAN network with respect to some important subset of Web-surfing traffic. This will make it possible to offer Web surfers improved service quality while stemming the rate at which capacity must be added.

Consider Figure 2.5.

Figure 2.5   Improving the QE Product by Combining Push Provisioning and Aggregate Traffic Handling

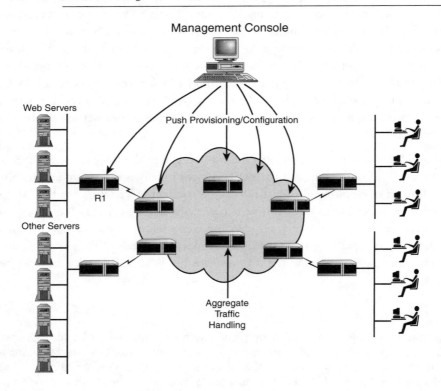

To improve the quality of certain Web-surfing traffic without adding further capacity, the network manager might configure R1 to recognize important traffic originating from the Web servers and mark it with an appropriate DSCP. Routers transmitting onto WAN links would be configured to grant the marked traffic relative priority.

This is quite an efficient approach because no resources are added to the network. However, while it provides a QoS that is better-than-best-effort (BBE), it still represents a relatively low QoS. It promises no quantifiable latency bounds. Latency might degrade significantly if an unusually high number of users decided to Web-surf simultaneously (thereby overwhelming the higher-priority queues in the routers). This condition would be especially severe if all simultaneous users were collocated. In this case, unusually high demands would be placed on a single WAN link. Thus, the QoS would depend on the number of simultaneous Web-surfing users and their location in the network topology. However, because Web-surfing does not demand particularly high service quality, this approach may be appropriate. The next example discusses the provisioning of higher-quality services.

2.4.3 *Supporting Higher-Quality Services in the LAN*

Consider an IP telephony application. Users of this application each require a guarantee from the network to carry 64Kbps, with a maximum end-to-end latency no higher than 100 milliseconds. A higher latency renders the service useless. Furthermore, users expect that an IP telephony session will not degrade in quality as the call progresses. Clearly, the IP telephony application requires a higher-quality service than the Web-surfing application. In a LAN environment, the higher quality may be offered effectively by using a combination of aggregate traffic handling and overprovisioning. This is illustrated in Figure 2.6.

| Figure 2.6 | Providing Telephony-Quality Service Using Push Provisioning and 802 user_priority |

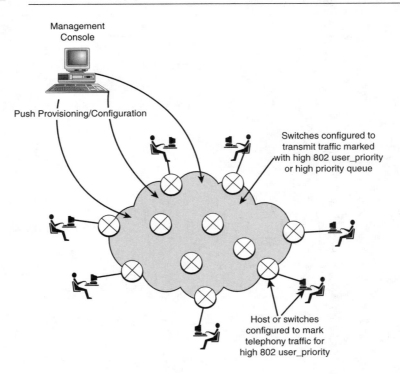

In this example, each switch in the LAN is configured with a high-priority queue and a standard queue. Switches or hosts at the periphery of the LAN are configured to recognize IP telephony traffic and to mark it with the appropriate 802 user_priority so that it is directed to the high-priority queues. Because bandwidth is relatively plentiful in the LAN, and because the bandwidth consumed by IP telephony sessions is relatively low, the high-priority queues will remain relatively underutilized and will offer the low-latency, high-quality service required. The simple combination of aggregate traffic handling and push provisioning raises the QE product enough to provide high-quality telephony service with only moderate overprovisioning.

2.4.4   *Supporting Higher-Quality Services in the WAN*

If it is necessary to support the same high-quality service across the WAN, the combination of push provisioning and aggregate traffic handling may not suffice. In Figure 2.7, two LANs are interconnected by a 1.5Mbps WAN link. Assume that push provisioning is used to configure the routers driving the WAN link (R1 and R2) to recognize telephony traffic and to direct it to a high-priority queue.

Figure 2.7   Supporting Telephony Service Across a WAN Link

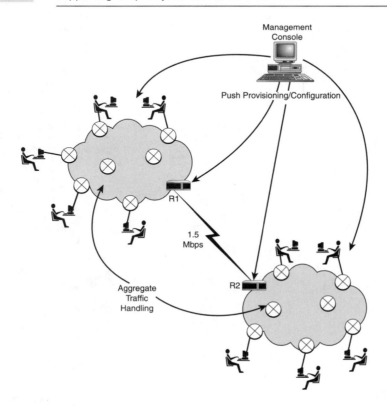

As long as telephony calls remain local to one of the LANs illustrated, capacity may be sufficient to provide high-quality service to all simultaneous telephony sessions. However, the WAN link is capable of supporting only a small number of simultaneous telephony sessions. Beyond some threshold, one additional telephony session will increase the utilization of the high-priority queue in R1 or R2 and will compromise the latency bounds provided by the queue. The marginal telephony session not only will experience compromised service itself, but also will compromise service to those sessions already in progress, as illustrated in Figure 2.8.

Figure 2.8   The Marginal Session Congests the WAN Link, Compromising Service to All

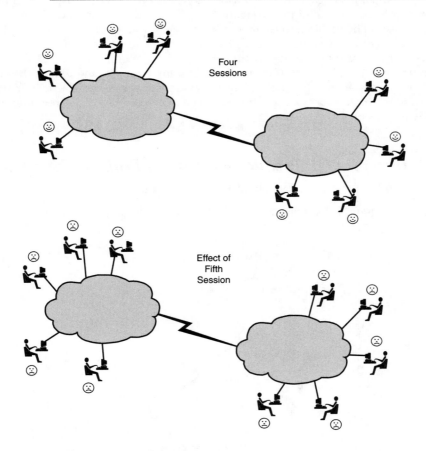

The service provided to telephony traffic in this example is of low integrity and low quality. This occurs because the simple push provisioning mechanism aggregates *all* telephony traffic into the high-priority queue indiscriminately.

To maintain a high QoS, the network manager may overprovision the WAN link to accommodate the worst-case number of simultaneously occurring telephony sessions. However, this is likely to be prohibitively expensive. Instead, the network manager can raise the QE product by employing a mechanism to restrict use of the high-priority queue to a limited number of telephony sessions. This can be achieved using QoS signaling for explicit admission control, as described in the following section.

Note

In theory, it is possible to achieve similar effects without QoS signaling, using only push provisioning and an *implicit* form of admission control. If R1 and R2 were made sufficiently intelligent, they could be designed to identify traffic associated with individual telephony sessions and could be configured to direct traffic only from the first N sessions to the high-priority queue (where N is the number of sessions that can be simultaneously accommodated without compromising service quality). To be generally effective, this requires cumbersome functionality in routers. Furthermore, there may be multiple such routers in the path. It is necessary to coordinate these routers so that they direct traffic from the same N sessions to the high-priority queue. It is quite complex to achieve such coordination using push mechanisms only.

2.4.5   Raising the QE Product of the WAN Link by Using Signaling

In Figure 2.9, R1 and R2 are capable of RSVP signaling.

Figure 2.9   Using Explicit Admission Control to Raise the QE Product of the WAN Link

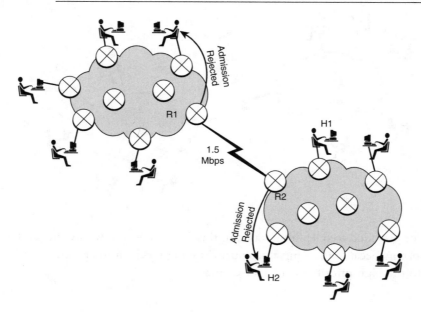

Hosts initiating telephony sessions generate signaling messages describing the session. R1 and R2 participate in RSVP signaling, explicitly admitting (H1) or rejecting (H2) each session based on the resources available. (Devices participating in signaling for the purpose of admission control are known as *admission control agents*). In this manner, routers can reject admission to sessions that would result in excess utilization of their high-priority queue (thereby protecting the integrity of pre-existing sessions, as illustrated in Figure 2.10).

Figure 2.10   The Marginal Session Experiences Low-Quality Service but Does Not Compromise the Quality of Service Available to Pre-existing Sessions

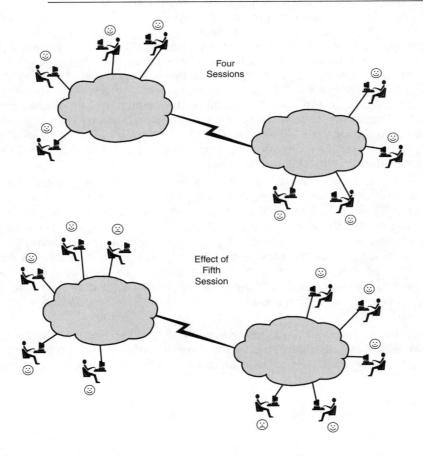

In a general topology, it may be necessary to coordinate admission control among multiple admission control agents along a traffic path. To this end, admission or rejection messages propagate along the traffic path so that all admission control agents are capable of coordinating the set of sessions admitted to their high-priority queues. Traffic from rejected sessions can then be redirected to the best-effort queue in each agent.

This approach combines per-conversation signaling and aggregate traffic handling to raise the QE product of the network. In the simple example illustrated, this approach is applied to the bandwidth-constrained WAN link. As a result, it is possible to provide high-quality telephony service (albeit to some limited number of simultaneous sessions) without over-provisioning the network.

Call Blocking

The approach described in the previous example raises the QE product by using signaling to block calls that would result in overutilization of high-priority resources. By doing so, it makes it possible to provide high-quality service to some limited number of calls. The utility of such an approach depends largely on the statistical distribution of telephony sessions over time. For example, assume that 1,000 potential IP telephony users are evenly distributed across the enterprise network. In the worst case, it will be necessary to support 500 telephony sessions across the WAN link at any point in time (two users per session). However, in most cases, the actual number of simultaneous sessions will be quite small. For example, if the number of simultaneous sessions is typically four, with occasional spikes to five and beyond, then the approach described works quite well. Admission control in the routers can be limited to admit capacity for four sessions. Occasionally, requests for a fifth or sixth session will be rejected, resulting in a blocked call or a busy signal.

To provide the same service quality without admission control, the network manager would have no choice but to increase the capacity of the WAN link. In fact, to *guarantee* the equivalent service quality without using admission control would require provisioning for 500 simultaneous sessions! This clearly would result in inefficient use of network resources. A middle ground could be struck, overprovisioning to a lesser degree. However, partial overprovisioning without admission control does not guarantee service integrity and quality. It assures these only to the extent that the provisioned threshold is not exceeded. If the statistics of call distribution over time are such that the provisioned threshold is exceeded, service will be compromised to all sessions at that time.

Note that the definition of high QoS does not preclude blocked calls. Rather, it stipulates that admitted calls should be provided good service with high integrity. If it is necessary to never block calls, there is no choice but to overprovision accordingly.

2.4.5.1 Issues Regarding the use of Signaling as a Mechanism for Raising the <u>QE</u> Product of a Network

Signaling in the context of RSVP will be discussed in depth in Chapter 5. Because it plays an important role in supporting a high QE product, however, certain related issues are discussed briefly in this section.

Signaling Costs

Signaling can improve the QE product of a network. However, this comes at a cost. Signaling itself requires network resources. Any form of signaling generates additional network traffic. Because of its soft state, RSVP signaling does so continually (albeit at low volumes). In addition, for the signaling to be useful, it is necessary for network devices to intercept signaling messages and to process them. This consumes memory and processing resources in the network devices. In addition to the impact of signaling on device resources, the processing of signaling messages in each device introduces latency. Hosts experience this latency as a delay in obtaining the requested QoS.

Signaling Density

In the example illustrated previously, only routers attached to the WAN link (R1 and R2) participate in signaling. Routers and switches within each of the LANs do not. Within the LANs, it is more cost-effective to provide the required service quality by overprovisioning than by requiring each device to participate in signaling.

In general, certain devices (including switches and routers) are obvious candidates to be configured as admission control agents. Typically, these are devices that are responsible for relatively bandwidth-constrained segments or subnetworks. Where resources are plentiful, it is rarely necessary to appoint admission control agents. Thus, the density of distribution of admission control agents can be reduced where compromises in efficiency can be tolerated. This reduces overhead at the cost of a reduction in QE product. This effect is illustrated in Figure 2.4.

Dense distribution of admission control agents improves the QE product of a network by improving the *topology awareness* of the admission control process. This effect is explained briefly in the related sidebar in this section. Signaling and topology awareness are discussed in detail in Chapter 5.

Signaling and Topology Awareness

Consider the simple network illustrated in Figure 2.11.

Figure 2.11   Sample Network

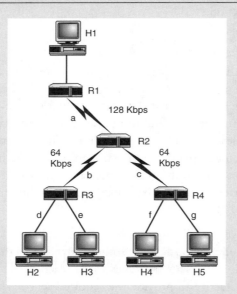

Assume that all routers illustrated participate in RSVP signaling. Now assume that a QoS session requiring 64Kbps is initiated between H1 and H2, and that another session requiring 64Kbps is initiated between H1 and H4. One RSVP request for 64Kbps would traverse R1, R2, and R3. Another RSVP request for 64Kbps would traverse R1, R2, and R4. The routers would admit these resource requests because they would not result in overcommitment of resources on any of the routers' interfaces. If instead H2 and H3 each attempted to simultaneously initiate a 64Kbps QoS session to H1, then R2 would prevent one of these sessions from being established in order to avoid overcommitting resources on segment b. More generally, R2 could admit two simultaneous requests for 64Kbps if one were for resources on segment b and the other for resources on segment c. However, if both were for resources on the same segment at the same time, one of the requests would not be admitted.

Thus, RSVP signaling makes it possible to admit or reject resource requests based on the *current* availability of resources in the specific devices whose resources would be required. This results from two facts. First, end systems generate RSVP signaling in real time as the need for resources arises. Second, the end systems address RSVP messages to the same address that data traffic is sent. As a result, the messages follow the data path and are available to each network device along the path. Throughout the rest of this book, this characteristic of RSVP signaling will be referred to as *topology-aware admission control*.

Push provisioning, by contrast, provides neither the dynamic nature nor the topology awareness of RSVP signaling. In push provisioning, resources are effectively preassigned to specific sets of traffic at the time classifiers are configured in network devices. Some volume of traffic will appear at each device and will match the installed classifiers, thereby claiming against allocated resources. The network manager has only limited knowledge regarding the volumes of traffic that will appear at each device. As a result, it is difficult to provide high-quality guarantees with push provisioning.

As mentioned before, the topology awareness supported by RSVP signaling is maximized when each device in the network acts as an admission control agent. Because this may be costly in terms of overhead, the network manager likely will limit the density of signaling-aware devices. The following example illustrates the effects this has on the QE product offered by the network illustrated in Figure 2.11.

Assume that the network manager reduces the density of signaling-enabled network devices by disabling the processing of QoS signaling messages in R2, R3, and R4. Only R1 now participates in signaling. In effect, it becomes the admission control agent for itself as well as the remaining routers in the network. In this case, the router's downstream interface has a capacity of 128Kbps (on segment a). If R1 were configured to apply admission control based on this capacity, it might admit requests of up to 64Kbps from both H2 and H3 simultaneously (or from both H4 and H5 simultaneously). This would overcommit the resources on segment b (or c), thereby compromising the service quality offered.

The service quality could be maintained if R1 was configured to limit admission of resource requests to 64Kbps. However, this would result in inefficient use of network resources because only one conversation could be supported at a time, when in fact two could be supported if their traffic were distributed appropriately. Alternatively, all 64Kbps links in the network could be increased to 128Kbps links to avoid overcommitment of resource requests, but the increased capacity would be used only if hosts H2 and H3 (or H4 and H5) required resources simultaneously. If this were only rarely the case, such overprovisioning would also be inefficient.

In general, a reduction in the density of admission control agents reduces the QE product that can be offered by a network. This is because the network manager has imperfect knowledge of network traffic patterns. In the previous example, if the network manager knew with certainty that hosts H2 and H3 (or hosts H4 and H5) never required low latency resources simultaneously, they could be offered high-quality guarantees without signaling and without incurring the inefficiencies of overprovisioning. In smaller networks, it is very difficult for the network manager to predict traffic patterns. In larger networks, it tends to be easier to do so because of the lower variance in traffic patterns. Thus, reductions in the density of signaling-aware devices tend to compromise the QE product less in large networks than in small networks.

Aggregation of Signaling Messages

In the case of standard RSVP signaling, messages are generated for each conversation in progress. In parts of the network through which a large number of conversations frequently occur, it is possible to aggregate per-conversation signaling messages into a smaller number of messages regarding aggregate resources. Aggregate signaling reduces demands on admission control agents and reduces overhead (as compared with per-conversation signaling). Of course, it also reduces the QE product.

2.5 Sharing Network Resources: Multiple Resource Pools

The general QoS-enabled network is required to simultaneously support applications with differing QoS requirements. Thus, in any part of the network, it must be possible to provide both low- and high-quality services. To this end, any physical subnetwork can be partitioned into a number of logical networks. The physical resources are allocated among the logical networks. Each logical network may be operated at a different point on the network's QE curve or even on a different QE curve.

2.5.1 Isolation Between Traffic Types Requiring Different Quality Service

High-quality services typically are made practical via the use of signaling and explicit admission control. Low-quality services may be offered by push provisioning, with no explicit admission control. To support both service types simultaneously in a single physical network, *policing* is required. Policing refers to the capability to prevent traffic from seizing resources to which it is not entitled.

Traffic admitted through the process of signaling and explicit admission control allows itself to be more readily policed than that which is not. The admission control process informs the network of the routes that will be used by admitted traffic. Resource requests for traditional IntServ services also inform the network of the specific quantity of resources that will be used by admitted traffic along the indicated routes. Thus, signaling requests offer the network policing parameters for the signaled traffic. The network then can ensure that the signaled traffic does not claim resources along routes other than those on which it is admitted and that the signaled traffic does not claim excess quantities of resources. (Note that policing may be applied on a per-conversation basis or on an aggregate basis).

By contrast, traffic that is not allotted resources as a result of signaling and explicit admission control does not offer policing parameters to the network. The network manager allots resources to this traffic by pushing classifiers to network devices, which qualify the traffic to receive certain resources. However, because the traffic offers no hint as to where it will appear in the network and at what volumes it will appear, the network manager is hard pressed to select appropriate policing parameters. Without policing, any traffic that appears at a network device and matches the preconfigured classifiers is capable of seizing resources.

To maintain the integrity of high-quality services, the network manager must prevent this rogue traffic from seizing resources that are required to support the high-quality services. Because this traffic offers no policing parameters, the network manager is left with no choice but to subjugate it to the traffic that is being offered high-quality services. This means that at network devices, traffic associated with high-quality services is policed and given prioritized access to resources. Traffic associated with lower-quality services is not policed but is given lower priority in its access to resources. In effect, traffic is divided into two *pools*.

Note

Because traffic associated with lower-quality services is subjugated to traffic associated with higher-quality services, it is not necessarily true that applications requiring lower-quality services are treated with less importance than applications requiring higher-quality services. For example, many network managers would balk at the notion that SAP/R3 traffic is treated less importantly than video-conferencing traffic. In general, this would be unacceptable.

The overall treatment of the application's traffic is determined not only by the priority granted to the application's traffic in any particular queue, but also by the size of the resource pool available to the application's traffic. Typically, only a small fraction of the resources available at network devices is available for reservation through explicit admission control, with the majority remaining available for traffic associated with lower-quality services.

Thus, although traffic associated with lower-quality services may briefly yield to latency-sensitive traffic associated with higher-quality services, the average amount of resources available to the lower-quality traffic is likely to be higher than that which is available to higher-quality traffic.

2.5.2 The Four Logical Networks

It is useful to recognize four logical networks within the general physical network. Each of these controls a certain (though not necessarily constant size) resource pool. Each may be operated on a different QE curve, and each offers a different general QoS to accommodate a different type of traffic. In general, traffic requiring higher qualities of service is policed so that it does not starve traffic requiring lower-quality services. The four logical networks can be described based on the type of traffic they serve, as follows.

- **Quantifiable traffic requiring high-quality guarantees**—This type of traffic requires a specifically quantifiable amount of resources along specific routes. These resources typically are allocated as a result of RSVP signaling, which quantifies the amount of resources required by the traffic flow in each part of the network. The highest-priority queues in network devices are reserved for this traffic. This traffic is subjected to strict admission control and policing. Examples of this type of traffic include IP telephony traffic and other multimedia traffic.

- **Nonquantifiable persistent traffic requiring high-quality guarantees**—This type of traffic requires resources that cannot be specifically quantified. However, it tends to be *persistent* in the sense that it consumes resources along a known route for some reasonable duration. Resources are allocated to this class of traffic as a result of RSVP signaling, which does not specifically quantify the resources required by the traffic flow. This signaling informs the network of the application sourcing the traffic, as well as the route taken through the network. This information facilitates prediction of traffic patterns, enabling reasonable quality guarantees. However, because resource requirements are not strictly quantified, resource consumption cannot be strictly policed, and this traffic is assigned to queues that are of lower priority than those available for quantifiable traffic. Examples of this type of traffic include client-server, session-oriented, mission-critical applications such as SAP and PeopleSoft.

- **Nonquantifiable, nonpersistent traffic requiring low- or medium-quality guarantees**—This type of traffic is relatively unpredictable because its resource requirements cannot be quantified and because its route through the network is fleeting and subject to frequent changes. The overhead of signaling cannot be justified for this type of traffic because it can provide little information to assist the network manager in managing the resources allocated to it. Because the impact of this traffic is so unpredictable, this traffic is forced to use queues that are of lower priority than those used by signaled traffic. As a result, only low-quality guarantees can be offered to such traffic. An example of this type of traffic is Web-surfing traffic.

- **Best-effort traffic**—This is all remaining traffic, which is not quantifiable and not persistent, and which does not need any QoS guarantees. The network manager must assure that resources are available in the network for such traffic, but no specific QoS must be provided for it. This traffic uses default FIFO queues and receives resources that are left over after the requirements of higher-priority traffic have been satisfied.

> **Note**
>
> Although it is implied that the resource pools are isolated from each other using strict priority queuing (see Chapter 3, "Queuing Mechanisms"), this is not necessarily the case. Other queuing schemes may be used as well, such as allocating relative shares of a link to different subsets of traffic, with no strict priority relationship between the queues.

2.6 Summary

QoS networks offer services to application traffic. Such services may be of high or low quality. *High-quality services* generally offer specific quantifiable service parameters and are of high integrity. *Low-quality services* offer little in the way of quantifiable parameters and/or are of low integrity. Different applications require different qualities of service.

Efficiency is a measure of the amount of bandwidth required in a network to support the demands of the applications making use of the network. When a network can be operated with less bandwidth, it operates more efficiently. When more bandwidth is required, the network operates less efficiently.

In general, the network manager is faced with a trade-off between the QoS that the network can provide and the efficiency with which the network can be operated. The more efficiently a network is operated, the lower the quality of services that can be offered. The less efficiently a network is operated (the more bandwidth is made available), the higher the quality of services that can be offered. Thus, the product of the average QoS that can be offered by the network and the average efficiency with which it is operated is a constant. This constant is referred to as the *quality/efficiency* (QE) *product* of the network.

The QE product of a network can be raised by enabling more sophisticated QoS mechanisms in the network. These mechanisms carry overhead, which must be weighed against the expected improvement in QE product. Network managers face this trade-off in each part of the network. Depending on the characteristics of different parts of the network, and depending on the demands on different parts of the network, different QoS mechanisms may be appropriate for that part of the network.

Because any subnetwork is likely to be required to support multiple service qualities, it is helpful to partition a physical subnetwork into four logical networks. These logical networks may each employ different QoS mechanisms to control a subset of the underlying physical resources. Traffic is assigned to a logical network based on the QoS that it requires.

PART II

QoS Mechanisms

Chapter 3   Queuing Mechanisms

Chapter 4   Integrated Services

Chapter 5   RSVP

Chapter 6   Differentiated Services

Chapter 7   The Subnet Bandwidth Manager and 802 Networks

Chapter 8   QoS over Layer 2 Media Other Than 802

Chapter 9   QoS Policy

Chapter 10   Putting the Pieces Together—End-to-End QoS

Queuing Mechanisms

Chapter 1, "Introduction to Quality of Service," described the role of traffic-handling mechanisms in providing network QoS. Queues and queue-servicing algorithms are critical elements of traffic handling and are the primary topics of this chapter. Queue-servicing algorithms are often complemented by metering, policing, and dropping schemes. Dropping schemes will also be discussed in this chapter. Metering and policing are discussed later in the book, in the context of the specific traffic-handling mechanisms to which they are relevant. They will be addressed only briefly in this chapter.

Queues form in network devices when traffic arrives at a device at a faster rate than it is forwarded to the next device. When queues form, queue-servicing algorithms determine the order and rate at which traffic is removed from the queues for forwarding. As such, these algorithms determine the QoS experienced by the queued traffic. This chapter discusses the formation of queues and the various queue-servicing algorithms that can be used to service these queues.

Note that this chapter focuses on the queuing and queue-servicing mechanisms themselves. These are the fundamental building blocks of QoS-enabled networks. Provisioning and configuration mechanisms must be used to enable the queuing mechanisms in network devices, to determine the appropriate parameters for these mechanisms, and to direct appropriate subsets of traffic to the various queues. The actual application of the various mechanisms discussed is addressed only briefly in this chapter. Application of the mechanisms is discussed further in later chapters, in connection with specific provisioning and configuration mechanisms.

3.1 Formation of Queues

Senders transmit network traffic into the network, where it is carried from network device to network device until it reaches its destination. Traffic arrives at the *ingress* interface of a network device. Hardware and software within the device then forward traffic from the ingress interface to an *egress* interface. From each egress interface, traffic is forwarded via some transmission medium, which carries the traffic to the ingress interface of the next network device in the path.

> **Note**
>
> Examples of transmission media include, but are not limited to, copper wire, fiber-optic cables, and wireless media.

This is illustrated in Figure 3.1.

Figure 3.1   Network Devices and Ingress and Egress Interfaces

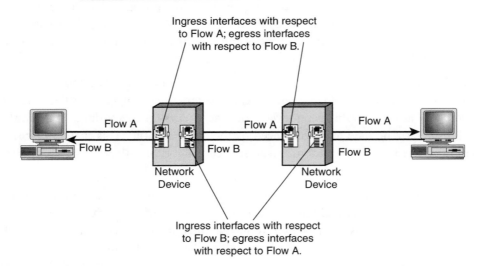

> **Note**
>
> Note that an interface is designated as an ingress or egress interface with respect to a specific unidirectional traffic flow. Thus, an interface may be both an ingress interface and an egress interface simultaneously, but with respect to different traffic flows. In *full-duplex* media, traffic flowing in one direction can be considered completely independently of traffic flowing in the opposite direction. On other media, traffic flowing in one direction may interfere with traffic flowing in the other direction, so the two cannot be considered in isolation.

3.1.1 *Queuing and Forwarding*

Figure 3.2 illustrates a simple network device that contains two *stages*. Each stage includes a set of queues and a forwarder. The queues represent device memory that is used to "hold" arriving traffic until it is forwarded. The forwarder removes traffic from the queues in the form of packets (or cells) and sends these packets to the next stage. In the simple device illustrated in Figure 3.2, the first stage includes queues on an ingress interface and a forwarder that carries traffic from the ingress interface queues to an egress interface. The second stage includes queues on the egress interface and a forwarder that carries traffic from the egress interface queues to the transmission medium that is connected to the next network device.

Figure 3.2   A Simple, Two-Stage Network Device

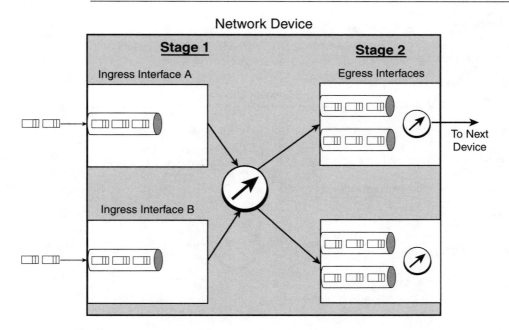

Network devices may vary considerably in terms of the number of stages, the number of queues that are formed at each stage, the depth of the queues, and other operating parameters. Often devices are designed so that the first-stage forwarder is capable of moving packets from an ingress interface to the correct egress interface at the maximum rate at which packets can arrive at the ingress interface. This requires forwarding logic that can process traffic at the rate at which it arrives, as well as a *nonblocking* backplane, which can carry traffic from ingress to egress interfaces at the rate at which it arrives. In this case, packets do not accumulate at the ingress interface—instead, they are always forwarded immediately to the egress interface. No queues form at the device's ingress interfaces.

3.1.2 Congestion

The situation at the egress interfaces of such devices may be quite different. Specifically, if multiple traffic flows arrive at different ingress interfaces, all destined for the same egress interface, the second-stage forwarder likely will be incapable of moving packets out of the device fast enough to prevent queues from building up on the egress interface. This is especially true if the transmission medium that carries packets to the next device has low capacity (also known as *bandwidth*). This condition is known as *congestion* and is illustrated in Figure 3.3.

Figure 3.3   Congestion at a Device's Egress Interface

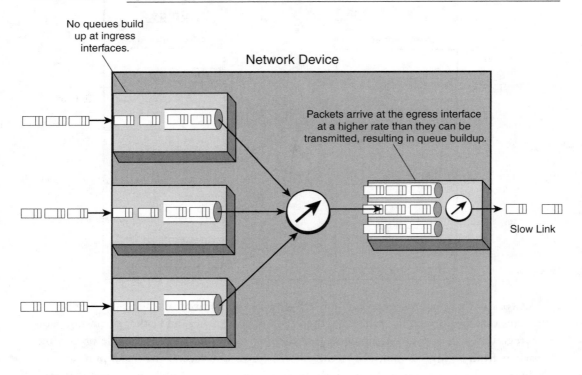

Note

Note that, although less common, congestion may also occur at the ingress interfaces of a device. Ingress congestion occurs either because traffic cannot be processed at the speed at which it arrives, or because it cannot be moved quickly enough across the backplane to the appropriate egress interface. Designing devices so that the performance of the ingress interfaces, the egress interfaces, and the backplane are all balanced can minimize ingress congestion.

The second-stage forwarder is analogous to an automobile traffic intersection at which traffic from a number of sources feeds into a single egress road. Queues form as automobiles wait their turn to clear the intersection. Traffic lights may be used to pace the rate at which traffic from different sources is allowed to pass through the intersection. In the network device, packets form queues on the egress interface as they wait their turn to be forwarded out the device. Queue scheduling algorithms then are used to pace the rate at which packets on different queues are forwarded out of the device.

In the simplest case, all packets on a congested egress interface form a single queue and are forwarded out the device in a first in, first out (FIFO) manner. In more sophisticated devices, traffic is separated into multiple queues by the process of classification (see the sidebar titled "Flows and Classifiers"). A queue-servicing algorithm determines the order and rate at which packets are forwarded from each of the queues. The combination of classification and queue-servicing strategy determines the QoS experienced by a particular traffic flow transiting the device. The remainder of this chapter describes various queuing strategies, queue-servicing algorithms, and their applications.

Although queuing may occur at multiple stages within a network device, the text generally discusses queues that are formed at the egress interface. Most of the principles discussed can be applied to any queuing stage.

Flows and Classifiers

In Chapter 1 (see the sidebar titled "Flows, Conversations, and Traffic Aggregates"), a traffic flow was described as a subset of all packets passing through a network device that has uniform QoS requirements. Thus, in a given network device, all traffic on a given flow will be carried on a corresponding queue and there can generally be considered to exist a one-to-one correspondence between a flow and a queue.

In network devices, classifiers are used to separate traffic into flows. These flows are then directed to the appropriate queues. Certain traffic-handling mechanisms require that traffic be separated into a large number of fine-grain flows, possibly as many as one per conversation. Other traffic-handling mechanisms separate traffic into fewer flows, aggregating multiple conversations into a small number of flows. In the former

continues

continued

case, many queues will be required and fine-grain classifiers will be required. In the latter case, fewer queues will be required. Classifiers may be (but are not required to be) coarser-grain.

3.2 Taxonomy of Queuing Mechanisms

For the purpose of this discussion, queuing mechanisms will be classified into several broad categories . The categories will be introduced in this section. Examples from each category will be discussed in depth later in the chapter. Categories of queuing schemes include the following:

- FIFO queuing

- Work-conserving queuing

- Non-work-conserving queuing

Dropping schemes will also be discussed, although these are not actually queuing mechanisms. Note that these categories are not strict; certain schemes may fall into multiple categories. For example, a single queue may be serviced in a manner that is both FIFO and work-conserving at the same time.

Often multiple queue-servicing algorithms may be in use simultaneously on the same interface. Note that dropping schemes are not queuing schemes. Nonetheless, they interact closely with queuing schemes and are an important aspect of traffic handling. Therefore, they are discussed in this chapter in connection with queuing schemes.

3.2.1 FIFO Queuing

FIFO is the simplest form of queuing. In FIFO queuing, all traffic is placed on the tail of a single queue, in the order in which it arrives. This is illustrated at the second stage forwarder in Figure 3.4. The forwarder removes packets one at a time from the head of the queue and transmits them onto the transmission medium. Because all traffic is queued on a single queue, all traffic is forwarded in the order in which it arrives at the queuing stage.

Figure 3.4   FIFO Queuing

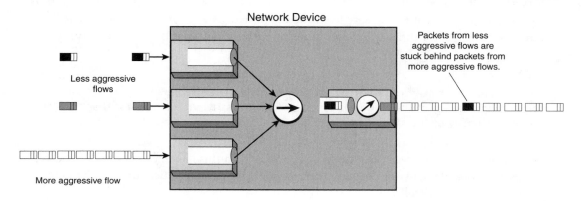

Queuing mechanisms are supposed to provide QoS by treating certain traffic preferentially over other traffic. Because FIFO queuing cannot alter the order in which packets are forwarded, the service experienced by a particular traffic flow depends entirely on the order in which packets on that flow arrive at the queuing stage, relative to packets on other flows. Thus, a high-bandwidth flow on which packets arrive very frequently will experience better service than a lower-bandwidth flow (on which packets arrive less frequently). Therefore, the FIFO queuing scheme is incapable of controlling the service allotted to a traffic flow and is of limited use in supporting QoS.

> **Note**
> Note that in FIFO queuing, the preservation of the FIFO ordering is *across* all flows. By contrast, in the queue servicing schemes discussed throughout this chapter, traffic is reordered *across* the scheduled flows, but generally remains FIFO *within* each flow.

3.2.2   Work-Conserving Queuing

In work-conserving queuing, packets are never held in queues if it is possible to forward them to the next stage. As long as the rate at which traffic is arriving at a stage is less than or equal to the rate at which traffic can be forwarded to the next stage, traffic will be forwarded immediately and no queues will form.

On the other hand, if traffic arrives at the stage at a rate higher than it can be forwarded, queues will form. The number of queues that actually form and the type of traffic directed to each queue will depend on the classification criteria used (see the sidebar titled "Flows and Classifiers"). As soon as capacity is available to forward traffic to the next stage, the queuing algorithm will select a packet from the appropriate queue, and the packet will be forwarded. It can be said that the clock or trigger that causes the next packet to be sent is the availability of a slot or capacity from the forwarder. As a result, work-conserving queue-servicing algorithms assure that available forwarding capacity never goes unused.

> **Note**
>
> This assumes that traffic arrives at an aggregate rate equal to or greater than the forwarding capacity of the stage. Of course, if traffic is arriving at a rate less than the forwarding capacity of the stage, capacity will go unused.

Work-conserving queuing is illustrated in Figure 3.5. In this illustration, each railroad car represents available network capacity. Each car carries a packet, indicating that the network capacity is used to its fullest.

Figure 3.5   Work-Conserving Queuing

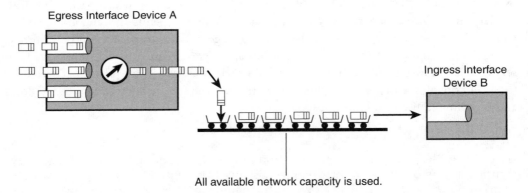

All available network capacity is used.

Work-conserving queue-servicing algorithms differ in terms of the scheme used to select the appropriate queue. For example, the simplest work-conserving queuing algorithm is *strict priority*. In a strict priority algorithm, queues are ordered in terms of priority. Lower-priority queues are serviced only when no packets are waiting on higher-priority queues. Strict priority queuing is common because it is very inexpensive to implement.

Work-conserving queue-servicing algorithms generally are used to share limited network capacity between flows that benefit from as much capacity (as high a bandwidth) as possible.

3.2.3   Non-Work-Conserving Queuing

In non-work-conserving queue-servicing schemes, forwarding capacity may purposefully be unused. These schemes use a clock to trigger the transmission of a packet (or a certain quantum of data) from a certain queue (usually for the purpose of forwarding traffic from the queue at a certain bit rate). For example, a non-work-conserving scheme may service a queue at a rate of one packet every 100 milliseconds. In this case, a timer will be set to expire every 100 milliseconds, and a packet will be forwarded from the queue each time the timer expires. The concept of non-work-conserving queuing is illustrated in the following diagram. Note that a real-time clock paces transmission of traffic from each flow. Network capacity is left unused (as indicated by the empty railroad cars).

| Figure 3.6 | Non-Work-Conserving Queuing |

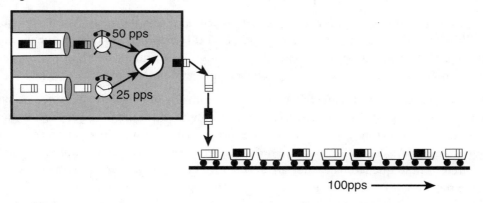

Non-work-conserving queue-servicing algorithms generally are used to limit the impact of a traffic flow on the part of the network to which it is being forwarded. This is analogous to the traffic lights that are used at highway on-ramps to control the pace at which traffic is allowed to enter the highway, thereby minimizing congestion on the highway. This application of non-work-conserving queuing can be considered a *policing* application because it is being used to limit the capacity available to an individual flow, in the interest of protecting a resource shared by multiple flows.

A common application of non-work-conserving queue-servicing schemes is in the pacing of multimedia traffic. Multimedia traffic (such as audio and video) can be consumed only at a limited rate. For example, it does not make sense to consume a 20Kbps audio signal at 40Kbps. Thus, non-work-conserving queue-servicing may be used to deliver an audio flow at a constant bit-rate equivalent to 20Kbps. This approach optimizes the use of network capacity, minimizes buffering requirements at the receiver, and has no adverse impact on the audio flow.

3.2.4 Dropping Schemes and Congestion Avoidance

Previous examples have focused on queue-servicing algorithms from the perspective of a forwarder that removes a packet from the head of a queue when it is ready to be forwarded. The packet is removed either when capacity is available (work-conserving queuing) or when a timer has expired (non-work-conserving queuing). Dropping schemes differ in the sense that they target packets for *dropping* rather than *forwarding*. Packets may be selected for dropping from their places in an existing queue or as they arrive, before they are enqueued. Dropping in this manner can help to avoid congestion.

Queues form in network devices as a result of congestion (or when non-work-conserving queuing schemes are used to purposefully create a bottleneck). In a functional network, the average rate of traffic arriving at a device over time is equal to the average rate at which traffic leaves the device. Thus, although queues may grow and shrink transiently, average queue lengths over time are expected to remain constant.

When queues grow in depth, device memory is required to hold the packets in the queues. In addition, the latencies experienced by packets held in deeper and deeper queues increase (and the QoS experienced by the packets decreases). When queue depth grows beyond a certain point, device memory is no longer available, and packets must be dropped.

Dropping schemes are designed to limit queue depths by intelligently selecting packets to be dropped as queue depths surpass certain preconfigured thresholds *before* device memory is exhausted and before congestion becomes problematic. As such, they can be considered *congestion-avoidance schemes*. Because dropping schemes reduce the amount of memory required to hold queued data, they are also referred to as *buffer-management schemes*. These schemes often are used simultaneously with the queuing schemes described previously (that service queues from their heads). One such dropping scheme is *random early detection* (RED), which will be discussed in the "An Alternative to Tail Dropping: Random Early Detection" section later in this chapter.

Figure 3.7 illustrates a queue with a high threshold and a low threshold. A dropper is shown selecting packets from the queue and then dropping them. When the queue depth reaches the low threshold, the dropper drops 5% of the queued packets. When the queue depth reaches the high threshold, the dropper drops 25%. A limited amount of memory is available for the queue (indicated by *max queue depth*); when this threshold is reached, no more packets can be queued. At this point, 100% of arriving packets will be dropped.

Figure 3.7 Dropping Schemes

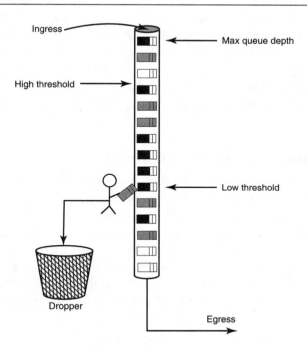

The dropping scheme illustrated selects the packets to be dropped at random. This scheme automatically penalizes the higher-bandwidth flows. Other dropping schemes favor certain flows over others. For example, Flows A and B may be targeted as soon as the low threshold is exceeded, while Flow C may be protected until the high threshold is exceeded.

3.3 Evaluation of Queuing Schemes

When evaluating the suitability of a queuing scheme, several criteria are of interest. First, the type of scheme must be appropriate for the task at hand. As described, work-conserving queuing schemes are designed to share available capacity optimally, while non-work-conserving schemes are designed to control the impact of a particular traffic flow on the network. Dropping schemes interact with queuing schemes. These control queue depth and, thereby, latency and drop probability. Each may be appropriate at different points in a network and for different types of traffic.

3.3.1 Processing Cost

Queuing schemes differ significantly in terms of the processing cost required to implement them. If the goal of a queuing scheme is to make effective use of forwarding capacity, this should be low cost to implement. If a processing scheme is expensive to implement, it may consume processing resources to the point that the total forwarding capacity of the network device is compromised. On rare occasions, it may be acceptable to compromise the total forwarding capacity to assure a particular flow a greater share of the capacity, but these cases are rare.

3.3.2 Bandwidth and Latency Guarantees

Queuing schemes provide QoS by controlling the forwarding capacity or bandwidth available to certain traffic flows and the latency experienced by packets on these flows. Egress interface capacity imposes an upper bound on the total rate at which traffic from all flows can be forwarded. One measure of a queuing scheme's effectiveness is the degree to which it can control the rate at which traffic on a particular flow is forwarded. An additional measure of a queuing scheme's effectiveness is the degree to which it can control the maximum latency experienced by a packet on a particular flow. This latency is the maximum amount of time that a given packet must wait before it is forwarded. Latency is generally a function of the interface capacity, the bandwidth provided to the corresponding flow, and the sequence in which the flows on the interface are serviced.

Jitter is another parameter that is affected by the choice of queuing mechanisms. Jitter refers to the *variation* in latency from packet to packet on the same flow.

3.4 Examples of Work-Conserving Queuing Schemes

As discussed previously, work-conserving queuing schemes are designed to use all available forwarding capacity by sharing it among a set of traffic flows. This section discusses several work-conserving queuing schemes.

3.4.1 Strict Priority Queuing

Strict priority queuing (also known as *priority queuing*) is the simplest of work-conserving queuing schemes. In this scheme, a set of queues is ordered according to priority. When capacity becomes available, the forwarder removes a packet from the highest-priority queue. If there are no packets on the highest priority queue, the forwarder removes a packet from the next highest-priority queue, and so forth. In this manner, a queue is serviced only when no packets are pending on any higher-priority queue.

Because priority queuing is so simple, it is inexpensive to implement. The complexity of priority queuing algorithms is $O(1)$.

Note

The notation $O(N)$ is read "order of N." It is a measure of *complexity* or processing cost. $O(1)$ indicates a constant processing cost. $O(N)$ indicates a processing cost that is directly related to N. $O(N^2)$ indicates a processing cost that is related to N-squared, and so forth.

Priority queuing is a very effective mechanism for handling extremely important traffic. In particular, it bounds the maximum latency for packets on the highest priority flow to P/r (where P is the largest packet size handled by the forwarder and r is the bit rate at which the forwarder can forward traffic).

Note

This latency bound is valid if there is a single high-priority flow. If there are multiple high-priority flows, they will compete with each other. Although a packet on a high-priority flow will be bound by P/r, a *specific* packet on a *specific* high-priority flow may experience a higher latency, as determined by the number of packets on other high-priority flows that are forwarded before it.

Figure 3.8 illustrates the worst-case latency of priority queuing. At time t_0, no packets are present on the high priority queue. Therefore, the forwarder forwards packets from the low-priority queue. At time t_1, packet 1 arrives on the high-priority queue. This packet would be transmitted immediately. However, the forwarder has *just* forwarded packet 5 on the low-priority queue for transmission. Because the forwarder cannot interrupt the transmission of a packet, packet 1 on the high-priority queue must wait for packet 5 on the low-priority queue to be transmitted before it can be forwarded for transmission. Thus, the packet on the high-priority queue has been delayed by the amount of time that it took for packet 5 from the low-priority queue to be transmitted.

Because packets on the highest-priority flow are always forwarded before packets on lower-priority flows, the fraction of forwarding capacity dedicated to the highest-priority flow is determined strictly by the rate of arrival of packets on this flow. As a result, if packets arrive for the high-priority flow at a rate equal to or in excess of the forwarding capacity of a device's egress interface, all forwarding capacity will be dedicated to the highest-priority flow. Although this result provides obvious benefits to the highest-priority flow, it also has the effect of *starving* all lower-priority flows.

Figure 3.8   Priority Queuing Latency

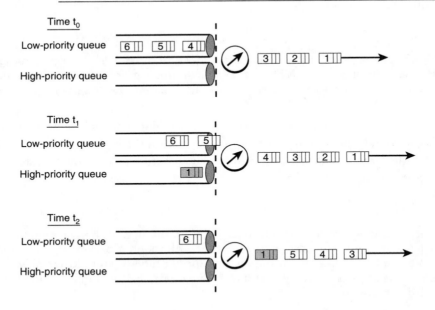

Because of its capability to starve traffic, strict priority queuing is rarely used in network devices and then only to a limited degree. One application of priority queuing is in optimizing service to critical *network control* traffic. This is traffic that is exchanged, typically at a low rate, between network devices and that is essential to the functioning of the network.

Another use of strict priority queuing is to service a single flow carrying user traffic that requires very strict latency control at a very low cost. In the first case, starvation of lower-priority traffic will occur only to the degree that critical network control traffic requires interface capacity. If this traffic is denied the capacity it requires, then the network is likely to fail and the starvation of all traffic becomes inevitable. In the second case, in which certain user traffic is given strict priority, the starving of lower-priority traffic is prevented by *policing* it. Typically, this is achieved by limiting the rate at which the user traffic is admitted to the high-priority queue to some low percentage of the interface's forwarding capacity. Packets arriving in excess of this rate may be discarded or delayed.

Strict priority queuing may be used in conjunction with other queuing schemes on the same interface. For example, a single high-priority queue may be created for network control traffic, while multiple lower-priority queues are created to share remaining capacity fairly among all lower-priority traffic flows, using an alternate queuing scheme.

3.4.2 Fair Queuing Algorithms

Earlier in this chapter, FIFO queuing was demonstrated to be *unfair* because it rewarded aggressive traffic flows at the expense of less aggressive flows. The QoS experienced by a traffic flow depends on the relative behaviors of the sources generating traffic on different flows. FIFO queuing in network devices therefore encourages greedy behavior on the part of traffic sources. This leaves the network manager helpless to control the allocation of shared network resources among different traffic sources.

Strict priority queuing is also unfair because it intentionally gives resources to higher-priority flows (with the possible consequence of completely denying resources to lower-priority flows). Strict priority queuing differs from FIFO queuing in that it takes the control of unfairness away from the traffic sources and yields it instead to the network manager. This is somewhat preferable because the network manager can be assumed to make decisions in the interest of all traffic sources. However, although priority queuing can be used to provide preferential treatment to traffic flows that can clearly be deemed higher priority, it is ill-suited to sharing resources fairly among flows that may have equal or similar priority. For example, it may be desirable to provide equal portions of forwarding capacity to all flows at a certain priority level. Alternatively, it may be desirable to provide certain flows relatively higher (but not unrestricted) shares of forwarding capacity.

Similar considerations apply to latency. Although FIFO queuing makes no guarantees regarding the latency on any particular flow, strict priority queuing provides very strict latency guarantees, but only for the highest-priority flow. Traffic on all other flows is subject to unlimited latency bounds.

A need exists for a queuing mechanism that is capable of more fairly controlling the relative forwarding capacity and latency guarantees that can be provided to individual flows. Mechanisms that meet this requirement are the various forms of *fair queuing*.

3.4.2.1 Nagle's Fair Queuing

The simplest form of fair queuing was proposed by Nagle [Nag87], [RFC 896]. In Nagle's scheme, a set of queues is serviced in rotation, in fixed order. In each *round*, a single packet is removed from the head of each queue and is forwarded. This scheme indeed promotes fairness among queues by assuring that a packet is forwarded from each queue in turn. See Figure 3.9.

Figure 3.9   Simple Fair Queuing

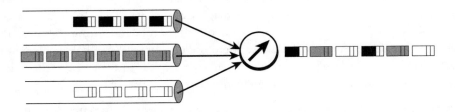

Nagle's fair-queuing algorithm is very simple. The complexity of the algorithm is $O(1)$. If all queued packets are of equal size, then Nagle's algorithm also allocates forwarding capacity among the queues with perfect fairness. In the case of N queues, packets from each queue will be forwarded at a rate equal to $^1/_{Nth}$ of the forwarder's capacity. In addition, Nagle's algorithm offers a latency bound that is determined strictly by the packet size and N. The maximum latency experienced by a packet is

$$(N - 1) \times P/r$$

Here, N is the number of queues or flows, P is the largest packet size handled by the forwarder, and r is the bit rate at which the forwarder can forward traffic.

Nagle's algorithm suffers from a number of problems, however. In packet-switched networks, packet sizes are not uniform. Consider an example in which data traffic (with an average packet size close to 1500 bytes) is placed on one queue and voice traffic (with an average packet size of 64 bytes) is placed on another queue. In this case, the simple fair-queuing algorithm will yield a significantly greater portion of the forwarder's capacity to the data queue. The ratio of capacity yielded to the two queues would be roughly 1500/64. This effect is illustrated in Figure 3.10.

Figure 3.10   Effect of Packet Size on Allocation of Capacity Using Simple Per-Packet Fair Queuing

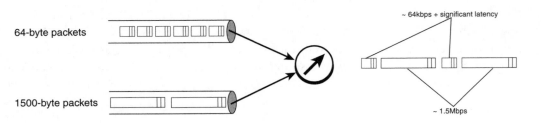

In this illustration, the two queues on the left are serviced in order, with one packet being removed from each queue in each round. However, because the packets on the lower queue are so much larger than those on the upper queue, packets from the lower queue consume a disproportionate share of the forwarding capacity. Furthermore, each small packet experiences significant latency because it must wait for a large packet to be transmitted.

Although latency bounds can be strictly predicted based on the number of queues and the maximum packet size, this may not be strictly controllable. The number of queues depends on the classification scheme used and may vary significantly. In addition, the dependency on maximum packet size is problematic. In the example described in the previous paragraph, the voice traffic would suffer unfair latency because of the large packet size associated with the data traffic.

3.4.2.2 *Bitwise Round Robin*

The deficiencies of Nagle's algorithm largely result from the fact that the unit removed from a queue (the unit *dequeued*) in each round is a packet. If it were possible to dequeue a single *bit* in each round, then the distribution of packet sizes would be irrelevant. Each queue would receive $1/_N$ of the forwarding capacity, regardless of packet size. Similarly, the latency experienced by a packet would be significantly improved and would not depend on the size of packets on other queues. This scheme is known as *bitwise round robin*.

Note

In ATM technology (which will be discussed in depth in Chapter 8, "QoS over Layer 2 Media Other Than 802"), the scheduled units are *cells* rather than packets. These are limited to 53 bytes in size and therefore offer a better approximation to bitwise round robin than packet-scheduling schemes.

Unfortunately, it is not practical to forward data in single-bit units. However, Demers, Keshav, and Shenker [DKS] have proposed a practical approximation to the bitwise round-robin algorithm, which enjoys many of the benefits of the theoretical algorithm. Because their scheme has served as the basis for most fair-queuing implementations, we will refer to it simply as *fair queuing*.

3.4.2.3 *Fair Queuing*

In this scheme, each packet is assigned a *completion time*. The completion time is the theoretical time at which the packet would be completely forwarded *if* all queues were serviced using a bitwise round robin scheme. The packet is then inserted into a list of packets that is sorted according to their completion time. The forwarder dequeues packets from the head of this list as capacity becomes available. Packets with an earlier completion time are forwarded before packets with a later completion time. The calculation of a packet's completion time is based on the number of flows, so the algorithm is still based on a presumption of a *logical* queue corresponding to each flow. Fair queuing is illustrated in Figure 3.11.

Figure 3.11   Fair Queuing

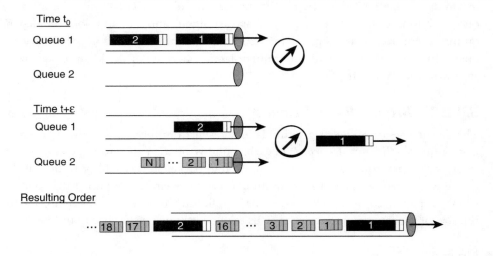

Figure 3.11 shows two queues. Packets on Queue 1 are 1000 bits in size. Packets on Queue 2 are 60 bits in size. At time t_0, two packets arrive on Queue 1. A very short time later (at time $t + \varepsilon$), some large number of packets arrives on Queue 2.

At time t_0, there are no packets on Queue 2, so the forwarder forwards the first packet on Queue 1. However, at time $t + \varepsilon$, the forwarder must decide how to order the remaining Queued packets. Assuming that in each round, 1 bit is forwarded from each queue, then the first packet on Queue 2 would be completely transmitted 60 rounds later. The second packet on Queue 2 would be completely transmitted 120 rounds later, and so forth. On the other hand, the next packet on Queue 1 would be completely transmitted 1,000 rounds later. Based on these completion times, the fair-queuing algorithm would order the first 16 packets on Queue 2 before the second packet on Queue 1, as illustrated.

This scheme has several appealing properties. It guarantees fairness in its allocation of forwarding capacity among different flows. In addition, it closely approximates the low-latency guarantees that are offered by the theoretical bitwise round robin scheme. In fact, the fair-queuing algorithm described by Demers, Keshav, and Shenker [DKS] can be used to reward flows that use less than their fair share of forwarding capacity by further reducing their latency bound.

> **Note**
>
> There is an implicit assumption here that *fair* is *good*. In certain cases, economic or other policy factors may invalidate this assumption.

This characteristic of fair queuing makes it particularly appealing in scenarios in which, for example, a number of voice flows and a number of data flows are serviced simultaneously. Consider that the voice flows are (by the nature of voice) rate-limited at their source. Most data flows (such as FTP) are not and will consume as much bandwidth as is available to them (subject to TCP flow control). Because traffic on a voice flow arrives at the queuing stage at a rate so much lower than traffic on a data flow, voice traffic will consume less than its fair share of the forwarding capacity. Rewarding the voice traffic for this behavior by lowering its latency is of great value to the latency-intolerant voice traffic. Several existing routers and switches implement fair queuing precisely for this reason.

Unfortunately, however, fair queuing is expensive to implement. Unlike previous algorithms described (which have a complexity of $O[1]$), fair-queuing has a complexity of $O(\log[N])$, where N is the number of queues. This cost results from the need to insert packets in a sorted list. Thus, it is impractical (barring significant improvements in hardware implementations) to implement fair queuing on high-speed forwarders.

3.4.2.4 Stochastic Fair Queuing

McKenney [MCK91] proposed hashing traffic from multiple flows into some limited number of queues to reduce N, thereby improving the efficiency of all fair queuing schemes for which complexity is a function of N. Although this approach does indeed improve the efficiency of such schemes, it also compromises the fairness guarantees offered. This is because traffic from multiple flows may hash to the same queue, so fairness between these flows is sacrificed. As such, stochastic fair queuing offers a trade-off between processing efficiency and degree of fairness achieved.

3.4.2.5 *Deficit Round Robin*

Shreedhar and Varghese [DRR] have proposed a variation on fair queuing known as *deficit round robin (DRR)*. DRR approximates the benefits of fair queuing (at least, in terms of fairness in the sharing of forwarding capacity), but at a significantly lower cost. Its complexity is $O(1)$.

The problem with the low-cost simple round robin scheme was that it did not account for packet sizes. Fair queuing accounts for packet size by computing a completion time that depends on the packet size. The greater the packet size, the later the completion time. The later the completion time, the farther back in the forwarding list the packet is inserted and the longer it waits to be forwarded. The complexity of fair queuing results from the work involved in determining where to insert a packet in the forwarding list. Fair queuing does not service flows in a round-robin manner.

By contrast, DRR does service flows in a round-robin manner. In each round, a fixed number of *credits* is added to each queue. The packet from the head of the queue is forwarded only if the size of the packet is equal to or smaller than the number of credits accumulated for the queue. If the packet is forwarded, the number of credits is reduced accordingly. This is the manner in which DRR accounts for packet size. Additional packets are forwarded from the head of the queue until the number of credits remaining is insufficient to forward the packet at the head of the queue (or until there are no packets pending). At this time, the number of credits is cleared to 0, and the next queue is immediately serviced.

If the packet at the head of a queue is too big to be forwarded (a credit *deficit*), credits are allowed to accumulate until, on a subsequent round, there are sufficient credits to forward the packet (refer to Figure 3.12).

Note

Note that DRR is a work-conserving scheme. If all queues are blocked because of insufficient credits, rounds are immediately processed to add sufficient credits to forward another packet.

Deficits are tracked and queues are eventually compensated for previous deficits. The number of credits added to a queue in each round is referred to as the *quantum*. The quantum has a significant effect on the behavior of the DRR algorithm.

Figure 3.12   Deficit Round Robin

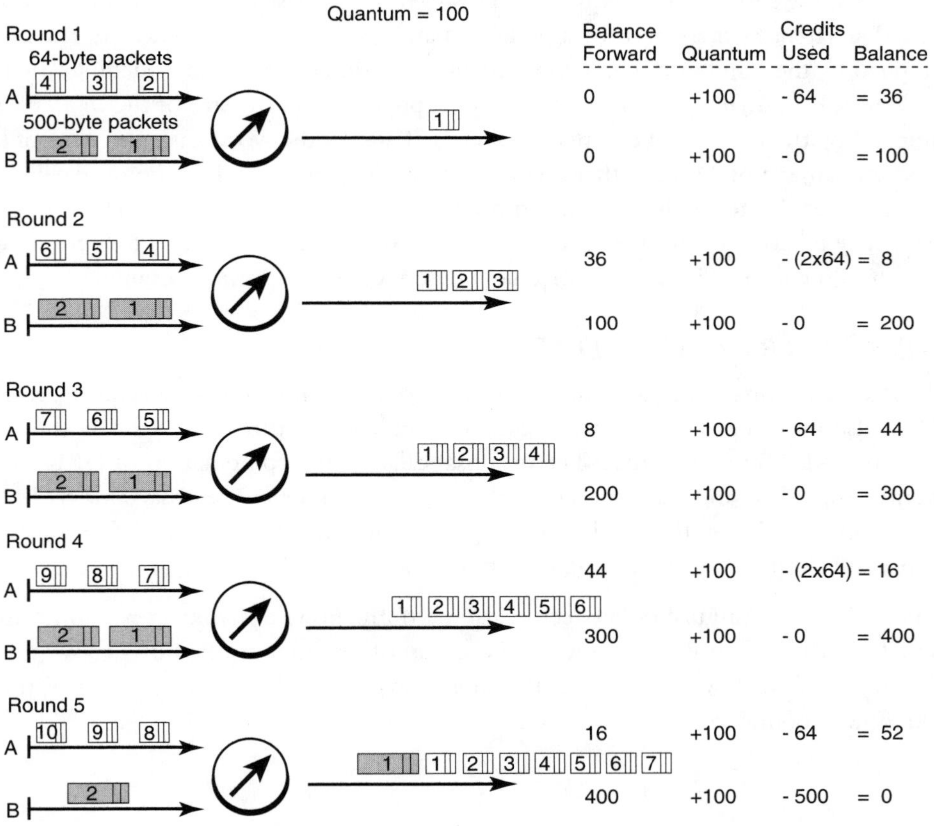

	Balance Forward	Quantum	Credits Used	Balance

Quantum = 100

Round 1
64-byte packets

A [4] [3] [2] →   0   +100   - 64   = 36

500-byte packets   [1]

B [2] [1] →   0   +100   - 0   = 100

Round 2

A [6] [5] [4] →   [1] [2] [3]   36   +100   - (2x64)   = 8

B [2] [1] →   100   +100   - 0   = 200

Round 3

A [7] [6] [5] →   [1] [2] [3] [4]   8   +100   - 64   = 44

B [2] [1] →   200   +100   - 0   = 300

Round 4

A [9] [8] [7] →   44   +100   - (2x64)   = 16
                    [1] [2] [3] [4] [5] [6]
B [2] [1] →   300   +100   - 0   = 400

Round 5

A [10] [9] [8] →   16   +100   - 64   = 52
              [1] [1] [2] [3] [4] [5] [6] [7]
B [2] →   400   +100   - 500   = 0

DRR can offer fairness comparable to fair-queuing (in terms of forwarding capacity). If the quantum selected is equal to (or greater than) the maximum packet size, then DRR is also significantly less costly than fair queuing. However, in the case of DRR, latency is compromised. The latency experienced by a packet on any given queue is bounded by the quantum multiplied by the number of competing queues. By comparison, in fair queuing, the latency experienced by a small packet is bounded by (approximately) the size of the *small* packet multiplied by the number of competing queues. Thus, in the worst case, the ratio of latency bound guaranteed by DRR to that guaranteed by fair-queuing is the ratio of maximum queued packet size to minimum queued packet size. The disadvantages of DRR in terms of latency may be even greater for flows that use less than their fair share of forwarding capacity (such as the latency-intolerant voice flow described in the previous example).

3.4.2.6   *DRR+ or Class DRR*

In [DRR], Shreedhar and Varghese propose a modification to DRR, which they refer to as DRR+ (also known as *class DRR*). The goal of this modification is to alleviate the poor latency bounds offered by DRR. The proposal calls for the combination of DRR with fair queuing. Shreedhar and Varghese argue that latency bounds are necessary for *real-time* (such as multimedia) traffic, while other types of traffic need a fair share of forwarding capacity but do not require strict latency bounds.

As such, DRR+ distinguishes between real-time traffic flows and *latency-tolerant* traffic flows. The DRR+ forwarder prioritizes the group of real-time traffic flows above the group of latency-tolerant flows. As a result, the latency experienced by packets on a real-time traffic flow is bounded to

$$((N \times P) + P') / r$$

Here, N is the number of real-time flows, P is the maximum packet size on the real-time flows, P' is the maximum packet size on the latency-tolerant flows, and r is the forwarding capacity.

DRR+ effectively subdivides traffic into two classes, with one class granted strict priority over the other class. Fair queuing is used to share capacity among flows within the high-priority class, while DRR is used to share capacity among flows within the low-priority class. Assuming that the majority of flows are in the lower-priority class, the majority of work done is $O(1)$. Thus, the combination of queue-servicing algorithms reduces processing burden while meeting the QoS requirements of both traffic types.

In general, DRR+ can be used with more than two classes. Combining several queuing schemes in this manner is not uncommon. In fact, most sophisticated QoS-capable network devices handle traffic using combinations of queuing schemes rather than a single scheme.

3.4.2.7   Weighted Fair-Queuing Schemes

The preceding discussion of fair-queuing schemes implied that forwarding capacity is shared fairly when each flow gets an equivalent share of the capacity. In the case that the classification and queuing schemes have no information regarding the nature of the various traffic flows, this approach might be reasonable. However, in general, implicit or explicit information regarding the various flows is available at network devices. This information can be used to share capacity among flows unequally.

> **Note**
>
> Unequal sharing should not be considered unfair sharing. For example, audio flows generally need less forwarding capacity than data flows but are also less latency-tolerant. A scheme that gives these flows less forwarding capacity and improved latency bounds (as compared with data flows) is a fair scheme.

When available information dictates unequal shares of forwarding capacity, *weights* can be applied to different queues in the various fair-queuing schemes. These weights can be used to determine the share of forwarding capacity allocated to each queue. This is known as *weighted fair queuing* (WFQ).

In the case of the fair-queuing algorithm devised by Demers, Keshav, and Shenker [DKS], these weights are used to bias the calculation of packet completion times. For example, if the packet completion time calculated is divided by the weight assigned to a queue, then queues with larger weights will be favored with increased shares of forwarding capacity and reduced latencies.

In the case of the DRR algorithm devised by Shreedhar and Varghese [DRR], weights can be used to manipulate the quantum associated with the different queues. For example, if the quantum is multiplied by the associated weight, then queues with larger weights will be favored with increased shares of forwarding capacity.

In practical implementations, weights generally are not used on a per-conversation basis. Rather, they are used to bias certain aggregate flows. For example, a router may assign all conversations that are identified and classified by RSVP signaling to a higher-weight queue than those conversations that are not.

3.5   Examples of Non-Work-Conserving Queuing Schemes

As discussed previously, non-work-conserving queuing schemes typically are used to control the impact of traffic on the network by limiting the rate at which it is forwarded to the network. This function will be referred to in the remainder of this chapter as *traffic shaping*.

Multimedia (or *real-time*) traffic lends itself quite naturally to traffic shaping. Although this traffic may be somewhat bursty, it generally has relatively quantifiable and limited resource requirements. Furthermore, it does not benefit from resources beyond those required. Other traffic does not naturally lend itself to traffic shaping; it tends to be very bursty, has no quantifiable resource requirements, and generally benefits from as much resource as can be allocated to it.

Non-work-conserving queuing typically is used to shape traffic either at the traffic source or in network devices near the periphery of the network. Because it is costly (in terms of processing power), it generally is not used in the core of the network, where speeds are higher, the number of traffic flows requiring shaping is higher, and processing power is at a premium. Real-time traffic usually is shaped at the source, based on the requirements of the source (such as *CODEC* profiles).

Note

CODECs (or coders/decoders) are devices that convert analog audio or video signals into packetized digital data (and vice-versa). They generally do so subject to certain quantifiable parameters.

Both real-time and non-real-time traffic may be shaped at various points within (but near the periphery of) the network, based on network policies. Real-time traffic generally is shaped by the transmitting host on a per-conversation basis. Non-real-time traffic usually is shaped in aggregate (across multiple conversations). For example, all traffic leaving a corporate site and traveling to an ISP may be shaped in a single aggregate class. Alternatively, the traffic may be subdivided into a number of smaller aggregates (such as by department or by type of traffic), each of which is shaped separately.

3.5.1 Shaping Parameters and Buckets

Non-work-conserving queuing schemes or traffic-shaping schemes shape traffic according to a set of parameters. A trivial shaping parameter would specify a single traffic rate to which a flow must be shaped. For example, it could specify that a flow should be shaped to 64Kbps.

Although such parameterization is indeed very simple, it is also impractical. All traffic, real-time or not, is bursty to some degree. Shaping is used to control the impact of bursts on the network, but it is not used to completely eliminate bursts. To account for the bursty nature of traffic, two shaping models are used: the *leaky bucket* model and the *token bucket* model.

3.5.1.1 *Leaky Bucket Model*

The leaky bucket model is illustrated in Figure 3.13. Traffic arriving at the queuing stage is inserted into the bucket from the top. A hole in the bottom of the bucket allows traffic to leak out at a fixed rate (r). This is the rate at which the forwarding stage would forward the traffic to the network. The bucket has a fixed size (B). Traffic arriving at a rate equal to or less than r will simply be forwarded at the rate at which it arrives (see Figure 3.13a). Traffic arriving at a rate in excess of the leak rate of the bucket will accumulate in the bucket (see Figure 3.13b). If traffic arrives at too high a rate, it eventually will overflow the bucket and will be dropped or discarded (see Figure 3.13c).

Figure 3.13	Leaky Bucket

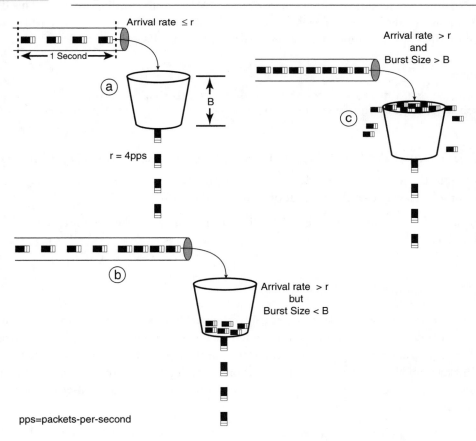

pps=packets-per-second

The leaky bucket model is attractive from the network's perspective because it has the effect of smoothing traffic that is delivered to the network. Traffic entering a leaky bucket queuing stage may arrive in bursts of back-to-back packets. These bursts are absorbed in the bucket and are dribbled out of the queuing stage at a maximum rate equal to the bucket's leak rate. Smoothing traffic in the network reduces demands on the memory required for buffer space in downstream network devices. If bursts were forwarded directly to the next queuing stage, these likely would have to be absorbed by buffers in the subsequent stage. In general, the relatively deterministic nature of smoothed traffic (versus the erratic behavior of bursty traffic) facilitates admission control decisions and enables the network resources to be managed more efficiently.

For example, assume that a network device has 1Mbps of forwarding capacity. This device can admit exactly 10 flows if each is sourced by a leaky bucket queuing stage with a leak rate of 100Kbps. Only minimal buffering will be required.

Note

Note that as traffic moves through network devices, its shape is distorted. Thus, to minimize buffering throughout the network, it is necessary to reshape it periodically.

Limitations of the Leaky Bucket When Applied to Application Traffic Sources

Although the leaky bucket model is ideal from the network perspective, it is less than ideal from the perspective of the application sourcing the traffic.

The leaky bucket model requires applications to parameterize their requirements using two parameters:

- The leak rate

- The bucket depth

Applications may specify a leak rate equal to the peak rate at which they source traffic. This would assure that none of their traffic would be discarded. However, applications generally source traffic at an average rate much lower than their peak rate. Requesting the network to make admission control decisions based on a peak rate would tend to result in an over-commitment of resources. The charge for this would be passed to the user of the application sourcing the traffic.

Alternatively, applications may specify a leak rate equal to their average rate. Although this would be less costly in terms of the resources committed by the network, it places a heavy burden on the application, requiring it to be very conservative in its specification of average rate (to select a high average rate) or to strictly control its burst behavior (to avoid passing any bursts to the network). An alternative to the leaky bucket, known as the *token bucket* model, is better suited to most applications.

3.5.1.2   Token Bucket Model

The goal of a shaping model used to shape application traffic should be to improve the predictability of the traffic from the network's perspective while at the same time accommodating typical application traffic patterns. The *token bucket* model assumes a bucket of depth B that is filled with tokens at a rate r. Each time a packet is available for forwarding, the forwarder must remove a token from the bucket. When no tokens are available, the forwarder must either drop packets or delay their forwarding. The token bucket model is illustrated in Figure 3.14.

| Figure 3.14 | Token Bucket |

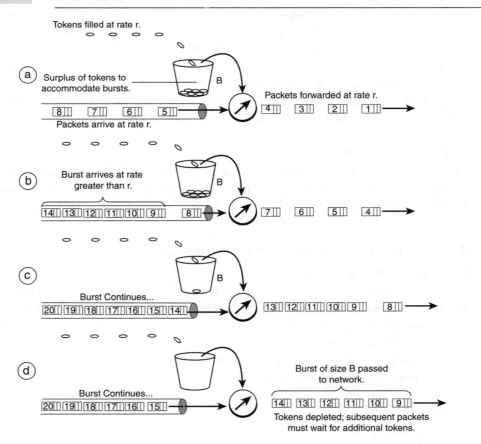

The bucket is filled with tokens at the rate r. In Figure 3.14a, packets arrive for transmission at the same rate. A surplus of six tokens is available in the bucket. Because tokens are available, packets can be forwarded to the network at the rate at which they arrive. Packets are arriving at the same rate that tokens are accumulating, so the token surplus is maintained.

In Figure 3.14b, a burst of packets is shown to arrive for transmission.

In Figure 3.14c, the first five tokens have been used to forward the first five packets of the burst to the network.

In Figure 3.14d, the last token is used to forward the sixth packet of the burst to the network. Packets are continuing to arrive in rapid succession, but the tokens are depleted. Therefore, the burst can no longer be forwarded to the network. Packets must be forwarded at the token rate until a surplus of tokens accumulates again.

The token bucket allows the application to pass bursts up to the bucket size to the network while limiting the long-term average rate at which traffic is passed to the network (to r). From the network's perspective, some predictability is lost in the sense that network devices may have to accommodate bursts. However, the size and frequency of bursts generated by any single application are limited by the token bucket parameters. Devices can leverage statistical multiplexing (see the accompanying note on statistical multiplexing) to admit traffic from multiple token bucket sources by providing some finite level of buffering.

Note

Statistical multiplexing is a method of combining multiple traffic sources, each with widely varying traffic patterns, into a single traffic flow. The resulting flow generally has more predictable traffic patterns and consequently can be serviced more efficiently.

3.5.1.3 The Combination of Token Bucket and Leaky Bucket

At first glance, the leaky bucket and token bucket models appear quite similar. The distinction between them is subtle. Each is parameterized by a bucket depth and a rate. The only difference between the two is that the leaky bucket absorbs the application's bursts at its input, smoothing them out before they are passed to the network. The token bucket, by contrast, passes the bursts directly to the network. Neither model will tolerate bursts in excess of the bucket size. Similarly, neither model will allow traffic to be passed to the network at an average rate exceeding r.

In most applications, the two models are combined as illustrated in Figure 3.15.

Figure 3.15 Token Bucket with Leaky Bucket

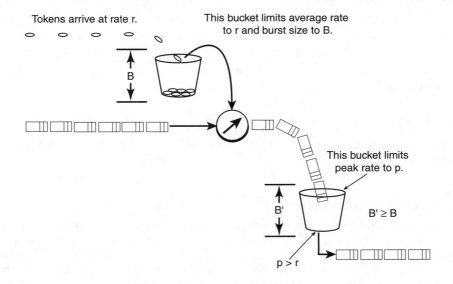

Tokens arrive at rate r.

This bucket limits average rate to r and burst size to B.

B

This bucket limits peak rate to p.

B'   B' ≥ B

p > r

Tokens are deposited in the token bucket at the average rate, *r*. Bursts of arriving packets up to size *B* can be forwarded immediately to the leaky bucket. Bursts in excess of *B* must be dropped or delayed because no tokens will be available to accommodate them. The leaky bucket that follows the token bucket can absorb the bursts passed by the token bucket, but it limits the rate at which these are passed to the network to a peak rate of *p*.

In this combination, the token bucket rate is set to the average rate at which the application sources traffic. The leaky bucket rate is set to the peak rate at which the application generates traffic (the burst rate). The resulting model is characterized by three parameters:

- The bucket depth (B)

- The average token rate (r)

- The peak rate (p)

The application is allowed to pass bursts of size *B* to the network as long as it does not exceed the average token rate. Within bursts, traffic will be limited to the peak rate. The network is guaranteed that, over a given time interval represented by *t*, the forwarder will forward no more than $B + (r \times t)$ units of traffic. It is further guaranteed that the forwarder will never forward traffic from this source at a rate exceeding *p* and that, on the average, it will forward traffic at the rate *r*.

This combination represents a practical compromise between allowing the application to burst and smoothing the flow of traffic to the network. Network devices are capable of applying statistical multiplexing effectively in making admission control decisions regarding flows that are forwarded by the combination token bucket and leaky bucket model. The combination model is so commonly used that it has come to be known as the *token bucket model* (even though, strictly speaking, the token bucket refers only to the front-end component, parameterized by B and r).

Note

A common variant on the model illustrated is the *dual-bucket* model, in which both stages are token bucket stages.

Shaping versus Discarding

As explained previously, neither the leaky bucket nor the token bucket is tolerant of bursts in excess of the bucket size. The same is true of the combination token bucket model. Traffic that arrives at a token bucket queuing stage when there are no tokens in the bucket must be discarded or detained until tokens accumulate. Detained packets must be stored in memory. Memory is a precious commodity in network devices that must be shared across all traffic sources. Consequently, network devices tend to discard excess traffic from a misbehaving source rather than storing it until tokens are available. In this manner, network devices use the token bucket model to *police* traffic. Note that in this example, the token bucket policer is a queuing stage that operates at the network device's *ingress* interface.

On the other hand, traffic sources may employ token bucket or leaky bucket *shapers* to prepare their traffic for submission to the network so that it will not violate the network's token bucket policer. An example of such a source is a host that generates application traffic. The application or the host's network stack may shape traffic to the token bucket parameters by queuing excess traffic in memory until tokens are available to forward it. In this case, the shaper is a queuing stage that operates at the host's *egress* interface. Generally, the use of a leaky bucket shaper as opposed to a token bucket shaper results in less loss at the subsequent policing stage.

3.6 *Link Sharing and Class-Based Queuing*

The various work-conserving queuing schemes described earlier in this chapter are all means of sharing limited forwarding capacity fairly among multiple traffic flows. They guarantee a *minimum* share of forwarding capacity (and, hence, a minimum bandwidth) to each traffic flow. On the other hand, the non-work-conserving queuing described shapes traffic, in effect imposing a *maximum* limit on the share of forwarding capacity granted to a traffic flow. The different types of queuing schemes serve traffic flows that have fundamentally different queuing objectives.

In most practical applications, it is desirable to accommodate both types of traffic flows. In addition, it is desirable to accommodate multiple levels of sharing hierarchy (as described in the following paragraphs). To this end, it is helpful to define *classes* of traffic flows. Each class has specific queuing objectives and a specific position in the sharing hierarchy. *Class-based queuing* (CBQ) is a formal framework for describing the relationship between these classes [CBQ].

3.6.1 *Sharing Hierarchy*

It is possible for example, to use WFQ to assure 30% of forwarding capacity to traffic from Dept. A and 70% of forwarding capacity to traffic from Dept B. This is achieved by assigning the queue for Dept. A's traffic a weight of 3 and the queue for Dept. B's traffic a weight of 7. When one of the departments is sourcing less than its share of traffic, the unused forwarding capacity will be available to the other department. In times of congestion, each department will be limited to its allotted share. As such, each department can *borrow* unused forwarding capacity from the other.

This example illustrates sharing forwarding capacity using a single level of hierarchy. It is often desirable to share forwarding capacity between traffic sources using multiple levels of hierarchy. For example, assume that WFQ is used to share forwarding capacity on a trans-Atlantic link between two companies. Assume further that within each company, it is desirable to share forwarding capacity between two departments. This is illustrated in Figure 3.16.

Figure 3.16   Single versus Multiple Levels of Hierarchy

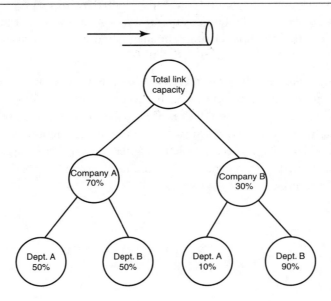

In this example, the sharing rules may be somewhat more complicated than for a single-level hierarchy. In particular, when one of the departments is sourcing less than its share of traffic, the unused forwarding capacity should be available to the other department *in the same company*. If the other department in the same company is incapable of taking advantage of the excess capacity, then the excess may be made available to departments *in the other company*. Borrowing is occurring at two levels.

- At the lowest level, there is borrowing between departments within a company.

- At a higher level, there is borrowing between companies. There is no easy way to express this hierarchy using simple WFQ.

3.6.2   Class-Based Queuing

As explained previously, class-based queuing is a framework that accommodates classes of traffic flows that have different queuing objectives and specific positions in a sharing hierarchy. This method of queuing assumes a combination of a subset of the fundamental queuing schemes described previously, each implemented by a *general scheduler*. The general schedulers apply one of the fundamental queuing schemes to a class of traffic, without regard to the position of the class in the class-based queuing hierarchy.

An *estimator* tracks the utilization of forwarding capacity by each class in the hierarchy. When a class is under capacity and excess capacity can be made available to other classes—or, alternatively, when a class is over capacity—the estimator invokes the *link-sharing scheduler*. The link-sharing scheduler runs in parallel with the general schedulers and enforces the borrowing constraints dictated by the sharing hierarchy. In this role, it may reconfigure one or more of the general schedulers as necessary, or it may directly regulate a class that is over capacity. Note that the link-sharing scheduler is required to be active only in times of congestion.

CBQ is generally quite complex and, therefore, computationally intensive. Recently, a number of high-performance switches have become available that support variations on CBQ in silicon. These sophisticated devices are capable of accommodating the different objectives of real-time traffic and non-real-time traffic simultaneously, at high speeds. Certain midrange devices are also available that offer software-based approximations of CBQ. These are limited to lower speeds and commonly are used to drive lower- and medium-rate WAN links.

3.7   Examples of Dropping Schemes

When congestion occurs, traffic cannot be forwarded and must instead be queued in the memory of network devices. Unless such congestion can be managed, device memory may be exhausted and packets arriving at a queuing stage must be dropped. In the simplest case, packets are dropped from the *tails* of the various packet queues. This is known simply as *tail dropping*. Tail dropping can result in drops of entire bursts of packets arriving in proximity.

3.7.1   Problems with Tail Dropping

Because of this behavior, tail dropping is problematic from a number of perspectives. For one, it tends to penalize bursty traffic flows without consideration for the average utilization by the traffic flow of its fair share of forwarding capacity. For example, a burst of traffic arriving when a queue is nearly full will mostly be dropped, even though the corresponding flow may not have contributed significantly to the filling of the queue.

In addition, tail-dropping causes a *global synchronization* effect when used with transport protocols that respond to packet drops. Consider TCP senders. A host sending traffic on a TCP connection or conversation will back off dramatically in response to dropped packets. If traffic arrives from a number of different TCP connections while queues are full, packets will be dropped from all connections, and all connections will back off simultaneously. As a result, the queuing stage will be underutilized until the connections ramp back up to capacity.

3.7.2   An Alternative to Tail Dropping: Random Early Detection

An alternative to tail dropping is to drop packets that are already queued rather than packets that would fall off the tails of queues. By dropping packets at random from different locations within each queue, the problems associated with tail dropping can be avoided. This approach is known as *random early detection* or *RED* [RED]. Simple implementations of RED begin selecting a certain percentage of packets for dropping at random when queues reach a certain configurable depth.

The randomness of this approach tends to distribute drops evenly across multiple connections. Thus, it avoids both the bias against bursty connections and the global synchronization effect described. It also offers the benefit of penalizing those traffic flows that are utilizing greater shares of the forwarding capacity, simply because they have more packets in the queue.

3.7.2.1 *Weighted Random Early Detection*

In *weighted random early detection* (WRED), different dropping behavior is applied to different traffic flows. The behavior applied to each flow is parameterized by queue depth thresholds and drop percentage. This is illustrated in Figure 3.17.

Figure 3.17   Weighted Random Early Detection Queuing

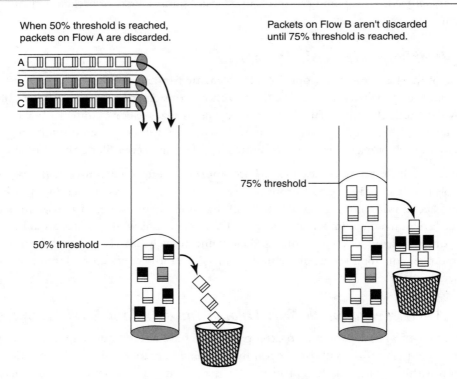

In this scheme, all traffic flows are considered to share a single queue (which may be a real queue or a virtual queue). Traffic is not dropped from a flow until the queue reaches a threshold depth associated with that flow. When the threshold is reached, a certain percentage of the flow's traffic is dropped at random. Flows that are associated with higher queue thresholds (and/or lower drop percentages) will experience improved QoS over flows that are associated with lower queue thresholds (and/or higher drop percentages). Not only will these flows experience lower drop probability, but they also will experience lower latencies because competing, less important traffic will be dropped sooner, maintaining lower average queue depths. In fact, because of the general reduction in queue depth, all traffic transiting the queuing stage will experience lower latency.

In sophisticated implementations of WRED, multiple thresholds can be designated for each flow, with a corresponding drop percentage. For example, a WRED scheduler could be configured to drop 5% of traffic from flow A when the queue reaches a depth of 1KB, 50% when it reaches 10KB, and 100% when it reaches 100KB. Considering that such parameters may be applied independently to multiple traffic flows, the resulting behavior can be both quite flexible and quite complex.

3.7.2.2 Suitability of Drop Schemes to Various Traffic Types

Drop schemes are generally best suited to traffic types that respond well to traffic drops. TCP senders handle packet drops as a routine indication of congestion, slow down in response, and resend dropped packets. UDP senders, by comparison, do not necessarily slow down in response to congestion and do not resend dropped packets. As a result, although drop schemes applied to UDP-type traffic may achieve certain network objectives, they also may significantly compromise the QoS experienced by the individual traffic flows. As a result, drop schemes such as WRED typically are applied only to TCP-type traffic (or other traffic that is responsive to packet dropping).

> **Note**
>
> Note that UDP is cited as a protocol that does not inherently respond to packet drops. It is possible that reliability layers above UDP would cause a particular traffic generator to respond to packet drops even when the underlying protocol is UDP. The effectiveness of dropping schemes is determined by the overall responsiveness of the traffic generator to dropping, not necessarily by the behavior of a specific protocol layer.

3.8 Application of Queuing Schemes

This chapter primarily has been concerned with descriptions of queuing schemes and only secondarily with their application. Applications of the queuing schemes are discussed in further depth in subsequent chapters, as various higher-layer traffic-handling mechanisms are described. The potential applications are so varied that it is difficult to categorize them or summarize them in one or two chapters. The following paragraphs provide some modest context and a very small set of examples of applications of queuing schemes.

3.8.1 Passive Configuration of Queuing Schemes

Chapter 1 discussed the need to configure traffic-handling mechanisms in network devices. For the most part, this amounts to configuring the queuing schemes described in this chapter. In certain cases, however, certain queuing schemes can be configured *passively*. This means that they require little, if any, active configuration. Instead, they simply are enabled in network devices out of the box or at the flick of a software switch.

For example, network devices can be programmed to distinguish individual conversations based on IP addresses and ports. These devices can then apply fair queuing to allocate forwarding capacity fairly between the conversations. Other passive mechanisms might use heuristics, for example, to identify flows with a preponderance of small packets and provide them with reduced latency. In another example, RED can be applied equally to all TCP traffic with generally beneficial effects.

Passive invocation of queuing schemes is characterized by neutrality across flows. Consider by analogy that rental apartments are usually painted white or beige. It is rare to find a rental apartment painted purple with pink polka dots. These apartments must appeal to the majority of consumers. Similarly, out-of-the-box queuing schemes cannot be biased heavily for or against a particular type of flow. Such biases are the realm of policies, which vary significantly from one situation to another and must be actively invoked under direct or indirect control of the network manager. As a result, passive use of queuing schemes tends to benefit the network as a whole, without striving to meet specific QoS objectives for specific traffic flows.

3.8.1.1 Actively Configured Queuing Behaviors

A fully QoS-enabled network, by comparison, does strive to meet specific QoS objectives for specific traffic flows. It configures queuing schemes actively. Classifiers must be configured to identify specific traffic flows. These must be associated with specific weights (or alternate queue-servicing parameters). Active configuration of queuing schemes tends to require extensive interaction with network devices. This may be achieved using push provisioning, in response to signaling, or by combination of the two methods (both were described in Chapter 1). As described previously, the provisioning and configuration of traffic-handling mechanisms (and the associated queuing behaviors) in an effective manner is a major consideration in the QoS-enabled network and is a major theme of this book.

3.8.2 Application Examples

The following examples illustrate both passive and active applications of some of the queuing schemes described. The short list of examples is by no means intended to be exhaustive. Rather, it is intended to illustrate the variation in potential applications.

3.8.2.1 Out-of-the-Box Fair Queuing at a Gateway

In the example shown in Figure 3.18, fair queuing is used passively to allocate valuable WAN link resources among multiple conversations and to reduce latency for low-bit rate audio traffic. Because of the audio traffic's low bandwidth requirements, it does not experience congestion. Furthermore, fair-queuing schemes may actually lower the latency experienced by the audio packets. Note that this functionality requires no particular configuration. The queuing scheme inherently favors low-bit rate traffic flows; it is ready out of the box.

Figure 3.18   Fair Queuing at a Gateway

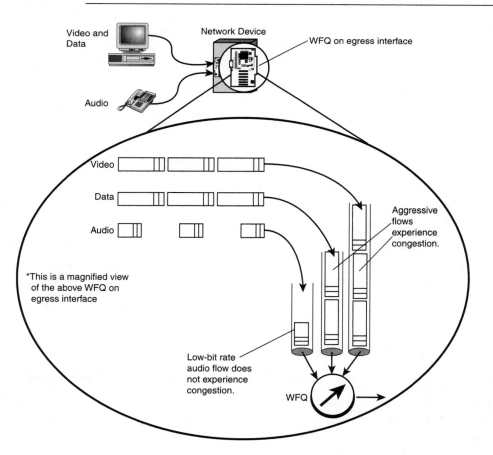

3.8.2.2 A Gateway with Active WFQ and Passive RED

In the example shown in Figure 3.19, a gateway router is actively configured to share WAN link forwarding capacity among multiple organizations. Capacity shares are allocated based on fees charged to each organization and thus are purposely unequal. In addition, RED is applied passively to all TCP traffic carried through the gateway. This avoids global synchronization (resulting in improved efficiency) and avoids penalizing bursty traffic.

Figure 3.19   Gateway with WFQ and RED

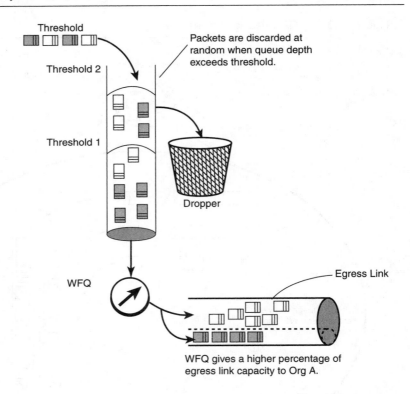

3.8.2.3 Host Generating Real-Time and Non-Real-Time Traffic

In the example shown in Figure 3.20, a host generates real-time traffic (Flow A) requiring low latency but only a limited share of available forwarding capacity. At the same time, it generates non-real-time traffic (Flows B, C, and D), which does not require low latency but benefits from as much forwarding capacity as is available. The non-real-time traffic is mixed using a work-conserving WFQ queuing stage. The real-time traffic is shaped to a peak rate of p using a non-work-conserving leaky bucket. This traffic is then fed into a strict priority-queuing stage, where it is mixed with the non-real-time traffic. The real-time traffic is assigned a higher priority than the non-real-time traffic. As a result, the real-time traffic receives a limited share of the forwarding capacity with very low latency. The non-real-time traffic receives all remaining capacity but no latency assurances.

Figure 3.20 Real-Time and Non-Real-Time Traffic

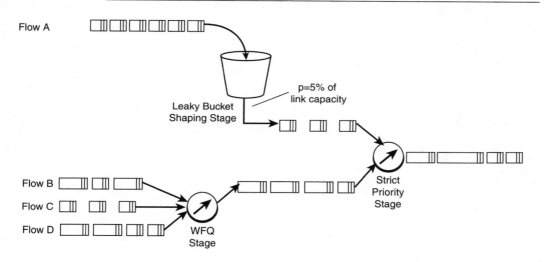

3.9 Summary

Queuing schemes are the fundamental building blocks of the QoS-enabled network. A large variety of queuing schemes exist. These can be loosely categorized into FIFO queuing, work-conserving queuing schemes, non-work-conserving queuing schemes, and dropping schemes. FIFO queuing is the simplest, default form of queuing in which traffic is forwarded through a network in the order in which it is submitted to the network. Work-conserving queuing schemes attempt to share network capacity fairly between a number of competing traffic flows without leaving any network capacity unused. Non-work-conserving schemes typically are applied to multimedia or real-time traffic and are used to limit the rate at which such traffic is forwarded, possibly allowing network capacity to go unused. Dropping schemes typically are applied to TCP-like traffic in an effort to improve network utilization and to prioritize certain TCP traffic flows above others.

In sophisticated QoS-aware network devices, multiple queuing schemes often are applied simultaneously to achieve multiple QoS objectives.

CHAPTER 4

Integrated Services

The Integrated Services (IntServ) working group of the IETF met for the first time in March 1994 at the Seattle IETF. The work produced by this group proposed (dare I say) a paradigm shift in the way that Internet service is viewed and formed the basis for most of the QoS work undertaken by the IETF in the subsequent four years.

The IntServ working group aimed to "transition the Internet into a robust integrated-service communications infrastructure" [INTSERV_WEB]. The transformed Internet envisioned by the IntServ working group would support audio, video, and other real-time and traditional data-traffic in a single network infrastructure. Note the focus on *high-quality* services (as defined in Chapter 2, "The Quality/Efficiency Product," in the section "The Quality of a Service").

To this end, the charter of the IntServ working group calls for the group to focus on the following:

- Defining the services to be provided by the Internet

- Defining interfaces to applications that enable them to express the end-to-end services required

- Defining interfaces to network elements that can be used to invoke the traffic-handling mechanisms corresponding to the required service (including admission control)

- Defining metrics by which the service provided by the routers can be validated

This chapter discusses the IntServ architecture in general. It discusses the components of the architecture—the IntServ *service model* and the *implementation framework*. A significant implication of the service model is that network resources must be explicitly managed, requiring resource reservation and admission control. This controversial requirement drove the development of the RSVP protocol, which is the topic of the next chapter. This chapter follows with a discussion of the types of applications served by IntServ and the specific services offered by the IntServ service model today (the *Controlled Load* and the *Guaranteed Services*). This chapter also discusses how these services might be provided using the queuing mechanisms described in Chapter 3, "Queuing Mechanisms," and assuming the resource reservation and admission control facilities of RSVP. The chapter ends with a discussion of the work of the *Integrated Services over Specific Link Layers* (ISSLL) working group of the IETF.

4.1 Overview of the IntServ Architecture

Figure 4.1 illustrates the concepts of the IntServ architecture that will be discussed in this chapter.

Figure 4.1   Concepts of the IntServ Architecture

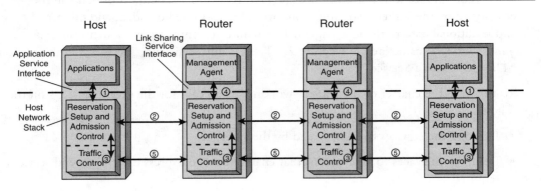

In (1) in the figure, applications issue a *service request* for a specific traffic flow across a *service interface*. Both routers and hosts include a network stack, which includes a *reservation setup agent*, *admission control*, and *traffic control*. In (2), the reservation setup agent on the host responds to the application service request by generating a *reservation setup protocol* service request message. This message traverses the network elements between sending host and receiving host (including the network stack in each host). Each network element determines, via the process of admission control, whether it has the resources to accommodate the traffic flow at the requested level of service. If it does, the network element configures traffic control (3) to recognize traffic on the flow and to service it accordingly. If all network elements are capable of supporting the service request, a *reservation* is in place and traffic on the flow is allotted the service requested (5).

Note that in (4), a *management agent* can be used to request service across a *link-sharing service interface*. This interface can be used (on a router or a host) to request service for aggregate traffic flows.

4.1.1 Integrated Services in the Internet: RFC 1633

In 1994, the IntServ working group produced an informational RFC defining the *IntServ architecture*: RFC 1633, written by Bob Braden, Dave Clark, and Scott Shenker [RFC 1633]. The proposed architecture has had a profound impact on subsequent QoS work. Many of the premises of the architecture were controversial at the time and continue to be so today.

> **Note**
>
> Much of the content of the following paragraphs closely mirrors the content in RFC 1633. This content is important because it lays the groundwork for the subsequent discussion. As such, it warrants explicit discussion in this book (as opposed to a mere "reference for the reader"). I expect that the authors of RFC 1633 will forgive the close reiteration of their work. The fact that the RFC structure and content is so closely mirrored here is testimony to the quality and clarity of the original work. To significantly depart from it would have done a disservice to the readers of this book.

4.1.2 Requirements Driving the IntServ Architecture and Their Implications

RFC 1633 begins by identifying the high-level requirements that drive the architecture. These are twofold:

- The IntServ architecture must provide service appropriate for *real-time* applications such as remote video, multimedia conferencing, visualization, and virtual reality (both for multicast and unicast).

- The IntServ architecture must provide the facilities for network operators to control the sharing of bandwidth on a particular link among different traffic classes (similar to the class-based queuing scheme described in Chapter 3). This will be referred to as link sharing.

The authors of the architecture recognize that the proposed changes to the service model of the Internet represent a major undertaking. However, they point out that the changes are merely an *extension* to the existing model, not a wholesale replacement.

Two elements exist in the IntServ architecture. The first is the integrated *service model*. The second is a reference *implementation framework*. The model describes the externally visible behavior of the architecture. It is separable from the underlying framework, which is concerned with the *implementation* of the model. Both are discussed in the following sections.

4.1.3 The IntServ Service Model

The IntServ service model describes the characteristics of the services that will be provided by an IntServ-capable network. These services are required to accommodate link-sharing requirements as well as the requirements of real-time applications. The services must support both unicast and multicast traffic flows.

The service characteristics are captured in the form of a service *interface*. The service interface separates the clients of the IntServ services from the providers of the services. Two types of clients are recognized. One type of client is an individual application traffic flow. The other is an aggregation (or class) of traffic flows. The service providers are the various underlying network link layers and QoS mechanisms. The IntServ clients use the service interface to request a certain service. The IntServ providers respond by committing (or not) to provide the requested service.

Figure 4.2 illustrates the concept of the service *interface*.

Figure 4.2   The IntServ Service Interface

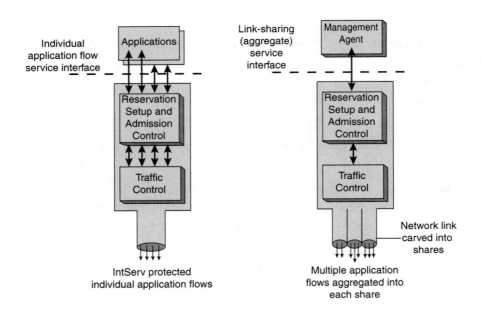

IntServ protected individual application flows

Multiple application flows aggregated into each share

Services committed to individual application flows are driven by the ergonomic requirements of the application. Services committed to aggregations of traffic flows are driven by resource sharing and economic requirements related to the management of resources in a subnetwork. The former category serves individual application users. The latter category enables link sharing and thus serves network managers. The two types of commitments correspond to the high level requirements of the IntServ architecture: satisfying the requirements of real-time applications and enabling link-sharing policies.

> **Note**
>
> The fact that the IntServ service interface was designed to support both link-sharing requirements and the requirements of individual application traffic flows is often overlooked. The prevailing perception is that IntServ focuses on the requirements of application traffic to the exclusion of link-sharing requirements. Indeed, the primary product of the IntServ working group is the definition of the *Guaranteed* and the *Controlled Load Services*, which are focused on application requirements. These will be discussed in detail later in this chapter.

4.1.3.1 *Abstracting the Network*

The purpose of the service interface is to provide a constant service model to the clients of the interface, regardless of the nuances of the specific underlying network link layers and QoS mechanisms. Thus, the service interface enables applications and network mechanisms to evolve independently. In this spirit, the Integrated Services over Specific Link Layers (ISSLL) working group of the IETF defines adaptation layers and mechanisms that can be used to enable different network link layers to provide the same service interface to applications. The ISSLL work will be discussed at the end of this chapter.

4.1.3.2 *Assumptions Underlying the IntServ Service Model*

The IntServ service model is based on the following assumptions:

- Adequate support of real-time applications requires service guarantees. These service guarantees, in turn, require reservations and explicit admission control.

- It is desirable to use a single Internet infrastructure to provide the best-effort service that we are accustomed to today, as well as the real-time services and link-sharing facilities proposed by the IntServ model. The alternative, of providing a separate network to support the IntServ model, is rejected.

- It is desirable to provide all services using the same existing protocol. At the time, both IP and CLNP were considered contenders. Today, CLNP is obviously not a contender.

- The *service model* must be consistent *end to end* to provide predictable behavior between communicating peers. The underlying implementation may vary across the Internet.

The first of these assumptions is by far the most controversial; it will be addressed in depth in the following sections. The remaining assumptions are less controversial and generally are accepted.

4.1.3.3 Reservations and Admission Control

Reservations and explicit admission control comprise a fairly heavyweight QoS mechanism that stands to add significant complexity to the network. The controversy surrounding this requirement is closely related to the quality/efficiency (QE) product discussed in Chapter 2. Basically, RFC 1633 argues that it is desirable to provide high-quality services and that, at least in parts of the network, efficiency is a significant concern. The astute reader will recognize this as a requirement for a high QE product. As explained in Chapter 2, a high QE product tends to require heavyweight QoS mechanisms. The justification for incurring the increased complexity of reservations and explicit admission control is therefore based on the requirement for a high QE product.

Two arguments are commonly presented against the need for a high QE product in the Internet:

- High-quality services are not required because applications can simply adapt to available network capacity.

- Efficiency is not a concern because bandwidth will be infinite.

The RFC dismisses these arguments on the grounds discussed in the next sections.

Applications Cannot Adapt to Arbitrary Network Conditions

Although the RFC acknowledges the value of applications that can adapt to network conditions, it refutes the notion that applications can adapt to *arbitrary* network conditions. According to the RFC, experiments show that users of conferencing applications find interaction to be impossible when network delays are multiple seconds. By definition, IntServ strives to accommodate such applications. Therefore, IntServ services must be capable of offering quantifiable delay bounds. The RFC concedes that some variation in the strictness of the guarantees provided by IntServ services is acceptable. However, it requires the service quality to be "sufficiently predictable that the application can operate in an acceptable way over a duration of time determined by the user."

Efficiency Is Important

With respect to efficiency, RFC 1633 assumes that it is not reasonable to rely on overprovisioned networks to provide the high-quality services defined. It acknowledges the rate of bandwidth proliferation but expects that in some regions of the network, inexpensive bandwidth will not be available for a long time. Even if the bandwidth were to become available, there will be economic incentives to not waste it.

Simple Prioritization is Insufficient

The RFC also dismisses a third argument presented by opponents of heavyweight QoS mechanisms. This is the argument that simple prioritization is a sufficient QoS mechanism to support the service requirements. The shortcomings of simple priority without admission control were discussed in Chapter 2 (in the section "Supporting Higher-Quality Services in the WAN"). The example illustrated in Chapter 2 shows that simple prioritization without admission control can result in degradation of service to all flows when too many flows are competing for the high-priority service. To avoid this condition, it is necessary either to provision sufficient high-priority capacity to accommodate all potential flows or to use explicit admission control. The first option amounts to overprovisioning. As argued previously, overprovisioning may be an acceptable approach in certain parts of the network, but it cannot be ubiquitously assumed. In cases in which overprovisioning cannot be assumed, explicit admission control should cause certain flows to receive a busy signal, to assure that other flows enjoy high-priority service for the duration of the session.

4.1.4 The Implementation Framework

The implementation framework defines the components that are required to support the services described by the IntServ model. These components are as follows:

- Packet scheduler

- Classifier

- Admission control

- A reservation setup protocol

The first three are lumped together under the category of traffic control (closely related to the more general concept of *traffic handling*, defined in Chapter 1, "Introduction to Quality of Service"). Traffic control functionality is implemented in network elements such as hosts, routers, and switches.

4.1.4.1 Packet Scheduler and Classification

These terms can be mapped directly to the elements that were introduced in Chapter 1 as the components that comprise *traffic handling*. The packet scheduler is the component that implements queue-servicing algorithms. Classification is the process by which traffic is identified and assigned to different queues in the packet scheduler.

It's important to point out that the IntServ architecture does not prescribe a particular classification granularity. IntServ is *commonly* discussed in connection with per-conversation classification. However, it does not *dictate* per-conversation classification.

4.1.4.2 Admission Control

The term *admission control* is used in different and often confusing contexts. The use of the term in this book is quite consistent with its definition as a component of the IntServ framework. In this context, admission control is an out-of-band process by which a network element (or a collection of network elements) decides whether sufficient resources are available to honor a new service request without compromising those service requests that have already been admitted.

Policing versus Admission Control

In certain cases, often in the context of DiffServ, the term *admission control* is used to refer to packet-by-packet *policing*. Policing is the process by which network elements monitor the arrival of packets on a flow and discard, delay, or demote the priority of packets that exceed a negotiated profile.

Policing is an *implicit* form of admission control, as opposed to the *explicit* form of admission control used in the context of IntServ. Explicit admission control is characterized by an out-of-band admission *request* to the network, followed by an admission control *decision* and an admission control *response* from the network. In this book, the term *admission control* will be used to refer to the explicit form unless mentioned otherwise.

In explicit admission control, the network element decides to either admit or reject the flow, explicitly. When it's admitted, the network element commits some level of resources (quantifiable or not) to the flow for some duration. By contrast, in implicit admission control, there is no a priori agreement between the network element and the application or the provisioning agent. Instead, senders submit packets, and the network element carries them if resources are available and polices them if resources are not available. Applications or network managers may detect that packets are being policed in one form or another as traffic succeeds or does not succeed in reaching a peer receiver. However, such detection is via implicit feedback, such as delayed or discarded packets.

IntServ defines admission control to be dynamic, in the sense that the negotiation process occurs each time that a "host requests some real-time service." In other cases, explicit admission control can be applied more statically. For example, a network element might be requested via provisioning to accommodate a certain traffic flow in *anticipation* of the arrival of traffic on the flow. The element may explicitly admit or reject the provisioning request.

The IntServ architecture recognizes that an admission control decision is the product of a decision based on the pure *availability of resources* as well as on *policies* regarding how available resources may be used. However, the IntServ work does not focus on policies. Instead, it focuses on the *admission control algorithms* that are used by network elements to determine admissibility of a request based on resource availability. It does not dictate or even specify admission control algorithms, but rather, offers guidelines for their implementation.

4.1.4.3 RSVP: The Reservation Setup Protocol

In discussing the assumptions underlying the IntServ model, the authors of the RFC conclude that "there is an inescapable requirement for routers to be able to *reserve* resources," and, further, that "an explicit *setup* mechanism is necessary." This is the IntServ requirement for a *resource reservation protocol*, which led to the development of the RSVP protocol. The RSVP protocol is discussed in depth in Chapter 5, "RSVP."

Note

Note that a setup *protocol* is not strictly required to support the IntServ service model. The protocol greatly simplifies the configuration of the IntServ traffic control mechanisms along a specific traffic path in a coordinated manner. However, in theory, it is possible to provide IntServ services by configuring the traffic control mechanisms in the required network elements using alternate means. For example, SNMP may be used to administratively configure IntServ mechanisms in these network elements [RFC 2213].

RSVP was originally developed to set up or to establish end-to-end *reservations* in the Internet. As such, it serves to invoke and to coordinate the admission control and reservation setup processes in a set of network elements along the traffic path of a flow. Transmitting hosts send RSVP messages through the network to receiving hosts. These respond by sending resource requests back toward the transmitter. The resource requests include a FLOWSPEC, which quantifies the requested resources. As these requests transit back toward the transmitter, network elements in the traffic path make an admission control decision. If all network elements along the path agree to admit the resource request, an end-to-end reservation is established. If any of the network elements are incapable of admitting the request, no reservation is established. The reservation model is illustrated in Figure 4.3.

Figure 4.3   Reservation Model

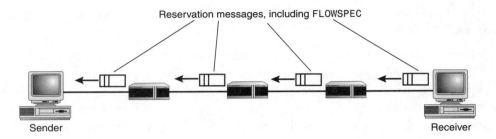

(a) Resource requests flow upstream

Reservation messages, including FLOWSPEC

Sender   Receiver

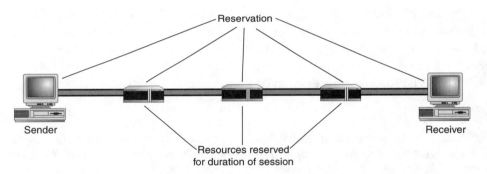

(b) Reservation is in place

Reservation

Sender   Receiver

Resources reserved
for duration of session

By reserving resources, network elements commit to making the resources available for the traffic flow. As a consequence, these resources cannot be guaranteed to other traffic flows until the initial reservation is *torn down* (or expired).

Packet Switching versus Circuit Switching

By reserving resources, RSVP in the Internet would effectively convert an exclusively *packet-switched* network to a partially *circuit-switched* network. The notion of using the Internet as a circuit-switched network borders on heresy to many Internet purists. Nonetheless, use of RSVP as originally designed would do so.

Networks can be categorized as circuit-switched or packet-switched. Circuit-switched networks set up a circuit to serve traffic sent from one point to another. The circuit is established either on demand (typically in response to some signaling protocol) or by provisioning. Each network element along the traffic path participates in setting up the circuit and dedicates resources exclusively to the circuit. Traffic submitted for a specific circuit at one end of the network is carried along the circuit to the other end of the network. Resources remain committed to the circuit until it is explicitly torn down, whether or not traffic is transmitted on it. The telephone network is an example of a circuit-switched network.

Packet-switched networks, by contrast, do not establish circuits. Instead, packets are marked with a destination address and are submitted to one end of the network. Network elements inspect each packet and determine dynamically which interface should be used at that time to carry the packet toward its destination. Network elements do not reserve resources exclusively for any particular circuit. Conventional data networks, such as Ethernet LANs and X.25 WANs, are examples of packet-switched networks.

One benefit often associated with circuit-switched networks is that, once granted, resources are guaranteed to be available for a traffic flow until the corresponding circuit is torn down (high-quality guarantees). By contrast, in a packet-switched network, because no resources are committed a priori, packets may experience congestion at various points in the network where resources are scarce.

Several disadvantages are involved in circuit switching. One of these is the call setup overhead—before packets can be transmitted on a circuit, the circuit must be established. Thus, latency is incurred whenever traffic is sent to a destination for which no circuit has been established. For session-oriented applications that endure for some period of time (such as video streaming), the setup latency might be negligible. However, for short transactions (such as DNS queries), this latency may be unacceptable. One way to avoid setup latency is to provision a permanent circuit a priori.

However, this leads to another disadvantage of circuit switching: When a circuit is established, resources usually are dedicated to that circuit. As a result, these resources cannot be offered to other traffic. If there is a lull in traffic sent on the circuit, the resources dedicated to the circuit may remain unused. This is not a problem for relatively constant-bit rate traffic flows that persist for some time (such as voice). However, it is an expensive way to use resources for bursty traffic or for erratic, short-lived flows. Note that certain circuit-switching technologies may actually make unused resources on one circuit available to another circuit (statistical multiplexing). However, in this case, the service provided by either circuit is not guaranteed (compromised in quality).

Furthermore, circuit-switched networks install per-circuit state in network elements along the circuit path and rely on these to free resources properly as circuits are torn down. Thus, they tend to be less robust and more prone to failure than packet-switched networks.

RSVP originally was developed to support the strict, quantifiable reservation model described previously. However, it has since been extended to support "softer" models. In these models, it may be used to request less quantifiable resources from the network, with corresponding lower-service quality expected from the network. Extensions to RSVP are discussed in Chapter 5.

4.1.4.4 Components of an IntServ Network Element

An IntServ-capable network element must include the classification, packet scheduling, and admission control functionalities that comprise IntServ traffic control. In addition, the network element must provide an agent that participates in the resource reservation protocol (an RSVP agent) and a management agent. The RSVP agent parses RSVP messages and extracts the FLOWSPEC for submission to the network element's admission control process. If a reservation is admitted, the classifier and packet scheduler are configured accordingly. The RSVP agent then generates the appropriate protocol messages, indicating admission or rejection of the request, to other network elements along the traffic path. The management agent is used to configure the classifier and packet scheduler for link sharing and to configure admission control policies. The elements of an IntServ switch or router are illustrated in Figure 4.4.

Figure 4.4   Elements of an IntServ Switch or Router

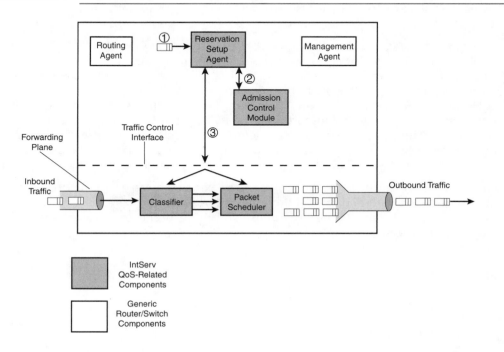

When a reservation setup message arrives (indicated as [1] in the figure), the reservation setup agent parses the message and passes it to the admission control module (2). If the request is admissible, then the reservation setup agent uses the traffic control interface (3) to configure the appropriate queuing parameters. The reservation setup agent also configures the classifier to recognize traffic on the admitted flow and to direct it to the appropriate queue.

The elements of an IntServ-compliant host are similar to those of a switch or router. However, unlike switches or routers, hosts do not forward traffic from one interface to another. Hosts forward traffic from applications to the network (transmitted traffic) and from the network to applications (received traffic). Hosts also include applications and an API by which these applications invoke the services of the RSVP agent. When a reservation is established for transmitted traffic, the RSVP agent configures traffic control elements on the host accordingly. Figure 4.5 illustrates the elements of an IntServ-compliant host.

Figure 4.5   Elements of an IntServ Host

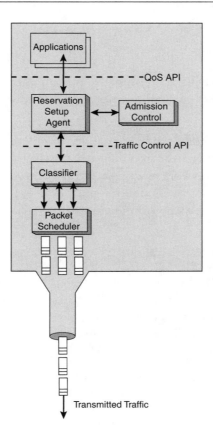

Figure 4.5 is very similar to Figure 4.4. However, the RSVP agent interacts with the application as well as the network.

4.2 The Services of the IntServ Model

The general notion of a service model and a service interface was discussed earlier in this chapter. This section discusses the specific services defined by the IntServ working group and the applications that they are designed to support. The section begins with a discussion of the application types that drive the service definitions and ends with a description of the services themselves.

4.2.1 Application Types and Their Requirements

The definition of the IntServ services was driven by an analysis of the requirements of different application types with respect to latency. RFC 1633 identifies three application types:

- Real-time-intolerant applications
- Real-time-tolerant applications
- Elastic applications

Both real-time application types are quantitative by nature; elastic applications are not. The requirements of the different application types are discussed in the following paragraphs.

4.2.1.1 Real-Time Applications

These applications are characterized by a sender that packetizes an audio or video signal and transmits it across the network as a packet stream. A receiver depacketizes the received traffic and converts it back into a continuous signal. The network inevitably delays individual packets to varying degrees. The variation in delay is referred to as *jitter*. (See the sidebar titled "Jitter Buffers").

Jitter Buffers

Jitter is illustrated in Figure 4.6.

In Figure 4.6, a sender samples an audio signal, generating packets at the rate of one every 20,000th of a second (a). As the packets are carried through the network, jitter distorts their temporal profile (b). For the receiver to reconstruct the original signal, it must render the packets at the same rate at which they were generated. For example, if an audio signal is sampled 20,000 times per second, then each sample must be available at most 1/20,000th of a second after its predecessor to properly reconstruct the signal. Because of jitter, received samples often are separated by more than 1/20,000th of a second.

Assuming that, on average, packets arrive at the rate at which they were generated, the receiver can compensate for jitter by using a number of techniques. It can simply render the packets as they arrive. Obviously, this will introduce distortion. It can also respond by holding the rate at which it renders constant, but ignoring and not rendering packets that miss their rendering time. This, too, will introduce distortion. Buffering at the receiver can minimize distortion. The receiver does so by simply reading the first few samples received into its buffer (the *jitter buffer*) before starting to play them. By doing so, the receiver always lags some amount of time behind the sender. If an individual packet is delayed in the network because of jitter, the receiver is unaffected as long as it still has samples to play in its jitter buffer. Provided that the jitter is bounded, the packet will show up sooner or later—hopefully before its rendering time.

To illustrate the operation of the jitter buffer, it is helpful to consider an extreme example. In this example, the receiver waits for the entire audio program to be downloaded before it begins to reconstruct it. In this case, the jitter buffer would need to have sufficient capacity to contain the entire program. In most cases, the jitter buffer is a small fraction of the program size, and it is necessary to buffer only a few samples to faithfully reproduce the original signal. The size of the jitter buffer depends on the jitter introduced by the network and the fidelity required in reconstructing the original signal. Note that the use of a jitter buffer intentionally introduces delay in the playback of the original signal.

| Figure 4.6 | Jitter |

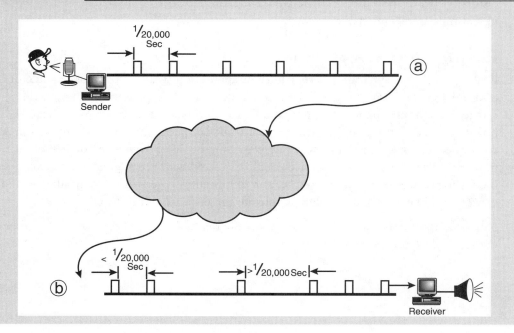

As explained in the sidebar, real-time applications handle jitter in the following ways:

- Using a jitter buffer (which introduces latency)

- Introducing distortion in rendering the original signal

- Using both of these methods

The original IntServ architecture recognizes that applications differ in both their tolerance for latency and their tolerance for distortion. However, for the purpose of defining *services*, the IntServ architecture focuses on the tolerance for distortion rather than the tolerance for latency.

Real-Time-Intolerant Applications

As such, the architecture defines real-time-*intolerant* applications as applications that are intolerant of distortion. Distortion can be avoided by using a jitter buffer that is sufficiently large to accommodate the worst-case jitter introduced by the network. The assumption is that distortion-intolerant applications are willing to use an arbitrarily large jitter buffer and to tolerate the associated delay to avoid distortion.

To enable such an application, the service interface must commit to guaranteeing an absolute maximum and minimum latency. The application can then use these parameters to determine the size of the jitter buffer that it must use to guarantee that there will be no distortion. RFC 1633 proposes the *Guaranteed Service* to accommodate the requirements of real-time-intolerant applications.

Real-Time-Tolerant Applications

Real-time-tolerant applications are defined as applications that are tolerant of some degree of distortion. The RFC suggests that most audio and video applications fall into this category. For these applications, the original RFC proposed the *predictive* service. The predictive service was to offer a fairly reliable, but not *perfectly* reliable, delay bound. As a consequence, the applications using the service might suffer from some degree of distortion. However, the predictive service could be offered with much greater *efficiency* than the Guaranteed Service and, therefore, at a significantly lower cost. As a result, users of the service could be expected to willingly tolerate the distortion introduced.

Note that the IntServ working group eventually rejected the predictive service in favor of the *Controlled Load Service*.

Distortion Tolerance versus Latency Tolerance

The focus on distortion tolerance versus latency tolerance is somewhat ironic. RFC 1633 states that most audio and video applications are expected to be somewhat tolerant of distortion. The only example of a distortion-intolerant application cited by the RFC is a circuit emulation application. At the same time, there is a clear need for distinguishing between applications that are latency-tolerant and applications that are latency-intolerant. Interactive multimedia applications (such as IP telephony and videoconferencing) are clearly latency-intolerant, while playback applications (such as video streaming and Internet radio) are clearly more latency-tolerant.

The common perception is that the *Guaranteed Service* is suitable for *latency*-intolerant applications because it offers *low* latency bounds, while the *Controlled Load Service* is suitable for latency-tolerant applications because it does not offer latency bounds. This was not the intent of the IntServ working group. In fact, the Guaranteed Service does *not* offer *low* latency bounds; it just offers *strictly guaranteed* latency bounds. Furthermore, to offer strict latency bounds, it must offer worst-case bounds, which are likely to be quite large. Thus, Guaranteed Service may not be suitable for latency-intolerant applications. On the other hand, although the Controlled Load Service does not *guarantee* latency bounds, it may actually provide quite low average latency.

Nonetheless, many people continue to associate Guaranteed Service with latency-intolerant applications such as IP telephony and Controlled Load Service with more latency-tolerant applications such as video streaming.

> **Note**
>
> Although many existing network elements support the Controlled Load Service, few support the Guaranteed Service *as defined*. It seems that there is little demand for the Guaranteed Service as originally defined. However, there is demand for services that are differentiated on the basis of latency tolerance (as opposed to distortion tolerance). Thus, it is likely that variations on the original Guaranteed Service will be implemented or that a different service will be proposed in its place. These variations may well offer *low* latency bounds. The expedited forwarding service (see Chapter 6, "Differentiated Services,") although not an IntServ service, is an example of such a service).

4.2.1.2 *Elastic Applications*

Elastic applications differ from real-time applications in that there is no inherent timing associated with the data. Voice that is packetized at 20KHz must be reconstructed at 20KHz. Elastic applications can tolerate jitter and latencies. Their utility to the user diminishes as latency and jitter increase, but not in the catastrophic manner that affects real-time applications. For example, the user of a Telnet session becomes progressively more annoyed as response time increases, but, across a broad population of users, there is no clear latency value above which Telnet becomes unusable. On the other hand, it has been shown that telephony service drops dramatically in its utility when the latency exceeds about 100 milliseconds.

Examples of elastic applications are numerous. RFC 1633 offers as examples Telnet, network file system (NFS), File Transfer Protocol (FTP), email, and others. The RFC proposes to "offer several classes of best-effort service to reflect the relative delay sensitivities of different elastic applications." However, these classes of service have not been defined within the IntServ framework to this date. On the other hand, these services are just the type of services most readily offered by DiffServ (see Chapter 6). Recently, the *Null Service* has been proposed as a mechanism for extending the IntServ service model and integrating it with DiffServ to support elastic applications.

4.2.2 The IntServ Services

The following paragraphs describe the characteristics of the two IntServ services that are proposed standards today. These are the *Controlled Load Service* [RFC 2211] and the *Guaranteed Service* [RFC 2212]. The *Null Service* [NULL_SERVICE] will also be described (even though, strictly speaking, it is not an IntServ service).

4.2.2.1 The Controlled Load Service

The Controlled Load Service offers an application's traffic flow the "appearance of a lightly loaded network."

Parameters Used to Request the Controlled Load Service

An application request for Controlled Load Service would specify that it is for the Controlled Load Service and also would specify the *profile* of the offered traffic for which the service is required. The traffic profile is expressed in the form of the token bucket model, described in Chapter 3. This model includes the following parameters:

- Average rate (r)
- Peak rate (p)
- Burst size (B)

The service request must also specify a *minimum policed unit* (m) and a *maximum packet size* (M). Packets smaller in size than m will be considered by network elements to be of size m. Packets larger in size than M will be considered as nonconforming to the profile specified by the application.

Note

The minimum policed size parameter is required to enable admission control algorithms to account for the effects of packet headers. For details on the use of this parameter, see the sidebar titled "Minimum Policed Size" in Chapter 12, "The GQoS API and the QoS Service Provider." Also see [RFC 2210].

Behavior of Controlled Load Service

If no network elements along the traffic path refuse admission to the service request, then the traffic flow is admitted. As a result, the application can expect that the specified quantity of traffic will enjoy the appearance of a lightly loaded network. According to [RFC 2211], this means that the following is true:

- A very high percentage of transmitted packets will be delivered to the receivers to which they are destined, and the percentage of packets not delivered will approximate the basic error rate of the medium.

- A very high percentage of transmitted packets will be delivered with a delay close to the minimum possible delay (speed of light delay plus serialization delay plus minimum processing delay).

Traffic in excess of the token bucket parameters is considered *nonconforming*. Controlled Load Service traffic is policed, which may result in best-effort or worse-than-best-effort treatment for that part of the traffic that is nonconforming or for all traffic on the flow. RFC 2211 states that nonconforming traffic must be handled as best-effort traffic if resources are available. However, it also recommends that the policing schemes used assure that nonconforming Controlled Load Service traffic (on flows that are not *rate-adaptive*) does not compromise best-effort traffic on flows that are rate-adaptive.

Note

Rate-adaptive traffic is traffic that responds to congestion by backing off. TCP traffic is generally rate-adaptive; UDP traffic is generally not. The concept of rate-adaptive traffic is discussed in Chapter 7, "The Subnet Bandwidth Manager and 802 Networks," under the heading "Use of TCP and Other Rate-Adaptive Protocols."

A service that offers the *appearance of a lightly loaded network* may seem to be fairly non-committal and, therefore, not all that useful. However, it is actually quite useful. The service offers the appearance of a best-effort network that is dedicated to the application's traffic flow. This means that the application can expect not to encounter congestion or packet drops. It does not mean that latency or jitter is bounded because latency and jitter are associated even with lightly loaded networks. However, if on the average, an application submits traffic at a rate conforming to that specified in the token bucket parameters, then it can expect the network to have the capacity to carry the traffic to its receiving peer in a reasonably timely fashion.

Suitability of Controlled Load Service to Applications

The Controlled Load Service is useful to serve applications that generate traffic at a quantifiable rate but that do not expect strict latency bounds. An example of such an application is a streaming video application. Streaming video applications generate traffic that can be characterized by a token bucket profile (as defined by the video *CODEC*).

These applications can tolerate some degree of jitter because the receiving peer can be expected to use a jitter buffer to absorb bursts and transient delays in the network. If the jitter occasionally exceeds the capacity of the jitter buffer, some degree of distortion may be introduced. The eye is fairly forgiving, so some degree of video distortion can usually be tolerated.

The Controlled Load Service may or may not be suitable for interactive audio traffic. Interactive audio generally requires lower latency than streaming video (because it is interactive). In addition, the ear tends to be less tolerant of distortion than the eye. Even though the Controlled Load Service makes no promises with respect to latency, it may be that it offers low enough latency characteristics most of the time to support a small jitter buffer at the receiver, thus bounding latency. However, if the capacity of the jitter buffer is exceeded, then distortion will be introduced.

Implementing the Controlled Load Service

To implement an IntServ service, it is necessary to implement both scheduling and admission control algorithms. RFC 2211 offers guidelines for the implementers of Controlled Load Service and suggests three scheduling schemes. In the simplest of these, a single, strict priority queue (see Chapter 3 for a discussion of strict priority queuing) would carry all Controlled-Load Service traffic. Admission control would be used to limit admission of Controlled-Load Service flows so that the strict priority queue is not overloaded and does not unacceptably starve best-effort traffic on the same interface. A separate policer would be necessary to enforce the limits prescribed by admission control.

A more sophisticated scheme would employ weighted fair queuing or class-based queuing (see Chapter 3) to place all Controlled Load Service traffic in a weighted queue or class of its own. Admission control would limit admission so that the weighted queue or class would remain lightly loaded. The advantage of this scheme is that the scheduler would inherently police the Controlled Load Service traffic, preventing the starvation of best-effort traffic without requiring a separate policer.

Yet another scheme would place each Controlled Load Service flow in a queue of its own, using weighted fair queuing. This approach is obviously performance-intensive. Its advantage is that it would use the scheduler to enforce traffic isolation between the different Controlled Load Service flows. This would obviate the need for per-flow policing. On the downside, it would not be capable of benefiting from the statistical sharing that could result when multiple flows are aggregated into a single queue or class.

Each of the scheduling schemes described requires admission control of some sort. A conservative approach to admission control might assume that each of the flows admitted consume resources as specified by the associated token bucket parameters. In this case, admission control would simply add the token bucket parameters across all admitted flows to determine when the capacity available for Controlled Load Service has been exceeded. (Of course, this scheme assumes that some form of policing is used to prevent a flow from consuming more resources than specified by the associated token-bucket parameters.)

A more liberal approach to admission control would assume that not all flows demand the worst-case resources specified by their token bucket parameters simultaneously. In this case, some degree of *statistical multiplexing* could be used to *oversubscribe* the total available capacity. Such statistical multiplexing is most likely to be effective when there are a large number of uncorrelated flows. This approach is likely to compromise service when the number of flows is small.

A third approach to admission control is to base it on measurement. A network element could measure the actual resources consumed by all admitted flows over some recent time period. This value could be used to adjust the theoretical load obtained by adding the token bucket parameters. Measurement may provide a hint of the degree of statistical multiplexing that can be tolerated before service is likely to be compromised.

4.2.2.2 *The Guaranteed Service*

The Guaranteed Service offers a strict delay bound to an application's traffic as long as the traffic does not exceed a specified profile.

Parameters Used to Request the Guaranteed Service

The profile of the *offered* traffic is specified using the same token bucket parameters associated with the Controlled Load Service (as well as m and M). To invoke Guaranteed Service, it is necessary to also specify the *desired service*. The desired service is specified in the form of a *rate* (R) and a *slack term* (S). The rate specified with the desired service (R) must be greater than or equal to the rate specified in the offered traffic profile (r). R implicitly specifies a desired latency as well as a desired rate. In other words, by requesting a higher desired bandwidth, an application can reduce the amount of time that it takes to transmit a fixed-size packet (considering only serialization delay and ignoring queuing delays) and, therefore, the latency of the packet. If R is large enough that latency would be reduced beyond what is required by the application, then the application quantifies this difference using the slack term. Network elements can use the slack term to relax resource allocation accordingly.

Behavior of Guaranteed Service

Per RFC 2212, the behavior that can be expected from the Guaranteed Service is "an assured level of bandwidth that, when used by a policed flow, produces a delay-bounded service with no queuing loss for all conforming datagrams." This is a pretty strong commitment compared to the weaker commitment of the Controlled Load Service. Guaranteed Service offers an *absolute* delay bound and *no* packet loss (due to queuing).

To offer this level of commitment, strict policing is required. At the edges of the network, nonconforming traffic should be treated as best-effort. It should also be marked as nonconformant so that it is treated accordingly at subsequent routers.

> **Note**
>
> Alternatively, nonconforming traffic may be delayed at the edge of the network so that it becomes conforming. This form of policing is non-work-conserving traffic shaping (see Chapter 3). Certain hosts police traffic submitted for Guaranteed Service in this manner.

Even though policing at the edges assures that traffic submitted to the network is conforming, the submitted traffic may become distorted as it moves through the network. For this reason, RFC 2212 actually recommends reshaping traffic at strategic points in the network.

In response to requests for Guaranteed Service, the service interface specifies that the network will inform the application of the maximum latency that it can expect to experience. This information is based on an accumulation of delay specifications from the network elements along the traffic path. Note, however, that the application does not have to settle for the delay bound offered. It may reduce the delay bound by increasing the R parameter or reducing the slack term in the desired rate specified with the service request.

Suitability of Guaranteed Service to Applications

As discussed earlier in this chapter, the delay bound assurance offered by the Guaranteed Service is particularly tempting when considering the requirements of latency-intolerant applications such as IP telephony. However, it is considerably more difficult and costly for a network element to offer proper Guaranteed Service than it is for it to offer Controlled Load Service. It can be expected that this cost will be passed back to the user of the service in one form or another.

Because the latency commitment is so strict, often the network cannot offer the application the latency that it requires unless the application specifies a very high R parameter (resulting in the reservation of resources to support a very high rate). This raises the cost of the service even further. In many cases, it may be possible for the Controlled Load Service to satisfy the requirements of the application at a significantly lower cost. As implied earlier in this chapter, it is still too early in the deployment cycle of IntServ to understand the utility and economic considerations of the Guaranteed Service versus the Controlled Load Service with respect to applications such as IP telephony. Further understanding will emerge as services and applications are deployed. Such factors as the types of CODECs used by applications, as well as user tolerance of distortion and latency, will likely be significant factors in how these services are used.

Obviously, certain applications (such as the control of a nuclear power plant) may absolutely require the delay bound assurances of the Guaranteed Service.

Implementing the Guaranteed Service

Implementation of the Guaranteed Service in a network element is significantly more complex than implementation of the Controlled Load Service. In particular, each network element implementing the Guaranteed Service must be capable of specifying absolute maximum bounds on the latency that it will introduce. This latency consists of three components:

- Queuing latency

- Rate-independent latency (denoted by D)

- Rate-dependent latency (denoted by C)

The first component is entirely determined by the queue-servicing scheme implemented in the network element. Whatever queuing scheme is used must be capable of guaranteeing an upper limit on queuing latency. The other two components are considered error terms. The rate-independent error term is the inherent latency of the network element or medium that is not dependent on traffic rate. An example of rate-independent latency offered by RFC 2212 is the worst-case latency incurred in waiting for a "slot" on a slotted or time-sliced medium. The rate-dependent latency is that latency introduced by the element or medium that is dependent on the specified flow rate (not the media rate). An example of a rate dependent latency is serialization delay of ATM cells.

The queuing latency component is determined by the queuing scheme and the associated parameters used by the network element. Work by Parekh and Gallagher [PG] has shown that if a source is shaped by a token bucket and is scheduled using weighted fair queuing (see Chapter 3), then it is possible to achieve an absolute upper bound on queuing delay. Thus, a common scheduling approach to offering Guaranteed Service is to create a separate queue for each Guaranteed Service traffic flow and to schedule among these queues using weighted fair queuing. Other queuing schemes may be used as long as they are capable of offering strict delay bounds.

As reservation setup messages move through the network, they inform network elements of the desired rate (R) for each Guaranteed Service flow and of the slack term for the flow. Network elements are required to configure their queuing mechanisms so that each flow can be serviced at the rate specified by R with a latency no worse than that implied by the combination of R and the slack term. If a finite slack term is specified, then a network element may compromise the latency it offers, consuming part of the "slop" allowed by the slack term. However, if it does so, it must update the slack term in the reservation setup message so that other network elements in the path are correctly informed of the remaining slack.

The error terms C and D are latency characteristics of each network element. The end-to-end queuing latency along a traffic path is increased by the sum of the latencies associated with these error terms at each network element. As reservation setup messages move through the network, they accumulate the latency (due to the C and D terms) introduced by each network element. Thus, network elements must be capable of quantifying their contribution to these terms and adjusting the cumulative terms accordingly in the reservation setup messages.

Admission control must be stricter in the case of Guaranteed Service than in the case of Controlled Load Service. Because the service offers absolute latency bounds, it must not admit new flows if there is any chance that they would compromise the service committed to previously admitted flows. Thus, measurement-based and other statistical admission control algorithms should not be used in the case of Guaranteed Service.

4.2.2.3   The Null Service

Over time, various other services have been proposed to the IntServ working group of the IETF. So far, no services other than the Controlled Load and the Guaranteed Service have survived the scrutiny of the working group leaders, and probably appropriately so. It seems that it would be appropriate to gain some experience with the existing services before defining new ones.

One service that may or may not be viewed as an exception is the *Null Service*, which has recently been proposed in the ISSLL working group of the IETF [NULL_SERVICE]. Note that this service was not proposed in the IntServ working group. The Null Service is quite unconventional because it does not specify any quantitative parameters relating to rate or latency of the traffic flow. Because it does not specify quantitative parameters, it is not amenable to the kind of quantitative admission control discussed so far. As such, it is quite different from the Controlled Load and the Guaranteed Services.

In RFC 1633, the IntServ working group proposed "to offer several classes of best-effort service to reflect the relative delay sensitivities of different elastic applications." The RFC explains further that this "service model allows interactive burst applications to have lower delays than interactive bulk applications, which in turn would have lower delays than asynchronous bulk applications." The RFC goes on to say, "In contrast to the real-time service models, applications using this service are not subject to admission control." The IntServ working group stopped short of defining this service model. Serendipitously, the definition of such a service model came years later, in the form of the Null Service.

The Null Service Interface

The service interfaces for Guaranteed and Controlled Load Services are fundamentally quite similar to each other. The application tells the network that it would like a certain quantity of service; the network does some arithmetic to determine whether the quantity is available and then either commits or does not commit to deliver the service. Many applications that are considered mission-critical by network administrators are incapable of quantifying their resource requirements. Examples of such applications are client/server database applications and Web transactions. For these applications, the quantitative type of service interface is inappropriate. These applications cannot tell the network what quantity of resources they need, so the network can hardly commit a specific quantity of resources in return. As such, even the *reservation* model is of dubious value for these applications. Of course, such *qualitative* applications could request the reservation of a specific quantity of resources. However, such a reservation likely would be used very inefficiently and either would yield marginal benefit or would incur significant cost.

An alternate service model would *prioritize* the access of such application traffic to resources but would not *reserve* a specific quantity of resources for the traffic. This implies a service interface in which an application asks for a certain priority for its traffic flows and the network then commits to deliver or not deliver the priority. In this case, admission control amounts to deciding whether the application's traffic is entitled to the requested priority. Because there are no objective quantifiable criteria on which to base this decision, admission control becomes purely a policy-based decision. The network decides what priority the application is entitled to based on the identity of the application, the specific type of traffic (the subset of the application), or the users sending and receiving the traffic. Thus, the service interface is of the form "Application identifies traffic flow to the network, specifying application name, subapplication name, and user. Network assigns priority to traffic."

Implementing the Null Service

Applications invoking the Null Service offer no quantifiable parameters, so their traffic can be expected to appear in any quantity at any time. Such traffic could easily wreak havoc with the commitments offered to Guaranteed and Controlled Load Service flows in the same network. To avoid this, network elements must either police traffic arriving on Null Service flows, assign it a priority lower than that assigned to traffic on Guaranteed and Controlled Load Service flows, or both. Obviously, it is difficult (although possible) to select quantifiable policing parameters for nonquantifiable flows. Therefore, a reasonable approach is simply to prioritize traffic on Null Service flows above best-effort traffic but below traffic on Guaranteed and Controlled Load flows. This could be achieved by using a queuing mechanism similar to the DRR+ scheme described in Chapter 3. For example, Guaranteed and Controlled Load Service flows would be assigned to the highest strict-priority class in the scheduler. Resources would be shared among these flows using weighted fair queuing (WFQ). All Null Service traffic would be assigned to a lower strict priority class.

Traffic submitted on the Guaranteed and Controlled Load Service flows is subject to quantitative admission control and to policing. This is important because it is necessary to prevent the Guaranteed and Controlled Load Service traffic from completely starving the Null Service traffic.

As stated previously, admission control becomes a matter of policy because there are no quantitative parameters on which to base it. However, there may nonetheless be a quantitative aspect to Null Service admission control. For example, consider that a network manager learns from experience that a certain speed link can support 30 SAP/R3 sessions at a certain priority level before that priority level becomes congested. In this case, the admission control policy implemented by the network would prioritize traffic from 30 SAP/R3 sessions and no more. All SAP/R3 traffic beyond the 30th session would be treated as best-effort. In this manner, Null Service admission control is based on the *number* of *concurrent flows* of a certain type.

4.2.2.4 Link-Sharing Service

Beyond the IntServ architecture RFC [RFC 1633], little is said about the IntServ concept of a link-sharing service. Nonetheless, network elements that offer IntServ services typically also offer a management interface by which certain link-sharing functionalities can be invoked. One form of link sharing can be provided by implementing the services described previously, but changing the classifiers to aggregate multiple conversations into a single flow. The scheme described to enable Null Service to be provided side by side with the Guaranteed and Controlled Load Services can also be extended to accommodate link-sharing goals.

4.3 Integrated Services Over Specific Link Layers

The IETF focuses on IP, which is a Layer 3 technology. Thus, the IntServ working group focused on the definition and requirements of services from a Layer 3 perspective. As a result, the service interface enables applications to express their service requirements without regard for the specific link layers over which their traffic would be running.

In reality, end-to-end paths in real networks consist of concatenations of a variety of link layers. Each link layer uses a specific medium and (if it does so at all) may provide QoS using different mechanisms. For example, on ATM media, a hardware *cell scheduler* supports QoS. On Ethernet, QoS can be provided using a software-based *packet scheduler*. (This scheduler may interact with or incorporate the Ethernet CSMA/CD mechanism).

The ISSLL working group was formed to develop mappings from the abstract expressions of QoS parameters used by IntServ, to the specific requirements of each link layer. This concept is illustrated in Figure 4.7.

So far, sub-working groups of ISSLL have focused on mappings for the following link layers:

- IEEE 802 networks (IS802)

- ATM (ISATM)

- Slow modem links (ISSLOW)

Figure 4.7   Mapping IntServ to Specific Link Layers

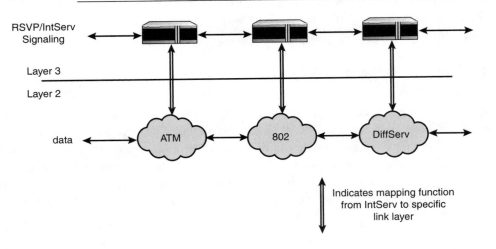

Recently, the ISSLL working group has begun to work on mappings of IntServ to DiffServ. Strictly speaking, DiffServ is not a link-layer mechanism. Nonetheless, many of the lessons learned in mapping IntServ to various Layer 2 network regions can be usefully applied when considering the support of IntServ on a DiffServ network. With the renewed interest in IntServ and the proliferation of new media, it is reasonable to expect that the IntServ working group will tackle additional link layers, such as cable modems, wireless media, and xDSL.

4.4   Summary

The IntServ architecture was developed with the goal of enabling the Internet to serve audio, video, and other real-time traffic side by side with traditional data traffic in a single network infrastructure. Many of the implications of the IntServ architecture were quite controversial. The IntServ work has had a significant and enduring impact on subsequent QoS work.

The IntServ working group of the IETF authored RFC 1633, which describes the IntServ architecture. The IntServ architecture includes a service model and an implementation framework. The service model describes the externally visible behavior of the architecture. The implementation framework describes how various QoS mechanisms can be constructed and applied to provide the services that comprise the service model. Applications request a certain service from the network using a service interface. The network responds by either committing or not committing to provide the requested service.

The services defined for standardization by the IntServ working group are quantitative services. They request specific quantities of resources from the network and expect these to be delivered with reasonably high integrity. To provide such services, it is necessary to reserve resources in network elements. This is one of the most controversial conclusions of the IntServ work. Detractors of IntServ argue that the complexity of resource reservation is not necessary. Proponents argue that it is necessary in order to raise the QE product of the network.

The implementation framework required to realize the service model includes the following components:

- Classifier

- Packet scheduler

- Admission control

- Reservation setup protocol

The classifier and packet scheduler provide traffic handling functionality, as defined in Chapter 1. Admission control is the process by which the network decides whether to commit to a specific service request. The resource setup protocol is the mechanism by which traffic handling is invoked and configured consistently across a set of network elements between senders and receivers. The need for a reservation setup protocol led to the development of RSVP.

The specific services that are standardized by the IntServ working group are the Guaranteed Service and the Controlled Load Service. Both are designed to meet the needs of real-time applications such as IP telephony and video streaming. The Guaranteed Service is specifically designed to provide strict latency bounds for traffic adhering to a specified profile. The Controlled Load Service offers the "appearance of a lightly loaded network" for traffic adhering to the specified profile. Although it may offer a low average latency, it cannot guarantee this latency. The Guaranteed Service can guarantee strict latency bounds, but it is likely to cost significantly more than a Controlled Load Service commitment for comparable service parameters.

Strictly speaking, the Guaranteed Service was designed for distortion-intolerant applications rather than latency-intolerant applications. It is not clear whether the Guaranteed Service is useful or necessary for latency-intolerant real-time applications. It may be possible to support both latency-tolerant and latency-intolerant real-time applications using the Controlled Load Service. On the other hand, it may be necessary to use the Guaranteed Service to support such latency-intolerant real-time applications as IP telephony. This issue will be better understood as real-time applications and IntServ services are more broadly deployed.

Although the IntServ service model leaves the door open for the standardization of additional services, the working group stopped with the definition of the Guaranteed and Controlled Load Services. Recently, the ISSLL working group of the IETF has proposed the Null Service. This service is suitable for applications that require prioritized service but are incapable of quantifying their resource requirements. The Null Service can be supported in network elements side by side with the Guaranteed and Controlled Load Services.

The ISSLL working group of the IETF focuses on the definition of adaptation layers and mechanisms that enable IntServ services to be supported by a broad variety of network elements and corresponding link-layer and physical media. So far, the ISSLL working group has defined how ATM, Ethernet (and other 802 media), and slow WAN links can support IntServ services. The ISSLL working group is also in the process of defining how DiffServ networks can support IntServ.

5

RSVP

RSVP was identified in Chapter 1, "Introduction to Quality of Service," as a signaling mechanism by which traffic handling can be configured coherently across a set of network elements. Chapter 2, "The Quality/Efficiency Product," discussed the merits of signaling in the configuration of traffic-handling mechanisms. In particular, the use of signaling for specific traffic can increase the quality/efficiency (QE) product of the network with respect to that traffic. This point was developed further in Chapter 4, "Integrated Services," in the context of the high-quality services offered by the Integrated Services (IntServ) framework. RSVP can also improve the general manageability of a QoS-enabled network by increasing the information available to the network-management system. As such, RSVP signaling is an important component in the mosaic of QoS mechanisms.

This chapter explains the operation of the RSVP protocol. It delves into the various extensions to RSVP and discusses various applications of the protocol and its extensions.

5.1 The History of RSVP

A lot can be learned about the appropriate role of RSVP in the QoS-enabled network by looking at its history. The following paragraphs describe the evolution of RSVP from its inception in 1993 to the present day.

5.1.1 The Birth of RSVP

In 1993 and 1994, Bob Braden, Dave Clark, and Scott Shenker were busily defining the IntServ architecture. (IntServ is described in detail in Chapter 4.) Their goal, captured in the charter of the IntServ working group of the IETF, was to define the requirements to "transition the Internet into a robust integrated-service communications infrastructure" [INTSERV_WEB]. The transformed Internet would support audio, video, and other real-time and traditional data-traffic in a single network infrastructure. To support the high-quality services envisioned by the IntServ working group, they identified the need for a reservation setup protocol. This was the impetus for the development of RSVP.

The first prototype of RSVP was developed in 1993 by a group of researchers at the Xerox Palo Alto Research Center (PARC) and the University of Southern California (USC). The group included Sugih Jamin, Lixia Zhang, and Scott Shenker. The goal of this group's work was to develop an "efficient, robust, and flexible signaling protocol for Internet QoS, supporting both multicast and unicast data flows" [RSVP_WEB]. This protocol eventually would meet the requirements outlined by the IntServ working group in [RFC 1633]. The group proceeded to enhance the prototype RSVP implementation and generated a draft of the RSVP protocol. This draft was introduced into the IETF standardization process at the Houston IETF meeting in 1994. The RSVP working group of the IETF was formed. Chaired by Lixia Zhang and Bob Braden, the RSVP working group assumed the significant task of developing the draft protocol to the status of proposed standard and eventually published RFCs (in 1997).

The Inextricable Intertwining of RSVP and IntServ

Not a week goes by that someone does not remind me of the importance of emphasizing the separate nature of RSVP and IntServ. In anticipation of the many tongue-lashings that will no doubt be directed my way, let me say it here loud and clear: RSVP is a *signaling protocol*. IntServ is a *framework for the definition and implementation of services*. They are *independently useful*. They even have separate chapters in this book.

That said, RSVP and IntServ are also inextricably intertwined. RFC 1633, which defines the IntServ architecture, states that "an explicit *setup* mechanism is necessary." It claims a "reservation setup protocol" as the "fourth and final component of the IntServ framework" and even goes so far as to give an overview of RSVP in RFC 1633. RFC 2210 discusses the use of RSVP with IntServ specifically. RSVP is particularly well suited to support the high-quality services defined by IntServ, and obtaining high-quality services tends to require topology-aware admission control. RSVP provides this by delivering service requests to the specific subset of network elements on the path from sender to receiver.

In many minds, the IntServ architecture and the RSVP protocol are one and the same: RSVP/IntServ. The term *RSVP/IntServ* will be used in this book to denote the original and popular model defined by the following characteristics:

- RSVP signaling is initiated by applications.
- RSVP signaling is on a per-conversation basis (5-tuple).
- RSVP invokes per-conversation traffic handling in IntServ-aware network elements to provide the IntServ Guaranteed or Controlled Load Service.

However, please note the following:

- RSVP can be used to invoke non-IntServ services (for example, the *Null Service*, which is described in Chapter 4).

- RSVP can be used to invoke bandwidth for aggregate traffic flows that include multiple conversations (for example, *aggregate RSVP*, which is described later in this chapter).

- IntServ services can be invoked without the RSVP protocol (for example, using SNMP and the IntServ MIB [RFC 2213]).

- IntServ services can be invoked on a per-conversation or aggregate basis (see the discussion of link-sharing in [RFC 1633]).

In other words, RSVP and IntServ can be applied in many different models other than the popular RSVP/IntServ model. This book discusses both the RSVP/IntServ model and alternate applications of IntServ and RSVP. In fact, due to a number of reasons (outlined in the following paragraphs), alternate applications of the two technologies are more likely to enjoy widespread deployment than the original RSVP/IntServ model.

5.1.2 The Rise and Fall of RSVP

As soon as the media caught wind of the RSVP and IntServ work progressing in the IETF, the celebrations began. RSVP/IntServ was hailed as the new panacea that would forever rid the Internet of all its troubles. Some seemed to believe that RSVP/IntServ would even go so far as to create much-needed bandwidth from thin air. The media hype and the excitement around it was sustained for some time. During this time, leading network equipment vendors and certain UNIX operating system vendors began to develop RSVP/IntServ implementations and to pitch the virtues of RSVP/IntServ to their customers. However, RSVP/IntServ failed to gain much practical support during these early years, for the reasons described in the following paragraphs.

5.1.2.1 Absence of Signaling Hosts

The use of RSVP (as originally envisioned) depended on signaling hosts. The majority of deployed hosts did not signal and had no clear plans to begin doing so.

5.1.2.2 No Support for Truly Mission-Critical Applications

RSVP/IntServ was targeted at quantitative applications such as audio and video applications. Although these were the topic of much excitement and anticipation, they were not the mission-critical applications that network managers had an urgent need to support in their networks. Network managers were far more interested in making enterprise resource-planning applications (such as the SAP/R3 enterprise resource planning application) work robustly on their network than they were in enabling new leading-edge applications.

5.1.2.3 *Perception That the RSVP/IntServ Model Is Not Scalable*

Scalability is an issue that has haunted the progress of the RSVP/IntServ model from its inception. Its original developers stated scalability as a target goal. Its early detractors cited scalability as the reason that RSVP/IntServ would never be broadly used. A number of scalability concerns are associated with the RSVP/IntServ model, as follows:

- The need to process per-conversation signaling in each network device

- The need to maintain per-conversation signaling state in each network device

- The need to apply per-conversation traffic handling in each device

- The need to maintain per-conversation traffic handling state in each device

Note that two fundamental scalability concerns exist. One is related to per-conversation traffic handling. The other is related to per-conversation signaling. The former is related more to RSVP than IntServ. The latter is related more to IntServ than RSVP. Neither is mandated by the corresponding technology (both allow aggregate applications). Nonetheless, these are the scalability concerns associated with the popular RSVP/IntServ model. Alternate applications of RSVP and IntServ (which will be discussed later in this chapter and in Chapter 6, "Differentiated Services") alleviate the scalability concerns associated with the original RSVP/IntServ model.

5.1.2.4 *Absence of Policy Mechanisms*

The premise of any QoS mechanism is that it alters the distribution of network resources with respect to consumers of network resources. Any such mechanism implies that there are policies governing which consumers benefit from the mechanism and which might be penalized by it. Before QoS mechanisms can be successfully deployed, it is necessary to support the implementation of specific policies with a corresponding security and accounting infrastructure. Although the RSVP protocol makes accommodations for such an infrastructure, it does not specify the infrastructure. In the early days of RSVP development, no such infrastructure was yet proposed (let alone ready for deployment). Had there been no other obstacles to the deployment of the RSVP/IntServ model, the absence of policy mechanisms may have been a minor obstacle to be overcome by clever network managers and creative scripting exercises. However, given the other obstacles listed, the absence of policy mechanisms became one more reason not to deploy the RSVP/IntServ model.

5.1.3 The Death Blow

In 1997, the RSVP version 1 protocol was advanced to the level of *proposed standard* in the form of RFC 2205.

> **Note**
>
> The IETF recognizes different types of documents with different status levels. Standards usually begin their lives as *Internet drafts*. Drafts may be *informational* or *standards track*. According to [RFC 2026], "Internet drafts have no formal status." When and if standard track drafts reach a certain level of stability and maturity, they may be progressed to the status of *proposed standard*—at that time, they become a Request For Comments (RFC). As an RFC matures, it graduates from proposed standard to *draft standard* and eventually to *Internet standard*. The various levels of standardization are described in detail in [RFC 2026]. The RSVP specification is currently a proposed standard. As it becomes more widely deployed, it will likely advance to the level of draft standard and, ultimately, Internet standard. To track its progress, see [STD1].

At the same time, the IETF released an applicability statement [RFC 2208] regarding the applicability of the RSVP/IntServ work done to date. This statement warned, "Wide-scale deployment of RSVP must be approached with care." It listed the following specific concerns:

- Scalability

- Security considerations

- Absence of policy control

Although the goal of the applicability statement was to adjust expectations, it unfortunately scared many would-be implementers and deployers away from any type of RSVP deployment. The media, always excited at the prospect of a new drama, jumped on the opportunity to pronounce RSVP dead on arrival and began searching for the new panacea.

5.1.4 The Renaissance of RSVP

Ironically, the birth of the next panacea, Differentiated Services (DiffServ), actually breathed new life into RSVP. DiffServ offered a scalable traffic-handling mechanism, but no signaling protocol. RSVP could make use of the DiffServ traffic-handling mechanisms to side-step the scalability issues associated with IntServ traffic handling, while at the same time raising the QE product of a DiffServ network (see Figure 2.3 in Chapter 2, and the discussion of DiffServ in Chapter 6). In addition, RSVP signaling provides classification information, which the DiffServ network can use to associate packets with users and applications. This combination of RSVP and DiffServ is addressed by the ISSLL working group of the IETF.

About the same time that DiffServ was emerging, Microsoft began to get serious about offering RSVP signaling and simple API support in Windows operating systems. This stood to significantly increase the number of RSVP signaling hosts. In addition, market leaders such as Microsoft and Cisco demonstrated the use of RSVP for nonquantitative mission-critical applications.

Meanwhile, the IETF was making progress in a couple of policy-related working groups. These include the *Resource Allocation Protocol* (RAP) working group and the *Policy Framework* (Policy) working group. Network equipment vendors were beginning to offer early policy-management systems.

> **Note**
>
> Because the RSVP protocol automatically configures traffic-handling mechanisms along the relevant traffic paths, RSVP actually simplifies the application of QoS policy. RSVP policy work has largely been completed in the form of COPS for RSVP (see Chapter 9, "QoS Policy," for further details on policy mechanisms). Much of the remaining work being tackled by the RAP and the Policy working groups is related to policy requirements for pushed (as opposed to signaled) provisioning.

Today it is evident that all the factors that initially hindered the deployment of RSVP are in various stages of resolution. The networking community is evolving the protocol to its needs in a manner that realizes its benefits while avoiding its shortcomings. The remainder of this chapter delves into RSVP concepts and explains the operation of the RSVP protocol. It focuses initially on the original RSVP/IntServ model. Next, it describes the evolution of the protocol and adaptations that have been developed to facilitate its deployment.

5.2   RSVP Concepts

Before delving into the detailed operation of the RSVP protocol, it is helpful to introduce certain fundamental concepts and terminology. These are introduced in the following paragraphs. Certain concepts will be discussed in greater depth later in this chapter.

5.2.1   The Notion of a Reservation

The notion of a *reservation* was discussed in Chapter 4, in the context of IntServ. The IntServ architecture correctly concluded that high-quality services can be realized efficiently only by *reserving* resources. (See the section "RSVP: The Reservation Setup Protocol," in Chapter 4, for a detailed discussion of the concept of a reservation.)

Note that the reservations obtained as a result of RSVP signaling are *simplex,* or unidirectional. A peer-to-peer telephone call, for example, requires two separate reservations: one from Host A to Host B, and another from Host B to Host A. In Figure 5.1, Host A is a sender on Reservation 1 and is a receiver on Reservation 2. Host B is a sender on Reservation 2 and is a receiver on Reservation 1. Each reservation reserves resources to carry traffic from sender to receiver.

Figure 5.1   The Unidirectional Nature of a Reservation

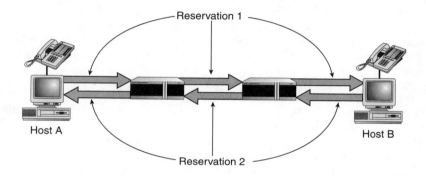

5.2.2   *Soft-State Model*

The Internet is designed to be resilient in the face of unreliable network nodes and, in particular, in the face of unreliable hosts. Because RSVP enables hosts to reserve resources through the Internet, great care must be taken to ensure that reserved resources will be freed in case the hosts that reserved them fail. Similarly, in the case of router failure or route changes, resources that will no longer be used must be freed in all affected routers.

With this in mind, RSVP was designed based on a *soft-state* model. This means that the reservation state in network devices expires automatically after some timeout period, unless it is continually *refreshed* by periodic signaling. This approach can be contrasted to the hard-state nature of alternative signaling protocols such as ATM signaling. In ATM signaling, explicit teardown messages are required to terminate reservations. A soft-state approach has advantages and disadvantages relative to the hard-state approach. To make a hard-state protocol resilient to node failures, each node must monitor the health of adjacent nodes using some sort of keepalive signaling. The soft-state approach does not require such keepalive signaling between adjacent nodes. However, because it refreshes each reservation periodically, it generates a higher volume of signaling traffic *per-reservation*. Nonetheless, this approach tends to shift complexity from the center of the network to the edges, in the general spirit of the Internet *end-to-end* philosophy.

The End-to-End Philosophy

RFC 1958 [RFC 1958], published in June 1996, is loftily titled "Architectural Principles of the Internet." It discusses some important principles and applies these to Internet protocol development and to Internet development in general. One of the principles espoused by this RFC (first described in [SALTZER]) is the *end-to-end* principle. The following excerpts from RFC 1958 summarize the end-to-end principle and its applicability to the soft-state nature of the RSVP protocol:

"The basic argument is that, as a first principle, certain required end-to-end functions can only be performed correctly by the end-systems themselves. A specific case is that any network, however carefully designed, will be subject to failures of transmission at some statistically determined rate. The best way to cope with this is to accept it, and give responsibility for the integrity of communication to the end systems.

"This principle has important consequences if we require applications to survive partial network failures. An end-to-end protocol design should not rely on the maintenance of state (i.e., information about the state of the end-to-end communication) inside the network. Such state should be maintained only in the endpoints, in such a way that the state can only be destroyed when the endpoint itself breaks (known as fate-sharing). An immediate consequence of this is that datagrams are better than classical virtual circuits. The network's job is to transmit datagrams as efficiently and flexibly as possible. Everything else should be done at the fringes."

A related aspect of the end-to-end philosophy is *transparency*. The transparency principle calls for packets to remain as unaltered as possible as they move through the Internet. In other words, the Internet should appear transparent from the perspective of the endpoints.

In applying the end-to-end philosophy to QoS in general (as opposed to RSVP in particular), it suggests that QoS should be controlled by hosts to the degree possible. At the very least, QoS should be controlled by the *cooperation* of hosts and network devices, certainly not by network devices alone, to the exclusion of hosts.

5.2.3 Receiver Orientation

A salient feature of the RSVP protocol is its receiver orientation. As explained in the previous section, in the traditional application of RSVP, resources are not actually reserved until the receiver responds to the sender's signaling messages. Thus, for the most part, the receiver controls the quantity of resources reserved on its behalf. This is important because the cost of a reservation is likely to be proportional to the quantity and quality of resources reserved and is likely to be borne (at least in part) by the receiver. In a multicast session, certain receivers may not be capable of receiving the full bandwidth offered by the sender(s). These receivers would opt for a lower quantity of reserved resources and, presumably, a lower cost. This is an example of *receiver heterogeneity*, which is enabled by the receiver orientation of RSVP. The value of receiver heterogeneity is debatable, however, and will be discussed in detail later in this chapter.

Note that despite the receiver orientation of RSVP, no action can be initiated on a reservation until the *sender* initiates the RSVP signaling cycle. The RSVP signaling cycle will be described in detail later in this chapter in the section "The Reservation Cycle."

5.2.4 IP Multicast

Another salient feature of RSVP is its support for IP multicast. One of the applications envisioned by the original developers of RSVP is a large-scale videoconference. Such a conference may have thousands of participants. These participants may join one multicast group to receive the conference audio traffic and then join another group to receive the conference video traffic. Multicast conferences with a large number of participants pose scalability problems because of the volume of RSVP messages that may be generated by all the participants. RSVP defines *merging rules* that merge reservations from multiple receivers to address the scalability problems of large multicast groups. Note that RSVP does not improve the scalability aspects of multicast technology itself. Instead, it leverages these so as not to compromise scalability when reservations are applied to multicast sessions.

5.2.5 RSVP Sessions

It is helpful to discuss traffic flows and RSVP reservations in the context of the RSVP *session* with which they are associated. The session is effectively the IP destination address and transport-layer port of the traffic served by a reservation. Because RSVP supports both unicast and multicast traffic flows, the session may represent a single receiver or a group of receivers joined to a single multicast group. In the unicast case, the session may represent, for example, the single receiving endpoint of an IP telephony conversation. In the multicast case, the session might represent a multicast address that carries a video program that is tuned to by a large number of receivers. From the perspective of an individual network device, a session is a useful abstraction with which to associate reserved resources. Note that sessions are *simplex*, or unidirectional. This means that a telephone call between two hosts is actually comprised of two sessions: one from Caller A to Caller B, and the other from Caller B to Caller A. Note also that sessions are defined by the destination (or destinations, in the case of a multicast session), not by the sender(s).

5.3 RSVP Messages and Basic Protocol Operation

The following section introduces the fundamental RSVP messages and explains the basic operation of the RSVP protocol. It is not intended to serve as a specification of the protocol, nor as an exhaustive description of its features and functionality. For these, see the many sources of information on RSVP, including [RFC 2205] and [YD]. This section focuses on the operation of the RSVP protocol with respect to single-sender, single-receiver, unicast sessions. Subsequent sections discuss the operation of the protocol in the context of multicast sessions (which is substantially more complex than the unicast case).

5.3.1 The Structure of RSVP Messages

As is the case with any network protocol, RSVP is based on the exchange of a set of *messages* between senders and receivers. RSVP messages carry a list of *objects*. Each object carries a specific set of related information. The message/object structure of RSVP makes it readily extensible. Additional objects can easily be defined and appended to standard messages. Devices that do not understand the new objects simply ignore them.

5.3.2 The Fundamental RSVP Messages: PATH and RESV

The fundamental messages comprising the RSVP protocol are PATH and RESV messages. Senders of QoS traffic issue PATH messages. Receivers respond with RESV messages (also known as *reservation* messages). The following paragraphs describe these messages in detail and illustrate how they are used to establish reservations.

> **Note**
>
> Throughout the remainder of this book, the terms *upstream* and *downstream* will be used in the context of RSVP. The term *downstream* will be used to refer to the direction from the sender of a traffic flow to the receiver. The term *upstream* will be used to refer to the opposite direction.
>
> Also note that, per the soft-state approach described previously, the primary RSVP messages are retransmitted (or "refreshed") periodically, as long as they remain valid.

5.3.2.1 PATH Messages

The process of establishing an RSVP reservation begins with the transmission of periodic PATH messages by a sending host. A PATH message identifies the host as the sender of a traffic flow and describes the characteristics of the traffic that the sender offers on the flow. It also specifies the session on which the traffic flow is being offered.

Composition of PATH Messages

Figure 5.2 illustrates the composition of an RSVP PATH message (see the text for a further discussion of the objects included in a PATH message):

- A standard RSVP header is placed at the head of the message.

- The SESSION object identifies the RSVP session to which the sender is sending.

- The RSVP_HOP object identifies the previous RSVP-aware hop from which the PATH message arrived.

- The TIME_VALUES object contains the refresh period used by the node generating the PATH message.

- The POLICY_DATA object contains policy data relating to the traffic generated by the sender.

- The SENDER_TEMPLATE object identifies the sender.

- The SENDER_TSPEC object describes the traffic that the sender transmits on the described flow.

- The ADSPEC object accumulates characteristics of the path from sender to receiver(s).

Figure 5.2   PATH Messages

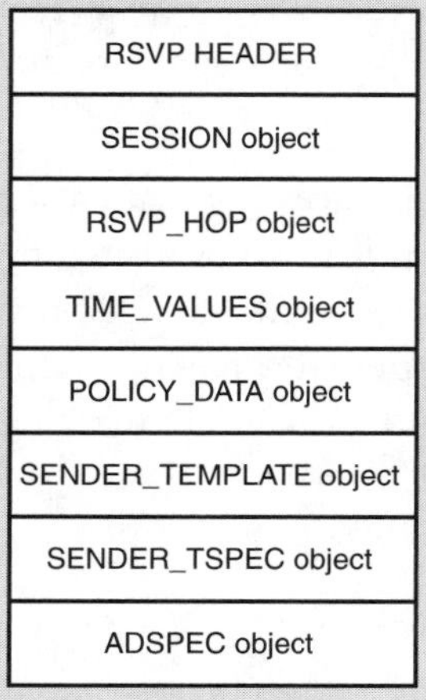

```
┌──────────────────────────────┐
│         RSVP HEADER          │
├──────────────────────────────┤
│        SESSION object        │
├──────────────────────────────┤
│       RSVP_HOP object        │
├──────────────────────────────┤
│      TIME_VALUES object      │
├──────────────────────────────┤
│     POLICY_DATA object       │
├──────────────────────────────┤
│   SENDER_TEMPLATE object     │
├──────────────────────────────┤
│    SENDER_TSPEC object       │
├──────────────────────────────┤
│        ADSPEC object         │
└──────────────────────────────┘
```

Marking the Downstream Path of the Data Traffic

The primary purpose of PATH messages is to mark the path through the network that is traversed by the associated data traffic flow. This is necessary to ensure that the RESV messages generated in response will flow upstream, through the same network devices that carry the data traffic downstream. In general, it cannot be assumed that data traffic sent from Host A to Host B would traverse the same network devices as traffic sent from Host B to Host A. Because RESV messages actually cause network devices to reserve resources, these must traverse the same set of network devices that carry the protected data traffic downstream.

To this end, PATH messages leave PATH state in each RSVP-aware network device as they progress downstream, including the destination receiver(s). This PATH state contains the address of the *previous-hop* device (which is carried in PATH messages in the form of the RSVP_HOP object). The previous-hop device is the immediately preceding RSVP-aware device on the downstream path.

Note

Note that the RSVP_HOP object may be used to specify *previous* hop (PHOP) or *next* hop (NHOP). The PHOP refers to the next hop upstream. The NHOP refers to the next hop downstream.

In this manner, PATH messages leave "breadcrumbs" that can be used to route RESV messages back upstream, through the same network devices that PATH messages traverse downstream.

Of course, for all this to work, it is necessary that PATH messages traverse the same path downstream as the data traffic that is to be protected by the associated reservation. This is assured by addressing PATH messages to the same destination address as the data to be protected. Standard routing then carries PATH messages along the same path as the data traffic. Figure 5.3 clarifies the role of PATH messages in marking the data path.

Figure 5.3   How PATH Messages Mark the Return Path for RESV Messages

(a) PATH messages sent downstream

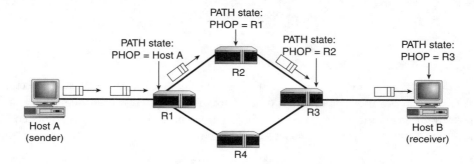

(b) RESV messages follow PATH upstream

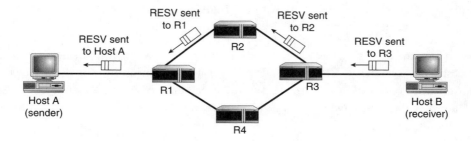

Characterizing the Offered Traffic

In addition to marking the path traversed by downstream data traffic, PATH messages advertise to the network and to receivers the characteristics of the traffic that is being transmitted on a traffic flow. These characteristics are described in the form of a SENDER_TSPEC object. In the original IntServ application of RSVP, the SENDER_TSPEC object uses a form of the token bucket model (see Chapter 3, "Queuing Mechanisms") to describe the transmitted traffic.

Note

Note, however, that although the token bucket model is useful for describing the quantifiable traffic traditionally associated with multimedia applications and the IntServ model, it is not useful for describing the type of nonquantifiable traffic generated by nonmultimedia applications. An alternate form of the SENDER_TSPEC object is used in the case of Null Service traffic (see Chapter 4 for an explanation of the Null Service).

Characterizing the Network Path

In addition to specifying the characteristics of the offered traffic, PATH messages accumulate information about the characteristics of the network equipment along the path transited by the PATH message (and by the corresponding data). This information is accumulated in the form of the ADSPEC object. The ADSPEC object accumulates information such as the following:

- Types of service that can be supported by network devices

- A snapshot of available resources at the time the PATH message is in transit

- The cumulative latency introduced by devices along the data path

- The maximum size of packet that can be protected by a reservation

- How many devices along a data path are IntServ-aware and whether any devices along the path are not IntServ-aware

Eventually, the PATH message reaches the receiver (or receivers) comprising the destination corresponding to the RSVP session. The information it carries informs the receiver(s) both of the nature of the offered traffic and of the capabilities of the RSVP-aware devices along the network path. Receivers may use this information to generate a response in the form of a RESV message.

Break Bits

Note that, as originally defined, the ADSPEC object includes *break bits*. A break bit exists for IntServ in general and for each of the IntServ services. The break bits are intended to notify receivers of any break in IntServ support on the path from sender to receiver. A break bit that is set indicates to a receiver that *at least one network device* on the path from sender to receiver does not support IntServ at all (the general break bit) or does not support one or another of the IntServ services (the per-service break bit). The break bits might be useful in a world in which nearly every device is RSVP/IntServ-aware. However, as will be discussed later in this chapter (in the section "Admission Control Agents"), it is likely that as QoS is deployed, only a small number of select network devices at congested locations will be RSVP/IntServ-aware. Thus, it is very unlikely that a receiver will ever receive an ADSPEC object indicating that *every* device on the path from sender to receiver is RSVP/IntServ-aware. Thus, the break bits probably have little practical value.

5.3.2.2 RESV *Messages*

When PATH state is established in a receiver, interested receivers may request a reservation to protect the offered traffic. A receiver does so by issuing a RESV message, as described in the following paragraphs.

Composition of the RESV *Message*

The RESV message composed by the receiver specifies the required service (for example, Guaranteed, Controlled Load, Null, or other) and (in the case of quantitative services) the quantity of resources that the receiver wants to reserve to protect the offered traffic (in the form of a FLOWSPEC object). The RESV message also specifies one or more senders and a *reservation style*. (These will be explained later in this chapter in the section "Reservation Styles".)

Composition of RESV Messages

Figure 5.4 illustrates the detailed composition of RSVP RESV messages (see the text for a further discussion of the objects included in RESV messages):

- A standard RSVP header is placed at the head of the message.
- The SESSION object identifies the RSVP session on which the receiver is reserving resources.
- The RSVP_HOP object identifies the previous RSVP-aware hop from which the RESV message arrived.
- The TIME_VALUES object contains the refresh period used by the node generating the RESV message.
- The RESV_CONFIRM object is an optional object indicating that the receiver wants to receive confirmation of a reservation.
- The POLICY_DATA object contains policy data relating to the identity of the receiver and the traffic for which resources are being reserved.
- The STYLE object is used to specify how reserved resources are to be allocated among multiple senders in a multicast session.
- The FLOWSPEC object describes and quantifies the resources to be reserved.
- The FILTER_SPEC object describes the subset of senders from which traffic is to be protected.

continues

continued

Figure 5.4   RESV Messages

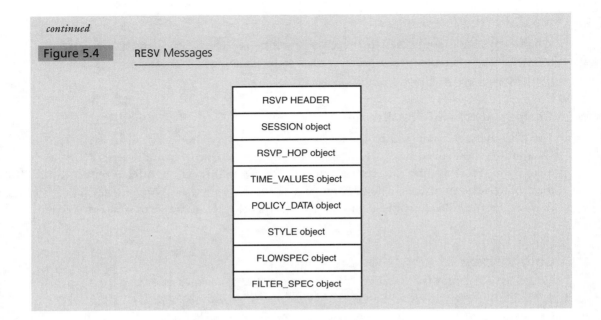

| RSVP HEADER |
| SESSION object |
| RSVP_HOP object |
| TIME_VALUES object |
| POLICY_DATA object |
| STYLE object |
| FLOWSPEC object |
| FILTER_SPEC object |

Processing the RESV Message

From the receiver, RESV messages are sent directly to the upstream RSVP-aware device in the data path (as indicated by the PHOP object in the receiver's path state). RESV messages flow upstream along the path marked by the incident PATH messages. As the RESV messages arrive at RSVP-aware devices along the data path, these devices process them.

Each device reviews the resource requests in the RESV messages. The quantity of requested resources and the requested service type are compared against the amount of resources available and the capabilities of the device. If sufficient resources are available, and if the device is capable of accommodating the resource request, the device may commit the requested resources at this time, installing RESV state. Note that the sending host also participates in this process. The network component of its operating system is the final network device in the path from sender to receiver. It, too, must verify that the resources are available in its layers of network software and hardware to accommodate the service requested in RESV messages.

In most cases, network devices will consider administrative policies in addition to the availability of resources before the resources are actually committed. Policy issues will be discussed later in this chapter in the section "Policy and Security."

Admission Control

The process of reviewing a resource request and deciding whether to commit the requested resources and install RESV state is also known as *admission control*. If a network device decides to commit resources to the request, the request is said to be *admitted*. Otherwise, it is considered *rejected*. When a device admits a request, it commits the requested resources, establishes RESV state, and forwards the corresponding RESV messages to the next RSVP-aware device in the upstream direction (per the PHOP object stored in its PATH state). When a device rejects a request, it does not forward RESV messages. Instead, it sends an error message downstream toward the requesting receiver, indicating the reason for the rejection. This message is known as a RESV_ERROR message.

Assuming that all RSVP-aware devices along the data path admit the resource request, RESV messages eventually will reach the sender that initiated the establishment of PATH state. At this time, a reservation is successfully installed. Note that, because the sender must periodically refresh PATH state by sending PATH messages, the receiver also must periodically refresh RESV state by sending RESV messages.

5.3.3 The Reservation Cycle

The previous section described the process of installing a unicast reservation between a single sender and a single receiver. The process begins with the periodic transmission of PATH messages by a sender toward a receiver for a specific session. When the first of these messages reaches the receiver, the receiver responds by beginning the periodic transmission of RESV messages back toward the sender. Each RSVP-aware device along the data path reviews the RESV messages. If the messages are successfully admitted, they will eventually reach the sender. The time at which the sender first receives a RESV message corresponding to the session is noteworthy. At this time, the sender can assume that a reservation is installed. It is helpful to refer to this process as a *reservation cycle* (illustrated in Figure 5.5). The reservation cycle is complete when the reservation is installed.

Figure 5.5   A Simple Reservation Cycle

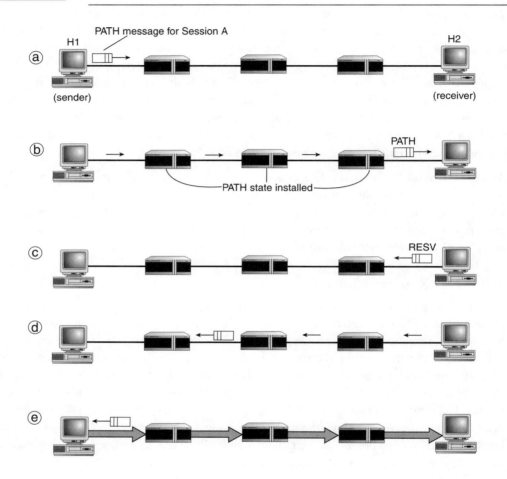

The following steps comprising the reservation cycle are illustrated in Figure 5.5:

1. Sender H1 transmits a PATH message for Session A.

2. The PATH message traverses the data path from sender to receiver, leaving PATH state for Session A installed in routers.

3. Receiver H2 responds with a RESV message for Session A.

4. Each router matches the RESV message with installed PATH state and admits the reservation request.

5. With the arrival of the RESV message at H1, the reservation cycle is complete, and a reservation is installed.

> **Note**
>
> Note that because of the soft-state nature of the RSVP protocol, both the sender and receiver (as well as intermediate RSVP-aware network devices) must periodically refresh reservations by issuing PATH and RESV messages, respectively. No one-to-one correspondence exists between the PATH messages issued by the sender and the RESV messages issued by the receiver. Instead, these are correlated through PATH and RESV state. As long as PATH state exists in a receiver and the receiver requires a reservation, it will issue periodic RESV messages. The same is true of intermediate RSVP-aware devices.
>
> Given the asynchronous relationship between PATH and RESV messages in different network devices, the notion of a reservation *cycle* is somewhat contrived. Nonetheless, it is a useful concept, at least in the case of single-sender, single-receiver, unicast sessions. In the case of multicast sessions, the notion of a cycle is less applicable, as will be discussed in the following section "Multicast Operation."

5.3.3.1   *Removing Reservations*

Reservations remain in place until they either time out due to a lapse in refreshes or until they are explicitly *torn down*. Senders may issue PATH_TEAR messages to remove PATH state. Receivers may issue RESV_TEAR messages to remove RESV state. Network devices may issue either message. Removal of PATH state or RESV state will tear down all associated reservations immediately.

Receivers and senders may issue RESV_TEAR or PATH_TEAR messages to quickly remove reservations and release associated network resources. Receivers and senders also can cause the removal of reservations by simply ceasing to refresh RESV state or PATH state. However, this approach would leave reservations in place for the duration of the timeout period, thus wasting resources.

Network devices typically issue RESV_TEAR or PATH_TEAR messages in response to error conditions or to effect policies that require the preemption of existing reservations.

5.4   *Multicast Operation*

One of the stated requirements in developing RSVP was the support of scalable QoS for multicast traffic. Much of the sophistication of the RSVP protocol is a consequence of this requirement. The previous section explained the relatively simple application of RSVP to unicast traffic. This section delves into the application of RSVP to multicast traffic.

5.4.1 Merging Reservations

Consider the following simple multicast scenario. A sender (H1) is offering an audio/video program to a multicast address. Any receiver interested in receiving the offered program may join the multicast group to which the program is offered. This is illustrated in Figure 5.6.

Figure 5.6	RSVP in a Multicast Tree

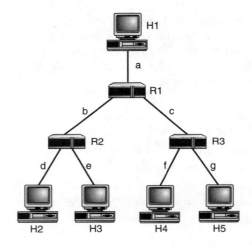

A multicast tree forms, with H1 at its root and receivers as leaves.

> **Note**
>
> A broad body of work, referred to simply as *IP multicast*, defines the algorithms and protocols that are used to form and join multicast trees (such as the tree illustrated in Figure 5.6) and to route multicast traffic. The details of this work are beyond the scope of this book. For further details on IP multicast, refer to [MCAST].

Assume that receivers H2 through H5 join the multicast group carrying the program offered by H1. The multicast data traffic will be delivered to the receivers over network segments a through g. The sending host will issue PATH messages on behalf of the sending application. These will be addressed to the same multicast address to which the audio/video data traffic is sent. As a result, PATH state will be established in R1, R2, and R3 and in H2, H3, H4, and H5 (assuming that these are all RSVP-aware).

Now consider that the receivers want to reserve resources for the offered traffic. To do so, they issue RESV messages in response. Consider, initially, H2:

1. H2 sends a RESV message toward H1.

2. When the message arrives at R2, the router commits resources on segment d.

3. R2 then forwards the RESV message upstream to R1.

4. When the message arrives at R1, the router commits resources on segment b.

5. R1 then forwards the RESV message upstream to H1.

6. Finally, H1 commits resources on segment a.

The reservation cycle is now complete, and resources are committed for the multicast session on all interfaces between H1 and H2.

Next, receiver H3 decides to request resources for the multicast session:

1. H3 sends a RESV message toward H1.

2. When the message arrives at R2, the router commits resources on segment e.

3. R2 then forwards the RESV message upstream to R1.

When the message arrives at R1, the router recognizes that it has already committed resources for the session of interest on the segment that serves H3 (segment b). Assuming that the resources already committed for the session are equal to the resources requested by H3, there is no need to reserve additional resources for the multicast traffic. R1 recognizes that the existing RESV state on segment b is adequate to accommodate the new request and *merges* RESV messages from H3 with existing RESV state. No additional action is required. No additional RESV message is forwarded upstream to H1.

Similar merging would occur as H4 and H5 decided to request resources for the session. Assuming that H4 is the next to issue a RESV message, this message would result in the commitment of new resources on segment f, by R3 and on segment c by R1. However, when the RESV message corresponding to H4 arrives at H1, the sender would merge the new request with existing RESV state on segment a.

When H5 issues a RESV message, it results in the commitment of new resources on segment g by R3 but is merged by R1 (because no new resources are required on segment c). No RESV message is sent to H1.

5.4.1.1 Merging, Scaling, and the Reservation Cycle

In describing the application of RSVP to unicast traffic, this chapter previously described a *reservation cycle*. In the application of RSVP to multicast traffic, however, reservation cycles are not clearly discernible. In the previous example, H1 issued a PATH message. H2 responded with a RESV message. The RESV message was carried all the way back to H1. With the arrival of the RESV message at H1, a reservation was installed and, in a sense, a reservation cycle was completed. However, when H3 issued a RESV message, the corresponding RESV message was merged by R1 and was never forwarded to H1. From the perspective of H3, the required resources were successfully reserved, but the "cycle" stopped short of completion.

Note that merge points maintain RESV state for the session in upstream devices by periodically issuing RESV messages corresponding to the session. However, they forward only a single RESV message in each refresh period on behalf of the session and all merged receivers; they do not refresh RESV state separately for each receiver in the session. This merging behavior is the key to the scalability of RSVP when applied to multicast sessions. (Note that other RSVP scalability issues are related to per-flow state and per-flow processing. These will be addressed separately.) If intermediate nodes did refresh state for each session individually, then the sender would receive RESV refresh messages for every receiver. This is clearly not scalable. Figure 5.7 illustrates the manner in which RESV messages are merged.

Figure 5.7   Merging RESV Messages

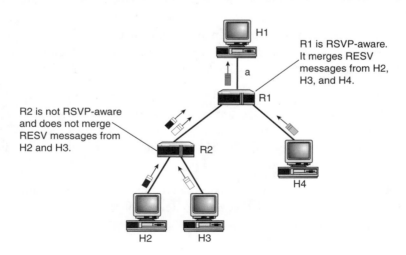

H1

R1 is RSVP-aware. It merges RESV messages from H2, H3, and H4.

a

R1

R2 is not RSVP-aware and does not merge RESV messages from H2 and H3.

R2

H4

H2   H3

In Figure 5.7, R1 is RSVP-aware, but R2 is not. Thus, R2 does not merge the RESV messages from H2 and H3. As a result, R2 passes the two sets of RESV messages to R1. Because R1 is RSVP-aware, it merges the RESV messages from H2, H3, and H4, forwarding only a single set of RESV messages to H1.

Reservation merging requires fairly sophisticated processing to handle all cases correctly. For example, if H2 were to issue a RESV_TEAR message for the session, R2 should not forward the RESV_TEAR message upstream (assuming that H3 is still issuing periodic RESV refreshes for the session). Additional complexity results when different receivers request different quantities of resources in their RESV messages.

5.4.1.2   *Receiver Heterogeneity*

Receiver heterogeneity is a much-touted feature of RSVP, which enables different receivers to request different amounts of resources for the same multicast session. The description of reservation merging described previously assumed that the receivers participating in the multicast session are homogeneous, in the sense that they each requested identical quantities of resources. However, the developers of RSVP envisioned that different receivers might request different quantities of resources in their RESV messages. This might happen if, for example, certain receivers are lower performance than others (and therefore are incapable of processing data at the full offered rate) or if certain receivers are attached via lower-performance network connections.

To accommodate such *heterogeneous* receivers, merging rules were defined to specify how to compare requests for different quantities of resources and how to determine a resulting merged quantity. (See Figure 5.8.)

Figure 5.8   Merging Requests from Heterogeneous Receivers

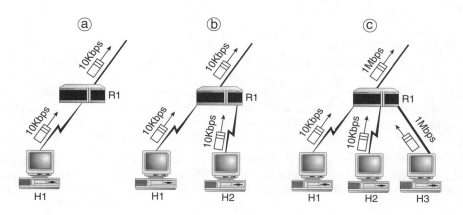

H1 and H2 are connected to R1 via a 28Kbps dial-up connection. H3 is connected via a 10Mbps Ethernet connection. In Figure 5.8a, H1 sends a RESV message requesting a reservation for 10Kbps. R1 forwards the RESV message upstream. In Figure 5.8b, the second receiver, H2, joins the multicast session and also requests a reservation of 10Kbps for the same session. R1 merges the RESV messages from H1 and H2, and continues to forward a single set of RESV messages upstream for 10Kbps. In Figure 5.8c, the third receiver, H3 joins the multicast tree. It requests 1Mbps. If approved, R1 then changes the merged RESV messages that it forwards upstream. The merged RESV messages will now request 1Mbps rather than 10Kbps.

The pragmatic value of this type of receiver heterogeneity is debatable. If traffic on the session of interest is offered at 1Mbps, and the reservation in place is only for 10Kbps (Figure 5.8a and b), then R1 will determine arbitrarily which subset of that traffic is protected in transmission to H1 and H2. The receivers are unlikely to be capable of making good use of an arbitrary subset of the offered traffic (see the accompanying sidebar, "Multilayer Encoding"). On the other hand, if traffic on the session of interest is offered at 10Kbps, then H3 would not request a reservation for 1Mbps. Receiver heterogeneity might be marginally more useful when considering latency parameters rather than bandwidth parameters.

However, specific variants on receiver heterogeneity might be quite useful. One such example is the case in which certain receivers issue RESV messages to request a sufficient amount of resources to protect all of a session's offered traffic while other receivers operate in best-effort mode (do not issue RESV messages). In this case, the best-effort receivers are willing to take the chance that they will be incapable of making good use of the received traffic. However, they incur no cost for doing so. An alternate application of receiver heterogeneity that might be useful arises in certain cases of *fixed filter* or *shared explicit* reservations in a multisender audio conference. This example will be discussed later in this chapter in the section "Reservation Styles."

Multilayer Encoding

It has been proposed that certain multimedia traffic streams be encoded with multiple "layers." In *multilayer encoding*, traffic is separated into high-frequency components and low-frequency components (or by using an alternate separation criteria). Less capable receivers would receive only the low-frequency components, producing an inferior-quality but still useable rendering of the traffic. More capable receivers would receive both the high- and low-frequency components of the offered traffic.

At first glance, it would seem that receiver heterogeneity can be usefully applied to multilayer encoded sessions. Less capable receivers would request only that quantity of resources required to protect the lower-frequency layers of the session's traffic, while more capable receivers would request resources sufficient to protect the entire session, including both the low- and the high-frequency components.

However, the problem with this approach is that routers supporting reservations for only the low-frequency components do not have the knowledge to separate the offered traffic in a manner that would protect the low-frequency component and discard the high-frequency component. Instead, these routers would install policers that would arbitrarily discard packets in excess of the reserved resources.

Multilayer encoding may be used very effectively in conjunction with RSVP reservations. However, it would seem that the preferred method for doing so is to separate the different layers into different sessions and to offer each layer on a different IP port. Thus, the receiving application could decide which layers it wanted to receive by issuing reservations for the corresponding sessions only. The routers would then protect the traffic corresponding only to those sessions for which reservations were in place.

5.4.1.3 Killer Reservation Problems

Under two identified conditions, RSVP multicast operation can lead to serious problems. These are referred to as *killer reservation* problems I and II. Killer reservation problems are forms of denial-of-service attacks. Both problems are addressed in the RSVP protocol specification. A correct implementation of the protocol will protect against killer reservation problems at the expense of increased state.

5.4.1.4 Free Rider Issues

A side effect of the merging behavior of multicast RSVP is the *free rider* effect. Consider the configuration in Figure 5.9, which is similar to the configuration illustrated in Figure 5.8.

Figure 5.9   The Free Rider Effect

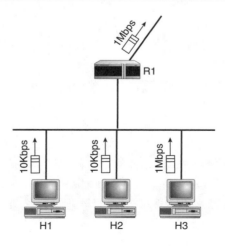

H1 and H2 request only 10Kbps. H3 requests 1Mbps. If R1 approves H3's request, it will forward the request for 1Mbps upstream and will reserve 1Mbps capacity on its downstream interface. Because this interface serves a shared Ethernet segment, H1 and H2 will both benefit from the full 1Mbps of traffic that is protected for H3. In an environment in which receivers are charged for the cost of resources they reserve, H1 and H2 would benefit at the expense of H3—they are free riders.

The free rider effect can arise in a number of realistic topologies; it generally is considered to be a benign side effect. If it is absolutely necessary to deny certain receivers free service, then the traffic flow may be encrypted at the application layer, and the key may be issued only to paying receivers. Alternatively, certain receivers could be blocked from joining certain multicast groups under control of IP multicast mechanisms.

5.4.2 Reservation Styles

In the multicast example illustrated in the previous section, a single sender sends to a single multicast session with multiple receivers. A different multicast scenario applies when considering a multiparty videoconferencing application. This scenario is illustrated in Figure 5.10.

Figure 5.10   A Multiparty Videoconference and Different Reservation Styles

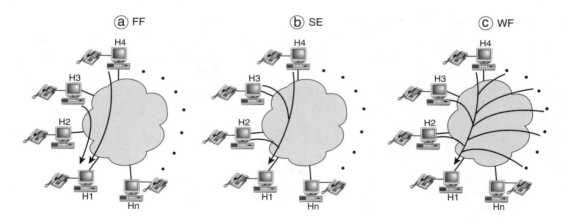

Note

The same scenario is illustrated three times, with a different reservation *style* in each case. Reservation styles are discussed in the next two sections.

In Figure 5.10, videoconference traffic is still sent to a single multicast session. However, any number of the receiving hosts may also be senders, resulting in multiple senders to the same multicast session. (In this example, each sender transmits 16Kbps of audio traffic to the multicast session.)

The added complexity of this example over the single-sender case gives rise to the notion of reservation *style*. Reservation styles allow receivers to request a specific amount of resources and to specify how those resources should be allocated among any number of the senders that are sending to the multicast session. The various styles are described in the following paragraphs. Note that merging behavior at interfaces serving multicast traffic depends on the style of the merged reservations.

5.4.2.1   Fixed Filter (FF)

Receivers use the fixed filter (FF) style to dedicate reserved resources along the path from each of a set of specified senders independently. A special case of the use of the FF reservation style is for unicast sessions. In this case, the set of senders includes a single sender, and the receiver dedicates all reserved resources to traffic originating from that sender.

In addition, receivers may use this style to specify a set of senders in a multicast session. FF is used for multicast sessions when it is essential to protect traffic from each specified sender, independently of the behavior of other senders that are sending to the same multicast session. An example of such a case is an audio conference in which a small number of important speakers must be heard with the best quality possible. In this case, receivers would each issue FF reservations for the multicast session, specifying each of the important senders. The total amount of resources requested would correspond to the total bandwidth sent by the specified senders. This case is illustrated in Figure 5.10a. H1 has requested FF reservations for traffic from H3 and H4. Each reservation is for 16Kbps, for a total of 32Kbps. The reserved capacity is sufficient to protect all traffic generated by H3 and H4.

5.4.2.2   Shared Explicit (SE)

Receivers use shared explicit (SE) reservations to share reserved resources among a set of senders when it is not important to protect each sender's traffic independently of other senders' behavior. For example, consider a multicast audio conference with a set of important senders. At any time, no more than some small subset of the important senders (N) is likely to be speaking. Thus, the receiver requests a reservation for a bandwidth of $N \times R$ (where N is the number of senders that the receiver is interested in receiving from simultaneously, and R is the rate at which each sender sends). In the reservation request, the receiver explicitly lists the set of senders from which it wishes to reserve resources. On occasion, some number of senders greater than N may speak simultaneously. In this case, the reserved resources are insufficient to protect the traffic from all simultaneous speakers. However, to protect all senders under all circumstances would require that the receiver issue FF reservations for all important senders. This may require considerably more resources than the SE alternative, so the receiver is willing to tolerate the occasional compromise in quality that results when more than N senders speak simultaneously.

This example is illustrated in Figure 5.10b. H1 requests a reservation for 32Kbps to be shared among senders H2, H3, and H4. H1 expects that, most of the time, only two of the three senders will transmit simultaneously. Therefore, the reservation of 32Kbps should protect the traffic generated.

5.4.2.3   Wildcard Filter (WF)

Receivers use wildcard reservations (WF) to indicate that they are willing to share reserved resources among any senders to the multicast session. This is appropriate when a large number of senders are equal in importance. Consider, for example, an audio conference with a dozen peers participating. It is reasonable to expect that no more than three speakers will attempt to speak at the same time. Thus, it is sufficient for a receiver to issue reservations for an amount of bandwidth to accommodate three simultaneous senders. The receiver has no preference as to which specific senders it reserves resources for because different subsets of the 12 senders may be speaking at any time. Thus, the receiver limits the amount of resources that it must reserve without limiting the set of senders that it protects. This example is illustrated in Figure 5.10c, in which H1 has requested a wildcard reservation for 48Kbps.

5.4.2.4   Summary of Style Types

The matrix in Figure 5.11 is excerpted from the RSVP proposed standard [RFC 2205].

This matrix identifies two distinct parameters of a reservation and characterizes each style in terms of these parameters. The parameters are as follows:

- Whether *distinct* reservations are created for different senders in the same session or whether a single reservation is *shared*

- Whether senders are selected based on an *explicit* list or whether all senders to the session are *implicitly* selected

Figure 5.11   The Style Matrix

Reservations / Sender Selection	Distinct	Shared
Explicit	Fixed-Filter (FF) Style	Shared-Explicit (SE) Style
Wildcard (Implicit)	None Defined	Wildcard-Filter (WF) Style

> **Note**
>
> Although the various reservation styles are most useful in the context of multicast sessions, one could imagine applying them in the case of multiple senders unicast sending to a single receiver.

5.4.3   Receiver Heterogeneity and Reservation Styles

Receiver heterogeneity may be particularly useful when considered in the context of FF and SE reservation styles. In this case, more capable receivers might reserve more capacity to be allocated to a larger number of simultaneous senders. Recall that the general problem with receiver heterogeneity was that routers would arbitrarily discard traffic for receivers that reserved less than the total bandwidth of traffic transmitted on a session. However, in the case of FF or SE reservations, routers will not discard traffic arbitrarily. Instead, they will discard the traffic of senders that were not specified in the reservation. Receiver heterogeneity is less interesting in the context of wildcard reservations.

5.5   Policy and Security

QoS policy is discussed in depth in Chapter 9. It is discussed briefly here, in the context of RSVP signaling. Security is closely related to policy and also will be discussed briefly in this section.

5.5.1   Admission Control Based on Policy

So far, discussions of admission control have focused on the capability of the admitting network device to provide the *resources* that would be required to accommodate the admitted flow. This type of admission control decision can be reduced to a simple matter of arithmetic—it is purely a *resource-based* decision. Because network devices can offer only limited resources, it is worthwhile to consider who or what gets to use these resources. At this point, the admission control decision becomes one of policy—it is a *policy-based* decision.

If QoS mechanisms are to be used to grant valuable resources to network users, then resource-based admission control (which doles out resources on a first-come, first-served basis) will not suffice. Instead, both policy- and resource-based admission control will be required. Although a resource-based admission control decision can be made in a network device, the policy component of an admission control decision will likely be outsourced to an external *policy server*.

Note

Outsourcing policy decisions may be necessary for a number of reasons. First, memory resources are often at a premium in network devices. Certain policies, such as lists of users entitled to resources, may be memory-intensive. (Policy processing may also be demanding on local processing resources.) Second, policy decisions may often benefit from high-level, cross-network coordination. Although RSVP offers explicit per-reservation coordination between specific network devices, policy servers can offer a looser and higher level of coordination.

Note that outsourcing policy decisions does not mean that each decision requires negotiation between a network device and a policy server. Much of the policy information necessary to make admission control decisions is likely to be cached in the network device in the form of a *local policy module*.

The policy server may be supported by a policy data store or directory, which contains the database of rules that comprise the QoS policies to be applied. The external policy components will be discussed in detail in Chapter 9. This section focuses on RSVP objects that support policy-based admission control.

Different policies may apply to the same users or applications in different regions of a network. For example, a corporate intranet policy might allow any user to consume resources on the LAN. However, it might limit the users who are entitled to consume resources on a precious WAN link. Because of its topology awareness, RSVP is well suited to the application of topology-dependent policies.

5.5.2 Policy Objects

Both RSVP PATH messages and RSVP RESV messages (as well as related error messages) may include policy objects. These may contain any information that is intended to be used to contribute to a policy-based admission control decision. The *Resource Allocation Protocol* (RAP) working group of the IETF has defined usage of the RSVP policy object for the purpose of securely identifying users or applications that are associated with a traffic flow. These are described in IETF RFCs [RFC 2752], [RFC 2872].

> **Note**
>
> Note that RSVP policy objects are not necessarily imited to identification of users and applications. However, these are the entities for which policy objects are currently defined.

A policy object that is included with an RSVP request specifies whether it is identifying a user or an application. It typically includes a *policy locator* and a *credential*. The policy locator takes the form of a *distinguished name* [RFC 1779]. It is a string that can be used to locate policies that are associated with the user or application in a directory or any appropriately structured database. The credential is included to securely authenticate the user or application, as described in the following section.

5.5.3 Security

It is important to validate that the policy locator identifying a user or application truly identifies that user or application. Without this level of security, Yoram Bernet playing Doom might identify himself as Bill Gates using SAP/R3. To this end, policy locators may be authenticated by a credential. Typical user credentials are the user's *Kerberos ticket* or *public key certificates*. Security considerations may also call for the user and application name to be encrypted so that malicious eavesdroppers cannot learn the names of users and applications using network resources.

Embedding an authenticated identifier in an RSVP message provides partial security. RSVP messages are still vulnerable to corruption or spoofing. For example, a malicious eavesdropper might extract the identifier from a legitimate RSVP message and copy it to an illegitimate message. Alternatively, the eavesdropper might modify an RSVP message carrying a valid identifier, thereby hijacking it to obtain resources on behalf of the eavesdropper. These problems are addressed by using an RSVP INTEGRITY object. The INTEGRITY object may be used to seal messages to prevent them from being tampered with.

> **Note**
>
> Issues surrounding security are complex and evolve rapidly. These are discussed briefly in relation to QoS policy in Chapter 9. Further details are beyond the scope of this book. For an in-depth treatment of security issues, see [SECURITY].

Figure 5.12 illustrates an RSVP message that contains POLICY_DATA objects identifying the user and application associated with the message, and an INTEGRITY object used to seal the message.

Figure 5.12   Identity and Integrity-Related Objects in an RSVP Message

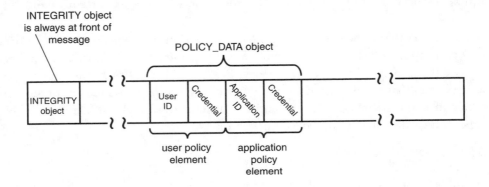

5.5.4   Policy Errors

Policy objects in RSVP messages may also be used to carry policy error codes. When a network element or a policy system rejects an RSVP request for resources as a result of policy, the rejecting entity uses the RSVP POLICY_DATA object to report a policy error that indicates the reason for rejection. Policy errors may indicate any number of conditions, including (but not limited to) a malformed policy object, an unrecognized user, or a recognized but ineligible user.

5.6   Enhancements to RSVP

Over time, proposals to enhance and extend RSVP have been submitted to the IETF. Some have resulted in modifications or extensions to the actual RSVP protocol. Some apply RSVP signaling to applications beyond resource reservation. These enhancements and extensions are discussed in this section.

Note

Note that much of the work described in this section is work in progress at this time and, therefore, is subject to change.

5.6.1 The SBM Protocol

The Subnet Bandwidth Manager (SBM) is discussed in detail in Chapter 7, "The Subnet Bandwidth Manager and 802 Networks." This chapter discusses the SBM-related adaptations to the RSVP protocol. These are necessary to optimize the behavior of RSVP in Layer 2 networks. Layer 2 networks pose several problems with respect to RSVP:

- By definition, Layer 2 devices do not recognize, let alone process, Layer 3 messages. RSVP messages are, strictly speaking, Layer 3 (or even Layer 4) messages.

- Layer 2 networks share resources among multiple senders. By contrast, RSVP was originally designed with full-duplex point-to-point links in mind. Resources on a given link in a given direction are dedicated to a *single* sender.

> **Note**
>
> Shared networks may be *physically* or *logically* shared. An Ethernet yellow wire, for example, is physically shared; each sender is connected to the same physical wire. A switch is logically shared. Although each sender is connected to the switch via a separate wire, the switch's internal resources are shared among the senders. There are various forms of logical sharing with switches maintaining more or less isolation between the sender's traffic. Regardless, from a *Layer 3 perspective*, all resources in a Layer 2 subnet are shared among all traffic flows.

Regarding the first point in the previous list, Layer 2 networks are growing in size, reach, and complexity. As a result, it is becoming more important for Layer 2 devices to play an active role in resource allocation. Layer 2 devices are becoming increasingly Layer 3–aware, and the once distinct lines between Layer 2 devices and Layer 3 devices are becoming increasingly blurred. Because some Layer 2 devices process Layer 3 messages and can play a role in resource allocation on Layer 2 networks, it is useful to define how these devices might participate in RSVP signaling and to identify any extensions to the protocol that would facilitate their participation. The SBM extensions do so.

As for the shared nature of Layer 2 networks, consider Figure 5.13.

Figure 5.13 RSVP in Shared Networks

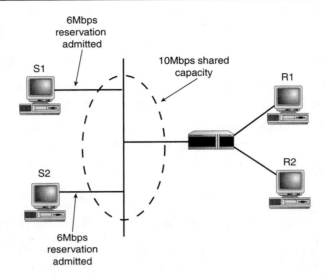

In this example, the shared subnetwork consists of a 10Mbps Ethernet segment. (Alternatively, the shared subnetwork might be a switch with a 10Mbps backplane.) Senders S1 and S2 are connected to the Ethernet segment via 10Mbps interfaces. Assume that a RESV request arrives from R1 for 6Mbps of traffic offered by S1. Admission control at S1 will verify that S1 has the capacity on its transmit interface to accommodate 6Mbps of traffic. The request will be admitted. Assume now that a similar request from R2 arrives at S2, also for 6Mbps. Admission control at S2 will also pass because S2's transmit interface has 10Mbps capacity. At this point, the shared 10Mbps subnetwork has been overcommitted. This problem arises because there is no RSVP-aware agent representing the limited resources of the shared subnetwork for the purpose of admission control. The SBM extensions to RSVP define the process of electing such a representative and enable it to be involved in the admission control process.

Thus, the SBM protocol results in the election of one or more *Designated Subnet Bandwidth Managers* (DSBMs), which participate in RSVP signaling to better allocate resources in Layer 2 networks. Although the DSBM itself may be quite complex, extensions to the RSVP protocol in support of the SBM are quite simple. If a Layer 2 subnetwork is managed by one or more DSBMs, then it is necessary for any device transmitting onto that subnetwork and participating in RSVP signaling to implement the protocol extensions. The SBM and related protocol extensions will be discussed in depth in Chapter 7.

5.6.2 *Aggregate RSVP Signaling*

Aggregate RSVP applies RSVP to bulk bandwidth reservation. Over time, several forms of aggregate RSVP have been proposed. The current prevailing model [AGGREG] applies the concept to DiffServ networks. Recall that DiffServ networks offer a certain behavior to traffic marked with a particular DiffServ codepoint (DSCP). To offer high-quality service guarantees without overprovisioning the DiffServ network (high QE product), it is helpful to reserve resources to be available to traffic marked with the appropriate DSCP. Aggregate RSVP can be used to reserve resources in this manner, as illustrated in Figure 5.14:

Figure 5.14   Aggregate Reservations Between Edges of a DiffServ Network

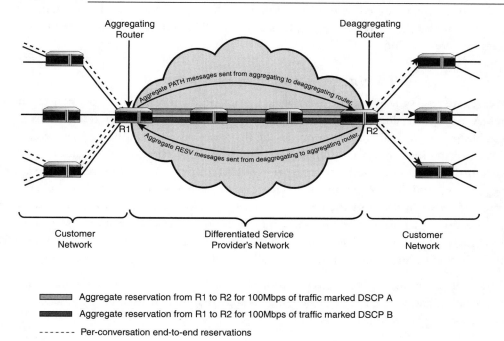

Aggregate reservation from R1 to R2 for 100Mbps of traffic marked DSCP A

Aggregate reservation from R1 to R2 for 100Mbps of traffic marked DSCP B

- - - - - - Per-conversation end-to-end reservations

The aggregate reservations are established between the peer routers at the edges of the DiffServ network. R1 is at the ingress to the DiffServ network and is referred to as the *aggregating router*. R2 is at the egress from the DiffServ network and is referred to as the *deaggregating* router. The region between them is the *aggregation region*. Two aggregate reservations are shown, each for a different DiffServ service level.

In addition, a number of conventional per-conversation RSVP reservations are shown. At the aggregating and deaggregating routers, these reservations are mapped to a certain DiffServ service level and to the corresponding aggregate reservation. In this example, the mapping is based on IntServ parameters in the per-conversation RSVP messages (such as IntServ service type and associated quantitative parameters).

In this model, routers internal to the aggregation region ignore per-conversation RSVP signaling messages (see the detailed discussion in the following sections). Instead, these process only aggregate RSVP signaling messages. As such, within the DiffServ network, both traffic handling and signaling are aggregated. This approach offers both a good QE product and improved scalability characteristics.

5.6.2.1   Identifying Aggregate Reservations

Conventional per-conversation RSVP reservations are identified by the IP addresses of the peer signaling hosts and the IP ports associated with the conversation. Aggregate RSVP reservations are identified by the IP addresses of the aggregating and deaggregating routers, and by the DSCP corresponding to the DiffServ service level provided by the aggregate reservation.

5.6.2.2   Establishing Aggregate Reservations

Aggregate reservations may be established automatically in response to per-conversation reservations traversing the aggregation region. Alternatively, aggregate reservations may be established by manual configuration. In the first case, the aggregating and deaggregating routers listen for per-conversation signaling messages traversing the aggregation region. As more resources or fewer resources are required for per-conversation reservations, the aggregating and deaggregating routers increase or decrease the aggregate resources reserved between them for the corresponding service levels. For performance reasons, the routers do not adjust aggregate reservations each time a per-conversation reservation is modified. Instead, various algorithms may be used to adjust the aggregate reservation from time to time by an amount sufficient to accommodate the required level of resources.

In the alternate case, aggregate reservations are established by manual configuration at the aggregating and deaggregating routers. This approach may be used in the absence of per-conversation reservations.

5.6.2.3   The Aggregate RSVP Protocol

Aggregating and deaggregating routers establish aggregate RSVP reservations between them using *aggregate RSVP messages*. These are very similar in nature to the conventional RSVP PATH and RESV messages. The only difference is that the RSVP SESSION object is enhanced to include the DSCP identifying the aggregate reservation.

An additional error code is defined in response to PATH messages. This code is sent by a deaggregating router to notify an aggregating router when to establish an aggregate reservation and to correlate per-conversation reservations with aggregate reservations.

In addition, a new IP protocol number is defined. When per-conversation RSVP messages enter the aggregation region of a DiffServ network, the conventional RSVP protocol number in the messages is changed. The rewritten value indicates to routers in the aggregation region that the message corresponds to a per-conversation reservation and should be ignored. The deaggregating router restores the conventional protocol number as the per-conversation message leaves the aggregating region. In this manner, the per-conversation RSVP messages are tunneled transparently through the aggregation region. On the other hand, the *aggregate* signaling messages that are exchanged between the aggregating and deaggregating router use the standard RSVP protocol number so that these are recognized and processed by the routers in the aggregation region.

5.6.3   RSVP over IP Tunnels

RSVP over IP tunnels shares many of the characteristics of RSVP aggregation. Both establish resource reservations that span a limited region of a network (as opposed to the end-to-end reservations of conventional RSVP signaling). In addition, both are capable of aggregating multiple per-conversation reservations. However, the two differ in motivation. Aggregate RSVP was designed to offer scalable resource reservation over DiffServ networks. On the other hand, RSVP over IP tunnels was designed to enable the operation of RSVP over existing IP-in-IP tunnels (hereafter referred to simply as tunnels).

Note

Note that many forms of tunneling exist. This section addresses IP tunneling specifically. Other forms of tunneling include MPLS, L2TP, PPTP, IPSec, and a variety of other acronyms). MPLS is discussed later in this chapter. Various work efforts are underway to address the interaction between QoS and other tunneling mechanisms. Most are too new to be discussed at this time.

IP Tunnels

The use of IP tunnels predates the development of RSVP. Tunnels are used to modify the routing behavior or service offered by a network. They are defined by their endpoints. At the ingress endpoint, the network device (typically a router, but possibly a host) *encapsulates* arriving IP packets in a second IP header (the tunnel header) and passes them to the next network device. Subsequent network devices process the packet based on the *outer* IP header (the *tunnel* header). The original packet header appears to these devices as part of the payload data. Eventually, the packet arrives at the tunnel egress device. This device removes the tunnel header, thereby exposing the original IP header.

continues

An example of the application of IP tunnels is illustrated in Figure 5.15.

In this example, hosts on two remote networks share the same address space (network 110.0.0.0). The two networks are interconnected by a larger provider's network. For a packet to transit the provider's network, it must be routed in the provider's address space. However, the remote customer networks do not participate in the provider's routing infrastructure. A tunnel between the two networks allows the customer's packets to be transported between the two remote networks transparently, without requiring the customer networks to be part of the provider's routing infrastructure. At the ingress points to the provider's network, the customer's packets are encapsulated in IP headers with addresses from the provider's address space. These are then routed through the provider's network. At the egress from the provider's network, the tunnel headers are stripped, and the packets are transmitted into the remote customer network.

Figure 5.15   IP Tunneling Used to Route Through a Foreign Routing Domain

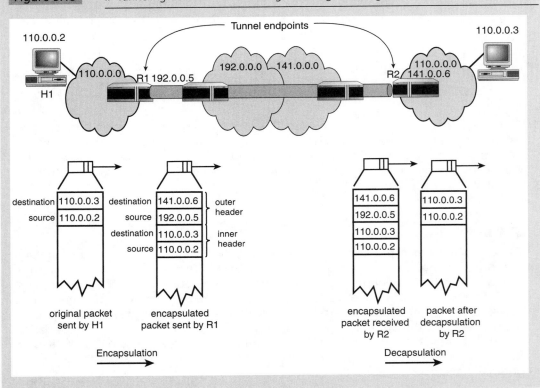

In the absence of additional protocol mechanisms, RSVP reservations are ineffective through IP tunnels for the following reason. When a host uses RSVP signaling to establish a reservation, it describes its traffic to the network by describing the IP addresses and ports in the headers of the packets for which resources are to be reserved. When packets are tunneled, they are encapsulated in a tunnel header with *different* IP addresses and ports. The signaling host is unaware of the tunnel header in which its packets are encapsulated. Devices in the tunnel see the tunnel header, not the internal one described in the RSVP signaling messages. Furthermore, devices in the tunnel do not see the RSVP signaling messages. Normally, these are detected by the RSVP protocol number in the IP header of the signaling messages. However, because the signaling messages are encapsulated, the RSVP protocol number in the inner header is invisible to the tunnel devices.

The remainder of this section addresses the problems of providing RSVP reservations over tunnels. The approach described is proposed in [RFC 2746]. From here on, the term *tunnel reservation* is used to refer to a reservation that exists between tunnel endpoints. The term *end-to-end reservation* (or *end-to-end conversation*) is used to refer to reservations or conversations that exist between peer hosts and that transit the tunnel. The router forming the endpoint of a tunnel closest to the sender of an end-to-end conversation will be referred to as the *tunnel ingress router*. The router forming the endpoint of a tunnel closest to the receiver of an end-to-end conversation will be referred to as the *tunnel egress router*.

This RFC recognizes three types of tunnels, differentiated by their level of support for RSVP reservations:

- **Type 1 tunnels**—This type of tunnel offers no QoS guarantees.

- **Type 2 tunnels**—This type of tunnel supports one or more tunnel reservations. Each tunnel reservation guarantees resources for traffic corresponding to multiple end-to-end conversations. As such, it is an aggregate reservation. In the simplest case, all end-to-end conversations are mapped to a single tunnel reservation. Multiple tunnel reservations may be used to provide multiple service levels. In this case, different end-to-end conversations map to different tunnel reservations.

- **Type 3 tunnels**—This type of tunnel provides a dedicated tunnel reservation for each end-to-end reservation.

Type 2 and Type 3 tunnels are illustrated in Figure 5.16.

Figure 5.16   Type 2 and Type 3 RSVP Tunnels

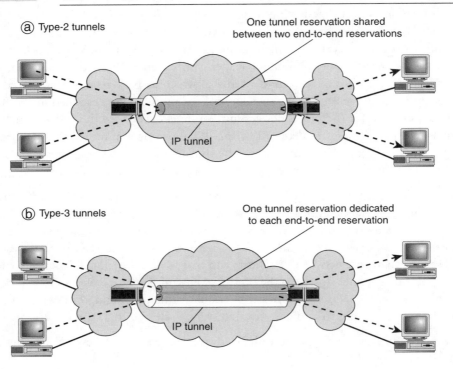

ⓐ Type-2 tunnels

One tunnel reservation shared
between two end-to-end reservations

IP tunnel

ⓑ Type-3 tunnels

One tunnel reservation dedicated
to each end-to-end reservation

IP tunnel

5.6.3.1   Identifying Tunnel Reservations

Conventional RSVP reservations are identified by peer host addresses and source and destination IP ports. Aggregate reservations are identified by the addresses of the aggregating and deaggregating routers and a DSCP. Tunnel reservations are identified by the addresses of the tunnel ingress and egress routers and a source UDP port.

At the tunnel ingress router, packets that are to be served by a specific tunnel reservation are encapsulated in a tunnel header that includes a UDP header containing the source UDP port that identifies the corresponding tunnel reservation. Packets that are to receive best-effort (BE) service in the tunnel are encapsulated with only an IP header, no UDP header. The tunnel ingress router encapsulates packets sent into the tunnel, associating them with tunnel reservations (or not) based on configured policies.

5.6.3.2   Establishing Tunnel Reservations

As is the case with aggregate RSVP, tunnel reservations may be established automatically, in response to end-to-end reservation signaling, or may be established by manual configuration, independently of end-to-end reservations.

5.6.3.3 Protocol for Establishing Tunnel Reservations

Tunnel reservations are established between tunnel ingress and tunnel egress routers using conventional PATH and RESV messages.

Tunnel egress routers use an object called a NODE_CHAR object to notify tunnel ingress routers of the existence of a downstream tunnel egress router that is capable of cooperating in the creation of a tunnel reservation. The NODE_CHAR object is appended to conventional end-to-end RESV messages arriving at the tunnel egress router from downstream receivers.

When the NODE_CHAR object is received by the tunnel ingress router, it removes the object before forwarding the RESV message upstream. It may also respond by creating an association between the end-to-end reservation and a tunnel reservation. It does so by appending a SESSION_ASSOC (session association) object to the corresponding end-to-end PATH messages. This object contains the UDP port of the corresponding tunnel reservation. When it receives PATH messages with this object, the tunnel egress router notes the association and removes the object before forwarding the PATH message downstream.

5.6.4 RSVP for MPLS

Multi-Protocol Label Switching (MPLS) is a technology that can be used to establish virtual circuits (VCs) in IP networks. (See the following sidebar on MPLS for an explanation of the technology.) One of the requirements of MPLS is the capability to negotiate and distribute labels that identify a particular VC. The MPLS working group of the IETF has proposed that RSVP be used to do so [RSVP_MPLS].

MPLS

ATM did not enjoy the level of penetration that its supporters might have hoped for. Nonetheless, many ATM concepts remain quite promising. One of these is the concept of switching discrete cells (or packets, to generalize) along a predetermined circuit. In conventional IP routing, a router inspects the destination address of each packet as it arrives at the router. It then applies a routing lookup to determine the interface to which the packet should be forwarded, to help it toward its ultimate destination. In ATM cell-switching, a sender requests a VC to a certain destination. ATM switches along the path from source to destination establish a VC and return an identifier to the sender. The sender then attaches this identifier to each cell transmitted to the destination. Within each device, the identifier is used to retrieve the forwarding interface appropriate for the VC. The identifier remains valid for the life of the VC.

In the years following ATM, a number of router vendors devised schemes by which IP routers could set up virtual circuits to be used in IP routing. These schemes would transparently establish temporary virtual circuits for commonly used paths. Routers

continues

along the path would cooperate to assign a *label* corresponding to a path. Participating hosts or routers close to a sending host would then tag packets with the appropriate label to help hasten it on its way. This approach became known as *label switching*. Early in the development of label switching, the approach was expected to offer performance enhancements over traditional IP routing.

As the label-switching approach gained popularity, the need to standardize the approach became evident. This led to the creation of the Multi-Protocol Label Switching (MPLS) working group of the IETF. The MPLS working group uses the term *label-switched path* (LSP) rather than *virtual circuit*. All packets marked with the same label are said to belong to the same *forwarding equivalence class* (FEC). The applications of MPLS extend beyond performance enhancement of a router's forwarding path. The establishment of LSPs can be used to direct packets along paths other than those that would be dictated by standard routing, for example, for load balancing or for circumventing troublesome routes (traffic engineering). MPLS can also be used to invoke specific processing for different groups of packets traversing the same route (different FECs), such as might be useful in providing QoS.

Today, MPLS VCs are not expected to offer significant performance advantages with respect to standard IP routing. Instead, proponents of MPLS cite the following advantages of the technology:

- Separation of routing space (as described previously in the section "RSVP over IP Tunnels")

- The capability to create *hierarchical* tunnels

- Ease of traffic engineering

For further information on MPLS, see [MPLS].

Note that MPLS and RSVP can cooperate in different forms. In one form, an LSP can be established for each RSVP-requested QoS flow. This usage is illustrated in Figure 5.17.

In Figure 5.17, H1 has established an RSVP reservation (RSVP Reservation 1) to H3, and H2 has established a separate RSVP reservation (RSVP Reservation 2) to H3. Within the provider's network, each of these reservations is supported by a separate LSP.

In an alternate form, the RSVP signaling protocol can be used to negotiate and distribute labels for LSPs. These LSPs may or may not then be used for QoS-related purposes. In the first form, MPLS serves RSVP. In the second form, RSVP serves MPLS. This section focuses on the second form. Although the second form may be used to assign labels to LSPs that correspond to RSVP-signaled reservation requests, it is more general in nature and can be used for many other applications as well.

Figure 5.17   Creating an LSP for Each RSVP Reservation

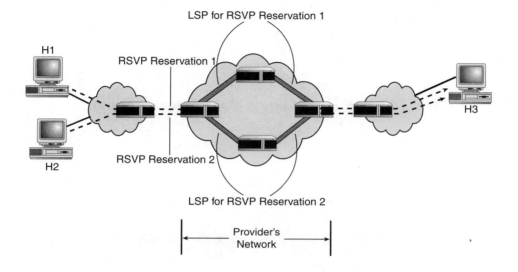

5.6.4.1   Basic Protocol Operation

For the purpose of negotiating labels, RSVP PATH messages can be augmented with a LABEL_REQUEST object. This object notifies downstream nodes that a label is required. Downstream nodes respond with a RESV message that is augmented with a LABEL object (carrying an assigned label). As the RESV message propagates upstream, routers in the LSP are notified of the label assigned to the LSP. When the RESV message reaches the node that originated the PATH message, the signaling cycle is complete and an LSP is established. The LSP extending from the originator of the PATH message to the originator of the RESV message is known as an *LSP tunnel*. LSP tunnels are typically established by administrative action. The use of RSVP to create an LSP is illustrated in Figure 5.18.

In Figure 5.18a, R1 sends an RSVP PATH message (administratively triggered) to R4 containing a LABEL_REQUEST object. In Figure 5.18b, R4 selects a label and responds with an RSVP RESV message containing the label (in a LABEL object). In Figure 5.18c, routers R1 through R4 have created an LSP identified by the label.

Figure 5.18 Using RSVP to Distribute the Label for an LSP

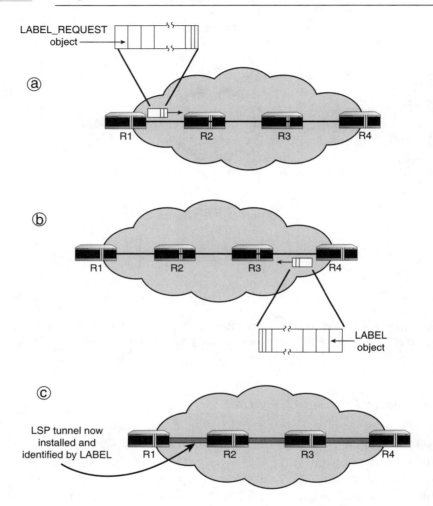

5.6.4.2 Using RSVP with MPLS for Quality of Service

PATH and RESV messages used to negotiate a label may also specify resource requirements using IntServ semantics. In this case, resources may be assigned to the entire LSP tunnel. In addition, a variation on the IntServ FLOWSPEC object is defined for MPLS. This is the *class-of-service FLOWSPEC* object. This object can be used to request treatment per the conventional *type-of-service* (TOS) octet per [RFC 1349] instead of actual resource reservations. As DiffServ changes the interpretation of the TOS octet, the interpretation of the class-of-service FLOWSPEC object can be expected to change accordingly.

5.6.4.3 Explicit Routing

In conventional RSVP, PATH messages are addressed to the session address and are routed via the same default route as data packets addressed to the session address. The extensions to RSVP defined by the MPLS working group of the IETF include an EXPLICIT_ROUTE object (ERO). The ERO can be included with PATH messages to force the PATH message to follow a specific route specified by the sender of the PATH message. This is a powerful tool that enables the traffic-engineering functionality of MPLS with RSVP. Using the ERO, the network administrator may force a route that has a high likelihood of satisfying required service objectives, or that optimizes resource utilization in the network or that satisfies goals of other administrative policies.

A complementary object to the ERO is the RECORD_ROUTE object. This object can be used to record the route along which an LSP tunnel is established. The RECORD_ROUTE object can also be used to request notification in the event of a path change.

5.6.5 Refresh Reduction, Node Failure Detection, and Related Optimizations

The soft-state nature of RSVP was discussed earlier in this chapter. The benefit of using soft state is that all RSVP-related state is guaranteed to eventually time out, thereby releasing any reserved resources. However, certain costs are incurred as a result of the soft-state approach. Soft state relies on continual refreshing of RSVP PATH and RESV messages. Refresh messages consume network bandwidth, which might otherwise be used to carry data.

It is important to put the refresh overhead in perspective. Consider a typical refresh interval of 30 seconds. Assume a PATH or RESV message size of 1KB. In this case, per-session overhead from message refreshes is about 2KB per 30 seconds (1KB each for PATH and RESV messages). This amounts to 66bps per session. For an audio session, this represents an overhead of less than 1%. For video sessions, the percentage overhead is even lower. Nonetheless, for large networks supporting a large number of RSVP sessions, it is worth investigating mechanisms that are capable of reducing the overhead associated with RSVP refreshes.

One mechanism for reducing RSVP refresh overhead is to increase the refresh interval. However, this approach is not without compromises. If a message requesting a change in the amount of reserved resources is lost, an adjustment cannot be expected until the next refresh period. Similarly, because RSVP does not refresh PATH_TEAR and RESV_TEAR messages, the loss of a single teardown message means that resources for the associated reservation are not freed until the reservation times out. The timeout period is typically equal to three refresh intervals. Thus, in a large network, increases in the refresh interval could result in a large pool of resources that are neither in use by valid reservations nor available for use by new reservations.

Various mechanisms for reducing overhead related to RSVP signaling are proposed in [REFRSH_REDUCT]. A related mechanism for detecting RSVP node failures is documented in [RSVP_MPLS]. These are described in the following sections. To aid in the description of these mechanisms, the term *trigger message* [REFRSH_REDUCT] will be used. A trigger message is a message that results in a change of state in a receiver; it differs from a *refresh message*, which simply serves to maintain existing state.

5.6.5.1 *Message Bundles*

To reduce the overhead associated with general RSVP signaling, [REFRSH_REDUCT] proposes bundling multiple RSVP messages into a single message *bundle*. Any RSVP messages that a node would send to its neighbor node may be bundled together. The benefits of bundling multiple messages in this manner are twofold:

- Reduction in bandwidth consumption due to the reduction in number of redundant headers that must be sent

- Reduction in the processing overhead required by the receiver due to the reduction in number of receive interrupts that must be processed

In a large network, the reduction in overhead due to message bundling between adjacent nodes may prove quite significant.

5.6.5.2 *Message IDs and* SRefresh *Messages*

Message bundling reduces overhead by handling messages in aggregate; it does not eliminate messages. SRefresh messages reduce overhead by actually eliminating redundant messages. In conventional RSVP operation, most of the messages generated are refreshes of existing PATH or RESV state. The useful information carried in these messages serves to "continue to maintain the state described in the PATH (or RESV) message that first established this state (the trigger message)." This information can be conveyed without transmitting all the information describing the state. To this end, the [REFRSH_REDUCT] draft defines a MESSAGE_ID object, which can be included in any RSVP message to identify the message. If a MESSAGE_ID object is included in each trigger message, then the state established by the trigger message can be subsequently refreshed simply by sending a special message containing the MESSAGE_ID of the trigger message. The message defined for this purpose is the SRefresh message. The SRefresh message carries one or more MESSAGE_ID objects identifying the trigger messages that describe the state to be refreshed.

5.6.5.3   *Rapid Refresh and Acknowledgements*

Message bundling and `SRefresh` messages reduce the overhead associated with RSVP signaling. However, the consequence of message bundling is that loss of a single bundle containing trigger messages may cause delays in state changes for multiple RSVP sessions. Consequently, it is important to investigate a means by which RSVP state changes can be rapidly and reliably signaled to peer nodes. One mechanism for doing so is described in [REFRSH_REDUCT]. This draft proposes that trigger messages (whether bundled or not) be protected against loss by rapidly retransmitting the message. In case the first trigger message is lost, a second one will follow close behind it.

At first glance, this approach would appear to violate the goal of reducing the overhead because of the increased frequency at which messages would be generated. However, this is not the case. The proposal requires that the trigger message include a `MESSAGE_ID` object with a flag set in the object header to request acknowledgement of the trigger message. Receivers of the trigger message are required to acknowledge the trigger message by returning a `MESSAGE_ID_ACK` object. In the common case, a trigger message would be acknowledged before it is retransmitted, with no adverse effect on the network. To protect against continual retransmission of trigger messages that are not acknowledged, the proposal dictates that a back-off mechanism must be used to quickly reduce the frequency at which the trigger message is generated.

5.6.5.4   *Slow Refresh Interval*

In addition to the reduction in overhead that results from use of the `SRefresh` message, further gains can be realized by lengthening the refresh interval between nodes so that refresh messages can be sent less frequently. As discussed previously, the potential downside of lengthening refresh intervals is the increased delay in state changes that results from lost trigger messages. However, the rapid retransmission of trigger messages moderates this downside. Consequently, it becomes reasonable to lengthen the refresh interval in a stable network.

5.6.5.5   *Failed Node Detection*

Although the rapid retransmission of trigger messages reduces the negative impact of a message lost in the network, it does nothing to address the sudden failure of a signaling node. Consider a node that is using a slow refresh interval to refresh reservation state in its peer. If the refreshing node fails suddenly, its peer will typically wait three refresh intervals before releasing the reserved resources. Because the two were communicating using a slow refresh interval, the consequences of this could be quite costly.

The mechanisms proposed effectively modify RSVP soft state to more closely resemble a hard-state protocol. As a consequence, it is necessary to introduce a keepalive protocol by which nodes can detect when peer nodes have failed. In response, these can rapidly reset state associated with the failed peer and can release resources. To enable the detection of peer node failures, [RSVP_MPLS] defines a HELLO message. The HELLO message may carry HELLO_REQUEST and HELLO_ACK objects and is used by nodes to detect peers that have failed or that have been reset.

5.6.6 DCLASS *and* TCLASS *Objects*

Two objects have been defined to assist in the use of RSVP with aggregate traffic handling. These are the DCLASS [DCLASS] and the TCLASS [RFC 2814] objects. These objects can be returned upstream toward senders, in response to PATH messages. Admission control agents may append one or both objects to RESV messages that have passed admission control. The DCLASS object specifies a DSCP to be used by upstream senders that perform DiffServ marking. The TCLASS object defines an 802.1p tag to be used by upstream senders that perform 802.1p tagging. In this manner, admission control agents can direct certain traffic flows to certain aggregate service levels. The DCLASS and TCLASS objects will be discussed further in Chapter 10, "Putting the Pieces Together—End-to-End QoS," and Chapter 7, "The Subnet Bandwidth Manager and 802 Networks." Their use is illustrated in Figure 5.19.

Figure 5.19   Use of the DCLASS and TCLASS Objects

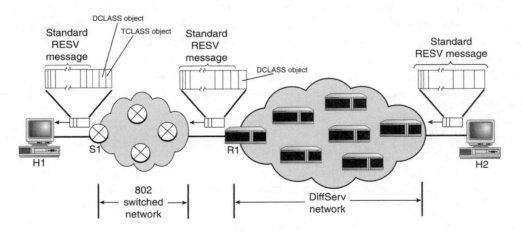

In Figure 5.19, H2 transmits standard RSVP RESV messages upstream for a certain session. R1 is the ingress router to the DiffServ network. It appends a DCLASS object to the RESV message. This object indicates to upstream senders the DSCP that should be used to obtain the requested QoS in the DiffServ network. As the RESV message propagates upstream, it transits the 802 switched network. S1 is the DSBM responsible for resource allocation in the switched network. S1 appends a TCLASS object to the RESV message. This object indicates to the device sending onto the 802 network what user_priority value should be used to obtain the requested QoS in the 802 network. The sender, H1, responds by marking traffic on the corresponding flow with the specified DSCP and user_priority (per the appended DCLASS and TCLASS objects).

5.6.7 RSVP with IP Security

IP security, commonly referred to as IPSec, is a mechanism for providing secure communications between peers [IPSEC]. It addresses the use of encryption and key exchange mechanisms. When a traffic flow is IPSec-encrypted, encryption is applied not only to the data payload, but also to part of the IP headers. In particular, IPSec obscures the standard IP protocol and source and destination IP port fields. (The addresses must remain unobscured so that routers that are not privy to encryption keys are capable of routing the encrypted packets.)

5.6.7.1 The Problem in Applying RSVP to IPSec-Encrypted Traffic

Recall that conventional RSVP/IntServ signaling describes traffic flows to the network using source and destination IP addresses and source and destination transport-layer ports. Network devices store these classification criteria so that they are capable of recognizing packets associated with a particular traffic flow, based on the fields in the IP packet header. This mechanism is obviously compromised when the ports are obscured. As a consequence, without modification, RSVP/IntServ cannot be used to tell routers how to differentiate among multiple encrypted flows between the same IP addresses.

5.6.7.2 RSVP Protocol Extensions Supporting IPSec

Because the transport-layer port numbers are obscured in IPSec encrypted traffic flows, alternate classification criteria are required. These are explained in [RFC 2207]. IPSec defines a field called the *Security Parameter Index* (SPI). The combination of SPI, destination address, and IPSec protocol type represents a unique *security association* (SA). When IPSec is used between RSVP-enabled hosts, it should be configured to generate a distinct security association for distinct traffic flows between the same pair of hosts. As a result, the SPI can be used to uniquely identify traffic flows.

The IPSec SPI is included in the RSVP `SENDER_TEMPLATE` and `FILTER_SPEC` objects instead of the source IP port included in conventional RSVP signaling. For the sake of generality, the SPI is referred to as a *generalized port identifier*. In addition, RFC 2207 defines the use of a *virtual destination port* (vDstPort). The vDstPort is used in the `SESSION` object in lieu of a destination port.

5.7   Issues in the Application of RSVP

The original vision of a majority of network devices participating in per-conversation RSVP signaling and applying per-flow traffic handling is unlikely to be realized. A new deployment model is emerging in which hosts signal RSVP for a set of applications (not limited to quantitative applications). Select admission control agents in the network participate in per-conversation RSVP signaling for the purpose of applying admission control. Other agents listen only to aggregate RSVP signaling. Yet other agents passively snoop RSVP to glean information about network traffic. This deployment model is described briefly in this section.

5.7.1   Admission Control Agents

In the conventional application of RSVP, each device in a traffic path participates in RSVP signaling and applies admission control. The admission control decision is based on the availability of resources on the interface controlled by the device. However, it is often not necessary for every device to participate in the admission control process. Instead, it is possible to partition a network into *admission control domains* (ACDs). There exists an *admission control agent* (ACA) associated with each ACD. The ACA is authorized to make admission control decisions on behalf of all devices and resources in the associated ACD. In the conventional application of RSVP, each router is both an ACD and the ACA for that ACD.

Consider the network illustrated in Figure 5.20.

In this network, there are two ACDs. One includes R1, R2, and R3. The other includes R4, R5, and R6. Only R1 and R4 are RSVP-enabled; R2, R3, R5, and R6 are not. In this example, R1 serves as the ACA for one ACD, and R4 serves as the ACA for the other ACD.

The resources available on R2 and R3's transmit interfaces (10Mbps) are less than those available on R1's interface (100Mbps). Similarly, the resources available on R5 and R6's transmit interfaces are less than those available on R4's interface. Because all traffic flowing through R1 also flows through R2 and R3 (and vice versa), R1 can accurately represent the resources available in its ACD. To this end, R1 should be configured based on a total capacity of 10Mbps (the most constrained interface in its ACD). Similarly, R4 can be configured as the ACA for itself and for R5 and R6.

Figure 5.20   Admission Control when a Subset of Devices Is RSVP-Aware

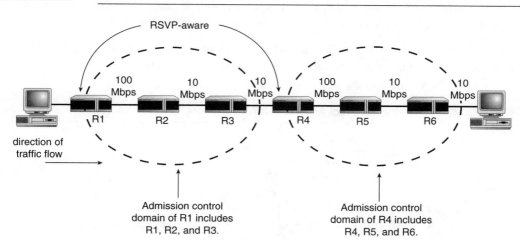

ACAs represent the resources of other network devices that do not participate in RSVP signaling. In the trivial and unlikely topology of the example in Figure 5.21, ACAs are capable of making accurate admission control decisions for their ACD. In more complex topologies, it may not be possible to do so because resource availability within an ACD varies depending on the specific paths traversed by different traffic flows within the ACD. In this case, ACAs must make admission control decisions based on imperfect information and assumptions regarding traffic patterns and resource availability within their domain. This concept will be explored further in the subsequent section.

As another example of ACAs, consider a router that participates in RSVP signaling and applies admission control over an ATM interface. This is illustrated in Figure 5.21.

In this example, R1's transmit interface capacity is defined by the characteristics of the ATM network to which it is attached. R1 is the ACA. The ATM network is the ACD. Reservation requests may arrive along multiple paths in the ATM network. Each path may have different capacities at different service levels. (As will be discussed in Chapter 8, "QoS over Layer 2 Media Other Than 802," IntServ service levels can be mapped to ATM service levels.) Note the following steps enumerated in Figure 5.21:

1. A reservation request is shown to arrive from the next RSVP hop, R2. For R1 to apply RSVP/IntServ admission control for resources on its ATM interface, it must determine whether a VC exists (or can be established) along the appropriate path in the ATM network at the appropriate service level.

2. R1 is shown to use ATM signaling to attempt to set up a VC appropriate for the requested QoS. Because of the relatively deterministic nature of ATM networks, R1 likely will be capable of making an accurate admission control decision.

3. The VC setup is shown to be successful; R1 admits the reservation request and forwards a RESV message upstream. As such, R1 serves as an admission control agent for the entire ATM network.

Figure 5.21   Admission Control Agent for an ATM Network

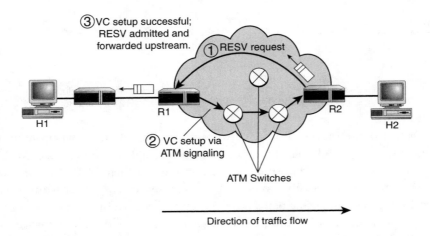

In this example, R1 is capable of invoking a link-layer admission control protocol (ATM signaling) that can be used to provide accurate admission control within its ACD.

Other examples of ACAs that may act on behalf of a number of RSVP-unaware network devices are DSBMs and ingress routers to DiffServ networks. (These generally are less capable of making accurate admission control decisions than discussed in the previous two examples.) DSBMs act as ACAs on behalf of Layer 2 networks in which varying numbers of devices may be RSVP-aware or unaware. Ingress routers to DiffServ networks act as ACAs on behalf of an entire DiffServ domain, based on the capacity specified in a service-level agreement that is in effect at the ingress.

5.7.1.1 *Signaling Density and QE Compromises*

The concept of an ACA applying admission control on behalf of other devices will be explored further throughout this book. This is a very powerful concept because it stands to significantly facilitate the deployment of RSVP (see the section "Signaling Density," in

Chapter 2). A reduction in signaling density reduces the number of devices that must be RSVP-aware. This means that networks can be upgraded piecemeal by upgrading only select devices at congested locations, rather than requiring all devices to be upgraded simultaneously. It also means that fewer devices need to provide the incremental processing power required to process RSVP signaling messages.

A reduction in signaling density often results in a compromise in the QE product. This effect was illustrated previously, in Chapter 2. It is illustrated again here so that it can be discussed in the current context. Consider the example in Figure 5.22, in which R1 acts as an ACA for the ACD, including R1, R2, and R3.

Figure 5.22   The QE Product Is Compromised as a Result of a Reduction in Density of RSVP-Aware Devices

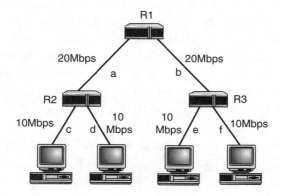

In this example, R1 serves R2 and R3 each via a 20Mbps-capacity link (links a and b). R2 and R3, in turn, each serve downstream receivers via one of two 10Mbps-capacity links (links c, d, e, and f). Optimal admission control would admit reservations up to 10Mbps on c, d, e and f. However, R1 is applying admission control on behalf of R2 and R3. When R1 receives a RESV message on link a, it cannot determine whether admitting the resource request would commit resources on links c or d. Similarly, when R1 receives a RESV message on link b, it cannot determine whether admitting the resource request would commit resources on links e or f.

R1's admission control strategy is bounded by two extremes:

- At one extreme, it could admit resource requests up to a total of 10Mbps each on links a and b. This is a conservative approach that would guarantee the quality of committed reservations because it would assure that no link is ever overcommitted. On the other hand, it would limit the efficiency of the network because it is possible to admit 20Mbps each on a and b, with no compromise in quality if the admitted reservations are for traffic balanced equally across c, d, e, and f.

- At the other extreme, R1 could take a liberal approach, admitting resource requests up to a total of 20Mbps each on links a and b. The problem with this approach is that it could result in the overcommitment of any of links c, d, e, and f if admitted reservations are for traffic that is not balanced equally between c and d on the one hand and between e and f on the other hand.

In the first case, R1's admission control strategy compromises efficiency. In the second case, it compromises quality. R1 could be configured to use resource limits somewhere between the two extremes described, thus selecting a different point on the QE curve. If the network administrator has special knowledge of traffic patterns, this knowledge could be used to configure R1 accordingly and to push the configuration to a higher QE product.

Varying configurations of ACAs and the devices they represent (the ACD) yield varying degrees of compromise in the QE product. ATM ACAs may use link-layer signaling and admission control in combination with RSVP admission control for a high QE product. DiffServ ingress routers can act as ACAs for a DiffServ network when configured with a static SLA. This combination of ACA and ACD bears the QE compromise exposed by representing a DiffServ network with a static SLA. DiffServ networks that support aggregate RSVP signaling may be capable of providing a dynamic SLA at the ingress router, thereby increasing the QE product offered by the DiffServ network and its ACA.

5.7.1.2 *Admission Control Agents at Select Congestion Points*

In the previous examples, signaling density was reduced by appointing a single ACA to represent an ACD that spanned many network devices. In many cases, signaling density can be reduced without unduly compromising the QE product by focusing only on congested parts of the network. In overprovisioned parts of the network, admission control is simply ignored. In these cases, an ACA may represent only a small number of network devices (possibly one) that are congested. Many other network devices may not provide admission control and may not be represented by an ACA at all.

For example, consider a typical enterprise network with a number of limited-capacity leased lines that connect remote sites to a relatively overprovisioned backbone. The routers serving the leased lines to remote sites act as ACAs only for the leased lines to which they are directly attached. Resources in the backbone are relatively plentiful and are not represented by an ACA. Thus, a small number of ACAs serving very small ACDs can increase the QoS guarantees that can be supported in the enterprise network without requiring an expensive increase in capacity.

5.7.2 Signaling for Qualitative Applications

The RSVP/IntServ model, with its Guaranteed and Controlled Load Services, is fundamentally *quantitative*. Applications signal the *quantity* of resources that they require at a certain service level. Network devices determine whether they can accommodate the requested *quantity* of resources. Many applications do not fit this model. These applications may be considered mission-critical by network managers, but they are incapable of quantifying their resource requirements. Examples of such applications are client/server database applications and Web transactions. For a subset of these applications, it may be quite useful to generate RSVP signaling to the network. Of course, to justify any form of signaling, the application will have to be persistent or session-oriented. Otherwise, by the time signaling is recognized by the network, the traffic described in the signaling messages may no longer be present on the network. Thus, client/server database applications may be prime candidates for signaling, and many Web applications would not.

Persistent applications of the sort described can generate RSVP signaling indicating the *Null Service*. (This service was described in Chapter 4.) Network devices and associated policy systems interpret Null Service signaling requests to mean, "I (the application) cannot (or will not) quantify my resource requirements. I will tell you what I am (application ID) and who I am (user ID), how to recognize me (classification criteria), and where my traffic will appear. You (the network) must decide how to treat my traffic." Requests for Null Service should therefore include at least an application ID in lieu of the quantitative parameters that would be included with Controlled Load or Guaranteed Service requests.

Although Null Service signaling does not offer the network information with which to apply quantitative admission control, it does offer the network information that can be very helpful in managing the application's traffic. This information includes an association of classification criteria with application ID, subapplication ID, and user ID. It also informs the network regarding the locations at which traffic associated with the application will appear and the current number of active sessions. Because no quantitative information is offered in the service request, it is not reasonable to expect quantifiable resource reservations from the network. Instead, the network will likely respond by applying a relative prioritization to the application's traffic, using certain aggregate traffic handling such as 802.1p or DiffServ service levels. In the case of 802.1p or DiffServ traffic handling, an admission control agent would likely append a DCLASS or TCLASS object to admitted RESV messages. These would specify the DSCP or 802.1p tag (respectively) to be used by upstream senders. This *prioritization* approach represents a fundamental departure from the conventional application of RSVP/IntServ to obtain quantifiable *reservations*.

Note that the Null Service may also be signaled by applications that *are* capable of quantifying their resource requirements but that defer to the network any role in defining the treatment that they would like to receive. In general, applications signaling using the Null Service are deferring their fate entirely to network policies.

5.7.3   RSVP Proxies

Various forms of RSVP *proxies* have been proposed. These would generate RSVP signaling on behalf of senders or receivers that are incapable of doing so. The following paragraphs discuss issues related to the use of proxies.

5.7.3.1   Advantages of Proxies

The primary advantage of a proxy is that it eliminates the requirement for hosts to implement the RSVP signaling protocol and for applications to be modified to invoke the RSVP signaling protocol. In addition, proxying at appropriate locations in the network can reduce the impact of RSVP signaling traffic on a network and can reduce the setup time required to establish a reservation. Consider the example in Figure 5.23.

Figure 5.23   Proxying for a Receiver

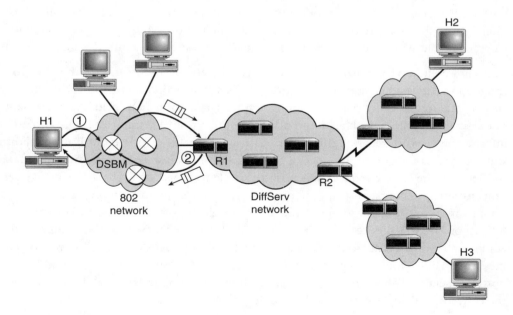

In this example, R1 proxies on behalf of receivers H2 and H3, as well any other receiving hosts that are downstream of R1. The following steps are illustrated:

1. H1 sends PATH messages that are terminated by R1.

2. R1 generates RESV messages in response.

As a result, PATH and RESV messages do not transit the network region between R1 and the receivers. Reservation setup times are reduced. In addition, none of the receivers need to support RSVP, and the receiving application need not be modified. Variants on this form of proxying are particularly well suited for client/server applications because they enable legacy client hosts and client-side applications, requiring only the server host and the application to be RSVP-capable.

5.7.3.2   Disadvantages of Proxies

A number of disadvantages must be considered carefully before deciding to use an RSVP proxy. When an application invokes RSVP signaling directly, it is capable of providing more granular and more robust information than a proxy is capable of providing. For example, quantitative applications are capable of describing exactly the resources that they require from the network. Furthermore, they are capable of updating these requirements dynamically, as they change. In addition, sending applications are capable of providing accurate and dynamic classification criteria, identifying various traffic flows.

These advantages are compromised when using proxies. The inability of a proxy to provide accurate quantitative information is less important in the case of qualitative applications that use the Null Service exclusively because no quantifiable parameters are associated with this service. However, the inability to provide accurate and dynamic classification criteria applies to proxies acting on behalf of sending hosts, whether they represent qualitative applications or quantitative applications. In the example illustrated, only the receiver is proxied, so the availability of robust classification criteria is not lost.

Another very significant disadvantage that results from the use of proxies is the topology awareness inherent in the conventional end-to-end RSVP model. The conventional RSVP model informs all interested devices along a traffic path of the nature of the traffic. It also enables any interested device to participate in admission control and in the application of policy to the relevant traffic flow. The closer to the sending host that a receiver proxy is located, the more the benefits of topology awareness are compromised. In the example illustrated, the location of the receiver proxy close to the sender largely eliminates the benefits of topology awareness. It may be appropriate to apply much different admission control strategies depending on whether the admitted session is between H1 and H2, on the one hand, or between H1 and H3 on the other hand. Because R1 proxies for both H2 and H3, it is impossible to apply different admission control criteria for the different receivers. If R2 were to proxy for H2 and H3, it would be possible to apply different admission control criteria for the different receivers. Thus, locating the proxy closer to the receiver can relieve the receiver of the need to support RSVP without compromising the benefits of topology awareness.

5.7.4 Snooping

Certain network devices may offer limited RSVP support in the form of RSVP *snooping*. Snooping devices are entirely passive from an RSVP perspective. They generate no signaling messages and transparently pass RSVP messages generated by other devices. However, they listen to RSVP messages. By doing so, they are capable of gleaning information from the network that can be used to enhance its manageability. In particular, many push-provisioning management systems offer the network manager the ability to manage traffic based on user IDs and application IDs. Within the management system, these must be correlated with fields in packet headers that network devices can recognize to apply the appropriate traffic handling. Snooping can be used to enhance the correlations between user and application IDs on the one hand, and classification criteria on the other hand.

5.8 Summary

RSVP is a signaling protocol that was invented in 1993 to address the need for a robust and scalable signaling protocol for Internet QoS. It was developed in close cooperation with the IntServ framework development. The RSVP/IntServ model initially was greeted enthusiastically. However, because of a number of concerns (primarily regarding the scalability of the per-conversation orientation of the RSVP/IntServ model), RSVP/IntServ quickly fell from grace. Subsequent progress in a number of related areas gradually has led to the renaissance of RSVP. In particular, the development of DiffServ aggregate traffic handling offers a scalable alternative to the per-conversation traffic handling initially associated with the RSVP/IntServ model.

The RSVP protocol is based on the exchange of PATH and RESV messages. Traffic senders generate PATH messages. These describe traffic to be sent and follow the same route taken by associated data traffic. PATH messages arrive at receivers. Receivers respond by sending RESV messages, which travel back toward the sender, along the path delineated by the PATH messages. In the conventional application of RSVP, RESV messages indicate the amount of resources that the receiver wants to reserve for the traffic flow described by the PATH messages. As the RESV message flows through network devices, these devices apply admission control by verifying whether they are capable of providing the requested resources.

Fundamental RSVP concepts include the following:

- A specific quantity of resources is reserved, available to each traffic flow.

- *Soft state*, RSVP state times out automatically unless it is periodically refreshed.

- *Receiver orientation*, receivers control the amount of resources reserved on their behalf.

- RSVP was designed with scalable *multicast* support as a goal, not an afterthought.

- *Sessions* are the fundamental identifiers by which traffic flows and reservations are correlated. The destination IP address and port (multicast or unicast) of a traffic flow define a session.

Policy and security are required components of any system that allocates resources. Support for these is built into the RSVP protocol via the inclusion of objects that identify and authenticate users and applications.

The RSVP protocol has been extended in a number of directions. Extensions include these:

- The SBM protocol extensions apply RSVP to Layer 2 networks.

- Aggregate RSVP can be used to reserve bulk resources across DiffServ networks.

- RSVP over IP tunnels describes extensions that make it possible to apply RSVP QoS to traffic transiting IP tunnels.

- RSVP can be used by MPLS as a label-distribution protocol. The combination can be used to traffic engineer MPLS tunnels to offer QoS.

- Various extensions combine to reduce the overhead associated with RSVP refreshes and to make the protocol more robust in the face of packet loss.

- IPSec extensions define how RSVP is modified to identify IPSec-encrypted traffic so that it can be served by QoS.

Pragmatic deployments of RSVP likely will differ from the pure RSVP/IntServ model initially envisioned. RSVP probably will be signaled on behalf of a range of persistent applications, including not just the quantifiable applications originally envisioned, but also many mission-critical qualitative applications (using the Null Service). Furthermore, only a small number of devices likely will be RSVP-aware. These admission control agents probably will be deployed at congestion points only and likely will make admission control decisions based on estimates of resources available in RSVP-unaware devices that they represent (admission control domains). Many devices (especially in large networks) probably will not provide the per-conversation traffic handling implied by the RSVP/IntServ model; instead, these devices will apply aggregate traffic handling. Admission control agents will effectively provide admission control to aggregate traffic-handling classes.

6

Differentiated Services

Differentiated Services (DiffServ) was introduced in Chapter 1, "Introduction to Quality of Service," as an aggregate traffic-handling mechanism. In the core of large networks, the sheer number of individual conversations that must be handled tends to make per-conversation traffic handling prohibitively costly. As a result, aggregate traffic-handling mechanisms such as DiffServ are particularly applicable to large networks. DiffServ networks offer a small number of traffic-handling classes in the network core. Traffic is expected to be marked and conditioned at the network edges as it is submitted to the DiffServ network. In this manner, the overhead associated with providing QoS is minimized in the core of the network and is instead pushed to the edges of the network, where it tends to scale better.

By combining DiffServ traffic handling with various provisioning and configuration mechanisms, it is possible to provide service guarantees spanning the range from low to high quality. This chapter will explain the evolution of DiffServ, the basic DiffServ architecture, and the components of DiffServ traffic handling and traffic conditioning. It will then show how various provisioning and configuration mechanisms can be used to offer various services.

6.1 The History and Background of Differentiated Services

In March 1996, Dave Clark delivered a talk at the Los Angeles IETF meeting. He described a simple mechanism for the provision of differing service levels to traffic that previously had been considered to need best-effort service only. Several talks later, in November 1997, Van Jacobson submitted an Internet draft titled, "A Two-Bit Differentiated Service Architecture for the Internet" (now [RFC 2638]). At the following IETF, in December 1997, Clark delivered a talk titled, "A Combined Approach to

Differential Service in the Internet." This talk discussed the work done by him and by Van Jacobson. It distinguished between traffic-handling *mechanisms* in network elements and the *services* that could be provided by these mechanisms. This talk and the November 1997 draft laid the groundwork for the DiffServ working group and for the specific DiffServ traffic-handling mechanisms that have been standardized thus far.

6.1.1 Formation of the DiffServ Working Group and Its Charter

The DiffServ working group met for the first time at the March 1998 IETF. The working group's charter called for the definition of "simple and coarse methods of providing differentiated classes of service." This would be achieved by defining a small number of *per-hop-behaviors* (PHBs) that would be used as building blocks from which services could be constructed. PHBs are various queuing behaviors in network devices (see Chapter 3, "Queuing Mechanisms," for a discussion of queuing behaviors) that can be invoked by the appropriate codepoints in packet headers. By supporting a small set of PHBs and parameterizing them appropriately, a variety of services could be provided in the network.

The charter also called for a "common understanding" regarding the use and interpretation of a set of codepoints and the corresponding behaviors. Since then, the charter has been updated to include the definition of a conceptual model for devices providing DiffServ and their traffic-conditioning elements. Initially, the charter specifically excluded the definition of services and work on signaling protocols.

> **Note**
>
> It wasn't until April 2000 (nearly two years after the creation of the working group) that the charter would be amended to allow discussion of services. The exclusion of services from the charter was intended to limit the scope of the working group and to focus it effectively in its early stages. Although it was effective in doing so, the orthodox exclusion of any discussion regarding services often (somewhat humorously) left working group members tongue-tied in discussions and (somewhat less humorously) created perceptions that perhaps DiffServ could not actually be used to provide services.

6.1.2 DiffServ and RSVP/IntServ

The birth of DiffServ followed the fall from grace of the RSVP/IntServ model. DiffServ was everything that RSVP/IntServ was not. Whereas RSVP/IntServ spoke about signaling for services, the DiffServ charter specifically excluded both signaling and the standardization of services. Whereas RSVP/IntServ spoke about fine-grain (per-conversation) service guarantees, DiffServ spoke about coarse service differentiation. Whereas RSVP/IntServ would offer strict guarantees for quantitative multimedia-type applications, DiffServ targeted more qualitative applications.

The radically different direction taken by the DiffServ working group is hardly surprising. To a large degree, this direction reflected a reaction to the perceived shortcomings of the RSVP/IntServ model of QoS. The DiffServ working group saw the complexity of the RSVP/IntServ model and decided that a simpler model was required. The group also saw that many of the applications that could benefit from QoS were not the leading-edge multimedia applications targeted by RSVP/IntServ and did not require the high-quality service guarantees that these did. DiffServ was a natural and logical successor to the RSVP/IntServ model.

6.1.3 *The Perspective of the DiffServ Provider*

The RSVP/IntServ model views QoS primarily from the perspective of the end-to-end service required by the end user of an application. DiffServ tends to look at QoS from the perspective of the service provider, offering bulk service to a peer service provider or to an enterprise network.

The perspectives are quite different. In the case of DiffServ, there is a need to handle large numbers of traffic flows in a scalable manner, without particular attention to any individual flow. In addition, the DiffServ provider is likely to be quite removed from the end user of the service. Thus, the DiffServ provider is most interested in the capability to offer various premium services to its immediate customer, to differentiate its offering from that of its competitors and to command a higher price.

The DiffServ provider prefers to deal in bulk capacity and to defer the problem of improving per-conversation service to the customer or to the customer's customer. This is a legitimate position for a large service provider to assume. However, it's important to realize that, in the end, the end users (or their agents) pay for network connectivity and enjoy (or suffer) the service offered. If the experience of the end user is not somehow improved by the provision of premium services in the DiffServ network, then the network-centric focus of DiffServ likely will compromise the success of the model.

6.2 *Differentiated Service Architecture and Concepts*

The DiffServ architecture offers a framework within which service providers can offer each customer a range of service levels that are differentiated on the basis of performance parameters such as latency and drop probability. A salient feature of DiffServ is its scalability, which allows it to be deployed in very large networks. This scalability is achieved by eliminating the overhead associated with fine-grain, per-conversation traffic handling in the core of the network.

Note

The DiffServ architecture pushes any fine-grain work to the periphery of the network. This work may be performed by the DiffServ provider or by the customer, depending on the agreement between the two. In either case, by pushing this work to the edge of the network, it is spread across a larger number of network devices, thereby reducing the performance demands on each device.

Key concepts of the DiffServ architecture will be described briefly in the next section.

6.2.1   Per-Hop Behaviors and DiffServ Codepoints

A per-hop behavior (PHB) is a behavior at a network device within a DiffServ network that can be formally defined and standardized. The IETF has standardized a set of PHBs that will be discussed in detail later in this chapter. The IETF does not standardize the underlying traffic-handling mechanism that is used to provide a PHB.

The most common way to invoke the behaviors offered by PHBs is by marking a *DiffServ codepoint* (DSCP) in the IP header of a packet. When the packet arrives at a device within the DiffServ network, the DSCP invokes a corresponding PHB to be applied to the packet. The DSCP is marked in the *DS field* (a combination of the fields formerly known as the *Type-of-Service* [TOS] field and the *IP precedence field*). See Figure 6.1 for an illustration of the DS field. Note that DiffServ supports legacy usage of the TOS field and the IP precedence field by the definition of the *Class Selector* PHB and the corresponding DSCPs. (See the section "The Class Selector PHB Group," later in this chapter).

Note

Depending on the agreement between the provider and its customer, the DSCP may be marked by the customer (before packets are submitted to the provider's network), by the provider (when packets are in the provider's network), or by both.

If the customer does not mark the packets, the network provider may classify packets at the network ingress, based on various fields in the packet headers or payloads. The provider may then mark these packets with an appropriate DSCP, based on the agreement between the customer and the provider. Alternatively, the provider may not mark the DSCP at all. Instead, devices in the provider's network may be configured to recognize specific subsets of traffic based on other fields in packet headers or payloads and to assign them a certain PHB directly.

For further discussion of customer marking versus provider marking, see the section "Customer Traffic Conditioning versus Provider Traffic Conditioning," later in this chapter.

 The DiffServ Codepoint

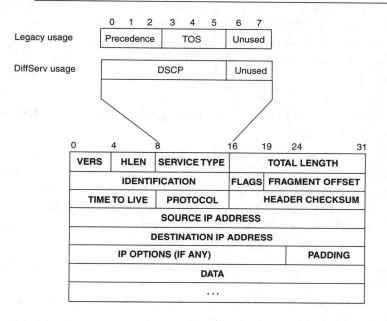

The DSCP, which is used to invoke the PHB, is nothing more than a codepoint. The IETF has standardized the usage of the DS field and has defined a small number of DSCPs that correspond to the standard PHBs. Because the DS field is 6 bits in size, it can accommodate 64 different DSCPs.

The DSCP space is divided into a *standard* space and an *experimental* space. The experimental space facilitates experimentation with new PHBs that may eventually be standardized. Although standard DSCPs can be expected to invoke the corresponding standard PHBs, the mapping of DSCP to PHB is implemented in each network device and is ultimately configured by the manager of the provider's network. In most cases, DSCP-to-PHB mappings will be configured consistently, at least within a given provider's network or domain. See the section "Providers, Customers, and Network Boundaries," later in this chapter, for a discussion of DiffServ domains.

6.2.2   Services versus PHBs

As implied by its name, the PHB invokes a traffic-handling mechanism in each network device (hop) independently. As such, PHBs alone do not offer services across a DiffServ network. However, the concatenation of many devices, each providing the requested PHB, coupled with explicit and/or implicit admission control (and various other traffic-handling functionality, as discussed in the next section) can yield a specific service between the edges of the DiffServ network. (See Chapter 4, "Integrated Services," for a discussion of implicit versus explicit admission control.) Although PHBs are at the heart of the DiffServ network, it is the *service* obtained as a result of marking traffic for a specific PHB that is of use to the customer.

6.2.3 Traffic Conditioning, Service Level Specifications, and Service Level Agreements

The admission control and related traffic handling that is required to yield a service is implemented primarily (but not exclusively) at the edges of the provider's network. This functionality is provided by *traffic conditioning* (TC) components. TC components will be described in detail later in this chapter. Briefly, these components condition traffic by marking, delaying, or discarding packets. In this manner, TC controls the amount of resources consumed by customer traffic in the provider's network.

Typically, the customer and the provider negotiate a profile describing the rate at which traffic can be submitted to the provider's network and specifying the service parameters that can be expected for traffic conforming to this profile. Packets submitted in excess of this profile may not be allotted the service requested. Traffic profiles and expected service parameters (both for conforming and for nonconforming traffic) are captured in the form of a *traffic conditioning specification* (TCS). The TCS is a subset of a broader specification, referred to as a *service level specification* (SLS). The SLS includes the TCS and additional parameters related to traffic handling beyond the fundamental TC parameters. For example, the SLS may also include information regarding network availability, encryption services, routing constraints, and so forth. Finally, the SLS is a subset of the *service level agreement* (SLA). The SLA includes the service specification in the form of the SLS, as well as business parameters such as the cost structure of the services provided. The concepts discussed in this section are illustrated in Figure 6.2.

| Figure 6.2 | DSCPs, SLAs, Traffic Conditioning, and PHBs |

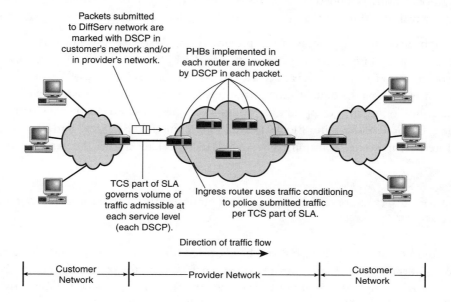

Packets submitted to DiffServ network are marked with DSCP in customer's network and/or in provider's network.

PHBs implemented in each router are invoked by DSCP in each packet.

TCS part of SLA governs volume of traffic admissible at each service level (each DSCP).

Ingress router uses traffic conditioning to police submitted traffic per TCS part of SLA.

Direction of traffic flow

Customer Network — Provider Network — Customer Network

6.3 Standard Per-Hop Behaviors

Three PHB groups have been standardized. A PHB group is a set of PHBs that are defined (at least in part) by their relationship to each other. This concept will become clearer with the introduction of the *assured forwarding PHB group* (AF), discussed later in this chapter. A special case of a PHB group is a single PHB group. The following sections describe the three standard PHB groups, *assured forwarding* (AF), *expedited forwarding* (EF), and the *class selector PHB group* (CS). The next section shows how these can be used as building blocks to create services.

6.3.1 The Expedited Forwarding PHB

The EF PHB is designed to provide a low-loss, low-latency, low-jitter, assured bandwidth service between two specific points at the edges of a DiffServ domain [RFC 2598]. Because this service appears as a leased line, it is often referred to as the *virtual leased line* (VLL) service. The EF PHB is based on the following simple principle: If the rate at which traffic is capable of departing a node exceeds the rate at which traffic arrives at the node, then no queue will form, and latency and jitter will be zero. As such, the specification of the EF PHB calls for a forwarding treatment that guarantees to EF marked packets a minimum departure rate, independent of other traffic that may be transiting the same node. In the interest of assuring bounded latency, this departure rate must be guaranteed over any time interval equal to or greater than the time it takes to transmit a packet at the guaranteed rate.

Although this behavior is necessary to provide the VLL service, it is not sufficient. The PHB guarantees a minimum *departure* rate for the EF marked traffic. To use this behavior to provide the VLL service, it is necessary to bound the *arrival* rate of EF marked traffic so that it is less than or equal to the guaranteed departure rate. This is achieved through traffic conditioning at the appropriate nodes in the network. For further discussion, see the "Using Traffic-Conditioning Blocks to Build Differentiated Services" and "Provisioning the Interior for Route-Constrained Services," sections later in this chapter.

Note

It is also necessary to bound the arrival of other (non-EF) traffic that competes for resources at the same interfaces.

The requirements of the EF PHB can be provided using a number of underlying traffic-handling mechanisms. A strict priority queue may be used for the EF marked packets as long as it is the highest-priority queue on the interface. Alternatively, a sufficiently weighted queue in a WFQ queuing scheme may be used (albeit with some compromise in QE product). In the case of a strict priority queue, it is important to bound the arrival of EF marked packets so that they do not starve lower-priority traffic. Other queuing schemes may also be used.

Note

Some controversy surrounds several aspects of the EF PHB and the VLL service. These include the exact definition of the service and whether the service can be provided if WFQ is used to implement the EF PHB. The VLL service is first described in [RFC 2598]. At the time of this writing, an additional draft, called "Virtual Wire Behavior Aggregate," is under consideration [VW_DRAFT]. This draft attempts to address some of the controversy and to clarify the use of the EF PHB to provide a VLL service.

This book cannot hope to resolve the controversy surrounding the VLL service. Some readers no doubt will recognize the description of the service as equivalent to their understanding of the service. Other readers will cry blasphemy and declare that the service described in this book as the VLL service is a bastardization of the one and only true VLL service. Regardless, this book will use the term *VLL service* to refer consistently to a service that emulates a leased line.

6.3.2   The Assured Forwarding PHB Group

Unlike the EF PHB, the AF PHB group is not intended to provide a latency-bounded service [RFC 2597]. The AF PHB group primarily addresses forwarding assurance by controlling the drop probability of AF marked packets at nodes implementing the PHB. The AF behavior calls for the forwarding of packets in four different *classes*. The forwarding behavior should be such that as long as arriving traffic marked for the class conforms to a specified profile, sufficient resources are available to forward the traffic. Within each class, packets may be marked for one of three drop probability levels. If arriving traffic marked for a class exceeds the specified profile, the PHB may begin to drop marked packets. However, it must always drop those packets marked for a higher drop probability before dropping packets marked for a lower drop probability.

Note

The different PHBs of the AF PHB group are denoted by AF_{xy}, where x denotes the *class* to which the PHB belongs and y denotes the drop probability associated with the PHB. Lower values of y indicate a lower drop probability.

The AF PHB group can be used to build services that offer a high assurance of delivery to traffic conforming to a specified profile and to provide control over which packets are dropped when the profile is exceeded. The specification of the AF PHB group does not define the relationships among the four classes. The AF PHB group is quite flexible and can be used to build a variety of service offerings.

Service providers may use the four classes to build tiered services. An example of such an offering is the hypothetical *Olympic service*. This service uses the different classes to offer relative average forwarding delays. For example, consider that three classes are implemented, yielding a *gold*, *silver*, and *bronze* service. The service can be constructed by designating three equally high-priority queues in network devices. One of the three queues is used for each class. Admission control is applied so that less traffic is admitted to the queue corresponding to the gold service than is admitted to the queue corresponding to the silver service. Similarly, less traffic is admitted to the queue corresponding to the silver service than is admitted to the queue corresponding to the bronze service. Because the queues are of equal priority, they will each receive equivalent shares of the link's capacity. However, because less traffic competes for this share in the gold queue than in the silver queue, traffic in the gold queue will be forwarded with a lower average delay than traffic in the silver queue. Similarly, traffic in the silver queue will be forwarded with a lower average delay than traffic in the bronze queue. See the appendix of [RFC 2597] for a discussion of the Olympic service.

The specification of the AF PHB group does not define the underlying traffic mechanisms that should be used to provide the required behavior. It does recommend, however, that a mechanism such as random early detection (RED)—see Chapter 3—be used to drop packets when necessary. The characteristics of RED can improve the stability of TCP flows using the AF PHB group while enforcing fairness among traffic corresponding to multiple conversations. The specification does require that packets not be reordered within a conversation. This is important because out-of-order packet arrival complicates processing at a receiver, increasing buffering requirements and compromising performance.

6.3.3 The Class Selector PHB Group

The *class selector* PHB group is standardized by the same RFC that standardized the usage of the DiffServ field of the IP header [RFC 2474]. This RFC recognized that the specification of a new usage model for what was formerly the IP precedence field could break legacy applications and network devices that make use of the IP precedence field. Few applications actually use this field, but some do. For example, network control traffic is often marked with IP precedence level 7, and many network devices handle such traffic accordingly.

The class selector PHB group specification identifies eight DSCPs (corresponding to eight PHBs within the same PHB group). The DSCPs are chosen so that they map directly to the legacy IP precedence field and can be interpreted by legacy network devices. The specification of the class selector PHB group requires that traffic marked for a higher precedence level be assured a higher or equal probability of "timely forwarding" than packets marked with a lower precedence level.

> **Note**
>
> Note that the class selector codepoints support legacy use of the IP precedence field. These codepoints span the TOS field as well as the precedence field. However, the TOS field is not recognized by implementations of the class selector PHB group.

> **The Default PHB**
>
> The *default* PHB offers best-effort service. It is invoked by the DSCP 000000, which is also the class selector PHB corresponding to the lowest level of IP precedence.
>
> Although typical usage of the default PHB is likely to be for best-effort service, certain DiffServ providers may actually allocate resources to the default PHB so that it offers service other than best-effort.

6.4   *Providing Services*

As discussed previously, the DiffServ working group of the IETF has focused on the definition of PHBs. The purpose of these PHBs is to serve as building blocks in the construction of services that DiffServ providers can sell to their customers. This section describes a general characterization of the services that might be offered across a DiffServ network. Subsequent sections will discuss the required traffic-conditioning components and how these can be configured or provisioned to yield specific services. Because DiffServ services are not yet widely available, the following text must be considered speculative rather than factual.

6.4.1   *Providers, Customers, and Network Boundaries*

Differentiated services are offered by a DiffServ *provider* to a DiffServ *customer*. The service is offered typically at the point that the customer submits traffic to the provider's network. This is the *ingress* point to the provider's network.

Note

Services may also be offered at egress points, as discussed later in this chapter in the section "The Scope and Extent of a DiffServ Service."

The service defines the manner in which the provider will carry the customer's traffic through the provider's network to the provider's egress points (and possibly beyond these). The service definition is captured in the form of the service level specification defined previously.

From an end-to-end perspective, network traffic generally traverses a concatenation of networks that may include hosts, home or office networks, campus or corporate networks, and several large *transit* networks. Transit networks carry traffic that mostly does not terminate or originate within the network. These are distinguished from *stub* networks, which carry traffic to and from termination points (hosts and servers and end users). Home and office networks are stub networks. These are typically customers of campus or corporate networks (small transit networks), which are in turn customers of large transit networks. DiffServ may be deployed within large transit networks as well as smaller campus and corporate networks, and, in special cases, all the way to individual hosts. As such, there may be numerous customer/provider boundaries at which the concept of a service applies.

At boundaries between peer transit networks, each network may act both as a customer of its peer and as a provider to its peer. As such, there are likely to be two service level specifications at these boundaries: one governing the service provided by Network A to Network B, and the other governing the service provided by Network B to Network A. At boundaries between transit networks and stub networks, the transit networks offer services to the stub networks, but the stub networks generally do not offer services to transit networks. Therefore, only a single (but possibly bidirectional) service level specification is required at the interface between a stub network and a transit network.

It is helpful to define a DiffServ *domain*. A domain is a set of contiguous nodes that operate with a common set of service provisioning policies, DSCP-to-PHB mappings, and PHB definitions. Contiguous DiffServ domains form a DiffServ *region*. The concepts of customer/provider boundaries, transit and stub networks, and domains and regions are illustrated in Figure 6.3.

Figure 6.3   Customer/Provider Boundaries, Transit and Stub Networks, and DiffServ Domains and Regions

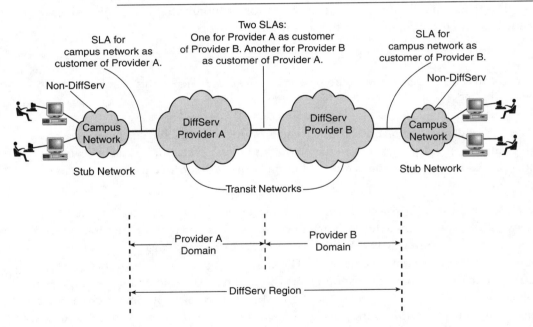

6.4.2   *Traffic Constraints and Quality of Offered Services*

In general, the services that can be offered at the DiffServ network boundary are related to the constraints that can be applied to the serviced traffic. This is true not just for DiffServ networks, but for any QoS mechanism. For example, if a customer specifies the ingress and egress points between which his or her traffic flows and specifies the exact profile of that traffic, then the provider can reserve the required amount of resources along the required routes specifically for that customer. The provider will configure the appropriate policing mechanisms to enforce the constraints that the customer has agreed to. That customer's traffic will be penalized if it strays from the declared route or if it exceeds the declared profile. Traffic that adheres to the declared route and profile can be allotted a relatively high-quality service.

Traffic that is less predictable cannot be offered as high quality a service.

> **Note**
>
> The term *predictable* is used to refer to both temporal and spatial variations in the traffic that do not follow a well-defined pattern. For example, traffic that is characterized by rapid and erratic variations in rate is not predictable from a temporal perspective. This traffic may also be referred to as *bursty* traffic. Traffic that may take rapidly varying paths through the network is not predictable from a spatial perspective.

For example, if the customer cannot provide a quantifiably bounded traffic profile, the provider cannot possibly guarantee to accommodate the traffic because, in theory, infinite resources may be required. Similarly, if the customer cannot specify the ingress and egress points that will be traversed, the provider must be ready to serve the customer's traffic at all ingress and egress points. To do so would require resources at all points instead of at a select few. Thus, providing high-quality service for unpredictable traffic tends to be prohibitively costly. In general, if all else is the same, the less predictable the traffic, the lower the service guarantees that can be offered.

Of course, a provider can offer high-quality guarantees even for unpredictable traffic by significantly overprovisioning the network. Alternatively, a customer may attempt to quantify bursty traffic by specifying the highest *expected* traffic rate. However, these approaches are inefficient. This is the quality/efficiency trade-off that was discussed in Chapter 2, "The Quality/Efficiency Product."

6.4.3   *Levels of Service Guarantees*

Chapter 2 suggested that a network provide a range of service guarantees by dividing network resources into multiple resource *pools*. It identified four such resource pools that would be available to support four general levels of service guarantees (including best-effort service). This section revisits the notion of discrete resource pools and corresponding service levels from the perspective of a DiffServ network and the service level agreements that can be offered. As explained previously, the more predictable the offered traffic, the higher the quality of the services that can be offered. The levels of service described here are distinguished along these lines.

Five service types are described: quantitative services, route-constrained qualitative services, route-independent qualitative services, best-effort service, and less-than-best-effort service. The first four correspond roughly to the four resource pools identified in Chapter 3.

6.4.3.1 Quantitative Services

These are services that offer quantifiable guarantees and that are targeted at quantifiable traffic. The VLL service described in the context of the EF PHB is one such example. Examples of quantifiable service guarantees are as follows:

- All traffic marked with the DSCP corresponding to EF and conforming to profile X will be delivered from DiffServ Ingress Point A to Egress Point B with a latency not to exceed 50msec.

- All traffic marked with the DSCP corresponding to AF_{xy} and corresponding to profile Y will be delivered from DiffServ Ingress Point A to Egress Point B with less than 0.1% drop probability and a latency not to exceed 1 second.

Note that both services are defined with respect to specific ingress and egress points from the DiffServ network. Unless the network administrator is willing to significantly overprovision the network, quantitative services can be offered only between specific ingress and egress points. Also note that both the profile of conforming traffic and the service parameters that can be expected are quantified.

> **Note**
>
> Although it is largely recognized that the provision of a useful service using the EF PHB requires the specification of both ingress and egress points between which the service is valid, it is not clear that this is true for the AF PHB group. DiffServ providers may choose to provide services based on the AF PHB group from a specified ingress point to unspecified egress points (or to a set of egress points). In this case, the quality of the services that can be offered is likely to be compromised relative to the quality of the services that could otherwise be offered.

6.4.3.2 Qualitative Services

Nonquantifiable traffic falls into two categories: that which is session-oriented and that which is not. Both types of traffic are sporadic and, therefore, unquantifiable. However, one type is session-oriented in the sense that the traffic persists between a defined set of endpoints for some amount of time. The other is nonpersistent or fleeting, in the sense that its patterns change rapidly and may include many endpoints.

An example of the first type of traffic is the traffic generated by client/server database applications. For example, consider the session between an airline ticketing agent and the central transaction server handling the ticket sales. Although the profile of traffic exchanged between the client and server is sporadic, sessions between the two may persist for an entire day. This type of traffic might, for example, make use of the Null Service described in the Chapter 4. An example of the second type of traffic is Web traffic solicited by any of a number of clients from any of a number of servers. Such traffic is not only not quantifiable, but it is also fleeting.

No clear line delineates persistent qualitative traffic from nonpersistent qualitative traffic. The two exist on a continuum. However, the distinction is useful from the perspective of providing services. This is because the provider can provision more efficiently for persistent traffic than for nonpersistent traffic. For example, a provider can offer increased resources to traffic between the central transaction server described previously and some small, specific number of client ticketing agents. The provider cannot afford to offer the same increased resources to transient users of a Web server. Simply put, the provider can offer more resources along constrained traffic paths than along arbitrary traffic paths.

Route-Constrained Qualitative Services

These are services that are offered for persistent nonquantifiable traffic. Such traffic can be expected to adhere to specific routes. Therefore, these services are offered between specific ingress and egress points. An example of such a service guarantee is:

> All traffic marked with the DSCP corresponding to AFij and conforming to Profile X will be delivered from DiffServ Ingress Point A to Egress Point B with low latency and low drop probability.

Note that the service provider constrained the profile of serviced traffic despite the fact that the traffic is not quantifiable. In general, for qualitative services, the profile is likely to be relatively liberal. This is because the latency and drop probability offered in return are relatively noncommittal. Because the route is constrained in this example, the service offering could be somewhat more quantifiable. For example, the provider might offer that 90% of the offered traffic will be delivered with a latency not to exceed 5 seconds. This is a far looser commitment than that offered in the case of quantifiable services.

> **Note**
>
> When a provider offers route-constrained services, the provider must enforce the negotiated route constraints. This may be done by the following ways:
>
> - Policing traffic at the customer's ingress based on destination address and expected routing
>
> - Policing at strategic network devices throughout the network, based on the customer from which the traffic originated

Route-Independent Qualitative Services

These are services that are offered for nonquantifiable nonpersistent traffic. It is not possible to assume routing constraints for such traffic. An example of such a service is as follows:

All traffic marked with the DSCP corresponding to AFpq and corresponding to Profile Y will be delivered from DiffServ Ingress Point A to any egress point with lower latency and lower drop probability than best-effort traffic.

Because the offered traffic is very unconstrained, the service guarantee is very noncommittal. In fact, the only guarantee offered in this case is that the serviced traffic is faring better than best-effort traffic. This is a *better-than-best-effort* (BBE) service.

6.4.3.3 Best-Effort Service

This is just the default service afforded to unmarked traffic. It is interesting to note that higher-quality services are predicated on the allocation of resources that would otherwise be available for best-effort traffic. Provisioning for higher-quality services must be done in a manner that does not *starve* best-effort traffic for resources.

6.4.3.4 Less-Than-Best-Effort Service

There is likely some value to providing a *less-than-best-effort* (LBE) service. For example, this service could accommodate early deployment of applications that are network hostile. An example of such an application is a UDP streaming media server. Streaming media applications tend to generate large volumes of traffic of a type that does not respond to congestion.

Network providers are reluctant to allow traffic from such applications to transit their networks because of the potential threat to other traffic. In the long run, all important application traffic will be marked for the appropriate service level and, if appropriate, will be prioritized above the aggressive streaming media traffic. However, an LBE service can enable streaming media traffic to be *de*-prioritized so that it is guaranteed not to wreak havoc with other unmarked network traffic. As a result, it can be allowed onto the network earlier rather than later. In this application, the LBE service should subjugate the streaming media traffic relative to pre-existing best-effort traffic. The LBE service can be implemented using the AF PHB group and need not be route-constrained.

6.4.3.5 Simultaneous Support for All Service Types

In general, DiffServ networks will support the five types of services defined simultaneously. Figure 6.4 illustrates a "Full-Service" DiffServ network offering four of the five service levels described.

Figure 6.4   The Full-Service DiffServ Network

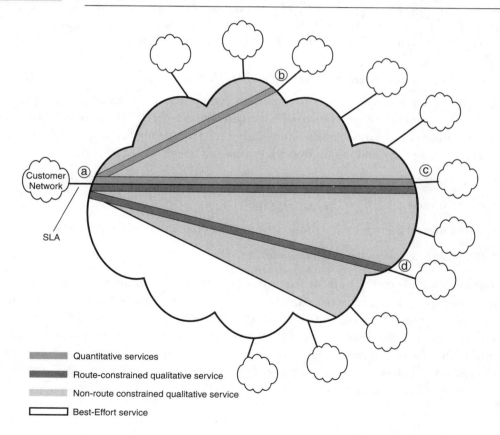

Quantitative services

Route-constrained qualitative service

Non-route constrained qualitative service

Best-Effort service

Figure 6.4 illustrates a DiffServ provider network (in the center) surrounded by numerous attached customer networks. A customer network attaches to the provider network at point a. The SLA at this point offers several services to the customer, as follows:

- Quantitative, route-constrained services to points b and c

- Qualitative, route-constrained services to points c and d

- Qualitative, non-route-constrained services to numerous connection points, as illustrated by the shaded region

- Best-effort service to all points served

The route-constrained services are available between specific endpoints. These appear as a mesh, spanning the DiffServ network. From the customer's perspective, the SLA at ingress point a offers a set of virtual private networks (VPNs) to specific remote egress points. The route-independent services permeate the entire DiffServ domain.

6.4.4 The Scope and Extent of a DiffServ Service

The *scope* of an offered service is an important component of the service specification. As demonstrated in the previous paragraph, certain services can be offered only between constrained ingress and egress points. Thus, these services have limited scope. Others may be offered between any endpoints. Examples of service scopes are listed here:

- From ingress point a to egress point b

- From ingress point a to any egress point

- From ingress point a to any of the set of egress points {b1, b2, and so on}

- From any ingress point to egress point b

The first example corresponds to the route-constrained services discussed previously, including the quantitative service and the route-constrained qualitative service. The second example corresponds to the route-independent qualitative service. The third example is a generalization of the first that might be appropriate, for example, for providing multicast quantitative service. It might also be appropriate for a semi-route-constrained service that offers a route-independent qualitative service with improved service for traffic destined to the set of specified egress points.

6.4.4.1 Agreements Governing Received Traffic

The fourth example of a service scope is quite different from the other three in the sense that it is based on a single egress point and specifies no ingress point. For the most part, DiffServ focuses on the service offered to traffic *submitted* to the DiffServ network. Services offer to forward the customer's traffic to its destination as long as the customer conforms to specified profiles and pays for the service. However, customers might wish to specify the treatment of various traffic *destined* to the customer. For example, a customer connected to a DiffServ network over a constrained link might want to prioritize traffic from specific ingress points and to discard unsolicited traffic.

The nature of services describing received traffic treatment is not well understood. Furthermore, it conflicts somewhat with an approach that offers guarantees regarding the *forwarding* of traffic. For example, if a service agreement offers to forward traffic from a customer at ingress point a to a customer at egress point b, but an agreement with the customer at egress point b calls for the discard of this traffic, one agreement must be violated.

6.4.4.2 Extent of a Service

The concept of extent of a service refers here to the number of DiffServ domains between service endpoints. In the simplest case, a service is offered across a single DiffServ provider's network. The service endpoints are all within the same DiffServ domain. In this case, the single DiffServ provider is responsible for meeting the guarantees offered by the service agreements that it negotiates with its customers. In the short run, DiffServ services are expected to be offered across a single DiffServ domain only.

In the long run, a DiffServ service will span multiple domains. A service agreement is offered to a customer at some ingress point in Provider A's network. However, the scope of the service may specify egress points in other Provider's networks or in other domains. In this case, Provider A must negotiate agreements with peer DiffServ domains to assure that the services offered by the provider can be delivered to the customer. If the egress points are in distant domains, then peer domains may in turn depend on agreements with their peers.

These agreements are particularly important with respect to the higher-quality services. Such services offer quantifiable service parameters that cannot be met unless sufficient resources are available across all DiffServ domains between the ingress and egress points specified for the service. Therefore, quantifiable services that extend across multiple domains require close cooperation between the DiffServ domains in terms of both routing and service level specifications at peering points.

On the other hand, the less quantifiable services—especially the BBE service types—do not require such close coordination. For these services, no quantifiable commitments are made and, therefore, no specific quantities of resources need to be provisioned. As long as peer domains agree to carry some of each other's traffic at better-than-best-effort priority, BBE type services can be accommodated regardless of their extent.

An additional complexity that arises when services are extended across multiple DiffServ domains is the interpretation of DSCPs. Domains either must agree to interpret DSCPs consistently at boundaries or must re-mark appropriately at ingress points.

6.4.5 Static versus Dynamic Service Level Specifications

Services may be static or dynamic. Initially, DiffServ services are expected to be static. Service level specifications for static services are instantiated as a result of negotiation between human agents representing provider and customer. A static SLS is first instantiated at the agreed-upon service start date and may periodically be renegotiated (over days or weeks or months). The SLS may specify that service levels change at certain times of day or certain days of the week, but the specification itself remains static.

Dynamic SLSs, on the other hand, may change frequently. Such changes may be triggered, for example, by changes in demand (as indicated by offered traffic load) relative to preset thresholds. Dynamic SLSs change without human intervention and thus require an automated agent and protocol. Aggregate RSVP, as described in Chapter 5, "RSVP," is one such protocol. Various researchers have proposed forms of *bandwidth brokers,* which operate at DiffServ network boundaries and support dynamic SLSs by monitoring or adjusting resource provisioning within a DiffServ network.

Dynamic SLSs require sophisticated automated provisioning mechanisms in the provider's network. Although these add complexity to the network, they also enable it to operate at a higher quality/efficiency product.

6.5 Traffic Conditioning

DiffServ networks construct services by implementing PHBs and by conditioning the traffic that is submitted to these PHBs. The PHBs are typically queuing schemes implemented on egress interfaces of network devices. Traffic conditioning is mostly implemented at ingress interfaces of network devices (although certain traffic-conditioning functions might be implemented at egress interfaces as well). (Note the distinction between ingress and egress interfaces with respect to a single device versus an entire DiffServ domain.) Traffic-conditioning components are combined to build *traffic conditioning blocks* (TCBs) to achieve various conditioning functions.

The following section describes each of the fundamental traffic-conditioning components in detail. Before delving into this level of detail, it is helpful to briefly explain at a high level the role of traffic conditioning functionality in providing a service. At ingress points to a DiffServ network, classifiers identify traffic submitted for each service level. Ingress traffic-conditioning components must at a minimum *police* submitted traffic.

Policing is the task of verifying conformance of traffic submitted for each service level to the corresponding profiles negotiated in the SLS. Excess traffic must be discarded or reduced in rate to force it to conform. Alternatively, it may be redirected to a lower service level. Policing protects the DiffServ network provider's resources. In addition to policing, ingress traffic conditioning may provide value-add services on behalf of a customer. Such value-add functionality might include marking the customer's traffic with the appropriate DSCP and preshaping the customer's traffic to conform to negotiated profiles.

As the conditioned traffic is carried beyond the ingress points to the core of the network, additional traffic-conditioning components may be used at strategic locations to verify that the traffic conforms to expected behavior. (See the section "Interior Provisioning," later in this chapter.) The role of traffic-conditioning components in providing DiffServ services is illustrated in Figure 6.5.

Figure 6.5   Traffic-Conditioning Functions in a DiffServ Network

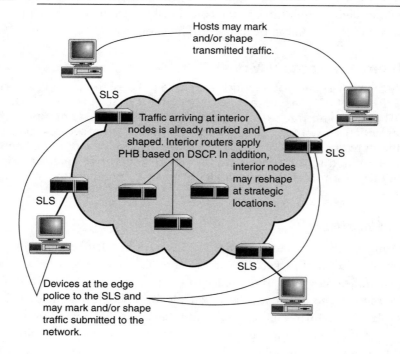

Hosts may mark and/or shape transmitted traffic.

Traffic arriving at interior nodes is already marked and shaped. Interior routers apply PHB based on DSCP. In addition, interior nodes may reshape at strategic locations.

SLS

Devices at the edge police to the SLS and may mark and/or shape traffic submitted to the network.

Note that the components described in the following text are logical representations of traffic conditioning functionality. These components do not literally represent specific hardware or software components, but rather abstractions of these.

6.5.1   Traffic-Conditioning Components

The primary traffic-conditioning components are listed here:

- Classifiers

- Meters

- Action elements (markers, shapers, droppers)

Traffic-conditioning components are described in an IETF draft titled "An Informal Management Model for DiffServ Routers" [CONCEPTUAL_MODEL]. (See the accompanying sidebar titled "The DiffServ Conceptual Model.") Formal definitions of traffic-conditioning components (such as those in the conceptual model draft) are in a state of flux. For example, certain sources consider classification to be a traffic-conditioning function, while others consider it to be outside the scope of formal traffic conditioners. As such, the following text focuses on the *functionality* of the various components listed, irrespective of the formal nomenclature. Although the specific nomenclature and definitions in this text may inevitably differ slightly from those in the conceptual model draft (or other sources), they are internally consistent and can be mapped to functionality defined in other sources.

The DiffServ Conceptual Model

To simplify the provisioning of network-wide QoS policies, the DiffServ working group of the IETF is defining a conceptual model for DiffServ routers [CONCEPTUAL_MODEL]. This model abstracts traffic-conditioning components and PHB elements. As a result, provisioning systems can use a common set of protocols and data structures to provision network devices of varying types from various vendors. Furthermore, the abstractions defined in the conceptual model are useful not only for strict DiffServ routers, but also for routers supporting RSVP and IntServ services.

6.5.1.1   Classifiers

Not surprisingly, classifiers classify traffic. Traffic arrives at a DiffServ network ingress point in the form of a stream of packets. Because the premise of a DiffServ network is that it offers *differentiated* services, it is necessary to separate arriving traffic into *different* traffic flows (corresponding to different classes), eligible for different treatment. This is the fundamental role of a classifier. Figure 6.6 shows a schematic representation of a classifier. It has a single input (at which the ingress packet stream is received) and multiple outputs, corresponding to the various subsets of traffic sorted according to the classification criteria.

Figure 6.6 Schematic Representation of a Classifier

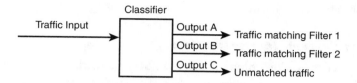

Two types of classifiers exist: *behavior aggregate* (BA) classifiers and *multifield* (MF) classifiers. These are described in the following sections.

Behavior Aggregate Classifiers

BA classifiers classify traffic solely on the basis of the DSCP in packet headers. These classifiers are useful when arriving packets have been previously marked with a DSCP. BA classifiers are typically used where it is necessary to control the rate at which traffic is submitted for a particular service level or simply to direct traffic submitted for a particular service level to a corresponding PHB at a device's egress interface.

Multifield Classifiers

MF classifiers classify traffic on the basis of any fields in submitted packets. An example of a simple MF classifier is a classifier that classifies based on some or all of the IP five-tuple (IP source address, destination address, source port, and destination port and protocol number). More complex MF classifiers might classify on fields much deeper into a packet, beyond the packet header. Certain sophisticated MF classifiers can even recognize session- or application-layer data in packets and might track session-layer protocol transitions.

MF classifiers are typically used near the ingress to a DiffServ network when it is necessary to recognize subsets of customer traffic and assign these to certain service levels. After the traffic is classified to the appropriate service level, traffic conditioners mark the corresponding DSCP and send the traffic on into the DiffServ network, where BA classifiers are used to handle the traffic from there on.

Filters

Classifiers are parameterized by filters. Filters specify the bit field to be used for classification and a mask. The mask specifies which bits of the bit field are significant for classification and which are not. As an example, a filter might specify that the source IP address field should be used for classification, but that only the high-order 16-bits of the field are significant. Filters may be applied in combinations—for example, a classifier may direct all traffic matching Filter A *and* Filter B to one output while all traffic matching Filter C *or* Filter D are directed to another output. Ambiguities can arise when packets match multiple filters. In these cases, classifiers may need to use precedence rules to resolve the ambiguity.

Classification Based on Ingress Interface

A very common classification criteria used in DiffServ networks is the ingress interface on which traffic is submitted. The ingress interface is often dedicated to a single customer and consequently can be used to identify that customer's traffic.

6.5.1.2 Meters

Meters are traffic-conditioning elements that measure the rate of submitted traffic and compare it against a temporal profile. Meters separate the submitted traffic according to its conformance to the profile used. Simple meters might separate traffic simply into conforming and nonconforming traffic. More sophisticated meters might recognize multiple levels of conformance. Figure 6.7 shows a schematic representation of a meter. It has a single input, which represents the submitted traffic stream. It has multiple outputs corresponding to traffic at various conformance levels, and it uses a metering profile.

Figure 6.7   Representation of a Meter

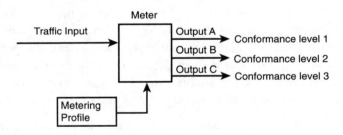

Meters are parameterized by *profiles*, which describe the temporal characteristics of conforming traffic streams. Examples of meters include token bucket meters, two-level token bucket meters, and average rate meters.

6.5.1.3 *Markers*

In the context of DiffServ networks, markers are used to mark a specific DSCP in a packet header. In many cases, traffic arrives at a DiffServ network premarked. In this case, a marker is used only if submitted traffic is found to be nonconforming and must be re-marked to a lower service level. In this role, it acts as a form of policing.

As an exception, when the interpretation of DSCPs by the provider's network differs from the interpretation by the customer's network, markers may be used to re-mark both conforming and nonconforming traffic.

In other cases, traffic may arrive at a provider's network unmarked. In this case, the SLS will typically include classification criteria describing the subset of the customer's traffic that is entitled to a certain service level. The provider will then typically use an MF classifier stage preceding a number of markers to mark the subsets of traffic accordingly.

Note

Note that the provider may never actually mark a DSCP in packet headers, using either alternate link-layer marking schemes, for example, or simply reclassifying the traffic using an MF classifier wherever necessary.

Figure 6.8 shows a schematic representation of a marker. It has a single input and a single output.

Figure 6.8   Schematic Representation of a Marker

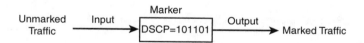

The marker is parameterized by the DSCP that it marks.

6.5.1.4 *Shapers*

Shapers alter the profile of submitted traffic by delaying certain packets, typically as a form of policing. A shaper is effectively a non-work-conserving queuing mechanism. Shapers are typically used to force a traffic flow that would otherwise be nonconforming so that it conforms to a particular profile. Figure 6.9 shows a schematic representation of a shaper. It has a single input and a single output.

Figure 6.9   Schematic Representation of a Shaper

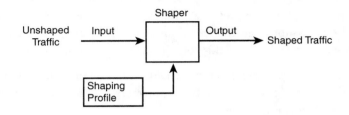

Shapers, like meters, are parameterized by a temporal profile. When a shaper uses the same profile as a subsequent meter, it assures that all submitted traffic will be deemed conforming by the meter. Note that because shapers delay traffic, they must queue packets. Queuing may have unwanted side effects such as increased latency and consumption of precious buffer space. In addition, shapers are expensive from a processing perspective, so shaping is a relatively rare form of policing and must be used carefully. Any shaper will have finite buffering resources and therefore will be incapable of handling the continual arrival of traffic at a rate that exceeds its shaping profile.

6.5.1.5 Droppers

Droppers simply drop packets. As such, they are used as a form of policing, typically to drop packets submitted to a network that are found to be nonconforming (by a meter). Figure 6.10 shows a schematic representation of a dropper. Note that droppers have no parameters.

Figure 6.10   Representation of a Dropper

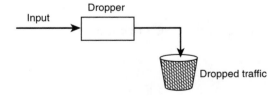

6.5.1.6 Multiplexers

Multiplexers are nodes that combine traffic from different sources. Figure 6.11 shows a schematic representation of a multiplexer.

Figure 6.11   Representation of a Multiplexer

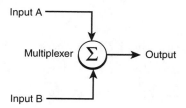

6.6   Using Traffic-Conditioning Blocks to Build Differentiated Services

The traffic-conditioning components described in the previous section are used to build traffic-conditioning blocks (TCBs). These provide traffic control functionality that is useful at specific points in the DiffServ network.

Traffic conditioning is most important at the edges of a DiffServ network. TCBs at DiffServ ingress points serve primarily to control the amount of traffic submitted to the network at each service level by each customer. In this manner, TCBs control the impact of submitted traffic on network resources. As a result, the provider is capable of offering service guarantees.

Traffic-conditioning blocks may be used to a lesser degree in the interior of the DiffServ network. In this case, they are used to ensure that traffic patterns remain within expected limits and do not starve network resources at strategic locations. The following section illustrates several examples of ingress TCBs and how these are used in the construction of services. The section "Provisioning the DiffServ Network," later in this chapter, describes the use of TCBs internal to the DiffServ network and also discusses the configuration of queuing behaviors, which are an integral part of any DiffServ service.

6.6.1   TCB Supporting VLL Service at the DiffServ Ingress

The following TCB is used at the ingress interface to a DiffServ network to support a VLL service. The VLL service uses the EF PHB to offer a low-latency, low-jitter, low-loss service, such as would be suitable for IP telephony, for example.

As explained previously, it is necessary to carefully control the rate at which traffic is submitted for the EF PHB at each node. Assuming that routing is well understood, it is possible to control the rate at which EF traffic arrives at each internal node by controlling the rate at which it is submitted at each ingress point. In this example, the customer is assumed to have premarked and preshaped traffic submitted for the EF PHB. Therefore, the sample TCB will not mark or shape packets. It serves merely to enforce the SLS negotiated with the customer, to protect the provider's resources. As such, it can be considered a *policing* TCB.

6.6.1.1   SLS Supporting the VLL Service

The VLL service offered is described by the following SLS:

```
/** Accept EF traffic to 2.X.X.X conforming to P1 **/

Traffic submitted by customer C1
    and marked with DSCP == EF
    and destination address in the subnet 2.X.X.X
    and conforming to profile P1
will be delivered to egress point B with a latency not exceeding 100 msec and a
drop-probability less than 1%.

/** Discard non-conforming EF traffic to 2.X.X.X **/

Traffic submitted by customer C1
    and marked with DSCP == EF
    and destination address in the subnet 2.X.X.X
    and not conforming to profile P1
will be discarded.

/** Accept EF traffic to 3.X.X.X conforming to P2 **/

Traffic submitted by customer C1
    and marked with DSCP == EF
    and destination address in the subnet 3.X.X.X
    and conforming to profile P2
will be delivered to egress point C with a latency not exceeding 100 msec and a
drop-probability less than 1%.

/** Discard non-conforming EF traffic to 3.X.X.X **/

Traffic submitted by customer C1
    and marked with DSCP == EF
    and destination address in the subnet 3.X.X.X
    and not conforming to profile P2
will be discarded.
```

```
/** Discard EF traffic to other egress points **/

Traffic submitted by customer C1
    and marked with DSCP == EF
    and destination address not in the subnet 2.X.X.X
    and destination address not in the subnet 3.X.X.X
will be discarded.

/** Traffic not marked for EF gets default service **/

Traffic submitted by customer C1
    and not marked with DSCP == EF
will be delivered with best-effort service.

/** Profile specification **/

P1:

Conforming traffic must not exceed 64 Kbps over any 5 msec interval.

P2:

Conforming traffic must not exceed 128 Kbps over any 2.5 msec interval.
```

This SLS guarantees low-latency, low-loss service for EF-marked traffic from the customer ingress point to either of two egress points. In this example, egress points are specified by destination subnet address. The customer's EF traffic is limited in rate and burstiness by the specified profiles, P1 and P2. Any traffic in excess of the profile may be discarded. Any traffic marked EF and not destined for one of the two specified egress points may be discarded. All traffic not marked for EF will be allotted best-effort service.

6.6.1.2   Schematic of the TCB

Figure 6.12 shows a logical representation of a TCB that enforces the SLS described previously. It should be constructed on the interface that serves as Customer C1's ingress interface to the DiffServ network.

It is assumed that the ingress interface on which the TCB is constructed is dedicated to Customer C1. If this were not the case, it would be necessary to preclassify traffic to determine the customer submitting each packet.

Figure 6.12 TCB01: Ingress TCB Supporting VLL Service

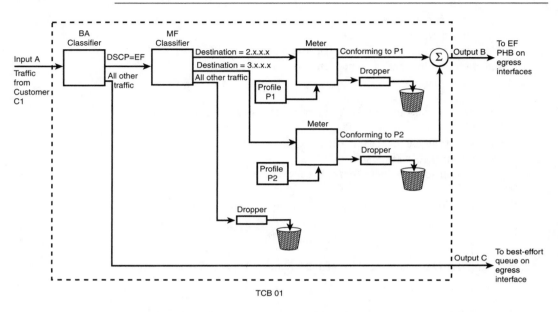

TCB 01

Because customer preclassification is not necessary, the first TC component is a BA classifier that separates traffic marked for the EF PHB from traffic that is not marked for the EF PHB. All traffic not marked for the EF PHB is directed to the best-effort queue at the appropriate router egress interface (as determined by routing).

Traffic that is marked for the EF PHB is directed to a second classifier that determines whether the traffic is destined for one of the two egress points for which the EF PHB is supported. Traffic marked for the EF PHB and not destined for one of the two allowed egress points is directed to a dropper, where it is discarded.

Traffic that is marked for the EF PHB and that is destined for one of the two supported egress points is submitted to a meter to verify conformance to the corresponding profile.

Traffic that is found to be nonconforming to a profile is passed to a dropper, where it is discarded.

Traffic that is found to be conforming is passed directed to the EF PHB queue at the appropriate egress interface of the router.

The TCB as a whole is named TCB01. It has a single input and two outputs. TCB01 will be reused in the next section.

6.6.2   TCB Providing VLL Service with Marking and Shaping

In the previous example, the ingress TCB serves only to protect the provider's resources by limiting the amount of resources claimed by the customer's traffic to those negotiated per the SLS. It is the customer's responsibility entirely to precondition traffic so that it is correctly marked and conforms to the SLS. The following example extends the previous policing TCB to provide value-add to the customer by marking and shaping on behalf of the customer.

6.6.2.1   Value-Add SLS for the VLL Service

The following SLS specifies marking and shaping functionality in addition to the basic policing functionality provided by the previous example.

```
/** Mark and shape traffic for port 5005 to 2.X.X.X **/

Traffic submitted by customer C1
    with UDP destination port 5005
    and destination address in the subnet 2.X.X.X
will be marked with DSCP == EF and
will be shaped to profile P1 and
will be delivered to egress point B with a latency not exceeding 100 msec and a
drop-probability less than 1%.

/** Mark and shape EF traffic for port 5005 to 3.X.X.X **/

Traffic submitted by customer C1
    with UDP destination port 5005
    and destination address in the subnet 3.X.X.X
will be marked with DSCP == EF and
will be shaped to profile P2 and
will be delivered to egress point C with a latency not exceeding 100 msec and a
drop-probability less than 1%.

/** Other traffic gets default service **/

Traffic submitted by customer C1
    with UDP destination port 5005
    and destination address not in the subnet 2.X.X.X
    and destination address not in the subnet 3.X.X.X
will be delivered with best-effort service.

Traffic submitted by customer C1
    and not for destination port 5005
```

```
will be delivered with best-effort service.

/** Profile specification **/

P1:

Conforming traffic must not exceed 64 Kbps over any 5 msec interval.

P2:

Conforming traffic must not exceed 128 Kbps over any 2.5 msec interval.
```

This SLS is suitable for a customer that runs an application that generates telephony traffic for destination UDP port 5005. The customer requires high-quality VLL service to support the telephony application between the ingress point of interest and Egress Points B and C. The customer purchases sufficient capacity at the EF service level to accommodate the expected average traffic rate to each of the egress points. However, the customer does not shape traffic and may occasionally generate bursts in excess of the negotiated capacity. The customer also does not mark traffic. Thus, the customer relies on the service provider to both mark and shape the submitted traffic.

6.6.2.2 Schematic of the TCB

Figure 6.13 shows a logical representation of a TCB that supports the SLS described previously. It should be constructed on the interface that serves as customer C1's ingress interface to the DiffServ network. The representation of the TCB separates the marking and shaping front end from the policing part of the TCB. The front end provides the value-add functionality. The policing part is identical to the TCB illustrated in the previous example (TCB01).

The first TC component is an MF classifier that identifies traffic addressed to port 5005 and destined for one of the two egress points allowed per the SLS. All traffic not addressed to port 5005 and one of the two egress points is directed to the best-effort queue at the appropriate router egress interface (as determined by routing).

Traffic that is addressed to port 5005 and destined for one of the two egress points is marked with the EF DSCP. Next, traffic is passed to one of two shapers. Traffic destined for subnet 2.X.X.X is shaped using profile P1. Traffic destined for subnet 3.X.X.X is shaped using profile P2. Following the shapers, traffic is submitted to the policing stage of the TCB.

Figure 6.13   Ingress TCB Supporting Marking and Shaping

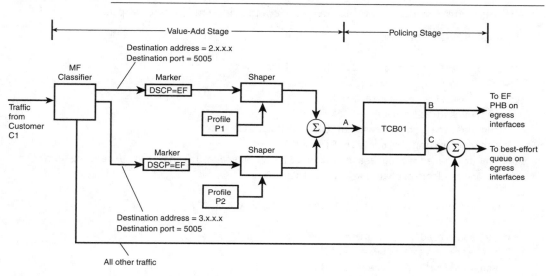

Note that the logical separation of the value-add stage from the policing stage of the TCB is solely for the purpose of clearly illustrating these separate functions. Representation and implementation of the TCB can be simplified considerably by combining functionality in the marking/shaping stage and the policing stage. The separate MF classifiers can be combined. In addition, the shapers preshape to Profiles P1 and P2. Therefore, it is not necessary to follow these with meters.

6.6.3   Ingress TCB Providing Olympic Services and BBE Service Using the AF PHB Group

The following TCB is used at the ingress interface to a DiffServ network to support a variety of services based on the AF PHB group. The gold and silver services are route-constrained. The third service is a better-than-best-effort route-independent service.

The Olympic services (gold and silver) are likely to be useful for multimedia playback applications. These applications require relatively high bandwidth for the duration of a program. However, thanks to buffering at the receiver, they have relatively relaxed latency requirements. For example, the BBE service might be used to provide improved service to route-independent traffic from a Web server.

6.6.3.1 SLS for Olympic and BBE Service

The following SLS describes the three services provided at the ingress point.

```
/** GOLD SERVICE **/

/** Accept AF11 traffic to 2.X.X.X conforming to P1 **/

Traffic submitted by customer C1
    and marked with DSCP == AF11
    and destination address in the subnet 2.X.X.X
    and conforming to profile P1
will be delivered to egress point B with an average latency not exceeding one
second and a drop-probability less than 1%.

/** Re-mark non-conforming AF11 traffic to 2.X.X.X **/

Traffic submitted by customer C1
    and marked with DSCP == AF11
    and destination address in the subnet 2.X.X.X
    and not conforming to profile P1
will be remarked to DSCP AF12 and
will be delivered to egress point B with a drop-probability less than 10%.

/** SILVER SERVICE **/

/** Accept AF21 traffic to 2.X.X.X conforming to P2 **/

Traffic submitted by customer C1
    and marked with DSCP == AF21
    and destination address in the subnet 2.X.X.X
    and conforming to profile P2
will be delivered to egress point B with an average latency not exceeding five
seconds and a drop-probability less than 1%.

/** Remark non-conforming AF21 traffic to 2.X.X.X **/

Traffic submitted by customer C1
    and marked with DSCP == AF21
    and destination address in the subnet 2.X.X.X
    and not conforming to profile P2
will be remarked to DSCP AF22 and
will be delivered to egress point B with a drop probability less than 10%.

/** Remark AF1X or AF2X traffic to other egress points **/
```

```
Traffic submitted by customer C1
    and marked with DSCP == AF1X or
    marked with DSCP == AF2X
    and destination address not in the subnet 2.X.X.X
will be remarked to DSCP 000000 and
will be delivered with drop probability and latency equal to best-effort traffic.


/** BETTER-THAN-BEST-EFFORT SERVICE **/

/** Accept AF31 traffic to any egress subject to P3 **/

Traffic submitted by customer C1
    and marked with DSCP == AF31
    and conforming to profile P3
will be delivered with drop probability and latency better than best-effort
traffic.

/** Remark AF31 traffic exceeding P3 **/

Traffic submitted by customer C1
    and marked with DSCP == AF31
    and not conforming to profile P3
will be re-marked to DSCP AF32 and
will be delivered with drop probability and latency equal to best-effort traffic.

/** Profile specification **/

P1:

Traffic must conform to a token bucket model parameterized by r = 1 Mbps, p = 10
Mbps, and B = 1 Mbyte.

P2:

Traffic must conform to a token bucket model parameterized by r = 4 Mbps, p = 10
Mbps, and B = 1 Mbyte.

P3:

Traffic must conform to a token bucket model parameterized by r = 10 Mbps, p = 10
Mbps, and B = 1 Mbyte.
```

This SLS accepts traffic for the gold or silver service, as long as it is destined for subnet 2.X.X.X. The gold service offers a high probability of low-latency delivery and a very low drop probability for traffic that conforms to P1. Traffic submitted for the gold service and that does not conform to P1 will experience a higher drop probability. The silver service offers the same low drop probability as the gold service. However, the latency offered is not as low as that offered by the gold service. A greater volume of traffic will be accommodated for the silver service, per P2. Traffic not conforming to P2 will be more likely to be dropped.

Traffic submitted for the BBE service will be delivered with a latency and drop probability that is better than that experienced by best-effort traffic.

6.6.3.2 Schematic of the TCB

Figure 6.14 shows a logical representation of a TCB that supports the SLS described previously. It should be constructed on the interface that serves as customer C1's ingress interface to the DiffServ network.

| Figure 6.14 | Ingress TCB Supporting Various AF-Based Services |

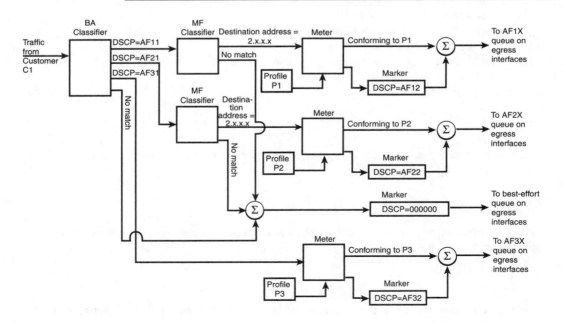

The first TC component is a BA classifier that identifies traffic marked for one of the three AF classes. Traffic marked for AF11 is directed to an MF classifier that verifies the destination address. Traffic directed to destination address 2.X.X.X is then forwarded to a metering stage. Traffic for AF11 that is not addressed to 2.X.X.X is re-marked for best-effort. The metering stage verifies conformance to P1. Conforming traffic is directed to the AF1X PHB directly. Nonconforming traffic is re-marked to AF12 and then directed to the AF1X PHB. Similarly, traffic marked for AF22 is tested for the correct destination address and then measured against P2, is re-marked as necessary, and is directed to the AF2X PHB. Re-marked traffic for either class is subjected to a higher drop probability as a result of RED action applied to the AF PHB queues. Traffic that is marked for either the AF1X or the AF2X classes but that is not destined to the approved egress point is treated as best-effort traffic.

Traffic marked for the AF3X class is measured against P3. Conforming traffic is directed to the AF3X PHB, regardless of its destination. Traffic that does not conform to P3 is re-marked before directing it to the AF3X PHB. It is subjected to a higher drop probability as a result of RED. Although this traffic may be provided better-than-best-effort service, it is not guaranteed.

Note

Note that the customer may actually pre-demote certain traffic by marking it for AFX2 (corresponding to a higher drop probability within a certain class). By doing so, the customer is effectively telling the network that this traffic is less important and should be dropped first in case of congestion. In this case, the DiffServ traffic-conditioning elements should not count such traffic against the profile for AFX1 traffic.

6.6.3.3 *Gold and Silver Services*

The gold and silver services are similar to the VLL service in the sense that they are route-constrained and make quantifiable commitments. Note that the commitments offered for gold and silver service by the SLS are looser than those offered for the VLL service. Only the *average* latencies are guaranteed, and they are much higher than those offered by VLL service.

Also, note that the gold service offers a lower average latency than the silver service. This is a result of the provisioning of the DiffServ network. Within the network core, the same queue weights are assigned to both classes of service. However, the rate of submitted traffic is policed at ingress points and at strategic points within the network core, to assure that the gold service is less loaded than the silver service. As a result, the average expected latencies are lower.

6.7 Provisioning the DiffServ Network

Conditioning traffic at the ingress to the DiffServ network is necessary to provide service guarantees. However, it is not sufficient. To provide service guarantees, it is also necessary to provision components internal to the DiffServ network so that they work in a consistent and predictable manner. This section discusses the provisioning of a DiffServ network.

For the purpose of this discussion, the term *provisioning* will be used to refer to the determination and allocation of the resources needed at various nodes in the DiffServ network. Provisioning includes the addition or removal of physical resources at various points (*physical provisioning*). Provisioning also includes the modification of operating parameters within existing physical network equipment to alter the relative share of the equipment's resources that are allotted to an aggregate class of traffic (*logical provisioning*). Provisioning may be applied to the links that interconnect network devices as well as to the network devices themselves. For example, a SONET link between two devices may be reprovisioned to a higher speed, or a twisted-pair cable may be replaced with a shielded twisted-pair cable.

6.7.1 Boundary Provisioning versus Interior Provisioning

It is helpful to distinguish between *boundary provisioning* and *interior provisioning*. Boundary provisioning refers to provisioning at ingress points to the DiffServ network to both constrain and accommodate the aggregate traffic that can be submitted at each service level (per the SLSs that are in effect at the ingress point). Interior provisioning refers to the provisioning of interfaces internal to the DiffServ network. This includes the allocation of resources among the supported PHBs. It may also include policing functionality to prevent unexpected misbehavior.

Note that boundary provisioning and interior provisioning cannot be distinguished strictly according to the location of the provisioned device in the network topology. Boundary provisioning is applied (logically, at least) to the *ingress* interfaces of boundary devices. Interior provisioning applies primarily (but not exclusively) to the *egress* interfaces of network devices, including devices in the network interior and at the boundary. This is illustrated in Figure 6.15.

Figure 6.15   Boundary Provisioning versus Interior Provisioning

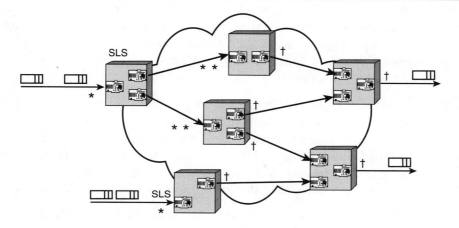

★   Boundary provisioning is applied at these interfaces to
      police and condition traffic as it enters the network.

†   Interior provisioning is applied at these interfaces to allocate
      transmit capacity among different service levels.

★ ★ Interior provisioning may be applied at these interfaces
      to prevent unexpected behavior (policing).

Note the usage of the terms *ingress* and *egress* with respect to *devices* versus entire *networks*. DiffServ networks have both ingress and egress interfaces. Likewise, network devices have both ingress and egress interfaces. An ingress interface to a DiffServ network is also an ingress interface for a certain device. Similarly, an egress interface from the DiffServ network is also an egress interface for a certain device. Within the DiffServ network, there are many *device* ingress and egress interfaces that are not *network* ingress or egress interfaces.

Simply speaking, SLSs drive boundary provisioning. Boundary provisioning in turn drives interior provisioning. In reality, the process is not quite an open loop. The resources available in the network interior limit the SLSs that providers can offer at different ingress points. Thus, the provisioning process typically iterates between the boundary and the interior.

6.7.2 Boundary Provisioning

The first TCB described in the previous section controls the impact of customer traffic on DiffServ network resources at each service level. The configuration of such policing TCBs at the various network ingress points is the logical component of boundary provisioning. The previous section also described a second TCB, incorporating value-add functionality that marks or shapes traffic on behalf of the customer.

Marking on behalf of the customer determines which subsets of the customer's traffic make use of the available resources. Shaping helps the customer to make better use of the available resources. Neither affects the aggregate resources provided to the customer at the various service levels. This is the role of the policing component of the TCB. For this reason, provisioning of the boundary deals with configuration of policing functionality. Value-add functionality such as marking and shaping is irrelevant from a provisioning perspective.

At a minimum, boundary provisioning requires the provider to assure that sufficient physical resources are available at the boundary to meet the requirements of all SLSs negotiated at each ingress point. For example, if the sum of the profiles supported at a particular ingress point across all service levels allows 10Mbps of traffic to be submitted, it is unacceptable to provision a T1 access link. A T3, however, would be sufficient.

Note

Note that providers tend to overcommit resources. So, a provider might in fact try to offer 10Mbps of service using a T1 link. The provider will get away with this practice to varying degrees, depending on the usage profiles of its customers and the strictness of the guarantees offered to the customers. This practice is known as *statistical multiplexing*. The provider bets that the customers will not all simultaneously require the maximum resources permitted per the SLS (or that they will be tolerant of occasional compromises in the service provided). If the provider wins the bet, the provider gets to sell more service at the same provisioning level, thereby increasing profits. If the provider loses the bet, the provider may lose customers.

After the physical provisioning is implemented, it is necessary to apply the appropriate logical provisioning. This is achieved by configuring policing TCBs to limit the aggregate amount of traffic accepted via the T3 access link at each service level and, in the case of route-constrained services, for the appropriate egress points.

6.7.3   Interior Provisioning

Provisioning the interior of the network requires physical provisioning similar to that required for boundary provisioning. Logical provisioning of the interior amounts to enabling the correct PHBs on the egress interfaces of network devices and allocating available physical resources among the various PHBs enabled at each interface. In addition, logical interior provisioning may include the configuration of policing TCBs at strategic locations in the network. These may be used to limit the impact of unexpected traffic loads or, in certain cases, to reshape traffic as it moves through the network.

For the purpose of provisioning the interior of the network, it is desirable to understand or to control the volume of traffic traversing each network node at each service level. The greater this understanding, the more efficiently the network can be provisioned while still meeting the requirements of the SLSs at the boundaries. It is feasible to understand the volume of traffic traversing each node if it is policed at the ingress based both on quantifiable parameters and on egress points (route-constrained traffic). This case is exemplified by the ingress policing TCB described for the VLL service.

Although the resulting traffic volumes cannot be anticipated at the interior of the network with perfect accuracy, it is possible to approximate them quite well, especially when routes are constrained using such mechanisms as MPLS LSP tunnels (see Chapter 5). It is therefore possible to provision internal network nodes reasonably well with respect to route-constrained traffic. Although such provisioning may be quite difficult in a large network, it is nonetheless a tractable problem.

On the other hand, many of the services offered by DiffServ networks will not be route-constrained. The corresponding traffic will not be restricted to specific egress points, let alone specific routes. Thus, interior nodes will have to be provisioned for these services without precise understanding of the corresponding volume of traffic that must be accommodated at each node.

Note that route-constrained services can be further divided into those that are quantitative and those that are qualitative. In general, it is simpler to provision for quantitative services than for qualitative services because the resource requirements are clearly quantifiable. The SLSs for qualitative services (whether route-constrained or not) often specify policing limits even though they may offer no quantifiable service guarantees. These limits may be used to guide provisioning for qualitative services. However, for qualitative services, the policing limits that may be enforced at network boundaries are often poor indications of the actual resources required in support of the service.

The interior provisioning of DiffServ networks can be quite complicated and is not well understood. It will likely evolve over time, starting from existing best-effort network provisioning techniques. The following paragraphs describe one possible approach to provisioning a DiffServ network. This example is presented primarily for the purpose of exploring the interesting issues; it is not presented as an authoritative discourse on DiffServ provisioning techniques.

6.7.3.1 Simultaneous Support for Route-Constrained and Route-Independent Services

It is necessary to be able to provision DiffServ networks to support both route-constrained and route-independent services simultaneously. Although the impact of route-constrained traffic can be controlled and anticipated quite accurately as a result of boundary provisioning, the impact of route-independent traffic cannot. Unexpected route-independent traffic bursts appearing at an internal node can consume unexpected amounts of resources. To preserve the high-quality service guarantees typically associated with route-constrained traffic, it is necessary to isolate the impact of fluctuations in route-independent traffic volumes in the DiffServ network.

One approach to this problem is to always subjugate route-independent traffic to route-constrained traffic. In this case, the two types of traffic must use nonoverlapping DSCPs. (Alternatively, but less likely, the two types of traffic might be separated by using MF classifiers, at a significant increase in complexity.) The PHBs invoked by route-constrained traffic must provide higher-priority access to resources than those invoked by route-independent traffic. Provisioning for route-constrained traffic must balance the overall capacity of interior interfaces with boundary provisioning at the network edges. This must be done to assure that the volume of route-constrained traffic appearing in interior nodes consumes only a limited fraction of the capacity available at these nodes.

6.7.3.2 Provisioning the Interior for Route-Constrained Services

As explained previously, based on boundary provisioning and knowledge of routing information, it is possible to estimate the volume of route-constrained traffic appearing at each node. When the resources required for this traffic at each node have been determined, provisioning of the node consists of installing or configuring interfaces of the appropriate capacity to easily accommodate the traffic that will traverse the node. Note that the phrase "to easily accommodate" is quite subjective. A number of factors must be considered when determining the appropriate capacity, given a certain volume of predicted quantitative traffic:

- Margin of error

- Statistical gain desired

- Capacity remaining for route-independent traffic (including best-effort and LBE traffic)

The first factor, margin of error, accommodates mistakes in computation, effects of transient route changes that are not otherwise accounted for, effects of traffic clustering as it moves through the network, and so on. The statistical gain desired refers to the degree to which a provider is willing to gamble that not all sources of route-constrained traffic will be simultaneously active at the limit dictated by boundary provisioning. This must be weighed against the penalty that the provider is willing to pay in terms of refunded charges or lost customers if unanticipated congestion compromises high-quality service guarantees. Finally, the provider must determine how much capacity will remain for route-independent traffic at each node. Thus, if it is determined that 1Mbps of route-constrained traffic might traverse a specific node, the provider might install a 10Mbps interface in the node. This would leave 9Mbps of capacity quite safely for route-independent traffic. In this case, the provider would be assuming that statistical gains that might be realized would be used to offset the margin of error that would compromise the resources available.

A simplistic example of provisioning for high-quality route-constrained services is illustrated in Figure 6.16.

Figure 6.16   Provisioning for Route-Constrained Services

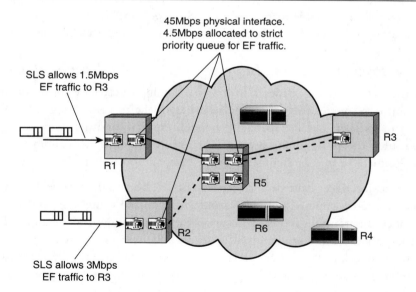

In this example, 45Mbps interfaces (T-3 links) are installed in each router during the physical provisioning phase. In this example, the EF PHB is offered by provisioning a strict-priority queue at each egress interface. Policers are configured to limit the amount of EF traffic at each egress interface to no more than 10% of the interface capacity (4.5Mbps).

In this example, based on this provisioning, two SLSs have been negotiated. One provides VLL service from R1 to R3, for 1.5Mbps. The other provides VLL service from R2 to R3, for 3Mbps. These services completely consume the 10% allocated on the egress interface of router R5 that is common to both routes. Additional VLL service could be allocated at R1 and R3. A 3Mbps capacity remains for VLL type service on the egress interface of router R1, and 1.5Mbps remain on the egress interface of router R3. However, if additional VLL service is to be offered at R1 or R3, it would have to be constrained to a route that does not use the fully allocated egress interface on R5. Alternatively, the egress interface of R5 could be physically reprovisioned or the network manager could accept the risk of allowing greater than 10% of its capacity to EF traffic, thereby reducing the capacity available for qualitative route-constrained and for non-route-constrained services. As it is presently configured, each egress interface retains 90% of its capacity to serve route-constrained qualitative services and non-route-constrained services.

In addition to installing or configuring the appropriate capacity at each interface, it may be desirable to configure policing TCBs to assure that the resources actually consumed by the higher-priority route-constrained traffic do not exceed expected limits. This is especially important if the provider is attempting to achieve a high degree of statistical gain or has not allowed for a reasonable margin of error. Such policing TCBs need not be configured at each interior node but should probably be configured at certain strategic nodes.

6.7.3.3 *Provisioning the Interior for Route-Independent Services*

One of the factors to be considered in the provisioning of capacity at internal nodes is the amount of resources that should be available for the relatively unpredictable route-independent services. Because route-independent traffic cannot be assumed to follow specific routes, this provisioning problem is far more difficult. Provisioning parameters must be estimated based on heuristics, experience, and possibly real-time measurement.

After physical interfaces have been selected to accommodate the resources required by the computed route-constrained traffic load and the estimated route-independent traffic load, additional configuration is required to support the route-independent traffic. This configuration amounts to PHB configuration. It includes the selection of relative weights for queues corresponding to different service levels, or the selection of RED thresholds or alternate logical resource provisioning parameters. The route-independent traffic is typically best accommodated using work-conserving queuing schemes.

Route-constrained quantitative traffic may be accommodated using either work-conserving or non-work-conserving queuing schemes. Regardless, the PHBs provisioned for this traffic should effectively isolate it from the effects of less predictable traffic. However, the configuration parameters that differentiate the various route-independent services may not provide such a degree of isolation among the qualitative services. Thus, it may be necessary to attempt to estimate the relative traffic arriving for each route-independent service and to anticipate the interaction between traffic of different route-independent services. Policing TCBs may be used at strategic interior nodes to provide some degree of isolation between different levels of route-independent traffic.

6.7.4 Static versus Dynamic Provisioning

So far, only static provisioning has been discussed. In the case that SLSs are static, static provisioning may be adequate for route-constrained traffic. However, because route-independent traffic is less predictable, it is likely to require dynamically changing resources at interior nodes, even when the SLS is static. For this reason, dynamic provisioning techniques are desirable and may improve the efficiency of network resource usage. In addition, dynamic provisioning is necessary to enable dynamic SLSs.

Dynamic provisioning may be based on signaling, measurement of current resource usage, or both. For example, a conventional RSVP router supports signaling-based dynamic provisioning. Hosts signal the router to request more or fewer resources, and the router adjusts accordingly. The host may or may not actually submit traffic at the rate at which it signaled it would, but the resources are committed in case it does. Measurement-based provisioning would adjust the resources committed in response to the traffic loads actually measured at the device. Although DiffServ services do not specify any form of signaled- or measurement-based provisioning, both may be useful.

6.8 Policy in the DiffServ Network

Policy will be discussed in depth in Chapter 9, "QoS Policy." This section briefly discusses policies in the context of DiffServ networks. Policies govern all aspects of DiffServ services. The following discussion focuses on those policies that allocate the resources of the DiffServ network among the various traffic flows traversing the network. Policies are applied primarily via the provisioning process described in the previous section. This section discusses the various mechanisms used to provision the network and effect network policies.

6.8.1 Policy Components

The targets of DiffServ policy mechanisms are the interfaces of network devices in the DiffServ network. Ultimately, the traffic-conditioning components and PHBs that are provisioned on these interfaces determine the service provided to network traffic. These interfaces *enforce* the provisioned policies. As such, they are referred to as *policy enforcement points* (PEPs). The notion of a PEP was introduced previously in Chapter 1 and will be discussed again in depth in Chapter 9. Network devices that handle traffic are PEPs regardless of whether they are considered in the context of DiffServ, IntServ, RSVP, or any other QoS mechanism.

Network devices are assisted by *policy servers*. These may be the same policy servers discussed in the context of RSVP policy and known also as *policy decision points* (PDPs). In the context of DiffServ, much of the provisioning information is pushed down to the network devices from these policy servers. This contrasts with the admission control decision outsourcing model described in the context of RSVP. The provisioning information that is pushed to the network devices includes the TCBs and PHB parameters described in previous sections.

Policy servers are often supported by a policy data store or directory, as described in the context of RSVP policy.

6.8.2   The Push Provisioning Model

The simplest model for effecting policies in a DiffServ network relies on push provisioning exclusively. In this model, the policy provisioning system constructs a model of the network topology, including each network device and the capacity of their interconnections. It then provisions the policing TCBs in boundary devices and provisions the PHBs and possibly additional policing TCBs in interior devices. Note that the policy provisioning system may also push value-add provisioning information (of the sort described in previous sections) to boundary devices.

The challenge of any approach to provisioning—and of the push approach in particular—is to provision devices across the network in a consistent manner that realizes the intended policies. (See the previous sidebar "The DiffServ Conceptual Model," which describes a conceptual model for network devices.) The reason that it is so difficult to effect policies using a push approach is that the policy provisioning system is not directly aware of routing within the network. Thus, it cannot reliably infer which interior devices are affected by the results of boundary provisioning. This problem is illustrated in Figure 6.17.

In Figure 6.17, the policy server pushes provisioning information to routers R1 through R6. The service provided to any traffic traversing R5 and R6 depends on the rate at which competing traffic arrives at these routers. The SLSs at R1 and R2 may both contribute traffic to R5 and R6. The policy server must understand the impact of allocating service at R1 and R2 on resources at R5 and R6. To this end, it must understand the various sources from which traffic arrives at R5 and R6. This is routing information that is not inherently available to the policy server.

Figure 6.17   The Difficulty of Push Provisioning

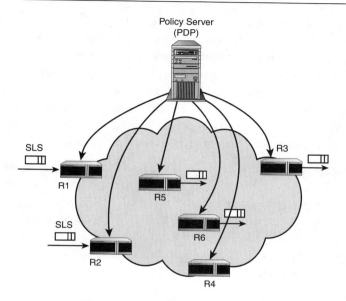

Push approaches can be supplemented by signaling and monitoring approaches, as described in the following paragraphs.

6.8.3   *The Signaling Provisioning Model*

Signaling approaches can enhance or facilitate the task of provisioning a DiffServ network to effect consistent policies. The principle of signaling approaches is that provisioning messages are transmitted between boundary nodes of the DiffServ network (as opposed to being pushed from policy servers). Aggregate RSVP, as described in Chapter 5, is an example of such a provisioning approach. MPLS traffic engineering is another example.

The signaling approach is particularly applicable to route-constrained quantitative services. It is somewhat less useful (although not useless) for route-constrained qualitative services and is not useful for route-independent service provisioning. On the other hand, this approach is ideal for supporting dynamic SLSs. The signaling approach to provisioning works well in conjunction with push provisioning. For example, policy servers can provision limits on the aggregate amount of resources to be available for route-constrained quantitative services at each interface. These limits are relatively static and are pushed down relatively infrequently (slightly more frequently than the physical provisioning time scale). As SLSs are negotiated, aggregate provisioning signaling messages are injected from the ingress point at which each SLS is negotiated to the egress points specified in the route-constrained services offered by the SLS.

The appeal of the signaling approach to provisioning is that these messages move *through* the network, using standard routing (as opposed to push provisioning, which is unaware of routing). As such, they transit the very set of devices that must provide resources to serve the corresponding data traffic. As these provisioning messages arrive at each device, they claim resources from the high-priority push-provisioned resource pool. If high-priority resources are exhausted at a particular node, the provisioning messages return an error toward the ingress point. The provider has the option of increasing the aggregate resources allowed at the node for route-dependent services or specifying a lower-capacity service at the SLS. As provisioning messages transit the network devices, these can update their policy servers regarding the current level of resource reservation.

Refer again to Figure 6.16. In this example, if the provider wanted to provision an SLS to provide 1Mbps of VLL service from R2 to R3, an aggregate RSVP request would be launched from R2 to R3, requesting 1Mbps for the EF DSCP. The request would be rejected at R5 because its egress interface is already fully allocated to its provisioned limit of 4.5Mbps for the EF DSCP. On the other hand, if the egress point for the new VLL SLS was R4, the aggregate RSVP request would likely traverse R6 instead of R5, and the request would not be rejected.

6.8.4 Provisioning Based on Real-Time Measurement

A third mechanism for the configuration of interior nodes is based on measurement of current traffic loads at key network nodes. Measurement-based configuration is less necessary for route-constrained provisioning because the corresponding traffic patterns are relatively predictable. However, it can significantly enhance the efficiency of provisioning for route-independent services. In this approach, network devices feed policy servers with current traffic load measurements. In response, policy servers recompute the parameters for the PHBs serving route-independent traffic and push the updated configuration information to the devices. Measurement-based configuration for route-independent services likely would be used in conjunction with signaling-based configuration for route-constrained services.

6.9 DiffServ with RSVP

The previous section illustrated the use of aggregate RSVP to aid in provisioning a DiffServ network at the time an SLS is instantiated. In addition, DiffServ can work well with *per-conversation* RSVP. The application of per-conversation RSVP to aggregate traffic handling (such as DiffServ) was first discussed in Chapter 2, in the section "Combinations of Traffic Handling and Provisioning and Configuration Mechanisms." This combination was identified in Chapter 2 as a particularly appealing combination in terms of its capability to offer a high QE product with relatively low overhead. The combination of per-conversation signaling with aggregate traffic handling is discussed at various points throughout the book. In the following paragraphs, it is discussed specifically in the context of DiffServ provider networks.

6.9.1 Admission Control

When a customer negotiates a static SLS at an ingress point to a DiffServ provider, the customer is allotted a limited amount of aggregate resources at a certain service level. The provider has little interest in how these resources are allocated among the various sources of that customer's traffic. It is in the customer's interest to use allocated resources carefully. For example, refer to Figure 6.18. Assume that the customer has negotiated 192Kbps of VLL service (invoked by the EF PHB) between the ingress point marked by R2 and the egress point marked by R3. For the sake of this discussion, consider only traffic sourced from Customer Network A and destined for Customer Network B. The same considerations apply to traffic in the opposite direction.

Figure 6.18   Using Per-Conversation Traffic Handling to Gain Admission to DiffServ Provisioned Services

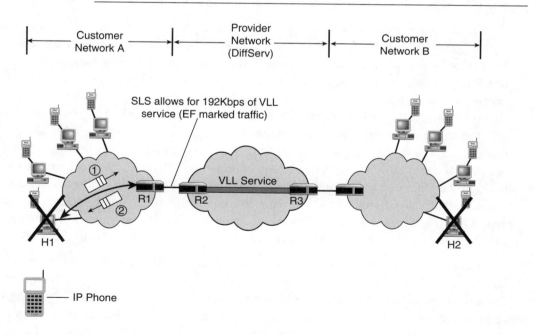

To maintain high-quality service, it is in the customer's interest to ensure that the negotiated capacity is not exceeded. Consider that three 64Kbps telephony terminals are currently generating traffic for the VLL service. The service is at capacity. If a fourth session were established, there would be 64Kbps excess traffic arriving at R2 for the VLL service. Because R2 polices are aggregate, without regard for individual conversations, the excess traffic would be discarded across all four sessions indiscriminately. As a result, service quality would be compromised to all.

Per-conversation RSVP can be used in this case to control admission to the VLL service. Assume that H1 sends a PATH message toward H2, requesting 64Kbps of *Guaranteed Service* (1). Either R1 or R2 could act as admission control agents. All that is required is that the router is capable of participating in RSVP signaling, that it is aware of the capacity available per the SLS, and that it is capable of mapping the Guaranteed Service request to the corresponding DiffServ service (in this case, Guaranteed Service maps to VLL service, which is invoked by the EF PHB). The router acting as admission control agent tracks available capacity and admits signaled service requests accordingly. Because the VLL service is currently at capacity, the PATH message requesting an additional 64Kbps is rejected with a PATH_ERROR. Note that R1 and/or R2 can act as admission control agents and, further, that admission control can be applied to PATH and/or RESV messages.

In general, routers that are both DiffServ-capable and RSVP-conversant can be used at ingress points to DiffServ networks to provide admission control to aggregate services. They must be provisioned with knowledge of the negotiated SLS and a mapping from RSVP-requested services to corresponding DiffServ services. Hosts in the customer network that use route-constrained services gain access to these services using per-conversation RSVP signaling. As these signaling messages arrive at DiffServ ingress routers, they can check admissibility per the limits specified in the SLS and current availability. In this manner, the DiffServ ingress routers act as admission control agents for the DiffServ network. If a request is admissible, the router allows the RSVP messages to continue through the DiffServ network unhindered. The router may also install value-add TCBs to recognize traffic associated with the specific conversation admitted and to mark it for the appropriate DiffServ service level. If a request is not admissible, the router will generate the appropriate RSVP error messages and will not allow the conversation in the TCB.

As described in Chapter 5, host-initiated per-conversation RSVP signaling can be used in conjunction with DiffServ edge-to-edge aggregate RSVP signaling to trigger changes in dynamic SLSs and the corresponding reprovisioning of the DiffServ network. Applying this approach to the example illustrated, if R2 were designated as an admission control agent, then the arrival of a request for a fourth session might trigger aggregate RSVP signaling between R2 and R3 for the purpose of increasing the capacity of the VLL trunk between them.

Typically, it is in the customer's interest to control which users and applications make use of the valuable DiffServ resources. To this end, the customer may attach policy servers to customer egress routers that connect to the DiffServ network. These can apply customer-specific policy to admit or reject per-conversation requests based on user and application before they are passed to the DiffServ ingress router. In certain cases, the provider may offer value-add services by installing customer-specific policy information in policy servers associated with the provider's ingress routers, obviating the need for these in the customer's network. In the previous example, either R1 or R2 would outsource admission control requests from the customer network to a policy server. Rather than admitting requests on a first-come, first-served basis, the admission control agent would then admit requests based both on available resources and on requesting user or corresponding application.

> **Note**
>
> In most cases, at least in early deployments, the DiffServ provider is unlikely to participate in per-conversation RSVP signaling from customers. Applying this to the previous example, R1 would provide the explicit admission control based on RSVP signaling with R2 simply policing in aggregate.

6.9.2   Traffic Classification

Regardless of whether per-conversation RSVP signaling is used for admission control to the DiffServ network, it can offer the network reliable classification information. Earlier in this chapter, a value-add TCB was described that recognized traffic based on destination IP port 5005 and that marked it for VLL service. In this case, destination port 5005 was assumed to indicate IP telephony traffic. In many cases, such reliable classification criteria are not available. Nonetheless, customers may rely on DiffServ ingress routers to recognize traffic associated with specific users or applications and to condition it accordingly.

When RSVP-capable routers are used at the ingress to the DiffServ network, they are capable of snooping per-conversation RSVP signaling messages from the customer and dynamically learning associations between users and applications and the corresponding classification criteria. Ingress routers can then work with associated policy servers to install value-add TCBs with the appropriate classification criteria. Both qualitative as well as quantitative traffic can benefit from this functionality.

In the example illustrated in Figure 6.19, H1 sends a PATH message that is intercepted (snooped) by R1 (1). The PATH message carries the following information:

- User ID = yoramb@microsoft.com

- Application ID = netmeeting

- Subapplication ID = voice call

- Required service type = Guaranteed Service

- Required bandwidth = 64Kbps

- Source port = 5004

- Source address = 2.3.4.5

- Destination port = 5005

- Destination address = 3.4.5.6

R1 extracts the user and application IDs and the classification criteria (source and destination ports and addresses) and forwards these (2) to the attached policy server. The policy server can now *bind* netmeeting voice calls to the corresponding classification criteria. This binding can be used by the policy server (3) when pushing configuration information to elements in (or at the periphery of) the DiffServ network.

Figure 6.19   Snooping RSVP Messages to Glean Classification Information

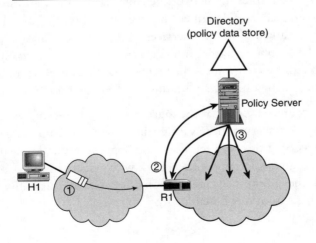

> **Note**
>
> Note that snooping can be applied to RESV messages just as it can be applied to PATH messages. Snooping PATH messages extracts information regarding the sender. Snooping RESV messages extracts information regarding the receiver.
>
> The Common Open Policy Service Protocol (COPS) is likely to be used by R1 to communicate to the policy server (in 2) and by the policy server to configure devices in the DiffServ network (in 3). For a discussion of the COPS protocol, see Chapter 9, "QoS Policy."

6.9.3 *The* DCLASS *Object*

The DCLASS object was discussed briefly in the context of RSVP (see Chapter 5). It is used to link RSVP signaling with DiffServ. Consider the example illustrated in Figure 6.18. R1 or R2 could install a TCB to mark traffic on admitted conversations for the EF DSCP. This requires the router to install MF classifiers to recognize individual conversations. Alternatively, the router may simply append a DCLASS object to RSVP signaling messages returned to the sending host. The DCLASS object carries a DSCP. It instructs upstream senders to mark this DSCP in the headers of packets transmitted on the per-conversation traffic flow.

6.9.4 *Mapping RSVP Signaled Services to DiffServ Services*

The DCLASS object effectively maps RSVP-requested services to a DSCP and, therefore, to a DiffServ service level. When DiffServ ingress routers act as RSVP admission control agents to a DiffServ network, they must apply such a mapping regardless of whether they actually do the marking themselves or use a DCLASS object to request that upstream senders do the marking.

The ISSLL working group of the IETF is responsible for developing the mapping from RSVP-requested services to DiffServ services. At the time of this writing, a mapping proposal is before the ISSLL working group. This proposal suggests mapping the IntServ Guaranteed Service to the DSCP corresponding to the EF PHB (for VLL service) and mapping the IntServ Controlled Load Service to one or more of the DSCPs corresponding to the AF PHB group (for a service similar to Olympic service).

Both the Guaranteed and Controlled Load Services require a route-constrained, quantitative service from the DiffServ network. A third service that may be requested by RSVP signaling is the Null Service. The Null Service is typically used to invoke route-constrained, qualitative service from the DiffServ network. Whereas the Guaranteed and Controlled Load Services imply specific DiffServ services, the very nature of the Null Service is that it does not request any specific service. Rather, it is used to provide information to policy servers in the DiffServ network, which in turn determine the appropriate DiffServ service level and the corresponding DSCP.

6.10   Issues in DiffServ

The following section addresses a number of miscellaneous issues surrounding the application of DiffServ.

6.10.1   Customer Traffic Conditioning versus Provider Traffic Conditioning

To provide DiffServ services, it is necessary to condition traffic before it is submitted to the DiffServ network. Traffic conditioning can be applied by the provider (at the network ingress point), by the customer (anywhere in the customer's network), or by both the provider and the customer. The determination of the appropriate level of traffic conditioning to be applied at different points in the network should be based on scalability issues and trust domains, as explained in the following paragraphs.

For scalability reasons, all traffic conditioning work should be pushed as far toward the edge of the network as possible. Devices at the edge of the network handle less traffic and therefore are less burdened by traffic conditioning. Devices near the core of the network handle more traffic and therefore are more burdened by traffic conditioning. This is true for all traffic conditioning tasks, but especially for per-conversation traffic conditioning.

As an example of the scalability concerns associated with traffic conditioning, consider a device at the ingress of a DiffServ network that is required to mark on behalf of the customer. Assume that the customer wants all its top-level executives to receive gold service and wants all mid-level executives to receive silver service. The provider must install a value-add TCB at the ingress to its network. The TCB must include classification criteria for each of the executives. In addition to being a management burden, this approach requires considerable MF classifier state and carries a processing burden.

It would be far preferable to allow the executive's hosts to mark their own traffic for gold or silver service. However, this approach raises trust issues. The provider should not trust the customer to control the amount of traffic marked for the gold and silver services. Any marked packet admitted to the provider's network consumes valuable resources in the network. Thus, the provider polices customer traffic to assure that the aggregate amount of resources consumed by the customer at each service level is limited to the amount allowed per the negotiated SLS. This is achieved by the use of a simple policing TCB for each customer. The TCB measures the rate at which DSCP marked packets are submitted and compares it against the corresponding profile. Excess traffic is discarded or otherwise penalized. Note that the policing TCB has no knowledge of individual conversations and the executives with which they are associated. It serves only to police to the *aggregate* profile negotiated per the SLS.

Generalizing from this analysis, the preferred approach to traffic conditioning is to push as much of the granular traffic conditioning work as far as possible toward the edge of the network. Traffic conditioning in the interior of the network should be limited to aggregate policing functionality. This policing functionality is necessary only at *trust boundaries* to enforce the agreement in effect at the boundary.

6.10.1.1 Trust Boundaries

Trust boundaries are interfaces between *trust domains*. Trust domains are domains in which network devices can be assumed to be operating with a common interest. Domain authorities can track down rogue devices within the trust domain and disable them.

The interface between a customer network and a provider network is an obvious trust boundary. Economic interests are at stake here. The provider sells the customer a limited amount of service. It is in the provider's interest to limit the resources provided to the customer. It is in the customer's interest to gain access to as much of the provider's resource as possible. The two do not operate with common interests. Figure 6.20 illustrates the customer/provider trust boundary.

Figure 6.20   Policing at the Customer/Provider Trust Boundary

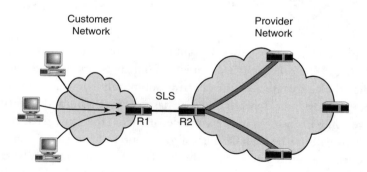

In this illustration, R1 acts as an admission control agent, admitting requests originating in the customer network up to the limit allowed by the SLS. R1 is in the customer's trust domain. Hosts are trusted within this domain to mark traffic only on admitted conversations. R2 is in the provider's trust domain. It polices marked traffic in aggregate, without regard for the individual conversations traversing it. R2 acts to protect the provider's network from use of resources beyond those negotiated in the SLS. R1 and the hosts in the customer network cooperate to make sure that the hosts in the customer domain use the negotiated resources effectively. Rogue hosts within the customer network may violate the trust of other hosts in the same trust domain but will not be capable of stealing resources from the provider.

Trust domains may also exist within the customer's network. For example, the customer may identify subnetworks corresponding to different departments. If traffic conditioning functionality is relegated to devices within these departments, the customer may configure DiffServ-capable devices with policing TCBs to assure that neither department claims more than its share of the aggregate resources allotted to it. This is illustrated in Figure 6.21.

| **Figure 6.21** | Trust Boundaries Within a Customer Network |

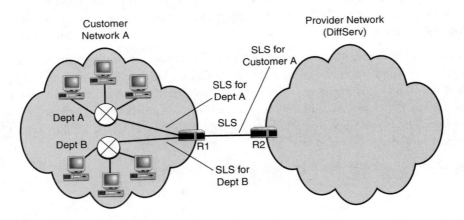

In this example, the customer network is subdivided into two subnetworks, one for Department A and the other for Department B. The network manager installs in R1 a TCB to police the aggregate amount of traffic submitted from each network for each service level. Rogue hosts may mark traffic that has not been admitted. However, these will steal resources only from hosts in the same department (the same trust domain). Hosts in one department will not be capable of stealing resources from hosts in another department. R2 polices the aggregate traffic submitted by the customer as a whole, without regard for the amount contributed by individual departments. In this manner, devices at trust boundaries police only at the granularity necessary, pushing finer-grain work closer to the edges. R1 polices at the granularity of a department. R2 polices at the granularity of a customer. Neither is required to recognize individual conversations.

It is important to understand the significance of policing at trust boundaries. Network providers are often alarmed at the notion of customers doing their own traffic conditioning because they fear that this allows customers to steal network resources. However, it is in the best interest of the provider to relegate as much traffic conditioning work to the customer as possible. The provider can protect its resources by aggregate policing.

6.10.1.2 Shaping versus Marking

Although the discussion of traffic conditioning has focused on marking, similar considerations apply to other traffic conditioning functions such as shaping. However, slight differences exist between shaping and marking. Within a trust domain, by definition, devices can be expected to mark responsibly. However, even if hosts shape traffic very carefully, traffic tends to lose its shape as it moves through the network. Therefore, it may be desirable to provide reshaping functionality at various points in the network that are not trust boundaries. Fortunately, shaping is required only for the highest-quality DiffServ services (such as the VLL service).

6.10.2 Mapping from DiffServ to Other QoS Mechanisms

A mapping of IntServ services to DiffServ services has been discussed at various points in this book. Mappings from DiffServ to services provided by other QoS mechanisms (such as 802.1p) have not been discussed. Suggestions surface from time to time that it would be valuable to generate such mappings. The author does not consider this a useful exercise. Consider the matrix that would result if service levels associated with each QoS mechanism were to be mapped to the corresponding service levels for every other QoS mechanism. A preferred approach would be to define a single set of high-level abstract services. These could then be mapped to corresponding services in each QoS mechanism. The result would be N mappings, as opposed to N^2 mappings. The two mapping options are illustrated in Figure 6.22.

To some degree, it can be argued that the high-level mapping exists already and that it is IntServ. The charter of the ISSLL working group seems to support this notion. However, the set of IntServ services does not include qualitative services. If it were to serve as the grand unifying service abstraction, qualitative services would have to be included.

Figure 6.22   Reducing the Number of Mappings Required

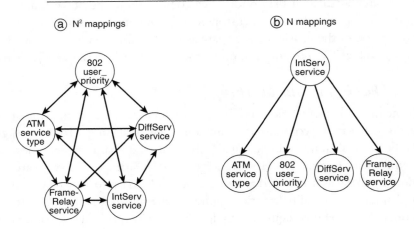

6.10.3 *Multicast*

At first glance, DiffServ appears to readily support multicast services. Multicast packets may be marked with appropriate DSCPs. These will simply be replicated with the marked DSCP at multicast branch points. However, multicast services may significantly complicate DiffServ provisioning for higher-quality services. Recall that these services are assumed to be route-constrained. In the case of multicast services, receivers may dynamically join the multicast group causing a proliferation of marked packets to appear in unexpected areas of the network. Besides wreaking havoc with route-constrained service provisioning, replicated packets may arrive at peer DiffServ domains that interpret DSCPs differently from each other.

As far as provisioning issues are concerned, the use of separate DSCPs for multicast traffic can at least provide isolation between multicast traffic (which can appear anywhere) and unicast traffic that can be route-constrained. Alternatively, policing TCBs can be used within the DiffServ network to restrict traffic for route-constrained services to certain multicast trees. Traffic straying from the provisioned trees can then be discarded or re-marked for lesser service.

With respect to differing interpretations of DSCPs at different peer domains, care must be taken to ensure consistent interpretation or appropriate re-marking at domain boundaries. The same can be said for unicast traffic, but the situation is exacerbated for multicast traffic.

6.10.4 IPSec and DiffServ

IPSec performs cryptographic calculations on all packets on a secured traffic flow. Fortunately, the DSCP is not included in these calculations. Thus, nodes in the DiffServ network may re-mark DSCPs as necessary, without concern that this will cause a security check to fail.

On the other hand, IPSec encryption obscures IP port numbers. This precludes MF classification in those parts of the network carrying encrypted traffic. Recall that MF classification may be used at various points in the DiffServ network (primarily at ingress points) to condition customer traffic. Because typical MF classification cannot be applied to IPSec-encrypted traffic, the network provider is faced with two choices. One choice is to relegate MF-dependent traffic conditioning to the customer. The other is to listen to RSVP signaling (where available) and to classify based on the SPI. (See Chapter 5 for a discussion of IPSec, RSVP, and the SPI.)

6.10.5 Tunneling and DiffServ

IP tunnels complicate DiffServ. If packets are marked with a DSCP before they are tunneled, network devices between the endpoints of the tunnel will not see the marked DSCP and will not provide the expected traffic handling. One mechanism to handle this condition is to copy DSCPs from inner headers to tunnel headers at the ingress to a tunnel. This would enable network devices between tunnel endpoints to handle tunneled traffic based on the original intended DSCP.

In certain cases, tunnel ingress nodes may purposely enforce tunnel-specific services by marking the DSCP in the tunnel header without regard for the DSCP in the internal header. In this case, the original DSCP is not honored in the tunnel but is preserved for use beyond the tunnel egress point.

6.11 Summary

Differentiated Services were proposed in their early form in 1996. In 1997, the IETF took on the role of standardizing Differentiated Services in the DiffServ working group. The salient features of DiffServ are its inherent simplicity and scalability. As such, it can be viewed as a response to the perceived complexity and scalability issues surrounding the RSVP/IntServ approach to QoS. Furthermore, DiffServ promised to address the needs of qualitative applications in addition to the quantitative applications that were the primary target of the RSVP/IntServ model.

The DiffServ framework describes a DiffServ domain consisting of a number of DiffServ-aware routers. Traffic submitted to the domain is marked at the edge of the domain with a DiffServ codepoint (DSCP) in packet headers. The DSCP invokes a particular per-hop behavior (PHB) in each of the DiffServ routers within the domain. Currently proposed PHBs include the expedited forwarding PHB, the assured forwarding PHB group, the class selector PHB group, and the default PHB. The concatenation of PHBs provided by the DiffServ routers, combined with traffic conditioning functionality at the edges, yields useful DiffServ services. Devices in the DiffServ network generally handle traffic based on DSCP only. They do not distinguish traffic belonging to one conversation from traffic belonging to another. Instead, conversations are aggregated by DSCP, hence the inherent scalability of the DiffServ approach.

DiffServ services can be categorized in various ways. Some provide strict quantifiable service parameters (high-quality services). Others provide much looser assurances (low-quality services). Some apply only to traffic between specific endpoints (route-constrained). Others apply from a given ingress point regardless of the egress point. Services are specified in the form of a service level specification that is negotiated at points at which customers submit traffic to the DiffServ network. Examples of DiffServ services include the high-quality virtual leased line service and the Olympic services. Many other services can be constructed using a variety of PHBs and appropriate traffic conditioning.

To provide useful services through the DiffServ network, it is necessary to condition the traffic submitted to the network at each service level. This is the role of traffic-conditioning mechanisms that are located primarily at the edges. At a minimum, these mechanisms police submitted traffic to protect the provider's resources. They may also be used to mark or otherwise condition traffic on behalf of the customer. Traffic conditioning is provided by traffic-conditioning blocks. These, in turn, are constructed from traffic-conditioning components, including classifiers, meters, shapers, markers, and droppers.

A variety of methods can be used to provision DiffServ networks. These include push provisioning, which is relatively static and relies on inferred routing information. Alternative methods use signaling between edges of the DiffServ network, measurement-based provisioning, and combinations of all methods.

This chapter discussed a number of issues surrounding DiffServ networks. One of these is the impact of trust boundaries and scalability concerns on the location of various traffic conditioning functionality. Other issues discussed related to the interaction between DiffServ and other technologies, including IPSec, multicast, and RSVP/IntServ.

7

The Subnet Bandwidth Manager and 802 Networks

The *IEEE 802 LAN/MAN Standards Committee* owns the task of standardizing LAN and MAN (and, recently, certain WAN) link-layer technologies. IEEE 802 is typically associated with LAN technologies, and these are the primary focus of this chapter. As such, the terms *802 networks* and *LANs* will be used interchangeably throughout the chapter. Various sub-committees of the IEEE 802 committee deal with different aspects of the various LAN technologies. These include different media such as Ethernet, Token Ring, and wireless, as well as media-independent aspects of LANs, such as addressing, management, and bridging protocols. A number of QoS mechanisms are available within the scope of 802 networks. Some of these are standardized; others are proprietary vendor-specific mechanisms.

To provide QoS in an end-to-end manner, it is necessary to coordinate QoS mechanisms across various media. Consistent with the goal of supporting end-to-end QoS, this chapter focuses on the more standard 802 QoS mechanisms as well as the abstractions and protocols that can be used to unify these across a heterogeneous IP network.

This chapter starts with a discussion of aggregate traffic handling in 802 networks, based on link-layer packet marking in the *802 user_priority* field. The chapter then delves into a discussion regarding the *SBM protocol*, which defines how RSVP signaling can be used in 802 networks. The role of the *DSBM* as an admission control agent and its impact on the quality/efficiency (QE) product of 802 networks will also be discussed. The chapter ends with a discussion of advanced QoS functionality in 802 networks and attached hosts.

7.1 user_priority

The IEEE 802 committee recognizes the concept of a *user_priority*, a value associated with the handling of traffic in an 802 network. Senders sending traffic onto 802 networks may specify a certain user_priority value. Devices in the 802 network such as bridges and switches are expected to handle traffic in accordance with the requested user_priority. At the receiving end, the user_priority value is indicated to the receiver.

> **Note**
>
> The 802 committee identifies the *MAC Service Interface*. This is the abstraction layer between the MAC layer and higher layers of the protocol stack in sending and receiving hosts. Strictly speaking, the *sender* resides above the MAC layer and may specify a particular user_priority across the MAC Service Interface. A given MAC layer may or may not support the user_priority.

The user_priority value is typically indicated in a packet header and invokes an aggregate traffic-handling mechanism. It is important to distinguish between user_priority and the underlying *traffic class*. The former is nothing more than a value marked in a protocol field. The traffic class is the underlying aggregate traffic-handling mechanism.

Various mechanisms exist for encoding the user_priority value in transmitted packets. For example, Token Ring packets may encode the user_priority value in its frame control (FC) octet. The IEEE specifies a consistent mechanism for encoding a user_priority value in an extension to the standard 802 packet format. This extension can be used with Ethernet, Token Ring, and other 802 media. The extended packet format includes an *802.1Q* header that carries (among other information) a 3-bit user_priority value (referred to as the *802.1p* bits). Note that the concept of user_priority does not dictate that the value actually must be carried across the network in transmitted packets. Alternatively, it may be assigned locally in each device, based on local policies and classification criteria that are coordinated via some out-of-band mechanism. However, in practical applications, the user_priority value is carried across the 802 network in the 802.1Q header. For further details on 802.1p and 802.1Q, refer to [802.1D-1998], [802.1Q-1998].

Figure 7.1 illustrates the format of the 802.1Q header and its location in the MAC header of an Ethernet packet.

Figure 7.1   The 802.1Q Header Format

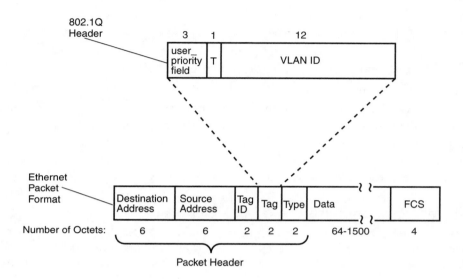

7.1.1 *Comparison to Differentiated Services*

LAN technologies such as bridging or link-layer switching operate at Layer 2—this differs from routing and IP layer protocol processing, which are Layer 3 technologies. The distinction between Layer 2 devices (such as bridges and switches) and Layer 3 devices (such as routers) is vanishing rapidly. Nonetheless, the terminology is still useful.

User_priority invokes traffic-handling mechanisms in Layer 2 devices. This is analogous to the differentiated service codepoint (DSCP), which invokes traffic-handling mechanisms in Layer 3 devices. Both user_priority and DSCPs invoke aggregate traffic-handling mechanisms because multiple flows are marked with the same user_priority value or with the same DSCP. The user_priority values are mapped to traffic classes at Layer 2 devices. By comparison, DSCPs are mapped to per-hop behaviors (PHBs) in Layer 3 devices.

However, while Differentiated Services (DiffServ) defines the specific behaviors that are invoked, the IEEE does not specify the behavior of the different traffic classes implemented by Layer 2 devices. Instead, the IEEE specifications state simply that implementations provide separate queues for each traffic class and that default implementations will use a strict priority queue-servicing scheme. Any number of traffic classes may be provided. At a minimum, two classes are required to provide anything other than best-effort (BE) service. There is not much point in providing more than eight classes because only eight distinct `user_priority` values can be indicated by the 3-bit `user_priority` value. Although strict priority is specified as the default behavior, more sophisticated devices might provide more sophisticated queuing schemes, such as round robin variants and weighted fair queuing. (See Chapter 3, "Queuing Mechanisms," for a discussion of queuing mechanisms.)

7.1.2 Providing Services Based on `user_priority`

Because of the similarities between `user_priority` aggregate traffic handling and DiffServ aggregate traffic handling, many of the same considerations apply in using these mechanisms to provide services. Lower-quality services can be supported with only loose coordination between devices in the Layer 2 network and without explicit admission control. Support for higher-quality services requires tighter coordination of resource allocation on the relevant end-to-end paths, as well as explicit, topology-aware admission control.

Is it Necessary to Raise the QE Product on LANs?

Many question the degree of QoS support required in LANs. Today, gigabit LANs are often overprovisioned with respect to traffic that requires high-quality guarantees (such as telephony traffic). This suggests that high-quality services can be provided by compromising efficiency and that there is no need to raise the quality/efficiency product of LANs by providing sophisticated QoS mechanisms. Instead, the simple aggregate traffic handling provided by `user_priority` is sufficient without requiring tight coordination of resource allocation among devices and without explicit admission control.

On the other hand, a number of observations suggest that there is value in enabling LAN administrators to raise the quality/efficiency product of their networks by supporting more sophisticated QoS mechanisms. For example, while telephony traffic does not require a significant fraction of the LAN *bandwidth*, the fraction that it does require must offer low *latency*. On a 1Gbps interface, effective queue depth must be limited to 10Mbits to offer a 10msec latency bound through the interface. This is roughly equivalent to 100–150 telephony conversations. Throw a couple of video conversations into the mix, and either queue depth grows to the point that latency is compromised or packets will have to be discarded. In practice, in busy LANs, significant delays may occur even in high-bandwidth switches.

This situation is exacerbated when considering emerging videoconferencing and video streaming applications. On the Microsoft campus, for example, daily meetings requiring the attendance of a large number of people are moving from the conference room to the corporate network. Videoconferences on this scale require significant bandwidth, with the result that the LAN appears less overprovisioned. The focus of videoconferencing is primarily the audio, so most users are willing to settle for relatively low-quality, low-bandwidth video. However, as *playback* streaming media finds the capacity available to offer improved quality video on demand within the campus network, more users find it to be a compelling application. The result is an exponential growth in bandwidth demand as both bandwidth per conversation and the number of conversations grows.

For these reasons, it is important to have the option to manage LANs in a manner that offers a high quality/efficiency product.

7.1.2.1 *Simple Use of 802* user_priority

In many cases, it is sufficient to operate 802 LANs at a low quality/efficiency product. This is either because the amount of resources available are such that the LAN can be considered over-provisioned with respect to applications requiring high-quality guarantees, or because it is not necessary to support high-quality guarantees through the 802 network. In this case, simple push configuration of Layer 2 devices is adequate.

In the simplest case, Layer 2 switches are configured to support as few as two traffic classes by providing a high-priority queue and a low-priority queue, serviced using strict priority. All traffic deemed entitled to lower user_priority values is directed to the low-priority queue. All traffic deemed entitled to higher user_priority values is directed to the high-priority queue. Because strict priority is presumed, it is advisable to police traffic submitted for the high-priority queue to ensure that it does not starve traffic submitted for the low-priority queue. The network manager may provision policing limits in a pushed manner in each Layer 2 device or, alternatively, only at the ingress to the Layer 2 network. Provisioning of the policing limits determines the relative distribution of network capacity between high-priority traffic and low-priority traffic.

In addition, it is necessary to associate a user_priority value with packets at the ingress to the Layer 2 network. This is analogous to the task of *marking* packets with a DSCP in DiffServ networks.

Simple use of 802 user_priority is illustrated in Figure 7.2.

In this illustration, all switches are configured for two traffic classes on each egress port: high priority and best effort. Packets with a user_priority value of 0–3 are directed to the best-effort class. Packets with a user_priority value of 4–7 are directed to the high-priority class. The high-priority class is served using a strict priority scheme. Switches S1 through S4 are configured to recognize telephony packets submitted from segments a through d (respectively) based on the corresponding IP source port and to mark them with user_priority 4. All other traffic is marked for user_priority zero. (Alternatively, the transmitting hosts could mark the telephony packets.)

Figure 7.2　　Simple Use of 802 `user_priority`

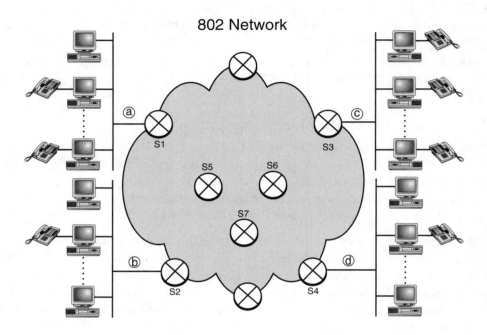

Policing is implemented by monitoring, at each switch egress interface, the aggregate volume of traffic arriving with `user_priority` values 4–7 and remarking to a `user_priority` value of zero any traffic in excess of 5% of the link capacity.

In this example, admission control is implicit. In the event of many simultaneous IP telephony users, it is possible to exceed the 5% capacity allocated for high-priority traffic at one or more interfaces. In this case, policing will compromise the quality of all telephony sessions traversing the interfaces, but best-effort traffic will not be starved.

Traffic Isolation in 802 Subnetworks

Newer 802 networks are typically constructed from intelligent multiport switches with a separate switch port dedicated to each sender. This is in contrast to legacy 802 networks, in which multiple senders share a single "yellow wire" segment or "dumb" hubs or bridges. The two cases are illustrated in Figure 7.3.

Figure 7.3	Newer 802 Networks Provide Superior Isolation Capability

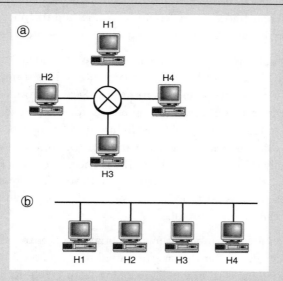

Assume that H1 is sending traffic marked with a high user_priority value to H2. At the same time, H3 is sending traffic with a best-effort user_priority to H4. In the case that each sender is isolated behind a dedicated switch port and that each switch supports traffic handling based on 802 user_priority (Figure 7.3a), traffic flows can be *isolated*. The switch will assure that traffic between H1 and H2 is protected from traffic between H3 and H4. However, in Figure 7.3b, multiple senders share a resource (the yellow wire segment) that is not capable of traffic isolation based on user_priority value. As a result, traffic between H1 and H2 is not protected from traffic between H3 and H4, even though the different traffic flows may be marked with different user_priority values.

The value of user_priority in supporting QoS in 802 networks can be realized only to the extent that senders are isolated by devices that can provide traffic isolation based on the user_priority value.

Determining the Appropriate user_priority Value

A number of mechanisms can be used to mark packets with the appropriate user_priority value. From the perspective of the Layer 2 network, the simplest option is to have Layer 3 devices (hosts or routers) mark the user_priority value as they transmit traffic into the Layer 2 network. Layer 3 devices would do so by appending an 802.1Q header including the appropriate user_priority value to each transmitted packet. An alternative approach is to have the Layer 2 ingress device to the Layer 2 network append the 802.1Q header with the appropriate user_priority value.

Regardless of whether the header carrying the user_priority value is appended by Layer 3 devices or Layer 2 devices, the challenge is in determining the appropriate user_priority value to use for different traffic. Hosts could be configured to append a certain user_priority value depending on the application or user sourcing submitted traffic.

Alternatively, routers or Layer 2 ingress devices can be configured to append a certain user_priority value based on classification information. (This is similar to the DiffServ approach, in which a router at the ingress to the DiffServ network is configured to mark submitted packets with a DSCP based on some classification criteria.) This approach suffers from the various classification problems discussed in Chapter 6, "Differentiated Services"—namely, difficulties in recognizing traffic associated with certain users or applications, especially in the case that the traffic is encrypted. One simple classification criterion that Layer 2 devices can use in marking traffic is the ingress port on which traffic is submitted. Because ingress ports are often associated with certain servers or certain users, this criterion can be quite useful.

Yet another approach for determining the appropriate user_priority value may be employed in the special case that packets submitted to the Layer 2 network are already marked with a DSCP. In this case, a static mapping from DSCP to user_priority may be applied either at the transmitting Layer 3 device or at the Layer 2 device at the ingress to the Layer 2 network. Taking this approach further, it could be argued that most higher-end Layer 2 devices today are capable of parsing IP headers and that most traffic today is IP traffic—so, therefore, Layer 2 devices should handle traffic based on DSCP. In this case, user_priority is irrelevant.

7.1.2.2 Using Signaling to Obtain a Higher Quality/Efficiency Product

As it becomes necessary to support increased traffic loads on 802 networks and at the same time to offer high-quality service guarantees, it is necessary to look beyond the simple usage of user_priority outlined in the previous section. The ISSLL working group of the IETF envisions a more sophisticated usage model when applying user_priority to support the Integrated Services (IntServ) Guaranteed and Controlled Load Services. This approach is outlined in a number of ISSLL RFCs, including [RFC 2816], [RFC 2815].

Briefly, the approach recommended by the ISSLL working group recommends the use of explicit signaling between Layer 3 devices and devices in the 802 network. This signaling is a form of the RSVP protocol that will be described in depth later in this chapter (see the section "Using RSVP with 802 Networks—the SBM and SBM Protocol"). In this approach, the standard RSVP messages signaled by hosts are modified slightly at the ingress to 802 networks. One or more Layer 2 devices in the 802 network process these messages. As a result, Layer 2 devices are capable of affecting admission control to various traffic classes and notifying Layer 3 devices of the appropriate user_priority value to append to submitted packets. Layer 2 devices determine the appropriate user_priority value based on the IntServ service type requested, associated quantitative parameters signaled in RSVP messages, and current resource availability. They indicate this value to Layer 3 devices by appending a TCLASS object (containing the user_priority value) to RSVP RESV messages.

(Note the analogy between the TCLASS object in 802 networks and the DCLASS object in DiffServ networks.) This approach relieves Layer 3 devices of the burden of determining the appropriate user_priority value. Instead, hosts request service using the same abstract IntServ types that are used to request RSVP reservations in RSVP-capable routers or to gain admission to DiffServ services in DiffServ networks. The 802 network responds with the appropriate user_priority value.

The signaling approach makes it possible to improve the quality/efficiency product of the Layer 2 network by supporting topology-aware explicit admission control. Signaling is also attractive because it provides the 802 network with the classification information necessary to associate traffic with users or applications, thereby facilitating policy-based management functionality in the 802 network. However, as stated previously, signaling is appropriate only for persistent traffic flows and carries an associated overhead in terms of the processing required. Furthermore, at present, signaling is not defined for qualitative services (other than the catchall Null Service). As such, 802 networks will likely support a combination of high-quality signaled services and lower-quality push-provisioned services.

Supporting a Range of Service Qualities

As discussed previously in the context of DiffServ networks, the 802 network can also be considered to consist of a small number of virtual networks (or resource pools) overlaid on a single physical network. Traffic classes and the corresponding user_priority values isolate these virtual networks from each other. Lower-quality traffic classes are likely to be used for lower-quality service guarantees. They do not require admission control and do not require close coordination between devices. Higher-quality traffic classes are likely to be used for higher-quality guarantees. Admission to these will be controlled via signaling, which also serves to closely coordinate Layer 2 devices across the 802 network.

7.1.2.3 Provisioning the 802 Network

The first task in QoS-enabling an 802 network is the provisioning of devices in the network. This process is similar to the process of provisioning a DiffServ network. First, devices must be selected. Then they must be populated with the appropriate capacity interfaces and interconnected to provide the desired topology.

When the physical provisioning phase is complete, logical provisioning commences. In this phase, interface capacity is carved up among a number of traffic classes, and the appropriate queue-servicing and traffic-conditioning parameters are applied. This establishes the virtual overlay networks described previously. At this point, the relatively static provisioning phase is complete, and the 802 network is ready for use. The challenge then becomes one of mapping traffic offered to the 802 network to the appropriate user_priority values and traffic classes.

7.1.2.4 Mappings

In [RFC 2815], the ISSLL working group addresses the problem of mapping traffic requiring a certain service to an appropriate user_priority, and then mapping the user_priority to an appropriate traffic class. The referenced RFC offers the mapping suggestion shown in Table 7.1.

Table 7.1   Mapping Service Requirements to user_priority Value

user_priority	Service
0	Default, assumed to be best-effort
1	Reserved, less-than-best-effort
2	Reserved
3	Reserved
4	Delay-sensitive, no bound
5	Delay-sensitive, 100ms bound
6	Delay-sensitive, 10ms bound
7	Network control

There are a number of interesting aspects to this suggested mapping:

- The first is to note that this is a mapping suitable for *quantitative* services (it specifies quantifiable delay bounds). It does not address the problem of mapping qualitative services.

- Another is that it does not actually map integrated service types to user_priority values. Instead, it maps traffic having different delay bound requirements to user_priority values.

- Finally, while user_priority values 4–7 imply increasing priority, user_priority values 0–3 do not.

Mappings for Qualitative Services

Because both the ISSLL and IntServ working groups have traditionally focused on the quantifiable integrated services, it is not surprising that the mapping does not address mappings of qualitative services. No formal abstractions for qualitative services have been defined yet. The closest approximation is the Null Service, which does not specify required service parameters so much as state that it defers to the network to choose the appropriate service level (in this case, traffic class). For those qualitative applications that generate RSVP signaling, devices in the 802 network may return the appropriate user_priority value in the TCLASS object, as described previously.

Referring to the mapping proposal suggested by the ISSLL working group, qualitative services might map to user_priority 4 (delay-sensitive, no bound). However, this user_priority value might be more appropriately used for traffic requiring the quantitative Controlled Load Service. If so, then in the interest of separating resources used by quantitative services from those used by qualitative services, it would be appropriate to designate one or more lower user_priority values (currently reserved) for traffic requiring qualitative services.

The Difficulty in Mapping Quantitative Integrated Services to user_priority

A problem occurs when attempting to map requests for IntServ services to user_priority. This is a consequence of the fact that IntServ requests are multidimensional. They request a certain bandwidth, delay, and service type. These service requests must be mapped to a set of user_priority values and traffic classes that by default are unidimensional (distinguished only by their relative priority).

The strict priority behavior of the 802 traffic classes can be applied to support the parameters associated with IntServ requests. To this end, the ISSLL working group considered two mapping approaches:

- In one approach, each IntServ service type maps to a specific user_priority value and traffic class.

- In the other approach, user_priority values and traffic classes are ordered according to delay-bound targets, and traffic requests for a specific IntServ type are dynamically mapped to a traffic class based on the corresponding quantitative parameters.

The working group concluded that the first approach is not sufficiently flexible and adopted the second approach. This approach requires admission control to verify that the aggregate rate of traffic submitted for any traffic class will not exceed the target delay bounds for the class. In addition, policing is required to ensure that senders do not submit traffic in excess of the rate indicated in the IntServ requests.

More sophisticated Layer 2 devices go beyond the default strict priority implementation of traffic classes. These devices offer sophisticated queuing schemes and additional quantitative configuration parameters, making it easier to support the multidimensional quantitative services.

The Ordering of user_priority Values

The proposed mapping from services to user_priority values illustrated previously suggests that best-effort maps to a user_priority value of 0. It then suggests that the user_priority value of 1 be reserved for less-than-best-effort traffic. A less-than-best-effort user_priority value can be used to mark traffic that exceeds negotiated admission control parameters and is therefore a candidate for demotion to a lower traffic class or discard. (Packets with no user_priority value marked are considered equivalent to a zero user_priority and are entitled to default, best-effort service.)

The mapping then reserves user_priority values 2 and 3 for future use. These may be applied to qualitative services that were not under consideration by the ISSLL working group.

The user_priority values 4 through 7 are clearly ordered in ascending priority. These are the user_priority values that are recommended for the support of the integrated services. The ISSLL working group intentionally chose to use values of 0 through 3 for best-effort or lower service, and values 4 through 7 for better-than-best-effort services. The reason for this is that simpler 802 devices are expected to support the range of user_priority values with only two underlying traffic classes. In this case, the IEEE recommends mapping user_priority values 0 through 3 to the lower-priority traffic class, and user_priority values 4 through 7 to the higher-priority traffic class. Thus, requests for better-than-best-effort service would be assigned to the higher-priority traffic class.

7.2   Using RSVP with 802 Networks—the SBM and SBM Protocol

Both user_priority values and the traffic classes to which they map provide the basic aggregate traffic-handling functionality to support QoS in 802 networks. This section discusses the use of RSVP signaling in providing enhanced services across 802 networks. The term *SBM* is used to refer both to an 802 admission control agent as well as to the protocol extensions necessary to communicate with this agent. This section first introduces the concept of the SBM as an admission control agent and then discusses the SBM protocol in detail.

7.2.1 The SBM as Admission Control Agent for 802 Networks

As discussed earlier in this chapter, there is value in enabling Layer 2 devices in an 802 network to participate in RSVP signaling. Participation in signaling can improve the quality/efficiency product of the 802 network. To this end, the ISSLL working group has defined the Subnet Bandwidth Manager (SBM) as an admission control agent for 802 networks. It may be implemented in Layer 2 devices internal to the 802 network. Alternatively, it may be implemented in a Layer 3 device that is attached to the 802 subnet. There may be a single SBM representing an entire 802 subnet, or there may be multiple SBMs representing the 802 subnet. Various SBM configurations are illustrated in Figure 7.4.

Figure 7.4 Various Configurations of SBMs as Admission Control Agents

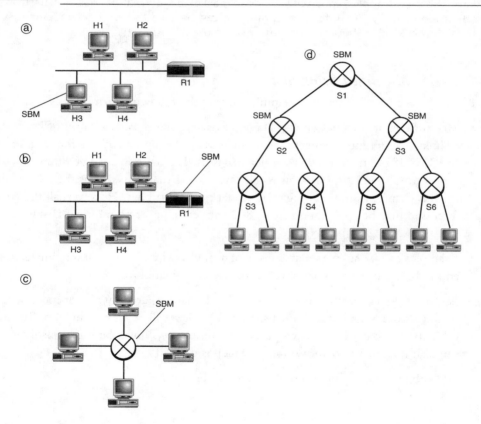

In Figure 7.4a, a shared Ethernet segment interconnects four hosts and a router. H3 is the SBM representing the shared segment. In Figure 7.4b, the same topology is illustrated, but R1 is the SBM for the segment. In Figure 7.4c, four hosts are interconnected via a switch. The switch is the SBM. In Figure 7.4d, a complex switch topology interconnects a set of hosts. S1, S2, and S3 are all SBMs, each for different parts of the 802 subnetwork.

As an admission control agent, the SBM participates actively in RSVP signaling traversing the 802 subnet.

> **Note**
>
> Note that an SBM can also be used to passively snoop signaling messages traversing the subnet. In this mode, the SBM is capable of gleaning classification information that correlates users and applications with fields in packet headers (but does not participate in admission control). The information gleaned can be used by policy management systems to facilitate push configuration of resources in the 802 subnet.

7.2.1.1   Managed Segments

Before proceeding further, it is helpful to clarify the following terminology:

- **802 subnet or 802 network**—These terms are used to refer to a set of Layer 2 devices or links that are interconnected without passing through a Layer 3 forwarding function. In [RFC 2814] the term *Layer 2 domain* is used. Note that a single 802 subnet may support multiple IP subnets (as is the case with virtual LANs). For the sake of simplicity, this chapter assumes a single IP subnet per 802 subnet. However, all the concepts discussed may be applied equally to 802 subnets supporting multiple IP subnets or multiple VLANs (virtual LANs).

  Examples of 802 subnets may consist of a single switch, a set of interconnected switches and hubs, an Ethernet coaxial cable, or any combination of these.

- **Segment**—This term refers to a physical link that is shared by one or more senders. Examples of a segment include a shared Ethernet (yellow wire or hub) or Token Ring cable, or a link between switch ports. The term *segment* will be used in isolation to distinguish it from a *managed segment*, which is defined next.

802 subnets and segments are illustrated in Figure 7.5.

Figure 7.5   802 Subnets and Segments

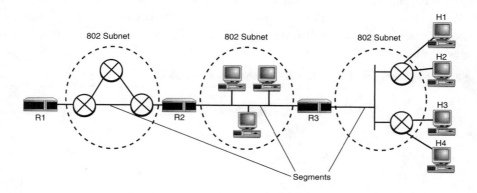

Three 802 subnets are illustrated in this figure. The leftmost subnet consists of three switches and the segments that interconnect them. The middle subnet consists of a single "yellow wire" segment. The rightmost subnet is a mix of shared segments and switches.

- **Managed segment**—This term refers to a combination of interconnected Layer 2 devices and segments that are managed by a single SBM. An 802 network may be subdivided into multiple managed segments. A managed segment may be further subdivided into multiple segments.

- **Designated Subnet Bandwidth Manager (DSBM)**—An SBM is a device that understands the SBM protocol and that is capable of providing SBM functionality. However, not all SBMs in an 802 network necessarily achieve self-actualization (actively participate in the SBM protocol and provide admission control functionality). For an SBM to act as admission control agent for a subnet, that SBM must be elected as the *designated* SBM for the subnet.

Entire 802 Subnet as a Single Managed Segment

In the simplest case, the SBM makes it possible for a single agent to intercept all RSVP messages transiting an 802 subnet. This agent is the DSBM for the subnet. If the 802 subnet consists of multiple Layer 2 devices, then the single DSBM provides admission control without explicit topology awareness. A single DSBM acting in this manner can improve the quality/efficiency product of the subnetwork to a limited degree. Increasing the density of DSBM distribution can further enhance the quality/efficiency product of the subnetwork. (See the section "Density of DSBM Distribution," later in this chapter, for further discussion.)

Figure 7.6 illustrates two examples of an 802 subnet that is managed by a single DSBM. In Figure 7.6a, one of the Layer 2 devices in the subnet (S1) is configured to act as the DSBM. In Figure 7.6b, one of the Layer 3 devices at the periphery of the 802 subnet (R1) is configured to act as the DSBM. In both cases, the 802 subnet is equivalent to the managed segment.

Figure 7.6 Examples of 802 Subnet Managed by Single SBM

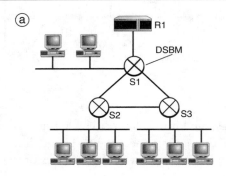

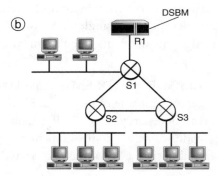

Multiple Managed Segments per Subnet

In the case that a single DSBM manages an entire 802 subnet, the managed segment and the subnet are equivalent. For further gain in quality/efficiency product, multiple SBM-capable devices can be used to manage a single 802 subnet. These SBMs effectively subdivide the 802 subnet into a number of managed segments. A single DSBM is then responsible for admission control to each of the managed segments of the subnetwork. This enables the network manager to configure different admission control limits for each of the managed segments. The result is finer control of the network resources and a higher quality/efficiency product. This case is illustrated in Figure 7.7.

Figure 7.7   An 802 Subnet Divided into Multiple Managed Segments

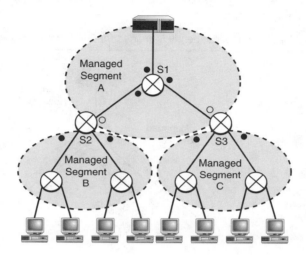

In this example, the 802 subnet is divided into three managed segments. S1 is the DSBM for Managed Segment A. S2 is the DSBM for Managed Segment B, and S3 is the DSBM for Managed Segment C. Note that S2 and S3 each straddle two managed segments. Neither of these switches as a whole can be considered to reside in either managed segment. Instead, the *interfaces* on each switch reside in one managed segment. DSBM is not a characteristic associated with a *device*, but rather with an *interface*. Thus, S2 is a DSBM on its interfaces in Managed Segment B but is not DSBM on its interface in Managed Segment A.

Note

The following notation is introduced in Figure 7.7 and will be used for the remainder of this chapter. A solid circle near an SBM interface indicates that the device is acting as a DSBM for the attached managed segment. An empty circle near an SBM interface indicates that the device is not acting as a DSBM for the attached managed segment.

Each Segment Managed Independently

Taken to the extreme, all Layer 2 devices in the 802 subnetwork can be SBM-capable. In a completely switched topology, this results in each segment being managed by its own DSBM. As a result, there is full topology awareness. A resource request is admitted only if each device and each link impacted by admission of the request can support its admission.

Although this approach offers the highest quality/efficiency product, the resulting efficiency is rarely required in 802 subnets. Figure 7.8 illustrates this scenario, in which each segment is also a managed segment.

Figure 7.8   Each Segment Independently Managed for Full Topology Awareness

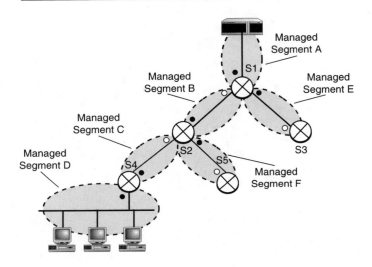

In this example, DSBMs manage segments as tabulated here:

- S1 is the DSBM for Managed Segment (MS) A and MS E.

- S2 is the DSBM for MS B and MS F.

- S3 is not a DSBM.

- S4 is the DSBM for MS C and MS D.

- S5 is not a DSBM.

7.2.1.2 *Density of DSBM Distribution*

In abstract terms, the granularity of independently managed segments corresponds to the density of admission control agents (in this case, DSBMs). The concept of the density of admission control agents and its impact on the quality/efficiency product of a network was introduced in Chapter 2, "The Quality/Efficiency Product," and can be applied to all types of networks, including 802 subnets.

Dense Distribution of DSBMs

Figure 7.8 represents a dense distribution of DSBMs. When all devices in the 802 subnet are SBM-capable, the resources on each segment are managed by a directly attached DSBM. Each DSBM is aware of the capacity and current resource consumption on each of the segments for which it is responsible for admission control. When an admission control request arrives at a DSBM, it can assess the impact of admitting the corresponding traffic flow. In this case, the DSBM can make perfect admission control decisions based on local knowledge.

Sparse Distribution of DSBMs

On the other hand, when not all devices are SBM-capable, DSBMs must make admission control decisions for segments to which they are not directly attached and on which they are not directly aware of resource availability. In this case, DSBMs must be configured with some overall notion of the capacity of the managed segments for which they are responsible. A conservative policy would configure the DSBM to admit resource requests up to the capacity of the slowest segment in the subnet. A liberal policy would configure the DSBM to admit resource requests up to some higher capacity. In either case, the DSBM cannot make perfect admission control decisions. This is illustrated in Figure 7.9.

Figure 7.9	A Single Admission Control Agent Acting on Behalf of Multiple Devices, Without Topology Awareness

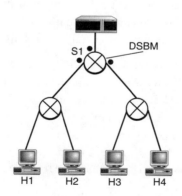

S1 is the DSBM. It admits flows between H1 and H2 as well as flows between H3 and H4. Although these flows impact separate resources, the DSBM must count them against the same admission control limits. This problem is equivalent to the problem presented in the "Signaling and Topology Awareness" sidebar in Chapter 2 (a *routed* network in which not all agents are RSVP-aware).

Intermediate Densities of DSBM Distribution

The previous two examples illustrate extreme cases. In the first case, every switch is SBM-capable. In the second case, a single switch is the DSBM for the entire subnet. In many cases, intermediate densities of DSBM distribution are most pragmatic. This example is illustrated in Figure 7.7. By choosing the appropriate density of DSBM distribution, the manager of an 802 subnetwork can choose the appropriate trade-off between the required quality/efficiency product and the cost of DSBM support.

7.2.1.3 SBMs and Traffic Handling

Generally, traffic handling in the 802 subnet is based on aggregate traffic classes. DSBMs admit traffic flows to particular traffic classes. Admitted traffic flows are then marked with the appropriate `user_priority` value by Layer 3 devices at the periphery of the 802 subnet. Traffic handling is based entirely on the `user_priority` value marked in each packet. Other than for the purpose of admission control, SBMs do not identify individual conversations. As such, this model is very similar to the model introduced in Chapter 6, in which certain devices provide per-conversation admission control to different DiffServ aggregates.

In certain cases, it may be desirable to handle RSVP-signaled traffic in the 802 subnet at a finer granularity than is possible based on `user_priority` alone. (Non-RSVP-signaled traffic generally does not require as high a quality/efficiency product and thus does not require finer-grain traffic handling.) This requires both that devices in the subnet have a traffic-handling mechanism that operates at a fine granularity (MF classifiers and corresponding policers or queuing mechanisms) and that the devices be both RSVP-aware and in the RSVP signaling path (to configure the traffic-handling mechanisms).

In Figure 7.10, S1 is the DSBM and the only RSVP-aware device. It is the admission control agent for the entire 802 subnet. Most traffic flows admitted by the DSBM will flow through devices that are not RSVP-aware. S1 admits (or rejects) the traffic flow from H1 to H2 (thereby determining the `user_priority` that will be used for the corresponding traffic). However, the admitted or rejected traffic is handled entirely by S2, S3, and S4. Because these switches are not RSVP-aware, they do not have the required information to handle traffic at a finer granularity than the `user_priority` values marked in the traffic.

If S2, S3, and S4 were RSVP-aware and had the appropriate traffic-handling mechanisms, they would be capable of applying finer-grain traffic handling. For example, they might police admitted conversations to assure that they are not seizing more than their share of the aggregate resources for a traffic class. These switches could even service each conversation with separate queues. Note that (although an unlikely scenario) the devices are not necessarily required to be SBM-capable, but they are required to intercept and parse RSVP messages.

Figure 7.10 Traffic Handling by Devices that Are Not RSVP-Aware

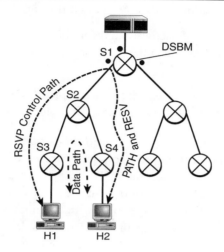

In the case that S1 is the DSBM and the only RSVP-aware device in the 802 subnet, QoS is provided by combining per-conversation admission control with aggregate traffic handling. In the case that S2, S3, and S4 are both RSVP-aware and have the fine-grain traffic-handling mechanisms, QoS may be provided by combining per-conversation admission control with fine-grain traffic handling. Combinations of different granularity of admission control with different granularity of traffic handling were discussed in Chapter 2. Various combinations result in varying quality/efficiency product in the 802 subnet. The increased quality/efficiency product that results from full per-conversation traffic handling is rarely required in an 802 subnet. However, some degree of per-conversation traffic handling may be very useful in certain cases. One such case is the handling of multicast branch points in the 802 subnet. This example will be discussed later in this chapter in the section "Receiver Heterogeneity and Multicast."

7.2.1.4 The DSBM Election Protocol—Formation of Managed Segments

As was explained previously, although all SBMs are capable of becoming DSBMs, not all do so. Typically, the network manager enables certain devices to become DSBMs. These devices spontaneously run an election protocol. The election protocol divides the 802 subnet into managed segments and results in the election of a single DSBM to manage each managed segment. DSBMs rely on a pair of special multicast addresses, which are used both in processing admission control requests as well as running the election protocol.

Two such multicast addresses are defined with the following characteristics.

- Packets addressed to these addresses are not passed through Layer 3 devices.

- Packets addressed to these addresses are intercepted by SBM-capable devices and are not passed through the device unless the SBM protocol entity in the device chooses to pass them.

- Packets addressed to these devices pass transparently through Layer 2 devices that are not SBM-capable (also known as *SBM-transparent* devices).

The two multicast addresses are known as the *DSBM Logical Address* and the *All SBM Address*. To participate in the election protocol, devices running for election send a message advertising their willingness to become DSBM addressed to the All SBM Address. These messages propagate to all Layer 2 devices in the *election scope* or *election domain* of the advertising SBM. The election messages propagate through SBM-transparent devices but are not propagated through SBM-capable devices. Thus, the distribution of SBM-capable devices determines the boundaries of the election domain, as illustrated in Figure 7.11. (Of course, the maximum extent of the election domain is the 802 subnet itself.)

Figure 7.11   Election Domains

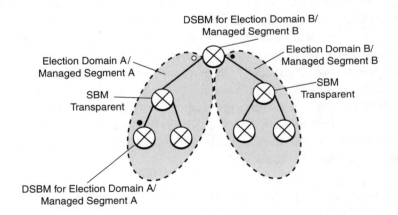

In Figure 7.11, the 802 subnet is subdivided into multiple election domains. Separate elections run within each domain, resulting in the election of a DSBM for the domain. Each election domain becomes a managed segment. In an 802 subnet with a dense distribution of SBM-capable devices, many DSBMs will be elected. If there is only a single SBM-capable device, the election scope is the entire 802 subnet and that device will become the DSBM for the entire subnet. If every device in the subnet is SBM-capable, then each segment will constitute an election domain and will be independently managed by a single DSBM. Each SBM-capable device participates in separate elections on each of its interfaces, so an SBM-capable device might become DSBM on multiple interfaces and might yield to other devices to become DSBM of the segments attached to other interfaces. In a topology that consists entirely of point-to-point connected switch ports with each switch being SBM-capable, each election domain consists of a link and the two switches that terminate it on each end. One of the two switches wins the election to become the DSBM for the link.

Note

In the case of full-duplex switch links, a DSBM likely will be elected separately for each direction of the link. One switch may act as DSBM for both directions. Alternatively, each switch may be elected the DSBM for one of the directions.

7.2.1.5 Election Priorities and Fault Tolerance

SBM-capable devices run for election with different priorities based on the type of device. Layer 2 devices run with the highest priority. Layer 3 routers are next in priority. Finally, hosts are lowest in priority. This prioritization is designed to result in the most topology-aware device winning the election for DSBM.

Devices that become DSBM periodically advertise their status to all SBM-capable devices in the election scope. If a DSBM fails, other devices will detect its failure and will run the election protocol to elect a new DSBM.

Note

Note that the appearance of a new device in the election scope with a higher election priority than the current DSBM will not displace the current DSBM unless or until it is disabled.

7.2.2 The SBM Protocol

The SBM protocol extends the utility of RSVP to 802 networks. As such, it must address the following problems:

- First, the protocol must define how Layer 2 devices participate in what is fundamentally a Layer 3 signaling protocol.

- Second, the SBM protocol must make it possible to account for resources on segments that are shared by multiple senders.

- Finally, the protocol must forward RSVP messages along the appropriate path in an arbitrary 802 network.

The first problem is relatively simple to address. The last two points warrant further discussion. These are best analyzed by reviewing the operation of conventional RSVP signaling in Layer 3 networks and then applying it to Layer 2 networks.

7.2.2.1 RSVP Operation in Layer 3 Networks

Consider the case of a fully routed Layer 3 network in which each router is RSVP-aware. An example of such a network is illustrated in Figure 7.12.

Figure 7.12   RSVP in a Layer 3 Network

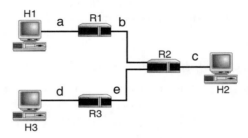

Note that the links a–e interconnecting the routers and hosts are bidirectional. However, resources consumed in one direction do not impact resources consumed in the other direction. In this case, only resources consumed in the direction from H1 to H2 (or H3 to H2) are of interest. For the purpose of this example, links a, b, d, and e have a capacity of 10Mbps in each direction. Link c has a capacity of 100Mbps.

Assume that H1 signals for a 6Mbps traffic flow to H2. It sends an RSVP PATH message addressed to H2. This message traverses the path H1 to R1 to R2 to H2. H2 generates an RSVP RESV message back toward H1. As it flows toward H1, the RESV message arrives at each device whose resources would be impacted by admission of the traffic flow (R2, R1, and H1, in that order). These devices evaluate the impact of admitting the flow and make an admission control decision based on the result. Assuming that no prior reservations are in place, R2 would commit 6Mbps on segment c, R1 would commit 6Mbps on segment b, and H1 would commit 6Mbps on segment a.

Assume now that H3 signals for a 6Mbps traffic flow to H2. At the completion of the signaling cycle, R2 will have committed an additional 6Mbps on segment c (for a total of 12Mbps committed on this segment), R3 will have committed 6Mbps on segment e, and H3 will have committed 6Mbps on segment d.

Admission of the first traffic flow would result in resources being consumed on segments a, b, and c, and on interfaces in H1, R1, and R2. The related RSVP messages arrive at each device whose resources are impacted by admission of the flow. Furthermore, an exclusive admission control agent takes responsibility for any consumed resource. Because H1 is the only sender onto segment a, it accounts for all resources on this segment. Similarly, R1 accounts for all resources on segment b, and R2 accounts for all resources on segment c. (Recall that only resources consumed in the direction from H1 to H2 are of interest.)

Admission of the second traffic flow is similar, with H3 taking responsibility for resources consumed on segment d, R3 for resources consumed on segment e, and R2 for the additional resources consumed on segment c.

Conventional RSVP signaling works in point-to-point routed networks because the following general conditions are met:

- Each segment, interface, or device on which resources will be consumed by admission of a traffic flow has an admission control agent that is responsible for it.

- Any resource request whose admission would impact resources on a particular segment, interface, or device arrives at the admission control agent responsible for that segment, interface, or device.

- The admission control agent at which a resource request arrives is the exclusive sender onto the impacted interface and segment, and has perfect knowledge of the current level of resources committed and available on that interface and segment.

As will be shown below, these conditions do not hold for general 802 networks.

7.2.2.2   RSVP in a Shared-Segment 802 Subnetwork

Now consider that R1 and R3 are connected to R2 via an 802 subnet instead of the point-to-point link in the previous example. This is illustrated in Figure 7.13.

Unlike the previous example in which each segment is a point-to-point link with only one sender, this example includes an 802 shared segment with a total capacity of 10Mbps (segment b). There are three possible senders onto segment b: R1, R3, and R2.

H1 again signals for a 6Mbps traffic flow to H2. As the RESV message flows back from H2 to H1, R2 commits 6Mbps on link c, R1 commits 6Mbps on segment b, and H1 commits 6Mbps on segment a. Now observe what happens when H3 signals for a 6Mbps traffic flow to H2. R2 commits an additional 6Mbps on segment c (for a total of 12Mbps), R3 commits 6Mbps on segment b, and H3 commits 6Mbps on segment d. Note that 12Mbps have been committed on segment b, which has a total capacity of 10Mbps. Both R1 and

R3 are aware that they are sending onto a 10Mbps interface, and so neither refuses a request for 6Mbps of capacity. They are not aware that they are sharing the 10Mbps interface and as a result they have overcommitted it. RSVP admission control fails to yield the desired results because the third condition listed above is not met; neither R1 nor R3 are exclusive senders on segment b, so neither has perfect knowledge of the current level of resources committed on the segment.

Figure 7.13   An 802 Subnet in the RSVP Path

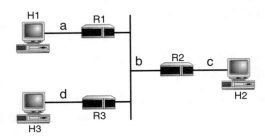

The problem illustrated in this example can be addressed by appointing a single admission control agent to be responsible for admission control for each shared resource. Thus, either R1, R2, or R3 can be appointed as the exclusive admission control agent responsible for segment b. The admission control agent would be aware that there is a total of 10Mbps capacity available on segment b and would review all admission control requests for resources on this segment. In the previous example, if the admission control agent admits the request for a 6Mbps traffic flow between H1 and H2, it would reject the subsequent request for a 6Mbps traffic flow from H3 to H2.

The SBM election protocol defines the mechanism by which either R1, R2, or R3 becomes the exclusive admission control agent (the DSBM) for the shared resource. The DSBM provides the means for accounting for shared resources. However, simply appointing a DSBM does not in and of itself solve the problem of extending RSVP to 802 networks. It is also necessary to cause admission control requests impacting resources under the control of the DSBM to be routed so that they arrive at the DSBM. Routing of RSVP messages in an 802 subnet will be discussed in detail in the next section. First, it is necessary to consider the 802 subnet in more general terms.

7.2.2.3   *RSVP in a Switched 802 Subnetwork*

In Figure 7.14, an RSVP-unaware switch with a 10Mbps backplane has replaced segment b from the previous example.

Figure 7.14   An RSVP-Unaware Switch in the Signaling Path

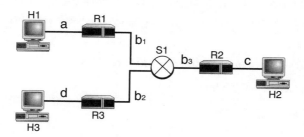

Resources in device S1 are impacted by admission of traffic flows between H1 and H2 (or H3 and H2). However, in the absence of alternate mechanisms, R1 and R3 would both act as admission control agents for the switch. However, neither is the exclusive sender to the device, and neither has perfect knowledge of the current level of resources committed in the device. This is the same problem encountered previously.

Again, the problem can be solved by considering the switch as a shared resource and appointing either R1, R2, or R3 as the admission control agent for the switch. This approach is based on a very simplistic view of the switch as a single shared backplane with a defined capacity. Although this may be appropriate for older switches, newer switches are more complex and cannot be viewed as a single shared backplane. The total capacity that can be accommodated by these switches may depend on the particular sets of ports that are carrying the traffic. (Although the switch in the example has only three ports, in general such switches will include many more ports.)

In the case that the switch is not a simple shared backplane, none of the routers surrounding it will have perfect knowledge of the current level of committed and available resources in the switch (because none of the routers is aware of the specific switch ports carrying admitted traffic). Therefore, it is advantageous to enable such switches to become DSBMs.

In general, then, the SBM protocol must allow for both switches in the 802 subnetwork or Layer 3 devices at the edges of the network (including both hosts and routers) to become DSBMs and to route RSVP signaling messages via the appointed DSBMs. Election of DSBMs and the notion of election domains has been discussed previously. The following section addresses routing of RSVP messages within the 802 subnetwork.

7.2.2.4 Routing RSVP PATH Messages Through the 802 Subnet

This section briefly describes the routing of RSVP PATH messages in an 802 subnetwork, in the context of a specific example. For a detailed discussion of this problem, refer to [RFC 2814].

Consider the 802 subnetwork illustrated in Figure 7.15.

Figure 7.15   A General 802 Subnetwork

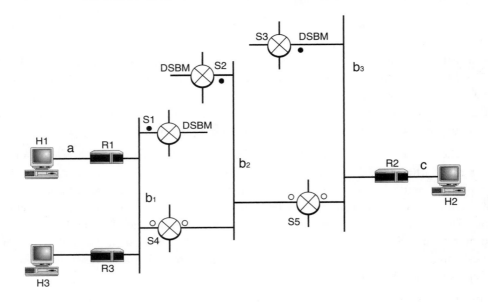

This 802 subnetwork consists of shared segments (marked b_1–b_3) and five SBM-aware switches (marked S1–S5). Multiple senders share each segment. Consequently, there is no natural single admission control agent for each of these segments. Instead, a DSBM has been elected to be the admission control agent for each of the segments. S1 is the DSBM for segment b_1, S2 is the DSBM for segment b_2, and S3 is the DSBM for segment b_3. However, note that none of the DSBMs is in the data path for the traffic flow from H1 to H2. In the absence of alternate mechanisms, conventional RSVP PATH messages would flow through the 802 subnet, without arriving at the designated admission control agents. Herein lies the problem that the SBM protocol must solve. Modifications are necessary to cause the RSVP PATH messages to flow through S1, S2, and S3 as the admission control agents responsible for the resources that would be consumed by admission of the traffic flow. As long as the PATH messages are routed correctly, RESV messages will follow these back through the admission control agents, and proper admission control can be applied.

In Layer 3 networks, each admission control agent stores the IP address of the previous hop from which the PATH message arrived. Similarly, in the Layer 2 network, each DSBM must store the address of the previous DSBM from which the PATH message arrived. Thus, each DSBM is configured with an IP address that is used to identify the DSBM and to create the path through the Layer 2 network.

In the Layer 3 network, each router looks at the destination IP address in each PATH message and uses Layer 3 routing to determine which interface to forward the message on. Switches in the Layer 2 network do not understand Layer 3 routing. Instead, these use Layer 2 address-forwarding tables to determine which port to forward messages on. Disregarding RSVP for a moment, R1 would forward data packets to H2 by addressing them to the IP address of H2 and the Layer 2 address of the next Layer 3 hop, R2. Within the 802 subnet, switches would route the packet based on the Layer 2 address of R2. As illustrated by the dashed line in Figure 7.16, the natural Layer 2 routing does not include the DSBMs.

Figure 7.16   The Natural Data Path from R1 to H2 Bypasses the Layer 2 Admission Control Agents

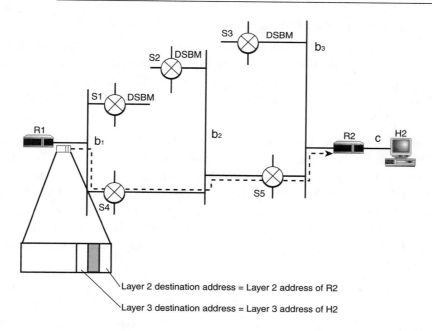

Layer 2 destination address = Layer 2 address of R2

Layer 3 destination address = Layer 3 address of H2

Therefore, R1 cannot simply address RSVP PATH messages to the Layer 2 address of R2. Instead, R1 must address RSVP PATH messages to the DSBM for segment b_1.

7.2.2.5 *Directing* PATH *Messages to the DSBM—SBM Clients*

To this end, the SBM protocol specifies that any Layer 3 RSVP-capable device must be capable of detecting when it is sending onto an 802 managed segment and must direct RSVP PATH messages to the DSBM that manages the segment. Such Layer 3 devices are known as *SBM clients*. SBM clients direct PATH messages to the DSBM by addressing them to one of the special multicast addresses (the DSBM Logical Address), described previously in the section "The DSBM Election Protocol—Formation of Managed Segments." The DSBM for each managed segment monitors this multicast address to receive PATH messages directed to the managed segment's DSBM.

Therefore, in the example illustrated, R1 addresses the PATH message (destined to R2 and ultimately to H2) to the DSBM Logical Address. Because the DSBM for each managed segment monitors this multicast address, the PATH message from R1 arrives at S1 (the DSBM for segment b_1). S1 can then install PATH state, noting R1 as the previous hop from which the PATH message arrived. However, at this point, S1 must determine how to forward the PATH message so that it proceeds along its path toward R2 and H2.

7.2.2.6 *Forwarding* PATH *Messages Beyond the DSBM*

When a DSBM receives a PATH message, it must continue to forward the message so that it arrives at the DSBM for the next managed segment along the route from sender to receiver. Forwarding the message according to standard Layer 2 forwarding (based on the Layer 2 address of the egress point from the 802 subnetwork) will do so, as described in the next paragraph.

In the example illustrated, S4 lies between S1 and the DSBM for the next managed segment. S1 therefore must forward the PATH message via S4. In the case of standard Layer 2 forwarding, packets destined for the receiver would contain the Layer 2 address of the egress point from the 802 subnetwork (R2). S1 would use this address to determine the appropriate egress port on which to forward the packet. However, in the case of the RSVP PATH message, the Layer 2 address of the egress point is no longer available from the packet header. The SBM client (R1) has overwritten the Layer 2 destination address field with the DSBM logical address.

For S1 (and other SBM-aware devices) to properly forward the PATH message, they must recover the Layer 2 address of the egress point. For this reason, the SBM protocol specifies that SBM clients must insert the Layer 2 address of the egress point in a special object in the RSVP PATH message. This object is known as the LAN_NHOP (next hop) object. The LAN_NHOP remains part of the PATH message as long as it remains in the 802 subnet. Any Layer 2 device can use this object to retrieve the Layer 2 address of the egress point from the 802 subnetwork and to determine the appropriate port on which to forward the PATH message. (The LAN_NHOP is removed from the PATH message after it leaves the 802 subnet.)

Thus, when R1 overwrites the contents of the Layer 2 destination address field, it must also insert a LAN_NHOP object containing the address of R2 into the PATH message that it addresses to the DSBM. When the PATH message arrives at the DSBM, S1 uses the LAN_NHOP object to determine the egress point from the 802 subnetwork and the appropriate port on which to forward the PATH message toward this point. S1 uses its standard Layer 2 forwarding tables to determine that the PATH message should be forwarded to the port sending onto b_1.

At this time, the destination address field in the PATH message still contains the DSBM Logical Address. Transmitting the PATH message to this address a second time would be futile because S1 is the only device on b_1 that monitors this address. (Recall from the section on the DSBM election protocol that because S4 is SBM-aware, it will not pass messages addressed to either the DSBM Logical Address or the All SBM Address.)

S1 could insert the address from the LAN_NHOP object into the destination address field of the PATH message. This would cause the message to be forwarded by S4 onto b_2. However, from there the PATH message would simply follow the data path through S5, toward R2 (missing S2 and S3, the DSBMs for segments b_2 and b_3). S1 must address the PATH message so that it flows through S4 and arrives at the DSBM for b_2 (S2). It does so by *forwarding* the message *as if it were* addressed to R2, but *addressing* the message toward the second of the special multicast addresses described previously, the All SBM Address. SBM-capable devices that are not DSBMs (as well as SBM client devices) monitor this multicast address so that they are capable of receiving the PATH messages. Thus, S4 receives the PATH message.

S4 then uses the LAN_NHOP object to determine the appropriate port onto which the PATH message should be forwarded. It forwards the PATH message onto b_2. Because S4 is *not* the DSBM for b_2, it addresses the PATH message to the DSBM Logical Address.

In this manner, the PATH message is forwarded through the 802 subnet, addressed alternatively to the DSBM Logical Address (by senders that are not DSBMs) and to the All SBM Address (by senders that are DSBMs). The progression of the PATH message through the 802 subnetwork is illustrated in Figure 7.17.

Figure 7.17   Progression of PATH Message Through 802 Subnetwork

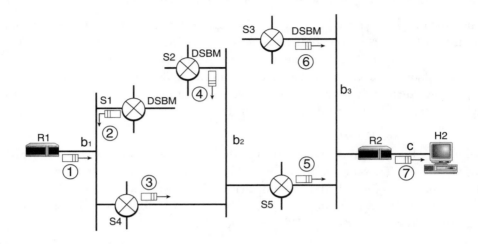

1. R1 addresses the PATH message to the *DSBM LogicalAddress* and sends it on b_1.

2. S1 intercepts the PATH message, stores R1's address as the previous hop, addresses it to the *AllSBMAddress* and sends it on b_1.

3. S4 intercepts the PATH message, addresses it to the *DSBMLogicalAddress*, and sends it on b_2.

4. S2 intercepts the PATH message, stores S1's address as the previous hop, addresses it to the AllSBMAddress and sends it on b_2.

5. S5 intercepts the PATH message, addresses it to the DSBMLogicalAddress, and sends it on b_3.

6. S3 intercepts the PATH message, stores S2's address as the previous hop, addresses it to the AllSBMAddress, and sends it on b_3.

7. R2 intercepts the PATH message, strips the SBM-specific objects from the message, addresses it to H2, and sends it on c.

When the PATH message has been carried correctly across the 802 subnet, RESV messages can be returned in the conventional manner. No special processing is required for these messages. The previous hop stored by R2 with its PATH state is the address of S3, the last DSBM on the path through the Layer 2 network. R2 sends RESV messages for the session to this address, just as it would in conventional RSVP processing. Similarly, S3 sends the

RESV message to S2, the DSBM for segment b_2, and S2 sends the RESV message to S1, the DSBM for segment b_1. Finally, S1 sends the RESV message back to R1, completing the reservation cycle. Actually, SBM-aware devices store the Layer 2 address of the previous hop, as described next in the context of the RSVP_HOP_L2 object. This eliminates the need for these devices to run ARP.

Note that 802 devices may append TCLASS objects to RESV messages as they propagate back toward senders. The use of TCLASS objects will be described in further detail later in the following section.

PATH messages for multicast sessions are handled in a similar manner, with minor differences. The multicast example will not be described in detail in this book. Instead, the reader is referred to [RFC 2814] for details on handling RSVP messages for multicast sessions in 802 subnets.

7.2.2.7 RSVP Objects Required for the SBM Protocol

Four new objects are defined to extend the RSVP protocol for use with the SBM:

- The LAN_NHOP object (described previously)
- The LAN_LOOPBACK object
- The RSVP_HOP_L2 object (described previously)
- The TCLASS object (described previously)

The first three are for use with RSVP PATH and PATH_TEAR messages. The TCLASS object may be included both in PATH and in RESV messages.

The LAN_NHOP object is used to store the egress point from the 802 subnet, as described previously. The LAN_LOOPBACK object is used to avoid looping of multicast messages in the 802 subnet. The use of this object is described fully in [RFC 2814]. The RSVP_HOP_L2 object is analogous to the RSVP_HOP object that is carried in conventional RSVP PATH messages to specify the previous hop from which a PATH message has arrived. The RSVP_HOP_L2 object carries the Layer 2 address corresponding to the previous hop. This obviates the need for Layer 2 devices in the 802 subnet to maintain mappings between Layer 2 and Layer 3 addresses and enables them to operate on Layer 2 addresses when directing the RESV message back toward H1.

The first three objects described are inserted by SBM clients as they send PATH or PATH_TEAR messages into 802 subnets and are removed by egress devices as the messages leave 802 subnets.

The TCLASS object may be generated by SBM clients but may alternatively be generated by DSBMs within the 802 subnet. If present, it is always removed from messages leaving the 802 subnet. The TCLASS object is used in admission control, as described further in the following section.

7.2.3 *Admission Control at DSBMs and the* TCLASS *Object*

Because of the SBM extensions to the RSVP protocol, PATH and RESV messages flow through each of the DSBMs responsible for resources that would be impacted by the admission of the corresponding traffic flow. Thus, these DSBMs are capable of participating in the admission control process. DSBMs are expected to track the availability of resources for which they are responsible and to refuse admission to traffic flows that would exceed available resources. DSBMs may do so by blocking PATH or RESV messages and by sending the corresponding error messages in response, just as conventional Layer 3 admission control agents do.

7.2.3.1 *Negotiating* user_priority *Values Using the* TCLASS *Object*

In assessing the impact of admitting a traffic flow, DSBMs must consider the user_priority with which the traffic will be marked. To manage its resources effectively and to assure that an admitted flow enjoys the expected service, a DSBM may force the traffic flow to use a particular user_priority. The TCLASS object is used to negotiate the appropriate user_priority for a particular traffic flow between the device sending the traffic onto the 802 subnet and Layer 2 devices handling the traffic in the 802 subnet.

A sender may propose a particular user_priority for a traffic flow by appending a TCLASS object specifying the user_priority value, to the PATH message generated for the flow. Alternatively, if no TCLASS object is inserted by the sender, a DSBM along the PATH may insert one. As the TCLASS object flows downstream toward the receiver, it is inspected by DSBMs along the PATH. If a DSBM is incapable of supporting the traffic class represented by the user_priority specified in the TCLASS object, it may modify the user_priority to a lesser value before forwarding the TCLASS object downstream. Otherwise, the DSBM is required to pass it on unmodified. As the TCLASS object propagates toward the receiver, it behaves much like the RSVP ADSPEC object, determining the highest user_priority value that may be supported along the path.

DSBMs en route to the receiver and the receiver itself are required to store the user_priority value from a PATH message's TCLASS object in the PATH state for the session. If a TCLASS object is present in the PATH message received at the receiver, then the receiver is required to include that TCLASS in the RESV message generated for the session. As RESV messages for the session flow back up toward the sender, DSBMs are required to forward the TCLASS object unchanged. If a RESV message is received at a DSBM without a TCLASS object, the DSBM is required to append a TCLASS object containing the user_priority value stored with the PATH state. Eventually, when the RESV message reaches the original sender, the sender must mark transmitted traffic with the user_priority value contained in the received RESV message.

In this manner, the TCLASS object is used to coordinate the selection of an appropriate user_priority value among all admission control agents along the 802 path. The negotiated value is then presented to the sender to effect the proper marking of packets transmitted into the 802 subnet. Special cases arise in multicast situations, when multiple TCLASS objects must be merged, either from multiple senders or multiple receivers. In the case that multiple senders insert TCLASS objects for the same session with different user_priority values, DSBMs may choose to modify one or more of the TCLASS objects to resolve the difference. In the case that a DSBM must merge TCLASS objects containing different user_priority values from different RESV messages, the ISSLL specifications require that the DSBM reject RESV messages.

Admission control in the 802 subnet can be quite complicated and is not well understood at the time of this writing. Therefore, ISSLL specifications regarding admission control and the use of the TCLASS object [RFC 2814], [RFC 2816] focus primarily on the protocol semantics. The specifications leave room for interpretation and innovation with respect to admission control algorithms and the selection of the appropriate user_priority value.

7.2.3.2 Receiver Heterogeneity and Multicast

The majority of Layer 2 devices, especially those that are not DSBMs, apply simple aggregate traffic handling based on the user_priority value specified in each packet. This results in certain compromises in the case of multicast scenarios, as illustrated in Figure 7.18.

In this scenario, both H2 and H3 receive traffic for the same multicast session, sourced by sender H1. H2 generates a RESV message to reserve resources for the session, while H3 does not. Note the multicast branch point at S1, within the 802 subnet. In a fully routed, RSVP-aware network, the router at the multicast branch point would maintain state identifying those individual traffic flows for which resources were reserved and would not dedicate resources to those for which resources were not reserved.

However, in the 802 subnetwork, the sender H1 will mark all traffic transmitted on the multicast session with a single user_priority value (determined by the TCLASS object selected by the DSBMs in the 802 subnetwork). Because switches handle traffic based on the user_priority value, it will be treated equally on all multicast branches in the 802 subnetwork. Specifically, S1 will prioritize traffic equally on segments c and e. As a result, resources will be dedicated to the multicast session, in Segments e and f, when, in fact, H3 is not entitled to these resources. At best, H3 gets a free ride. At worst, resources in the branch serving H3 are not available for other sessions and other receivers.

Figure 7.18   Multicast Branch Point in the 802 Subnet

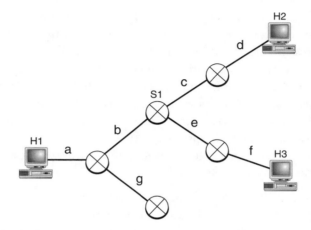

The only way to remedy this condition is by requiring S1 to store the state necessary to distinguish those flows that do have reservations from those flows that do not. By doing so, S1 is capable of demoting (by re-marking) the `user_priority` value in traffic destined to receivers that do not have reservations. This approach compromises the scalability of the aggregate traffic-handling approach to providing QoS in the 802 subnet. S1 now must store the classification information necessary to recognize specific flows and must treat them specially (rather than simply handling traffic according to the 802 `user_priority` value). However, the gains in efficiency that can be realized by enabling this functionality at a small number of key multicast branch points in the 802 subnet may justify the compromise in scalability.

7.3   *Supporting Heterogeneous Senders on 802 Subnets*

802 subnets are traditionally considered *shared* networks. Older 802 technologies such as yellow-wire Ethernet cables or simple hubs actually share physical resources. These cables or hubs have no notion of which traffic is entitled to higher priority and are incapable of protecting higher-priority traffic from lower-priority traffic. They are incapable of providing any means of traffic isolation (see the sidebar "Traffic Isolation in 802 Subnetworks," earlier in this chapter). Any device choosing to send onto these shared networks will consume physical resources that will not be available to other senders.

Newer 802 subnets are constructed from 802 switches that dedicate a separate port to each sending device. These switches are not shared physically and therefore are generally able to provide traffic isolation at least between senders and often between different traffic classes of a single sender (based on user_priority).

As 802 subnets differ in their capability to enforce traffic isolation, senders differ in their sending behavior. Certain sender operating systems generate signaling, requesting permission to mark traffic with certain user_priority values before doing so. Other senders may mark traffic without requesting permission. Others yet, have no notion of signaling or of user_priority values; these just send traffic when they have traffic to send. Senders may exhibit any combination of these behaviors.

To add to the mix, applications and protocols differ in their use of network resources. Certain applications running on operating systems that understand signaling may refrain altogether from sending traffic on a flow that has not been admitted to the network. The UDP protocol, which is typically used for multimedia streaming applications, is greedy in the sense that it will attempt to use as much of the available network resources as the application above it requires. On the other hand, the TCP protocol and other rate-adaptive protocols are sensitive to network congestion. These are socially conscious in the sense that they generally back off and lower their transmission rate when the network is congested. The following section describes how this mix of network devices, operating systems, applications, and protocols can be supported simultaneously in a manner that enables the network manager to retain control of network resources.

7.3.1   Legacy 802 Subnets

Legacy subnets are those subnets that are constructed from devices that cannot provide traffic isolation. These rely on the behavior of attached senders to use resources responsibly. For the most part, a network manager concerned with providing QoS services can be expected to upgrade its 802 subnets to use devices that are capable of traffic isolation. However, there may be certain instances in which some degree of QoS must be supported on legacy networks. These are discussed in the following section.

7.3.1.1   Use of TCP and Other Rate-Adaptive Protocols

When senders transmit traffic using the TCP protocol, they will generally share network resources fairly between them. TCP cannot in itself offer a network manager a mechanism for preferentially granting resources to different traffic flows, but it will generally preclude resource starvation for all traffic flows. In addition, when TCP and non-TCP traffic exist simultaneously on the 802 subnet, TCP senders will generally yield to non-TCP senders. Other rate-adaptive protocols exist besides TCP (though none is as commonly used as TCP). From here on, TCP and other such well-behaved protocols will be referred to collectively as *rate-adaptive* protocols.

7.3.1.2 Advanced Host Functionality

With the appropriate host operating system or application support, resources on legacy 802 networks can be assigned preferentially to certain traffic sources. The combination of legacy subnets with advanced function hosts is likely to be even less common than legacy subnets with legacy hosts, but it is worth considering this scenario further.

Consider the example illustrated in Figure 7.19.

Figure 7.19   Legacy 802 Subnet with Advance Function Senders

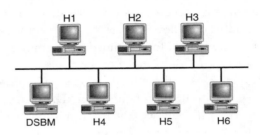

In this example, the network manager has deployed a single SBM, which wins the election to serve as the DSBM for a legacy subnet. (The DSBM functionality may be provided by a router sending onto the subnet or by a host sending onto the subnet.) The network manager configures the DSBM with an admission control limit to be used in admitting signaled resource requests. This limit will typically be some fraction of the subnet capacity. So, for example, on a 10Mbps subnet, the provisioned limit might be 1 or 2Mbps. On a 100Mbps subnet, it might be 10 or 20Mbps.

This example actually provides reasonable control of the network if all senders sending non-rate-adaptive traffic signal for permission to send such traffic and refrain from sending if permission is denied. This approach does not require that every sender participate in signaling. For example, it can be used to control a number of video streaming servers so that they make use of the network without overwhelming available resources.

The key to this approach is that non-rate-adaptive senders behave correctly. This is a tall order. Correct behavior can be enforced by operating systems that signal on behalf of applications. Alternatively, applications using non-rate-adaptive protocols may use QoS APIs provided by the operating system (see Chapter 12) to affect signaled requests and to refrain from sending if their request is denied.

This approach is not likely to be popular with application writers. Experience shows that the greedy application is more likely to gain network resources than the well-behaved application. As a result, there is little incentive to refrain from sending. Furthermore, in the case that 802 subnets are not legacy subnets and are capable of traffic isolation based on user_priority, the application *should* be allowed to send regardless of whether its resource request was approved. As long as the sending device does not mark rejected traffic for a high user_priority value, then best-effort service can be supported for the rejected application's traffic without compromising resources that are allocated to admitted traffic.

The author's belief is that, within reasonable limits, the operating system should provide the application with the information necessary to behave responsibly, without preventing it from transmitting traffic altogether. Applications that behave responsibly are more likely to be deployed by network managers. Applications that do not behave responsibly are less likely to be deployed. Deployability, as determined by network managers, will ultimately motivate application writers to behave responsibly. To this end, the host operating system should provide APIs to applications that enable them to detect when sending traffic on a rejected traffic flow is likely to adversely impact network resources and when it is not. By using this API, the application can optimize its use of network resources while remaining well-behaved.

NonResvSendLimit

Whether or not an application should be allowed to send in the absence of a reservation depends on the capability of the network to provide traffic isolation. In subnets built from 802.1p-capable switches with dedicated switch ports for each sender, applications are free to send even if their traffic has not been admitted via signaling. The operating system will prevent their traffic from being marked with a user_priority value other than best-effort, and the traffic will not adversely impact network resources. On the other hand, in legacy 802 subnets, such traffic isolation means are not available and applications should refrain from sending traffic that has not been explicitly admitted. The decision as to whether applications should be allowed to send in the absence of approved reservations is really a matter of network policy.

Furthermore, this is not a simple binary decision. It may be that a certain amount of non-rate-adaptive traffic can be tolerated even in legacy subnets and even in the absence of an approved reservation. For example, a network manager might decide that it is acceptable to allow IP telephony applications to send without explicit admission, whereas the higher-bandwidth streaming video applications should be precluded from doing so.

Because decisions as to how much traffic applications should or should not be allowed to send in the absence of an admitted reservation is a network policy decision, it is desirable to provide a means by which the network manager's policy can be reflected to behaving applications through the QoS API on advanced function hosts. The DSBM is ideal for this purpose. Because the DSBM periodically announces its presence on the 802 subnet, it is also capable of periodically advertising a limit on the bandwidth that applications should be allowed to send in the absence of a reservation. This parameter is called the NonResvSendLimit. (The NonResvSendLimit specifies *per-flow* limits in the form of a token bucket profile. See [RFC 2814] for further details.) It is configurable on a per-DSBM basis by the network manager.

In the case that the DSBM serves a network capable of traffic isolation, it can advertise a NonResvSendLimit of infinity. In the case that it serves a legacy network that is not capable of traffic isolation, it can be configured to advertise a NonResvSendLimit of zero or some other small number. All SBM capable hosts on the 802 subnet are capable of obtaining this value and reflecting it as appropriate to applications.

Obviously, the use of finite but small NonResvSendLimits on a legacy network is not foolproof. The actual amount of resources consumed may be much larger than expected if a large enough number of senders send simultaneously. In addition, to the extent that routers send non-rate-adaptive traffic onto the legacy subnet, resources may be compromised beyond the level expected (unless the routers also heed the NonResvSendLimit). However, the capability to advertise a NonResvSendLimit and the cooperation of host operating systems and applications provides yet another tool to aid network managers in maintaining control of their network resources.

7.3.1.3 *Modern 802 Subnets*

Advanced 802 subnets dedicate switch ports to senders and are capable of traffic isolation based on user_priority. In such environments, applications may send without reservation. The network enforces the allocation of resources to the various traffic flows that coexist in the 802 subnet.

Two general approaches exist for providing QoS support in this environment: aggregate traffic isolation and per-conversation traffic isolation. These approaches were compared briefly earlier in this chapter. They are revisited here for the sake of completeness.

Aggregate Traffic Handling Based on 802 user_priority

In this approach, devices in the 802 subnet isolate traffic based on user_priority but do not recognize individual conversations and do not isolate traffic between conversations. The network manager configures one or more DSBMs with aggregate limits that are reasonable for each traffic class in the managed segment for which each DSBM is responsible. For example, consider an 802 network consisting of a single switch with a 1Gbps capacity backplane. In this case, the switch is enabled to become a DSBM and might be configured to admit no more than 100Mbps of traffic for user_priority 5 and no more than 200Mbps of traffic for user_priority 3. As long as host operating systems and routers sending onto the subnet do not mark user_priority 3 or 5 on traffic flows that have not been explicitly admitted, the network manager is able to control the utilization of high-priority resources in the 802 subnet.

If a host or router misbehaves, marking a user_priority value of 3 or 5 for traffic that is not entitled to be so marked, then the amount of traffic competing for high-priority resources is greater than that allowed by the network manager. Because devices in the 802 network do not recognize individual conversations, rogue senders cannot be isolated and service is compromised to all traffic flows using these priority values, regardless of whether they are well behaved. (Rogue senders do not compromise service to traffic flows using higher priority values.)

Per-Conversation Traffic Handling

In most cases, aggregate traffic handling with signaled admission control should be capable of providing adequate QoS in an 802 network. Rogue senders would have to resort to hacking the operating system. However, in certain cases in which strict traffic isolation is required, devices in the 802 subnet may be required to track individual conversations and to police on a conversation-by-conversation basis. In this case, each such device would have to become a DSBM to monitor per-conversation signaling. This approach is costly in terms of processing overhead and is unlikely to be commonly deployed.

7.4 Summary

user_priority is expected to be the most common approach to QoS traffic handling in 802 subnets. user_priority values ranging from 0 to 7 are marked in the Layer 2 headers of packets submitted to the 802 subnet. Switches in the 802 subnet then provide aggregate traffic handling based on the user_priority value marked in each packet. This mechanism is analogous to the use of aggregate traffic handling based on DSCP in DiffServ networks.

The manager of an 802 subnet is faced with similar considerations as the manager of a DiffServ network when considering the allocation of resources by push provisioning versus configuration in response to RSVP signaling. However, in an 802 network, over-provisioning tends to be less expensive than in the typically wider-area DiffServ networks.

Therefore, 802 networks can typically provide adequate-quality service with a lower density of admission control agents and simpler admission control algorithms than DiffServ networks.

When signaling is used to gain access to prioritized resources in 802 networks, it is necessary to designate SBMs as devices that are capable of assuming responsibility for admission control to the 802 subnet. These devices will then run an election to determine which of them will actually assume responsibility for admission control to different parts of the 802 subnet. Those that win the election become designated SBMs (DSBMs).

For DSBM devices to participate in signaling, it must be possible for them to intercept signaling messages transiting the 802 network even though they may not naturally be in the data path (and, therefore, will not naturally be in the RSVP signaling path). DSBMs do so by advertising their presence on the 802 subnet via multicast messages. Senders on the 802 subnet are required to detect the presence of a DSBM and to address RSVP PATH messages to the DSBMs instead of the session destination address used in conventional RSVP signaling. Such senders are referred to as SBM clients. Minor extensions to the RSVP protocol describe the behavior of SBM clients and the manner in which SBM-aware Layer 2 devices forward RSVP messages across the 802 network. These extensions specify a small number of SBM specific objects that are inserted into standard RSVP messages. With the exception of election protocol-related messages, no new RSVP messages are required for the SBM protocol.

The TCLASS is one of the SBM-specific objects defined for use in 802 subnets. SBM-capable Layer 2 devices may append the TCLASS object to RESV messages that are sent toward senders onto the 802 subnet. The TCLASS carries a user_priority value that the sender should use to mark traffic on an admitted flow. The TCLASS object is analogous to the DCLASS object in DiffServ networks.

Aggregate traffic handling based on user_priority can support a reasonable level of QE product in many 802 subnets. Signaling can be used to control admission to different traffic classes in order to raise the quality/efficiency product of the 802 subnet and to facilitate management of resources based on user and application IDs. It is possible to apply the concept of the SBM and the SBM protocols to support per-conversation traffic handling at each Layer 2 device for an even greater quality/efficiency product. However, this level of complexity can rarely be justified, given the relatively low cost of bandwidth in 802 subnets.

QoS over Layer 2 Media Other Than 802

To provide end-to-end services, QoS mechanisms may be desirable in any intermediate subnetwork. So far, this book has discussed the details of Layer 3 QoS mechanisms in RSVP/IntServ-aware, routed subnetworks and DiffServ routed subnetworks, and Layer 2 mechanisms in 802 subnetworks. Many of the existing subnetworks can be categorized either as a wide area routed network or a local area 802 network, and they support QoS via the mechanisms discussed in previous chapters. However, certain Layer 2 subnetworks that are not 802 networks support low-layer QoS mechanisms specific to the particular subnet media. Examples of such subnetworks are ATM networks, Frame Relay networks, slow dial-up links, cable modem networks, P1394, wireless, and others. It is desirable for Layer 3 (and higher-layer) QoS mechanisms to utilize the underlying Layer 2 QoS mechanisms appropriate for the media over which they are operating.

This chapter discusses QoS mechanisms in some of the widely deployed Layer 2 subnetworks, including ATM, Frame Relay, and relatively slow dial-up links. Because RSVP was presented in Chapter 4, "Integrated Services," as a high-level, abstract signaling protocol that can unify disparate QoS mechanisms, special emphasis is placed on the integration of RSVP and the Layer 2 QoS mechanisms described. In particular, the work of the ISSLL working group of the IETF in mapping RSVP and Integrated Services (IntServ) to ATM (ISATM) and to slow dial-up links (ISSLOW) will be discussed. In addition, because Differentiated Services (DiffServ) is a fairly abstract Layer 3 mechanism, the Layer 2 mechanisms described in this chapter can also be used to support DiffServ QoS, which in turn may be controlled by RSVP signaling.

8.1   ATM and QoS

Asynchronous Transfer Mode (ATM) is a Layer 2 technology that arrived on the scene in the late 1980s. In many ways, it promised the ultimate QoS functionality. The combination of cell scheduling at the link layer, circuit switching, and a specialized signaling protocol (ITU standard Q.2931) were to offer a variety of services including (among others) best-effort, high-bandwidth variable bit rate service, and low latency, constant bit rate service.

> **Note**
>
> ATM cells are small, fixed-size (53 bytes) link-layer packets or frames. Higher-layer packets (such as IP packets) are *segmented* into these cells at an ATM transmitter and then are *reassembled* at the receiver.

ATM deployment fell short of expectations. For one, it is not ubiquitously deployed. ATM technology can be found today primarily in the large backbone networks. It is used mostly by large service providers and to a lesser degree in large campus networks. It does not typically extend to the home or the desktop (except for certain custom applications in the context of ADSL). For another, it has been deployed in a manner that does not leverage ATM's QoS capabilities. Typical ATM networks provide permanent circuits akin to traditional leased lines with no particular attention to QoS requirements.

Despite this state of affairs, numerous schemes and examples illustrate the application of ATM technology in QoS-enabling networks. This section first introduces fundamental ATM concepts and then describes the schemes by which they can be applied to support the QoS-enabled network.

8.1.1   Fundamental ATM Concepts

The fundamental ATM concepts include the decomposition of data packets into small cells, scheduled by hardware (in the data plane) and the signaling and switching intelligence to provide QoS-enabled circuits (in the control plane). These are described in further detail in this section.

8.1.1.1   Scheduling Cells

Chapter 3, "Queuing Mechanisms," described various traffic-handling schemes. For the most part, these used queue-servicing algorithms to transmit *packets* on an interface in a specific order. Such packet-scheduling schemes impose a constraint on the best-case latency bound that can be offered on the interface. To clarify this point, assume that a packet of the maximum allowable size from Flow A has just been submitted for transmission on the interface. Some infinitesimally small time later, a high-priority packet arrives on Flow B.

This packet must wait P/r seconds before it can be transmitted (P is the maximum allowable packet size in bits per second, and r is the interface transmission rate). As a result, when the unit of scheduling is the packet, the best latency bound that can be guaranteed is proportional to the maximum allowable packet size on the link. In the case of IP networks, packets that are passed to the link layer (Layer 2) may be as large as 64KB (although most Layer 2 media impose significantly smaller maximum packet sizes). These are generally not fragmented by Layer 2 links.

When IP packets are submitted to an ATM link layer, they are *segmented* into cells. These cells are 53 bytes in size (significantly smaller than the maximum packet size supported by most media). ATM network devices schedule on a *cell-by-cell* basis, as opposed to a *packet-by-packet* basis. As a result, ATM networks are capable of offering very low latency bounds (for a given line rate). This approach is analogous to the description of ISSLOW scheduling, which is discussed later in this chapter. When the ATM cells arrive at the egress point of the ATM network, they are reassembled into packets. The process of segmenting and reassembling packets at ATM ingress and egress points is known as *segmentation and reassembly* (SAR).

The ATM Cell Tax

One of the often-cited disadvantages of ATM is known as the ATM *cell tax*. Each ATM packet requires a header, describing the circuit with which the cell is associated and various other required parameters. Because the ATM cell is so small, a significant fraction of each packet is used for this header. As a result, this fraction cannot be used for data. Depending on the way in which packets are mapped to cells, this cell tax can typically range from 10 to 20% overhead. This overhead compromises the efficiency with which network resources can be used.

However, the complaints about ATM cell tax are somewhat misleading. Voice over IP technology can waste 40 bytes of header to send 20 bytes of data, *regardless* of the underlying link layer. Achieving low latency on any packetized media requires small packets or cells at the cost of increased overhead.

8.1.1.2 Circuit Switching and Signaling

ATM is a circuit-switched technology. Before data can be exchanged over an ATM link between two peers, a circuit must be set up between the peers. This circuit typically spans a number of intermediate ATM *switches*. In ATM terminology, the circuit is known as a *virtual circuit* (VC). At each ATM switch, a number is assigned to the circuit. Subsequently, as cells are transmitted on the circuit, they are marked with this number (the *VC identifier*, or VCI).

VCs may be *permanent* (PVCs) or *switched* (SVCs). PVCs are established in a relatively static manner by management intervention. SVCs are set up dynamically by signaling messages from ATM endpoints. In the case of SVCs, the transmitting peer generates signaling messages that are sent toward the receiving peer. These messages identify the receiving peer and describe the type of service required for the circuit. Each ATM switch along the route between the two peers reviews the messages. Each switch determines whether the circuit request is admissible (based on link-layer policies and resource availability) and, if so, how to route it onward toward the receiving peer. If the request is admissible at all switches along the path, the SVC is established.

VCs may be *point-to-point* (P-P) or *point-to-multipoint* (P-MP). P-P VCs carry traffic from a single sender to a single receiver. P-MP VCs carry traffic from a single sender to a set of receivers. P-MP VCs require ATM devices to replicate cells for transmission to each endpoint.

The circuit-switched nature of ATM is in stark contrast to traditional Layer 3 IP networking. IP itself is completely connectionless—packets are routed toward their destination one at a time, based on the destination address in the packet header. When TCP is used over IP, the concept of a connection exists, but it is between the sender and the receiver only. The intervening network devices have no knowledge of its existence.

Benefits of ATM's Connection Orientation and Signaling

The connection-oriented nature of ATM offers certain benefits. These are most apparent in the case of SVCs (that are established dynamically via signaling) but are also apparent in the case of PVCs. At connection setup time, the sender (whether an SVC or a PVC) or the network manager can ask for specific QoS parameters. Switches along the circuit path review the request and admit it, subject to resource availability. If the resources are available (and the requester is entitled to these resources), the request is admitted, a circuit is established, and resources are committed to it. Subsequent circuits will be established only to the extent that they do not compromise the service offered to existing circuits. Switches are the admission control agents that admit or reject requests for service in the ATM network. The process of admitting or rejecting a request for a specific service level is referred to in ATM terminology as *connection admission control* (CAC).

Compromises Arising from ATM's Connection Orientation

However, there are compromises to the connection orientation of ATM. For one, as is the case with any circuit-switched network, when resources are committed to a circuit, they are not available for use by other traffic (the degree to which this is true varies based on the specific ATM service type). This problem is alleviated in the case of SVCs. However, in this case, there is the obvious overhead associated with signaling. It requires processing resources in network devices and in hosts. In addition, because data cannot be sent until a circuit is established, the first packets sent to a new destination may incur significant latency.

Statistical Multiplexing

This particular issue is less significant in the case of ATM than it is, for example, in the case of traditional leased lines. ATM is actually somewhat of a hybrid between circuit-switched and packet-switched technology. Whereas leased lines and other traditional circuit-switched approaches tend to dedicate resources exclusively to the circuit, ATM affords some flexibility in doing so. Because ATM switches are really switching on a cell-by-cell basis, they are capable of taking advantage of lulls in resource demands on a particular circuit and shifting those resources to other circuits.

As such, ATM networks are well suited to *statistically multiplexing* resources among multiple circuits offering different service types. This feature enables ATM networks to offer both the QoS available in circuit-switched networks and the efficiency of resource utilization associated with packet-switched networks. The degree to which statistical multiplexing can be applied to ATM networks depends on the specific mix of ATM services being offered.

Analogy to RSVP/IntServ

Ironically, ATM's circuit orientation mirrors the RSVP/IntServ model. The notion of a reservation is inherent both to ATM and to IntServ. ATM employs a protocol to establish reservations; the RSVP protocol can be used to establish reservations. The RSVP notion of a reservation is quite a bit looser than that of ATM. Senders do not require an RSVP reservation to be in place before sending traffic. In addition the IP packets sent on an RSVP session are not routed on a circuit, but rather are based on destination address. Nonetheless, the commonality between the two protocols' reservation orientations makes ATM in many ways very suitable to supporting RSVP-style QoS.

In addition to the inherent connection orientation shared by ATM Layer 2 technology and RSVP Layer 3 technology, the two share a common multicast capability. Although ATM's support for multicast is somewhat awkward, it is useable for the support of RSVP multicast sessions. The mapping of RSVP to ATM will be explored in depth later in this chapter, in the sections "Mapping RSVP and IntServ to ATM VCs" and "Managing VCs to Support RSVP QoS."

8.1.2 *Mapping IP to ATM*

ATM cells and ATM signaling are Layer 2 concepts. The ATM layer is ultimately used to support higher-layer protocol traffic. Note that certain applications are written to *native* ATM (using no intermediate protocols), but these tend to be nonstandard applications that are not broadly deployed. The vast majority of traffic carried over ATM networks today is IP traffic.

Some of the challenging issues surrounding the application of ATM to higher-layer protocols such as IP include the determination of when to create a VC between two endpoints, what service type the VC should be, and when it should be torn down. Because IP is generally a connectionless and best-effort protocol, it offers little help to the underlying link layer in making this determination. The following paragraphs initially describe the various service types that are offered by ATM VCs and the traffic to which they are suited. Later, the text tackles the problem of determining when to establish and when to tear down VCs.

8.1.2.1 *ATM Service Types*

VCs are established for specific service types. The required service type is specified in sender-originated signaling messages that set up the VC. Most service type specifications must include quantitative parameters that further describe the required service (such as token bucket parameters). The description of service types that follows will show that the quantitative ATM services map reasonably well to the abstract IntServ services described in Chapter 4. However, because of the quantitative nature of certain ATM services, they may not map as well to the qualitative DiffServ service types.

ATM services focus on resource *reservation*, setting aside a fixed amount of resources. For the most part, they lack the concept of *prioritization*. So, although it is a simple matter to set up a VC to carry 384Kbps of traffic with low latency, it is difficult to divide an ATM link between a number of VCs with a strict-priority relationship between them. Similarly, it is difficult to implement a weighted fair queuing type scheme using ATM services.

ATM networks apply traffic-conditioning functions similar to those described in Chapter 5, "RSVP," in the context of DiffServ. However, whereas DiffServ networks police, shape, and schedule on a packet-by-packet basis, ATM networks do so on a cell-by-cell basis. The function of policing is referred to in ATM networks as *usage parameter control* (UPC).

> **Note**
>
> ATM includes the notion of *cell loss priority* (CLP). Packets marked for CLP will be dropped before other packets during congestion. As such, CLP is analogous to the different drop-priority levels in the AF PHB group.

Constant Bit Rate (CBR)

Constant bit rate service is fairly self-explanatory. A CBR VC carries traffic at a constant rate with generally low latency and low drop probability. Required latency bounds and drop probabilities are specified in the form of *cell transfer delay* (CTD) and *cell loss ratio* (CLR), respectively. CBR service is parameterized by the *peak cell rate* (PCR), which is the constant rate at which traffic will be carried. Traffic offered in excess of the PCR is policed. Policing of nonconforming traffic in ATM networks takes one of two forms; nonconforming cells may be dropped immediately or, alternatively, may be marked for *cell loss priority* (CLP), indicating that this cell may be dropped later in the network if congestion is encountered.

Strictly speaking, CBR service does not necessarily offer low latency. It offers to deliver data at a constant rate. As such, it can be used whenever synchronization of the traffic source and destination is required. For example, CBR is well suited to carry constant rate streaming video. Typically, CBR service also offers quite low latency and therefore is also suitable for interactive traffic, such as telephony. CBR service is often used to emulate traditional telephony circuits (*circuit emulation service*) or leased lines. As such, it can be used to carry any kind of traffic that a leased line might be used for. Note, however, that CBR dedicates resources to a VC that cannot be reclaimed for other VCs (except, to a limited degree, for the less deterministic services described later in the chapter). For this reason, it tends to be expensive and tends not be cost-effective for bursty traffic. In addition, CBR service requires per-VC policing or shaping, which is costly in terms of performance.

CBR service maps well to the IntServ Guaranteed Service. It also maps well to the DiffServ virtual leased line (VLL) service and can be used to emulate the EF PHB (see Chapter 6, "Differentiated Services," for a discussion of the EF, or expedited forwarding, PHB).

Real-Time Variable Bit Rate (rtVBR)

Real-time VBR is suitable for many of the same applications as CBR but is generally more cost-effective. VBR, whether real-time or not, is designed to accommodate traffic that varies in rate. Most traffic is not constant in rate but tends to be somewhat bursty. This is true for compressed voice and video. VBR service allocates resources statistically, based on the assumption that across a large number of VCs, bursts will be uncorrelated. As a result, VBR service can be offered at a significantly lower cost than CBR service. Real-time VBR service is parameterized by a peak cell rate (PCR), a *sustained cell rate* (SCR), and a maximum burst size. The token bucket parameters associated with IntServ services map naturally to these ATM parameters. In addition, real-time VBR service offers a bounded cell transfer delay (bounded latency).

Real-time VBR service maps well to the IntServ Guaranteed Service. It can also be used to emulate the more quantitative applications of the DiffServ AF PHB group—specifically, route-constrained services with quantitative admission control. (For a discussion of the AF, or assured forwarding, PHB group, see Chapter 6.)

Non-Real-Time Variable Bit Rate (nrtVBR)

Non-real-time VBR differs from real-time VBR only in the absence of delay bound parameters. It is suitable for the transport of variable bit rate traffic that requires a corresponding amount of bandwidth but that is tolerant of varying delay bounds. As such, it may be used for streaming video or audio. It may also be used for qualitative traffic that requires better-than-best-effort service. It is not suitable for interactive audio such as telephony. Non-real-time VBR is parameterized by a PCR, an SCR, and a maximum burst size. Because the guarantees that it offers are less stringent than those of the real-time VBR service, it supports a greater degree of statistical multiplexing and can be offered at a lower cost.

Non-real-time VBR maps well to the IntServ Controlled Load Service. It can also be used to support the DiffServ Olympic services that are based on the DiffServ AF PHB group. (See Chapter 6 for a discussion of the DiffServ Olympic service.)

Available Bit Rate (ABR)

As implied by the name, available bit rate service offers varying bandwidth and delay, depending on current network conditions. It assures a minimum bandwidth known as the *minimum cell rate* (MCR), but it provides higher bandwidth as resources are available. It offers no guarantees regarding CLR. ABR service should not be used for any traffic that is delay-sensitive. It may be used to provide better-than-best-effort service.

Because ABR service does assure an MCR, it can be mapped to the IntServ Controlled Load Service. In doing so, the MCR is selected to be equal to the token rate (r) of the controlled load token bucket parameters. ABR can also be used to emulate certain uses of the AF PHB group.

Unspecified Bit Rate (UBR)

UBR offers no quantifiable service. It offers the same level of service that is associated with traditional best-effort service. As such, it is widely used.

8.1.3   Using ATM to Provide QoS

This section describes various applications of ATM technology in the support of QoS. Although ATM networks are ideally suited to this purpose, their full potential is rarely exploited. The ISSLL working group of the IETF has formalized the use of ATM networks to support the RSVP/IntServ model. Other than this, there are various custom applications of ATM to support QoS, but no standard ones.

As described earlier in this chapter, ATM provides the underlying technology necessary to support QoS in its capability to create VCs for particular service levels with associated quantitative parameters. However, there are few guidelines on when to establish VCs of a given type to support higher-layer QoS requirements. Similarly, there are few guidelines on the mapping of higher-layer QoS requirements to specific quantitative parameters of a VC. The challenges in using ATM to support higher-layer QoS include the following:

- Determining when to establish VCs and when to tear them down

- Determining the appropriate service type for which to establish a VC

- Determining the quantitative parameters appropriate for the VC

- Directing the appropriate subset of higher-layer traffic to the appropriate underlying VC

8.1.3.1   Common Usage—Point-to-Point PVCs

The most common usage of ATM is in providing a single point-to-point PVC between two endpoints at a fixed capacity. Many carriers use ATM in this manner to offer a service similar to leased-line service or Frame Relay circuits. The customer is offered a PVC between specified endpoints with a certain rated capacity and a certain service type (typically CBR). In this application, there is no question as to when to establish the VC. PVCs are created up-front at service provisioning time just as leased lines or Frame Relay circuits are established. Because there is only a single PVC between the two endpoints, there is also no question as to which VC should be used to carry a given higher-layer QoS flow.

From a QoS perspective, such service is no different than leased-line service or Frame Relay circuits. If a customer wants to use this service to support different service levels between sites, the customer must multiplex traffic corresponding to different QoS flows on the single PVC. QoS can be supported at Layer 3 using IntServ or DiffServ packet scheduling and admission control approaches. In this model, the total capacity of the underlying ATM PVCs may be reflected to higher-layer QoS components for the purpose of admission control. However, there is no awareness at the ATM layer of the distinct QoS flows that are scheduled above it. This usage is illustrated in Figure 8.1.

Figure 8.1   Using Point-to-Point PVCs to Provide QoS

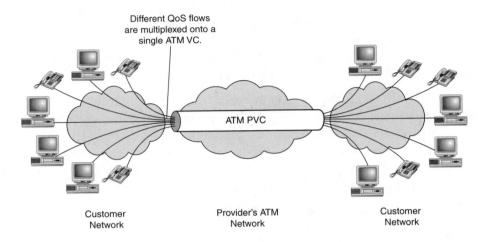

This application of ATM as an underlying technology offers no direct QoS-related benefit to the user of the service. However, it may enable the service provider to manage the network more efficiently and more dynamically than would be possible in the case of traditional leased lines or Frame Relay networks. As a result, it may offer certain indirect QoS-related benefits to the user. For example, the provider may respond to changes in demand for resources between certain endpoints of the provider network by increasing or decreasing the capacity of the VC. Such changes might be triggered by per-conversation RSVP messages arriving at the edges of the ATM network or by changes in traffic arrival rates, and can be effected by administratively or automatically reprovisioning the PVC.

8.1.3.2 Multiple Point-to-Point VCs

A slightly more sophisticated use of ATM in supporting QoS relies on provisioning multiple PVCs between two endpoints. These PVCs may be of the same or of different service types. The customer uses the different PVCs to support higher-layer QoS flows having different service requirements. Because PVCs are used, there is no question as to when to establish a VC. However, because multiple VCs are used, the customer must determine which VC should be used to carry different higher-layer traffic flows. This demultiplexing or mapping function is typically provided by some sort of edge device at the ingress to the ATM network. If the edge device is RSVP-aware, it may listen to RSVP signaling to identify different traffic flows. It then maps each flow to the appropriate VC based on the signaled QoS parameters. Simpler devices map higher-layer packets to underlying PVCs based on the DSCP or 802.1 user_priority marked in a packet.

In one application of this approach, two equivalent PVCs may be provisioned between peer sites. The edge device directs a limited amount of high-priority traffic between the sites to one PVC and then directs the remainder of traffic to the other. Using this approach, the customer obtains different service characteristics by controlling the loading of each PVC. This usage is illustrated in Figure 8.2.

Figure 8.2   Providing Different Service by Controlling Relative Loading of Equivalent VCs

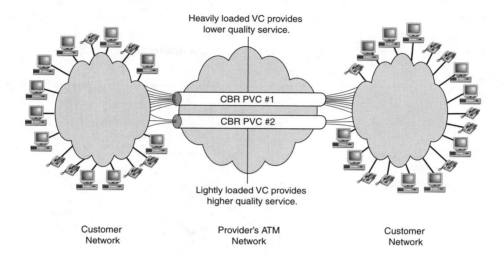

An alternate approach is to negotiate PVCs for different service types between peer sites, such as a CBR PVC and a UBR PVC. The customer then uses the CBR PVC for traffic requiring higher-quality service and the UBR PVC for best-effort traffic. The use of multiple ATM PVCs to support QoS in this manner are illustrated in Figure 8.3.

Figure 8.3   Using Multiple PVCs of Different Types to Support Different Service Qualities

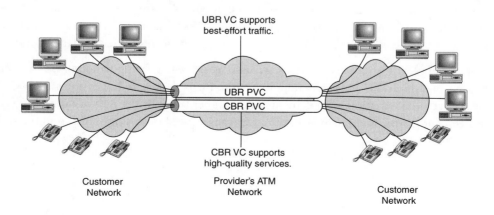

8.1.3.3 *Using Soft PVCs to Support Aggregated QoS Flows*

Most ATM service providers today do not offer end-to-end SVC service. To do so would require them to process customer-generated signaling messages. This would increase the complexity of the customer/provider interface and would expose the provider to malicious or erroneous customer-generated signaling messages. Instead, providers offer only a PVC service interface to the customer. In certain cases, the provider may present a PVC interface to the customer while using SVCs within the provider's network. This approach enables the provider to realize some of the benefits of SVCs (such as dynamic reprovisioning of the network), without rendering the network vulnerable to signaling from the customer. This is referred to as the *soft PVC* model and is illustrated in Figure 8.4.

Figure 8.4	Soft PVCs

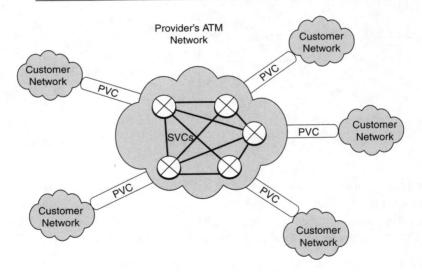

From the customer's perspective, the soft PVC model is no different from the end-to-end PVC model described previously. However, soft PVCs make it easier for the service provider to adjust the capacity of the customer's service in response to changes in demand.

In the examples illustrated so far, VCs are used as aggregate traffic-handling mechanisms. In the case of a single VC between endpoints, all traffic is aggregated onto the same VC, and any service differentiation is implemented at a higher layer. In the case of multiple VCs between endpoints, multiple conversations are aggregated onto some small number of VCs.

8.1.3.4 *Mapping QoS Flows to Dedicated VCs*

ATM networks may also be used to provide per-conversation traffic handling. In this case, each higher-layer conversation is mapped to a dedicated VC having the QoS characteristics appropriate for the conversation. Because individual conversations tend to be fleeting in nature, PVCs are not well suited to this approach. Instead, SVCs should be set up and torn down as necessary. Although this mode of operation provides superior traffic isolation between flows, it also carries the performance and scalability concerns associated with per-conversation traffic handling and signaling.

8.1.3.5 *Mapping RSVP and IntServ to ATM VCs*

When per-conversation traffic handling is deemed appropriate, the device at the edge of the ATM network must use some means to detect the start and stop time of each conversation and to determine the appropriate parameters with which to establish the corresponding VC. RSVP signaling is ideally suited to this approach. It provides clear indications of the start and stop time of higher-layer QoS flows. It also provides quantitative parameters describing the required QoS for each flow.

The ISSLL working group has published a number of RFCs discussing the mapping of RSVP signaling and IntServ parameters to the creation of ATM VCs with the appropriate ATM service type and parameters [RFC 2382], [RFC 2379], [RFC 2381], [RFC 2380]. These documents address two components of this mapping: the mechanics of establishing and tearing down the appropriate VCs (*VC management*), as well as the mapping from IntServ service parameters to ATM service parameters (*QoS translation*). An in-depth treatment of the topic of mapping RSVP/IntServ to ATM is beyond the scope of this book, but a brief overview is presented in the following paragraphs. For further details, refer to the relevant RFCs.

8.1.3.6 *Managing VCs to Support RSVP QoS*

One model for VC management in support of RSVP assumes the existence of PVCs between all communicating endpoints. One advantage of this model is that no VC setup latency is incurred in the transmission of RSVP control messages or data on RSVP flows. However, this model does not lend itself to the provision of a dedicated VC per RSVP flow. As a result, it offers poor traffic isolation between flows. In addition, because of the relatively static nature of PVCs, this model does not exploit one of the key advantages of ATM: the capability to dynamically adjust the required resources along a given path. This results in inefficient use of network resources. In this sense, the PVC model is no different in its support for RSVP than traditional point-to-point networks. The remainder of this section focuses on an alternate model, which uses SVCs in support of RSVP.

At first glance, there appears to be an inherent incompatibility between the receiver-centric nature of RSVP and the fact that senders typically create ATM SVCs. However, there is actually no incompatibility. In standard RSVP operation, senders commit resources on each RSVP-aware interface as the RESV message arrives at the interface. In a similar manner, RSVP-aware ATM edge devices are capable of creating VCs to the downstream egress point of the ATM network from which RESV messages arrive. These edge devices may be Layer 2 devices implementing ATM LAN Emulation (LANE, discussed later in this chapter in the section "IP over ATM and LAN Emulation") or may be ATM-attached routers. The operation of ATM-attached routers with respect to RSVP is simpler than that of LANE edge devices. The operation of ATM-attached routers in support of RSVP is illustrated in Figure 8.5.

Figure 8.5   ATM-Attached Routers Create ATM VCs in Response to RESV Messages Arriving from Downstream

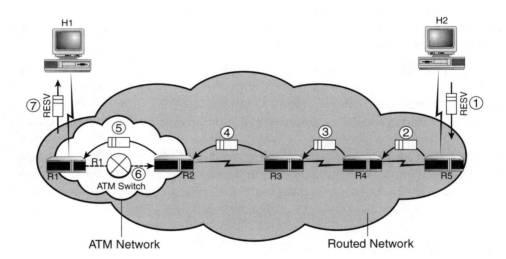

Note

In the case of ATM-attached routers, the downstream egress point from the ATM network typically coincides with the downstream next IP hop. In this case, the VC established by the sender terminates at the egress point from the ATM network. There are various scenarios (that are beyond the scope of this discussion) in which this may not be the case.

Figure 8.5 illustrates an end-to-end path that consists of a non-ATM network, concatenated with an ATM network. An RSVP PATH message has been sent from H1 to H2. In (1), H2 responds with an RSVP RESV message. When this message arrives at R5, the router reserves resources on its downstream interface. The RESV message is then sent upstream to R4, R3, and R2, in sequence. Each of these reserves resources on its downstream interfaces as the RESV message arrives. R2 and R1 are ATM-attached routers. When R2 forwards the RESV message upstream, it is intercepted by the previous (upstream) Layer 3 RSVP-aware hop, which is R1 (5). R1 must reserve resources downstream, on its ATM interface. It does so by establishing a VC to the next (downstream) RSVP-aware hop, which is R2 (6). The intervening ATM switches participate in the establishment of the VC but are unaware of the RSVP messages that triggered the VC establishment. In (7), R1 forwards the RESV message upstream toward H1, in conventional RSVP fashion.

A number of interesting issues arise when considering the management of SVCs in support of RSVP reservations. These are discussed in the following paragraphs.

Multicast Models

ATM does not naturally lend itself to multicast in the manner that LAN networks do. ATM networks support multicast by explicitly establishing many point-to-point VCs or one or more point-to-multipoint VCs (one for each multicast sender). This mode of multicast support creates a number of challenges when applied to RSVP.

First of all, there is a concern with respect to RSVP message implosion. In a large ATM network with many receivers, the number of receiver-generated RESV messages arriving at the ATM ingress node may overwhelm the available processing resources. This is illustrated in Figure 8.6.

Figure 8.6 illustrates a large ATM network with many directly connected receivers. The receivers generate RESV messages that are sent upstream. The next RSVP-aware hop in the upstream direction is the ATM-attached router, R1. In a fully routed network, the ATM switches illustrated within the ATM network would be routers. These would merge RESV messages (as described in Chapter 5) so that only some small number of RESV messages would arrive at R1. However, in the ATM network illustrated, the ATM switches are RSVP-unaware. Consequently, each receiver's RESV message arrives at R1, potentially overwhelming the edge device.

Of course, this problem exists in large ATM networks regardless of whether they support RSVP. Consequently, it is expected that the network will be engineered accordingly.

Figure 8.6   RESV Message Implosion

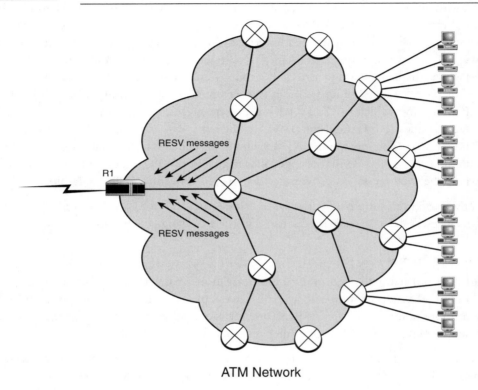

ATM Network

Another challenge in the support of RSVP multicast is RSVP's receiver heterogeneity. Receivers joined to a single RSVP multicast session may have different QoS requirements. In the simplest case, there may be two groups of receivers: those requiring QoS and those satisfied with best-effort service. In more complicated cases, different receivers may require reservations for a range of different capacities. The ISSLL RFCs describe four different approaches in support of heterogeneous multicast reservations.

In the *full heterogeneity* model, a separate P-MP VC is established from the ATM ingress point for each level of QoS required. Although this model supports each receiver's service requirements exactly, it may result in significant waste of resources because it requires the device at the ATM ingress point to replicate traffic onto each of the P-MP VCs. The full heterogeneity model is illustrated in Figure 8.7.

Figure 8.7 Full Heterogeneity Model

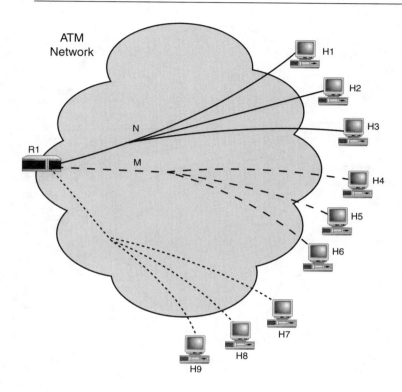

In Figure 8.7, H1 through H3 issue reservations for *N* resources. H4 through H6 issue reservations for *M* resources (where $N > M$). H7 through H9 are best-effort receivers and do not issue reservations at all. To accommodate this receiver heterogeneity, the ATM-attached router R1 creates three multicast VCs, one with a capacity of M, another with a capacity of N, and a third best-effort VC.

A more efficient model is the *limited heterogeneity* model. In this model, exactly two P-MP VCs are created at the ATM ingress point. One is a best-effort VC; the other is a QoS VC. The cost of the increased efficiency of this model is that only a single level of QoS is supported. If a single receiver wants to increase the capacity of its reservation, its success depends on the availability of equivalent resources to every other receiver in the session. The limited heterogeneity model is illustrated in Figure 8.8.

Figure 8.8   Limited Heterogeneity Model

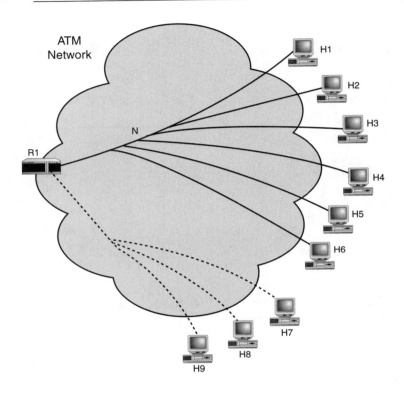

In Figure 8.8, a single P-MP QoS VC is created to accommodate all QoS receivers (H1 through H6). It is created with a capacity of N, to accommodate the most demanding receivers. In addition, a single best-effort P-MP VC is created to accommodate the best-effort receivers.

The *homogeneous* model simply establishes a single P-MP VC at the service level required by the most demanding receiver. This model is illustrated in Figure 8.9.

In this model, there is no best-effort VC. Receivers H1 through H9 are all supported with a single P-MP VC with the capacity to support the most demanding receiver.

The homogeneous model is similar to RSVP operation over LANs in the sense that it allows *free riders*. A free rider is a receiver that requests either very few resources or best-effort service, but benefits from a higher service level requested by another receiver in the same session. The free rider may benefit from resources paid for by another receiver. Although this may in itself be a tolerable problem, there may be more dire problems with the homogeneous approach. In particular, if resources are not available to support any receiver's requirements, the reservation request may fail, resulting in no VC being established. As a result, receivers will not even be capable of receiving best-effort service. This is not a problem in non-ATM networks because best-effort service is always available.

| Figure 8.9 | The Homogeneous Model |

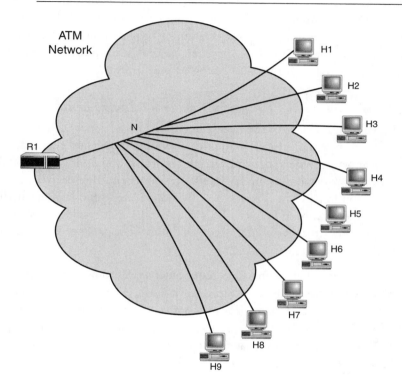

To address this problem, a variation on the homogeneous model is proposed: the *modified homogeneous* model. In the modified homogeneous model, a single P-MP QoS VC is created to all receivers, if possible. If it is not possible to serve all receivers with the same QoS, a best-effort VC is created to any receivers that cannot be served with the required QoS. In this case, the modified homogeneous model degenerates to the limited heterogeneity model described previously. The modified homogeneity model offers the benefit of the homogeneous model in that less cell replication is required in the ATM network when all receivers can be served with a single P-MP VC, yet it does not suffer from the potential denial of best-effort service. Of course, when it is not possible to serve all receivers with a single P-MP QoS VC, additional replication will be required to serve the best-effort receivers.

The fourth model proposed for the support of RSVP multicast is referred to in the RFCs as the *aggregation* model. This model assumes a mesh of relatively high-capacity pre-existing PVCs spanning the ATM network. These may be limited to P-P VCs (in which case, they are managed much as point-to-point links are managed in traditional leased-line or Frame Relay networks) or may include P-MP VCs. In this case, multiple multicast flows with differing QoS requirements are simply multiplexed over the PVC mesh. This model was discussed previously in the sections "Common Usage—Point-to-Point PVCs" and "Multiple Point-to-Point VCs." This approach carries with it both the benefits and the compromises associated with PVCs, as discussed previously.

Receiver Transitions and Changes in Resource Requirements

Two additional issues surface in the management of VCs to support RSVP multicast. One issue is that of receiver transitions. As multicast group membership changes, it is possible that a receiver must be added (or removed) to (or from) one multicast VC and removed (or added) from (or to) another multicast VC. In this event, the receiver may experience a transient condition in which it is receiving either duplicate traffic or none at all. Guidelines call for receivers to be moved between VCs in a manner that results in the receipt of duplicate traffic rather than no traffic. Receivers must be capable of handling the resulting transient traffic duplication.

The other issue is that of changing QoS requirements. Although RSVP naturally supports changing QoS requirements on an existing reservation, ATM does not. To modify the QoS between two ATM endpoints, it is necessary to tear down the existing VC (or, in the case of P-MP VCs, a branch of the VC) and to set up a new VC with the required QoS parameters. This complicates VC management and leads to various transient conditions similar to those associated with receiver transitions.

Carrying RSVP Signaling Messages

A number of options are available for handling RSVP control messages. Two primary approaches are possible. In one, RSVP control messages are handled on the same VC as data traffic. In the other, a separate VC is created to handle RSVP control messages. In selecting the preferred approach, the following issues should be considered.

If RSVP control messages are carried on the same VC as data traffic, they should be carried on a data VC that offers a preferred class of service. However, these VCs generally police nonconforming traffic. Consequently, if excess data traffic is submitted on these VCs, it may cause RSVP traffic to be deemed nonconforming and to be discarded. Discarding of RSVP control messages could result in the VCs being torn down and re-established frequently. This is clearly undesirable.

The alternate approach, in which dedicated VCs are created to carry RSVP traffic, could require a significantly larger number of VCs than might otherwise be necessary. In addition, a setup latency would be experienced by RSVP control messages as the corresponding VC is being established.

Regardless of which approach is used, it will be necessary to establish at least UBR or ABR VCs in advance of RSVP signaling to carry routing traffic, multicast joins, the first RSVP messages for a session, and other miscellaneous traffic.

8.1.3.7 QoS Translation

The previous paragraphs discussed issues related to the management of QoS VCs. The other component of the RSVP-to-ATM mapping relates to the determination of the appropriate ATM service types and QoS parameters to support an RSVP request for a specific service and associated parameters. The table in Figure 8.10 tabulates the recommended mappings from IntServ service types to ATM service types, per [RFC 2381].

Figure 8.10   IntServ-to-ATM Service Type Mappings

IntServ service type \ ATM service type	CBR	rtVBR	nrtVBR	ABR	UBR
Guaranteed	✓	✓	✗	✗	✗
Controlled Load	Note 1	Note 1	✓	✓	✗
Best-Effort	Note 1	Note 1	✓	✓	✓

Note1: These ATM services can be used to support the required IntServ service. However, these are not the most efficient service mappings. See [RFC 2381] for further details.

8.1.4   IP over ATM and LAN Emulation

IP over ATM and LAN emulation (LANE) are two basic mechanisms for mapping traditional network services to ATM networks. These mechanisms were developed initially with no concern for particular QoS requirements. IP over ATM enables the use of ATM media to support IP traffic and deals with such issues as the resolution of IP addresses to ATM addresses, routing of IP traffic, and when to set up and tear down VCs. LANE describes how ATM networks can be used to provide traditional LAN functionality, suitable for any higher-layer protocol. LANE deals with issues such as the provision of LAN multicast services using ATM as well as when to set up and tear down VCs.

Because the developers of these mechanisms were not initially concerned with QoS, they both assumed a model of a single VC carrying all traffic between endpoints. As edge devices detect traffic addressed to an endpoint to which there is no existing VC, a new VC is created. After a period of inactivity on the VC, it is automatically torn down. This approach does not lend itself to supporting the multiple varying levels of QoS that may be required between a single pair of endpoints. Certain implementations of IP over ATM evolved to enable the creation of multiple VCs between endpoints by applying heuristics based on the monitoring of traffic between the endpoints. The second version of LAN Emulation (LANE 2.0) acknowledges the need to support QoS by establishing multiple VCs between endpoints, but it says nothing about when and how to create these VCs. The guidelines for supporting RSVP/IntServ-style QoS recommended by the ISSLL working group of the IETF may be applied both to IP over ATM and to LANE models.

8.2   Frame Relay and QoS

Frame Relay is a wide-area link-layer technology that came on the scene in the late 1980s and early 1990s. It is particularly interesting from a QoS perspective because it is one of the few commonly available network services that relies on shared infrastructure (with the commensurate cost savings) for which providers offer a service level agreement (SLA) that commits to certain QoS parameters. The other obvious example of such a service is wide-area ATM service. ATM and Frame Relay wide-area services are similar in many respects. The next subsections introduce basic Frame Relay concepts and how these can be applied to support higher-layer QoS mechanisms such as DiffServ and RSVP/IntServ. Note that, unlike ATM, the IETF has not defined a model for using Frame Relay to support IntServ.

8.2.1   Overview of Frame Relay

Frame Relay networks are built by interconnecting a mesh of leased lines and Frame Relay switches, as illustrated in Figure 8.11.

Figure 8.11   A Frame Relay Network

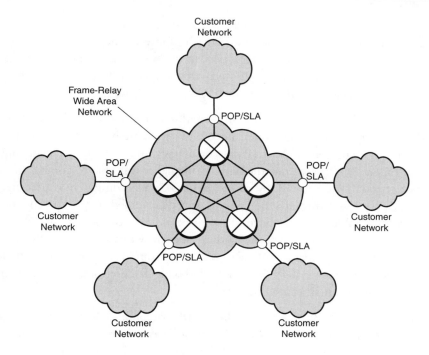

Customers negotiate point-to-point service with the Frame Relay provider. To support the service, the provider provisions a Frame Relay *virtual circuit* (VC) on the physical leased-line mesh between the provider's endpoints (*points of presence*, or *POPs*) that are physically closest to the customer's endpoints. These VCs are very similar to ATM VCs. However, they carry packets or frames (occasionally packet fragments) rather than cells. The service offered by the provider is characterized by an SLA that specifies quantitative QoS parameters. The provider is able to support the SLA by policing customer traffic at the ingress to the Frame Relay network and by controlling the path along which the customer's traffic flows.

Note

Note that, similar to ATM networks, most Frame Relay networks today support only PVCs. A small number of Frame Relay networks do support SVCs.

8.2.1.1 Comparison Between Frame Relay Networks and Routed Networks

At an abstract level, this type of network provides functionality very similar to that provided by a DiffServ network consisting of a mesh of interconnected routers and offering service characterized by static SLAs. However, at the time that Frame Relay began to proliferate, there were advantages to Frame Relay that enabled it to offer higher performance and more deterministic performance than an IP-routed network.

For one, frames were switched rather than routed. As in ATM networks, the frames were switched based on a local VC identifier marked in the frame header. At the time, the hop-by-hop routing lookup required for IP networks was slower than frame switching. For another, in Frame Relay networks, the network manager was able to control the path that frames took through the network by provisioning VCs accordingly. In routed networks, at the time, the path taken through the network was determined by the current state of the network's routing tables and was beyond the direct control of the network manager. For this reason, it was easier to control the loading of each switch in a Frame Relay network than it was to control the loading of each router in a routed network. Consequently, the service provided by a Frame Relay VC could be relatively deterministic in comparison to the service offered by an IP routed network.

In the years since Frame Relay was introduced, IP switching, MPLS, and related technologies are making it possible both to route IP traffic at ever-increasing speeds and to apply sophisticated traffic engineering to control the loading of IP routers or switches. Consequently, the advantages of Frame Relay over IP-routed networks are disappearing.

8.2.1.2 Comparison Between Frame Relay Networks and Leased-Line Networks

A customer might consider obtaining similar service characteristics simply by interconnecting sites via traditional leased lines, as illustrated in Figure 8.12.

Although such a network would indeed offer higher and more deterministic service than a routed network, this approach may be very inefficient when compared to a Frame Relay network. The source of the inefficiencies is the dedicated nature of the leased lines. Leased lines each offer a strictly defined capacity between the customer endpoints. If the capacity is not fully utilized at all times, it is wasted. In the case that the customer has strictly defined and unchanging bandwidth requirements between each pair of endpoints, this may not be a problem. However, this is rarely the case, especially when the network is used to carry data traffic.

Figure 8.12   A Leased-Line Network

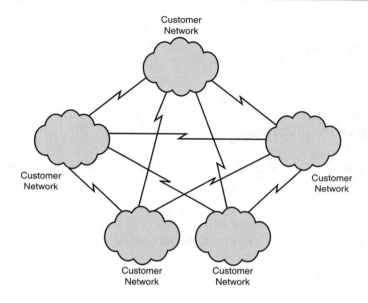

In a Frame Relay network, each leased line and each switch is shared among multiple VCs (and often among multiple customers). When resources are unused by one VC, they are available for use by another VC. The economies of scale of Frame Relay networks and the capability to share resources between VCs make it possible to provide service at a significantly lower cost than an equivalent simple leased-line configuration.

In addition to the improved efficiencies of Frame Relay networks over simple leased-line networks, they are also significantly more flexible than leased-line networks. It is a simple matter to add, drop, or modify services between a specific pair of endpoints, simply by reconfiguring VCs.

8.2.2   QoS in the Frame Relay Network

The QoS offered by Frame Relay networks is quite simplistic and therefore easy to deploy and support, yet has proven to be extremely useful. Frame Relay QoS parameters are captured in the form of an SLA and are described in the following paragraphs.

8.2.2.1 Committed Information Rate

The basic QoS parameter of a Frame Relay SLA is the *committed information rate* (CIR). This is the average rate at which the provider commits to carry the customer's traffic (usually over some specified time interval). The customer is allowed (and, in fact, is expected) to exceed the CIR rate quite frequently. When conditions in the network are such that it can accommodate excess traffic on a VC without compromising the CIR committed on other VCs, the excess traffic is carried. However, as congestion builds in the network and it is less capable of accommodating traffic in excess of the CIR, it attempts to throttle excess traffic, eventually discarding it.

8.2.2.2 Congestion Notification and the Discard Eligible Bit

Switches in the Frame Relay network use interface queue depths as an indicator of congestion or of impending congestion. As queue depth builds above a certain threshold, they begin to mark congestion notification bits in frame headers. These bits are the *forward-explicit congestion notification* (FECN) and *backward-explicit congestion notification* (BECN) bits. These bits are available to senders as an indication that network conditions are degrading to the point that excess traffic will start to be penalized.

Explicit Congestion Notification

Explicit congestion notification (ECN) is a topic that has received much attention in the TCP/IP community. Most traffic on the Internet uses either UDP or TCP over IP. Yet these protocols provide no explicit means by which congestion conditions in one area of the network can be communicated to other areas of the networks or to the hosts generating the traffic. Hosts using TCP can learn of congestion in the network as indicated implicitly by packet loss. However, intermediate network devices do not operate at the TCP layer and remain unaware of congestion elsewhere in the network. Similarly, hosts are incapable of detecting congestion encountered by UDP traffic using the unreliable UDP protocol.

Hosts respond to congestion indicated by TCP packet loss by dramatically reducing their transmission rates. Network devices, unaware of congestion downstream, do not respond at all. If it were possible to provide a more explicit indication of congestion to other network devices and to hosts, it is possible that these could respond to congestion in a manner that results in more efficient utilization of network resources. To this end, researchers have suggested the use of an ECN bit in the IP packet header. Network devices would mark this bit when congested; hosts and other network devices would respond accordingly. ECN is likely to claim 1 or both of the 2 unused bits in the same byte in which the 6-bit DSCP is marked. For further information on ECN, see [RFC 2481].

If network congestion continues to worsen, switches begin to discard traffic to alleviate the congestion. It is important that they do so by discarding only traffic that is submitted in excess of negotiated CIRs. To this end, it is the responsibility of the Frame Relay ingress device to enforce each VC's CIR by tagging frames submitted in excess of the CIR. This tag takes the form of setting a bit in the frame header known as the *discard eligible* (DE) bit. Under congestion conditions, switches discard only frames marked as discard eligible. Packet discards are a firm indicator to hosts that they are exceeding the available capacity of the network. In the common case that hosts are using the TCP/IP protocol (or other rate-adaptive protocols), they usually respond to discarded packets by throttling back their transmission rate.

8.2.2.3 Burst Sizes and Excess Information Rate

Most Frame Relay SLAs specify three parameters in addition to the CIR. These are the *committed burst size* (Bc), the *excess information rate* (EIR), and the *excess burst size* (Be). These parameters are explained in the following paragraphs.

The committed burst size serves to further qualify the provider's commitment beyond the CIR. A CIR alone does not constrain the size of bursts that the customer can submit to the network. Depending on the type of traffic for which the service is being used, it may be desirable for the customer to be able to submit large bursts to the Frame Relay network. However, large bursts can consume a disproportionate share of the provider's resources. Therefore, it is in the provider's interest to limit the allowable burst size, in so smoothing offered traffic and controlling the demands on the provider's resources. The committed burst size specifies the size of a burst that the provider commits to carry. Traffic bursted in excess of Bc may be discarded.

The EIR and the excess burst size specify additional thresholds for customer traffic. Because the provider is not obligated to carry anything beyond the CIR and the Bc, you might ask why it is useful to specify additional thresholds. The reason is that providers often use the second set of thresholds to afford a layer of protection to resources that might otherwise be abused or shared unfairly between customers. Specifically, traffic exceeding the CIR or the Bc is marked discard eligible at the ingress to the network and may be discarded *if congestion is encountered deeper in the network*. However, by the time this excess traffic reaches a congested node and is discarded, it has already consumed resources between the network ingress and the discarding node. Abusive senders may submit so much excess traffic that they consume an unfair portion of the network resources, contributing unfairly to congestion and thereby compromising the service allotted to other traffic. To preclude this effect, ingress nodes will usually unconditionally discard traffic submitted in excess of EIR and Be.

8.2.2.4   *The Token Bucket Model*

The policing model described for Frame Relay SLAs is, in effect, a variation on the token bucket model described in Chapter 3, in the context of traffic-handling mechanisms and again in Chapter 6, in the context of DiffServ policing mechanisms. In particular, it is equivalent to a two-stage token bucket in which the first stage determines the CIR and the Bc, and the second stage determines the EIR and the Be. This two-stage token bucket model can be used to shape traffic before it is submitted to the Frame Relay network or to police traffic at the ingress to the Frame Relay network.

8.2.2.5   *Characterizing the Frame Relay Service*

Certain parameters characterize the QoS provided by the provider when the customer meets the constraints specified by the SLA. These are the *frame transfer delay* (FTD) and the *frame delivery ratio* (FDR). The FTD specifies the latency from the submission of the first bit of a frame at the network ingress to the receipt of the last bit of a frame at the network egress. Different providers may measure the FTD slightly differently. However, regardless of the exact measurement method, it provides an indication of the average latency that can be expected between the VC endpoints.

The FDR measures the ratio of frames dropped between the ingress and egress points of the VC. This ratio is typically measured separately for frames conforming to the CIR and the Bc and excess frames. The FDR should be very low for conforming frames and may be quite a bit higher for nonconforming frames.

8.2.3   *Using Frame Relay to Provide QoS*

The basic service provided by Frame Relay VCs can be used to support higher-layer QoS services in a number of ways. The next subsections describe the use of Frame Relay VCs to offer DiffServ QoS and to support RSVP/IntServ-style QoS.

8.2.3.1   *DiffServ and Frame Relay*

Because of the popularity of the Frame Relay SLA model, early implementations of DiffServ attempt to offer a similar service model. In particular, DiffServ traffic conditioners have been proposed to support the Frame Relay notions of CIR, Bc, EIR, and Be using the AF PHB group. For further details, see [RFC 2698], [RFC 2697].

8.2.3.2 RSVP/IntServ and Frame Relay

The simplest application of Frame Relay in support of RSVP/IntServ treats a Frame Relay VC as a well-characterized point-to-point link. Multiple RSVP flows are multiplexed over the VC, and Layer 3 packet scheduling and admission control are applied over the link. Packet scheduling and especially admission-control algorithms would differ slightly when applied over a Frame Relay link as opposed to a more strictly characterized leased-line link. Specifically, admission control would tend to be more permissive, exploiting the excess capacity available in the case of Frame Relay.

In a more sophisticated application of Frame Relay to RSVP/IntServ-style QoS, the customer may negotiate two VCs between a pair of endpoints, offering different service frame transfer delay characteristics. RSVP flows may then be directed by the edge device to the appropriate VC, depending on the specified IntServ latency parameters.

8.2.3.3 Voice over Native Frame Relay

Certain vendors have rolled out voice over Frame Relay access devices (VFRADs). These convert PBX-sourced telephony traffic into frames that are then sent to their destination over Frame Relay VCs. The voice frames are multiplexed with data traffic over the same VC. The obvious benefit of this approach is the capability to support voice and data with a single enterprise network. VFRADs use QoS mechanisms such as directing voice frames to a high-priority queue and fragmenting the data frames to control latency. This latency control mechanism is especially important on lower-speed links and will be described in detail (in a non-frame-relay specific contect) in the following section.

8.3 QoS on Low-Bit Rate Links

Low-bit rate links (less than T1 or 1.544Mbps) present an especially challenging environment from a QoS perspective. These types of links are important because they appear in the end-to-end path of a very significant proportion of network users. A large proportion of Internet users connect to their service providers via dial-up plain old telephone service (POTS) modems typically ranging in bandwidth from 28.8Kbps to 56Kbps. Because the bandwidth of these links is so low, efficiency of bandwidth usage is a major concern. As shown in Chapter 2, "The Quality/Efficiency Product," if it is necessary to support high-quality services through these links while maintaining efficient use of the link resources, then QoS mechanisms are required to raise the quality/efficiency (QE) product of these links. The especially high level of efficiency required on these links requires a high QE product, necessitating fairly sophisticated QoS mechanisms.

8.3.1 Supporting Different Qualities of Service

Not all traffic requires high-quality guarantees. Adaptive best-effort traffic generally makes do with lower-quality service and simply adapts to the low bandwidth available on low-bit rate links. Sophisticated QoS mechanisms are not required for this traffic.

Certain mission-critical, qualitative applications have limited capability to adapt and often falter over slow links. Simple Layer 3 packet scheduling is often sufficient to support these.

Supporting higher-quality services such as are required by voice and video is problematic. Admission control and Layer 3 packet scheduling may be sufficient to accommodate limited audio traffic alone. However, mixing voice and data on the same link is difficult. The problem lies not necessarily in the sharing of *bandwidth* between the two, but rather in the *latencies* that can result from the link sharing. Addressing the latency problem requires traffic-handling mechanisms beyond admission control and simple Layer 3 packet scheduling. Of course, video traffic presents its own challenges in that it generally requires significant bandwidth.

The ISSLOW subworking group of the IETF ISSLL working group has done work on the problem of providing IntServ over slow links. This work can be applied to other QoS service models. The next section discusses issues in supporting QoS over low-bit rate links and tells how these can be addressed in a manner that supports higher-layer QoS services.

8.3.2 Bandwidth Constraints and Admission Control

Simple bandwidth constraints present the obvious challenge. Slow links are (by definition) the slowest part of the network that is encountered on many end-to-end paths. Consequently, these links are often the limiting factor in providing end-to-end QoS. Because high-quality QoS flows often require a large proportion of the bandwidth available on these links, only a small number of flows can be supported at a time. For example, a 56Kbps modem link can support only a single voice call with some background data traffic. A T1 link interconnecting two corporate sites might be used to support two or three voice calls at a time in addition to background data traffic.

> **Note**
>
> Of course, when a T1 link is used exclusively to carry telephony traffic, it can be very efficiently divided into discrete channels using *time-division multiplexing* (TDM) and can carry up to 24 voice calls. However, when the link is required to support mixes of packetized IP traffic including large and relatively bursty data packets, the percentage of the link that can be used for high-quality service is significantly lower.

Because of the low number of flows that can be supported, statistical multiplexing and the requisite overprovisioning is not an option. Instead, explicit admission control is desirable to support high-quality service.

8.3.2.1 Admission Control Agents

By appointing the edge devices that serve low-bit rate links as RSVP-aware admission control agents, it is possible to provide explicit admission control to these links. Two examples of applying admission control agents to slow bit rate links are illustrated in Figure 8.13.

Figure 8.13   Two Examples of Admission Control Agents on Low-Bit Rate Links

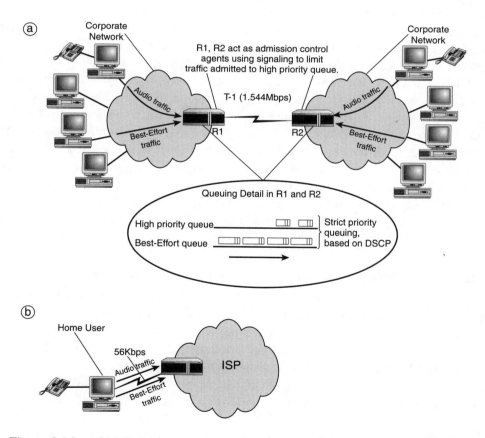

In Figure 8.13a, a T-1 link interconnects routers at two corporate sites. The routers transmitting onto this link (R1 and R2) are RSVP-aware and are each configured with a strict-priority queue and a best-effort queue. Access to the priority queue is available for a limited aggregate rate of high-quality traffic (for example, 192Kbps) and is invoked by marking high-priority packets with the appropriate DSCP. Hosts signal their bandwidth and service requirements for a traffic flow to gain admission to the priority queue. R1 and R2 act as admission control agents, admitting traffic to the queue up to the provisioned aggregate bandwidth limit of 192Kbps. (R1 is the admission control agent for traffic transmitted from left to right. R2 is the admission control agent for traffic transmitted from right to left.) The provisioned limit is sufficient to accommodate three simultaneous 64Kbps voice calls. Once admitted, packets corresponding to the voice calls are scheduled using strict priority. In this example, link-specific traffic handling mechanisms may not be required.

In Figure 8.13b, a single home user is connected to an ISP via a dial-up modem link at 56Kbps. Only a single voice call can be supported on this link. If the edge device interconnecting the link to the ISP's network is RSVP-aware, it should serve as an admission control agent. However, its role in supporting QoS differs somewhat from the role of the admission control agent in the previous example. The link in this example is dedicated to a single user. The link in the previous example is shared between a large number of potential users. In the case of a dedicated link, improper admission control will compromise only the single user of the link. In the case of the shared link, improper admission control will compromise all users of the link. For this reason, it can be argued that admission control is less important on the dedicated link. However, as will be shown subsequently, RSVP signaling awareness on this link can be very useful in identifying traffic requiring specific QoS. In fact, traffic handling on the dedicated link is of greater importance than admission control: Special traffic handling is required to support audio traffic on this link. Appropriate link-layer traffic handling will be discussed later in the section "Traffic Handling to Minimize Latency."

8.3.2.2 *Compression and Its Impact on Admission Control*

Many of the devices sending onto slow links alleviate bandwidth limitations by compressing transmitted traffic. Compression is attractive because it can buy significant gains in efficiency of bandwidth usage. However, it tends to wreak havoc with admission control. In typical RSVP signaling, the sending application specifies the bandwidth required to carry the traffic that it generates. Compression is typically implemented in the sending operating system but may also be applied at multiple points in the network. A sending operating system may slightly modify the bandwidth specified in an RSVP signaling message to accommodate for protocol header overhead, but it does not have the information necessary to account for the effects of compression on the required bandwidth at various points in the network. This is because efficiency of compression varies widely from link to link, depending on the compressed data and the particular compression scheme employed.

A conservative option is simply to apply admission control based on the unmodified RSVP-specified parameters. However, this approach is very wasteful when there are significant compression gains to be had and can even result in the rejection of an admission-control request that could otherwise be accommodated.

Compressibility Hints

An alternate approach [COMPRESS] enables the application to provide a compressibility hint. This hint is an estimate of the compressibility of the data that the application is sending. The hint is carried in the sender's RSVP messages. Routers in the network can then use this hint to estimate the local effect of applying compression on the local admissibility of the request. Note that the bandwidth requirement indicated by the application and included in the RSVP SENDER_TSPEC object remains unmodified. This bandwidth requirement is converted to an *effective* bandwidth requirement at each node, based on local compression parameters.

Header Compression

In addition to various data compression techniques, header compression can yield significant bandwidth gains. Audio packets often contain 20 to 40 bytes of payload data. Considering that each packet may require a 20-byte IP header, up to 50% of a link's bandwidth could be reclaimed if it were possible to eliminate packet headers. Like data, headers can be compressed at various layers in the network stack and at various nodes in the network with varying effects. The ISSLOW working group of the IETF has documented various approaches to link-layer header compression [RFC 2688].

8.3.3 Traffic Handling to Minimize Latency

In addition to bandwidth constraints, low-bit rate links present latency problems. From the time a 1500-byte packet is submitted to a 28.8Kbps link, to the time it clears the link, approximately 400msec have elapsed. In many network interfaces, the unit of traffic passed to the network hardware is a single packet. When the packet is handed to the hardware, the link is committed. Consequently, if a small audio packet is submitted to the hardware for transmission, just after a large data packet was submitted to the hardware, the audio packet may experience an unacceptable latency. This effect is often called the *head-of-line blocking* problem and is illustrated in Figure 8.14.

Figure 8.14   Head-of-Line Blocking

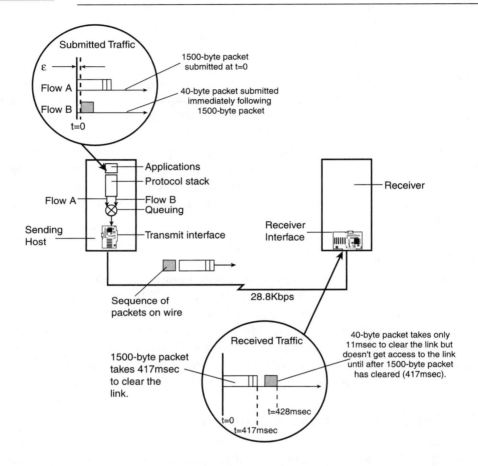

> ### Note
> Although head-of-line blocking is illustrated here in the context of a host, it applies equally to any intermediate node transmitting onto a slow link.

The submitted traffic timeline shows a 1500-byte packet submitted to a 28.8Kbps sending interface at time t=0. A 40-byte packet is submitted immediately thereafter, at time t=ε. The received traffic timeline shows the 1500-byte packet clearing the link at t=417msec ($(1500 \times 8)/28800 = .417$). Because the 40-byte packet was submitted after the 1500-byte packet, it cannot access the link until it is clear at t=417msec. Although it takes this packet only 11msec to clear the link, it is not received until t=428msec (417 + 11 = 428).

> **Note**
>
> The packet sizes used refer to the actual datagram size submitted to the link. The available payload after accounting for various protocol headers may be significantly less.

The ISSLOW documents specify two mechanisms for reducing the latency that results from head-of-line blocking. These are described in the following paragraphs.

8.3.3.1 *Multilink Fragmentation*

Most network interface hardware handles traffic on a packet-by-packet basis. The network software stack hands a packet to the hardware, and the hardware sends the packet on the network link. When that packet is sent, the next packet is handled. On these interfaces, it is impossible to interrupt the transmission of a packet.

Therefore, to minimize the effect of head-of-line blocking, it is desirable to pass only very small packets to the network interface hardware. By doing so, the link is never committed for a long period of time. If an application submits a packet that requires low latency, it can be rushed to the front of the packet queue (using a strict priority Layer 3 packet scheduler) and can be submitted to the link as soon as the previous packet clears. This is illustrated in Figure 8.15.

Figure 8.15 compares the arrival time of a 40-byte packet submitted to a 28.8Kbps link *just* (t=ε) after a 1500-byte packet, both when fragmentation is applied and when it is not. When the 1500-byte packet is not fragmented, the 40-byte packet must wait 417msec for the 1500-byte packet to clear the link before it gains access to the link. It clears the link 11msec later, at 428msec (as described previously). However, when the 1500-byte packet is fragmented into 40-byte fragments, the 40-byte packet waits only for the *first fragment* to clear the link before it gains access to the link (at 11msec). The 40-byte packet clears the link 11msec later, at 22msec. The net reduction in the latency perceived by the 40-byte packet is 406msec (428 –22). The 1500-byte packet does experience an increase in latency due to the interleaving of the 40-byte packet on the link. The net increase in latency experienced by the 1500-byte packet is 11msec (428 –417). This evaluation neglects any overhead associated with fragmentation.

However, forcing all traffic into small packets is problematic. As packet sizes are reduced, the ratio of header information to useful payload information increases. This further compromises the efficiency of resource usage on the slow link, which is obviously undesirable. IP layer headers are quite large, exacerbating this effect. In addition, the cost in inefficiencies of IP-layer fragmentation would be borne by all links in the path from sender to receiver. IP-layer fragmentation is therefore not a good approach. Instead, link-layer fragmentation is desirable.

Figure 8.15   Fragmenting to Avoid Head-of-Line Blocking

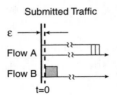

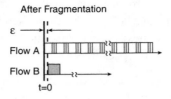

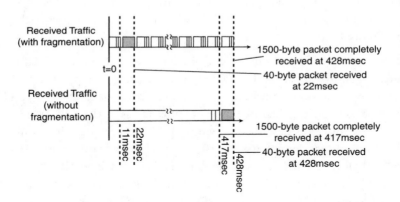

As it happens, the *Point-to-Point Multilink* protocol supports link-layer fragmentation that is appropriate for slow links. This protocol introduces only minimal packet overhead, thereby enabling efficient use of the link resources. The ISSLOW working group has documented the application of multilink fragmentation to the problem of reducing latency on slow links. The approach is to fragment all packets above a certain size at the link layer (packets smaller than the fragment size obviously do not need to be fragmented). The fragment size then determines the minimum latency that can be guaranteed.

Overhead versus Fragment Size

Even though packets requiring low latency may be submitted for transmission relatively infrequently, all packets submitted must be fragmented. This is because the low-latency packets may appear at any time, and the link must not be committed when they appear. Consequently, the per-fragment header overhead, as small as it may be, is borne by every fragment of every packet transmitted on the link. To reduce this overhead, it is necessary to increase the fragment size. However, increasing the fragment size compromises the latency guarantees that can be supported. A good rule of thumb for supporting audio traffic over slow links is that the fragment size should be equal to the size of an audio packet. This means that an audio packet need never experience latency greater than would be required to transmit a single other audio packet. Fragment sizes on the order of 40–120 bytes tend to yield a good trade-off between latency and overhead on slow modem links (28–56Kbps).

Packet Scheduler over Fragmenter

The multilink fragmenting approach does not obviate the need for Layer 3 packet scheduling. This function must be implemented before the fragmenting function, as illustrated in Figure 8.16.

Figure 8.16 Packet Scheduling over the Fragmenter

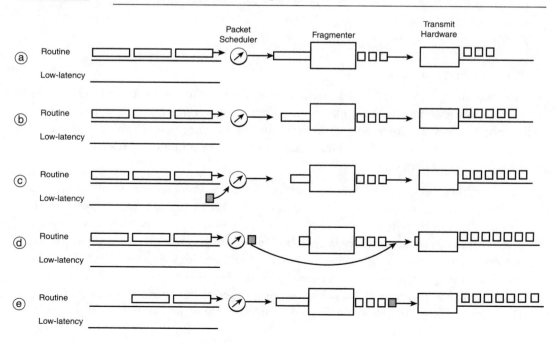

In Figure 8.16a and Figure 8.16b, large packets submitted on the routine queue are passed to the packet scheduler and then to the fragmenter. The packets are fragmented in the fragmenter and then are submitted to the transmit hardware for transmission. In Figure 8.16c, a small packet is submitted on the low-latency queue. It is rushed to the front of the transmit queue by the packet scheduler, as shown in Figure 8.16d. It bypasses the fragmenter Figure 8.16e and is put at the head of the queue for the transmit hardware. A routine fragment has just been submitted to the transmit hardware, so the prioritized packet must wait for this fragment to clear the link Figure 8.16e.

To understand the overall effects of link-layer fragmentation, it is necessary to look at the Layer 3 packet scheduler and the fragmenter as a system.

In the simplest case, the packet scheduler uses strict priority scheduling to always place low-latency packets at the front of the Layer 3 packet queue. Below the packet scheduler, the fragmenter contains two queues: a *fragmenting* queue and a *nonfragmenting* queue. Low-latency packets are rushed through the Layer 3 packet scheduler and are passed immediately to the nonfragmenting queue from which they are transmitted onto the link at the next opportunity. As a result, these can always be assured a bounded worst-case latency.

However, no assurances are provided to fragmented packets. These are subjected to whatever Layer 3 queue-servicing algorithms are in place to handle those traffic flows that are not of highest priority. The only effect of the fragmenter on these packets is that their transmission time may be increased due to the interleaving of one or more nonfragmented packets.

Levels of Preemption

The combination of Layer 3 packet scheduler and fragmenter, as described, offers two levels of latency control. The high-priority nonfragmented packets experience a strictly bounded latency. Fragmented packets are assured no latency bound. This configuration is quite useful. For example, it enables a slow link to offer simultaneous telephony-quality service as well as data transfer service.

However, this configuration does have its limitations. Consider, for example, using a link to carry audio, video, and data traffic. Ideally, the packet-scheduler/fragmenter combination would offer three levels of latency control. Strict low-latency bounds would be guaranteed for audio packets, higher-latency bounds would be guaranteed for video packets, and no latency bounds would be guaranteed for data traffic. Using the simple configuration illustrated previously, video packets could be scheduled by the Layer 3 scheduler. The scheduler would prioritize these below the audio packets but above all other packets. The video packets would have to be placed into the fragmented queue when passed to the fragmenter. This scheme offers no latency guarantees to the video packets beyond those that would be offered using only the Layer 3 scheduler. If a video packet was submitted to the scheduler just after a data packet had been passed to the fragmenter, the video packet would wait for the entire data packet to be fragmented and sent before it could be sent.

This is because the simple fragmenter fragments only a single packet at a time. If the fragmenter is to offer any latency control to the video traffic, it must be capable of interrupting its fragmentation of a data packet to intersperse fragments of a video packet. As a result, packets from more than one packet may be interspersed on the link. This is illustrated in Figure 8.17.

Figure 8.17   Multiple-Layer Fragmentation

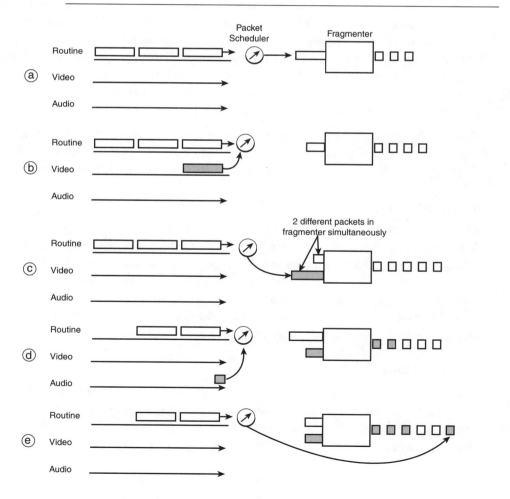

In Figure 8.17a, routine packets are being scheduled and fragmented. In Figure 8.17b, a video packet is submitted. The strict priority scheduler passes it to the front of the packet queue, for submission to the fragmenter Figure 8.17c. In Figure 8.17c, Figure 8.17d, and Figure 8.17e the routine packet and the video packet are both in the fragmenter simultaneously. In Figure 8.17d, an audio packet is submitted. It is rushed through both the packet scheduler and the fragmenter.

This mode of operation requires added complexity in the fragmenter. The simple fragmenter discussed previously need not track associations between fragments and packets. Because only a single packet is fragmented at any time, a receiver simply reassembles fragments in the order received until a complete packet is assembled (at which time it is handed to the layer above it). However, if the fragmenter fragments more than a single packet at a time (as illustrated in Figure 8.17), the receiver needs information by which to correlate received fragments with the packets from which they originated. This requires an identifier in each fragment header to associate it with its original packet. So, although multiple levels of fragmentation offer a second level of latency control, this requires a more sophisticated fragmenter and reassembler at the receiving end, as well as the commitment of additional header bits. The use of a fragmenter to support multiple fragmented *classes* simultaneously is specified in the form of the *multiclass extension to multilink PPP* [RFC 2686].

Early implementations of the multilink fragmentation scheme use the simple fragmenter to support a single level of link-layer latency control. Whatever latency control is offered to fragmented traffic is limited by the constraints of the layer 3 packet scheduler.

Prefix Elision

Link-layer fragmentation can be used in a manner that reduces somewhat the overhead of link-layer protocol headers. This is achieved via a method known as *prefix elision*. For example, consider that all fragments of a certain packet have some number of bytes in common at the front of their headers. The fragmenting sender could indicate to the receiver that all fragments associated with this packet should be considered to have the same first byte (or more) as this packet. This eliminates the need for the common bytes to actually be carried on the wire more than once.

8.3.3.2   Suspend/Resume Approach

The suspend/resume approach is an alternate approach to latency reduction at the link layer. This approach can be used whenever it is possible to interrupt (or suspend) a packet that has been submitted for transmission. Because a packet can be suspended *after* it has been committed, there is no need to fragment all packets *a priori*, substantially reducing link-layer overhead. Suspend/resume approaches require sufficient header information available to mark the boundaries of the suspended packet so that it can be properly reassembled. There are two implementations of the suspend/resume approach, described in the following subsections. However, because the requirement for specialized hardware, the suspend/resume approach is not commonly used.

Software Suspension

Certain network interfaces provide a byte-level interface (as opposed to the more common packet-level interface) between the transmitting software stack and the hardware that puts data on the link. Because of the obvious overhead associated with this approach, such interfaces are increasingly scarce. However, when a byte-level interface is available, software is capable of suspending the transmission of a latency-tolerant packet in favor of a latency-intolerant packet.

Hardware Suspension

Hardware suspension is supported by certain specialized hardware. This approach maintains the efficiencies of a packet-oriented interface between the transmitting software stack and the hardware, but it allows the software to suspend the transmission of a latency-tolerant packet by signaling the hardware.

8.3.3.3 Identifying Fragmentable versus Nonfragmentable Flows

Regardless of the approach used to provide low-latency bounds on slow links, some classification mechanism is required to identify the traffic that is non-latency tolerant and to differentiate it from the traffic that is latency-tolerant. Classification mechanisms are discussed in the following paragraphs.

RSVP

Clearly, if the device transmitting onto the slow link is RSVP-aware, then sufficient information is available to identify traffic flows that are latency-intolerant and to classify packets belonging to these flows. In fact, the device need not be an active participant in RSVP signaling; it need only snoop RSVP messages to glean classification information and the quantitative parameters associated with a flow. Guaranteed Service flows are likely to require the latency bounds offered by whatever ISSLOW mechanism is in place. Controlled Load Service flows are less likely to require the benefits of the latency-bounded link-layer service. To the extent that Controlled Load Service Traffic is admitted to this service, it must be done in a manner that does not interfere with the strict latency bounds offered for guaranteed traffic.

Heuristics

Often, the device transmitting onto the slow link is not RSVP-aware. In this case, heuristics may be applied to attempt to recognize traffic that is latency-intolerant. For example, streams of small packets arriving periodically at rates in the range of 8–64Kbps are likely to correspond to audio flows and to require low latency. Heuristics such as these are not guaranteed to be 100% effective, but they are also not required to be.

DiffServ Codepoints and `user_priority` Values

Another mechanism for identifying latency intolerant packets is by the DSCP or `user_priority` value marked in packet headers. The problem with this approach is that these marks do not necessarily correlate clearly with latency tolerance.

8.4 Summary

True end-to-end QoS requires support in the many different subnets and media types that may occur along arbitrary end-to-end paths. Earlier chapters discussed link layer-independent abstractions of QoS mechanisms, including IntServ and DiffServ, and mechanisms specific to the common 802 link layer. This chapter discussed link layer-specific mechanisms for ATM, Frame Relay, and slow WAN links.

The ISSLL working group of the IETF has defined ATM-appropriate mechanisms to support IntServ services under the heading of ISATM. The ATM link layer is in many ways ideally suited to provide high-quality QoS. It uses hardware to schedule cells at a very fine granularity. Furthermore, it has a native notion of different service types that correspond quite well to the quantitative services offered at higher layers. Cells are transmitted through ATM networks on virtual circuits. Establishing and tearing down these circuits at the right time, between the right devices, is referred to as VC management. VC management is one of the challenges of mapping higher-layer QoS services to ATM. Another challenge is in determining the appropriate ATM service type and associated quantitative parameters to support higher-layer QoS parameters. ATM does not lend itself readily to multicast. Supporting multicast RSVP/IntServ-style QoS on ATM is therefore particularly challenging.

Frame Relay is a commonly used wide-area technology that offers cost-effective high-performance connections with deterministic, quantifiable QoS. It is typically used to connect peer sites in an enterprise network. Customers are offered an SLA that offers to carry traffic conforming to a set of token bucket parameters, with a certain average latency. Frame Relay edge devices can map higher-layer QoS parameters to one or more underlying Frame Relay VCs.

The ISSLOW subworking group of the IETF working group has addressed the problem of supporting IntServ over slow link layers. Slow links are commonly encountered in end-to-end paths. One of the primary problems presented by these links is their impact on latency due to head-of-line blocking. In addition, varying link-specific compression schemes make it difficult to do admission control over these links. To tackle the impact of head-of-line blocking on latency, the ISSLOW recommends one of two approaches. These include link-layer fragmentation, per the PPP Multilink protocol, or the use of suspend/resume-capable network interfaces.

QoS Policy

Policy is arguably the most elusive component of QoS. Working groups in the IETF have been struggling to architect the grand unified network policy system for years. Vendors are producing complex policy systems. Numerous books and articles are written on the topic. Yet somehow, the goal of the grand unified policy system remains unrealized. This chapter attempts to define the concept of policy from the QoS perspective. It then explains the role of the policy management system and describes the components of such a system. Next, the chapter describes the different types of QoS policies that are applied in a QoS network. Finally, it shows how the policy management system can be used to apply the policies described.

9.1 Defining the Concept of Policy

The difficulty in converging on a standard approach to policy is largely attributable to the lack of a clear definition of the concept. Policy has come to mean many different things to different people. I won't claim to finally be the one to provide the "correct" definition of policy—that would be far too arrogant. Instead, in the interest of progress, I will offer a definition of policy that is admittedly biased and limited in scope.

In the context of this book, policy is defined as follows:

> A high-level description of the quality and efficiency objectives to be met by the network under discussion

This definition is reminiscent of the discussion of the quality/efficiency (QE) product in Chapter 2, "The Quality/Efficiency Product." It says that QoS policy embodies the decisions that will be made by the network manager regarding the qualities of service that will be supported through the network and the manner in which the network will use various QoS mechanisms or overprovisioning to support these service qualities.

Much of this chapter will discuss issues relating to the implementation of a *policy management system*. A policy management system is defined as follows:

> A system of components and tools that work together to manage a network in a manner that realizes certain high-level objectives as specified by QoS policies

The foremost value of a policy management system is that it presents a high-level interface that enables QoS policy objectives to be expressed in *human* terms. It then automates (or at least facilitates) the compilation of these objectives into the jumble of different machine configurations that need to be installed across the network.

9.1.1 Examples of QoS Policy Objectives

A network manager invited to specify QoS policy objectives at the highest level might specify a policy of the form, "Provide a range of service qualities while using network resources optimally." The ideal policy system might then provide the network manager with a button labeled Double-Click to Provide a Range of Services While Using Network Resources Optimally. Obviously, such a system is impractical. At the very least, the network manager will have to provide a more refined definition of the service objectives. The policy system may then be capable of helping by offering different options for realizing these objectives, guided by the requirement to do so efficiently.

The following list offers examples of the type of high-level service objectives that might be specified as part of QoS policy:

- Provide telephony-quality service for entitled users of telephony applications across and beyond the enterprise network

- Support high-quality streaming video to all employees within the enterprise network

- Provide adequate bandwidth to assure that nightly backups between the New York and London offices always complete by 7 a.m.

- Assure that network performance does not hinder the capability of the accounting department to produce month-end financial reports on schedule

9.1.2 Features of a Policy Management System

To simultaneously meet all these objectives, it is necessary to coordinate QoS components across a large network. So far, this book has discussed various low-level QoS components such as traffic-handling mechanisms, queuing algorithms, signaling protocols, and so forth. These can be managed, for example, to prioritize one traffic flow over another at a specific network node or, with the use of RSVP, even to assure that a particular flow is guaranteed the service that it needs across the network. Yet these are *low-level* as well as *local* mechanisms. They are low-level in the sense that they require interaction with detailed, machine-specific configuration parameters. They are local in the sense that they pertain to resource usage at one particular node or for one particular flow. A policy management system enables the more high-level, global management necessary to simultaneously realize high-level objectives with network-wide implications across the entire set of network users.

Key aspects of a policy management system include these:

- **Centralized management**—The network manager must be capable of effecting network-wide management policies from a single location. The network manager must not be required to configure each network device individually.

- **Abstraction of management data**—The policy management system must abstract the complexity of the myriad low-level QoS mechanisms that exist in each network device. The network manager should be presented with a simple high-level view of these mechanisms.

- **Rule compilation**—The policy management system should enable the network manager to express desired policies in the form of high-level rules. It should then compile these rules into configuration information and actions appropriate for each device.

- **Automation**—The policy management system should automate the task of policy management by distributing configuration information, responding to changes in resource requirements, and alerting the network manager only when human intervention is required.

- **Status monitoring and reporting**—The policy management system should report network status to the network manager. The manager relies on such information to test the efficacy of policies applied to the network.

> **Note**
>
> Policy has been discussed so far in the limited context of QoS. A general discussion of policy would include such aspects of network management as address allocation, security, routing policies, and so forth. In the interest of tackling policy in a tractable manner, this chapter is concerned only with the QoS aspects of network management.

9.1.3 Policy Taxonomy

Before delving into the components of a policy system and their use, it is helpful to explore the type of QoS policies that would be realized. Different policies govern different sets of resources and different traffic flows on different time scales. In the following paragraphs, taxonomy for different types of policies is introduced.

9.1.3.1 Categorization of Policies by Time Scale and Scope

This section categorizes policies by time scale and scope. It introduces the concepts of static global policies, semi-static policies, and dynamic policies.

Static Global Provisioning Policies

Static global policies are policies that affect the operation of the network in general, without regard for specific allocations of resources among specific traffic flows. Chapter 2 explained the concept of the QE product of a network. One of the most important global policies that a network manager considers is the operating point of the network on the set of possible QE curves. Is it a goal of the network to support high-quality services? What capacity is required in different parts of the network? To what degree can it be overprovisioned? Is it less expensive to support high-quality services by enabling certain QoS mechanisms than by overprovisioning? As discussed in Chapter 2 (in the section "Sharing Network Resources: Multiple Resource Pools"), it is possible to superimpose a number of logical networks, each operating at a different point on a different QE curve, on a single physical network. How will physical resources be allocated between the logical networks? Recall that these are the type of policy issues that were discussed in Chapter 6, "Differentiated Services," in the context of provisioning a DiffServ network. These are global QoS policy issues that can be applied to any type of network. A policy management system should help the network manager consider these issues and provision the network accordingly.

Global policies such as these tend to be fairly static. It is impractical to frequently change the amount of capacity available in a region of a network or to decide suddenly to support telephony-quality guarantees when these have never been supported in the past. As such, these policies differ from the more dynamic policies described in the following sections. A complete policy system should support both dynamic and static policies. However, different subsets of the policy system likely will be used to effect the static policies than will be used to effect the dynamic policies.

From a procedural perspective, global policies are applied in two forms:

- **Hardware installation**—The selection and installation of hardware devices, their interfaces, and the links that interconnect them

- **Push provisioning**—The configuration of the traffic handling and signaling mechanisms that will be enabled in each device, and the parameterization of these to create the superimposed logical networks corresponding to the high-level resource pools

Semi-static Policies

Semi-static policies govern resource allocations that are more local than the static global policies described previously and that persist for shorter periods of time (more dynamic). These policies are typically applied in a pushed manner in anticipation of certain observed traffic patterns or usage requirements. (See the section "Pushed versus Signaled Mechanisms," in Chapter 1, "Introduction to Quality of Service," for a discussion of *pushed* versus *signaled* provisioning and configuration mechanisms.)

For example, a DiffServ provider might decide as a matter of static global policy that 10% of network capacity is to be available for high-quality quantitative services. Semi-static policies would then govern the fraction of this capacity that is available to each of the provider's customers. Semi-static policies might also limit the regions of the network in which resources are available to each customer (as is the case for route-constrained services). The allocation of resources from different pools among different customers is formalized in the form of service level agreements (SLAs) or similar agreements that may be more or less dynamic. These are negotiated as customers come, are cancelled (returning resources to the pool) as customers go, and are renegotiated as an individual customer's resource requirements change—hence the distinction between semi-static policies and the less dynamic static global policies.

In general, semi-static policies include any push-provisioned policies that allocate resources to aggregate traffic flows. To be clear, static global policies also use push provisioning to allocate resources to aggregate traffic flows. However, the aggregates created in the application of static global policies are very coarse-grained. These are aggregates corresponding to the logical network or resource pool granularity. By contrast, the aggregates created in the application of semi-static policy are at the per-customer or finer granularity.

Dynamic Policies

To support high-quality services for quantitative traffic, it is often necessary to guarantee (or reserve) a specific quantity of resources to an individual traffic flow in a specific set of devices, for the duration of a session (such as a telephony session). When a session is over, the resources should be freed so that they are available to other sessions. These types of services are often supported by the interaction of end-to-end signaling with the policy management system, subject to dynamic policies.

Note

Note that the association of dynamic policy with quality services does not mean that the more static policy types are excluded from the allocation of high-quality services. Rather, it means that dynamic policy is used only for the allocation of higher-quality services and is not required for the allocation of the lower-quality services.

For illustration, static global policy sets aside a network-wide pool of resources for high-quality services. Semi-static policy can be used to create high-quality virtual leased lines across the network for use by customer networks. Dynamic policy may then be used to divvy up the resources of a virtual leased line among individual conversations. Dynamic policy is not typically used to divvy up lower-quality resources.

Just as semi-static policy was shown to operate at a finer granularity than static global policy, dynamic policy tends to operate at a finer granularity than semi-static policy.

Dynamic policies are put in place to provide high-quality resources to be available to individual conversations, corresponding to specific users and applications in specific parts of the network. Signaling then dynamically claims resources against these allocations. Note that the dynamic policies themselves don't necessarily change frequently. Rather, the application of these policies requires dynamic interaction between network devices and *policy servers* (defined in the section "Layers and Components of a Policy System," later in this chapter), resulting in rapid reallocation of network resources.

To illustrate this point, consider a policy that supports guaranteed resource reservations to a set of telephony users. The policy might state that all executives should be entitled 128Kbps each of low-latency service for telephony sessions. This policy might persist for many months. However, the telephony sessions that it provides for are fleeting. The policy management system will be required to interact with network devices as telephony sessions come and go by reallocating resources. It is important to distinguish between the lifetime of a policy and the frequency at which a policy must interact with and modify parameters in network devices. Dynamic policies may have long lifetimes even though they act dynamically.

Note that the distinction between dynamic and semi-static policies is somewhat blurred. Dynamic policies may be applied to qualitative traffic flows as well as quantitative traffic flows. Similarly, pushed semi-static policies may be used to allocate resources for fleeting high-quality sessions. In general, however, dynamic policies require more frequent interaction between network devices and policy servers, and tend to be used to support higher-quality services than their semi-static counterparts.

Relationship of Static, Semi-static, and Dynamic Policies

It is helpful to summarize with a brief discussion of the relationship between the different types of policies described so far. At the highest level, static global policies determine the overall capacity of the network and divide the network into coarse-grained resource pools or logical networks. At the next level, semi-static policies divide the resources of each logical network among customers, groups of applications, or other such medium-grain consumers. (Although semi-static policies can be used to allocate resources at as fine a granularity as the per-conversation level, they are not generally used to do so.) At the lowest level, dynamic policies are used to allocate resources from the higher-quality resource pools to individual, fleeting conversations. This relationship is illustrated in Figure 9.1.

Figure 9.1   Relationship Between Static, Semi-static, and Dynamic Policy

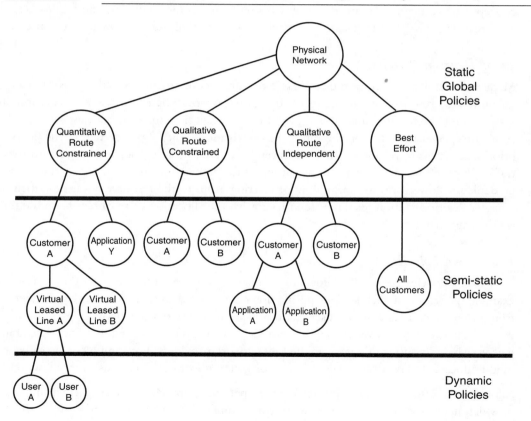

9.1.3.2 Other Categories of Policy

Policies may be categorized according to other criteria that are orthogonal to time scale and scope. These are described in the following sections.

Reservation Policies

Certain policies provide for *reservation* of resources. Others provide for *prioritization* of resources. Reservation policies allow resources to be reserved for or dedicated to specific traffic flows. (The notion of a reservation is discussed in Chapter 4, "Integrated Services," in the section "Overview of the IntServ Architecture.") These are the kinds of policies that grant resources for a telephony session or for streaming a video. Reservation policies guarantee a specific amount of resources for the duration of a session. Referring back to the concept of resource pools introduced in Chapter 2, reservation policies tend to allocate resources from the pool that serves quantifiable traffic requiring high-quality guarantees.

Prioritization Policies

Many traffic flows do not have quantifiable resource requirements. Strictly speaking, to guarantee the resource requirements of such flows, it would be necessary to reserve infinite resources for them. Of course, this is prohibitively expensive. Instead, policies can be applied to *prioritize* traffic on these flows. Prioritization policies give certain traffic flows prioritized access to resources. As long as resources are available, they are assigned to these traffic flows. However, if resources are required for higher-priority traffic flows, they may be denied to lower-priority traffic flows. Referring again to the resource pools described in Chapter 2, prioritization resources tend to govern the allocation of resources to traffic that is not quantifiable.

User-Based Policies

User-based policies govern the allocation of resources based on user or user group. For example, policies may dictate that specific users are entitled to specific resources distinct from other users. Less granular user-based policies may differentiate between groups of users, such as executives versus non-executives, or employees versus guests. Even less granular user-based policies might be applied by network providers. For example, a provider might allocate different resources to traffic originating from different customer networks.

Allocation of resources based on user is a very natural approach to policy in environments in which users pay for network resources. An example of such an environment is an ISP network offering dial access to home users. In other environments (such as an enterprise network), users may not pay directly for resources.

Application-Based Policies

In a large enterprise network, individual employees do not pay directly for resources. Instead, the enterprise finances the network. In these environments, all employees may be considered equally entitled to resources. However, the enterprise may have certain policies regarding how these resources are to be used. For example, such policies may dictate that network resources are to be available to engineering applications or marketing applications, but not to games.

Time-of-Day Policies

Many policies may incorporate time-of-day dependencies. For example, a policy might specify that certain users or applications are entitled to certain resources only during business hours. The term *time-of-day* should not be interpreted too literally. Alternate time-of-day policies might actually specify policies based on day of the week or month. In general, time-of-day policies are policies that have different effects at different times. Note that both dynamic and semi-static policies may also be time-of-day policies. The policies themselves do not change with time. Rather, the application of the policies changes.

9.1.4   The Value of a Policy Management System

The primary value of a policy management system is in its capability to simplify the work of the network manager. Strictly speaking, the network manager could manage the network in a manner that realizes high-level QoS objectives without a policy system. As long as the various network devices implement the necessary traffic-handling mechanisms and provide means to configure these, policies can be implemented to meet the necessary QoS objectives.

However, the complexity of the management task is daunting. Networks generally include a hodgepodge of network devices, supporting different functionality from different vendors. End-to-end services require that these all be configured consistently. A good policy management system abstracts the complexity of the underlying network from the manager. It enables the manager to express policies at a high level and converts these into sets of configuration files and commands that are installed or issued to the appropriate network devices. With this in mind, the next section of this chapter describes the components of a policy management system.

9.2   Layers and Components of a Policy System

The application of network policies requires the cooperation of many types of network devices that operate at different layers. At the lowest layer, the switches and routers that carry traffic through the network must enforce the policies. At a higher layer, devices are required to convert abstract policies into device-specific configuration information. At a higher layer yet, there is a need for a reasonably centralized management interface and a data store to hold policy-related data. Such data includes anything from network topology information to device profiles, to lists of users and applications and the resources to which they are entitled. This section offers taxonomy for the different layers of a network management system. It also describes the protocols used by these layers to communicate among themselves.

Note

The policy layers described are abstract, functional layers. These correspond roughly, but not strictly, to specific components and devices. The blocks in Figure 9.2 represent both the layers and the typically corresponding components. In certain cases, a single physical component may operate at multiple layers, or the functionality of a single layer may be distributed among multiple physical components.

The policy-related working groups of the IETF and the Desktop Management Task Force (DMTF) have been struggling with terminology, so the distinction between the underlying functional layers is often obscured. The terminology used in this book and illustrated in Figure 9.2 corresponds to the terminology used in the IETF working groups at a certain snapshot in time. These terms are offered as placeholders; they may not perfectly describe the underlying functionality represented. Where they do not, it will be noted. Every effort will be made to focus on the appropriate layers of abstraction and the corresponding functionality, rather than on the terminology.

The basic functional layers standardized by the IETF and the corresponding components are illustrated in Figure 9.2.

Figure 9.2 illustrates the following:

- The *policy enforcement* point (PEP)—This layer represents switches and/or routers that enforce policies by forwarding packets with varying levels of service

- The *policy decision* point (PDP)—This layer reviews raw policies from the policy data store and converts these into device configuration information for the policy enforcement components. It also reviews resource requests and determines how to handle these based on policies in the data store. This functionality is often provided in a *policy server*.

- The *policy data store*—This layer stores the raw policy data.

- The *management* or *user interface*—This is the interface by which the network manager interacts with the policy system.

Figure 9.2   Layers of a Policy Management System

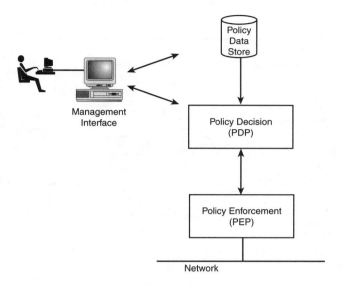

9.2.1 *Policy Enforcement Point*

No packet moves through the network until a host network stack, switch, router, or similar network device decides to forward it. As such, these devices are the ultimate enforcers of all network policies. Therefore, they comprise the policy enforcement layer and are known as *policy enforcement points* (PEPs). PEPs comprise the lowest layer in the pyramid that is the policy management system. PEPs are also the most numerous component. The functionality of interest in a PEP includes the traffic-handling mechanisms available and the protocols by which these can be provisioned or configured. These vary from vendor to vendor and from device to device.

In general, a PEP contains several interfaces that are interconnected by a switching or routing fabric. (Host-based PEPs may contain only a single interface.) Each interface has a certain capacity for forwarding traffic. Traffic-handling mechanisms on the interface determine how this capacity is distributed across traffic flows. In the interest of simplifying policy management, it is useful to define an abstract model of a PEP, as well as abstract policy interfaces to it. One such definition has been developed in the form of an informational draft in the DiffServ working group of the IETF [MODEL]. Although the conceptual model draft was developed in the context of DiffServ, it is general enough to be applied to other QoS mechanisms as well. The block diagram in Figure 9.3 illustrates the major components of a PEP as described in the conceptual model draft.

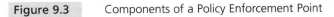

Figure 9.3   Components of a Policy Enforcement Point

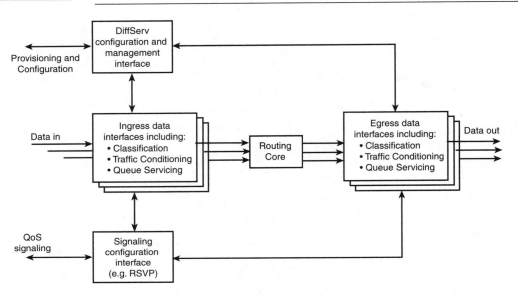

The illustration represents a switch- or router-based PEP. (Obviously, in the case of a host-based PEP, certain elements would differ.) Note that there are elements of routers and switches that are not directly related to QoS policy. The elements of a router that understand routing protocols and that determine which outbound interface to use to forward a packet are not necessarily or directly related to QoS policy. In Figure 9.3, the box labeled *routing core* represents these. Therefore, although these reside in the same physical box as the PEP, they are not part of the PEP. Similarly, some policy elements that may not directly relate to enforcement of QoS policies also might reside in the same physical box as the PEP. These also are not part of the PEP.

The Host as a PEP

It is an often overlooked fact that hosts are PEPs. The host network stack must allocate resources to transmit or receive network traffic. Many hosts may use simple *first in first out* (FIFO) queuing and may not differentiate among traffic flows. However, other hosts may include sophisticated traffic-handling mechanisms. The network stack of these hosts is therefore capable of enforcing policies and is an important component of the policy management system.

9.2.2 Policy Decision Point

Above the PEP in the policy pyramid, the next functional block is the *policy decision point* (PDP). The term *decision point* is a carryover from the days in which QoS policy consisted exclusively of "deciding" whether to admit or reject an RSVP reservation request. Today, PDPs do much more than this; in many cases, they may not actually make decisions as much as "compile" policies (although in some abstract sense, this functionality can be considered to be making decisions). Instead, the PDP is the layer that converts high-layer abstract policies into low-layer interactions with PEPs. These interactions may take the form of pushing unsolicited configuration information to a PEP or may take the form of responding to signaled requests from the PEP. Approving or denying an RSVP reservation request is an example of the latter type of interaction.

> ### Note
>
> As noted previously, the terms *PDP* and *PEP* identify functional layers rather than physical boxes. In most cases, a policy server "box" provides PDP functionality, and a switch or router "box" provides PEP functionality. As such, *in the context of policy*, this book uses the terms *PDP* and *policy server* interchangeably. Similarly, it will often use the term *PEP* to refer to a box that is a switch or a router. In case one of the terms is used to refer strictly to the logical functionality (and not its physical embodiment), or vice versa, this will be noted.

The following paragraphs discuss the positioning of PDP functionality in the policy management system and communications between PDPs and PEPs. Subsequent sections will delve further into the operation of a PDP.

9.2.2.1 Distribution of PDPs

The work associated with PDP functionality may be quite burdensome and may require considerable storage and general processing capacity. PEPs are often built to be as lightweight as possible and to perform specific forwarding tasks with great efficiency. Thus, in many cases, it would be inappropriate to burden PEPs with PDP functionality. Add to this the fact that the realization of a higher-layer policy might require configuration of a large set of PEPs by a single PDP. All this points to the preference (though not necessity) for implementing a PDP in a separate device from the PEP. In large deployments, a single PDP likely will manage multiple PEPs (as illustrated in Figure 9.4).

Figure 9.4   A Single PDP Manages Multiple PEPs

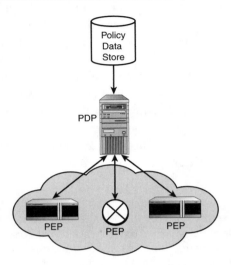

In certain cases, PDP functionality may reside in the same device as the PEP. For example, certain high-end switches or routers might include the processing and storage power required to support PDP functionality (functionality that includes operating with a broader view of the network). In this case, implementing the PDP in the same device as the PEP reduces the number of hardware devices that must be installed and managed.

9.2.2.2   The Interface Between a PDP and a PEP

In general, PDPs and PEPs will not reside in the same hardware device. Instead, the PDP will reside in a policy server, external to the PEP. In the interest of promoting interoperability between policy servers and PEPs from multiple vendors, it is desirable to standardize an interface between the two. Several elements exist in this interface. One of these is the conceptual model of the PEP's functionality, discussed previously. Another is the protocol that a policy server uses to communicate with the PEP. The third element of the interface is the specific set of data structures exchanged in the communication between the two. Obviously, when a PEP and a PDP are co-resident in the same device, interoperability between the two is implicit and standard protocols are not required.

9.2.2.3   Common Open Policy Service Protocol

A number of protocols are in use for communicating between PEPs and policy servers. The emerging standard protocol for policy server/PEP communication is the *Common Open Policy Service Protocol* (COPS). COPS was defined initially with the very specific goal of providing a standard protocol by which a PEP can outsource the admission control decision on an RSVP request to an external policy server. Since then, COPS has expanded and has become the center of quite a bit of controversy.

At the center of this controversy is a tug-of-war between proponents of COPS and devotees of *Simple Network Management Protocol* (SNMP). SNMP has been around for many years and is ubiquitous in network devices. Appropriately, SNMP devotees questioned the need to invent new protocols for managing the QoS aspects of network devices. See the accompanying sidebar "The Strange Debate of SNMP versus COPS" for further details on the SNMP versus COPS debate.

The Strange Debate of SNMP versus COPS

Simple Network Management Protocol (SNMP) is a protocol that was created in the late 1980s for the purpose of fault and configuration management of IP network nodes [RFC 1157]. SNMP relies on network nodes to present status information and to accept configuration information in the form of standardized schemas that are known as *management information bases* (MIBs).

Some of the requirements for the management of QoS mechanisms in IP networks could not readily be met by the relatively ancient SNMP protocol. One such requirement was to be capable of outsourcing an RSVP admission control decision from a PEP to an external policy server. The COPS protocol was initially created for this purpose. As DiffServ gathered steam, it became desirable to extend COPS so that it supported DiffServ management requirements. This would allow both DiffServ and RSVP/IntServ QoS mechanisms to be managed using a common protocol and infrastructure. The extensions to COPS that were required to support DiffServ provisioning are known as COPS/PR (COPS for provisioning), distinct from COPS/RSVP (COPS for RSVP).

The expansion of the scope of COPS was a source of much consternation and grumbling among those in the IETF who had been raised on SNMP. Rightfully so, IETF leaders sought to check the proliferation of new management protocols that would fragment the management framework that had been largely dominated by SNMP. They called for a comparison of SNMP and COPS to determine whether it was really necessary to create a new protocol suite for the management of QoS mechanisms. This comparison was captured in draft form in late 1999.

This draft defines *network-wide configuration* as opposed to *device local configuration*. According to the draft, although the relatively simple networks of the past could be adequately managed on a device-by-device basis, the increasing complexity of network functionality required the introduction of a level of management abstraction. This abstraction level would enable a network manager to declare network-wide policies (not limited to QoS) that can automatically be translated into device local configuration information and pushed to a large number of devices. This approach is known as *policy-based management.*

continues

COPS/PR brings with it the concept of a *policy information base* (PIB). PIBs are analogous to MIBs. The creators of COPS claimed in the draft that although SNMP and MIBs are well suited to the requirements of device local configuration, COPS and PIBs are necessary to meet the higher-level requirements of policy-based management.

Specific reasons cited in support of this claim include these:

- PIBs are defined to contain (higher-level) network-wide policies/configuration data, while MIBs continue to be used to define (lower-level) device-local data. The low-level granularity of MIBs is awkward.

- Because of the higher level of abstraction offered by COPS/PR and PIBs, the same policies can be pushed to a device via COPS more efficiently than via SNMP (in terms of both bandwidth and number of messages).

- COPS uses TCP and is thus inherently reliable. Existing versions of SNMP use UDP.

- COPS supports message sizes up to 64KB. SNMP, as originally defined, is limited to messages of 484 bytes.

- COPS was created with security as an integral requirement. By comparison, security was added to SNMP as an afterthought and is therefore relatively cumbersome. It likely will be difficult to overcome the inertia of the installed base of unsecured SNMP systems.

Not surprisingly, proponents of SNMP argued in the same draft that SNMP mostly meets the requirements of policy-based management and that, where it does not, it can easily be extended to overcome the deficiencies.

The SNMP/COPS comparison exercise culminated in a rather odd *de´tente*. The Resource Allocation Protocol working group of the IETF was encouraged to continue to work on COPS/PR. (The COPS/RSVP work was largely finished at this time.) At the same time, it was asserted that policy-based management *could* be done with SNMP and that an IETF working group would be created with the charter of extending SNMP to support the requirements of policy-based management. At the time this book is being written, work is wrapping up on COPS/PR, and the SNMPCONF working group of the IETF is addressing the needs of SNMP for policy-based management.

COPS *for RSVP*

COPS was first designed as a protocol to be used by PEPs to *outsource* admission control decisions on RSVP messages. When an RSVP message arrives at an RSVP-aware PEP, the PEP must decide whether to admit the message and allow it to continue on its path, or to reject it and return the appropriate error to the originator of the message. Admission control decisions can be applied to PATH or RESV messages. In effect, two decisions must be made on any message. One is a resource-based decision; the other is a policy-based decision.

The resource-based decision is based strictly on the availability of resources on the relevant device interface. The policy decision is based on policy that ultimately governs the use of available resources by different users for different application traffic.

> ## Note
>
> Note that criteria other than user and application may be used in the policy-based decision. Such criteria might include, for example, location, address type (multicast versus unicast, service type, and so on). However, in most cases, these criteria are either implicit (for example, location is implied by the location of the specific PEP from which the decision is being requested) or indications of the user or application (for example, a certain address implies a certain user or user group).

The resource-based decision can often be resolved quite simply. If the resources specified in the RSVP request are less than the resources currently available at the relevant interface, the request can be admitted. Otherwise, it must be rejected. This decision can usually be made locally, in the PEP. On the other hand, the policy-based decision is more complex. It requires extracting the user and application identification (if present) from the RSVP message and comparing these against the appropriate policy rules.

Resolving requests against policy rules typically requires access to a database of user and application information. To further complicate matters, user identifiers must often be authenticated using a security mechanism to avoid malicious abuse of network resources. As a result, the policy-based decision is often outsourced to an external policy server. Note that this does not necessarily mean that each and every RSVP message triggers an outsourced policy decision. Typically, a caching strategy is employed between the PEP and the policy server to minimize the need for PEP/policy server exchanges and the latency in processing RSVP messages that pass through the PEP.

The usage of COPS for RSVP is described very briefly here. For further details on COPS for RSVP, refer to the IETF RFCs [RFC 2748], [RFC 2749], [RFC 2750].

When a PEP receives an RSVP message it packages the RSVP message in a COPS *request* message and sends it to the policy server. The policy server responds with a COPS *decision* message. The decision message indicates to the PEP whether policy deems the RSVP request admissible. The decision message may also cause the PEP to modify certain objects in the RSVP message (or to add certain objects, known as replacement objects, to the RSVP message) before forwarding an admitted request (*replacement objects*), or it may trigger certain error messages if a request is rejected.

COPS for Provisioning

With the advent of DiffServ, it became clear that managing a PEP would entail more than the simple decision outsourcing model of COPS for RSVP. In a pure DiffServ model, management takes the form of pushing configuration information from a policy server down to a PEP. Such information typically includes information to configure classifiers, policers, markers, schedulers, and queuing parameters, among others. In short, this involves all the traffic conditioning information described in Chapter 6 on DiffServ.

In the interest of using a single common protocol for all aspects of QoS management of a PEP, the developers of COPS for RSVP decided to apply the same protocol to DiffServ provisioning. This usage of COPS is captured in a variant of the protocol known as *COPS for provisioning*, or *COPS/PR*. This application of COPS triggered the SNMP versus COPS debate (described in the previous sidebar "The Strange Debate of SNMP versus COPS"). Although it could be argued that SNMP did not lend itself readily to a request/decision model, it is harder to argue that SNMP does not lend itself to the strict provisioning model required for DiffServ. Nonetheless, as described in the sidebar, some aspects of COPS make it particularly suitable for both models, and so it endures.

9.2.2.4 *SNMP and CLI*

COPS is a relatively new protocol that has been developed in the last couple years specifically to address the relatively recent requirements associated with QoS management. SNMP and CLI are older protocols that preceded the development of QoS and gained the status of standard and de facto standard long before COPS was conceived.

SNMP is in wide use, primarily for the purpose of *monitoring* the status of network equipment and network interfaces. Many standard SNMP MIBs exist today. Examples of MIBs include Ethernet interface MIBs and TCP/IP protocol MIBs. SNMP enables a management entity to query a network device for a set of MIBs. Such queries are referred to as SNMP *gets*. In addition, SNMP supports *set* operations. SNMP sets are used to configure (as opposed to monitor) parameters in network devices. In practice, SNMP is less used for set operations than for get operations. The reason for this is that early versions of SNMP did not provide the security mechanisms necessary to protect devices from malicious misconfiguration. The security concerns surrounding SNMP account for one of the reasons that it has not been readily embraced as a QoS management protocol. Nonetheless, the broad availability of SNMP MIBs for monitoring is likely to make SNMP an important component in policy server/PEP communications.

The term *command-line interface* (CLI) refers to a generic command-line interface used for the purpose of monitoring and configuring network devices. Various vendor-specific command-line interfaces are in use today. However, because of the rapid increase in popularity of Cisco's network equipment, Cisco's CLI has become a de facto standard, familiar to most network managers and referred to simply as CLI. Due to the popularity of CLI, many vendors of policy management systems use this interface to communicate with PEPs. In addition, PEP vendors other than Cisco often offer a look-alike interface.

9.2.2.5   *Inter-PDP Communication*

Some debate circulates about the degree of direct communication required between PDPs. From the previous illustration of the components of a policy system, it is clear that PDPs communicate with the PEPs below them and with the data stores above them. Implicit inter-PDP communication results from the fact that multiple PDPs share a common data store and that the PEPs served by one PDP communicate via RSVP with the PEPs shared by another PDP (and, somewhat less explicitly, by the passage of in-band DSCP values from one PEP to another). For example, if one PDP causes a PEP to reject an RSVP request, then other PDPs along the same data path learn of the rejection via RSVP signaling along the path. Thus, inter-PEP communication provides implicit inter-PDP communication.

However, relying on RSVP or the passage of DSCPs between PEPs on the one hand, or on a central data store on the other hand as the exclusive means for inter-PDP communications can be quite limiting. RSVP messages are not spontaneously generated by PDPs (with the possible exception of certain proxy creations). In-band DSCPs do not offer very rich interaction. The central data store is typically a repository for relatively static information and cannot be used to exchange dynamic information between PDPs. As a result, it is possible that PDPs will use some means of direct inter-PDP communication. This further complicates the policy management system, as illustrated in Figure 9.5.

Figure 9.5 illustrates the inherent inter-PDP communication that results from the passage of RSVP messages through each PEP along a network path and from each PEP to its corresponding PDP. It also illustrates an additional potential inter-PDP communication mechanism in which PDPs communicate directly with each other, without going through their associated PEPs and the RSVP protocol.

Figure 9.5   Inter-PDP Communication

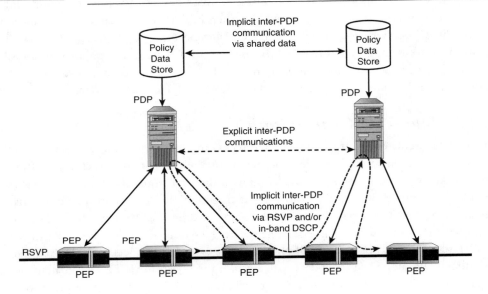

9.2.3 *Policy Data Stores and Directories*

A data store resides at the peak of the policy management system pyramid. The data store contains all the information required to apply network policies. Such information may include the following:

- **Network topology information**—Represents the devices in the network, their interfaces, and the connections between them.

- **Device and interface capacity and capability information**—Represents the capacity of the various devices and interfaces, and the functionality available on the interface (signaling capability, traffic-handling capabilities, and so on).

- **Allocations of resources (per static global policy) among resource pools at each interface**—Represents allocation of each interface capacity among the various resource pools described in Chapter 2.

- **Transnetwork services**—Represents parameters of services offered in the network (such as virtual leased-line services) and the SLAs representing these to customers.

- **Policies governing access to resources based on users**—Indicates which users and user groups are entitled to resources in different parts of the network at different times.

- **Policies governing access to resources based on applications**—Indicates which applications or parts of applications are entitled to resources in different parts of the network at different times.

This list is representative but not exhaustive. The application of the information described will be discussed in the section "Applying Policies," later in this chapter. The following subsections describe the data store itself in further depth.

9.2.3.1 Requirements of the Data Store

A data store that is suitable for storing QoS policy data has certain requirements. These are described in the following paragraphs.

Central Write, Distributed Read

The network manager must be able to administer policies from a single central location, regardless of the location of the participating PDPs. This location may change from time to time, depending on the location of the network manager; however, at any time, the network manager should not be required to move between sites to administer network policy. Therefore, it is necessary to present the network manager with a centralized view of the network policy data.

At the same time, the policy data must be accessible to PDPs that are distributed across the network. Therefore, it is necessary to distribute the policy data across a broad physical region. These requirements can be accommodated by a logically centralized but physically distributed data store. Such a data store has the benefits of improved scalability and fault tolerance. It also alleviates the need for PDPs to maintain wide-area connections to access a central data store. In any case, distributed data stores are often available because they are required for purposes other than network QoS policy management. A common form of distributed data store is a *directory*. Directories will be shown to be quite suitable for use as a policy data store. The concept of the distributed directory and its role in policy management is illustrated in Figure 9.6.

Figure 9.6 shows three PDPs serving six PEPs. The PDPs access policy data via the servers marked S1 and S2. These are *directory servers* (see the section "Directory Servers," later in this chapter). The directory servers may be geographically dispersed. Directory data (illustrated in the form of the triangle) is distributed across multiple such directory servers. These servers each cache relevant pieces of the directory data in attached storage devices.

One of the consequences of using a distributed directory as a data store is that data cannot be updated instantaneously, across all nodes of the directory. The process of distributing directory data updates is known as *replication*. Because replication is not instantaneous, devices that rely on the directory must tolerate transient conditions during which data is inconsistent between different directory nodes. Such inconsistencies will tend to be exacerbated the more frequently data is changed. Thus, directories are more suitable for relatively static policy data. More dynamic policy data must be maintained in the policy servers, PEPs, or alternate data stores. In addition to the data consistency limitations of distributed directories, they tend not to support atomic transactions or relational queries. Fortunately, these are not strict requirements of a policy data store.

Figure 9.6   Using a Directory as a Distributed Data Store

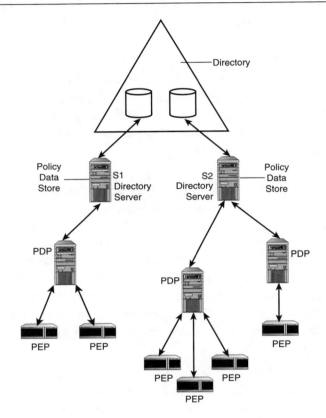

Security and Fault Tolerance

Because the data store contains usernames and mission-critical information, it must be both secure and fault-tolerant. The distributed nature of a directory makes it relatively immune to local faults, providing fault tolerance. However, it also compromises security. Data is vulnerable to snooping and spoofing as it is replicated between directory nodes. In addition, the vulnerability of a single node to direct malicious attacks on the node is multiplied by the number of nodes when considering the vulnerability of the directory as a whole.

Efficient Data Storage Model

Directories typically store large volumes of heterogeneous data. Consider the amount of data that is associated with a 20,000-employee enterprise. Besides network data, there are employee records, accounting data, inventory data, and so on. Often, overlap exists between data consumed for different purposes. For example, both payroll and network policies may associate data with individual employees or groups of employees. Any individual data consumer needs to be able to access specific data relevant to the specific consumer without tediously wading through pools of irrelevant data. To make data access efficient, data must be structured efficiently. Typically, this is achieved through a hierarchical data storage model.

Reusability of Management Data

In a large enterprise, the network manager must handle unwieldy volumes of information, such as lists of 20,000 employees and lists of hundreds of deployed applications. It is desirable that this data be at least consistent with—and preferably shared between—the various management applications used in the enterprise, whether these pertain to QoS, to server privileges, or to payroll information. A central enterprise directory facilitates such sharing of data. At a minimum, it obviates the need for the network manager to input the list of employees (because presumably the list is already available for the purpose of payroll management or other applications). Beyond this, it enables the network manager, for example, to use the same groupings of employees by organizational units that are used for other aspects of organizational management.

9.2.3.2   Elements of the Directory

The following paragraphs describe the various elements that comprise the directory.

Directory Servers

The directory data is distributed among a number of *directory servers*. These are physical devices, typically server-class PCs with a significant capacity for data storage (such as hard disks). Directory servers are located in topological proximity to the consumers of the data that they hold. This strategy reduces the need for PDPs to access policy information over relatively low-bandwidth WANs. As a result, PDPs have fast access to policy information. The relatively slow nature of WAN links then impacts replication (which, by its nature, is a relatively slow process) rather than PDP access.

Schemas

Because the directory contains data that is consumed by different devices from different vendors (in the context of QoS policy management, these are primarily PDPs), it is important to have a common representation of the data. As shown previously, different types of policy data exist. For each type of policy data, different sets of data structures will be appropriate. Structures corresponding to different types of policy will likely be interrelated. The content and form of these different structures comprise a *model* for representing the data. The different data models are known as *schemas*.

Standard schemas promote interoperability. Standard schemas would enable PDPs from different vendors to make use of the same policy data. Well-designed schemas represent the underlying data in a simple and intuitive form. This form resides between the user interface (from above) and the hardware (from below). As such, the schemas are reflected in the user interface. To the extent that these are simple and standard, they can simplify the user interface and the work of the network manager. The policy framework working group of the IETF has been tasked with the standardization of schemas to be used for network policy management in general and for QoS management specifically.

Data Access Interface

Assuming that schemas exist to describe the structure of data in the directory, it is necessary to use a protocol to store and retrieve this data. *Lightweight Directory Access Protocol* (LDAP) is a commonly accepted protocol designed to efficiently access directory data. LDAP likely will emerge as the standard protocol by which PDPs access policy data from a directory form of policy data store. Of course, directories are not mandated. Certain systems may use alternate database systems, in which case, the corresponding database access protocols would be used.

User Interface

The data access interface discussed previously is a relatively low-level interface used to directly manipulate the data in the directory. The user interface is a higher-level interface that is presented to the network manager. It may be closely related to the data access interface and to the schemas used for data representation in the directory. However, it must present a user-friendly, abstract view of network policies to the network manager.

It is reasonable to consider the user interface as residing immediately above the data store in the abstraction that is the policy pyramid. For this reason, the user interface is discussed here in the context of the data store or the directory. In this model of a policy management system (illustrated in Figure 9.7a):

1. The network manager installs data into the directory.

2. The data is retrieved by the PDPs.

3. PDPs pass the data to the PEPs to effect the policies.

This model suffers from certain limitations. Specifically, the interaction between the network manager applying policies and the PDP, which understands these policies, is restricted by the nature of data exchange via a general-purpose directory. All data must be expressed in the format of the data store. PDPs cannot apply sanity checks to data and feed back the results in real time (although the management console may be capable of applying limited sanity checks); in general, the user interface offers little, if any, support for dynamic monitoring or configuration.

| **Figure 9.7** | Alternate Models of a Policy System User Interface |

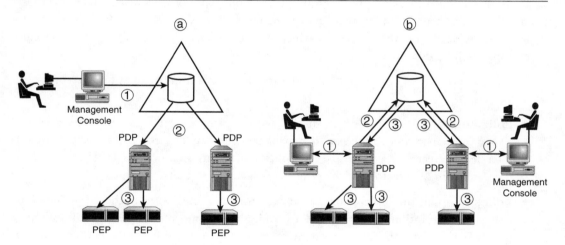

In an alternate model (illustrated in Figure 9.7b), the following occurs:

1. The network manager accesses the policy system via a user interface offered by a PDP.

2. The PDP then relays data, as appropriate, to be stored in the directory.

3. PDPs retrieve information from the directory to be pushed to their PEPs.

Note that this approach supports monitoring of the network via the user interface in real time (as indicated by the bidirectional arrows between the management consoles and the PDPs, as well as between the PDPs and the PEPs). Although this approach eliminates the problems illustrated previously, it raises problems of its own:

- How is data consistency maintained?

- Is the network manager required to communicate with multiple PDPs?

- If not, which PDP should the network manager communicate with?

- Is a replication protocol between PDPs required, or is it sufficient for the front-end PDP to use the directory to replicate policy data?

In the subsequent section on applying policies, the first model is assumed. However, it is still not clear which model will become standard in the long run. It is possible that both models will co-exist.

9.3 Applying Policies

Previous sections of this chapter described the various types of QoS management policies and the components of policy management systems. This section brings these concepts together by describing the process by which different policies are actually applied. Specific examples will be described.

The application of policy can be considered to consist of a number of abstract steps, as follows:

- **Policy authoring**—In this stage, the policy management system user interface presents a view of the network to the network manager. The network manager then uses the user interface to create, or author, a set of policies. The authored policies are likely stored in the data store or directory of the policy management system.

- **Policy compilation**—In this stage, the policy servers convert the authored policies into a set of configuration information. This configuration information is targeted both at the PEPs that are distributed across the network and at the policy servers that maintain connections to the PEPs.

- **Policy installation**—In this stage, the policy servers install the configuration information created in the previous stage. Much of the information is "pushed" into the PEPs. Different configuration information may be pushed to different PEPs, depending on their location and role in the network. Other configuration information remains in the policy server to be used to handle outsourced decisions.

- **Status reporting**—PEPs respond to configuration by reporting results to policy servers. These, in turn, report results to the network manager. Status reporting continues beyond the initial installation phase. Lower-level devices in the policy pyramid may continually offer information regarding the status of network resources to layers above them.

9.3.1   The Format of Authored and Compiled Policies

Many of the policies related to QoS can be authored at an abstract level in the following fundamental form:

traffic description : service

The first part of the policy describes a set of traffic to which a specific service is to be provided. The second part describes the service to provide (in a broad sense rather than at a specific PEP). These policies are then compiled into this lower-level form:

classification criteria : action

Within PEPs, the specific subsets of traffic described in the abstract expression of the policy are identified by classification criteria. The classification criteria may be very coarse-grained, such as a DSCP or a source IP subnetwork, or may be fine-grained, specifying, for example, a single conversation. The service specified in the abstract expression of policy may take the form of a reservation or a prioritization, for example. The broad service is provided by enabling certain local actions in PEPs. For instance, such actions may include the creation of a reservation (in the IntServ sense, as described in Chapter 4), the application of policing parameters, queuing parameters, marking, and so forth. Different actions may have to be enabled in different PEPs, depending on their location in the network.

The formats illustrated are very fundamental. Useful policies will likely call for various *conditions* to be met for certain traffic to be provided certain service. For example, a service may be provided to the specified traffic only at a certain time of day or only to a certain amount of traffic. Conditions can be expressed as part of the traffic description or as part of the service to be provided. Time-of-day conditions might compile into instructions to enable, disable, or modify the policy based on time of day. Conditions limiting the amount of traffic entitled to a service might compile into metering actions (see Chapter 6 for a discussion of the term *metering*).

Generally, the policy management system enables the network manager to author policies in the high-level abstract form and then compiles these into low-level detailed classification criteria and actions.

Note that not all policies take the form described here. Physical provisioning (described in the following section) is one exception. Similarly, the logical provisioning of certain equipment for different modes of operation (such as aggregate versus per-conversation traffic handling) is another exception. The form described is particularly applicable to semi-static and to dynamic policies, and somewhat less to static global policies.

9.3.2 Applying Static Global Provisioning Policies

Static global provisioning policies were described earlier in this chapter. In addition, static provisioning was discussed in Chapter 6, in the context of DiffServ. Provisioning policies such as these are relatively static and therefore are applied infrequently. The application of static global policies entails both physical provisioning and logical provisioning. The distinction between physical and logical provisioning was first explained in Chapter 6.

9.3.2.1 Physical Provisioning

Physical provisioning refers to the process of selecting the appropriate hardware devices, interfaces, and interconnects. The policy management system described in this chapter is not likely to be used in the physical provisioning process. Instead, capacity-planning tools are generally used. These help the network manager to physically provision a network to meet target capacity requirements. That said, there is substantial overlap between the functionality required for capacity planning and for policy management. As such, there is a trend toward providing both sets of functionality in a common package.

Note that decisions made during the physical provisioning phase will determine the QE curves applicable to the network and the operating points of the network on the QE curve. For example, selecting equipment that supports sophisticated QoS mechanisms will generally enable operating curves that support a high QE product. The degree of overprovisioning or underprovisioning of capacity will then determine where on the QE curve the network operates. A policy of overprovisioning will compromise efficiency in favor of the QoS that can be supported. A policy of underprovisioning will compromise service qualities in favor of efficiency. If the QE product is high enough, it will be possible to offer high-quality services with minimal overprovisioning.

9.3.2.2 Logical Provisioning

Because the *physical* component of static global provisioning is outside the scope of the policy management system, this chapter concentrates instead on the *logical* component of static global provisioning. Recall from Chapter 2 that a single physical network can support several superimposed virtual networks, each characterized by a different QE product.

The logical component of static global provisioning refers to the process of allocating physical network resources among the different virtual networks by creating different resource pools. The following resource pools were identified in Chapter 2:

- Resources available to quantifiable traffic requiring high-quality guarantees

- Resources available to nonquantifiable persistent traffic requiring high- to medium-quality service

- Resources available to nonquantifiable, nonpersistent traffic requiring medium- to low-quality service

- Resources available to best-effort traffic

Figure 9.8 illustrates the use of static global policies to create the resource pools described.

Figure 9.8   Using Static Global Policies to Divide a Network into Resource Pools

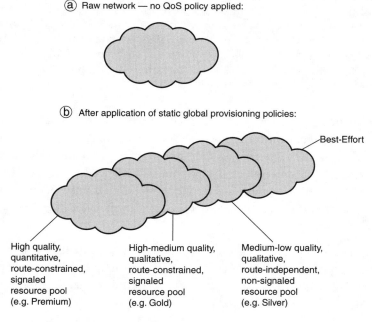

ⓐ Raw network — no QoS policy applied:

ⓑ After application of static global provisioning policies:

Best-Effort

High quality, quantitative, route-constrained, signaled resource pool (e.g. Premium)

High-medium quality, qualitative, route-constrained, signaled resource pool (e.g. Gold)

Medium-low quality, qualitative, route-independent, non-signaled resource pool (e.g. Silver)

Authoring Static Global Provisioning Policies

A policy management system facilitates the process of static global provisioning by first presenting a map of the network topology to the network manager. It then guides the network manager in authoring policies that determine the allocation of resources in different regions of the network, among different resource pools. Presented with the network topology, the network manager must decide which quality of services are to be supported through different parts of the network. The next policy decision that must be made concerns the relative amount of resources that should be applied to the different quality services (and hence allocated to the corresponding resource pool) in each part of the network.

For example, for best results, only a small fraction of network capacity should be allocated for high-quality quantitative services. Overallocation of resources to the high-quality service pool tends to compromise lower-quality services.

Note

In addition, dedicating a large proportion of a link's capacity to a single resource pool tends to reduce the quality of the service that can be supported by the pool, specifically in terms of the latency guarantees that can be offered. Consider, for example, a high-quality service that is supported using strict priority. If only 5% of a 100Mbps link's resources are dedicated to this service, and if admission control is properly applied, then traffic using the high-priority service will never compete with more than 5Mbps of competing traffic. On the other hand, if 50% of the link's resources is dedicated to the high-priority service, then traffic using the high-priority service will compete with up to 50Mbps of competing traffic. From the perspective of the average bandwidth available, the two cases are equivalent. However, from the perspective of latency assurances, they are not.

Thus, the network manager may decide to allocate 5% or 10% of capacity in each region of the network to the highest-quality resource pool. The policy management system might offer suggestions to the network manager. For example, it might suggest that more resources can safely be allocated to this pool in higher-speed regions of the network (such as LANs) without unduly compromising the service. In a similar manner, the policy management system would guide the network manager in the allocation of resources to lower-quality resource pools.

The policy management system should help abstract the concept of resource pools. It might name the pools in a manner that suggests their usage. For example, the high-quality, quantitative pool might be considered to offer *premium* service, with lower-quality pools offering *gold*, *silver*, and *bronze* services.

Compiling and Installing Static Global Policies

When the network manager has authored the static global policies, it is necessary to compile these into configuration information and to install this information into PEPs. Policy servers compile these policies into information appropriate for the types of PEPs present in different parts of the network. For example, to create the high-quality resource pool (described previously) in a DiffServ domain, the policy servers might generate the following configuration information for each PEP:

- Enable DiffServ mode operation.

- Enable the EF DSCP in each PEP, to be used for high-quality services. (See Chapter 6 for a discussion of the EF, or *expedited forwarding*, PHB.)

- Create a strict priority queue (or alternate prioritization mechanism) in each PEP to serve EF-marked traffic.

- Configure policing mechanisms in some subset of the PEPs to assure that no more than 10% of an egress link's capacity is used for the EF DSCP.

Note

Note that this example decomposes the process of creating an EF PHB (and parameterizing it to support a certain quality resource pool) into four fine-grained steps. Assuming DiffServ router support, the four fine-grained steps might be replaced with a single macro of the form "Create an EF PHB with the Following Parameters."

In an 802 LAN, policy servers would generate similar configuration information, appropriate for 802 PEPs:

- Enable four 802 traffic classes in each switch.

- Map user_priority value 0x05 to the highest-priority traffic class.

- Configure policing mechanisms in some subset of the switches to ensure that no more than 10% of an egress link's capacity is allowed into the highest-priority traffic class.

In PEPs in which strict priority queuing is not available, policy servers might configure a heavily weighted queue in a *weighted fair queuing* (WFQ) scheme instead.

In certain regions of the network, it might be appropriate to enable conventional RSVP/IntServ–style operation. In this case, the following configuration information would be generated:

- Enable select PEPs to participate in RSVP signaling (to act as admission control agents).

- Configure RSVP admission control limits for each IntServ service type, in each RSVP-enabled PEP.

- Enable WFQ or alternate traffic handling in each PEP in support of RSVP/IntServ.

As a variant on the conventional per-conversation RSVP/IntServ model, PEPs might be enabled to participate in RSVP signaling but to apply DiffServ style aggregate traffic handling. This mode of operation will be discussed in further detail later in this chapter, in the section "Dynamic Policy Applied with Aggregate Traffic Handling."

The compilation and installation of static global provisioning policies is illustrated in Figure 9.9 for three different types of PEPs.

Figure 9.9   Compilation and Installation of Static Global Configuration Information

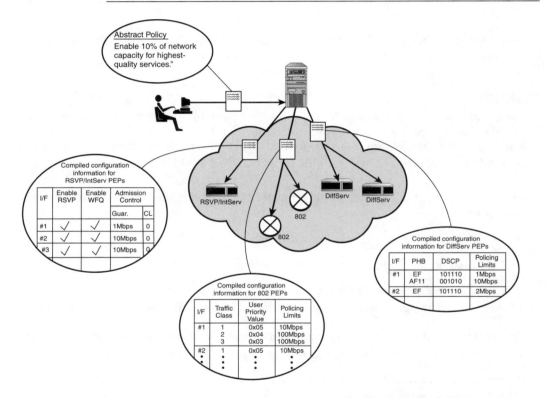

The three different PEPs correspond to the three examples described previously, as follows:

- **RSVP/IntServ–aware devices**—For these PEPs, the policy compiles into commands to enable RSVP, enable WFQ, and configure quantitative limits for explicit admission control.

- **802 devices**—For these PEPs, the policy compiles into mappings from user_priority values to traffic classes (configuration of the traffic classes is not explicitly illustrated in the figure), and the configuration of implicit admission control limits for the amount of traffic that will be admitted to each class.

- **DiffServ devices**—For these PEPs, the policy compiles into mappings from DSCPs to PHBs (configuration of the PHBs themselves is not explicitly illustrated in this figure), and the configuration of implicit admission control limits for the amount of traffic that will be admitted to each PHB.

Note that, for each PEP, compiled configuration information is likely to be generated on a per-interface basis.

> **Note**
>
> The IETF policy working group is currently debating the value of the concept of *roles* in policy application. A role would define a set of interfaces of a certain type, all of which get treated identically by the policy system. So, for example, policy might identify a role of *high-speed LAN interface*. In this case, compiled configuration information might be generated for a specific role and then pushed to all interfaces matching that role.

In general, compilation of the sort of static provisioning policies described in this section focuses on the overall mode of operation of the PEP and on queuing parameters. Queuing parameters are typically (but not necessarily) installed on a PEP's egress interfaces. Queues are created with relative priorities or weights, to accommodate the distinct resource pools or service levels specified by the policies. Associated classification and policing criteria may be installed on ingress interfaces. However, in the case of static global policies, these tend to be coarse-grained and very simple.

During installation of compiled policy, PEPs may respond, indicating that there are insufficient resources on a certain interface or that a certain traffic-handling mechanism is not available. Policy servers would have to respond accordingly, informing the network manager if they are incapable of accommodating the specified policies.

> **Note**
>
> To optimize interaction between devices and their PDPs, it is helpful for devices to be capable of reporting device capabilities to their PDP. For example, PDPs could benefit from knowing ahead of time which devices are capable of RSVP signaling and which are not. Such capability reporting functionality is supported via COPS/PR.

9.3.2.3 *Participation in Signaling and Traffic Handling Mode*

The choice of QE product required in different parts of a network will dictate which PEPs are required to participate in aggregate signaling or per-conversation signaling, and which can ignore signaling messages (as well as additional details regarding the handling of signaling messages).

The choice of QE product also dictates which PEPs implement aggregate traffic handling and which implement per-conversation traffic handling. Policy servers should aid the network manager in attaining the required QE product in each part of the network by configuring PEPs to participate or not participate in per-conversation or aggregate RSVP signaling, and to enable the appropriate traffic-handling mechanisms. The impact of the operating mode of the PEP (in terms of signaling participation and traffic handling) on the QE product is tabulated in Figure 2.3 in Chapter 2.

9.3.3 Applying Semi-static Policies

When network resources have been allocated to the various resource pools described in the previous section, these pools can be further subdivided for use by different traffic aggregates. For example, a large provider might divide resources among peer providers or enterprise or campus customer networks that are paying for the provider's network resources. Within an enterprise network, resources may be divided among corporate departments, other user groups, or groups of applications.

The provisioning of semi-static policies is more dynamic than the static global provisioning described previously, but it is nonetheless relatively static when compared with finer-grain dynamic allocation policies. The effect of applying semi-static policies is illustrated in Figure 9.10. In the specific example illustrated, resources are shared among customers of a provider's network.

Note

Note that the total allocation of resources at this stage need not add up to exactly 100%. In the case of resource pools that offer lower-quality services, the pool may be oversubscribed (exploiting the potential of statistical multiplexing). In the case of resource pools that offer higher-quality services, allocations must not exceed 100% and may be lower than 100%.

Figure 9.10   Using Semi-static Policies to Share Resource Pools Among Customers

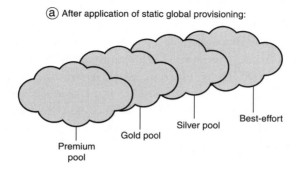

(a) After application of static global provisioning:

Premium
pool

Gold pool

Silver pool

Best-effort

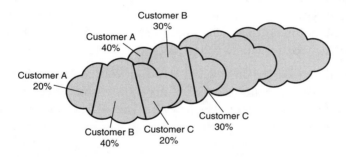

(b) After application of semi-static provisioning:

Customer B
30%

Customer A
40%

Customer A
20%

Customer C
30%

Customer B   Customer C
40%   20%

The allocation of any resource pool among traffic aggregates can be changed without requiring reallocation of overall network resources among the high-level resource pools. Over time, a network manager may observe that there are insufficient resources in a pool to satisfy demand. This might lead to adjustments in static global provisioning. These adjustments may be physical (such as the addition of physical resources to the network). Alternatively, these adjustments may be logical (such as the reallocation of resources among pools).

Semi-static policies are typically pushed policies in the sense that they are pushed from policy servers to PEPs. These policies are typically pushed in anticipation of traffic patterns and resource requirements. As such, they can be contrasted with signaled dynamic policies that are typically effected as individual traffic flows come and go. (See Chapter 1 for a discussion of pushed versus signaled provisioning and configuration information.)

9.3.3.1 Examples of Semi-static Policies

The following are examples of semi-static policies:

- The manager of a DiffServ provider network negotiates SLAs with managers of customer networks. An SLA specifies aggregate amounts of resources (from the provider's network) to which a customer is entitled. Because the provider's network offers resources from different pools to support different service levels, the SLA reflects this by specifying aggregate resources available to the customer at each service level separately. As the network manager negotiates SLAs, the manager is basically doling out the resources available in each pool among its customers. Policies determine how much of a particular pool's resources are allocated to each customer in different parts of the network.

- Within an enterprise or campus network, formal SLAs might not be negotiated. However, administrative policies might determine certain allocations of resources among groups of network users. For example, a certain enterprise might choose to implement a policy that offers accountants prioritized access to resources during the last five days of each month. Such a policy might be implemented to facilitate end-of-month financial report generation and payroll work.

- Certain applications have the potential to abuse network resources. For example, the network game Doom brought a number of networks to their knees when it first became popular on the Microsoft campus. The news and advertising application Pointcast wrought havoc with many enterprise networks as it gained popularity. Network managers often must resort to extreme measures, prohibiting the deployment of such applications. A preferable approach would be to use QoS policies to limit the impact that these applications have on network resources.

9.3.3.2 Authoring Semi-static Policies

Semi-static policies nearly always conform to the abstract format described earlier in this chapter in the section "The Format of Authored and Compiled Policies." For example, a semi-static policy might be authored in this form:

All traffic of the SAP/R3 application is entitled to silver service.

The policy management system will compile this policy to low-level configuration information, as described in the following section. However, the authoring interface presented to the network manager should remain abstract. It should enable the network manager to describe useful traffic aggregates such as customers, users, user groups, and applications in plain text. It should also enable the network manager to express services in abstract form.

9.3.3.3 Compiling and Installing Semi-static Policies

The compilation of semi-static policies converts the abstract expressions of traffic aggregates into classification criteria. It converts abstract expressions of services into traffic-conditioning actions and parameters appropriate for different PEPs. The policies are then installed by pushing the appropriate classification criteria and traffic-conditioning actions and parameters to different PEPs in the network.

To this end, the policy management system maintains tables mapping user-friendly representations of useful traffic aggregates to the corresponding classification information. It also maintains tables of abstract service names and the corresponding DSCPs, 802 user_priority values, and other traffic-conditioning parameters necessary to provide the service.

Note

Note that the mappings from applications, users, and other traffic aggregates to classification criteria may or may not be static. In many cases, these might change each time an application starts up or each time a user gets a new IP address. Furthermore, applications may use multiple ports for different subsets of their traffic. In all these cases, various mechanisms can be exploited to help the policy management system maintain its internal mappings. RSVP signaling is an obvious and very straightforward way of feeding useful classification information to policy systems. Other mechanisms are also used but smack somewhat of Rube Goldberg machines. Examples are policy systems that communicate with DHCP or DNS servers to glean mapping information.

The policy management system must also understand the network in which it installs policies. It must have a minimal understanding of the network topology (the more accurate, the better), and it must understand the capabilities of the various PEPs under its control.

Compiling and Installing an Application-Centric Policy in an Enterprise LAN

The high-level policy described in the previous section called for all SAP/R3 traffic to be provided silver service. Consider the installation of this policy in an enterprise LAN. The policy might compile into the following low-level configuration information to be pushed to switches at the periphery of the LAN:

All traffic from source TCP/IP port 5304 must be marked with user_priority 0x03.

This assumes that IP port 5304 can be used as the classification criteria by which SAP/R3 traffic can be identified. It also assumes that PEPs in the core of the LAN have been provisioned (using static global policies) to provide silver service for packets marked with 802 user_priority 0x03. The compilation and installation of this policy is illustrated in Figure 9.11:

Figure 9.11   Compiling and Installing an Application-Centric Policy in an Enterprise LAN

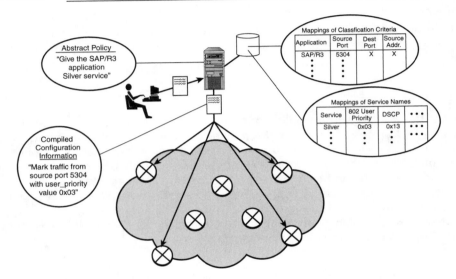

The example illustrated is quite simplistic. There is no concept of admission control in the application of this policy. Excessive amounts of SAP/R3 traffic might overwhelm the silver service. In the absence of the appropriate static global policing policies in the core, this traffic might also compromise traffic entitled to lower service levels (such as best-effort traffic). Although semi-static policies are appropriate for managing medium-quality services, higher-quality services can be provided more efficiently using dynamic policies (that incorporate signaling and explicit admission control).

This example is also simplistic in the sense that it applies policy only to a single type of PEP with a single traffic-handling mechanism. In this example, all PEPs are 802 switches and use 802 user_priority to prioritize traffic. In real networks, there are likely to be a variety of PEPs with differing functionality.

Adding a Customer to a DiffServ Network

Another application of semi-static policy is in the addition of a new customer to a DiffServ provider's network. When a customer is added to a DiffServ network, the customer and the provider negotiate an SLA describing the service that the customer can expect. The

SLA can be expressed in the form of a high-level policy. Consider for example, the following policy:

> Provide customer A 2Mbps of gold service (invoked by DSCP 0x05) from ingress R1 to egress R2.

Figure 9.12 illustrates the compilation and installation of this policy in the DiffServ network.

Figure 9.12   Installing a User-Centric Semi-static Policy Across a DiffServ Network

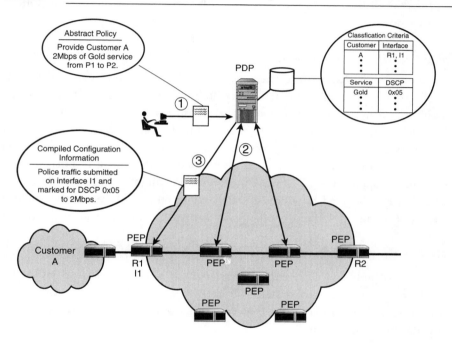

The policy is conveyed to a central PDP in (1). In (2), the PDP verifies that sufficient resources remain available to provide gold service along the traffic path from R1 to R2. This requires the PDP to have some knowledge of routing within the DiffServ network so that it can identify the devices that will be impacted by traffic flowing from R1 to R2. Presumably, the PDP is aware of the resources that have already been allocated for gold service in the core of the DiffServ network (by the application of static global policies). If resources are not sufficient, the PDP must reject the new semi-static policy. If resources are sufficient, the PDP can proceed to compile and install the appropriate classification and policing information (3) for the PEP R1. This information takes this form:

> Police traffic submitted on R1, interface I1 (from Customer A), destined for R2 and marked for DSCP 0x05, to 2Mbps.

The classification criteria include the interface on which traffic is submitted, as well as the DSCP mark in the traffic's IP header. (In this example, the traffic is assumed to be marked *before* it is submitted to the network.) The traffic-conditioning action is the policing. (In reality, policing actions are likely to require a more complex profile such as a token bucket model.)

If resources are not available to support the new semi-static policy, the network manager may modify the static global policies to allocate additional resources for gold service in PEPs in the core of the network. Alternatively, the network manager may negotiate a lesser SLA with Customer A.

Complex Classification Criteria

Semi-static policies tend to require finer-grained configuration information than static global policies. The classification criteria associated with these policies may be quite complex, requiring relatively large amounts of storage and fast processing in PEPs. For example, consider a policy that states that executives are entitled to silver service for accounting applications. Unless all executives share a common address space, the classification criteria might compile to a long list of IP addresses logically "anded" with a list of IP ports identifying the set of accounting applications. The classification criteria might be significantly simplified if all executives were allocated IP addresses on the same subnet. However, this could prove awkward topologically and might conflict with or preclude alternate address groupings.

Conflicting Classification Criteria

Because of the complexity of classification criteria that is often associated with semi-static policies, the policy management system will likely be required to resolve conflicts at policy compilation time. An example of the type of conflict that is likely to arise is illustrated by the following two compiled policies:

All traffic on source TCP/IP port 5305 gets marked AF11.

All traffic from source subnet 2.3.0.0 gets marked AF31.

These create a potential conflict in handling traffic on source port 5305 from subnet 2.3.0.0. How should such traffic be marked? The policy management system should detect the potential conflict. It may offer a strategy for resolving the conflict, such as prioritizing TCP/IP port matches over IP address matches. Alternatively, it may require the network manager to resolve the conflict.

Effect of Classification Criteria on Resource Consumption

Many semi-static policies will configure traffic-conditioning components to mark traffic that meets certain classification criteria for a certain DSCP or user_priority value (or alternate aggregate traffic-handling mechanism such as an aggregate ATM VC). As part of the compilation process, the policy management system should consider the effect of each policy on resource consumption at each node and across the network. (This process is illustrated in step 2 of Figure 9.12.)

In general, as classification criteria are added, more traffic becomes eligible for a limited set of resources. This traffic may interfere with other traffic directed to the same service level or might starve traffic directed to a lower service level. Without signaling- or measurement-based feedback, the policy system generally will not have the intelligence to estimate the volume of traffic that will actually match installed classification criteria. However, it can assist the network manager by generating warnings. For example, a warning might be generated when policies are installed that direct additional traffic to a previously committed service level. Similarly, warnings could be generated for policies resulting in very coarse-grain classification criteria (as these would tend to direct higher traffic volumes).

Policing for Semi-static Policies

Policy compilation often results in the installation of policing functionality at various nodes (as illustrated in Figure 9.12). Policies specifying SLAs, for example, require policing information to be installed at network ingress nodes. Further policing may be configured internally to isolate the impact of different traffic aggregates on each other. The policing that is installed in response to semi-static policies differs from policing that is installed for the more static global policies. The latter is put in place to carve up the network into different resource pools. The former is put in place to limit the amount of resources that any customer or other traffic aggregate can seize *within* a resource pool. As such, policing for semi-static policies will tend to be finer-grained and more complex.

The configuration of policing parameters requires careful attention. Because qualitative applications cannot commit to specific quantitative limits on the traffic that they generate, policing of such traffic should not be overly aggressive. Policing of qualitative traffic should be of a form that gracefully and gradually degrades service rather than abruptly discarding all traffic above a certain threshold. Such policing can be achieved on a per-service-level basis by using various buffer management and work-conserving queuing schemes such as random early detection (RED) and WFQ, respectively (see Chapter 3, "Queuing Mechanisms," for a discussion of queuing mechanisms). It is more difficult to use these queuing mechanisms to police on a finer-grain basis. To do so would require hierarchical queuing (such as class-based queuing, or CBQ), as illustrated in Figure 9.13.

Figure 9.13 Hierarchical Queuing Used to Isolate Traffic Aggregates Within a Service Level

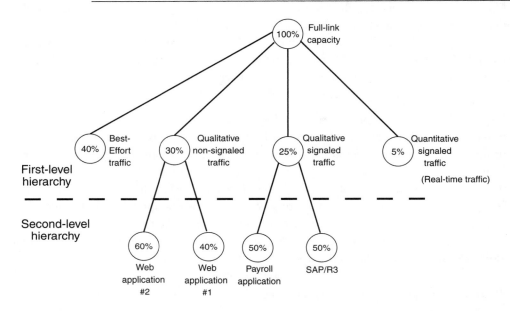

In Figure 9.13, 5% of the link is allocated to real-time, quantifiable traffic. Subflows within this category can be policed to quantifiable limits and accommodated via quantifiable reservations. By contrast, the remainder of the link is allocated to qualitative traffic that cannot be policed to quantifiable limits and cannot be accommodated via quantifiable reservations. Instead, remaining link capacity that is subdivided between applications or users is accommodated using a work-conserving form of hierarchical link sharing.

The compilation and installation of semi-static policies tends to focus on classification criteria and marking and policing at a PEP's ingress interfaces. For the most part, semi-static policies can remain independent of the egress interface queuing parameters that implement the static global policies. Similarly, semi-static policies result primarily in the configuration of PEPs near the periphery of a network region and less in configuration of PEPs in the core of a network region.

9.3.4 *Applying Dynamic Policies*

Dynamic policies differ significantly from the relatively static policies discussed so far. First and foremost, dynamic policies are almost always applied based on signaling along traffic paths. Static policies are almost always pushed in a top-down manner. Whereas static policies are usually applied to aggregate traffic flows, dynamic policies are usually applied to individual traffic flows. Dynamic policies are required to efficiently provide high-quality quantitative services. Lower-quality services can be accommodated by either dynamic or semi-static policies.

Note

Note that these are general guidelines, not hard rules. There are exceptions. For example, the semi-static, pushed policies discussed in the previous section can become quite dynamic when augmented by measurement-based feedback mechanisms.

9.3.4.1   The Operation of Dynamic Policy

Dynamic policies take the familiar form of descriptions of traffic aggregates and the services to which they are entitled. As such, at a high level, dynamic policies may seem quite similar to semi-static policies. However, unlike semi-static policies (which require potentially large tables of classification criteria and the corresponding actions to be pushed down to PEPs), dynamic policies are maintained primarily in the policy servers. Dynamic policies are often not even compiled into lists of classification criteria, but rather remain in abstract form.

The difference between semi-static and dynamic policies is best illustrated by contrasting the operation of the two types of policies in terms of the corresponding PDP/PEP interactions. In the case of semi-static policies, compiled configuration information is pushed down from the PDP to the PEP on a semi-static time scale (such as monthly, weekly, or perhaps hourly). For example, the semi-static policy illustrated in Figure 9.12 pushes compiled configuration information to the PEP when the DiffServ provider and the customer renegotiate their SLA. In the case of semi-static policies that require complex classification criteria (such as "All Executives Are Entitled to Silver Service for Accounting Applications") the compiled configuration information may be quite voluminous. Compiled configuration information resides in the PEP for relatively long periods of time. Whenever traffic arrives, it is compared against the classification criteria in the PEP and is handled accordingly.

By contrast, dynamic policies usually operate in response to RSVP signaling messages. These arrive at PDPs (via PEPs) and announce the imminent arrival of traffic. RSVP signaling messages typically describe traffic corresponding to a single conversation and request service for that conversation. In response, PDPs may do nothing more than approve or reject the service request. Alternatively, they may respond by pushing down a small amount of compiled configuration information to the PEP, corresponding to the conversation described in the signaling message. (See the sidebar "Overlap of COPS/PR and COPS/RSVP" later in this chapter).

> **Note**
>
> Note that the distinction in time scale between semi-static and dynamic policies applies to the *operation* of the policy (in terms of PDP/PEP interaction), not to the *authoring* of the policy. In both cases, the policies may be *authored* on relatively static time scales.

The operation of dynamic policy will be discussed initially in the context of the conventional RSVP/IntServ model. However, dynamic policies can also be applied to variations on this model. These variations will be discussed subsequently.

Applying Dynamic Policy to the Conventional RSVP/IntServ Model

Figure 9.14 illustrates the operation of dynamic policy in the context of the conventional RSVP/IntServ model discussed in Chapters 4 and 5.

Figure 9.14   Interaction Between PEP and PDP to Effect Dynamic Policy for RSVP/IntServ

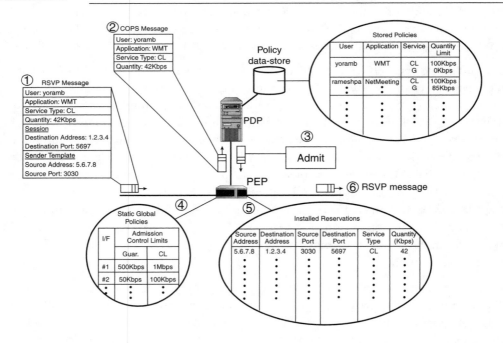

In this example, no classification information is stored in the PEP beforehand. The following steps occur:

1. When a host requires high-quality service for a traffic flow, it generates an RSVP signaling message describing the traffic flow and the desired service. The message arrives at the PEP.

2. The PEP extracts the classification criteria describing the specific flow and stores them temporarily. Contents of the signaling message are then passed up to the policy server, using COPS. This information includes the application and user identity associated with the traffic flow (contained in RSVP policy objects), the required IntServ service type, and the quantity of resources required.

Note

The COPS message typically includes the entire RSVP message. However, for the purpose of making a policy decision, only a subset of the information in the RSVP message may be required.

The example illustrated is abstracted somewhat. In reality, there is not necessarily a single RSVP message that contains the information necessary to make the policy decision. Instead, there are PATH and RESV messages. Each contains different information. Depending on the policies authored, one or both messages may be required to make a policy decision.

The stored policies illustrated specify quantitative resource limits for the cross-product of specific users *and* specific applications. In most cases, policies will likely be authored to control resources for users *or* applications. Because of the sheer number of policies that would result, policies based on the cross-product of users *and* applications likely will be too cumbersome to manage.

3. The policy server compares the request in the signaling message against the dynamic policies stored. It may also apply security mechanisms to authenticate the user identity. The policy server returns the results of the comparison to the PEP, using COPS (3). Rejections are usually accompanied by an RSVP policy error, explaining the reason for rejection.

4. When the PEP receives the result, it acts accordingly. If the request was permitted by the PDP, the PEP will apply admission control (against limits configured previously by static global policy) to assure that resources are available to handle the admitted flow.

Note

Alternatively, the PEP may apply resource-based admission control following Step 1 before it sends the COPS message to the PDP.

5. If resources are available in the PEP, it will install the corresponding reservation. In the RSVP/IntServ model, this amounts to configuring per-conversation classification and policing information for the admitted traffic flow and configuring queuing parameters to assure that the admitted flow enjoys the requested service. The classification

criteria and traffic-conditioning parameters can be extracted from the same RSVP message that was initially received by the PEP. Note that traditional RSVP/IntServ reservations are installed only in response to RSVP RESV messages. RSVP PATH messages may invoke related processing at the PEP and PDP, but they do not trigger the installation of a reservation in the RSVP/IntServ sense. See Chapter 5, "RSVP," for additional detail.

6. The PEP then forwards the RSVP signaling message on its path.

If the request was rejected, no reservation will be installed, and the PEP will generally block the RSVP signaling message and return the appropriate error to the originator in an RSVP policy object. For a list of policy errors, see the accompanying sidebar "Policy Errors."

Policy Errors

The following list contains some of the common policy errors that may be generated by PDPs and/or PEPs. It is not exhaustive.

- UNSUPPORTED_CREDENTIAL_TYPE—The form of authentication credential is not recognized.

- INSUFFICIENT_PRIVILEGES—The flow identified is not entitled to the resources requested.

- EXPIRED_CREDENTIAL—The authentication credential is no longer valid.

- ERR_PREEMPT—A previously approved flow has been pre-empted by a higher-priority flow.

- ERR_PDP—PDP is unavailable.

- ERR_RSVP—A malformed RSVP request occurred.

- ERR_SERVICE—IntServ service type was rejected.

Dynamic Policy Applied with Aggregate Traffic Handling

In the example illustrated in Figure 9.14, the application of the dynamic policy resulted in the configuration of per-conversation classification, policing and queuing information in the PEP. This is often not practical. A PEP in the core of a large network that is required to support many flows is unlikely to provide per-conversation traffic handling because of scalability constraints. Instead, it likely will use a small number of queues to aggregate many conversations into a small number of service levels or traffic classes. This is aggregate traffic handling per DiffServ or 802 user_priority. By combining per-conversation signaling and dynamic policy with aggregate traffic handling, it is possible to offer a high QE product without incurring the overhead of the full per-conversation RSVP/IntServ model. (See Chapter 2, Figure 2.3.)

In one realization of this model, the application of dynamic policy requires no configuration of traffic-handling mechanisms in the PEP. This model relies instead on preconfigured static global policies and trusted hosts (or alternate devices that mark and shape or police traffic upstream). This is illustrated in Figure 9.15.

Figure 9.15   Interaction Between PEP and PDP to Effect Dynamic Policy Combining Per-Conversation Signaling with Aggregate Traffic Handling

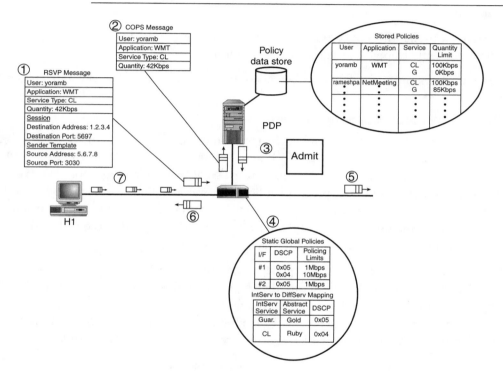

The example in Figure 9.15 is quite similar to that illustrated in Figure 9.14. Steps 1 through 3 are identical. However, the response of the PEP differs in this example from the example illustrated in Figure 9.14. In the previous example, the PEP responded to the PDP's decision to admit a traffic flow by verifying that resources are available to accommodate the flow and by installing an RSVP/IntServ reservation. In this example, the PEP verifies the availability of resources, but it does not install a reservation. In fact, it configures no additional classification or traffic conditioning in response to the admission of the traffic flow. Instead, the PEP applies an admission control decision against previously installed static global policies, based on a *mapping of the requested IntServ service type to DiffServ service levels.*

This functionality is based on the assumption that the admission of an RSVP request for a traffic flow for a certain IntServ service type will result in the marking of traffic on that flow for a corresponding DiffServ service level. The traffic might be marked by the host that generated the RSVP or, alternatively, by an upstream router. In this example, the upstream device marking the traffic on the flow is trusted to do the following:

- To not mark traffic with a DSCP other than best-effort unless the traffic flow was admitted

- To mark traffic with the correct DSCP corresponding to the requested IntServ service (per the same mapping specified in global policies)

- To not mark traffic on the flow in excess of the quantity specified in the initial request

Policing and Marking with Dynamic Policy

In the example illustrated in Figure 9.15, upstream devices are trusted to mark traffic only to the extent that it is admitted via RSVP signaling and dynamic policy. PEPs likely will police the *total* traffic submitted for a particular DSCP (per static global policies). However, they do not, in this case, police each flow that was admitted to a DiffServ service level. If upstream markers mark traffic on individual flows in excess of the quantity admitted at the PEP, then the excess traffic will be discarded or demoted at the PEP without regard for the specific traffic flow with which it is associated.

If upstream markers are not trusted, policy might call for PEPs to police traffic on a per-conversation basis or to remark traffic (thereby ignoring upstream marking) at the PEP on a per-conversation basis. Either approach requires that per-conversation classification information be compiled and pushed to the PEP. However, neither requires per-conversation queuing to be configured in the PEP. Queuing remains on an aggregate basis.

The degree of per-conversation work performed by a specific PEP is a matter of static global policy and is related to trust and scalability issues.

Note

Note that certain complications arise when handling multicast flows. Multicast flows may require some degree of fine-grain classification and traffic conditioning in the network to handle subsets of receivers that are entitled to different qualities of service. See the related discussion in Chapter 7, "The Subnet Bandwidth Manager and 802 Networks," in the section "Receiver Heterogeneity and Multicast."

Using the DCLASS *Object to Override IntServ/DSCP Mappings*

In another variation on the model illustrated in Figure 9.15, policy might direct traffic flows to particular DiffServ service levels on a dynamic basis.

In the example of Figure 9.15, dynamic policy amounted to the admission or rejection of an RSVP request, based on the following:

- The quantity of resources requested at a particular service level

- The availability of resources at that service level in the PEP (per static global policies)

- Dynamic policies regarding the entitlement of the requesting user or application to resources at the requested service level

Dynamic policy can be taken a step further by allowing the PDP to supply an RSVP DCLASS object (see Chapter 5 for a discussion of the DCLASS object) to the PEP. The DCLASS object directs the device marking the traffic flow to use a particular DSCP (as opposed to relying on the global mapping of IntServ service types to determine DSCPs). The PEP appends the DCLASS object to the RSVP RESV message that is sent upstream toward the marking device (see Figure 5.20). The marking device is then expected to mark in accordance with the DCLASS object. If the PEP does the marking (as described in the previous section), then the DCLASS object may remain local to the PEP.

This mode of operation is particularly relevant to the Null Service (see Chapter 4 for a discussion of the Null Service). Recall that this service type is for use by a broad range of qualitative applications that do not readily lend themselves to the standard quantitative IntServ services. Although there are somewhat natural (if debatable) mappings from the Guaranteed and Controlled Load IntServ Services to DiffServ PHBs (and the corresponding DSCPs), there is no obvious mapping from the Null Service type to a particular DSCP. Thus, in the case of qualitative applications and the Null Service, the choice of DSCP becomes entirely a matter of policy. Dynamic policies are likely to associate specific DSCPs with specific qualitative applications. This enables a network manager to prioritize qualitative applications relative to each other, as appropriate for the managed network.

Note that policy systems may use the TCLASS object in the same way that the DCLASS object is used. TCLASS objects affect upstream 802 user_priority markers (as opposed to DSCP markers).

Overlap of COPS/PR and COPS/RSVP

It is interesting to compare the use of COPS/PR and COPS/RSVP in the support of semi-static and dynamic policies. COPS/RSVP was proposed before DiffServ and before the associated push-provisioning mechanisms were broadly considered. The semantics of successful COPS/RSVP admission control can roughly be expressed as follows (see Figure 9.14):

- Intercept RSVP message at PEP.

- Store copy of RSVP message in PEP.

- Use COPS/RSVP to pass RSVP message to PDP for decision.

- PDP approves admission control and returns approval to PEP using COPS/RSVP *decision object*.

- PEP installs RSVP reservation by configuring classifier (per information in RSVP SESSION and SENDER_TEMPLATE objects) and policing and queuing parameters (per information in RSVP FLOWSPEC and SENDER_TSPEC objects).

- PEP forwards RSVP message.

With the arrival of DiffServ, it became clear that a push-provisioning protocol would be useful, so COPS/PR was proposed. The semantics of push provisioning using COPS/PR are as follows (see Figures 9.11 and 9.12):

- PDP uses COPS/PR configuration messages to pass compiled classification criteria to PEP.

- PDP uses COPS/PR configuration messages to pass corresponding compiled traffic-handling parameters to PEP.

In both cases, the net effect is that classifiers and corresponding traffic-handling parameters are configured in the PEP under control of the PDP. In the case of COPS/PR, the classification parameters and the traffic-handling parameters are compiled in the PDP and are *explicitly* pushed to the PEP. In the case of COPS/RSVP, the PDP merely approves a request from the PEP. In doing so, it authorizes the PEP to configure its own classification and traffic-handling parameters, thereby *implicitly* configuring these.

Given that PEPs and PDPs are required to support a range of service qualities subject to both dynamic and semi-static policies, PDPs likely will use both COPS/RSVP and COPS/PR to communicate with PEPs. In retrospect, there is commonality to the semantics of each that could be used to combine COPS/RSVP and COPS/PR. In particular, dynamic policy could be effected via the following semantics:

- Intercept RSVP message at PEP.

- Use COPS/RSVP to pass RSVP message to PDP for decision.

- PDP approves admission control and configures classification criteria and traffic-handling parameters in PEP explicitly, using COPS/PR configuration messages.

- PEP forwards RSVP message.

In this usage, classification criteria and traffic-handling parameters are configured explicitly by a PDP, using COPS/PR whether these are associated with semi-static provisioned policy or with dynamic signaled policy and RSVP. The difference between the semi-static and dynamic cases is that in the dynamic case, the PDP's action is prompted by an unsolicited COPS/RSVP message from the PEP. In the semi-static case, the PDP's action is prompted by a push-provisioning event. This approach merges elements of COPS/PR and COPS/RSVP. The benefits of this merge are a reduction in protocol complexity and a recognition that both signaling and push provisioning result in the configuration of classification information and allocation of resources in the same device.

9.3.4.2 Other Aspects of Dynamic Policy

Dynamic policies may be applied in various models. Different applications of dynamic policy require that the corresponding PEPs be configured to operate in different modes. For example, in the previous sections, the following PEP configuration options were discussed:

- Operate in conventional RSVP/IntServ mode, installing reservations in response to admitted traffic flows

- Operate in a mode that combines RSVP with DiffServ, using only aggregate traffic handling

- Use aggregate queuing, but apply per-conversation marking or policing

These configuration options are a matter of static global policy and would typically be pushed to the PEPs at the time that these policies are compiled and installed. Additional configuration options are relevant to the application of dynamic policy. These options tend to be more dynamic in the sense that they may be applied differently depending on the user or application requesting resources. As such, they are part of the dynamic policies themselves. These are described in the following paragraphs.

Applying Policy on PATH and/or RESV Messages

Recall that RSVP signaling includes PATH messages, which are sent from sender to receiver, and RESV messages, which are sent from receiver to sender. Presumably, the application identification information is the same for PATH and RESV messages corresponding to the same session. However, the user identification is likely different.

Dynamic policies include a specification as to whether they should be applied based on RESV messages, PATH messages, or both. A policy that is applied based on PATH messages only, determines who may *transmit* traffic at a particular service level. A policy that is applied based on RESV messages only, determines who may *receive* traffic at a particular service level. Policies that are applied to the cross-product of PATH and RESV messages determine admissibility of a traffic flow based both on the sender *and* the receiver.

Receiver Proxying

Receiver proxying for RSVP was discussed in Chapter 5. In receiver proxying, a PEP along the traffic path intercepts the sender's PATH message and returns a RESV message in response. Receiver proxying is useful for legacy client/server applications in which it is a relatively simple matter to upgrade a small number of servers to support signaling, but it is impractical to upgrade all clients.

When the proxying PEP is closer to the receiver, the topology-awareness benefits of RSVP signaling are still leveraged. When the proxying PEP is closer to the sender, these benefits are lost, but response times are reduced because signaling messages travel shorter distances. As such, selecting where to proxy for different applications is a matter of policy. The decision whether to proxy is typically based on application. It is a matter of dynamic policy. PDPs implement the network manager's policies regarding proxying for specific applications by directing the appropriate PEP to proxy in response to PATH messages that are associated with certain applications.

Modifying RSVP Objects in the Policy Server

COPS for RSVP [RFC 2748] specifies that a policy server may offer *replacement objects* for certain RSVP objects. Specific replacements may be dictated by dynamic policies. For example, policies may specify that certain applications are entitled to certain quantitative parameters other than those requested. In this case, the policy server might replace an incident RSVP FLOWSPEC with an alternate FLOWSPEC. (Note that the corresponding protocol processing required in the network can be quite complicated.)

9.3.4.3   Identity Objects and Policy Locators

RSVP signaling messages may include policy objects identifying the user or application associated with a traffic flow. This is a very powerful aspect of dynamic policies and signaled QoS in general. The RAP working group of the IETF has authored a number of drafts that describe the format and usage of these objects [RFC 2752], [RFC 2872]. These are discussed in further detail in the following paragraphs.

The Identity Object

IETF drafts specify the format of a POLICY_DATA object. This object includes *policy elements*. Two types of policy elements are defined:

- One type of policy element is used to identify the *user* associated with a traffic flow.

- The other policy element is used to identify the *application* and *subapplication* associated with a traffic flow.

Each policy element contains an Identifier (known as the *Policy Locator*) field and a *Credentials* field. The Credentials field is used to *authenticate* the associated identity element. Authentication is a security-related process that will be described in further detail later in this section.

Policy elements also include a *Policy Error* field and a *Digital Signature* field. The policy server may insert an error code in the Policy Error field to communicate the reason for a policy-based admission control failure to other network devices and to hosts. The Digital Signature field is used to contain additional authentication information in certain cases.

The Policy Locator field is in the form of an X.500 *distinguished name*. This format is commonly used in directories and in the LDAP protocol. It enables the policy locator to be readily parsed in a hierarchical manner. The contents of the policy locator differ between the user identity element and the application identity element, as described subsequently.

Credentials may be in the form of a Kerberos ticket or a public key certificate. Use of the credentials will be described subsequently.

Use and Content of Policy Locators

Policy locators are used as indices into the policy data store. As RSVP messages are passed to policy servers, these extract the policy locator from the message. The policy locator is then used to index into the data store to find the policy corresponding to the user or application. Note that policy may vary from subnet to subnet, so the policy locator may be combined with a subnet or interface identifier to locate interface-specific user or application policy. This is illustrated in Figure 9.16.

The capability to identify the interface from which a request is originating is an important component of policy. Resources on certain interfaces likely will be considerably more expensive than on other interfaces (WAN versus LAN, for example).

Figure 9.16   Combining Policy Locators with Subnet Identifiers to Index into the Policy Data Store

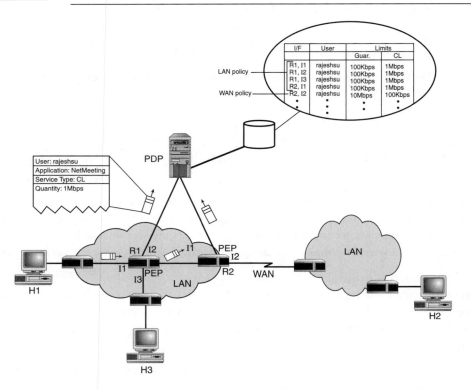

In Figure 9.16, both R1 and R2 are PEPs that are configured as admission control agents and are supported by the same PDP. The PDP maintains separate connections to each PEP and (using COPS) is capable of identifying the specific interface on the PEP from which a signaled request is directed. In the scenario illustrated, H1 generates an RSVP request for resources along the path to H2. The RSVP request is intercepted at both PEPs. The PDP locates different policies for the same user, depending on the specific PEP and interface from which the request was directed to the PDP. Note that the policy for the WAN interface (R2/I2) is more restrictive than the policy for the LAN interfaces (R1/I1, R1/I2, R1/I3, and R2/I1). Because the requested resources (1Mbps) exceed the quantity allowable for the user at R2/I2 (100Kbps), the request will be rejected at R2 and the corresponding rejection messages will be signaled along the path, preventing the installation of the requested reservation between H1 and H2.

On the other hand, if H1 generated the same request for resources to H3, the request would be processed only at R1, and only LAN policies would apply. The request would be admitted.

> **Note**
> Network managers are unlikely to author per-user, per-interface policies. The quantity of data required to express such fine-grain policies would be prohibitively large. Instead, network managers tend to author subnet policies that apply across all users and then to designate a small number of individual users or user groups that are exceptions to the general policy. (For examples of per-subnet policies, see the description of Microsoft's Admission Control Server in Chapter 14, "The Microsoft Admission Control Service.")
>
> In general, subnet policies may apply to the part of a network having a particular range of IP addresses, a LAN, a WAN link, or other various forms of subnetworks.

Policy Hierarchy

Policy data stores may structure policies in various forms. Typically, there is a hierarchical structure to the policies. For example, there may be a default policy that is applied to *any* traffic flow for which the policy locator does not locate a matching user policy (unauthenticated users), and a different default policy for any user that can be authenticated. At a lower level of the hierarchy may be default policies specific to authenticated and unauthenticated users on a particular subnet. If a user is authenticated on a particular subnet, different policies may be applied based on the user group to which the user belongs, or even specific to the individual user. However, as noted previously, network managers are unlikely to generate a large number of user-specific policies. The hierarchical policy structure described is illustrated in Figure 9.17.

Figure 9.17	Hierarchical Structure of a Policy Data Store

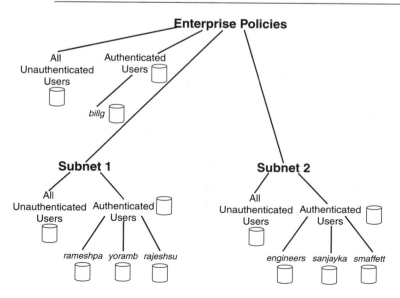

The structure illustrated in this figure is based on user. It resembles the policy structure used by the Microsoft Admission Control Server (described in Chapter 14). Policy may alternatively be structured based on application or on both user and application. (In the case that policy is based on both user and application, it is necessary to define which criterion takes precedence.) The parsing rules used to locate the policy that best matches a policy locator or a set of policy locators (in the case that both user policy locators and application policy locators are used) may be quite complex.

The user policy locator recommended in the related IETF work [RFC 2752] is relatively simple: It is an X.500 string containing the distinguished name of the user. Typically, this is the same name that is used to identify the user for other enterprise policies, such as email routing, file access privileges, and so on. This simplifies management of resources across the enterprise because user groups formed for file access permissions, for example, may be reused for network resource permissions.

The application policy locator is slightly more complex. It is also an X.500 string, composed of hierarchically related subelements identified by keywords. Keywords identify such information as the application, the version number, and the subflow of the application. An example of an application policy locator is shown here:

```
APP=netmeeting, VER=3.0, SAPP=video
```

Note that *SAPP* refers to the subflow of the application. Application policy locators should use some form of globally unique identifier (GUID) to avoid namespace collisions. The GUID would identify the application vendor in the following form:

```
GUID=http://www.Microsoft.com/application_id
```

This subelement would be prepended to the previous policy locator.

Policy Contents and Evaluation

When the policy is located in the data store, it may take different forms. For example, policy may take the form of quantitative resource limits to be applied to a specific user or group of users. All users that are members of a particular group may be entitled each to a maximum of 100Kbps of resources at the Guaranteed Service level and 1Mbps of resources at the Controlled Load Service level on a particular subnet. There may be limits on the number of flows allowed for each user. There will likely be limits on the total resources that can be allocated on any given subnet, regardless of user.

In the case of quantitative requests, the policy server must use the policy locator to parse the policy data store, find the appropriate policies, and evaluate them to return a simple admit/reject decision. In the case of qualitative requests, there are no quantifiable parameters on which to operate. In this case, evaluation of policy may result in a DCLASS object that is returned by the policy server to the PEP.

Populating Policy Locators and Corresponding Policies

Previous sections described how policy locators are used at run time to locate corresponding policies in a policy data store. This assumes that the policy locators and the corresponding policies have been created beforehand. In large enterprises, user policy locators are typically created in the data store at the time a new employee is hired or at the time a new policy system is installed. The users are typically structured in groups (such as by job category or by seniority or management level). Various policies are associated with the users. One set of policies is network-related.

Application policy locators may be installed at the time an application is deployed in the enterprise. The Desktop Management Task Force (DMTF) is in the process of defining a *content information model* (CIM) that includes a standard set of schemas describing applications. Some subset of this model would specify the policy locators that might be generated by the application. At the time a new application is deployed, policy servers should be capable of learning the set of policy locators (such as by querying an instance of the application for its CIM structure) and storing them at the appropriate place in the directory. The policy system could then inform the network manager of the existence of new policy locators and prompt the manager to create the policies corresponding to each of the new policy locators.

In the absence of other mechanisms for explicitly entering policy locators, policy systems could populate the data store with policy locators at run time, as these appear on the network. The first time a new policy locator appears in signaling messages, the policy management system could inform the network manager of the appearance of a new user or application on the network, and prompt the network manager to enter the corresponding policies.

9.3.4.4 Security: Authenticating Identity Objects

Security concerns require that the policy management system be capable of *authenticating* identity information. Because certain users or applications may be entitled to more resources than others, there is incentive for less privileged users or applications to misrepresent themselves as more privileged users or applications. The process of authentication verifies that an identity object truly represents the identity of the requestor. As an analogy, banks use signatures to authenticate the issuer of a check.

The Credentials field is used for the purpose of authentication. Three types of credentials are discussed in the related IETF drafts. These include *simple* (no authentication), *Kerberos*, and *public key*. In the case that simple credentials are used, there is no authentication mechanism and the policy locator is in clear text.

Kerberos is an authentication mechanism in widespread use that is based on a shared secret in the form of *keys* or *tickets*. To use Kerberos credentials, both the requestor of resources (the host) and the policy management system must obtain a ticket from a key distribution center. (The details of Kerberos, keys, and key distribution are beyond the scope of this book. See [SECURITY] for further details on Kerberos.) The host uses its ticket to encrypt the policy locator. It then constructs the policy element to be transmitted in an RSVP message by inserting the encrypted policy locator in the Policy Locator field of the policy element and then inserting its Kerberos ticket in the Credentials field of the element.

When the policy management system receives the RSVP message, it extracts the host's Kerberos key. It is able to use its own key, in conjunction with the key extracted from the RSVP message, to "crack" or decrypt the policy locator. The process of encrypting and then decrypting the policy locator using the two Kerberos keys provides authentication and offers the added benefit of encrypting the user policy locator. Authentication is provided because the Kerberos system assures that only the identified user can access the corresponding Kerberos key. In this manner, the key acts as a sort of signature.

Public key systems work in a similar manner, using credentials instead of keys. The Digital Signature field in the policy identity element is used for public key–based authentication systems. Public key systems also provide the benefit of encrypting the policy locator string.

9.3.4.5 *Security: Integrity*

Authentication mechanisms offer a significant improvement in security. However, they do not prevent a class of security problems, including *cut-and-paste* or *replay* attacks. In a cut-and-paste attack, a malicious agent may monitor RSVP messages on a network and extract policy objects containing authenticated identity elements. The agent may then paste these policy objects into its own resource requests. Such an attack would enable the agent to claim resources using a false identity. Even if mechanisms were put in place to prevent the malicious agent from extracting the policy object from an RSVP message, the agent might copy the entire message and replay it in a different part of the network or at a different time, again obtaining resources using a false identity.

[RFC 2747] specifies the format of an INTEGRITY *object*. This object is used to prevent cut-and-paste and replay attacks by verifying that an RSVP message has not been tampered with. The INTEGRITY object contains a *hash* and a *hash algorithm*. The sender of an RSVP message uses the hash algorithm and a secret key (shared with the message receiver) to generate a hash over the contents of the entire message. The receiver of the message may use the key to regenerate the hash and verify that the message has not been tampered with.

Note that INTEGRITY objects do not encrypt the contents of the RSVP message. The INTEGRITY object as described prevents cut-and-paste attacks, but it does not prevent replay attacks. To prevent replay attacks, the sender includes a sequence number in each message (which is also incorporated into the hash). The sequence number in subsequent messages must be monotonically increasing. Thus, a replay attack would cause a receiver to receive multiple messages with the same sequence number, betraying the attack.

9.3.4.6 *Merging and Translating Policy Objects*

Policy objects and the related security mechanisms were described in the context of unicast RSVP sessions within a single administrative domain. Complex issues arise when considering the application of these mechanisms to multicast sessions or across administrative domains. These are addressed in the following paragraphs.

Merging Policy Objects in Multicast Sessions

In multicast RSVP sessions, the processing of identity objects presents a challenging problem. As multiple receivers send RESV messages toward the root of a multicast tree, they are merged according to standard RSVP processing rules. The merge rules are quite clear with respect to the quantitative parameters in the FLOWSPECs of the RESV messages. However, it is not clear how policy objects should be merged. One approach would simply concatenate the identity elements from the merged messages at each merge point and pass the concatenated object up toward the root of the tree. As the policy object progresses toward the sender, it would increase in size, including the identity elements from each receiver at a lower point in the multicast tree. Policy servers at each location would then have the option of applying policy based on any of the merged policy locators. For example, policy may be applied based on the least restrictive policy matched or the most restrictive policy matched.

Unfortunately, this approach to handling multicast session policy suffers from serious scalability problems. Multicast sessions might include thousands of receivers; as a result, a merged policy object quickly becomes unwieldy and consumes excessive resources on the network. This problem is illustrated in Figure 9.18.

Figure 9.18   The Effect of Multicast Merging on RSVP Policy Objects

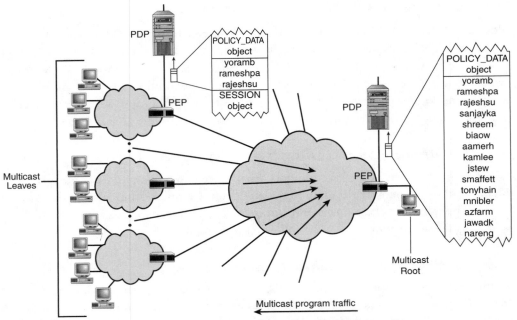

Mechanisms could be devised to replace policy locators at each policy server encountered along the multicast tree, with some new policy locator representing the merged policy locators. However, it is not clear how to do so while preserving the utility of the policy locators.

Translating Identity Objects

Consider Figure 9.19, in which an RSVP message traverses multiple administrative domains on its path from H1 to H2.

The end-to-end path of interest includes the domain of the enterprise originating the RSVP message, the domain of a provider or transit network, and the domain of the enterprise receiving the message. The sending host may insert, for example, a user identity element identifying the particular user in the originating enterprise. If a globally unique distinguished name is used, then it may be possible to meaningfully parse this identifier in the transit and receiving domains. However, these domains will not likely be interested in the specific user from the originating domain. The transit network, in particular, is interested not in applying policy based on the end user, but rather in applying policy based on the enterprise customer to whom it is selling network services. Applying policies in the transit domain based on the end user causes serious scalability and accountability problems.

Figure 9.19   Policy Object Translation at Domain Boundaries

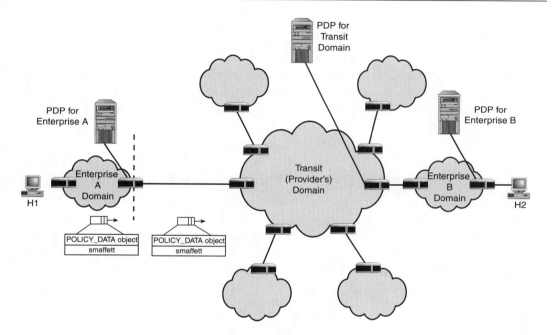

This issue can be tackled by translating policy objects at domain boundaries. For example, a policy server at the egress of the originating enterprise domain could translate the policy object to identify the enterprise customer as a whole, rather than the individual user within the enterprise. In Figure 9.19, the PDP for Enterprise A translates the policy objects in outgoing RSVP messages to identify Microsoft as opposed to the individual user within Microsoft. Policy servers within the transit domain would then act on these translated policy objects.

This addresses certain scenarios, but not others. For example, consider that the two enterprise networks are of the same administrative authority (for example, geographically dispersed offices of the same enterprise customer). In this case, the receiving domain may want to apply policy based on the end user identity. However, this identity has been lost due to the translation. If the end user identity is not to be lost, then the policy server in the originating domain must concatenate the enterprise customer identity to the user identity rather than replacing the user identity with it. This presents problems of its own, including scalability concerns (although not nearly as severe as in the multicast case) as well as complexities in determining the appropriate policy objects to be operated on by different domains.

Security Implications

The security implications of multicast or of multiple administrative domains are exceedingly complex. The security mechanisms described previously are based on shared secrets and key distribution mechanisms. Secrets shared by all members of a multicast tree rarely remain secrets, however. Secrets shared by multiple administrative domains are similarly unreliable. Various security mechanisms and key distribution systems can be used to address these problems. However, these are beyond the scope of this book.

9.3.4.7 Implementing Dynamic Policies Without Signaling

It is possible, although generally suboptimal, to achieve the effects of signaling and dynamic policies without actually signaling. This approach requires complex hardware support in the PEP. For example, assume that the policy is to admit up to 100Kbps of EF-marked traffic on a specific link. A list of entitled users and applications and the corresponding classification criteria is available in the policy system. This could be achieved without signaling, in the following manner.

The list of classification criteria corresponding to the users or applications entitled to EF service, on the particular link, is pushed down to the PEP by the PDP. (Note that this list could be quite large. An alternative approach would allow the list to be maintained in the policy server, but this approach would require the PEP to contact the policy server each time that a packet arrives at the PEP. Some hybrid of the approaches would cache limited amounts of classification criteria in the PEP.)

When a packet marked for EF and matching the classification criteria arrives at the PEP, the PEP identifies this as a new conversation. The PEP then begins to monitor traffic arriving on the conversation to gauge the conversation's bandwidth. The PEP subtracts this bandwidth from the available 100Kbps and considers the new conversation admitted. The conversation remains admitted as long as traffic arrives on the conversation and the conversation's bandwidth requirements remain relatively constant.

When an EF-marked packet arrives on a new conversation and matches the list of classification criteria, the PEP again begins to monitor the traffic arriving on this conversation. If its bandwidth is less than or equal to the remaining bandwidth available for EF traffic on the link, then this conversation, too, is admitted.

The process repeats until the 100Kbps of bandwidth available for EF traffic is committed. At this point, the PEP remarks (or otherwise polices) any additional EF-marked traffic arriving for the link.

The mechanism described theoretically realizes most of the benefits of signaled QoS and dynamic policy. It admits traffic to the high-priority service from the list of entitled users and applications. It maintains the integrity of admitted conversations by tracking conversations and refusing admission to additional traffic that would compromise the quality of admitted traffic. (Without tracking traffic on a conversation-by-conversation basis, the PEP stands to discard traffic in excess of the allowed 100Kbps indiscriminately. In doing so, it would compromise the QoS experienced by all conversations, thereby wasting all EF resources on the link.)

Unfortunately, this approach suffers from numerous problems. It requires sophisticated hardware in the PEP, with the capability to track conversations and monitor their resource requirements. It also requires the storage of large amounts of classification criteria in the PEP (consider a policy that admits three simultaneous telephony sessions from a list of 10,000 entitled users).

Finally, consider that, without end-to-end signaling, admission control may not be coordinated across a network. So, if there are two PEPs in the path between two subnetworks, each implementing a similar admission control mechanism, each PEP might admit the first three conversations matching configured classification criteria. However, because the two PEPs are not guaranteed to see the same traffic at the same time, it is possible that one PEP would admit Conversations A and B, while the other PEP would admit Conversations B and C. Because neither Conversation A nor Conversation C is admitted along the full path, neither will be assured the required quality, and the resources allocated to them will be wasted at each of the PEPs. (This problem was illustrated first in Chapter 1, Figure 1.3.) Of course, this problem can be avoided by use of the omniscient bandwidth broker, which by definition communicates with the two PEPs and knows enough to coordinate their actions. The bandwidth broker will be discussed in further detail later in this chapter, in the section "Administrative Domains and Bandwidth Brokers."

9.3.5 Host Resident PEPs

For traffic that is not session-oriented, it simply does not make sense to signal to the network. Consider, for example, fleeting transactions such as login messages or clicks on a Web site. The traffic generated in these examples is so fleeting (nonpersistent) that by the time a signaling message could be sent to the network and an action taken in response, the traffic described in the signaling messages would no longer exist. Nonetheless, it may be important to offer this nonpersistent traffic prioritized access to network resources.

This can be achieved through the process of push-provisioning configuration information compiled from semi-static policies. Of course, in general, this approach assumes that classification criteria can be defined by which the traffic of interest can be identified. As discussed previously, this is often nontrivial.

9.3.5.1 Coordinating the Allocation of Resources to Nonpersistent Traffic with the Allocation of Resources to Signaled Traffic

It is important that the allocation of resources to such nonpersistent traffic be coordinated with the allocation of resources to traffic that requires high-quality services. For example, because nonpersistent traffic may appear in unpredictable volumes in unanticipated parts of the network, it should not be allowed to use the same DSCP as telephony traffic. Otherwise, it might compromise the integrity of high-quality service guarantees that were offered for signaled telephony sessions through explicit signaled admission control. Thus, allocation of resources to nonpersistent traffic is ideally governed by the same policy system that allocates resources for high-quality services in the same network. This is readily achieved when the marking of nonpersistent traffic is driven by the same PEPs and PDPs that reside in the network and that drive policies for higher-quality services as well.

9.3.5.2 Allocating Resources to Nonpersistent Traffic by Marking in Hosts

In some scenarios, it is desirable to mark nonpersistent traffic in hosts. This approach can circumvent the difficulties of correlating classification criteria with users and applications. If a network manager wants to prioritize login traffic or certain traffic associated with a particular Web page, it may be impossible to determine the classification criteria that should be configured in network-based PEPs such as switches and routers (especially if the traffic is encrypted). Because no signaling messages are generated for either type of traffic, PDPs cannot glean the classification criteria from signaling messages. The sending host, however, *is* capable of identifying the traffic associated with the login process or a Web page because the corresponding applications reside on the host. By incorporating the host into the policy management system, the network manager can author policies of this form when it might otherwise be impossible to do so:

> Prioritize login traffic by marking it with DSCP A, and prioritize traffic from Web page 1234 by marking it with DSCP B.

9.3.5.3 *Incorporating the Host into the Policy Management System*

The preceding discussion shows that it is sometimes desirable to mark traffic in hosts, but that such marking should be coordinated with the policy management system that controls the actions of PEPs and PDPs in the network. The logical conclusion is that the host should be made part of the policy management system. This notion was raised early in this chapter when it was suggested that the host is basically the first PEP in the network. This is illustrated in Figure 9.20.

Figure 9.20	The Host as PEP

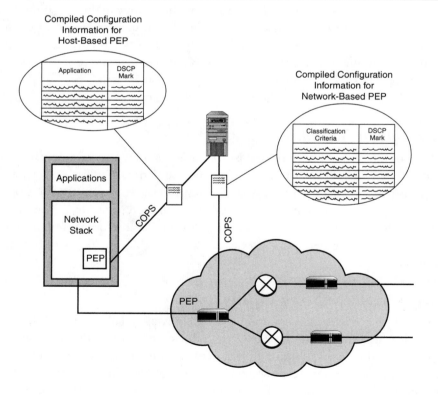

As do all other PEPs in the network, the host resident PEP communicates with a policy server using COPS. The nature of communications between a host resident PEP and its policy server likely will differ from the communication between a network-based PEP and its policy server. In particular, a policy server configures a network-based PEP to mark traffic by pushing to the PEP both the classification criteria and the corresponding mark. On the other hand, the policy server configures the host-based PEP to mark traffic by pushing the application or user name and the corresponding mark.

> **Note**
>
> Note that scalability concerns are associated with this approach. Due to the large number of hosts, this approach places a significant load on policy servers, as compared with an approach in which the policy server serves only switch- and router-based PEPs. In addition, the amount of network traffic exchanged between PEPs and PDPs may increase substantially.

9.4 Administrative Domains and Bandwidth Brokers

This section discusses policy issues that surface at administrative domain boundaries. Bandwidth brokers are also discussed in this context because they are often considered to implement interdomain functionality. A fair amount of work has been done on the relationship between intradomain resource allocation policies and interdomain resource allocation policies [TWO_TIER]. An in-depth discussion of this work is beyond the scope of this book. Instead, a brief survey of the issues will be presented.

9.4.1 Domain Boundary Issues

A number of interesting policy-related issues surface at administrative domain boundaries. Some of these, as they relate to the merging and translation of policy objects, were discussed earlier in this chapter. In many cases, domain boundaries are the locations at which customers are delineated from providers and at which currency of one form or another changes hands. Service level agreements are negotiated at interdomain boundaries, and policies in each domain determine how traffic from neighboring domains is handled in that domain.

9.4.1.1 Accounting and Billing

This book does not address accounting and billing issues related to QoS. However, it does acknowledge the existence of these issues and the important role that they play in deploying QoS-enabled networks. Although trial networks might be deployed without accounting and billing mechanisms, large-scale deployment of QoS enabled networks will not happen until robust accounting and billing mechanisms are in place. Fortunately, the underpinnings for these mechanisms are reasonably well understood. Many of these have been discussed in this chapter, in the context of policy. In particular, the policy servers described are capable of monitoring and controlling network resource usage and of correlating resource usage with customers (either peer networks or end users).

Several billing- and accounting-related issues have been identified that require further work. These include translation or aggregation of policy objects at domain boundaries, as well as interdomain security issues.

9.4.1.2 Admission Control Policies

Various forms of admission control must be supported at domain boundaries. These govern the amount of resources in a provider domain that each customer is granted at each service level. In the simplest cases, static DiffServ-style SLAs are implemented. These are typically supported by simple policies in the provider domain that discard or demote traffic exceeding the specified limits.

In more sophisticated networks, dynamic SLAs may be supported. These allow the SLAs at domain boundaries to be dynamically renegotiated, whether based on explicit signaling or implicit mechanisms (such as changes in monitored traffic patterns).

In cases in which end-to-end services must be supported across multiple domains, it may be necessary to coordinate resource allocation across multiple interdomain boundaries.

9.4.2 Bandwidth Brokers as Admission Control Agents

In all scenarios described previously, admission control agents are required. Per the general discussion of admission control agents (ACAs) in Chapter 5, these represent defined regions of a network and manage resources within the region of the network that they represent. ACAs also negotiate with customers requiring resources within the region that they manage and allocate resources to those customers.

Certain groups within the QoS community (including the Internet2 and its Q-Bone initiative) define *bandwidth brokers* (BBs) as follows:

> A BB manages network resources for IP QoS services supported in the network and used by customers of the network services. A BB may be considered a type of policy manager in that it performs a subset of policy management functionality.

As such, BBs provide general functionality equivalent to that of an ACA. Figure 9.21 illustrates the standard view of the bandwidth broker and its role in a multidomain network.

Figure 9.21   Bandwidth Brokers and a Multidomain Network

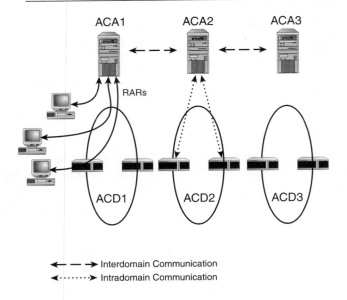

In this illustration, three bandwidth brokers (ACA1, ACA2, and ACA3) are each appointed to be responsible for one of the three domains (ACD1, ACD2, and ACD3, respectively) of the multidomain network illustrated. The bandwidth brokers are responsible for provisioning resources at different service levels within each domain and for communicating among themselves to broker access to resources between domains. Hosts or management entities near the edges of the network typically initiate resource requests (RARs). These requests specify the type and amount of required resources and the endpoints between which the resources are required. These requests are sent to the bandwidth broker representing the domain at the network edge. The bandwidth broker inspects each resource request and may determine that additional bandwidth brokers in other domains need to be involved in admitting the resource request. In this case, the bandwidth broker will signal to the appropriate adjacent bandwidth broker in a peer domain.

9.4.2.1   *The Bandwidth Broker and Its Relation to RSVP*

Ironically, traditional RSVP provides much of the functionality of a bandwidth broker in a completely distributed manner. The bandwidth brokers, as illustrated, are required to track resource availability in various parts of the domain for which they are responsible. They must process admission control requests, understanding the impact that the admission of a request would have on the resources in their domain, and then take action on the request. This is exactly what RSVP does.

There is some merit to exploring alternate mechanisms for implementing the admission control and resource provisioning functionality provided by traditional RSVP. As has been discussed throughout this book, the complete distribution of admission control functionality across every device in the network is probably excessive (see Chapter 2's section "Signaling Density"). It makes a great deal of sense to centralize admission control to some degree, appointing a small number of ACAs. The benefits of complete distribution of admission control in terms of improved QE product are outweighed by scalability concerns and the complexity of supporting admission control functionality in every device. Some degree of centralization affords significant improvements in scalability and management in exchange for a limited compromise in QE product. In addition, the traditional distributed admission control model of RSVP does not properly support qualitative services and admission control for nonpersistent traffic.

However, it is not clear that the degree of centralization implied by the bandwidth broker model is appropriate. The bandwidth broker model tends to centralize admission control and resource management functionality for an entire domain in a single entity. It is worth discussing the tradeoffs that result from centralization of admission control and resource management functionality.

9.4.2.2 Tradeoffs Resulting from Centralized Admission Control and Resource Management Functionality

As this functionality is centralized, related processing requirements are shifted from multiple distributed devices to a small number of centralized devices. This includes processing related to parsing signaling messages and performing admission control calculations. On a less tangible note, but still important, the number of managed devices is also reduced.

Assume that there are N devices in a domain and that P represents the total amount of processing capacity required in each device. Assume that p represents the amount of processing capacity required in each device that is related to admission control and resource management functionality. A crude analysis suggests that the centralized bandwidth broker is required to provide $N \times p$ processing power and that the processing required in each device can be reduced from P to $P - p$. Obviously, this analysis is quite crude. There are economies of scale to be realized from centralizing the admission control and resource management functionality that are difficult to quantify.

However, a major issue has been overlooked in this analysis: topology awareness. As discussed throughout this book, one of the benefits of traditional RSVP signaling is that it provides perfect topology awareness implicitly. In traditional RSVP, each resource request is delivered to each device whose resources would be impacted by admission of the request. Each device evaluates the request based on current resource availability. When admission control functionality is centralized, an ACA is appointed to evaluate a resource request based on the following:

- Its knowledge of the resources currently available in the devices for which it is responsible

- Its knowledge of the impact that the admission of the request would have on these devices

This knowledge is rarely perfect. To the degree that the knowledge of the ACA is imperfect, it is necessary to overprovision the resources in its domain of responsibility or to compromise the quality of services that can be supported through the domain (to compromise the QE product).

Discussions of BBs are often based on assumptions of omniscience. The hypothetical bandwidth broker is endowed with near-perfect knowledge of network topology, resource availability, and routing tables so that it is capable of rigorously analyzing any resource request.

Note

The words *bandwidth broker* were first uttered by Van Jacobson and have since gained mythical significance. Although no one has quite articulated yet just how the bandwidth broker will be endowed with the omniscience attributed to it, bandwidth broker zealots are faithfully toiling to create one. Other, perhaps more pragmatic, folks consider the omniscience requirement to be an insurmountable obstacle and prefer alternate approaches.

Indeed, most descriptions of BBs assume that they are monitoring current levels of resource availability and that they participate in the routing protocol within the domain for which they are responsible. When analyzing the tradeoffs of centralized versus distributed admission control and resource management functionality, it is important to consider the additional processing power that must be provided in the BB to participate in the domain's routing protocol and to track resource usage. This functionality not only requires additional processing capacity, but it also tends to be quite complex and error-prone. Requirements for perfect topology awareness in the BB can be relaxed in exchange for overprovisioning (or compromising service qualities) in the associated domain.

Oddly, proponents of the centralized bandwidth broker model often dismiss or diminish usage of RSVP. This is particularly strange because it seems that recent work on RSVP and aggregated RSVP supports a model in which the protocol can be used in a manner that affords great flexibility in choosing the degree of centralization of admission control that is desired. Degree of centralization is determined simply by enabling fewer or more network devices to participate in RSVP signaling. The bandwidth broker approach seems to advocate a new set of inter-BB protocols and little flexibility with respect to choosing the appropriate degree of centralization.

9.5 *Summary*

Policy is defined as a high-level description of the quality and efficiency objectives to be met by the network under discussion. A policy management system is defined as a system of components and tools that work together to manage a network in a manner that realizes certain high-level objectives as specified by QoS policies. The system does so by implementing certain policies. Several types of policies may be implemented. Static global policies dictate the long-term physical provisioning of the network and the logical allocation of network resources into different resource pools. Semi-static policies are push-provisioned policies that allocate resources to aggregates of traffic flows. Dynamic policies are typically used to allocate resources for high-quality services to traffic flows corresponding to individual conversations of limited duration. Network managers typically use policies to allocate resources at varying levels to particular users or groups of users, or to particular applications. The value of a policy management system is its capability to simplify the task of the network manager by presenting an abstract, high-level user interface and by coordinating the configuration of QoS mechanisms across many disparate devices throughout the network.

Policy systems consist of network devices, also known as policy enforcement points (PEPs); policy servers, also known as policy decision points (PDPs); and policy data stores (which are often in the form of distributed directories). These are typically structured as a pyramid, with a large number of PEPs forming the base of the pyramid, a small number of policy servers controlling these PEPs, and a smaller number of directory nodes (or a single centralized data store) containing the policy data used by the policy servers (see Figure 9.6). Policy servers and PEPs typically communicate using two forms of COPS (COPS/PR and COPS/RSVP). Policy servers may communicate among themselves using various protocols. Policy servers typically communicate with the data store using LDAP.

Dynamic policies differ significantly from static global policies and from semi-static policies in that they tend to be based on end-to-end RSVP signaling. They are used primarily to support higher-quality services. Dynamic policies can be used in various ways, combining per-conversation or aggregate signaling with per-conversation or aggregate traffic handling to obtain different levels of QE product from the network.

A powerful aspect of dynamic policies based on signaling is the capability to authenticate users of resources based on identity objects in the RSVP signaling protocol. In addition, dynamic policies can be used to support complex policies based on cross-products of users, user groups, and applications that may vary from subnet to subnet.

Many interesting policy-related issues surface at interdomain boundaries. Many of the requirements at interdomain boundaries can be supported by creative use of the RSVP protocol. Certain groups have defined the concept of bandwidth brokers. These are agents that represent the resources within an administrative domain and that manage the allocation of resources within the domain as well as to peer agents in other domains.

CHAPTER 10

Putting the Pieces Together— End-to-End QoS

Previous chapters discussed the various elements that comprise the QoS network. These include traffic-handling mechanisms appropriate for a variety of media; mechanisms for the configuration of traffic-handling, including push provisioning and RSVP signaling; and, finally, the elements of a policy management system. This chapter brings these elements together, illustrating their role in a full-service, end-to-end, QoS-enabled network.

Because QoS is a nascent technology and not yet widely deployed, much of the content of this chapter should be considered speculative rather than definitive. Furthermore, the examples in this chapter illustrate a network at a fairly advanced stage of QoS deployment. Networks will not typically become fully QoS-enabled overnight. Rather, simple QoS mechanisms are likely to be enabled initially and only in the most congested regions of the network. Over time, increasingly sophisticated mechanisms will be enabled across more of the network.

The chapter begins by introducing a sample network consisting of a number of subnetworks of different types. The subnetworks are members of corresponding administrative domains. Next, the chapter discusses the various mechanisms used to provide traffic handling, configuration and provisioning, admission control, and policy-based management in each of these subnetworks. These QoS mechanisms will be discussed in the context of the specific applications that must be supported in each of the networks.

10.1 The Sample Network

The QoS deployments discussed throughout this chapter will be considered in the context of the network illustrated in Figure 10.1. This sample network is a simplistic view of a cross-section of the Internet. The purpose of the cross-section illustrated is to include sufficient variety to address a breadth of deployment issues. The Internet is a concatenation of many subnetworks that vary by media type, number and type of network devices, capacity, geographical span, administrative authority, and other characteristics. This chapter cannot possibly address all the subnetwork types that exist in the Internet. In reality, the subnetworks of the Internet and the interconnections between them are often more complicated, more varied, and less structured than the sample network illustrated. Nonetheless, the examples in this chapter can illustrate many of the QoS issues that arise in real networks.

Figure 10.1   The Sample Network

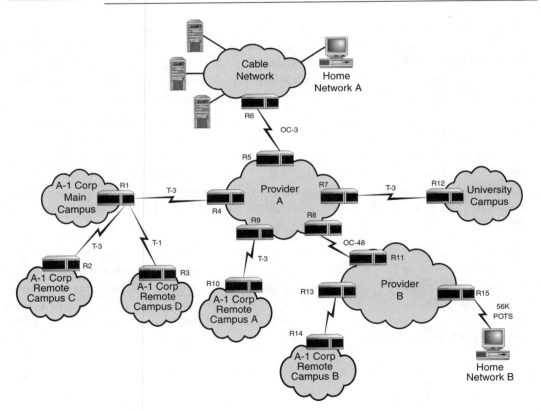

10.1.1 Overview of the Subnetworks of the Sample Network

The following paragraphs describe the sample network at a high level. They describe its decomposition into subnetworks and the interconnections between these subnetworks. Subsequent sections describe each of the sample subnetworks in detail and cover the QoS mechanisms deployed in these subnetworks.

The sample network consists of the following subnetworks:

- A-1 Corporation main campus network

- A-1 Corporation Remote Campus Networks A to D

- University main campus network

- Provider Networks A and B

- Home Networks A and B

- Cable network

10.1.1.1 A-1 Corporation Subnetworks

A-1 corporation operates a main campus network that serves thousands of users in a small geographical area. The main campus network is interconnected to Remote Campus A and B networks via DiffServ-enabled VPN services (see the accompanying sidebar "Virtual Private Networks") offered by Provider Network A and Provider Network B.

Virtual Private Networks

Virtual private networks (VPNs) use the public Internet to provide customers with the appearance of a private network.

In the past, corporations and other organizations that needed to interconnect geographically disparate sites typically purchased private leased lines or used various forms of semiprivate circuit-switched networks (such as X.25 and Frame Relay). Leased lines (and, to a lesser degree, X.25 and Frame Relay circuits) can be very expensive and usually require long lead times for initial installation and any subsequent changes in capacity. Much of the cost of these forms of interconnection is attributable to the dedicated and private nature of the resources provided.

With the proliferation of the public Internet, an opportunity arises to significantly reduce the costs required to interconnect geographically disparate sites. Sites can simply be connected to the nearest public Internet provider at a relatively low cost. However, this approach presents two primary problems. The first is security. Although leased lines and even Frame Relay or X.25 networks are relatively immune to malicious eavesdropping, the public Internet is not. The second problem is QoS. Leased lines act

continues

as dedicated wires that guarantee a specific capacity between endpoints. X.25 and Frame Relay circuits guarantee a minimum capacity (as described in Chapter 8, "QoS Over Layer 2 Media Other Than 802"). However, the Internet as it exists today offers no guarantees beyond best-effort delivery.

Internet service providers recognize the opportunity presented by this state of affairs. With the appropriate security and QoS mechanisms, it should be possible to leverage the Internet infrastructure to offer secure, private interconnections at a specific contracted QoS. These interconnections could be provided at a cost far below that of traditional leased-line service (or similar services). Those providers that can offer such VPNs should be capable of passing some fraction of these savings to their customers and realizing the remaining fraction as profit. IPSec has come a long way toward addressing the security and privacy requirements of VPNs. The QoS mechanisms discussed in this book—most notably, DiffServ—address the service quality requirements.

For more information on VPNs, refer to New Riders Publishing's *Windows 2000 Virtual Private Networking*, by Thaddeus Fortenberry.

The main campus network is connected to Remote Campus D via a T-1 leased line and to Remote Campus C via a T-3 leased line. The main campus network and Remote Campuses A to D are all in the same administrative domain.

10.1.1.2 University Network

The university campus network is similar to A-1 Corporation's main campus network. It serves thousands of users, and its connection to the world is via Provider Network A. Provider A offers DiffServ services to the university campus network. The entire university campus network is operated as a single administrative domain.

10.1.1.3 Provider Networks

The two provider networks are large routed networks. They offer connectivity to the campus networks (via T-3 access lines), the cable network (via an OC-3 link), each other (via OC-48), and individual home users (via the POTS network). Provider A's network listens to signaling from its customer networks. Provider B's network does not. The two provider networks are each operated as independent administrative domains.

10.1.1.4 Cable Network

The cable network is connected to Provider A via an OC-3 (155Mbps) connection. It serves several thousand home users via cable modem connections. It contains a number of content servers from which it sources various Web content as well as video-on-demand services.

10.1.1.5   Home Networks

Home Network A is connected to Provider A via a relatively high-bandwidth cable network. Home Network B is connected to Provider B via a much lower-capacity plain old telephone service (POTS) network.

> **Note**
> Digital subscriber loop (DSL) is a technology that offers high-bandwidth connectivity to homes over existing POTS wire. DSL competes with cable modem technology in many areas. Although DSL QoS is not addressed in this book, it does warrant mentioning.

The term *home network* might seem like overkill for a single modem-attached PC. However, with the advent of HDTV and the explosion of digital consumer electronics, we can expect to see a proliferation of sophisticated home networks interconnecting multiple PCs, audio/video devices, and Internet appliances. These will require high-bandwidth connections as well as high-quality services within the home and to the Internet.

10.2   A-1 Corporation's Main Campus Network

A-1 Corporation's main campus network is the most complex subnetwork discussed in this chapter. As such, this subnetwork will be discussed in depth. Subsequent discussions of other subnetworks will build upon the groundwork laid in this section.

Figure 10.2 illustrates the internal structure of A-1 Corporation's main campus network.

At its center is an ATM backbone switch. The backbone switch interconnects a number of routers (only three are illustrated) via OC-3 links. Two of the routers illustrated (R16 and R17) each serve a separate building on the main campus. About a thousand users in each building connect to these routers via two levels of Ethernet switches. All Ethernet connections are 100Mbps. The other router illustrated (R1) serves to connect the main campus network to remote campuses and the Internet, via a combination of private leased lines and VPNs. These range in speed from T-1 to T-3 rates.

The subnetworks of the main campus network are discussed separately in the following paragraphs.

Figure 10.2   The Main Campus Network of the A-1 Corporation

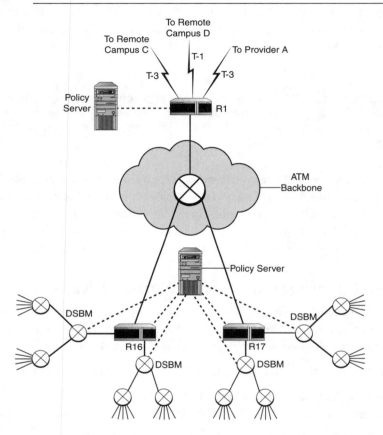

10.2.1   Building Networks

Each building network is built from one or more two-level switch hierarchies. The top-level switch in each hierarchy is connected to the building router. This network structure is illustrated in Figure 10.3.

Note

Note that typically a structured switched network would be designed with redundant interconnects or redundant switches for the sake of fault tolerance. In either case, traffic would be shared between redundant routes (using some form of intelligent load balancing), or the spanning-tree algorithm would prune the network to disable redundant routes unless they become necessary. Such redundancy tends to complicate the discussion of QoS-related functionality. For this reason, redundancy is not addressed in this discussion.

Figure 10.3   The Building Networks

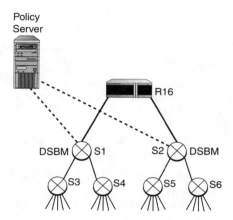

10.2.1.1 *Switched Subnetwork Requirements*

The switched subnetworks are required to support standard best-effort service within the buildings and between buildings. Mission critical applications such as email and enterprise resource planning (ERP) applications must be adequately served. In addition, all buildings are required to support IP telephony and limited videoconferencing and video streaming (noninteractive, playback only) within and between buildings. Hosts generate RSVP signaling for Guaranteed and Controlled Load Services on behalf of interactive audio and streaming audio/video traffic, respectively. Hosts generate RSVP signaling for the Null (qualitative) Service on behalf of email, ERP, and certain other persistent, qualitative, mission-critical traffic.

> **Note**
>
> *Persistent* traffic is traffic that is associated with sessions that persist for some amount of time between well-defined endpoints. *Nonpersistent* traffic is traffic for which a session cannot be clearly identified. It consists of brief exchanges between a potentially large and changing set of endpoints. Signaling is useful for persistent traffic, but not for nonpersistent traffic.

Nonpersistent, mission-critical traffic may be marked for prioritized service either by host resident policy enforcement points that are integrated with the building's policy management system (see the section in Chapter 9, "QoS Policy," titled "Incorporating the Host into the Policy Management System") or, alternatively, by classification and marking in network devices (network-based application recognition). This category includes such traffic as login messages, name-resolution messages, and similar low-volume, bursty transactions that can benefit from prioritization.

Note that the scenario described is a relatively advanced scenario. In many early deployment scenarios, some mission-critical applications do not invoke QoS signaling and cannot be recognized in the network. See the accompanying sidebar titled "The Incremental Deployment Dilemma" for a discussion of such scenarios.

The Incremental Deployment Dilemma

In the deployment scenarios discussed in this chapter, all important applications are considered to be QoS-enabled. This means either that they invoke QoS signaling or that it is possible to recognize and mark their traffic (either in the host or in the network) for prioritized access to network resources in accordance with their importance to the network manager. In general, this will not be the case. Certain applications will be QoS-enabled sooner than others.

What happens when certain applications deemed most important by the network manager cannot yet be supported by QoS mechanisms? What are the consequences of deploying applications that *are* QoS-enabled simultaneously with more important applications that *are not* QoS-enabled?

One need not look far for such an example. Consider a deployment scenario in which IP telephony and video applications generate RSVP signaling and are fully QoS-enabled, but email, which is considered mission-critical, is not. Even in the absence of any QoS mechanisms, the network manager may be reluctant to allow deployment of multimedia applications. These tend to generate nonadaptive traffic that may starve adaptive mission-critical applications for resources. Certainly, then, there is little incentive to deploy QoS mechanisms that will give these applications even higher priority than they would have if they were required to compete with mission-critical traffic on equal terms. Can QoS mechanisms be used at all in cases such as this?

The answer is yes. QoS mechanisms can be used to actually *lower* the priority of the less important traffic generated by QoS-enabled applications. One mechanism for doing so is to configure policy servers to admit signaling requests from QoS-enabled applications up to a certain limit, and to respond with a DCLASS or TCLASS object corresponding to the appropriate priority level. (See the section in Chapter 6, "Differentiated Services," titled "DiffServ with RSVP," or the section in Chapter 7 "The Subnet Bandwidth Manager and 802 Networks," titled "Using Signaling to Obtain a Higher Quality/Efficiency Product.") When this limit is exceeded, traffic of QoS-enabled applications can be *demoted* to less-than-best-effort priority by *admitting* the corresponding requests at the policy servers and returning a DCLASS and TCLASS object corresponding to *less-than-best effort* priority. (In 802 networks, a user_priority value of 1 typically invokes less-than-best-effort service.)

In this manner, a limited amount of traffic from QoS-enabled applications may be prioritized, while excess traffic is demoted to a lesser priority than best-effort, thereby protecting non-QoS-enabled traffic. This approach is particularly useful in the case that the QoS-enabled applications are aggressive multimedia applications that generate nonadaptive traffic. Creative network managers may employ this or other approaches to support incremental deployments, combining QoS-enabled and non-QoS-enabled applications simultaneously.

10.2.1.2 Traffic-Handling Configuration in the 802 Switched Subnetworks

Each switched subnetwork is operated using 802 user_priority aggregate traffic handling. Switches are configured for the following priority levels:

- **Highest**—For traffic marked with user_priority value 6. This priority level is used for IP telephony traffic (or other interactive audio traffic) requiring the latency bounds of Guaranteed Service. Note that user_priority value 7 may actually invoke higher-priority service than user_priority 6. However, this value is typically reserved by the network manager for network control-type traffic.

- **High**—For traffic marked with user_priority value 5. This priority is used for video traffic or noninteractive streaming audio that is more latency-tolerant than interactive audio.

- **Medium**—For traffic marked with user_priority 4. This priority is used for certain persistent nonquantifiable traffic such as subsets of traffic between email clients and servers, or between ERP clients and servers.

- **Better-than-best-effort (BBE)**—For traffic marked with user_priority 3. This priority is used for nonpersistent traffic that requires the protection of a better-than-best-effort service.

- **Best-effort (BE)**—For unmarked traffic or for traffic marked for user_priority 0. This priority is used for default, non-QoS-enabled traffic.

- **Less-than-best-effort (LBE)**—For traffic marked for user_priority 1. This priority is used for multimedia traffic in excess of the admitted limit. The LBE priority level is designed to protect best-effort traffic from aggressive multimedia traffic in excess of the admitted amount.

The policy servers illustrated (in Figures 10.3 and 10.2) are used to push configuration parameters to the switches in each building. In addition to creating the priority queues corresponding to the six priority levels listed here and associating these queues with the corresponding user_priority values, policers must be configured.

Policing is a feature of more sophisticated switches. Policers limit the amount of traffic admissible to the medium- and high-priority queues at each switch's egress interface. The policers are not aware of individual conversations. Instead, they police based strictly on the user_priority value. Policers limit traffic marked for user priorities 5 and 6 to no more than 5% of the capacity of each interface. Policers re-mark traffic in excess of these limits to user_priority 1. This policing strategy provides high-quality service to a limited quantity of multimedia traffic, expected to be sufficient to accommodate standard usage patterns.

However, if actual multimedia traffic levels exceed expected levels, the excess traffic is forced below best-effort to protect best-effort traffic from aggressive multimedia traffic.

10.2.1.3 Admission Control Agents in the 802 Network

The top switches in the hierarchies in each building network (S1 and S2, in Figure 10.3) are SBM-aware and are enabled to run for the election of DSBM. (See Chapter 7 for a discussion of the Subnet Bandwidth Manager and DSBM.) Because the remaining switches in each building are of lower functionality and are not SBM-aware, S1 and S2 will in fact become DSBMs. Switches acting as DSBMs are controlled by an attached policy server and are configured using COPS or SNMP. Hosts and routers are well-behaved SBM clients (meaning that they detect the presence of a DSBM on the shared network and direct RSVP PATH messages to the DSBM).

DSBM Policies for IP Telephony and Video Traffic

DSBMs apply dynamic policies (under control of the attached policy servers) to RSVP requests corresponding to IP telephony, video, and qualitative, persistent applications. Policies for IP telephony and video traffic admit requests for quantitative services subject to per-user and total per-subnetwork limits.

> **Note**
>
> The term *subnetwork* is used here to refer to the subnetwork that includes all switches and segments in the DSBM's admission control domain. (In Figure 10.3, for example, one subnetwork consists of S1, S3, S4, and the segments to which they are attached.) This subnetwork is not a *subnet* in the IP addressing sense of the term. Instead, it is equivalent to a *managed segment* (see Chapter 7 for a discussion of managed segments).

Per-user limits prevent any single user from using more than that user's fair share of the subnetwork's high-priority queues. Per-subnetwork limits prevent oversubscription of the subnetwork's high-priority queues across all users. In addition, policies restrict usage of the high-priority queues to authenticated users only. (Authenticated users are users recognized by the corporation's security system.)

DSBMs enforce the policies for IP telephony and video traffic by rejecting requests for resources above the applicable permitted limits. Hosts and routers sending onto the switched subnetworks are trusted to cooperate by marking traffic on admitted flows for the appropriate user_priority value (per a default mapping from the requested service type) and to mark traffic on rejected flows for best-effort service.

> **Note**
>
> Certain hosts are trusted to mark traffic based on the results of RSVP signaling. Traffic on admitted flows is marked based on a default mapping from the requested service type to a corresponding `user_priority` value and DSCP. Traffic on rejected flows is marked best-effort. This is explained in depth in Chapter 13, "The Traffic Control API and Traffic Control Components," in the context of Windows hosts.

If individual senders misbehave by marking traffic on rejected flows for higher priority than that to which they are entitled, they may compromise service to other traffic in the same priority level. However, because of the per-service-level policers configured on each switch's egress interface, traffic from misbehaving hosts will not compromise lower-priority services.

Note that a single DSBM acts as the admission control agent for each switched subnetwork hierarchy. Because switched subnetworks contain additional non-SBM-aware switches, the single DSBM does not operate with perfect topology awareness. The QE product of the switched subnetwork is compromised because the low density of admission control agents. (See the section "Sparse Distribution of DSBMs," in Chapter 7.) As a result, the DSBM must be configured with admission control limits based on a reasonable estimate of traffic patterns and volumes within the switched subnetwork.

DSBM Policies for Qualitative Signaled Traffic

Dynamic policies for qualitative signaled traffic (such as email and ERP traffic) differ from those for quantitative traffic. In particular, because this traffic is not quantifiable, the *amount* of traffic generated is not directly limited. In certain cases, it may make sense to apply quantitative limits to qualitative applications. However, in this example, policies limit the *total number of flows* admissible. Also, because qualitative applications signal for the Null Service, and because there is generally no default mapping from the Null Service to a specific `user_priority` value, the DSBM returns a TCLASS object (provided by the policy server) upstream. The TCLASS object directs senders to mark traffic on admitted flows for the appropriate `user_priority` level (see Chapter 7 for a discussion of the TCLASS object).

> **Note**
>
> Note that, in this example, the DSBM does not provide DCLASS objects. DCLASS objects generally control resource usage in Layer 3 networks, and the DSBM in this example is responsible for resource usage in the switched Layer 2 networks only. That said, there is a tendency toward convergence of Layer 3 and Layer 2 functionality in a single device. In general these devices may generate DCLASS objects.

An example of a policy for qualitative traffic might be a policy that allows each authenticated user to mark traffic on a single email flow for user_priority 4. An additional policy might allow each authenticated user to mark traffic corresponding to a single subflow of an ERP application (such as a subflow that represents a time-critical transaction) for user_priority level 4. Users would be prohibited from prioritizing traffic on more than one flow per application at any time.

10.2.1.4 *The Host's Role*

Hosts generate signaling for the applications described previously and cooperate with the subnetwork DSBM by marking traffic on admitted flows in accordance with default mappings (for quantitative traffic flows) or based on a returned TCLASS object (for nonquantitative traffic flows). Note that if a DCLASS object is also received in a RESV message, hosts will mark the corresponding DSCP. However, in this example, DCLASS objects are not generated by the DSBM. Traffic on rejected flows must not be marked or must be marked for best effort (user_priority 0).

In addition, hosts communicate with policy servers in the switched subnetwork to mark traffic corresponding to nonsignaled applications. Subnetwork policy servers push a list of nonsignaled traffic flows (identified by sending application and subapplication) that are entitled to prioritization, and the allowable marks to cooperating hosts. (See the section "Incorporating the Host into the Policy Management System," in Chapter 9.) Hosts mark the corresponding traffic for the appropriate user_priority (user_priority 3, in this example) and DSCP (for the class selector PHB corresponding to IP precedence 2, in this example). Policy servers assure that the marks issued for nonsignaled traffic do not overlap with marks used for higher-quality services.

Both modes of operation are illustrated in Figure 10.4.

In (1), the policy server is shown pushing marking instructions for nonsignaled traffic to H1, using COPS/PR. An example of instructions that might be pushed is, "Mark DNS queries with user_priority 0x03."

Separately, in (2), the policy server is shown using COPS/RSVP to return a TCLASS object (indicating user_priority 0x04, 0x05, or 0x06) in response to host-initiated RSVP signaling (the PATH message is not illustrated). The TCLASS object is carried back to the host in an RSVP RESV message (3).

Figure 10.4 Host Interaction with Policy Servers to Effect Packet Marking

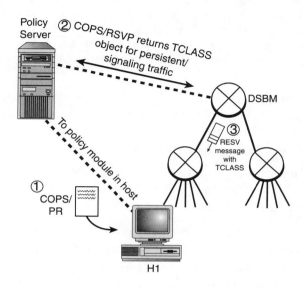

10.2.1.5 *Simpler Configurations of the Switched Subnetworks*

The deployment scenario described in the previous sections is quite sophisticated. Effectively six different priority levels are configured in each switch. DSBMs act as admission control agents by participating in signaling for both quantitative and qualitative applications. In addition, hosts and policy servers interact to enable prioritized marking for nonsignaled application traffic, in accordance with centralized policies. This degree of sophistication offers a high QE product. However, if the switched network can be considered overprovisioned with respect to the quantity of traffic generated by deployed applications, then a high QE product may not be necessary. Reasonable quality can be obtained using simpler QoS mechanisms.

For example, a simpler configuration would configure just two priority levels in the subnetwork switches, and no admission control agents (DSBMs). All traffic marked for a user_priority value above a certain threshold would be directed to the high-priority level. All traffic marked for a user_priority value below the threshold would be directed to the low-priority level.

> **Note**
>
> It could be argued that a scenario in which *all* switches in the subnetwork act as DSBMs is actually simpler from a management perspective. In this case, all DSBMs might be configured to allocate a certain percentage of the links under their control. This would eliminate the need to manually select a single per-subnetwork limit that is appropriate for the entire subnetwork. This approach also has the advantage of offering a higher QE product.

Many possible scenarios may be enabled between the extremes of the two priority level/no admission control agent scenario and the six priority level/DSBM scenario.

10.2.1.6 Deploying Down-Level Hosts

In most early deployment cases, it is necessary to support down-level hosts that are not capable of signaling or of marking user_priority values and DSCPs. There are several mechanisms by which these hosts can be supported side by side with QoS-enabled hosts.

In the simplest case, down-level hosts are simply allowed on the network with the expectation that they are incapable of marking traffic for prioritized treatment. As a result, traffic from these hosts will be treated as best-effort traffic. Privileged users, requiring the benefits of QoS prioritization, are required to upgrade to more sophisticated hosts.

Even though such down-level hosts may not mark traffic for prioritization, they may send sufficient quantities of traffic into the network to compromise services provided to QoS-enabled hosts. In this case, down-level hosts must be isolated behind switches that are configured to police their traffic. Such switches would be deployed as necessary, at the lowest level of hierarchy, in each building. All down-level hosts would be connected to the network via ports on the policing switches. These would simply limit the aggregate traffic transmitted into the network by down-level hosts. Excess traffic would be discarded, shaped to a lower rate, or marked by the switch for LBE service.

In certain cases, it may be necessary to actually prioritize certain traffic from down-level hosts. In these cases, the hosts would also be isolated behind special switches. These must be configured (for example, via COPS/PR) to recognize the traffic that is eligible for prioritization, based on the corresponding classification criteria. This traffic would be marked for the appropriate user_priority level and would be policed to configured limits, to prevent it from compromising service to other traffic. The first-hop switches described may even be used to mark DSCPs on behalf of down-level hosts.

Figure 10.5 illustrates the deployment of down-level hosts behind isolating switches.

Figure 10.5 Isolating Down-Level Hosts

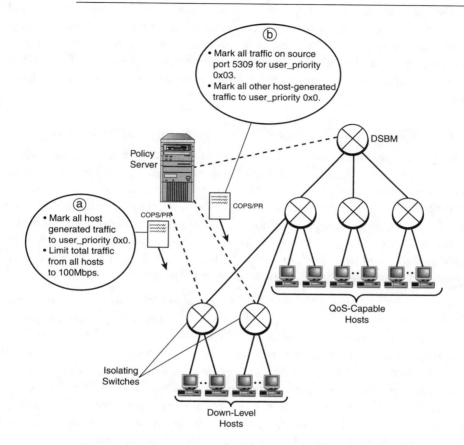

In Figure 10.5a, the isolating switch is configured to clear user_priority values from down-level hosts to user_priority 0 (best-effort) and to police the total amount of traffic submitted by down-level hosts. In Figure 10.5b, the isolating switch is configured to actually mark specific traffic for prioritized treatment.

10.2.1.7 Network-Based Application Recognition

In the deployment of down-level hosts, certain policies may require that switches be configured to recognize traffic based on certain classification criteria and to mark, prioritize, and police it accordingly. As discussed in Chapter 6, in the context of push provisioning, it is not always possible to classify traffic in the network. (An obvious example is when traffic is encrypted.) When it is possible to identify traffic in the network, this mechanism can sometimes be used to support down-level hosts and certain nonsignaled traffic in general (even from QoS-enabled hosts) quite effectively.

Such network-based application recognition should be used very carefully in marking traffic for the higher-quality quantitative services. Specifically, such marking of nonsignaled traffic must be implemented with an understanding of the amount of marked nonsignaled traffic that will be injected into the network and the routes that it will take through the network. Failure to do so will compromise the high-quality service provided to signaled traffic because of the relatively unpredictable load presented by competing nonsignaled traffic.

10.2.1.8 Configuration Via the Policy Management System

To simplify the provisioning and configuration of the switches in the building subnetworks, the network manager uses a policy management system. The network manager first authors a static global policy to provision all switches for the six priority levels to be invoked by the corresponding user_priority marks, as described previously. In addition, the policy calls for the provisioning of policers to limit the amount of traffic admitted on any egress interface for user_priority levels of 4 or higher to no more than 5% of the interface capacity (and to re-mark excess traffic for user_priority 1). The policy servers then push this provisioning information to each of the switches.

Next, the network manager authors policies for signaled QoS. The network manager is required to select quantitative limits both for the total amount of quantitative traffic admissible in each admission control domain, and per-user or per-application limits. These limits apply to traffic generated by the IP telephony and videoconferencing and streaming applications. In the case of the building subnetworks described, admission control domains include a complete switch hierarchy. Total limits for the domain must be selected to prevent overutilization of the high-priority resources in the domain. Per-user limits should be selected to enable specific users or user groups to make use of these resources. Resource requests corresponding to other users or user groups will be rejected.

In addition, the network manager must author policies for *qualitative* signaled applications. These policies must specify a per-user and total limit on the number of admissible flows (and the users or user groups entitled to prioritization). The policies must also specify the TCLASS object to be returned for admitted flows.

Finally, the network manager must create policies for nonsignaled traffic. In the case of appropriately enabled hosts (see discussion of host resident PEPs in the section "Incorporating the Host into the Policy Management System," in Chapter 9), the network manager must generate a list of nonsignaling applications entitled to prioritization and the marks to which they are entitled. These must then be pushed down from policy servers to the policy-enabled hosts. Down-level hosts must be isolated behind policing switches. Policies must be pushed to these switches to limit the traffic transmitted by down-level hosts at various priority levels, to protect the integrity of the high-quality services provided to other traffic. In certain cases, classification criteria must be installed to recognize and prioritize nonsignaled traffic eligible for prioritization (whether originating from down-level hosts or not).

10.2.2   *The ATM Backbone*

Routers (such as R1, R16, and R17, in Figure 10.2) connect the switched building sub-networks to the ATM backbone and to the wide area network beyond. The routers operate as sophisticated ATM edge devices, establishing SVCs of the appropriate type, as required. The routers also act as admission control agents to the ATM backbone and beyond, to the wide area network. The following paragraphs describe the QoS mechanisms enabled within the ATM backbone. For general information on the support of QoS in ATM networks, refer to Chapter 8.

10.2.2.1   *Traffic Handling in the ATM Backbone*

Within the ATM backbone, a separate VC is created for each traffic flow requiring quantitative services. In general, these may be created by routers using ATM signaling (SVCs) or by provisioning (PVCs). A constant bit rate (CBR) VC is created for each interactive audio flow (IP telephony and the audio component of videoconferencing traffic). In IntServ terms, these are Guaranteed Service flows. A variable bit rate (VBR) VC is created for each streaming audio or streaming video flow. In IntServ terms, these are Controlled Load Service flows. Thus, at any time, there may be multiple CBR and VBR VCs between any pair of routers.

In addition, a single unspecified bit rate (UBR) VC is created on demand between each pair of routers. This VC carries all nonsignaled traffic, as well as all traffic corresponding to *qualitative* signaled flows. Within each UBR VC, routers prioritize traffic based on DSCP. The mapping from different types of traffic flows to ATM VCs that occurs at each edge router is illustrated in Figure 10.6. Note that each signaled quantitative traffic flow has a corresponding VC, whereas all qualitative traffic flows and nonsignaled traffic flows are multiplexed onto a single UBR VC by scheduling components in the edge router (R16, in this example).

Figure 10.6   Mapping Different Traffic Flows to ATM VCs

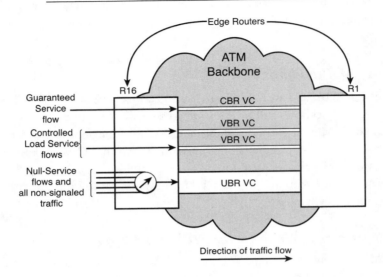

A mesh of VCs connects the edge routers at the periphery of the ATM backbone. This mesh is illustrated in Figure 10.7.

Note

Note that the ATM backbone consists of multiple interconnected ATM switches. These are not explicitly illustrated. Also note that four routers are illustrated. R1, R16, and R17 correspond to the routers illustrated in Figure 10.2. R18 has been added to Figure 10.7 only to illustrate the variety of VC configurations that is possible.

In the mesh illustrated, a UBR VC exists between each pair of routers. In addition, the following CBR and VBR VCs have been established:

- Two CBR VCs between R18 and R17

- One CBR VC between R16 and R17

- Three CBR VCs between R1 and R16

- One VBR VC between R1 and R17

- One VBR VC between R16 and R17

Figure 10.7 SVC Mesh in the ATM Backbone

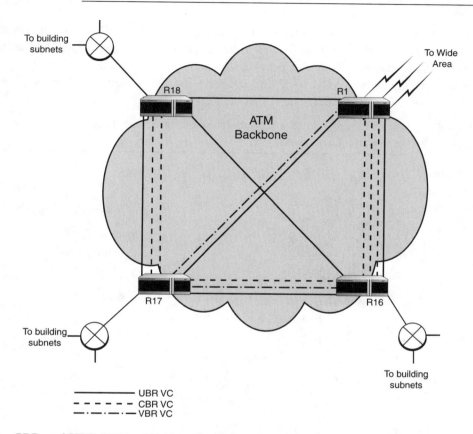

On CBR and VBR VCs, traffic is policed on a per-conversation basis. Traffic that is found to be nonconforming to the signaled profile is marked by edge routers as discard eligible and may be dropped in the case of congestion within the ATM network. No policing is applied to UBR VCs.

Note

Few large-scale ATM networks are operated with genuine SVCs. The use of SVCs as described in this chapter can increase the QE product of the network. However, it also increases the complexity of the network (in terms of related hardware and software, not in terms of network management, which is likely to be reduced in complexity). If sufficient capacity is available in the ATM network, it may be possible to provide adequate quality service without requiring SVCs.

10.2.2.2 Edge Devices and Admission Control Agents in the ATM Network

Routers interconnecting the switched building subnetworks to the ATM backbone (such as R16 and R17) act as ATM edge devices in the sense that they establish and tear down VCs in the ATM network. They also provide admission control functionality, both for resources consumed in the ATM backbone and for resources consumed in the switched subnetwork to which they are attached. This is illustrated in Figure 10.8.

| Figure 10.8 | Routers Provide Admission Control for Resources Both in the ATM Backbone and in the Building Subnetworks |

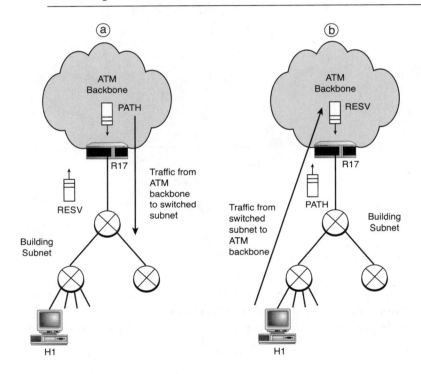

In Figure 10.8a, R17 acts as an admission control agent for resources consumed in the switched subnetwork by traffic from senders in the ATM backbone or beyond. In Figure 10.8b, R17 acts as an admission control agent for resources consumed in the ATM backbone, by traffic from senders in the switched subnetwork. Admission control functionality in both directions will be discussed separately.

> **Note**
>
> For the sake of simplicity, only two interfaces are illustrated (in Figure 10.8) on R17: one in the ATM backbone, and the other in the switched subnetwork. In Figure 10.2, however, R17 is shown to have two interfaces that serve switched subnetworks. As such, R17 also provides admission control between the two switched subnetworks that it serves.

In either direction, the router applies *explicit* admission control for all *signaled* traffic (both quantitative and qualitative) by participating in signaling. The router may also police certain *nonsignaled* traffic, thereby providing *implicit* admission control (see Chapter 4, "Integrated Services," for a discussion of policing versus explicit admission control).

10.2.2.3 UBR VCs

Routers on the ATM backbone establish CBR or VBR VCs to peer routers also on the ATM backbone, to carry traffic on signaled quantitative flows. These are established in response to RSVP signaling. VCs must also be established to carry best-effort and other nonsignaled traffic. To this end, routers establish UBR VCs *on demand* to peer routers on the ATM backbone.

Whenever an edge router receives a packet from a switched subnetwork that is destined toward a remote network, the router checks to see whether the packet is on a quantitative traffic flow that is served by a pre-established CBR or VBR VC. If it is not, then the router determines whether a UBR VC exists to the peer router. If a VC exists, the packet is directed to the existing VC. If no VC exists, the router establishes a UBR VC to the peer router. The UBR VC then remains in place until no UBR traffic is detected for some configurable period of time (the timeout period). As a result, a mesh of UBR VCs is likely to be in place between peer routers at any time.

> **Note**
>
> The discussion of UBR VCs in this context is quite simplistic. In practice, various algorithms of differing complexity may be used to establish and tear down UBR VCs on demand. In many cases, because these VCs do not actually commit resources, they may be established as PVCs under administrative control rather than on demand.

This VC mesh carries best-effort traffic, nonsignaled QoS traffic, and *qualitative* signaled traffic. In addition, the UBR VCs carry traffic on quantitative flows until the appropriate CBR or VBR VC can be established. (Thus, the first few packets of a quantitative conversation may receive only UBR service.)

10.2.2.4 Explicit Admission Control for Resources Consumed in the ATM Backbone

Figure 10.8b illustrates the role of the edge router, R17, in controlling resources consumed in the ATM backbone. R17 applies admission control to RSVP PATH messages that are generated by senders on the switched subnetworks and to RSVP RESV messages that are generated by receivers on the other side of the ATM backbone. PATH messages are admitted only if dynamic policy entitles the sending user (or application) identified in the PATH message to send onto the backbone. Assuming that the sender is admitted, the PATH message is allowed to continue on its way, eventually reaching the receiver.

Note

In conventional RSVP usage, resources are committed on RESV messages, which originate from the *receiver*. However, as discussed in Chapter 9, in the section "Applying Policy on PATH and/or RESV Messages," admission control can also be applied to PATH messages to control the behavior of the *sender*.

Receivers (or proxies for these) in the ATM backbone or beyond respond to PATH messages by generating RESV messages. Admission control on the RESV messages varies depending on the type of service requested.

RESV *Admission Control for Quantitative Services*

The RESV message carries a request for a specific type of service. If a quantitative service is requested, the router will first determine whether the requesting receiver (user) is entitled to the requested quantity of resources for the application identified in the RESV message. Dynamic policies governing the amount of resources to which different user groups are entitled on the backbone network may differ from those governing the switched networks within the building.

Assuming that the requested resources are admissible by policy, the router will then invoke local traffic control. In response, local traffic control will attempt to establish a VC across the ATM backbone to the next router in the downstream traffic path, for the appropriate service type (CBR for Guaranteed Service requests, VBR for controlled load requests) and the appropriate token bucket parameters. If VC establishment is successful, then the request may be considered admitted and the RESV is allowed to continue on its path upstream toward the sender. The router stores classification information mapping the admitted conversation to the corresponding ATM VC. The admission control process for quantitative requests is illustrated in Figure 10.9.

Figure 10.9   Admission Control for Quantitative Resources Consumed in the ATM Backbone

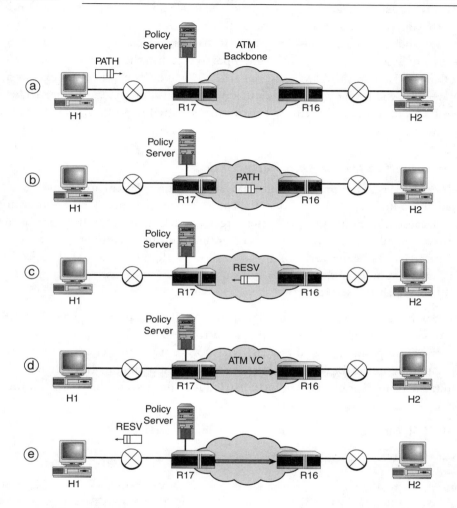

In Figure 10.9a, H1 sends a PATH message describing quantitative traffic that it is sending to H2, on the other side of the ATM backbone. R17 inspects the PATH message and compares it against dynamic policies in the PDP. The PATH message is admitted and is forwarded on its way (Figure 10.9b). (Admission control is also applied at R16. However, this will be discussed later, in the section "Explicit Admission Control for Resources Consumed in the 802 Switched Subnetworks.")

Assuming that it is admitted downstream, the PATH message eventually reaches H2. H2 responds with a RESV message. In Figure 10.9c, the RESV message is shown to be flowing upstream (having passed admission control at R16). In Figure 10.9d, R17 inspects the RESV message and checks for admissibility against dynamic policies in the PDP. Assuming that the RESV message is admissible, R17 attempts to establish the ATM VC illustrated. If resources are available in the ATM backbone, the VC will be established successfully and the RESV message will be allowed to continue on its way, as illustrated in Figure 10.9e. At this time, R17 will route traffic sent by H1 (on the admitted flow) to the ATM VC in the ATM backbone.

RESV *Admission Control for Qualitative Services*

When RESV messages requesting the Null Service (qualitative service) are received at a router sending onto the ATM backbone, the router applies only policy-based admission control. (Because no quantitative parameters are associated with this traffic, there is no resource-based admission control.) Policies regarding the admissibility of qualitative requests in the backbone network are similar to those in the switched subnetworks. In particular, a limited number of traffic flows corresponding to certain users and applications are admitted to a prioritized service.

Recall that traffic corresponding to signaled qualitative flows is prioritized within UBR VCs. To this end, routers applying admission control on these flows append a DCLASS object to the corresponding RESV messages. The DCLASS entitles the sending host to mark the corresponding traffic for the class selector PHB corresponding to IP precedence 3. As a result, the router's traffic control prioritizes this traffic above other traffic on the UBR VCs.

Figure 10.10 illustrates admission control for qualitative services.

Note

Note (in Figure 10.10) that RESV messages transit DSBMs in the switched subnetworks before reaching sending hosts. DSBMs may append an additional TCLASS object to the RESV messages, but they will not modify the DCLASS object because it does not affect resource usage in the switched subnetwork for which they are responsible.

Admission control with respect to PATH messages is similar for both quantitative and qualitative services. PATH admission control was illustrated previously, in Figures 10.9a and 10.9b. Admission control with respect to RESV messages differs between qualitative and quantitative services. As such, Figure 10.10 illustrates the admission control process beginning with the receipt of a RESV message for qualitative (Null) service.

Figure 10.10 Admission Control for Qualitative Resources Consumed in the ATM Backbone

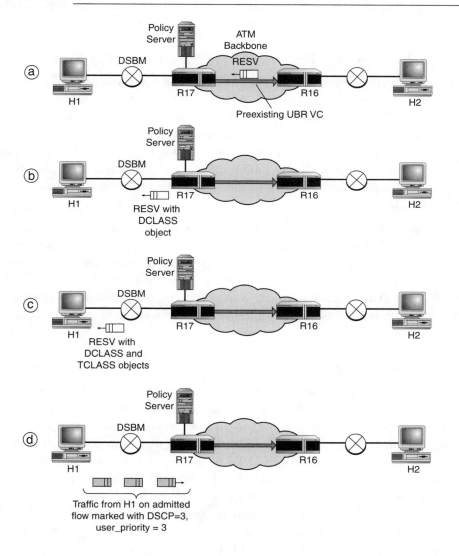

In Figure 10.10a, the RESV message is shown to be returning from H2. R17 reviews the RESV message and locates the corresponding dynamic policy in the PDP. Based on the requesting user and application, the PDP admits the request and provides the appropriate DCLASS object (indicating the DSCP corresponding to IP precedence 3). In Figure 10.10b, R17 has forwarded the RESV message, toward the sender, H1, with a DCLASS object appended. In Figure 10.10c, the DSBM has admitted the flow and has appended a TCLASS object to the RESV message. In Figure 10.10d, H1 is shown to be sending traffic on the admitted flow. The traffic is marked based on the DCLASS and TCLASS objects received with the RESV message.

10.2.2.5 Nonsignaled Prioritized Traffic in the ATM Backbone

Signaled traffic is allotted resources in the ATM backbone via the process of explicit admission control, as described in the previous section. In addition to signaled traffic, there is nonpersistent traffic that is entitled to prioritized service in the ATM backbone but that is not signaled. As described earlier in this chapter (in the section "Switched Subnetwork Requirements"), this traffic is marked based on pushed semi-static policy, either by host resident policy modules or by switches and routers in the switched subnetworks. Nonpersistent traffic eligible for prioritized service is marked with a DSCP equivalent to IP precedence 2.

Nonpersistent traffic that is marked in the switched subnetworks arrives at the edge routers destined for the ATM backbone. This traffic is not re-marked at the edge routers. (See the discussion of the trust model in the next section.) The edge routers use priority queuing (or alternate scheduling mechanisms) to schedule this traffic on the appropriate UBR VC. The UBR VC is shared among signaled qualitative traffic, nonpersistent prioritized traffic, and best-effort traffic. Nonpersistent prioritized traffic is serviced at a priority above best-effort traffic but below signaled qualitative traffic.

10.2.2.6 Trust Model

Within the switched subnetworks described in the previous section, hosts are trusted to mark traffic in accordance with the results of signaled admission control or in accordance with semi-static policies that are pushed to host-resident policy modules. Traffic is policed in aggregate only. However, within the ATM backbone, this is not the case. Traffic submitted for the high-quality CBR and VBR VCs is policed on a per-conversation basis. Consequently, it is impossible for an unauthorized host to seize more than its fair share (per dynamic policy) of these high-quality services. On the other hand, the edge routers maintain no per-conversation classification information corresponding to the signaled qualitative traffic flows or the nonsignaled traffic. As a result, hosts may consume disproportionate shares of resources on the ATM backbone UBR VCs.

Policing may be introduced to control the amount of UBR resources consumed by each host's traffic (or by the traffic generated by certain groups of hosts). In the simplest case, policy servers may configure aggregate policers on each edge router's ingress interface (the interface connected to the switched subnetwork) to limit the total amount of traffic offered for each prioritized DSCP from each switched subnetwork. These policers must be tolerant of bursts over short time periods to accommodate qualitative traffic (that tends to be bursty by nature). The policers are required only to assure that the average contribution over time of prioritized traffic from each switched subnetwork does not exceed the appropriate amount.

Note that the ingress policing described is different from the aggregate *egress* policing described in the switched subnetwork. Ingress policing assures that resources are shared equally among the different sources of prioritized traffic. Egress policing, by comparison, assures that the sum total of high-priority traffic on any interface does not starve lower-priority traffic on that interface.

A more sophisticated usage of ingress policing in the ATM backbone would leverage the classification information offered by host signaling for qualitative traffic to install per-conversation classifiers and policers at ingress interfaces. However, because typically no quantifiable traffic profile is offered for qualitative traffic, it tends to be difficult to apply per-conversation policing. In the absence of per-conversation policing, aggregate policing ensures fair distribution of resources among switched subnetworks, leaving the allocation of resources among hosts within a subnetwork as a matter of trust to be enforced as necessary by the manger of the switched subnetwork.

10.2.2.7 Explicit Admission Control for Resources Consumed in the 802 Switched Subnetworks

In addition to serving as admission control agents for the ATM backbone, routers such as R16 and R17 provide explicit admission control functionality to control resources consumed in the switched subnetworks to which they are attached (see Figure 10.8a). DSBMs in the switched subnetworks also play a role in admission control to the switched subnetworks.

In Figure 10.8a, R17 applies admission control to RSVP PATH messages that are generated by senders in the ATM backbone and beyond. R17 also applies admission control to RESV messages that are generated by receivers in the switched subnetwork. PATH messages are admitted only if dynamic policy entitles the sending user (or application) identified in the PATH message to send into the switched subnetwork. Assuming that the sender is admitted, R17 forwards the PATH message on its way toward the receiver in the switched subnetwork. The PATH message is routed through the DSBM for the switched subnetwork and then on to the receiver. The receiver responds with a RESV message.

As the RESV message returns toward the router, the DSBM applies admission control and appends a TCLASS object, which entitles the traffic flow to a certain traffic class in the 802 network. The router then reviews the RESV request subject to dynamic policies for admissibility to the switched subnetwork. For *quantitative* services, these policies specify the *quantity* of traffic originating from certain users or applications that may be admitted to the switched subnetwork. For *qualitative* services, the policies specify the receivers that are eligible to receive prioritized traffic and the number of flows that may be admitted for each receiver. Because the router is admitting traffic to the 802 subnetwork, where DSCPs are ignored, the router does not append a DCLASS object to RESV messages.

Assuming that the router admits a RESV request from a receiver in the switched subnetwork, it uses the TCLASS object appended by the DSBM. The TCLASS object indicates the appropriate user_priority value with which the router should mark traffic on the corresponding flow as it is sent into the switched subnetwork. As such, the router must store per-conversation classification information corresponding to each quantitative flow admitted to the switched subnetwork.

Note

Policies may be structured to apply more restrictive admission control at the router than at the DSBM. Policies applied at the router restrict the amount of traffic from *outside* the switched subnetwork that is admitted to high-priority traffic classes within the switched subnetwork. On the other hand, policies applied at the DSBM are applied to all signaled traffic in the switched subnetwork, whether originating from outside the subnetwork or from inside the subnetwork.

With respect to quantitative traffic, the difference in policies may manifest in the form of lower admission control limits provisioned in the router than in the DSBM. With respect to qualitative traffic, the difference in policy may manifest in the form of lower user_priority values allowed by router policy than those allowed per the DSBM generated TCLASS. When the user_priority value specified in router policy conflicts with that allowed by the DSBM, policy typically calls for the router to mark traffic based on the lower of the two user_priority values.

Figure 10.11 illustrates the admission control process by which traffic originating from outside a switched subnetwork is admitted to the appropriate 802 traffic class in the switched subnetwork.

Figure 10.11   Admission Control to 802 Traffic Classes in the Switched Subnetworks

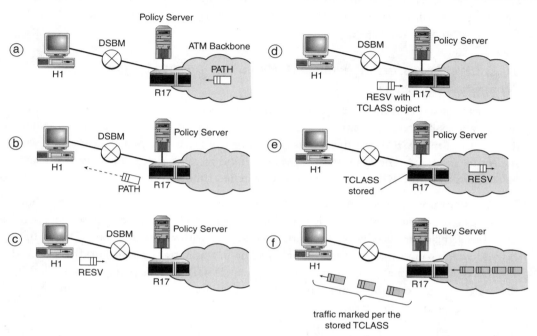

In Figure 10.11a, a PATH message is sent from a sender outside the switched subnetwork. The PATH message is admitted subject to dynamic policies that govern senders (that are not themselves on the switched subnetwork) onto the switched subnetwork. R17 forwards the PATH message toward the receiver (H1), via the DSBM (Figure 10.11b). Upon arrival, the receiver responds with a RESV message specifying the desired service type and quantity of resources (Figure 10.11c). As the RESV message transits the DSBM, the DSBM admits the request and applies a TCLASS object mapping the corresponding traffic flow to the appropriate traffic class in the 802 subnetwork. (Alternatively, the DSBM may append a TCLASS object to the PATH message, with the expectation that the receiver will copy the object to the RESV message that it generates.)

The RESV message continues on its path upstream, delivering the TCLASS object to R17 (Figure 10.11d). R17 applies admission control, subject to dynamic policy, to determine whether to admit the requested quantity of resources (in the case of quantitative services) for the receiving user at the service level requested. R17 admits the RESV request and forwards the RESV message upstream toward the sender. The TCLASS object is stripped off the RESV message and is stored with the relevant session state. R17 also stores the classification information corresponding to the admitted flow (Figure 10.11e). Assuming that the RESV request is admitted at all upstream admission control agents, traffic arriving on the corresponding flow will be marked with the appropriate user_priority value (Figure 10.11f) from the stored TCLASS object.

10.2.2.8 Translation from DSCP to user_priority for Nonsignaled Traffic

In the case of signaled traffic, edge routers maintain per-conversation classification information and associated user_priority values for each conversation. user_priority values are derived from the DSBM (via the TCLASS object) or from dynamic policies associated with the router interface. The user_priority value is used to mark traffic transmitted on signaled flows from the ATM backbone to the switched subnetwork.

In the case of nonsignaled traffic that arrives at the edge router from the ATM backbone, no associated user_priority value is stored in the router. However, remote senders may mark nonsignaled traffic eligible for prioritized service with a corresponding DSCP. In this case, the edge router marks a user_priority value in traffic transmitted into the switched subnetwork based on a mapping from the incident DSCP. This mapping is controlled by the policy servers to ensure consistency with the use of user_priority values throughout the A-1 Corporation's network.

Figure 10.12 illustrates the marking of user_priority value in nonsignaled prioritized traffic arriving from the ATM backbone for transmission onto switched subnetworks.

Figure 10.12 Marking of Nonsignaled Prioritized Traffic as It Is Transmitted onto a Switched Subnetwork

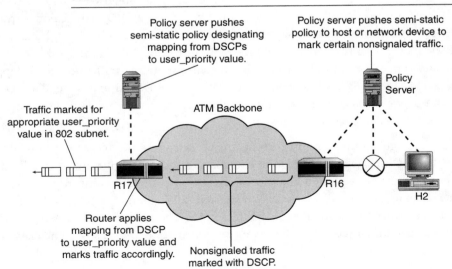

10.2.2.9 Configuration of Edge Routers via the Policy Management System

In the example illustrated, the same policy system that controls the switches in the building subnetworks also controls the edge routers that straddle the boundary between the ATM backbone and the switched subnetworks (such as R16 and R17). In other cases, separate policy systems may be used. In controlling these routers, policy servers must apply policies governing both the transmission of traffic from the switched subnetworks onto the ATM backbone as well as the transmission of traffic from the ATM backbone onto the switched subnetworks (as illustrated in Figure 10.8). These policies have been referred to in the preceding paragraphs; they are summarized in the following sections.

Policies Regarding Transmission onto the ATM Backbone

The following policies are applied to traffic transmitted onto the ATM backbone:

- Enumeration of sending and receiving users and applications entitled to quantitative services (CBR or VBR VCs) in the ATM backbone, including per-user and per-application limits (number of VCs and total capacity)

- Total capacity of any sending or receiving ATM interface that may be dedicated to CBR or VBR VCs

- Enumeration of sending and receiving users and applications entitled to prioritized service on UBR VCs in the ATM backbone and the specific DCLASS to be returned on associated RESV messages

- Policing parameters controlling the amount of traffic admitted to UBR VCs for each DSCP

- Rules regarding the replacement (or not) of DCLASS objects in RESV messages received from outside a switched subnetwork as they are forwarded to senders within the switched subnetwork

- Direction to the edge router to act as a receiver proxy for specific applications or subapplications

Policies Regarding Transmission onto the Switched Subnetwork

The following policies are applied to traffic transmitted from the ATM backbone onto the switched subnetworks.

- Enumeration of sending users and applications external to the switched subnetwork that are entitled to high-quality quantitative resources (and the corresponding 802 traffic class) within the switched subnetwork

- Enumeration of receivers within the switched subnetwork that are entitled to high-quality quantitative resources (from the corresponding 802 traffic class) within the switched subnetwork, for traffic originating from outside the switched subnetwork

- Mappings from DSCP to user_priority values for packets arriving for transmission onto the switched subnetwork and not corresponding to a signaled flow

10.2.3   The Interface to the Wide Area Network

Referring back to Figure 10.2, Router R1 connects the A-1 Corporation's main campus network to geographically remote networks and to the Internet at large (via Provider A). This section discusses the role of this router in providing QoS for traffic carried between hosts in the A-1 Corporation's main campus and peers in the remote networks or in the larger Internet.

The role of R1 differs from the role of R16 and R17 in several important aspects. For one, whereas R16 and R17 control access between the ATM backbone and the relatively resource-*rich* switched local area subnetworks, R1 controls access between the ATM backbone and relatively resource-*poor* wide area networks. For another, it controls accesses to resources that are outside the administrative domain of A-1 Corporation.

R1 connects the A-1 Corporation main campus network to remote networks and the Internet via three separate interfaces, as follows:

- A T-3 leased line to Provider A. This line provides service to Remote Campuses A and B, as well as the larger Internet.

- A T-3 leased line to Remote Campus C.

- A T-1 leased line to Remote Campus D.

The following sections focus on QoS functionality provided to traffic transmitted from the main campus network onto the wide-area leased lines. The section titled "Admission Control and Policies Governing Resources Consumed in A-1 Corporation's Main Campus Network" later in this chapter discusses QoS functionality provided to traffic transmitted from the wide-area leased lines onto the main campus network.

10.2.3.1   Traffic Handling on Remote Interfaces

Remote Campus C is larger than Remote Campus D and, therefore, is served by a T-3 leased line, offering a capacity of 45Mbps. The interface to Provider A is also via a T-3 leased line. The leased line to Remote campus D, on the other hand, is a T-1 with a capacity of only 1.5Mbps. The difference between the two line rates calls for different traffic-handling mechanisms and policies being applied on the different lines.

Six service levels are offered on the remote links:

- **Guaranteed Service**—For IP telephony, interactive audio, and other traffic that is highly sensitive to delays

- **Controlled Load Service**—For video traffic and noninteractive (streaming) audio

- **Qualitative prioritized service**—For signaled qualitative traffic

- **Better-than-best-effort service**—For nonsignaled qualitative traffic

- **Standard best-effort service**—The service applied by default to all traffic that is not otherwise classified.

- **Less-than-best-effort service**—For signaled traffic deemed to be nonconforming

Note that the six service levels offered on the remote links correspond to the six service levels in the switched subnetworks (see the previous section "Traffic-Handling Configuration in the 802 Switched Subnetworks").

Per-Conversation Traffic Handling on the Slow Leased Line

On the relatively slow T-1 interface, conventional, per-conversation RSVP/IntServ functionality is enabled. As a result, R1 installs per-conversation classification state and the corresponding per-conversation policing and queuing for signaled quantitative traffic flows. This approach provides high-quality Guaranteed Service for IP telephony traffic and good traffic isolation among competing IP telephony flows. As will be discussed subsequently, video traffic is precluded from this relatively slow link because of its high bandwidth demands.

On the slow leased line, qualitative signaled traffic and nonsignaled prioritized traffic are handled in aggregate, based on DSCP, as described next.

Aggregate Traffic Handling on the Leased Lines

On the T-3 interfaces, the overhead of per-conversation policing and queuing is more processing-intensive than on the relatively slower T-1 interface. In addition, the degree of traffic isolation (and the QE product in general) that is afforded by per-conversation policing and queuing is not required. As a result, the A-1 Corporation network manager has chosen to use aggregate traffic handling (which is less processing-intensive) and to be slightly more conservative in the admission of high-quality traffic flows (so that the links appear slightly overprovisioned with respect to these flows). Aggregate traffic handling on these links is provided exclusively based on the DSCP in packets transmitted on the links.

On the T-1 link, high-quality quantitative traffic is handled on a per-conversation basis; however, lower-quality traffic is handled in aggregate, based on DSCP.

Note that the queuing strategy and the interpretation of DSCPs on the interfaces serving Campuses C and D are entirely within the control of A-1 Corporation's network managers. However, services offered via Provider A are subject to the provider's traffic-handling mechanisms and interpretation of DSCPs. In the general case, a DSCP translation function may be required at the corresponding interface. Translation may be applied at the egress interface of R1 or at the ingress interface of Provider A's router. In either case, the SLS in place at the interface between the A-1 Corporation main campus network and Provider A should specify the DSCP values to be used to obtain each service.

Policing

As explained previously, traffic forwarded onto the private T-1 leased line for Guaranteed or Controlled Load Service is policed based on per-conversation classification criteria signaled in RSVP messages.

> **Note**
>
> Recall from Chapter 6 (in the section "Traffic Conditioning") that policing is the task of verifying and enforcing conformance of a traffic flow to a corresponding profile. In general, policing may force conformance by re-marking nonconforming packets, discarding them, or detaining them until they become conforming (known as shaping). The specific manner in which policing is applied at a specific interface depends on the ownership of the interface (customer or provider), the type of traffic flow being policed, and other factors.

Traffic forwarded onto the T-1 leased line for per-conversation, quantitative traffic is policed using standard RSVP/IntServ policing functionality (as described in Chapter 4). Traffic forwarded onto the T-1 leased line for qualitative signaled or nonsignaled traffic is policed in aggregate (by shaping based on DSCP) or not at all. Figure 10.13a illustrates traffic policing tables on the T-1 interface for both high- and medium-quality services.

Traffic forwarded onto the T-3 leased lines for Guaranteed or Controlled Load Service is policed in aggregate based on total capacity allowed for the corresponding DSCP. Traffic on Guaranteed Service flows is expected to be shaped at the source, but it may be reshaped by R1. Traffic on Controlled Load Service flows will be policed by demoting nonconforming traffic to the best-effort DSCP (also by R1). Traffic forwarded onto the T-3 leased lines for qualitative signaled and nonsignaled services is policed by shaping to long-term average (sufficiently long to accommodate the burstiness of the qualitative traffic) or not at all. Finally, all traffic offered to Provider A is also policed in aggregate, based on DSCP, at the ingress to the provider, per the negotiated SLA (re-marking nonconforming traffic on Controlled Load Service and lesser-quality flows, discarding nonconforming traffic on Guaranteed Service flows). The configuration tables for the policing functionality described are illustrated in Figure 10.13.

Figure 10.13 Policing Parameters Affecting Remote Links

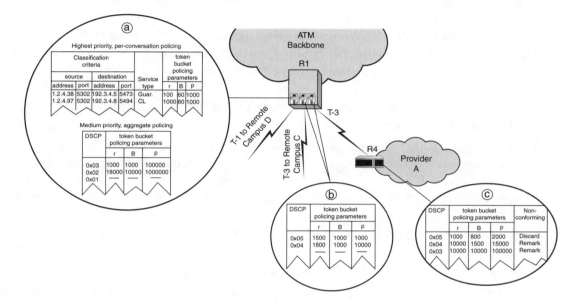

Note

Note that the tables illustrated in Figure 10.13 affect traffic sent *from* the A-1 Corporation main campus *to* the wide area network. The variables *r*, *p*, and *B* are used in a number of figures in this chapter. These represent the token bucket average rate, peak rate, and bucket size, respectively. These are discussed at length in Chapter 3, "Queuing Mechanisms," in the section "The Combination of Token Bucket and Leaky Bucket."

In Figure 10.13a, two policing tables are illustrated for the T-1 link. The top table illustrates per-conversation policing parameters that are installed for RSVP-signaled quantitative traffic flows. The bottom table illustrates aggregate policing parameters that are installed for RSVP-signaled qualitative (Null Service) traffic flows and for nonsignaled prioritized traffic. In policing packets based on these tables, R1 would first look for a match against per-conversation classification criteria in the top table. If no match were found, it would then classify based on DSCP in the bottom table.

The policing table illustrated in Figure 10.13b is representative of the tables that would be installed on both of the R1 interfaces that are transmitting onto the T-3 links. These tabulate aggregate policing parameters to be applied to all traffic on a specified DSCP. Different parameters likely would be tabulated for each of the two T-3 links.

The policing table illustrated in 10.13c is used by Provider A at the ingress to the provider's network. It prescribes policing per the SLA negotiated between A-1 Corporation and Provider A. Of course, these are aggregate, per-DSCP limits. As explained later in this chapter in the section "Dynamic versus Static Services," certain entries in this SLA are static, while others may change dynamically.

10.2.3.2 Admission Control and Policies Governing Resources Consumed on Remote Links

R1 (from Figure 10.2), in cooperation with its associated policy server, provides explicit admission control functionality for all signaled requests initiated in the main campus network for resources in the wide area network. Such admission control functionality is similar to that applied to signaling requests affecting resources only within the main campus network. However, policies affecting the wide area network tend to be more restrictive than those within the main campus network. These are described in the following sections.

Admission Control on the T-1 Private Leased Line

Prioritized resources on this link are extremely valuable because of its relatively low capacity. Policies enable a very limited total quantity of traffic for the high-quality Guaranteed and Controlled Load Services on this line at any time. Admission control for these services is limited to 10% of the total line capacity. This constraint enables the admission of a small number of RSVP requests for low-bandwidth IP telephony conversations at any time, but it rejects RSVP requests corresponding to the higher-bandwidth video applications. All rejected traffic is marked for lower-than-best-effort priority to prevent it from starving best-effort traffic.

In addition to pure resource-based admission control as described previously, policies determine the set of users and applications that are entitled to the high-quality services on the T-1 leased line. The set of users entitled to these services on the T-1 leased line is significantly restricted with respect to the set of users entitled to equivalent services within the campus local area.

Because requests for qualitative service by definition do not quantify the requested resources, these are not admitted based on quantitative traffic profiles. Instead, these are admitted based on a total number of qualitative flows admissible on the leased line at any time. Because traffic for qualitative services is handled based on DSCP, admission control to these services requires that R3 append a DCLASS object to the corresponding RESV messages arriving from the remote side of the leased line. These inform the sending host of the appropriate DSCP to use when marking traffic on qualitative signaled flows.

DSCPs and DCLASS Objects Across Domain Boundaries

Note that in Figure 10.10, edge routers transmitting from the ATM backbone onto the switched subnetworks append a DCLASS object to RESV messages received from the ATM backbone or beyond (as prescribed by associated policies). These may conflict with DCLASS values appended by the upstream router serving the wide area links, as illustrated in Figure 10.14. This is a general problem that may occur when multiple devices in a traffic path append DCLASS objects.

There are several ways in which to handle this problem. In one approach, DCLASS objects and DSCPs are assumed to have only local (per administrative domain) significance. In this approach, DCLASS objects are interpreted and acted upon by upstream markers only in the local domain (and are likely removed from RSVP messages before they are forwarded across domain boundaries). This approach also requires that DSCPs are translated as data packets traversing domain boundaries.

In an alternate approach (the *cumulative* approach), DCLASS objects and DSCPs are both ordered and are interpreted consistently across domain boundaries. In this approach, the DCLASS object can be used to arrive at a marking decision that reflects the cumulative result of multiple policies along the traffic path. Thus, packets can be marked differently based on the traffic path that they will traverse through a network. This approach is illustrated in Figure 10.14.

In Figure 10.14a, a RESV message is generated by a receiver on the far side of one of the widearea links, for a traffic flow originating from H1. In Figure 10.14b, the router serving the wide area links appends *DCLASS1* to the RESV message. In Figure 10.14c, policy for the edge router serving the switched subnetwork (R17) prescribes DCLASS2 to be appended to the RESV message. However, policy for R17 dictates that R17 accumulate the DCLASS value by appending a DCLASS object containing the *lesser* of the DSCP values from DCLASS1 and DCLASS2 as it forwards the RESV message upstream.

Although this specific example illustrates the cumulative approach, it is unlikely that this approach will be broadly deployed across administrative domains. It is more likely to be deployed within a single administrative domain.

continues

Figure 10.14 Accumulating DCLASS Values

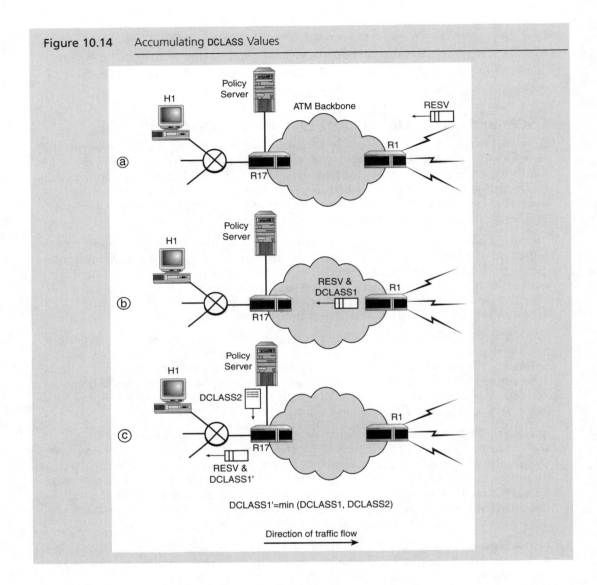

Admission Control on Faster Leased Lines

Admission control on the faster leased lines is similar to that implemented on the slower T-1 line, with several exceptions.

With respect to quantitative traffic, admission control is per-conversation and is based on the quantity of resources requested, the quantity available at the corresponding service level on the particular leased line, and the requesting user and application. On the leased line connected to Provider A, the admissible quantities are specified by the SLAs that are enforced by the provider's ingress router. On the private leased line, admissible quantities are determined at the network manager's discretion. High-quality resources on the faster lines are generally limited to some small fraction of the line's capacity, just as they are for the slower T-1 line. However, because the capacity of these lines is quite a bit higher than that of the T-1 line, there is generally sufficient capacity to admit video traffic as well as telephony traffic.

Requests for admission to qualitative service levels are handled on these lines in much the same manner as described with respect to the slower T-1 line. Because all traffic on the faster lines is handled based on DSCP, admission control agents for these lines are required to return a DCLASS object for all signaled traffic.

Per-Conversation Admission Control to High-Quality Aggregate Traffic Classes on Private Leased Lines

The leased lines between A-1 Corporation's main campus and its remote campuses are the hot spots of A-1 Corporation's network. Bandwidth on these lines is scarce and costly. The leased lines must be run efficiently and must provide high-quality quantitative services. Thus, on these lines, it is important to enable a high QE product. On the T-1 line, this is achieved by using the full RSVP/IntServ model with per-conversation signaling and per-conversation admission control. On the T-3 lines, the network manager combines aggregate traffic handling with per-conversation signaling. Aggregate traffic handling is preferable to per-conversation traffic handling due to scalability concerns. The use of per-conversation signaling enables the network manager to do the following:

- Prevent admission of too much traffic to the high-priority aggregate traffic-handling class on the leased line. (Admission of too much traffic to this class would compromise the quality offered by the class.)

- Control which users and applications make use of the valuable high-priority resources on the leased line.

The operation of per-conversation signaling, in conjunction with aggregate traffic handling to control resource usage for quantitative services on the leased lines, is illustrated in Figure 10.15.

Figure 10.15   Per-Conversation Admission Control to High-Quality Traffic Aggregates on Private Leased Lines

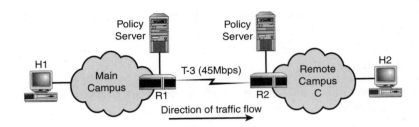

(a) Network-wide mappings from IntServ to DSCP

IntServ	DSCP
Guaranteed	CS5
Controlled Load	CS4

(b) Policies in effect at R1 (for interface serving T-3 leased line)

Total per-subnet limits:

DSCP	r	p	B
CS5	4.5Mbps	4.5Mbps	4500bytes
CS4	9Mbps	18Mbps	10,000bytes

(c) Per-user limits:

	Service	r	p	B
Any Authenticated user	Guaranteed	500K	500K	1500
	Controlled Load	1Mbps	1Mbps	3000
Unauthenticated users	Guaranteed	100K	100K	1500
	Controlled Load	200K	200K	3000

In Figure 10.15, R1 acts as the admission control agent for traffic transmitted from left to right across the T-3 private leased line between the A-1 Corporation's main campus network and Remote Campus C. (For the purpose of this discussion, only traffic flowing from left to right is considered. The same analysis can be applied in the opposite direction.) R1 has been configured to provide aggregate traffic handling based on DSCP. As such, it effectively operates in DiffServ mode. It uses strict priority queuing, as follows:

- **DSCP corresponding to the CS5 PHB**—Highest-priority service

- **DSCP corresponding to the CS3 PHB**—Second-highest-priority service

> **Note**
>
> The CS5 and CS3 PHBs belong to the *class selector* family of PHBs. These are described in detail in Chapter 6. In this chapter, the notation CS'X' is used to refer to the corresponding class selector PHB or the DSCP used to invoke the corresponding class selector PHB. Furthermore, class selector PHBs denoted by CS'X' are invoked by the same DSCP that would be used to invoke IP precedence 'X' and invoke the same behavior that would be expected from IP precedence 'X'.

Within the A-1 Corporation's network, the class selector PHBs are used. Within the provider DiffServ networks, these may be mapped to more sophisticated PHBs (such as expedited forwarding and assured forwarding PHBs). This mapping is discussed later in this chapter in the section "Provider Networks."

(Additional DSCPs are recognized and invoke lower-quality services. However, for the purpose of this discussion, only the two high-quality quantitative services are considered.)

Policers are configured in R1 to enforce the per-subnetwork aggregate limits tabulated in the table in Figure 10.15b. The policers limit the amount of traffic eligible for the highest-priority service to about 10% of the link capacity. They limit the amount of traffic eligible for the second-highest-priority service to about 20% of the link capacity. These limits prevent the starvation of lower-priority traffic and ensure that the higher-priority service offers relatively low latency.

R1's traffic-handling mode, the mapping of DSCP to priority queues, and the aggregate policing limits are all provisioned as static global policy (see Chapter 9 for a discussion of different policy types). Additional static global policy throughout the A-1 Corporation's network maps IntServ services to DSCPs per the table in Figure 10.15a. The mapping is in effect both at hosts and at routers. The mapping maps the IntServ Guaranteed Service to the CS5 DSCP, and maps the IntServ Controlled Load Service to the CS4 DSCP.

Dynamic policy at R1 restricts per-user usage of the prioritized resources on the T-3 link. Per the table in Figure 10.15c, authenticated users are each entitled to consume about one-ninth of the total resources available at each of the two service levels. Unauthenticated users are entitled to considerably less.

Hosts are trusted to mark traffic for best-effort service by default (DSCP = 0). Hosts are allowed to mark traffic for prioritized service only on *signaled flows that have been admitted*. On these flows, traffic must be marked per the global mapping from IntServ service type to DSCP. In addition, hosts are trusted to mark traffic for prioritized DSCPs at the rate specified in the signaled request.

In operation, hosts on the main campus network (such as H1) that require high-quality service to Remote Campus C transmit RSVP PATH messages toward the remote host (H2). The remote host responds with an RSVP RESV message specifying the IntServ service type desired and the quantity of resources desired. For the sake of discussion, assume a session from H1 to H2 for 200Kbps of Guaranteed Service (for example for interactive audio). Assume also that the users on both H1 and H2 are authenticated users.

When the RESV message arrives at R1, it applies admission control as follows:

- **Check the availability of resources on the T-3 line, at the requested service level—** Per the mapping, Guaranteed Service corresponds to the CS5 DSCP. Per static, global policy, a total of 4.5Mbps is available for this DSCP on the T-3 line. Some portion of this may already have been allocated to other sessions. R1 must track how much of the capacity for each DSCP is allocated at any time. If sufficient capacity remains, then from a resource-only perspective, the request expressed in the RESV message is admissible.

- **Check the availability of resources for the requesting user—** R1 must check against the per-user limits specified by dynamic policy to verify that the requesting user is entitled to the requested resources on the T-3 line. R1, in cooperation with the policy system, must track per-user allocations to ensure that sufficient capacity remains available to the user at any time. If sufficient capacity remains for the user, then from a per-user policy perspective, the request is admissible.

Note

Note that for the sake of brevity, only the average rate, r, is discussed in the resource check. All token bucket parameters must be considered in admission control.

If the request is admissible both from the resource perspective and from the user policy perspective, then the request can be admitted. R1 and the policy system must adjust their notion of the current allocations, and the RESV message can be sent toward the sender.

Upon reaching H1, the RESV message entitles the sender to mark traffic based on the global mapping from service type to DSCP. Therefore, traffic is marked with the CS5 DSCP. The host ensures that no more than 200Kbps of traffic will be marked on the admitted flow.

This example illustrates the use of aggregate traffic handling in combination with per-conversation signaling, to yield a high QE product on the private leased line between the main campus network and Remote Campus C. A similar strategy can be used to yield a high QE product between the main campus network and Remote Campus A or Remote Campus B. The application of this strategy when a provider network exists between the two campuses is discussed next.

SLA at the Interface to Provider A's Network

Traffic forwarded to Provider A's network is handled subject to the SLA negotiated between the A-1 Corporation and the provider. This SLA offers services that vary in type and extent. The following services are offered:

- **Static, quantitative, route-constrained**—(See the discussion in Chapter 6, in the section "Levels of Service Guarantees," for an explanation of route-constrained services.) These services offer a fixed, quantifiable amount of high-quality resources between Provider A's ingress and Remote Campus B.

- **Dynamic, quantitative, route-constrained**—These services offer a variable, quantifiable amount of high-quality resources between Provider A's ingress and Remote Campus A.

- **Qualitative, route-constrained**—These services offer qualitative service for traffic between Provider A's ingress and Remote Campus A, and between Provider A's ingress and Remote Campus B.

- **Qualitative, route-independent**—These services offer qualitative service between Provider A's ingress and any egress point.

These services are illustrated in Figure 10.16 from the perspective of the A-1 Corporation's network.

Figure 10.16   Services Offered by SLA with Provider A

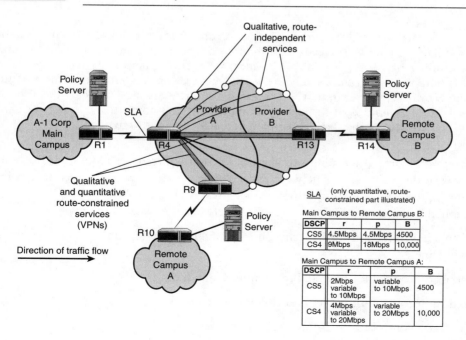

> **Note**
>
> For the sake of simplicity, DSCPs in the SLA are expressed as DSCPs for the class selector PHB. As explained later in this chapter (in the section "Provider Networks"), Provider A and Provider B implement the expedited forwarding (EF) and the assured forwarding (AF) PHBs, not the class selector PHBs. Therefore, DSCPs are translated at provider network boundaries.

From the perspective of the A-1 Corporation, the SLA provides two VPNs: one to Remote Campus A and the other to Remote Campus B. (The term *VPN* is used here in the abstract sense, as discussed earlier in this chapter in the sidebar "Virtual Private Networks." The abstract usage may differ somewhat from specific VPN product offerings.) Both VPNs offer a mix of high-quality, quantitative services and medium-quality, qualitative services. The amount of quantitative service provided by the VPN to Remote Campus A can be modified dynamically between some minimal base level and some maximum limit. The amount of quantitative service provided by the VPN to Remote Campus B is fixed. In addition, to the two VPNs, the SLA offers low-quality qualitative service to any point on Provider A's network (route-independent service).

Details as to how the services are actually provided by Provider A and Provider B will be discussed later in this chapter, in the section "Provider Networks". This section assumes that the services are provided and discusses the details of admission control to the services.

> **Note**
>
> Note that services offered to Remote Campus A commit resources that are entirely under the control of provider A. However, services offered to Remote Campus B commit resources that are not under direct control of Provider A. To offer quantifiable services between A-1 Corporation's main campus network and Remote Campus B, Provider A must negotiate with Provider B to ensure that the necessary resources are available between Provider A and Remote Campus B. Such peering arrangements will be discussed in further depth later in this chapter, in the section "Peering Between Provider Networks."

Referring to Figure 10.16, admission control for signaled resource requests at the boundary between the main campus network and Provider A's network is provided by a combination of egress router R1 and Provider A's ingress router, R4. Both routers are provisioned based on the SLA that is in place between the two.

From an admission control perspective, it is helpful to separate admission control along the following lines:

- Admission control for the VPN to Remote Campus A

- Admission control for the VPN to Remote Campus B

- Admission control for the route-independent service

Because the VPN to Remote Campus B offers fixed (static) amounts of resources for the high-quality services, it is analogous to the private leased line between the main campus and Remote Campus C. Admission control to the high-quality services on this VPN is therefore analogous to the admission control described previously in the section "Per-Conversation Admission Control to High-Quality Aggregate Traffic Classes on Private Leased Lines." Refer back to Figure 10.15 for an illustration of admission control to the private leased line between the main campus and Remote Campus C. Figure 10.15b (total per-subnetwork limits) is equivalent to the static part of the SLA (in Figure 10.16) that describes the high-quality services between the main campus and Remote Campus B. For the purpose of admission control for the VPN to Remote Campus B, this static part of the SLA can be provisioned in R1 as the total allowable per-subnetwork limits. R1 can then act independently as the admission control agent for the VPN, providing explicit admission control based both on per-user policies and per-subnetwork resource limits. R4 is not required to participate in signaling for admission to this VPN. Instead, it provides only implicit admission control for the VPN by policing per the SLA.

While the VPN to Remote Campus B offers fixed amounts of resources, the VPN to Remote Campus A offers dynamically variable amounts of resources (ranging between some prenegotiated minimal base level and maximum limit). This is reflected in the SLA for Remote Campus A. By offering dynamically variable amounts of resources, the SLA can be negotiated for the average expected resource requirement of the customer, rather than the peak resource requirements. The SLA is automatically increased up to the limit during periods of peak demand and is reduced back to the base level as demand diminishes. This frees the provider to commit otherwise unused resources to additional customers (based on some sort of call-blocking probability model). As a result, customers pay less for their service. The sophisticated functionality offered by such a dynamic SLA requires Provider A to be capable of dynamically reallocating resources within its network. (To this end, Provider A employs aggregate signaling between R4 and R9, as discussed later in this chapter, in the section "SLAs and Admission Control in the Provider Networks.")

In the case of the VPN to Remote Campus B, a fixed amount of quantitative resources was committed. The corresponding static part of the SLA could be configured into R1, enabling it to provide both resource- and policy-based explicit admission control. However, in the case of the VPN to Remote Campus A, this is not the case. Because the quantitative resources offered change dynamically, R1 and R4 must both participate in explicit admission control to the VPN. R1 still applies the per-user, policy-based admission control. It relies on R4 to apply the resource-based admission control, based on the current level of resources available in the provider's network. To do so, R4 must participate in per-conversation RSVP signaling originating from the main campus.

> **Note**
>
> The use of RSVP for admission to DiffServ networks in various forms is described in depth in Chapter 6, in the section "DiffServ with RSVP."

Provider A's ingress router does not apply admission control to RSVP requests for qualitative services. These are admitted or rejected exclusively by the customer's egress router, based on user, application, and policies specifying the maximum number of simultaneous flows allowable to specific egress points.

No signaling is generated for qualitative, route-independent service. This is nonsignaled, nonpersistent traffic, and it is policed on the fly, if at all.

Special Handling of Policy Objects at the Leased Line to the Provider's Network

Policies within the A-1 Corporation are based on policy objects recognized within the corporation's administrative domain. These include user identities and application identities that are recognized within this domain. These policy objects are of little use beyond the corporation's administrative domain, in the various ISP networks and in the Internet at large.

Therefore, admission control agents forwarding RSVP signaling messages beyond the corporation's domain may append a higher-level policy object identifying the corporation's administrative domain as a whole. As a result, any admission control agents external to the A-1 Corporation's domain that participate in per-conversation RSVP signaling are capable of applying policies based on the administrative domain sourcing the traffic, without regard for the particular user or application within the domain. See the section in Chapter 9 titled "Translating Identity Objects" for further discussion of this issue.

10.2.3.3 Admission Control and Policies Governing Resources Consumed in A-1 Corporation's Main Campus Network

The previous section described admission control affecting traffic transmitted from A-1 Corporation's main campus onto the wide-area network. This section describes admission control affecting traffic forwarded from the wide-area network onto the main campus network. A number of special cases are considered, as illustrated in Figure 10.17 and described in the following sections.

Figure 10.17   Issues in QoS for Traffic Received from the Wide Area

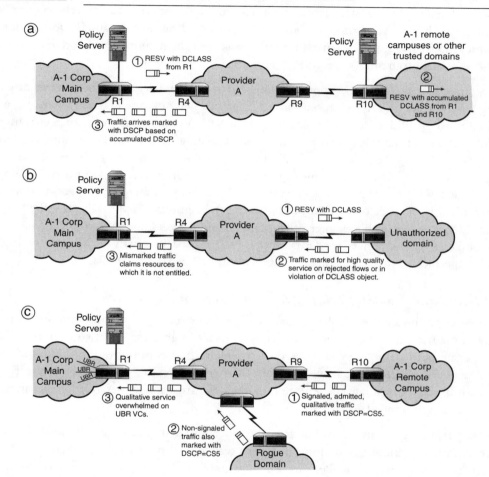

Handling Signaled Requests for Traffic Originating in the Wide Area

Refer briefly to Figure 10.1. RSVP signaled resource requests arrive at R1 (A-1 Corporation's ingress router) for traffic originating in the wide area, beyond A-1 Corporation's main campus network. These requests may correspond to traffic originating from a remote campus of the A-1 Corporation or from a remote campus in a separate administrative domain (a foreign domain). In the former case, admission control policies can be based on policy objects identifying users and applications that are recognized within the A-1 Corporation administrative domain. (Note that these resource requests will also include higher-level policy objects identifying the A-1 Corporation as the source administrative domain.) In the latter case, foreign user and application policy objects will not be recognized by the A-1 Corporation policies. Special policies may be applied for any foreign traffic. Alternatively, policies may be applied based on the identity of the foreign administrative domain sourcing (or relaying) the traffic.

Assuming that policy checks approve admission of *quantitative* signaling requests originating from outside the A-1 Corporation main campus network, the ingress router, R1, will attempt to establish a per-conversation CBR or VBR VC to the appropriate peer router within the main campus network. Traffic corresponding to *qualitative* signaling requests will be carried on the appropriate UBR VC. For qualitative signaled requests, R1 will append a DCLASS object to RESV messages as they return from receivers in the main campus network toward the remote wide-area sender. These may be merged with DCLASS objects prescribed by policy closer to the sender (using the cumulative approach, described in the sidebar earlier in this chapter titled "DSCPs and DCLASS Objects Across Domain Boundaries"). The remote sender is expected to mark packets with the accumulated DSCP value specified in the DCLASS object. This is illustrated in Figure 10.17a.

Policing and Mapping Traffic Originating in the Wide Area

A number of interesting challenges arise when considering the handling of traffic originating in the wide area and destined for receivers in the main campus network. In most cases, aggregate traffic handling will be used to provide resources to this traffic within the campus network. When traffic arrives on one of the private leased lines connected directly to one of the A-1 Corporation's remote campuses, the trust model described earlier in this chapter can be applied.

However, traffic on the leased line from Provider A may originate outside the A-1 Corporation's administrative domain. In this case, different trust models than those described earlier may apply. Policing will have to be applied to prevent abuse of resources within the A-1 Corporation administrative domain by senders on remote networks in different administrative domains. See Figure 10.17b for an illustration of marked traffic sent on a signaled flow from an unauthorized domain.

In addition, marking for nonsignaled traffic is easily controlled within a single administrative domain to prevent conflict with higher-priority marks. Even when crossing domain boundaries, DCLASS objects can be used to request the appropriate DSCP marking (or translation) for traffic on *signaled* flows. However, when marked traffic on nonsignaled flows crosses domain boundaries, marking conflicts and inconsistencies may arise and can be quite difficult to resolve. This is illustrated in Figure 10.17c.

> **Note**
>
> Protection against unauthorized traffic arriving from Provider A's network may be offered by SLAs governing *received* traffic. See the section "Agreements Governing Received Traffic," in Chapter 6.

The resolution of such issues is not well understood. Interdomain QoS is recognized to be one of the more challenging problems in QoS deployment. Techniques for tackling various interdomain problems are discussed throughout the book in the context of the various QoS mechanisms.

10.3 A-1 Corporation's Remote Networks

The remote campus networks of the A-1 Corporation are significantly smaller than the main campus network. They range in size from tens of users (Remote Campus D) to hundreds of users (Remote Campuses A to C). These campuses are discussed in the following sections.

10.3.1 Remote Campus D

Remote Campus D is illustrated in Figure 10.18.

Figure 10.18   Remote Campus D

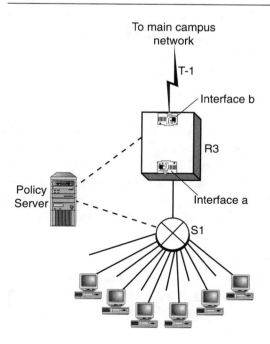

This network consists of a single switch, a router connecting it to the remote network, and a local policy server.

> **Note**
>
> Note that in particularly small networks, PDP functionality may be embodied in a switch or a router rather than in a separate policy server.

10.3.1.1 Traffic Handling in Remote Campus D

From a traffic-handling perspective, there are two zones in the remote campus network. One of these is the switched zone. The other is the T-1 leased line to the main campus network.

Traffic Handling in the Switched Zone

Within the campus network, the QoS for a particular traffic flow is determined exclusively by the resources allocated to that flow in the switch. The relatively simple switch employed in this network provides only two levels of priority. Traffic marked with 802 user_priority 0 to 3 is directed to the standard-priority queue. Traffic marked for 802 user_priority 4 to 7 is directed to the high-priority queue.

The switch is relatively overprovisioned with respect to the number of users in the network. Therefore, there is no danger of resource starvation. However, competition with large data packets in general and with nonadaptive video traffic specifically may compromise IP telephony service quality.

Recall that (per corporate-wide policies) the default user_priority for admitted IP telephony traffic is user_priority 6, and the default user_priority for admitted video traffic is user_priority 5. Because the threshold between the high- and low-priority services in the switch is between user_priority values 3 and 4, IP telephony and video traffic would compete for resources in the same priority level. Therefore, dynamic policies are authored in the policy server to admit a relatively large number of IP telephony flows, but to limit admission to video traffic to a small number of flows. Qualitative signaled traffic also competes at the same priority level. However, this traffic is expected to be adaptive (based on TCP) and will also be limited in terms of the number of admissible flows.

Traffic Handling on the T-1 Link

Because of the relatively low number of conversations accommodated on the T-1 interface, it is practical to support RSVP signaling and per-conversation traffic handling on this interface. Weighted fair queuing (WFQ) is enabled on the interface. Relatively high weights are assigned to traffic on RSVP-admitted quantitative flows. Remaining traffic flows are handled using a lower weight, in aggregate, based on DSCP. These include RSVP-signaled qualitative traffic flows; nonsignaled, prioritized qualitative traffic, and best-effort traffic.

10.3.1.2 *Admission Control in Remote Campus D*

The switch used in Remote Campus D is less capable than those employed in the main campus network. As such, it is not RSVP-aware. The router is RSVP-aware and is also SBM-enabled. Because it has no competition on the network, it wins the election for DSBM on interface a. As DSBM, it applies admission control for any flows that would consume resources in the local-area switched network. It also applies standard RSVP admission control on interface b. RSVP admission control on interface b affects all signaled traffic flows originating in the local area network that would consume resources on the wide-area T-1 link. Recall that R1 provides admission control for traffic flows originating on the main campus and destined for receivers on Remote Campus D.

The following policies govern admission control at the Campus D router (R3).

- Admit requests for IP telephony traffic flows that remain local to the switched network for all authenticated users.

- Admit requests for IP telephony traffic flows originating from the remote campus and destined for the main campus, up to a specified total bandwidth.

- Admit requests for video traffic flows that remain local to the switched network, up to a specified total bandwidth.

- Reject all requests for video traffic flows originating from the remote campus and destined for the main campus.

- Admit requests for signaled qualitative traffic that remains local to the switched network for all authenticated users. Assign these user_priority 4.

- Admit limited requests for signaled qualitative traffic originating from the remote campus and destined for the main campus. Append to these a DCLASS that specifies the DSCP corresponding to IP precedence 3.

Note that policies in the remote network for qualitative signaled traffic apply only to certain applications. For example, signaling for the ERP applications discussed previously originates from servers on the main campus and is terminated by RSVP receiver proxies on the main campus. The ERP clients on the remote campus do not respond to server-initiated signaling, nor do they initiate signaling of their own. Therefore, there are no policies in the remote campus that apply to signaling requests for ERP traffic. Other qualitative applications, on the other hand, may rely on receivers to respond, or may be symmetric in the sense that hosts on the remote campus initiate signaling for traffic transmitted from the remote campus to the main campus. In these cases, policies may be applied at the remote campus.

10.3.2   Remote Campus A Through C Networks

These are larger networks than those of Remote Campus D. They are similar to the main campus network in the sense that they are constructed of a number of interconnected switched networks. The topology of Remote Campus A is illustrated in Figure 10.19 (Remote Campuses B and C have a similar topology).

Figure 10.19   Remote Campus A

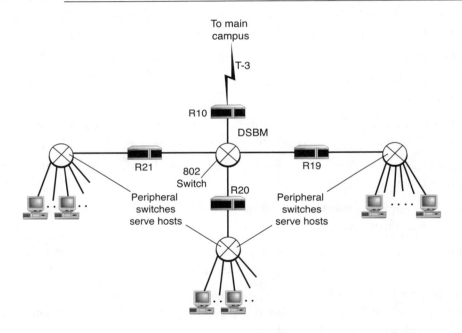

Remote Campuses A to C provide QoS based on the same principles discussed so far with respect to the main campus and Remote Campus D. For the sake of brevity, the following sections will not repeat the details discussed in previous sections. Instead, they briefly discuss the differences between the implementations discussed so far and those implemented in Remote Campuses A, B, and C.

10.3.2.1 QoS Within the Remote Campus Networks

Unlike the main campus network (in which the routers are interconnected via ATM VCs), the routers in these networks are interconnected by a high-capacity 802 switch. This switch offers traffic handling per the six priority levels identified previously in the context of the main campus switched networks. It also acts as a DSBM to provide admission control for traffic flows traversing the switched core.

The peripheral switches also provide six levels of prioritization. However, these are not SBM-capable. Instead, the routers R19 to R21 act as DSBMs for each of the peripheral subnetworks.

10.3.2.2 QoS Between the Remote Campuses and the Wide Area

Routers R10, R14, and R2 provide connectivity to the main campus network for Remote Campuses A, B, and C, respectively. These routers handle traffic transmitted on their wide-area link in a similar manner as their peer routers on the main campus networks. As such, they provide six priority levels for traffic aggregates marked with the corresponding DSCPs. Unlike the router in Remote Campus D, these routers do not offer any per-conversation traffic handling.

R2, R14, and R10 implement policies regarding admission control to signaled traffic in a manner similar to that provided by R1 on the main campus. Because of the relatively high capacity (T-3) available between these campuses and the wide area, policies permit the admission of some amount of video traffic onto the wide-area links.

10.4 University Campus Network

The internal structure and QoS mechanisms of the university network are very similar to those of the A-1 Corporation's main campus network. However, unlike the A-1 Corporation, which connects a number of remote campuses via VPN QoS services, the university has no specific remote peer networks. In addition, policies affecting usage within the university network are quite different from those that are implemented in the A-1 Corporation networks. The university campus network is illustrated in Figure 10.20.

This network consists of an ATM backbone network, interconnecting a number of building networks.

Figure 10.20 High-Level View of the University Campus Network

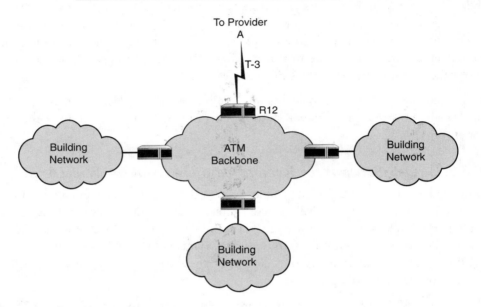

10.4.1 Building Networks

The university network is subdivided into building networks in the same manner as the A-1 Corporation main campus network. Each building network is constructed of a switched hierarchy as illustrated in Figure 10.3. Two fundamentally different types of policy are applied in these networks, depending on the particular type of building. One type serves dormitory building networks, from which students may connect their own PCs to the university network. The other type serves lab building networks, classroom building networks, and administrative building networks. The resources and privileges afforded within and between dormitory networks are more restricted than those afforded within and between the other building networks.

10.4.1.1 Dormitory Networks

QoS is used within the dormitory networks primarily for the purpose of providing adequate quality for video content that is distributed from servers in administrative buildings. Various video programming is made available to students in this manner.

Switches within the dormitory networks handle traffic using two levels of prioritization (similar to switches in A-1 Corporation's Remote Campus D). Policies implemented in the dormitory routers and DSBMs reject requests for high-priority service that are initiated by senders in the dormitories. As a result, all traffic sent by these senders competes for best-effort service. On the other hand, these policies admit requests for high-priority service *from* certain approved video servers in the administrative buildings *to* authenticated receivers in the dormitory networks.

To this end, switches re-mark all `user_priority` fields to `user_priority` value 0 in traffic originating from the dormitories. Similarly, routers reset DSCPs on all traffic originating from the dormitory building networks. Such re-marking behavior is appropriate because of the weak trust model inherent in a university dormitory environment. DSCPs and `user_priority` values originating from outside the dormitory networks but within the university network are honored subject to aggregate policing limits.

10.4.1.2 Labs, Classrooms, and Administrative Building Networks

These networks are slightly more sophisticated than the dormitory networks. They offer the same six levels of service that are offered within the A-1 Corporation main campus network. Policies allow use of the high-quality services for entitled users by various videoconferencing applications, video streaming applications, signaled qualitative applications, and nonsignaled qualitative applications. In addition, limited high-priority resources are available to authorized users for experimentation within and between lab networks.

10.4.2 The University Backbone

The university backbone network interconnects the various building networks by an ATM fabric. Unlike the corporate backbone, which establishes switched VCs on demand, the university backbone uses PVCs. A full mesh of UBR PVCs is statically configured among all building networks. In addition, a limited mesh of CBR and VBR PVCs is statically configured among certain administrative, classroom, and lab building networks. A small number of VBR PVCs is also statically configured from certain administrative buildings to the dormitory networks for the purpose of carrying video content to these networks. The use of PVCs in the backbone is illustrated in Figure 10.21.

For the sake of simplicity, only three representative building networks are illustrated in Figure 10.21. R22 connects the university backbone network to a laboratory network. R23 connects the university backbone to an administrative network, and R24 connects the university backbone to a dormitory network.

A full mesh of UBR PVCs interconnects all building networks. The laboratory network and the administrative network are also interconnected by a CBR and a VBR PVC. A VBR PVC from the laboratory network serves the dormitory network.

Figure 10.21 Use of PVCs in the University Backbone Network

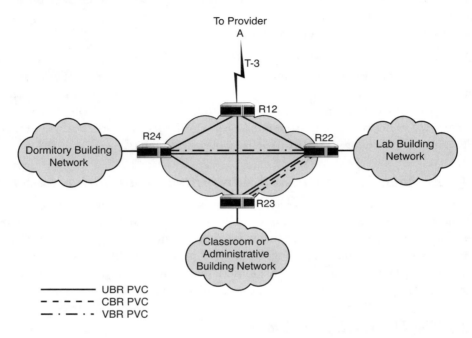

10.4.2.1 *Admission Control in the University Backbone*

Because of the use of PVCs rather than SVCs, admission control in the university backbone differs from admission control in the corporate backbone described previously. For the purpose of admission control, routers interconnecting the various buildings regard the CBR and VBR PVCs as fixed-capacity leased lines between the buildings. Quantitative admission control requests are then approved or rejected by the routers, subject to the remaining resources available on the CBR or VBR PVC between the sending router and the receiving router. UBR VCs are used in the same manner as they are used in the A-1 Corporation's main campus. Traffic entitled to prioritized qualitative service is scheduled at a higher priority on the same UBR VC as other traffic, based on DSCP.

10.4.3 *Connecting the University Network to the Wide Area*

Provider A provides all connections between the university network and the wide area. Because the university designates no specific peer networks, the provider offers no route-constrained services. The provider does offer a route-independent prioritized qualitative service to traffic originating from the university network to arbitrary endpoints, as described in the following section.

10.4.3.1 Prioritized Qualitative Service from the University Campus

The SLA between the university and Provider A allows for a certain amount of traffic originating in the university's network to be carried at a better-than-best-effort priority level. This traffic must be marked with the appropriate DSCP for Provider A's network. The better-than-best-effort DSCP used within the campus network may therefore be re-marked to the appropriate DSCP for the wide area. To prevent abuse of this priority level both within the university campus and in the wide area, traffic is policed at the router serving the building from which the traffic originates (as described earlier in this chapter, in the section "Dormitory Networks").

10.4.3.2 Prioritized Traffic to the University Campus

Certain senders from the wide area may send traffic from quantitative signaling applications to receivers in the university network. Consider, for example, a videoconferencing sender in A-1 Corporation's campus network, establishing a session with a peer in the university network. Because the SLA at A-1 Corporation's connection to Provider A does not allow quantitative service to the university network, the corresponding admission control requests will be rejected. The signaling sender will be notified of the admission control failure and will not be entitled to prioritized service to the university network. (The sender will likely send the traffic anyway. However, the traffic will not enjoy prioritized service.)

On the other hand, route-independent qualitative service will be provided to certain qualitative traffic originating from the corporate network (or similar remote networks) and destined for the university campus network.

10.5 Provider Networks

The networks of both Provider A and Provider B are large networks, consisting of a large number of routers interconnected by wide-area, high-capacity fiber optic lines, as illustrated in Figure 10.22.

Each network provides numerous interconnections to campus networks (such as the A-1 Corporation's network or the university network) and to individual users (typically connected via a POTS or a cable modem network).

Traffic handling in both provider networks is provided using aggregate DiffServ-style services. Provider A is somewhat more sophisticated than Provider B in that it uses aggregate signaling for certain internal provisioning, participates in per-conversation signaling for explicit admission control (at certain boundary routers), and offers dynamic SLAs. Provider B, by comparison, offers only static SLAs.

Figure 10.22   Provider Networks

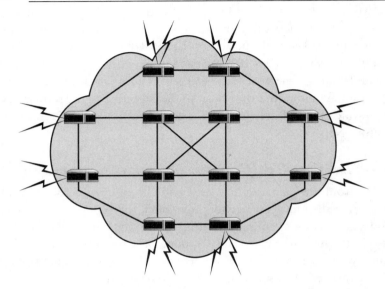

The following sections briefly describe the capabilities of the two provider networks in terms of traffic handling and admission control. In general, these networks are based on the functionality described in Chapter 6, on DiffServ networks.

10.5.1 Traffic Handling in the Provider Networks

Within the provider networks, customer traffic is handled in aggregate, based on DSCP. The networks offer a high-quality, virtual leased-line service, which is provided using the EF PHB. In addition, they offer four levels of prioritized service based on the AF PHB group. The four service levels are ordered by timeliness of forwarding. In other words, lower latencies can be expected for the higher service levels than for the lower service levels. Recall that the customers of the provider networks mark traffic using DSCPs from the class selector PHB group. Therefore, it is necessary to re-mark traffic at provider network ingress and egress points, based on a mapping between the class selector PHB group on the customer side, and the EF and AF PHB group on the provider side.

Traffic submitted for CS5 (which maps to the EF PHB) is strictly policed to SLAs at ingress points. Excess traffic is simply discarded. At various points within the network, EF traffic may be reshaped in aggregate by the provider.

> **Note**
>
> The high quality of service allotted to EF-marked traffic depends on it being strictly shaped. Even if traffic is shaped at its source, it can lose its shape as it progresses through a sequence of network hops. Periodic reshaping helps prevent this from happening.

Traffic submitted for the lower-class selector PHBs is re-marked to corresponding levels within the AF PHB group. Traffic submitted for CS4 is mapped to the highest service level in the AF PHB group and is policed to the quantitative limits specified in the SLA. Excess traffic is re-marked to a higher drop probability within the same service level. As a result, traffic marked in the customer network for CS4 enjoys a service similar to IntServ Controlled Load Service in the provider networks. Traffic marked in the customer network for CS3 and CS2 is mapped to the second and third service levels in the AF PHB group. These service levels are very loosely policed so that packets are dropped only during times of extreme congestion.

10.5.2 SLAs and Admission Control in the Provider Networks

SLAs are in place at the boundaries between customer networks and the provider networks (and at the boundary between Provider A and Provider B). As described earlier, in the section "SLA at the Interface to Provider A's Network," the SLAs offer a variety of services distinguished by type and extent. The SLA between A-1 Corporation's main campus network and Provider A is illustrated somewhat abstractly in Figure 10.16. Figure 10.23 illustrates a representative SLA in somewhat more detail.

Figure 10.23   The SLA in Place Between the A-1 Corporation's Main Campus and Provider A

	Submitted DSCP	Remap to DSCP for PHB	Service DiffServ	Service IntServ	To Egress	Policing Limits	Type
Quantitative Route-Constrained	CS5	EF	VLL	Guaranteed	Remote Campus A	TB1	Dynamic to TB1'
	CS5	EF	VLL	Guaranteed	Remote Campus B	TB2	Static
	CS4	AF1x	—	Controlled Load	Remote Campus A	TB3	Dynamic to TB3'
	CS4	AF1x	—	Controlled Load	Remote Campus B	TB4	Static
Qualitative Route-Constrained →	CS3	AF2x	BBE1		Remote Campus A & B	TB5	
Qualitative Route-Independent →	CS2	AF3x	BBE2		All	TB6	—

Although the table in this figure is somewhat simplistic, it illustrates a number of important points:

- The two highest service levels are quantitative and route-constrained. They are policed to specific quantifiable limits and are provided only to specific egress points, as designated.

- The highest service level is invoked at the provider network boundary by the CS5 DSCP. It is re-marked to the DSCP corresponding to the EF PHB internal to the provider network. It offers the DiffServ virtual leased line (VLL) service, which also supports the IntServ Guaranteed Service.

- The second-highest service level is invoked at the provider network boundary by the CS4 DSCP. It is re-marked to the DSCP corresponding to the AF11 PHB internal to the provider network. It offers a DiffServ service equivalent to the IntServ Controlled Load Service.

- The amount of resources offered to Remote Campus B for the two highest service levels is fixed, per the token bucket profiles denoted by TB2 and TB4.

- The amount of resources offered to Remote Campus A for the two highest service levels is dynamic. The minimum available is denoted by the token bucket profiles TB1 and TB3. However, these may grow up to the amounts specified by TB1' and TB3'.

- The qualitative signaled service invoked by CS3 is available to both Remote Campus A and Remote Campus B. It is a signaled service, providing better-than-best-effort service (BBE1), but with no guarantees. It is re-marked to the DSCP corresponding to the AF21 PHB. The profile TB5 is a lenient profile that guarantees no end-to-end resources but that is used strictly for policing at the ingress to Provider A.

- The lowest quality of the prioritized services offered by Provider A is invoked by the CS2 PHB. It is a nonsignaled prioritized service (BBE2) offering better-than-best-effort service but less than the BBE1 service. It is re-marked to the DSCP corresponding to the AF31 PHB. It offers no guarantees. It is policed to the loose profile specified by TB6 and is available to any destination.

10.5.2.1 Dynamic versus Static Services

As discussed earlier in this chapter, the quantitative services provided between the A-1 Corporation's main campus network and Remote Campus A are *dynamic* services. This means that the agreement between the customer and the provider guarantees a certain minimum capacity at the specified service level, but that it may be adjusted, up to a higher limit, depending on current demand and availability. Provider A is capable of offering dynamic services between A-1 Corporation's main campus network and Remote Campus A because these services rely exclusively on the availability of resources within Provider A's network and because Provider A is capable of dynamically reprovisioning its network. By contrast, services between A-1 Corporation's main campus and Remote Campus B rely on resources in Provider B, which is not capable of dynamically reprovisioning its network. As a result, Provider A offers only *static* services to the A-1 Corporation for traffic carried to Remote Campus B.

Note

Strictly speaking, Provider A *could* offer dynamic services between the A-1 Corporation's main campus network and Remote Campus B. The SLA at the interface between Provider A and the A-1 Corporation's main campus network would indicate a base level of resources and a maximum level of resources (as illustrated in the SLA in Figure 10.16). Provider A would have to negotiate a *static* commitment with Provider B for the *maximum* amount of resources offered in its SLA at its interface to the A-1 Corporation's main campus. The resources committed within Provider A could still vary between the base level and the maximum limit. The viability of such a service would depend on the dynamic range of the service and specific economic considerations.

10.5.2.2 *Admission Control*

As part of its support for dynamic services, Provider A participates in per-conversation signaling from its customer networks. By monitoring this signaling, it is capable of determining when it is necessary to reprovision the quantitative route-constrained services that it offers.

In addition, it is capable of offering explicit admission control to the customer network that reflects the current quantity of available resources within the provider's network. When signaled requests from the customer network exceed the current capacity of the provider's network to the specified destination for the specified service level, the provider may initiate aggregate RSVP signaling between the endpoints of the service to increase the available capacity (up to some prenegotiated limit). Similarly, when the available capacity between a pair of endpoints at a particular service level is not used for some time, the provider may initiate aggregate RSVP signaling between the endpoints to reduce the available capacity. The use of aggregate RSVP signaling in this manner is illustrated in Figure 10.24. (Aggregate RSVP was described in Chapter 5, "RSVP," in the section "Aggregate RSVP Signaling.")

Figure 10.24 Reprovisioning on Demand Using Aggregate Signaling

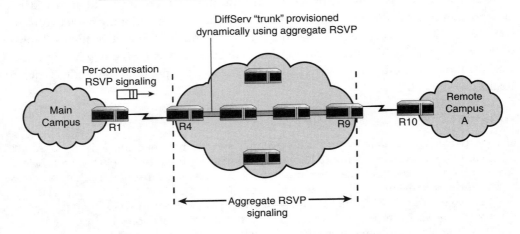

Figure 10.24 illustrates a DiffServ "trunk" provisioned dynamically between R4 and R9 using aggregate RSVP signaling. Per-conversation RSVP signaling messages arriving from customer networks can trigger aggregate RSVP signaling within the provider's network to reprovision the DiffServ trunk for a specific service level, on demand.

10.5.2.3 Provider Networks That Are Not Signaling-Aware

Unlike Provider A, Provider B's network does not participate in any form of external QoS-related signaling. It simply provisions fixed-capacity services, specified by a static SLA, and polices submitted traffic from each customer to the specified capacity. This is the nature of the service that it offers to A-1 Corporation's Remote Campus B.

If explicit admission control is required to these services, signaling-aware admission control agents in the customer network must provide it. This mode of operation was illustrated earlier in this chapter, in Figure 10.15. The specific admission control scenario illustrated in Figure 10.15 relates to the admission of signaled traffic from A-1 Corporation's main campus network to Provider A's network for statically provisioned services to Remote Campus B. The same scenario applies to the admission of traffic from Remote Campus B for statically provisioned service in the opposite direction.

10.5.2.4 Peering Between Provider Networks

Note that the SLA between Provider A and the A-1 Corporation's main campus network commits to carry traffic from the A-1 Corporation's main campus network to its Remote Campus B. However, the provision of such service depends on the availability of resources in Provider B's network. Because these resources are not in the administrative domain of Provider A, the provider must rely on a *peering* agreement between the two providers. This agreement is captured in the form of an SLA between the two provider networks. Such peering agreements are typically negotiated for large traffic aggregates. Providers then can resell fractions of this capacity and negotiate SLAs with customers for service that transits multiple provider networks. This concept is illustrated in the general network illustrated in Figure 10.25.

Figure 10.25   Reselling Capacity Negotiated in Peering Agreements

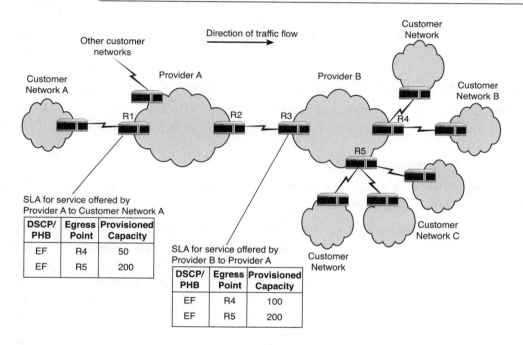

In the example illustrated, Provider A has negotiated with Provider B to carry 100 units of EF traffic from the ingress point (R3) to egress point R4, and 200 units of EF traffic from the ingress point to egress point R5. (Both R4 and R5 offer connectivity to multiple customers that Provider A is interested in serving.) Presumably, traffic within the allowed capacity will be offered VLL service. Provider A can now resell this capacity to its customers.

In the example illustrated in Figure 10.25, Provider A offers Customer Network A 50 units of EF traffic capacity from its ingress point (R1) to R4, and 200 units from its ingress point to R5. As such, Provider A has resold half of its capacity for EF traffic to R4 and all of its capacity for EF traffic to R5. It still has 50 units of EF traffic capacity to R4, which can be resold to other customer networks.

> **Note**
>
> For the sake of simplicity, the provisioned capacity entries in the SLAs are parameterized by a scalar. In reality, capacities are represented using more complex parameter sets, such as the r, p, and B parameters of a token bucket model.

Because Provider B does not dynamically reprovision capacity between its edges, it offers a strictly static SLA to Provider A. Consequently, Provider A can offer only static SLAs to customers for service to egress points served by Provider B. If both Provider A and Provider B were capable of dynamically reprovisioning capacity between their edges, then by extending aggregate RSVP signaling (or alternate signaling) between R2 and R3, Provider A would be capable of offering dynamic SLAs to its customer for egress points served by Provider B's network.

10.5.3   Policy and Provisioning in the Provider Networks

Provisioning of DiffServ networks was discussed in depth in Chapter 6. It will be described here briefly in the specific context of the ISP networks illustrated.

10.5.3.1   Provider B's Network

Provider B's network is managed entirely by push provisioning from a centralized policy server, as illustrated in Figure 10.26.

No devices in this network participate in RSVP signaling (neither per-conversation nor aggregate). The network manager authors static global policies to control the amount of resources allocated for each service level on each interface. These policies create logical networks for each service level that are superimposed on the physical infrastructure. As SLAs are negotiated with customers, the network manager then authors semi-static policies to provision policers and re-markers at the customer interfaces. These limit the amount of traffic that is accepted from each customer at each service level.

The network manager must be careful to not negotiate SLAs that cannot be supported by the internal provisioning of the network. To do so, the network manager (with or without the aid of the policy server) must learn and must consider the network topology. This provisioning approach is relatively static and hinders Provider B from being capable of offering dynamic SLAs.

Figure 10.26   Management of Provider B's Network by Push Provisioning from a Central Policy Server

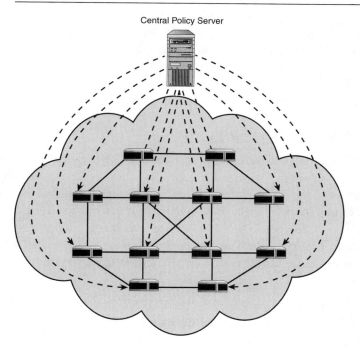

Central Policy Server

10.5.3.2 *Provider A's Network*

Provider A's network is provisioned by a combination of policy servers and edge-to-edge aggregate RSVP signaling. In the first step, the network manager authors static global policies to determine the amount of resources available at each device interface for each service level. This step is similar to the logical provisioning of Provider B's network.

After the network has been subdivided into logical networks for the different service levels, the network manager can negotiate SLAs with customers. As SLAs are offered for quantitative services, policy servers are used to inject aggregate signaling messages for the corresponding services from the ingress point at which the SLA is negotiated to the specified egress point. These messages claim resources at the appropriate interfaces against those previously provisioned for high-quality services. When dynamic SLAs are offered, the aggregate signaling messages injected by the policy servers may vary based on the arrival of per-conversation resource requests from hosts outside the provider's network. Policy servers control the amount by which dynamic SLAs can be reprovisioned based on per-customer policies.

As SLAs are negotiated for nonsignaled, qualitative services, the network manager uses policy servers to provision the appropriate policers and re-markers at the customer interfaces.

10.5.4 Services Provided to Other Customer Networks

So far, the discussion has focused on the services provided by the providers to campus networks, primarily those of the A-1 Corporation. Similar service is provided to the university campus network. The primary difference between the service provided to the A-1 Corporation networks and the university network is that no quantitative services are provided to the university network. The remainder of this section discusses the services provided to POTS-connected end users and to end users with cable modems.

10.5.4.1 POTS-Connected End Users

Provider B offers all POTS-connected end users a choice between standard and premium services. As users dial in to Provider B's network, policy servers provision classification criteria and markers in the dial-in access devices for customers that have selected premium service. As a result, all traffic from these customers is marked for AF handling. The particular AF service level assigned is the same service level that is used to handle nonsignaled qualitative traffic from the larger campus networks (mapped from the CS2 DSCP). Traffic originating from customers that are offered standard service is marked to CS0, for best-effort service.

Note that the congestion experienced by the POTS-connected end users is usually in the direction from the traffic sender toward the end user. The mechanism described prioritizes traffic in the other direction, from the end user toward the sender. This may be useful in peer-to-peer applications in which the end user is both a sender and a receiver (such as NetMeeting-style videoconferencing), but it is of limited use in content provider applications in which the end user accesses data on remote content servers (such as Web surfing and video-on-demand). In these cases, the end user relies on the content-providing sender to obtain prioritized service from the provider (as will be described in the context of the cable network). Alternatively, the signaling model can be used to enable receivers to request prioritization for specific traffic flows sent from specific senders. However, it will likely be some time before large providers respond to signaling from individual POTS-connected end users.

In the model described, providers may offer a single prioritized service for all traffic originating from a given end user. In an alternate model, the provider may allow the end user to send certain traffic at a prioritized service level and to send other traffic at the standard best-effort level. This service model relies on the end user to mark traffic for prioritized treatment and polices the marked traffic to some negotiated limit in the dial-up access device. Obviously, for this model to work, hosts must be capable of marking the appropriate traffic for the higher service level.

10.5.4.2 Cable Modem-Connected End Users

Other end users are connected to Provider A via the cable network illustrated. For these end users, the cable network is effectively their network provider. Therefore, these users will be discussed in the following paragraphs, in the context of the cable network.

10.6 The Cable Network

Note

Cable modem standards for QoS are still under definition. This section speculates at an abstract level how QoS might be provided in a cable modem network in a manner that supports end-to-end services at various levels of quality.

The cable network is illustrated in Figure 10.27.

Figure 10.27   The Cable Network

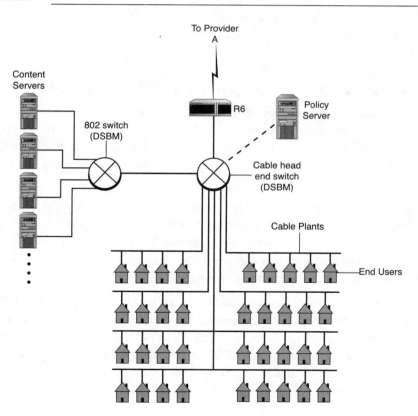

The cable network is in part a switched network and in part a shared network. A switch is located at the head end. This is not a switch in the conventional, 802 sense (although it may provide prioritization similar to 802 user_priority). Rather, it switches traffic among multiple cable plants, each of which is shared by many end users, using cable network-specific media access control mechanisms. The details of QoS mechanisms in cable networks are beyond the scope of this book and will be discussed only briefly in this section.

Link-layer QoS mechanisms in the cable plant can be used to provide dedicated or prioritized resources from the head end to individual end users and in the reverse direction, from individual end users to the head end. In addition, the head end switch is capable of providing multicast services to groups of end users.

A number of large Web and video content servers are located at the head end. These are connected to the head-end switch via a conventional, multigigabit-capacity 802 switch. The servers provide content both to cable modem end users and to end users elsewhere in the Internet. Within the 802 switch, traffic is handled based on 802 user_priority.

The cable modem network is connected to Provider A and the Internet at large via R6. This router handles traffic between the cable network and Provider A in aggregate, based on DSCP.

10.6.1 Services and Traffic Handling Within the Cable Network

The low-level media access mechanisms provided by the cable head-end switch and the end-user cable modem hardware are well suited to offering QoS. Quantitative services can be supported by reserving specific quantities of resources at the cable link layer. Qualitative services can also be provided by scheduling traffic at different priorities for the remaining unreserved resources.

Because of its inherent capability to support QoS, the cable network supports a broad range of services to its end users. It supports IP telephony service and video-on-demand within the cable network by emulating the Guaranteed and Controlled Load Services, respectively. It also can support qualitative services, giving certain end users prioritized access to Web content on the network's Web servers.

The services offered within the cable network cannot necessarily be extended at the same quality beyond the cable network (because the less predictable nature of the less structured provider networks). In certain cases, the cable network may extend telephony service by connecting the cable head end to the POTS network and providing gateway functionality. This functionality is not provided in the network illustrated in this section.

10.6.2 *Admission Control Agents in the Cable Network*

Within the cable network, RSVP signaling is used to obtain quantitative service. Hosts that want to obtain high-quality services for IP telephony or for video traffic must generate the appropriate RSVP signaling. Hosts include policy objects identifying the subscriber requesting the service. Admission control agents in the cable network admit the requests based on resource availability and on policies that specify the privileges to which the requesting subscriber is entitled.

Several admission control agents exist within the cable network. One of these is the cable switch, which is the DSBM for the cable plants to which the subscribers are attached. The 802 switch is also an admission control agent, providing admission control functionality within the 802 region of the cable network. Finally, the router R6 provides admission control for services between the cable network and Provider A.

10.6.2.1 *Admission Control in the Cable Plants*

The cable head-end switch is the DSBM for the cable plants. As a result, it intercepts all RSVP messages sent to or from subscribers. It applies dynamic policies as directed by its policy server. Requests that pass policy approval are then passed to the cable switch link layer. At this stage, the cable switch negotiates with the cable modem adapters in the subscriber's host to establish the appropriate link-layer service. This process is analogous to the use of the ATM UNI link-layer signaling to establish ATM VCs in response to RSVP requests. In the case of cable networks, a cable-specific signaling protocol is used. One such protocol is itself a variant of RSVP specified by the Data over Cable Service Interface Specification (DOCSIS). A detailed discussion of cable signaling protocols is beyond the scope of this book. The coordination of Layer 3 RSVP signaling and the cable-specific signaling protocol is illustrated in Figure 10.28.

The following signaling steps are illustrated in Figure 10.28:

1. End user H1 generates an RSVP PATH message describing quantitative traffic to be sent to a receiver outside the cable network.

2. The remote receiver responds with a RESV message, requesting a specific quantity of resources at a specific service level.

3. Assuming that policy- and resource-based admission control pass at all downstream admission control agents, the RESV message arrives at the cable head-end switch. It applies policy-based admission control and then uses cable modem-specific link-layer signaling to allocate resources between H1 and the cable head end.

Figure 10.28 Coordination Between RSVP Signaling and Cable-Specific Link-Layer Signaling

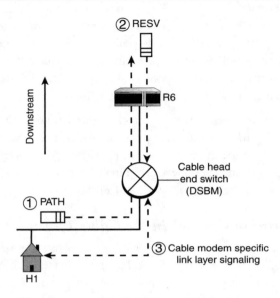

10.6.3 Nonsignaled QoS Within the Cable Network

The cable head-end switch supports nonsignaled QoS based on user_priority values marked in subscriber packets. Depending on the policies enforced, specific subscribers may be entitled to mark a certain amount of traffic for service at one or more levels of better-than-best-effort service. Alternatively, policies may install classifiers and markers to prioritize all traffic or some subset of traffic originating from specific subscribers.

10.7 Summary

This chapter demonstrated the integration of the various QoS mechanisms discussed in the previous chapters by describing the provision of various QoS services across a variety of interconnected subnetworks. These subnetworks include corporate campus networks, university networks, DiffServ-based large provider networks, cable networks, and end users connected via POTS or cable modem service.

Most of the networks offer several levels of aggregate traffic handling, based on DSCP or user_priority. In simpler networks, fewer service levels are offered. On certain, relatively low-capacity links, quantitative services are supported using conventional, RSVP/IntServ per-conversation traffic handling. On higher-capacity links, RSVP per-conversation signaling is used for admission control, but traffic is handled in aggregate. Certain qualitative services are offered in response to signaling. Others require no signaling but rely instead on marking by sending hosts or on network-based application recognition.

Each of the subnetworks contains admission control agents that are managed by policy servers. Many of these agents provide explicit admission control by participating in RSVP signaling. All provide some degree of implicit admission control simply by policing traffic based on DSCP or `user_priority` values.

A number of interesting issues arise at domain boundaries, whether between ISPs and networks of end users or between peer ISPs. These include varying degrees of support for signaling (and the resulting capability to provide more or less dynamic service agreements), the applicability of policy objects from one administrative domain in another administrative domain, the need to remap DSCPs between domains, and others. As a result of the complexity of interdomain QoS, it is often impossible to extend services across domains at the same quality as can be offered within domains. Peering agreements between ISPs allow some level of services to be provided across multiple administrative domains.

PART III

Windows QoS Mechanisms

Chapter 11   The Microsoft QoS Components

Chapter 12   The GQoS API and the QoS Service Provider

Chapter 13   The Traffic Control API and Traffic Control
Components

Chapter 14   The Microsoft Admission Control Service

11

The Microsoft QoS Components

So far, this book has discussed QoS mechanisms in general. In the following chapters, the focus shifts to the specific QoS mechanisms implemented in Windows operating systems, primarily (but not exclusively) Windows 2000. Note that this book should not be used as a specification of QoS functionality in Windows operating systems. For detailed specifications, refer to the various Windows documentation, much of which is listed in Appendix B, "References."

Two primary sets of components exist. One set resides in the host protocol stack and serves in the context of a sending or receiving host. The other set includes the Subnet Bandwidth Manager (see Chapter 7, "The Subnet Bandwidth Manager and Other Layer 2 Media," for a discussion of the SBM), the Admission Control Service (ACS), and Active Directory. These components provide policy management functionality. Both sets of components will be briefly introduced in this chapter and will be discussed in depth in the following chapters.

11.1 Components Residing in the Host Operating System

Figure 11.1 illustrates the components residing in the host operating system.

These can be subdivided into user-level components and kernel-level components, as discussed in the following paragraphs.

Figure 11.1   QoS Components in the Host Operating System

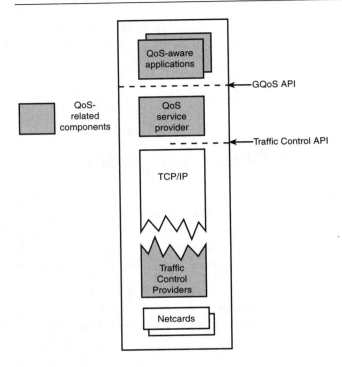

11.1.1   User-Level Components

User-level components include the following:

- QoS-enabled applications
- The GQoS application programming interface (GQoS API)
- The QoS service provider
- The traffic control API

The following sections discuss these in more detail.

11.1.1.1   QoS-Enabled Applications

Applications are illustrated at the top of the host protocol stack. These are QoS-enabled applications in the sense that they explicitly invoke QoS functionality via a set of QoS APIs. QoS mechanisms are also available to support non-QoS-enabled applications on the host operating system. However, the benefits of QoS are optimally realized when the application actively participates in network QoS.

Examples of existing QoS-enabled applications (at the time of this writing) include the following:

- **NetMeeting**—A Microsoft videoconferencing application

- **TAPI-3**—A Microsoft infrastructure that supports third-party videoconferencing and telephony applications

- **Windows Media Technology**—Microsoft's streaming media application

- **IP/TV**—Cisco's streaming media application

- **MSMQ**—Microsoft's message-queuing service

- **SAP/R3**—SAP AG's enterprise resource planning application

Note that the applications listed include both quantitative and qualitative applications. All the applications described are also persistent (as defined in previous chapters). At present the Windows APIs support explicit QoS invocation by persistent applications only. Any application that is persistent in nature and that is important from a QoS perspective is a good candidate for QoS enabling.

Extensions are currently under development to add support for nonpersistent QoS-enabled applications. These will be available in future releases and/or service packs of Windows operating systems.

11.1.1.2 The Generic QoS API

Applications that invoke QoS explicitly do so via the GQoS API. The GQoS API is supported on Windows 2000 and, to a lesser degree, also on Windows 98. The acronym *GQoS* stands for *Generic Quality of Service*. The use of the term *generic* here is significant: The generic nature of the API relieves the application of the need to understand the specific underlying QoS mechanisms that will be invoked on its behalf. This simplifies the API and reduces the marginal amount of work required to invoke QoS from an application. For example, applications need not understand the nuances of RSVP, DiffServ, or user_priority values. The interface provided by the API is *generic*.

On the other hand, the GQoS API also provides extensions to support those applications that are QoS-savvy and interested in close control of the QoS mechanisms that are invoked on their behalf.

At this time, the GQoS API is Winsock-focused. In particular, certain fields in certain Winsock 2 calls enable the application to request QoS on its own behalf. The marginal work of modifying an application that already uses Winsock 2 to invoke QoS is trivial. Winsock 2 is a natural API for those applications most likely to require QoS in the near future. Extensions are currently under development to add support for emerging applications that use APIs other than Winsock 2—in particular, Web applications and applications using the universal run time (URT) API.

Winsock

Windows operating systems offer a network API known as *Winsock*, which applications use to obtain network services from the operating system. Winsock is based on Berkeley Sockets, which is an API that was popularized in Berkeley UNIX. At the time of this writing, the version of Winsock that is most widely distributed and used is Winsock 2. For details on Winsock, see [QUINN].

The services presented to applications via the Winsock API are provided by Winsock service providers that cooperate with other parts of the operating system network stack. One such service provider is the QoS service provider.

11.1.1.3 The QoS Service Provider

When applications invoke the GQoS API, the QoS service provider responds. This is the focus of QoS intelligence in the host. The QoS service provider offers the following functionality:

- Generates RSVP signaling on behalf of the application

- Provides policy support by authenticating the user

- Invokes traffic control functionality on behalf of the application, based on local policies or network responses to signaling

- Provides the abstraction layer between the complex underlying QoS mechanisms and the generic QoS API

- Provides feedback to applications regarding the status of QoS in the network

The GQoS API is implemented as a Winsock 2 service provider. However, unlike most service providers, it acts only in the control path, not in the data path. The operation of the QoS service provider is discussed in depth in Chapter 12, "The GQoS API and the QoS Service Provider," in the section "Behavior of the QoS Service Provider." It is described briefly here.

Brief Description of the QoS Service Provider Operation

Applications use the GQoS API to indicate to the QoS service provider that they require QoS. Quantitative applications include quantitative parameters. Qualitative applications do not generally include quantitative parameters, but they do insert application and sub-application identifiers.

For quantitative, transmitting applications, the QoS service provider invokes traffic control immediately to cause transmitted traffic to be shaped to the profile requested by the application. Such shaping is considered *nongreedy traffic control*. Depending on local policies, the QoS service provider may also begin to generate RSVP signaling to the network on behalf of the application.

RSVP signaling provides the network with information that may include the user and the application associated with the signaling, as well as the service level required and the resources required at that service level. If the network approves the signaling requests generated by the QoS service provider (as indicated by the return of an RSVP RESV message to the sender), then the QoS service provider will begin to mark packets on the corresponding flow for prioritized treatment. The marks are intended to invoke the level of service approved by the network. Such marking is considered *greedy traffic control*. In this manner, the QoS service provider unifies RSVP signaling with DiffServ and 802 marking. The invocation of greedy and nongreedy traffic control by the QoS service provider is illustrated in Chapter 12, in Figure 12.8.

For certain applications, policy may dictate that the QoS service provider does not signal. In this case, local policies may allow the QoS service provider to invoke greedy traffic control without requiring network approval via RSVP signaling. Greedy traffic control may be invoked in this manner via the traffic control API (TC API), as described later in this chapter. This functionality supports nonpersistent applications. However, direct use of the TC API bypasses policy management.

For transmitting qualitative applications, traffic shaping is not invoked. Instead, the QoS service provider generates signaling for the Null Service and marks traffic on the corresponding flow based on the DCLASS and TCLASS values returned from the network.

Another QoS Service Provider—Intel's PC RSVP

Intel has produced a QoS service provider known as *PC RSVP*. This service provider is very RSVP-centric, compared to the more generic Microsoft QoS service provider. Although it was not initially written to the GQoS API, it has since been modified to be somewhat interoperable with this API. Consult Intel for details regarding the level of interoperability offered by PC RSVP.

PC RSVP offers only a subset of the functionality offered by the QoS service provider. Although developers writing for Windows 2000 and Windows 98 are advised to design to the Microsoft QoS service provider, the PC RSVP service provider may offer a reasonable solution for legacy operating systems such as Windows 95 and NT 4.

11.1.1.4 The Traffic Control API

The traffic control API (TC API) provides an interface by which user-level software can invoke traffic control functionality. Because the TC API is inextricably intertwined with the traffic control functionality itself, it will be addressed in further detail in Chapter 13, in the context of traffic control. it is described briefly here. Note that the TC API is available only on Windows 2000. It is not available in Windows 98 (however, limited traffic marking functionality is available in certain releases of Windows 98).

The traffic control API separates traffic control providers from traffic control consumers, as illustrated in Figure 11.2.

Figure 11.2   Traffic Control Consumers and Providers

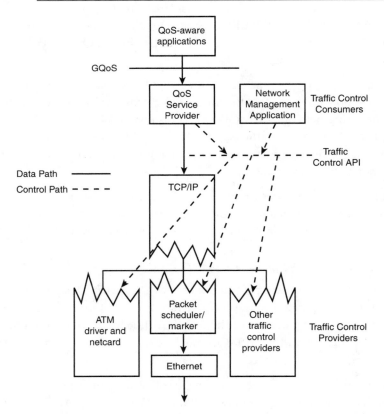

Traffic control providers are mostly kernel components that can provide traffic control functionality.

> **Note**
>
> Windows, like most operating systems, includes *user-level* components and *kernel-level* components. User-level components tend to be "closer" to applications and to the user. Kernel-level components tend to be low-level services that are embedded deep within the bowels of the operating system. Kernel-level components have privileged access to hardware and other low-level resources, and are not directly available to users. In Figure 11.2, components above the line marked Traffic Control API are user-level components. Components below this line are kernel-level components.

Traffic control functionality includes such functions as packet classification, shaping or queuing traffic (whether by cells, packets, or other quanta), marking traffic for prioritized treatment, low-level signaling (such as ATM UNI signaling), and so on. Examples of traffic control providers include ATM drivers, 802 LAN packet scheduling drivers, and so forth.

Traffic control consumers are software components that require traffic control services. The primary traffic control consumer is the QoS service provider. In addition, network-management applications may be written to directly invoke the TC API on behalf of applications that are not QoS-enabled and that therefore are incapable of invoking the services of the QoS service provider. Note that applications that invoke the TC API directly do so without the benefit of the policy-enforcement mechanisms provided via the QoS service provider. In other words, direct invocation of the TC API may sidestep the process of obtaining permission from the network before invoking greedy traffic control. For this reason, the TC API is available only to applications with administrative privileges. It must be used with caution to avoid compromising QoS that *is* granted subject to network policies.

> **Note**
>
> One might ask why network-management applications would not invoke QoS on behalf of other applications via the GQoS API and the QoS service provider. The reason is that, due to the nature of Winsock, different applications cannot easily share sockets among themselves. Thus, a network-management application could not control QoS on a socket that is being used by another application to send data.

The TC API Primitives

The following primitives are the primary primitives of the TC API:

- **Add Flow and Modify Flow**—This primitive creates or modifies a set of characteristics that are applied to a traffic flow. Such characteristics include scheduling or queuing parameters and DSCP or 802 `user_priority` marks.

- **Add Filter**—When a flow is created, a filter can be added to it. The addition of the filter determines the set of packets that are directed to the flow and are subjected to the parameters with which the flow is created (classification parameters).

The TC API includes other calls. However, these provide the majority of the API functionality. The effect of these API calls is shown in Figure 11.3.

Figure 11.3   Creating Flows and Adding Filters

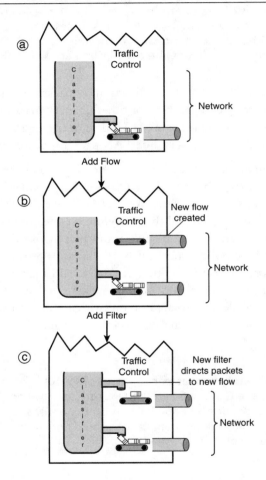

Note

Note that the module labeled *classifier* represents an instantiation of the filters that are added to a flow. (Classification functionality is implemented by a module known as the generic packet classifier.) The pipes illustrated each represent a separate traffic flow. Traffic from all pipes is combined (using certain queuing disciplines) before being placed on the network.

Despite the apparent simplicity of these primitives, the TC API is actually quite complex. Flows can be created with sophisticated shaping and queuing behaviors. For GQoS-enabled applications, the QoS service provider abstracts the complexity of the underlying traffic control functionality from the application. Those applications that invoke the TC API directly are expected to be quite sophisticated.

11.1.2   Kernel-Level Components—The Traffic Control Providers

The majority of traffic control functionality is provided by kernel-level components. In actuality, traffic control can be subdivided into one or more network kernel drivers, the generic packet classifier, and the traffic dynamic linked library (DLL), as illustrated in Figure 11.4. This Figure is similar to Figure 11.2, but shows added detail in the kernel components. Three specific traffic control providers are illustrated: ATM, Ethernet and WAN. Also note the generic packet classifier.

Figure 11.4   The Traffic DLL and Traffic Control Providers

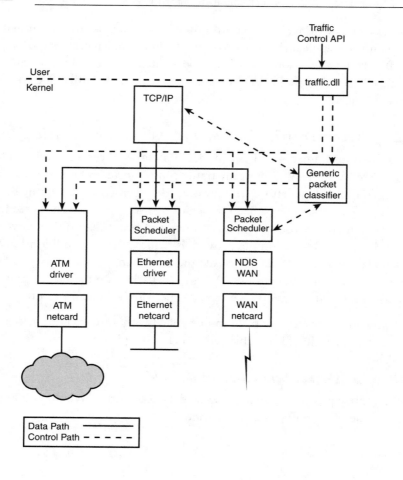

The traffic DLL resides partly in user space. It responds directly to TC API calls and translates these into the various calls understood by the underlying traffic control drivers. Together, these drivers and the traffic DLL constitute the traffic control providers.

11.1.2.1 Traffic Control Functionality

Traffic control providers provide the following functionality.

- Packet classification (implemented by the generic packet classifier).

- Traffic scheduling (shaping and queuing).

- DSCP and 802 user_priority marking.

- Link-layer signaling functionality (as appropriate).

- Specialized link-layer mechanisms such as ISSLOW. (See Chapter 8, "QoS over Layer 2 Media Other Than 802" for a discussion of ISSLOW.)

Note that, as of this writing, traffic control functionality applies to transmitted traffic only. No traffic control is applied to received traffic. In future enhancements to the operating system, traffic control functionality will also be applied to received traffic. Such functionality may be used to police traffic arriving at a receiver or to prioritize one type of received traffic over another.

11.1.2.2 Greedy Traffic Control and Nongreedy Traffic Control

Certain traffic control functionality is considered *greedy*, and certain traffic control functionality is considered *nongreedy*. Nongreedy traffic control includes functionality that does not assign a certain traffic flow network resources at the expense of other traffic flows. For example, shaping a traffic flow to 3Mbps on an Ethernet interface is not greedy. The traffic flow receives no more network resources as a result of being shaped than it would if it were not shaped. In fact, its impact on the network is reduced, leaving additional network resources available to other traffic flows. On the other hand, marking packets for a high 802 user_priority or an advantageous DSCP *is* greedy. Packets on the marked traffic flow are allocated resources in the network that would otherwise be available to other traffic flows.

In general, nongreedy traffic control can be applied without consulting network policies. Greedy traffic control should be subjected to network policies.

11.1.2.3 The Packet Scheduler and ATM

Two traffic control providers are available by default as part of Windows 2000: the *packet scheduler* and the ATM traffic control provider.

The packet scheduler is a software layer that resides in the data path between transport- and network-layer protocols from above, and media drivers from below. It identifies traffic flows generated by the protocol stack and schedules packets among these flows as they are passed down to the media driver. It is capable of implementing complex queuing algorithms, including both work-conserving and non-work-conserving mechanisms. It generally operates over LAN interfaces such as Ethernet, Token Ring, FDDI, or any interface that presents itself as a LAN interface. In certain cases, it is also capable of providing ISSLOW scheduling over WAN interfaces. In addition to scheduling, the packet scheduler helps to mark packets for DSCP and 802 `user_priority` values as appropriate.

Another traffic control provider is the IP over ATM module. ATM interfaces provide hardware-level cell scheduling. The IP over ATM layer can be used with the traffic DLL to link this cell scheduling with the requirements of the traffic control consumer. In addition to scheduling support, the IP over ATM layer uses ATM signaling to establish virtual circuits (VCs) of the appropriate service type to support the requirements of the flows created by the traffic control consumer.

11.2 Policy Enforcement Components—the SBM and the ACS

The components described thus far are components that reside on the sending or receiving hosts. Certain Microsoft QoS components do not reside on hosts, but reside instead in the network. These are used to enforce network policies. These components include the SBM and the ACS.

11.2.1 Functionality Provided by the SBM and ACS

Unlike routers and switches, Microsoft components are typically not in the data path of network traffic and, strictly speaking, are incapable of enforcing network policies with respect to data traffic. As such, they cannot be considered policy enforcement points (PEPs) in the strictest sense (see Chapter 9, "QoS Policy," for a discussion of PEPs and PDPs). Nonetheless, it is possible to insert Microsoft components in the QoS control path and to enforce network policies indirectly by impacting signaling. As a result, applications and network devices that heed the results of signaling will enforce policies with respect to generated or forwarded traffic.

Recall the policy-enforcement role of the PEP that was described in Chapter 9. A transmitting host generates resource requests directed toward a peer receiver. Unhindered, these requests typically arrive at the receiver, which then generates return messages in response. If the return messages arrive at the sender, the sender considers its request admitted and approved, subject to network policy. As a result, Windows 2000 hosts invoke greedy traffic control (as described earlier in this chapter). Any device that is capable of intercepting and modifying or rejecting the resource requests (or the responses to them) is capable of effecting policy via the process of admission control, thereby controlling the impact of the host on the network.

Traditional routers and switches are well suited to provide such policy-enforcement functionality because they are in the data (and, therefore, the signaling path) by default. For Microsoft components to participate in the process of admission control, they must be capable of inserting themselves into the signaling path even though they typically are not in the data path. The SBM provides a convenient mechanism for achieving this in 802 networks. Recall from Chapter 7, "The Subnet Bandwidth Manager and 802 Networks," that the SBM is capable of causing all RSVP signaling messages on a LAN to be directed through it by winning the election to be the DSBM for the subnet.

Because the SBM is capable of intercepting the signaling messages, it is capable of applying resource-based admission control, which is standard SBM functionality. Moreover, it can hand off the signaling messages to a process that applies admission control based on policy parameters. This is the basis for the policy functionality offered by Microsoft QoS components. Microsoft offers a basic SBM. In addition, it offers the *Admission Control Service* (ACS), which is the process that works with the SBM to apply admission control based on policy parameters. The combination of SBM and ACS is illustrated in Figure 11.5. Note that the ACS relies on policy data stored in Active Directory to make its policy-based admission control decision.

Figure 11.5 The SBM/ACS Combination

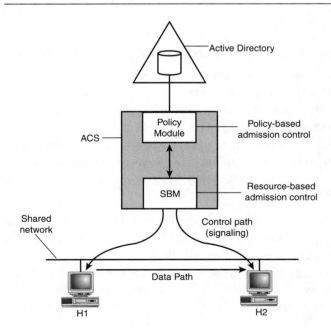

One obvious deficiency of the SBM/ACS combination is its incapability to enforce policy in topologies that are not shared (from a Layer 3 perspective). It is intended to be used in shared topologies such as LANs. The SBM mechanism can be leveraged only in these topologies. Note that limited ACS functionality is available as part of the Microsoft *RRAS* routing platform. As such, the RRAS platform can offer PEP functionality for certain non-shared network applications. This is illustrated in Figure 11.6.

Figure 11.6   ACS on a Router, Without the SBM

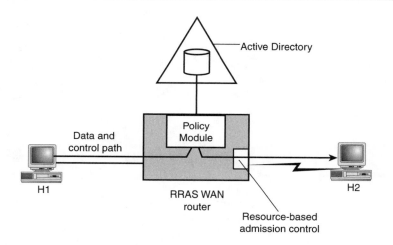

11.3   *Summary*

This chapter provides a brief overview of the Microsoft QoS-related components. These include applications, the GQoS API, the QoS service provider, the traffic control API, and traffic control components, all of which reside on sending or receiving hosts. In addition, Microsoft provides a Subnet Bandwidth Manager (SBM) and a policy enforcement point (PEP) in the form of the Admission Control Service(ACS).

Applications use the GQoS API to invoke QoS on their on behalf. The QoS service provider responds to the GQoS API, signaling the network as appropriate and invoking traffic control via the TC API. Network-management applications may call the TC API directly. Traffic control components provide primarily traffic scheduling and marking functionality, functions that are considered nongreedy and greedy, respectively.

The SBM and the ACS are capable of providing both resource- and policy-based admission control. Policy-based admission control relies on Active Directory as the policy data store.

12

The GQoS API and the QoS Service Provider

The Generic QoS (GQoS) API is used by QoS-aware applications to invoke the services of the QoS service provider. The QoS service provider generates RSVP signaling on behalf of the application, invokes traffic control in accordance with policy, and provides status to the application on the state of network QoS.

This chapter delves into the details of the GQoS API and its interaction with the QoS service provider. This is not an API specification. For a detailed API specification, see [GQOS_SPEC].

12.1 Overview of the GQoS API

The GQoS API was designed to abstract the services provided by the QoS service provider so that applications are capable of invoking QoS without a detailed understanding of QoS mechanisms. At the same time, the API makes it possible for applications that are more QoS-savvy to exert close control over complex aspects of QoS. The following sections provide a brief overview of the API. The subsequent section explains the API usage and the QoS service provider's behavior in further depth.

12.1.1 Winsock Orientation

In the interest of simplifying the invocation of QoS, the GQoS API is built on the Winsock 2 API. Winsock 2 is similar to UNIX Sockets (BSD) and for many years has been the primary API by which Windows applications invoke network services.

12.1.1.1 Service Providers

Winsock2 defines the notion of *service providers*, which can be layered on top of each other to provide stacked network functionality. Applications invoke network services by requesting a service provider. Most applications request the services of a *base service provider*, to provide simple TCP/UDP/IP connectivity. QoS applications request the services of the *QoS service provider*. As a result, the QoS service provider is layered over a *base* service provider, as illustrated in Figure 12.1.

Figure 12.1   The QoS Service Provider

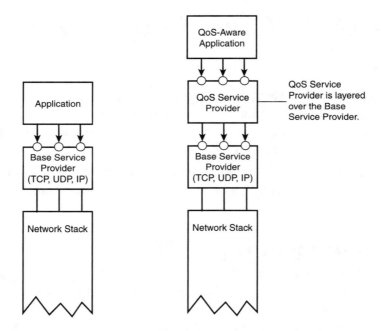

12.1.1.2 Sockets

Applications use the Winsock 2 interface to open a *socket* for each connection (represented by the circles in Figure 12.1). In its most abstract form, a connection is represented by a source and a destination address, and by a source and a destination *service access point* (SAP), which demultiplexes traffic among potentially multiple flows between the same source and destination addresses. Although Winsock 2 is supposed to be protocol-independent, it has come to be used primarily for the TCP/IP protocol. In this book, it will be considered in that context. In the context of TCP/IP, a socket is represented by the IP 5-tuple, which includes a source and a destination IP address, a source and a destination IP port (the SAP), and the protocol identifier (TCP vs. UDP). A degree of complexity is added by the fact that the destination address may be a multicast address. In this case, a single socket may connect multiple senders with multiple receivers.

Winsock 2 allows applications to control the creation of sockets to various destinations and then to transmit or receive traffic over these sockets. As such, there is both a *control plane* and a *data plane*. QoS functionality is invoked in the control plane. The QoS service provider is not active in the data plane. This is an important consideration from a performance perspective. It is illustrated Figure 12.2.

Figure 12.2   The QoS Service Provider Is Active only in the Control Plane

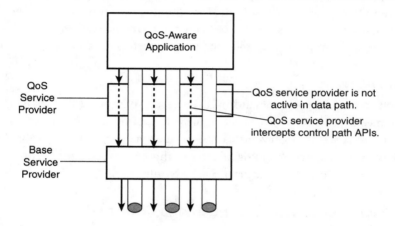

As illustrated, data passes directly through the QoS service provider with no performance impact. The QoS service provider intercepts only control traffic.

12.1.1.3   QoS Calls and Parameters

The control plane Winsock 2 APIs that are most interesting from a QoS perspective include the following:

- **WSASocket**—Creates a socket over a specified service provider (or stack of layered service providers).

- **WSAConnect**—Connects the created socket to a peer socket (may be used both for connection-oriented protocols as well as nonconnection-oriented protocols).

- **WSAAccept**—Accepts a connection request from a peer socket (for connection-oriented protocols).

- **WSAJoinLeaf**—Joins a sender or a receiver to a multicast session.

- **WSAIoctl**—Used to issue many socket control commands. In the context of QoS, this call is used to asynchronously modify QoS parameters on a socket.

- **WSAGetQoSByName**—May be used in certain cases to retrieve a template for quantitative parameters to be used when invoking QoS.

The use of these APIs will be discussed in depth later in this chapter in the section "Usage of the GQoS API."

The first version of Winsock had no notion of QoS. In the early 1990s, Winsock 2 was created. Winsock 2 included a new parameter for the WSAConnect, WSAAccept, and WSAJoinLeaf calls. This parameter is the QualityOfService data structure, which can be used to specify the required QoS behavior on a socket. In addition, a new control command was defined for use with WSAIoctl. This is the SET_QOS command. It, too, carries the QualityOfService data structure and can be used to modify QoS parameters on a socket at any time.

Notification Events

In addition to the control commands just described, Winsock 2 defines *notification events*. These are mechanisms by which a service provider can notify applications of changes in network status. A set of QoS events can be notified via use of the FD_QOS event notification. These events will be described in detail later in this chapter (see the sections "QoS Status and Event Notification" and "Registering for Notifications").

12.1.2   Relation to RSVP and Traffic Control

Although the GQoS API is designed to be independent of specific underlying QoS mechanisms, it embodies those aspects of RSVP that are considered generically useful. As such, it is designed to trigger the generation of signaling messages to the network whenever these can be used to enhance the capability of the network to offer QoS.

As discussed in previous chapters, RSVP signaling can be used to the benefit of any persistent application, whether it is qualitative or quantitative by nature. Signaling beyond the host is not practical for nonpersistent applications. In the initial releases of the GQoS API, on Windows 98 and on Windows 2000, the choice of whether to trigger signaling is left to the application. In future enhancements to the API, the choice of whether to signal beyond the local host will be based on policy information distributed from policy servers.

The RSVP orientation is evident in various aspects of the GQoS API, especially in those parameters that are used by QoS-savvy applications to invoke more complex functionality from the QoS service provider.

12.1.2.1 *Triggering* PATH *and* RESV *Messages*

When RSVP signaling is appropriate, the QoS service provider generates PATH and RESV messages automatically, based on certain triggers from the GQoS API and from the network. The trigger from the API is generally both an indication by the application that it is interested in QoS and the availability of sufficient information to generate the signaling messages. In most cases, there is a correspondence between a socket on which RSVP signaling is invoked and an RSVP *session* (see Chapter 5, "RSVP," for a definition of an RSVP session).

The interaction between the GQoS API and the generation of RSVP signaling messages will be described in further detail later in this chapter.

12.1.2.2 *Traffic Control Invocation*

Regardless of whether RSVP is invoked, certain traffic control functionality may be invoked in response to the GQoS API. This functionality may include traffic scheduling, packet marking, and link-layer signaling. The QoS service provider invokes traffic control on behalf of the application by creating a flow with the desired scheduling and marking characteristics and then by adding a filter to that flow. The filter specifies the IP 5-tuple corresponding to the sending IP port and address and the receiving IP port and address (the RSVP session) associated with the socket created by the application. Note that in Windows 2000, traffic control is invoked with respect to transmitted traffic only. There is no traffic control for received traffic. In Windows 98, only limited traffic control is invoked.

Quantitative applications provide quantitative parameters that are translated by the QoS service provider into scheduling parameters for the flow. Marking parameters for the flow are based on the service type requested by the application and the response from the network. These may be applied both to qualitative and to quantitative flows.

When traffic control is invoked by the QoS service provider on behalf of an application, the filter is a unique 5-tuple corresponding to a single socket. This effectively provides per-conversation traffic handling. The QoS service provider is not intended to invoke aggregate traffic handling on a host. If it is necessary to do so, the traffic control API can be invoked directly. In this manner, it is possible to specify masked filters corresponding to multiple conversations (aggregate traffic handling).

12.2 *Usage of the GQoS API*

This section discusses the various API calls and data structures and their usage. The next section "Behaviour of the QoS Service Provider" describes the resulting behavior of the QoS service provider.

12.2.1 *Creating a QoS Socket*

The first step for an application using the GQoS API is to create a QoS socket. This process is described in the following sections.

12.2.1.1 WSAEnumProtocols

The first step in creating any Winsock 2 socket, whether QoS-enabled or not, is to select the appropriate service providers. In response to the WSAEnumProtocols call (illustrated in *Listing 12.1*), Windows returns a list of WSAPROTOCOL_INFO structures, which describe the characteristics of the available service providers. On Windows 98 and Windows 2000, the returned list of service providers will include QoS-enabled service providers. The XP1_QOS_SUPPORTED flag (in the dwServiceFlags1 parameter of the WSAPROTOCOL_INFO structure, also illustrated in Listing 12.1) can be used to identify these service providers. The WSAPROTOCOL_INFO structure also specifies the protocol provided by the service provider. The QoS service providers are of the Internet address family (iAddressFamily = AF_INET) and are available for either UDP (iProtocol = IPROTO_UDP) or TCP (iProtocol = IPROTO_TCP). When the application has located the service provider meeting its needs, it can proceed to create a socket using that service provider.

Listing 12.1   Prototype of the WSAEnumProtocols Function and the WSAPROTOCOL_INFO Structure

---

```
int WSAEnumProtocols(
    LPINT lpiProtocols,
    LPWSAPROTOCOL_INFO lpProtocolBuffer,
    ILPDWORD lpdwBufferLength
);
```

lpProtocolBuffer points to a list of WSAPROTOCOL_INFO structures. One such structure is illustrated below.

```
typedef struct _WSAPROTOCOL_INFO {
    DWORD                dwServiceFlags1;
    DWORD                dwServiceFlags2;
    DWORD                dwServiceFlags3;
    DWORD                dwServiceFlags4;
    DWORD                dwProviderFlags;
    GUID                 ProviderId;
    DWORD                dwCatalogEntryId;
    WSAPROTOCOLCHAIN     ProtocolChain;
    int                  iVersion;
    int                  iAddressFamily;
    int                  iMaxSockAddr;
    int                  iMinSockAddr;
```

```
    int             iSocketType;
    int             iProtocol;
    int             iProtocolMaxOffset;
    int             iNetworkByteOrder;
    int             iSecurityScheme;
    DWORD           dwMessageSize;
    DWORD           dwProviderReserved;
    TCHAR           szProtocol[WSAPROTOCOL_LEN+1];
} WSAPROTOCOL_INFO, *LPWSAPROTOCOL_INFO;
```

12.2.1.2 WSASocket

Next a QoS socket is created by calling the WSASocket API with a pointer to the WSAPROTOCOL_ INFO structure corresponding to the QoS service provider. Note that the Windows QoS service provider may be invoked in *overlapped* mode. This mode enables asynchronous calls on the socket (so that the application does not have to wait for each socket call to complete before proceeding to the next call). To do so, it is necessary to set the WSA_FLAG_OVERLAPPED flag (in the dwFlags parameter) with the call to WSASocket (see Listing 12.2).

Listing 12.2	Prototype of the WSASocket Function

```
SOCKET WSASocket(
    int af,
    int type,
    int protocol,
    LPWSAPROTOCOL_INFO lpProtocolInfo,
    GROUP g,
    DWORD dwFlags
);
```

12.2.2 Using the QoS Socket

If successful, the call to WSASocket will return a handle to a QoS socket. This socket can now be used to establish a QoS session. Depending on the type of session—unicast vs. multicast, connection-oriented (TCP) vs. connectionless (UDP)—different calls are used to establish the session and to specify the appropriate QoS parameters. The following paragraphs describe the usage of the various calls in establishing different session types. The QoS parameters specified in the calls will be described later in this section under the heading "The QoS Parameters."

12.2.2.1 WSAIoctl(SIO_SET_QOS)

There are two methods for specifying the QoS parameters to be associated with a socket. One of these includes QoS parameters with the calls that are used to control session establishment (WSAConnect, WSAAccept, WSAJoinLeaf). This method achieves the dual purpose of establishing a session and specifying QoS parameters in a single call. The other method issues an *IO control call* (Ioctl) on a socket, which does nothing more than specify the QoS parameters to be applied to the socket. IO control calls are issued on sockets via the WSAIoctl call. The specific IO control call that is used to supply QoS parameters on a socket is denoted by WSAIoctl(SIO_SET_QOS). To invoke it, the dwIoControlCode parameter should be set to SIO_SET_QOS. In addition, the lpvInBuffer parameter should point to the QualityOfService structure illustrated in Listing 12.3.

The WSAIoctl(SIO_SET_QOS) call and one of the session establishment calls may both be used to request QoS on the same socket. In this case, the most recently supplied QoS parameters (whether supplied via WSAIoctl(SIO_SET_QOS) or one of the session establishment calls) are associated with the socket.

Listing 12.3	Prototype of the WSAIoctl Function

```
int WSAIoctl(
    SOCKET s,
    DWORD dwIoControlCode,
    LPVOID lpvInBuffer,
    DWORD cbInBuffer,
    LPVOID lpvOutBuffer,
    DWORD cbOutBuffer,
    LPDWORD lpcbBytesReturned,
    LPWSAOVERLAPPED lpOverlapped,
    LPWSAOVERLAPPED_COMPLETION_ROUTINE lpCompletionRoutine
);
```

12.2.2.2 WSAAccept

In unicast TCP sessions, there are two communicating peers. One of these is the *active* peer, and the other is the *passive* peer. Typically (though not necessarily) the passive peer is the sender and the active peer is the receiver. The active peer calls WSAConnect to initiate a connection to the passive peer. The passive peer listens for an indication from the service provider that a remote peer is initiating a connection. The passive peer accepts the connection by calling WSAAccept.

In its call to WSAAccept, the passive peer defines a callback function (lpfnCondition). The QoS service provider will call this function to obtain the QoS parameters for the accepted connection (see Listing 12.4). In the typical case, in which the passive peer is the sender, the callback function should provide sending QoS parameters. If the passive peer is the receiver, the callback function should provide receiving QoS parameters. The prototype for the callback function is defined in the Winsock 2 specifications (and in the GQoS specifications).

> **Note**
> Note that the CONDITIONPROC type and the CALLBACK type (in Listing 12.4) refer to the same function prototype.

Listing 12.4   Prototype of the WSAAccept Function and the Callback Function

```
SOCKET WSAAccept(
    SOCKET s,
    struct sockaddr FAR *addr,
    LPINT addrlen,
    LPCONDITIONPROC lpfnCondition,
    DWORD dwCallbackData
);
```

lpfnCondition points to a function of type CALLBACK, listed below.

```
int CALLBACK ConditionFunc(
    IN LPWSABUF lpCallerId,
    IN LPWSABUF lpCallerData,
    IN OUT LPQOS lpSQOS,
    IN OUT LPQOS lpGQOS,
    IN LPWSABUF lpCalleeId,
    OUT LPWSABUF lpCalleeData,
    OUT GROUP FAR *g,
    IN DWORD dwCallbackData
);
```

12.2.2.3 WSAConnect

The WSAConnect call may be used to invoke QoS functionality for either TCP sessions or UDP sessions. In the case of TCP sessions, it is invoked by the active peer to establish a connection. At that time, it may be used to provide the QoS parameters for the session. QoS parameters are provided via the lpSQOS parameter that points to an LPQOS structure. (See Listing 12.7 for the prototype of the LPQOS structure).

> **Note**
>
> Note that there is an `lpGQOS` parameter in addition to the `lpSQOS` parameter in the `WSAConnect` call. The `lpGQOS` parameter remains from the early days of Winsock 2. It was initially intended to specify QoS for a socket group. (It is not supported.)

The active peer is typically the receiver and therefore typically includes *receiving* QoS parameters. If the active peer is the sender, the `WSAConnect` call should include *sending* QoS parameters.

`WSAConnect` (see Listing 12.5) is commonly used to establish TCP sessions, which are connection-oriented by nature. It is not typically used to establish UDP sessions, which are connectionless. However, in certain cases, the `WSAConnect` call is a convenient method for establishing a UDP session and invoking QoS parameters simultaneously. The `WSAConnect` call can be issued on a UDP sending or receiving socket to specify the address of the remote peer and the QoS parameters to be used on the socket. This method is appropriate when the UDP socket is used to communicate with a single peer. If the UDP socket is expected to receive from more than one peer or is to be used to send to more than one peer, then `WSAConnect` must not be called on the socket. `WSAConnect` will constrain the socket to the single peer specified in the `WSAConnect` call. If a single UDP socket is to be used to communicate with multiple peers, it is necessary to provide QoS parameters using the `WSAIoctl(SIO_SET_QOS)` call rather than the `WSAConnect` call.

Listing 12.5	Prototype of the `WSAConnect` Function

```
int WSAConnect(
    SOCKET s,
    const struct sockaddr FAR *name,
    int namelen,
    LPWSABUF lpCallerData,
    LPWSABUF lpCalleeData,
    LPQOS lpSQOS,
    LPQOS lpGQOS
);
```

12.2.2.4 WSAJoinLeaf

`WSAJoinLeaf` (see Listing 12.6) is called by sending applications to configure a socket for sending to a multicast session or by receiving applications to configure a socket for receiving from a multicast session. A single application may join a multicast session both as a sender and as a receiver. Applications may include QoS parameters with their call to `WSAJoinLeaf` (in the `lpSQOS` parameter) to invoke QoS for the multicast session. `WSAJoinLeaf` is used with UDP sockets only.

| Listing 12.6 | Prototype of the WSAJoinLeaf Function |

```
SOCKET WSAJoinLeaf(
    SOCKET s,
    const struct sockaddr FAR *name,
    int namelen,
    LPWSABUF lpCallerData,
    LPWSABUF lpCalleeData,
    LPQOS lpSQOS,
    LPQOS lpGQOS,
    DWORD dwFlags
);
```

12.2.3   QoS Status and Event Notification

The QoS service provider can be used to asynchronously notify the application of certain QoS-related events on the network. The type of events that are asynchronously notified by the QoS service provider are signaling-related events. In addition, QoS applications may call the service provider to retrieve the currently configured QoS parameters. The status and event mechanisms are described in the following paragraphs.

12.2.3.1   WSAAsyncSelect *and* WSAEventSelect

These are standard Winsock 2 event notification mechanisms. They can be used to request notifications of QoS events by the QoS service provider. The application indicates its interest in QoS events specifically, by setting the FD_QOS flag in its call to WSAEventSelect or WSAAsyncSelect.

12.2.3.2   WSAIoctl(SIO_GET_QOS)

Upon notification of a QoS event, the application uses the WSAIoctl call (specifying SIO_GET_QOS as the Ioctl type) to retrieve the QoS status notification. As an alternative to WSAEventSelect or WSAAsyncSelect, the application may issue an overlapped call to WSAIoctl(SIO_GET_QOS).

12.2.3.3   WSAGetQoSByName *and Related Calls*

This call can be used by an application to determine the appropriate parameters to use when invoking quantitative QoS. A number of *templates* are stored in the operating system. Each template is associated with a name (such as the name of the type of CODEC for which it is appropriate). The application may retrieve the template with the appropriate QoS parameters by specifying the corresponding template name in its call to

WSAGetQoSByName. The application may then use the retrieved parameters to request QoS from the QoS service provider. If no template name is specified in the call to WSAGetQoSByName, a list of available template names will be returned.

> **Note**
>
> Caution must be used when relying on WSAGetQoSByName. Many CODECs generate variable bit rate data. Thus, the QoS parameters appropriate for the actual data transmitted may deviate from parameters provided in corresponding templates. Templates should generally not be used for variable-rate CODECs.

Related API calls are available to manage the list of stored templates. These include WSCInstallQoSTemplate and WSCRemoveQoSTemplate.

12.2.4 The QoS Parameters

Most of the QoS-related calls convey QoS parameters between the application and the QoS service provider. In most cases, these parameters are expressed using the same QoS data structure, as illustrated in Listing 12.7.

Listing 12.7   The QualityOfService Structure

```
typedef struct _QualityOfService {
    FLOWSPEC  SendingFlowspec;    //flowspec for data sending
    FLOWSPEC  ReceivingFlowspec;  //flowspec for data receiving
    WSABUF    ProviderSpecific;   //provider-specific parameters
} QOS, FAR * LPQOS;
```

This structure includes a pair of flow specifications (flowspec). (The flowspec structure is illustrated in Listing 12.8). One flowspec is used for sent traffic, and the other is used for received traffic. In addition, the structure includes a ProviderSpecific buffer. In simple cases, all necessary information is contained in the flowspecs. In more complicated uses of the API, additional parameters and directives may be included in the ProviderSpecific buffer.

12.2.4.1 The Flowspecs

The QoS structure includes a SendingFlowspec structure and a ReceivingFlowspec structure. These structures are identical. Depending on the particular use of the structure, one or both may actually contain useful information. The other may be unspecified.

The information that may be specified in the `flowspec` structure includes a number of quantitative parameters that correlate to the token bucket specification and the latency requirements or characteristics of the corresponding flow. In addition, the `flowspec` structure contains a `ServiceType` parameter, which is used to specify the service type required for the flow (and may be used to specify additional qualifying parameters). The set of possible service types includes the IntServ Guaranteed and Controlled Load Services, as well as the Null (also known as the Qualitative) Service.

The `flowspec` structures are illustrated in Listing 12.8.

Listing 12.8	The Flowspec Structure

```
typedef struct _flowspec {
    uint32          TokenRate;          // in bytes/second
    uint32          TokenBucketSize;    // in bytes
    uint32          PeakBandwidth;      // in bytes/second
    uint32          Latency;            // in microseconds
    uint32          DelayVariation;     // in microseconds
    SERVICETYPE     ServiceType;        // guaranteed, predictive, etc.
    uint32          MaxSduSize;         // in bytes
    uint32          MinimumPolicedSize  // in bytes
} FLOWSPEC, *PFLOWSPEC,  FAR * LPFLOWSPEC;
```

The elements of the `flowspecs` are described in the following paragraphs.

Token Bucket Parameters

The first three parameters should be familiar from the token bucket model described in Chapter 3, "Queuing Mechanisms." These include the `TokenRate`, `TokenBucketSize`, and `PeakBandwidth` parameters.

The `TokenRate` parameter corresponds to the average rate of a QoS traffic flow. The `TokenBucketSize` parameter corresponds to the burst size (or bucket size) on the traffic flow. The `PeakBandwidth` parameter corresponds to the peak rate of the traffic flow. In constant-rate applications, `TokenRate` and `PeakBandwidth` will be equal. Quantitative applications are expected to specify at least the `TokenRate` parameter and may specify the `TokenBucketSize` and `PeakBandwidth` parameters in addition. If they do not, the QoS service provider will attempt to derive default values for these.

When these parameters are specified in the sending `flowspec`, the QoS service provider will include these parameters in related signaling messages (RSVP `PATH` messages) and will invoke traffic control to schedule traffic in accordance with the parameters. When these parameters are specified in a receiving `flowspec`, no local traffic control will be invoked, but the parameters will be included in related signaling messages (RSVP `RESV` messages).

In the interest of simplifying the task of the application, the GQoS API is designed to allow defaulting of most of the quantitative parameters by specifying `QOS_NOT_SPECIFIED`. The QoS service provider will derive values for unspecified parameters.

Senders selecting a quantitative service type are required to specify only the `TokenRate` parameter (in addition to the service type). Senders selecting the qualitative service are expected to specify `QOS_NOT_SPECIFIED` for all quantitative parameters.

On receivers, quantitative parameters specified by the receiving application are copied to the `RESV` messages generated for the session. The receiving application is not required to specify any quantitative parameters. If it does not, the QoS service provider will simply assume that the receiver is satisfied with the quantitative parameters offered in the `PATH` messages for the corresponding session and will echo these values in the `RESV` messages.

Other Quantitative Parameters

Additional quantitative parameters include `Latency`, `DelayVariation`, `MaxSDUSize`, and `MinimumPolicedSize`. The `Latency` and `DelayVariation` parameters may be used to specify the latency and latency variation that can be tolerated by packets on the flow. These are relevant for Guaranteed Service flows only. The `MaxSDUSize` corresponds to the equivalent IntServ parameter and specifies the maximum packet size that can be expected to enjoy prioritized treatment. `MinimumPolicedSize` corresponds to the equivalent IntServ parameter. See the accompanying sidebar "Minimum Policed Size" for guidelines on setting this parameter.

It is not necessary to specify any of these parameters; the QoS service provider can derive all of these. Applications should specify these only if they want to exert fine-grain control.

Minimum Policed Size

This parameter (denoted here by *m*) warrants further discussion. It is used by the QoS service provider and is signaled to the network for use by network elements participating in RSVP signaling. These network elements and the QoS service provider use *m* to compute overhead introduced by packet headers. Applications declare a flow rate to the QoS service provider and to the network. This flow rate describes the application-generated *data* traffic.

However, the sending host's IP stack appends transport- and network-layer (TCP/IP or UDP/IP) headers to each packet generated by the application. Low-layer network software at the sending host and at intermediate nodes adds additional link-layer headers. These headers add overhead that increases the effective flow rate that must be committed in the network. If this overhead is not considered by the network at the time that a resource request is admitted, then the network will not commit sufficient resources to accommodate the flow. Therefore, it is desirable for the network to consider the amount of overhead required at the time that a reservation is made.

However, the overhead depends on the distribution of packet sizes that will be submitted. If the application submits a preponderance of small buffers (as would be the case with an interactive voice application), then header-related overhead is quite significant. On the other hand, if the application submits a preponderance of large packets, then header-related overhead is not significant. The parameter *m* enables the application to offer hints to the network regarding the impact of header-related overhead.

Given that the network uses *m* to estimate overhead, if the application selects too low a value for *m*, the network will expect higher overhead and will be more likely to reject the resource request (or charge more for it). On the other hand, if the application selects too high a value for *m*, the network will expect lower overhead and will configure its policers accordingly. This may result in traffic being policed excessively, to the detriment of the application.

RFC 2210, on the use of IntServ with RSVP, recommends that *m* be set to the minimum packet size generated by the application and explains that all packets smaller than *m* will be policed as if they were of size *m*. It also stipulates that an application transmitting only a low percentage of small packets might choose to set the value of *m* to a value larger than the minimum packet size. This would more accurately reflect the overhead that should be expected.

The QoS service provider uses the value of *m* to adjust the token bucket parameters signaled to the network by the QoS service provider, so that it accounts for transport- and network-layer (but not link-layer) overhead. The following formula applies:

$$P_{sig} = P_{gqos} \times (1 + Oh/m)$$

Here, the following applies:

- P_{sig} refers to the actual token bucket parameter signaled to the network.

- P_{gqos} refers to the token bucket parameter requested by the application via GQoS.

- Oh is the amount of per-packet header overhead (28 for UDP sockets, 40 for TCP sockets).

- m is the `MinimumPolicedSize` parameter provided by the application via GQoS.

As a result, the token bucket parameters signaled to the network are not the same as those requested by the application. This adjustment is applied to the `TokenRate`, `PeakBandwidth`, and `TokenBucketSize` parameters.

The ServiceType *Parameter*

In addition to the quantitative parameters, the flowspec structure includes a ServiceType field. This field has a number of uses. Its primary use, not surprisingly, is to allow the application to select a type of service from the network and from local traffic control. The service types that can be selected are listed here:

- **Guaranteed (SERVICETYPE_GUARANTEED)**—Recommended for interactive voice and other latency-sensitive applications. The Guaranteed Service enables the application to request a delay bound. In response to a request for Guaranteed Service, the QoS service provider signals an RSVP/IntServ request for Guaranteed Service. It also invokes traffic control in a manner that shapes the transmitted traffic flow strictly to the quantitative parameters specified by the application.

- **Controlled Load (SERVICETYPE_CONTROLLEDLOAD)**—Recommended for streaming-media, noninteractive applications. The Controlled Load Service produces the effect of a lightly loaded network. In response to requests for Controlled Load Service, the QoS service provider signals an RSVP/IntServ request for Controlled Load Service. It invokes traffic control in a manner that tolerates bursts in excess of the profile specified by the application, but it marks excess traffic so that it may be reduced in priority in case of congestion.

- **Qualitative (SERVICETYPE_QUALITATIVE)**—Recommended for applications that are incapable of quantifying their traffic profiles using the token bucket model. These applications specify only the qualitative service type and the MaxSDUSize. They are also expected to identify themselves to the network by providing an application identifier in the provider-specific buffer (see the discussion later in this section).

- **Best-effort (SERVICETYPE_BESTEFFORT)**—Applications specifying this service type can expect best-effort service.

For further guidelines, see the discussion of the suitability of different service types to different applications in Chapter 4, "Integrated Services," in the sections "Suitability of Controlled Load Service to Applications" and "Suitability of Guaranteed Service to Applications."

Specification of the ServiceType field by the application has different meanings on senders and receivers. Sending applications use the ServiceType field to specify one or more services that may be appropriate for the corresponding flow. The sending application may use the *bit-mask* portion of the ServiceType field to identify one service or a specific set of services that are appropriate. Alternatively, it may use the *value* portion of the field to identify a single service or to specify GENERAL_INFORMATION (indicating that any service type is appropriate). Generally, it is recommended that sending applications specify a single service type based on the guidelines in the previous list.

Whereas senders may offer a range of potential service types, receivers must specify a single service type in which they are interested.

In addition to the four service types listed, the following may be specified in the value portion of the `ServiceType` field:

- **NO_TRAFFIC**—Applications that are interested in QoS only for transmitted traffic or only for received traffic should indicate this value in `ReceivingFlowspec` or `SendingFlowspec` (respectively). This suppresses the invocation of QoS in the corresponding direction.

- **NO_CHANGE**—Applications may want to modify QoS parameters in one direction but not in the other direction, or to modify QoS parameters specified in the provider specific buffer, but not in either of the `flowspecs`. By specifying this value in the `ServiceType` field of `SendingFlowspec` or `ReceivingFlowspec`, the application can cause the QoS service provider to ignore the parameters in the corresponding `flowspec`, thereby leaving them unchanged.

Applications may also use the following control flags in the bit-mask portion of the `ServiceType` field:

- **SERVICE_NO_TRAFFIC_CONTROL**—This flag suppresses the invocation of traffic control by the QoS service provider. It is for use by applications that want to do their own traffic scheduling.

- **SERVICE_NO_QOS_SIGNALING**—This flag suppresses the generation of signaling messages for the corresponding traffic flow by the QoS service provider. It can be used by nonpersistent applications for which signaling cannot be justified. In future releases, the decision whether to signal for a particular application's traffic flow will be determined by downloadable policy. Note that packets will not be marked for prioritized treatment on flows on which signaling has been suppressed.

12.2.4.2 The Provider-Specific Buffer

In many cases, applications will be capable of obtaining adequate QoS by minimal use of the `flowspec` structures, leaving the QoS service provider to control the detailed aspects of QoS functionality. In certain cases, the application may want to exert closer control over the operation of the QoS service provider. In these cases, it may use the provider-specific buffer to exert additional control. The provider-specific buffer itself is unstructured. The GQoS API defines a number of structures that can be supplied in the provider-specific buffer. The application must compose these structures and may concatenate multiple objects in the provider-specific buffer with its call to any of the QoS-related APIs. Structures defined for the provider-specific buffer enable the application to invoke the following functionality:

- **Application and subapplication policy identity element specification**—Applications may provide an object describing the application and the subapplication corresponding to a traffic flow. The QoS service provider includes these as application identifiers in the policy information signaled in RSVP messages. This functionality is especially important for applications invoking the qualitative service type, but it can be used by any application, qualitative or quantitative.

- **Override of default signaling behavior**—The QoS service provider generates RSVP signaling based on numerous assumptions regarding the intent of the requesting application. QoS-savvy applications can override the default behavior, forcing specific signaling behavior by specifying the appropriate objects in the provider-specific buffer. One example of this is the capability to override the default RSVP reservation styles assumed by the QoS service provider.

- **Override of default traffic control invocation**—The QoS service provider also invokes traffic control based on a number of assumptions. QoS-savvy applications may provide objects in the provider-specific buffer to alter the manner in which traffic control is invoked by the QoS service provider.

- **Retrieval of QoS events**—In addition to using the provider-specific buffer to supply information from the application to the QoS service provider, the provider-specific buffer may be used to retrieve information from the QoS service provider regarding the state of QoS in the network.

12.3   Behavior of the QoS Service Provider

The previous section focused on the GQoS API and its usage. This section describes the operation of the QoS service provider in response to the API.

12.3.1   RSVP Signaling Behavior

Whenever an application provides a non-null `QualityOfService` structure with a call to the GQoS API, the QoS service provider assumes that this is a request for QoS and for the associated signaling. (There are exceptions—if the application specifies `SERVICE_NO_QOS_SIGNALING`, `SERVICE_BESTEFFORT`, or `SERVICETYPE_NOTRAFFIC`, the QoS service provider understands this to mean that the application is suppressing QoS functionality to one degree or another.)

Assuming that signaling is not suppressed, the QoS service provider will begin to generate RSVP signaling messages as soon as it has sufficient information to do so. PATH messages are generated when an application invokes QoS for transmitted traffic. RESV messages are generated when an application invokes QoS for received traffic. This is illustrated in Figure 12.3 and Figure 12.4.

Figure 12.3 Generation of PATH and RESV Messages When One Application Instance Invokes QoS for Transmitted Traffic Only and the Other Invokes QoS for Received Traffic Only

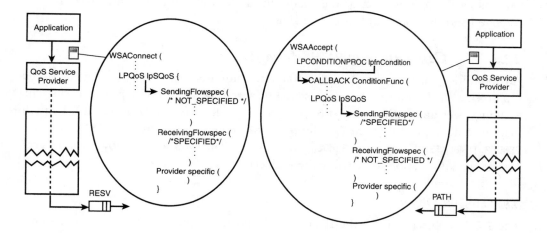

Figure 12.4 Generation of PATH and RESV Messages When Both Application Instances Invoke QoS For Both Transmitted and Received Traffic

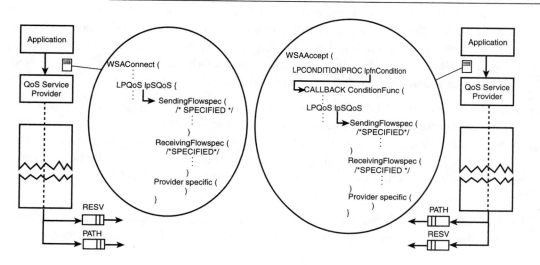

Figure 12.3 and Figure 12.4 illustrate the generation of PATH and RESV messages in response to application calls to WSAConnect and WSAAccept. Figure 12.3 illustrates a client/server application in which the client application instance specifies QoS for received traffic only and the server application instance specifies QoS for transmitted traffic only. In Figure 12.4, both application instances specify QoS for both received and transmitted traffic. The RSVP messages generated by each QoS service provider reflect the invocation of QoS by each application instance.

The following sections describe the conditions under which signaling messages are triggered and the content of those signaling messages.

12.3.1.1   Generation of PATH Messages

An application may request QoS for traffic transmitted on a socket by calling any of the QoS-related APIs and specifying a SendingFlowspec. The QoS service provider will generate PATH messages on behalf of the corresponding traffic flow as soon as it has sufficient information to do so. Recall (from Chapter 5) that PATH messages include a SESSION object, a SENDER_TEMPLATE object, and a SENDER_TSPEC object. The QoS service provider must accumulate the information to generate these objects.

The SESSION Object

The SESSION object includes the IP address, IP port, and protocol ID of the peer to which the application is sending. Winsock 2 applications typically provide this information when calling one of the connection-oriented APIs, WSAConnect, WSAAccept, or WSAJoinLeaf. The information is then stored in association with the corresponding socket. When using connection-oriented TCP sockets, the application typically calls either WSAConnect or WSAAccept. In this case, the QoS service provider can retrieve the peer address information associated with the socket and can use it in the generation of SESSION objects for PATH messages. In the case of UDP multicast sessions, the information for the SESSION object can be derived directly from the multicast session specified with the call to WSAJoinLeaf.

However, in the case of UDP unicast sessions, the application typically does not call WSAConnect (or any other connection-oriented Winsock 2 API). As a result, the QoS service provider may not have access to the peer address information required to generate a session object. There are two ways in which a sending application can provide the necessary information to enable the QoS service provider to generate the SESSION object for UDP unicast sessions:

- The first is to call WSAConnect on the corresponding socket. This provides the QoS service provider with the address information of a single peer (specified in the WSAConnect call).

- In certain cases, a sending application may want to use a UDP socket to send to *multiple* peers. In this case, the application is not likely to call WSAConnect on the socket. Instead, it is likely to call WSASendTo for each transmitted buffer, explicitly specifying the address of the receiving peer with the API call. The QoS service provider does not intercept calls to WSASendTo and, therefore, will not provide QoS for the corresponding sessions. In this case, the sending application can invoke QoS for receiving peers by calling WSAIoctl(SIO_SET_QOS) and including the QOS_DEST_ADDR object in the associated provider-specific buffer. The QoS service provider will use the address included in the QOS_DEST_ADDR object to generate the SESSION object.

The SENDER_TEMPLATE *Object*

The SENDER_TEMPLATE object specifies the source IP address and IP port associated with the transmitted traffic flow. Winsock 2 typically associates a source port and address with a socket as a result of a *bind* by the application. Many applications issue a bind call to specify a source port and address. In certain cases, the application will not specify a source port in its call to bind, or may not call the bind API at all. In these cases, Winsock 2 binds implicitly, selecting a source port and an appropriate source address from the addresses associated with the sending host. In any case, the information required to generate the SENDER_TEMPLATE object is eventually associated with each sending socket. However, in certain cases of implicit binds, this information may not be available until the application calls one of the connection-oriented APIs.

The SENDER_TSPEC *Object*

The SENDER_TSPEC object includes the quantitative QoS parameters describing the traffic transmitted on a flow. The QoS service provider derives these directly from the SendingFlowspec structure that is provided by the application. The application may provide the SendingFlowspec using any of the connection-oriented APIs or, alternatively, may do so by calling WSAIoctl(SIO_SET_QOS).

Quantitative applications are required to specify at least the ServiceType and TokenRate parameters of the SendingFlowspec. Qualitative applications need specify only the ServiceType parameter.

Timing

The QoS service provider generally begins to send PATH messages as soon as it understands that the application is interested in QoS for its transmitted traffic and as soon as the service provider can derive the necessary information described previously. The necessary information amounts to the source and destination IP addresses and ports, the service type, and other quantitative parameters that are provided in the SendingFlowspec. The source and destination IP addresses and ports are derived from the socket context. This information is typically available after a socket has been connected via a call to one of the connection-oriented APIs. The service type and other quantitative parameters are derived from the SendingFlowspec.

Figure 12.5 illustrates the timing of the generation of PATH messages with respect to application calls.

Figure 12.5   Timing of the Generation of PATH Messages

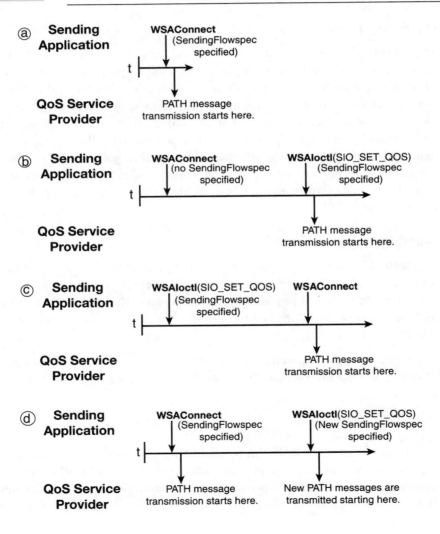

In the simplest case (Figure 12.5a), the SendingFlowspec is passed to the QoS service provider with a call to one of the connection-oriented APIs, and the QoS service provider can begin to generate PATH messages immediately. In certain cases, the application may call one of the APIs to establish a connection, without passing a SendingFlowspec at that time. In that case, the SendingFlowspec may be passed to the QoS service provider at a later time, by calling WSAIoctl(SIO_SET_QOS). In this case, the QoS service provider will begin to generate PATH messages at that time (Figure 12.5b). In other cases, the application may provide a SendingFlowspec in advance of a call to one of the connection-oriented APIs (Figure 12.5c). In these cases, the QoS service provider stores the associated parameters but must wait to generate PATH messages until addressing information is associated with the socket (typically as a result of one of the connection-oriented calls).

In all cases, WSAIoctl(SIO_SET_QOS) may be issued at any time to change the QoS parameters that are signaled in the PATH messages (Figure 12.5d).

The QoS service provider stops generating PATH messages when the socket is closed, shut down, or disconnected, or when the application indicates that it is no longer interested in QoS signaling. The application may do so by passing a SendingFlowspec specifying SERVICETYPE_NOTRAFFIC or SERVICE_NO_QOS_SIGNALING.

12.3.1.2 *Generation of* RESV *Messages*

As is the case in the generation of PATH messages, the QoS service provider generates RESV messages on behalf of a receiving application as soon as it understands that the application is interested in QoS for its received traffic and the service provider has sufficient information to generate the RESV messages. The RSVP signaling protocol requires that PATH state be present at the receiver before RESV messages can be issued. Thus, one prerequisite for the generation of RESV messages is the presence of PATH state for a session at the receiving QoS service provider. Whereas the generation of PATH messages can be triggered as a result of events occurring on the transmitting host, the generation of RESV messages depends on events at the receiving host and the prior receipt of PATH messages from the network.

RESV messages include an RSVP SESSION object, a FLOWSPEC object, and a FILTER_STYLE object. This information must be accumulated on the receiving host before the QoS service provider can begin to generate RESV messages.

The SESSION *Object*

The SESSION object specifies the IP destination address and port to which the QoS traffic is being transmitted. When a unicast receiving application binds to a specific socket, a port and an address are associated with that socket. Thus, the QoS service provider can retrieve the information required to generate a SESSION object from the socket context. Simply put, for unicast receivers, the SESSION object that is transmitted in RESV messages contains the address and the port of the receiving socket.

Multicast receivers call WSAJoinLeaf to indicate the multicast session for which they want to receive traffic. Thus, in the case of multicast receivers, the QoS service provider obtains the RSVP SESSION object from the multicast address specified in the receiving application's call to WSAJoinLeaf.

The FLOWSPEC Object

The FLOWSPEC object specifies the service type requested by the receiver and the quantitative parameters of the QoS to be applied to the received traffic. When the receiving application calls one of the QoS APIs, this information may be provided in the ReceivingFlowspec field.

However, to simplify the requirements on the receiving application, receivers are not required to specify the quantitative parameters in the ReceivingFlowspec. In the absence of receiver-specified quantitative parameters, the QoS service provider assumes that the receiver is interested in the same quantitative parameters that are offered in the SENDER_TSPEC in the incident PATH messages for the corresponding session. In this case, the QoS service provider simply copies those parameters into the FLOWSPEC object in the RESV messages. In certain cases, the receiver may want to override the default behavior of the QoS service provider and to specify quantitative parameters other than those offered in the sender's PATH messages. These cases are described in the section "Application Considerations," later in this chapter.

The FILTER_SPEC Object

The FILTER_SPEC object specifies a set of traffic sources from which the receiver is interested in QoS. For unicast sessions, the FILTER_SPEC identifies a single sending peer. For multicast sessions, the FILTER_SPEC may indicate traffic from various subsets of sending peers. The FILTER_SPEC may be complicated by the variety of reservation *styles* that are possible. See Chapter 5 for a discussion of reservation styles.

As is true for other parameters that must be included in RESV messages, the QoS service provider attempts to deduce the appropriate FILTER_SPEC to generate on behalf of the receiving application without requiring the application to explicitly specify it.

Matching PATH and Sessions in the QoS Service Provider

When a receiving application indicates interest in QoS for received traffic, the QoS service provider stores state for the corresponding session. The session state is defined by the IP address and port on which the application receives traffic. This information is available to the QoS service provider as soon as the socket is bound (or, in the case of multicast sessions, as soon as the receiving application has called WSAJoinLeaf to specify a multicast session).

The QoS service provider also stores PATH state, just as RSVP-aware network devices do. PATH state is created when a PATH message for a new session arrives at a QoS service provider. The PATH state includes the session to which the PATH message is addressed.

When PATH state and session state exist for the same session, the QoS service provider detects matching PATH state. When matching PATH state is detected, the QoS service provider can extract the SENDER_TEMPLATE from the PATH state. The SENDER_TEMPLATE specifies the traffic source and thus can be used to generate a FILTER_SPEC, to be included in RESV messages corresponding to the session.

If the receiving socket is a TCP socket, then at some time, the receiving application specifies a single sending peer from which it intends to receive traffic. At that time, the QoS service provider uses the address of the specified sending peer to generate the FILTER_SPEC included in RESV messages. It also specifies a fixed-filter reservation style.

On the other hand, if the receiving socket is a UDP socket, the QoS service provider may be somewhat more promiscuous. Receiving applications may choose never to connect a UDP socket. For unconnected unicast UDP sockets, the QoS service provider generates RESV messages for any matching PATH state. In this case, the QoS service provider specifies the wildcard filter reservation style in the corresponding RESV messages. If the receiving application does choose to connect the UDP socket at some later time, then the QoS service provider will at that time limit the generation of RESV messages to the sender to which the socket is connected. In this case, it specifies the fixed-filter reservation style in the corresponding RESV messages.

Note

Note that there is a side effect that results from the use of WSAConnect on a UDP receiving socket. Specifically, any traffic received from senders other than the one specified in the call to WSAConnect will be discarded. If a receiving application wants to constrain the generation of RESV messages to a specific sender but does not want to lose traffic from other senders, it should call WSAIoctl(SIO_SET_QOS) instead of WSAConnect. It should specify the sender's address in a QOS_DEST_ADDR object included in the associated provider-specific buffer.

Overriding the Defaults

The previous paragraphs described the default generation of the FILTER_SPEC object by the QoS service provider. To summarize briefly, the default behavior is as follows:

- **TCP socket**—Fixed-filter reservation style specifies connected peer

- **Unconnected unicast UDP**—Wildcard-filter reservation style

- **Connected unicast UDP**—Fixed-filter reservation style specifies connected peer

- **Multicast UDP**—Wildcard-filter reservation style

These defaults are generated based on the QoS service provider's assumptions regarding the intent of the application and based on the information available at the time that a RESV message is generated. Applications may override the defaults by including an RSVP_RESERVE_INFO structure in the provider-specific buffer that is included with the QoS API call. The Style parameter in this structure determines the reservation style that will actually be used and the set of senders (in the case of non-default fixed-filter or multicast shared explicit reservations) that will be specified in the RESV messages generated.

Timing

As is the case with PATH messages, RESV messages are generated as soon as the QoS service provider understands that the receiving application is interested in QoS protected traffic *and* sufficient information is available to generate the RESV message.

The QoS service provider assumes that a receiving application is interested in QoS as soon as the application provides a ReceivingFlowspec with one of the QoS APIs. The information necessary to generate RESV messages amounts to SESSION, FLOWSPEC, and FILTER_SPEC objects. As described previously, the information necessary to generate a SESSION object is available as soon as the receiving socket is bound (unicast) or the receiving application has called WSAJoinLeaf (multicast). The information necessary to generate the FLOWSPEC object is available as soon as the application calls any of the QoS APIs that includes a ReceivingFlowspec. Finally, the information necessary to generate the default FILTER_SPEC object is available as soon as there is matching PATH state and session state. Figure 12.6 illustrates two possible timing sequences for a simple case of QoS invocation on a receiver.

Figure 12.6   Timing of the Generation of RESV Messages

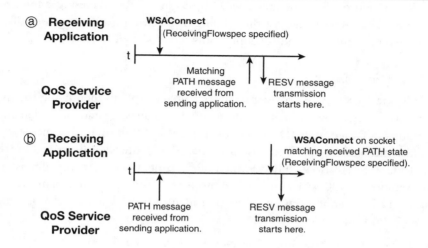

In both cases, the receiving application calls WSAConnect (specifying a ReceivingFlowspec) to connect to a specific sender. In Figure 12.6a, the WSAConnect call is issued first, followed by the arrival of a matching PATH message from the specified sender. The receiver's QoS service provider begins generating RESV messages upon receipt of the PATH message. In Figure 12.6b, the PATH message from the sender arrives first, followed by the application call to WSAConnect (with a ReceivingFlowspec specified). In this case, the receiver's QoS service provider begins generating RESV messages following the application's call to WSAConnect.

Note that information generated in the FLOWSPEC and FILTER_SPEC objects may be modified during the course of a session. Specifically, calls to WSAIoctl(SIO_SET_QOS) can be used to modify the FLOWSPEC parameters. Calls to WSAIoctl(SIO_SET_QOS) with a provider-specific buffer can be used to choose a nondefault reservation style and to select a particular set of senders. Similarly, the act of connecting an unconnected UDP socket will modify the reservation style and will specify the connected peer as the QoS sender.

12.3.1.3   Receiver Proxies

Receiver proxies were defined in Chapter 5. In certain cases, devices in the network may proxy on behalf of the receiver. In this case, the receiving application need not call the GQoS API. The QoS service provider on the receiving host is inactive. This is inconsequential from a traffic control perspective because there is no traffic control on receivers. However, from a signaling perspective, the receiving host loses the capability to modify the signaled QoS parameters and loses the capability to receive in-band notifications regarding the state of QoS for the session.

12.3.1.4 Generating Policy Objects

The QoS service provider generates policy objects in the RSVP messages transmitted to the network. These specify at least the sending or receiving user and, optionally, the sending or receiving application and subapplication.

User Identification

By default, the QoS service provider includes a policy element identifying the user corresponding to a traffic flow in the related signaling messages. The identity element contains the Windows NT login user ID (in the form of an X.500 distinguished name). The user ID is authenticated and encrypted using Kerberos credentials (as described in Chapter 5 and in [RFC 2752]), also included in the policy element. This functionality is available only on Windows 2000. On Windows 98, no user identity policy element is generated. See Figure 12.7 for an illustration of the user identity policy element that is generated by Windows 2000 hosts.

Figure 12.7 Policy_Data Object Generated by Windows 2000 Hosts

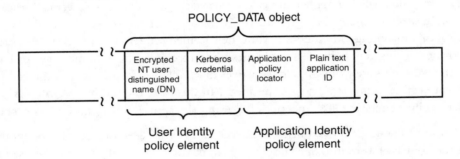

Application Identification

The QoS service provider does not identify applications to the network by default. However, it is recommended that applications include an application identifier and a subapplication identifier in the provider-specific buffer of the QualityofService structure. The QoS service provider includes these in the application identity policy element within RSVP signaling messages sent for the corresponding flow (see Figure 12.7 for an illustration of the application identity policy element that is generated by Windows 2000 hosts). The subject of application identification will be discussed further in the section "Application Considerations," later in this chapter.

12.3.2 Information Provided to Applications by the QoS Service Provider

The QoS service provider offers QoS-related information to applications through three mechanisms:

- **Registering for notifications**—Applications can use the GQoS API to request notification from the QoS service provider regarding changes in the QoS state in the network or the service provider.

- **Querying for current state**—Applications can query the QoS service provider for current QoS-related state.

- **Generating responses to QoS API calls**—The QoS service provider offers immediate feedback to applications in response to erroneous or malformed API calls.

The following sections describe the various mechanisms by which the QoS service provider offers information to applications. The nature of this information and its significance to the application are discussed in depth in the section "Application Considerations," later in this chapter.

12.3.2.1 Registering for Notifications

Two mechanisms exist by which applications may register a request for the QoS service provider to notify it regarding changes in QoS state. One is by calling WSAAsyncSelect or WSAEventSelect to register for the FD_QOS event notification. When a change occurs, the QoS service provider notifies the application. The application is expected to call WSAIoctl(SIO_GET_QOS) to learn the exact nature of the change.

Alternatively, the application may issue an overlapped WSAIoctl(SIO_GET_QOS) request, specifying a completion routine. When a change occurs, the QoS service provider calls the completion routine and provides information regarding the change in the buffer provided with the call to WSAIoctl(SIO_GET_QOS).

12.3.2.2 Queries from Applications to the QoS Service Provider

Applications may query the QoS service provider regarding current state by calling WSAIoctl(SIO_CHK_QOS). The application must specify a query code, as described in the section "Application Queries to the QoS Service Provider" later in this chapter.

12.3.2.3   Responses to API Calls

The QoS service provider may provide miscellaneous error indications in response to any of the QoS API calls.

12.3.3   Traffic Control Invocation

Unless the SERVICE_NO_TRAFFIC_CONTROL flag is set in the SendingFlowspec, the QoS service provider will invoke traffic control on sending hosts. There is no traffic control on receiving hosts. Traffic control functionality amounts to scheduling the transmission of data, marking transmitted data packets or cells for a certain priority level, and any link layer-specific mechanisms (such as ATM signaling) that may be required to provide traffic control on the medium on which the host transmits.

12.3.3.1   Greedy and Nongreedy Traffic Control

Traffic control can be subdivided into *greedy* and *nongreedy* functionality. Shaping or scheduling packets in accordance with the SendingFlowspec parameters is nongreedy because, regardless of how much shaping is applied, the transmitting adapter will not send traffic at a rate higher than it would if the traffic were not shaped. Consequently, shaping reduces the demand on network resources downstream. On the other hand, marking is greedy behavior. This is because marking certain packets for higher-priority service than others will result in the allocation of resources in the network to those packets, at the expense of other packets.

It is important to distinguish between greedy and nongreedy traffic control functionality because the QoS service provider invokes these under different conditions. Specifically, nongreedy traffic control can be invoked as soon as the QoS service provider learns the relevant quantitative parameters from the application. However, to maintain the integrity of the assurances provided by the network to other flows, greedy traffic control must not be invoked without the approval of the network, subject to network policies and the availability of resources. Thus, greedy traffic control is invoked only after successful admission control in the network (as indicated by the arrival of RESV messages at a sending host).

12.3.3.2   Interpreting Traffic Control Parameters in the QoS Service Provider

The QoS service provider must map relatively abstract traffic control parameters provided by a sending application to specific parameters to be included in the call to the traffic control API. As is the case with signaling, the QoS service provider tries to deduce appropriate traffic control parameters from the context of the application's API call. QoS-savvy applications may override the QoS service provider's default traffic control behavior, as described in the section "Application Considerations," later in this chapter.

Behavior of the QoS Service Provider When Traffic Control Is Disabled

In certain cases, applications may disable the invocation of traffic control. As a result, the QoS service provider will not invoke any traffic control functionality.

Selecting Default Traffic Control Parameters

The only traffic control parameter that must be provided by the sending application is an estimate of the average sending rate (the TokenRate). If the token bucket size and the peak rate are not explicitly specified by the application, these will be defaulted by the QoS service provider. The token bucket size will be defaulted to the MTU size for the corresponding interface, and the peak rate will be defaulted to the media rate (for example, to 10Mbps on an Ethernet interface). Note that these defaults will be used both in the invocation of local traffic control and in the generation of signaling messages to the network.

Note that the DelayVariation and Latency parameters have no impact on the invocation of traffic control. These affect only the signaling messages generated by the receiving host.

Modifying the Shaping Rate

By default, the QoS service provider invokes local traffic control to schedule transmitted traffic in accordance with the parameters requested by the application and signaled to the network. In certain cases, the application may request the QoS service provider to override the local traffic-scheduling parameters without altering the parameters signaled to the network. The QoS service provider will do so only if the overriding parameters are less aggressive than those signaled to the network. Otherwise, it would be violating its contract with the network in a greedy manner.

12.3.3.3 The ShapeDiscard Mode

When the QoS service provider creates a traffic control flow, the flow is created with a certain ShapeDiscardMode. By default, the QoS service provider selects the ShapeDiscardMode based on a mapping from the service type specified by the application. This mode determines the shaping behavior applied by traffic control. The impact of the shaping mode will be discussed in further depth in Chapter 13, "The Traffic Control API and Traffic Control Components."

12.3.3.4 Marking Behavior

As explained previously, marking is considered greedy traffic control behavior and, as such, is invoked only with network approval. The QoS service provider considers the arrival of a RESV message at a sender an indication that the network has admitted a request to a specified service level, so it approves the appropriate marking of conforming traffic on the flow.

Two types of marks are typically applied—the network-layer mark in the IP header and the link-layer mark. The host IP stack applies the network-layer mark in cooperation with the packet-scheduler component of traffic control. This is the DiffServ codepoint, or DSCP. The netcard driver applies the link-layer mark in cooperation with the packet scheduler. In the case of Ethernet netcards, the link-layer mark is an 802 user_priority. In the case of other media, the netcard driver may map the 802 user_priority to whichever marks are appropriate for the medium.

Note that the packet scheduler is required to participate in the marking of packets because it determines whether a packet conforms to the specified quantitative parameters. If a packet does not conform, the packet scheduler must cause it to be marked with the corresponding non-conforming mark.

Mappings

Although the QoS service provider controls the marking of packets by invoking traffic control, it does not directly select the mark to be applied. Rather, the QoS service provider invokes traffic control for a certain service type. A mapping is then applied by the traffic control components to derive the appropriate mark from the service type. See Chapter 13 for details regarding the mapping of service types to marks. Until a flow is admitted by the network, the QoS service provider invokes traffic control specifying the best-effort service type (regardless of the service type actually requested by the application).

As a result, packets on these flows will be marked for best-effort service (nongreedy traffic control). After the flow is admitted by the network, the QoS service provider modifies the service type specified (via the traffic control API) to match the service type requested by the application. At this time, packets will be marked for prioritized service (greedy traffic control). This behavior is illustrated in Figure 12.8.

Referring to Figure 12.8, note the following steps:

1. In Figure 12.8a, the application requests QoS from the QoS service provider, via the GQoS API.

2. The QoS service provider requests *nongreedy* traffic control via the traffic control API. As a result, traffic is scheduled but not marked for priority.

3. At the same time, the QoS service provider begins signaling RSVP PATH messages to the network.

4. Sometime shortly thereafter, Figure 12.8b illustrates an RSVP RESV message returning from the network, indicating successful admission control in the network.

5. In response, the QoS service provider invokes *greedy* traffic control via the traffic control API. As a result, traffic is both scheduled and marked for priority at this time.

6. At the same time, the QoS service provider notifies the application that its request has been approved.

Figure 12.8   Timing Related to the Invocation of Greedy and Nongreedy Traffic Control.

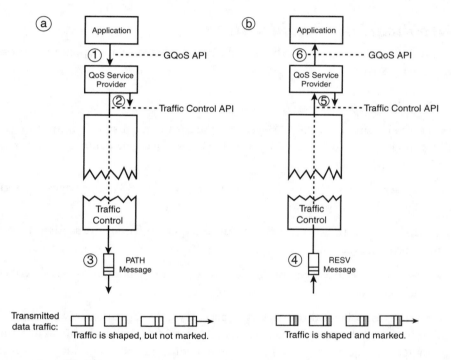

For further details on the invocation of traffic control by the QoS service provider, see the section "The Interaction of the QoS Service Provider and Traffic Control," in Chapter 13.

There are two mechanisms to override the default mappings from service type to mark. One of these is to modify the default mapping table in each host. This table is maintained in the registry and may be modified programmatically (whether locally or by remote administration from Active Directory). This override mechanism is applied by the traffic control components without the involvement of the QoS service provider. The other override mechanism is more dynamic and does involve the QoS service provider. This mechanism allows the network to modify the mark used for a particular traffic flow by appending DCLASS or TCLASS objects to RESV messages. The DCLASS object modifies the DiffServ codepoint mark, and the TCLASS object modifies the user_priority mark. The QoS service provider passes these objects to traffic control when the RESV message is received, thereby overriding the default mapping that would otherwise be used.

Note that the default mark for qualitative service is the same mark that maps to the best-effort service. Thus, traffic on qualitative flows is marked only if the network returns a DCLASS or TCLASS object to the sending host.

12.4 *Application Considerations*

This section discusses certain issues that should be considered by the application programmer using the QoS APIs.

12.4.1 *Service Types*

The ServiceType parameter in the FLOWSPEC structure is the most significant parameter specified by applications calling the GQoS APIs. The service type parameter determines the following behavior:

- The IntServ service type that is signaled to the network in RSVP messages (no signaling is generated for best-effort flows).

- The priority at which the corresponding traffic is queued within the sending host's traffic control provider (see the next chapter on traffic control for further details).

- The ShapeDiscard mode applied by traffic control on the sending host (as described in the previous section).

- The DiffServ codepoint and the 802 user_priority used to mark traffic on the corresponding flow (see the next chapter on traffic control for further details). Note that if a DCLASS or TCLASS object is returned from the network, the corresponding mark is determined by the DCLASS or TCLASS object, not by the service type.

Service types for use by applications include Guaranteed, Controlled Load, Null, and best-effort. (Note that the GQoS API refers to Null Service as qualitative service. The terms are used here interchangeably.) These have been described previously. Guaranteed Service should generally be used for traffic that is latency-intolerant. Controlled Load Service should generally be used for traffic that requires the appearance of a lightly loaded network but that is tolerant of some latency. Null Service should generally be used by applications that cannot quantify their resource requirements but that benefit from some medium-quality service assurances.

Applications should select a service type based on their needs. Requests for more demanding service types are less likely to be admitted to the network than requests for less demanding service types. In addition, hosts are likely to be charged more (via whatever charging mechanisms exist) for more demanding services.

12.4.2   Quantitative Applications

Quantitative applications are applications that are capable of quantifying their resource requirements. These are typically multimedia applications. These applications request the Guaranteed or Controlled Load Service types.

12.4.2.1   Quantitative Traffic Control Parameters Specified by Sending Applications

Quantitative sending applications must specify at least the TokenRate parameter in the SendingFlowspec in addition to one of the quantitative service types. The TokenRate parameter should indicate the expected average sending rate of the application. If the token bucket size and peak rate are not explicitly specified by the application, these will be defaulted by the QoS service provider, as described previously.

It is recommended that applications specify all token bucket parameters whenever possible. In the case of multimedia applications that use fixed-rate CODECs, the application may use the WSAGetQoSByName call to determine the appropriate parameters to include in the traffic control call. In the case of nonfixed-rate CODECs, the application must determine the token bucket parameters to be used.

Sending applications are not expected to specify the DelayVariation and Latency parameters in the SendingFlowspec.

12.4.2.2   Quantitative Traffic Control Parameters Specified by Receiving Applications

The QoS service provider must specify certain quantitative parameters in the RESV messages that it generates on behalf of quantitative applications. If a receiving application does not specify quantitative parameters, the QoS service provider simply uses the parameters offered in the PATH messages generated by the corresponding sender.

In the case of unicast sessions, there is little reason for the receiver to request QoS parameters other than those described by the sender, so the receiver need not specify quantitative parameters in the ReceivingFlowspec. The utility of overriding the default quantitative parameters offered by the sender arises in certain multicast scenarios. Consider the case of a multiparty videoconference (as described in Chapter 5). Certain receivers may want to reserve sufficient capacity to receive traffic from multiple senders simultaneously. Thus, if each sender specifies a token rate of r in its SENDER_TSPEC, receivers may want to specify $N \times r$ in the FLOWSPEC generated, to protect traffic from N senders simultaneously.

Other cases in which receivers may want to modify the parameters offered in the SENDER_TSPEC have to do with the trade-off between token rate and delay when the receiver requests Guaranteed Service. This allows receivers to exert some control over the size of the buffer required at the receiver. Details of this trade-off are beyond the scope of this discussion. For further information, refer to [RFC 2212].

12.4.3 Qualitative Applications

Certain applications cannot readily quantify their resource requirements using the token bucket parameters available. These applications should request qualitative service. In response, the QoS service provider will specify the Null Service in its signaling messages to the network. These applications do not specify any quantitative parameters in the SendingFlowspec or the ReceivingFlowspec.

12.4.3.1 Application and Subapplication Identifiers

Applications that request qualitative service must specify application identifiers and subapplication identifiers. This is the only information that the network can use to determine how to handle the corresponding traffic. The network typically responds to requests for the Null Service by returning a DCLASS and/or TCLASS object to cause the traffic to be marked for the appropriate service level. Applications that do not specify indentifiers will likely be provided only best-effort service by the network.

Application identifiers should specify the name of the application. Subapplication identifiers include the version of the application and serve to differentiate subflows of the application that should receive different QoS. The selection of subapplication identifiers used by an application should be based on a careful analysis of the different types of traffic generated by the application and the different QoS requirements of each type of traffic.

An application may choose to modify the subapplication identifier associated with a socket if it modifies the type of traffic submitted on that socket during the life of the socket. This can be done by calling WSAIoctl(SIO_SET_QOS) with the new subapplication identifier specified in the associated provider specific buffer. The network may then adjust the QoS provided to the corresponding traffic. This mechanism can be used to accommodate relatively slow and infrequent changes in traffic types. It cannot be used, for example, to accommodate packet-by-packet changes in traffic type. Signaled QoS is not suitable for applications that must frequently change the type of traffic submitted on a socket (and the type of service allotted to that traffic).

12.4.3.2 *Populating Policy Management Systems with Application and Subapplication Identifiers*

The Microsoft Active Directory can be used to manage qualitative traffic based on application and subapplication identifiers. The Active Directory management infrastructure provides mechanisms by which management utilities can query applications (at deployment time) for the application identifiers and subapplication identifiers that they may use at run time. Applications facilitate management of their traffic by supporting these mechanisms via WMI.

12.4.4 *Persistent versus Nonpersistent Applications*

Signaled QoS is suitable for *persistent* applications. These are applications that are session-oriented in the sense that they generate traffic flows that persist for some period of time between a well-defined set of hosts. For example, telephony and video applications are clearly persistent because they persist for the duration of a phone call or a video clip between two peers or between a server and a client. SAP/R3 and other qualitative client/server applications are also persistent. Although their traffic may be bursty, it is possible to define a session between a sender and a receiver.

Certain applications are *nonpersistent*. Such applications generate only brief bursts of traffic to a given destination after which no additional traffic is generated or the destination of the traffic changes. Examples of such applications include network logon or certain modes of Web browsing. Signaled QoS is not suitable for these applications because it takes a finite amount of time to establish signaling state in the network. By the time signaling state is established for such applications, their traffic is no longer present on the signaled path. The GQoS APIs and the QoS service provider will be modified to handle nonpersistent applications post-Windows 2000. To be QoS-ready, nonpersistent applications should call the GQoS API specifying the qualitative service type with signaling disabled (by setting the SERVICE_NO_QOS_SIGNALING flag in SendingFlowspec).

12.4.5 *The* ShapeDiscard *Mode*

Local traffic control applies a certain ShapeDiscard mode, as determined by the specified service type. Applications may override the default mapping from service type to ShapeDiscard mode by including the appropriate object in the provider-specific buffer. The ShapeDiscard mode will be described in further detail in chapter 13.

By default, the *shape* mode is invoked only for Guaranteed Service flows. The shape mode warrants further discussion. In this mode, traffic control components delay traffic submitted by the application in the kernel so that it conforms to the token bucket profile specified by the application. In other words, the kernel forces transmitted traffic to conform to the token bucket parameters specified by the application. Applications selecting Guaranteed Service (or forcing shape mode for other service type flows) must be aware of this behavior. If the sending application consistently exceeds the token bucket parameters specified, traffic will back up in the kernel, consuming increasingly more nonpaged pool. Although there are safety mechanisms in traffic control to prevent disruption to the operating system, this behavior may clearly have undesirable side effects.

12.4.6   Disabling Traffic Control

Traffic control is invoked on senders by default whenever a SendingFlowspec is provided to the QoS service provider. Applications may disable the invocation of traffic control by setting the SERVICE_NO_TRAFFIC_CONTROL flag in the SendingFlowspec. This feature is provided for applications that want to cause signaling to be generated to the network but that want to maintain control over the scheduling of their traffic. Because packet marking and link layer-specific QoS mechanisms are also provided by traffic control, disabling it prevents marking by the transmitting host and may alter the behavior of certain link layer-specific mechanisms.

Note that whereas applications may be capable of providing coarse-grain scheduling on their own behalf, they are generally precluded from marking packets (because this is greedy behavior). It is generally not recommended that applications disable traffic control.

12.4.7   Interpretation of Information from the QoS Service Provider

Note that applications cannot use the information available from the QoS service provider to determine with certainty just what QoS the network is providing. Applications using the GQoS API should continue to use any mechanisms at their disposal for determining the quality of service allotted to their traffic (such as in-band performance measuring, Real-Time Control Protocol [RTCP], and so on). Feedback from the QoS service provider regarding the state of the network is useful primarily for the purpose of determining when the network has admitted a signaling request for QoS and how network policies are being applied to the application's traffic. These will be clarified further in the following paragraphs.

12.4.7.1 Indicated Status Codes

When applications call WSAIcotl(SIO_GET_QOS), the QoS service provider returns an RSVP_STATUS_INFO structure in the provider-specific buffer. This structure contains a high-level Winsock2 status code as well as extended codes that provide more detailed information. The following types of information are indicated via the status codes:

- **Indication at a receiver regarding the presence of PATH state from a sender that corresponds to the receiving socket**—This can be interpreted as an indication that there is a sender interested in providing QoS-protected traffic to the receiving application.

- **Indication at a sender regarding the arrival of a RESV message corresponding to a transmitted traffic flow from one or more receivers**—This can be interpreted as an indication that a receiver (or a proxy) has indicated interest in the offered traffic and that the network has admitted the flow for which the sender has signaled. The admission indication can also be obtained at the receiving application.

- **Indication that there are no remaining senders (or receivers)**—This indication complements the previous indications by notifying the application that the last sender (or receiver) has ceased to send (or be interested in receiving) QoS-protected traffic.

- **Indication regarding failure to admit a flow**—A flow may be refused admission because of a lack of resources, policy reasons, conflicting reservations styles (see Chapter 5), and various other errors. Applications can determine the general reason for admission control failure from these indications.

12.4.7.2 Additional Status Information Indicated via the Provider-Specific Buffer

The QoS service provider often offers more detailed feedback to the application in the provider-specific buffer in the form of a list of objects contained in the RSVP_STATUS_INFO structure. This structure may contain the RSVP ADSPEC object and RSVP policy objects indicating the reason for policy decisions applied in the network. (See Chapter 5 and related RSVP protocol specifications for information regarding these objects.)

The ADSPEC object can be retrieved by applications on indication that PATH state is present. The QoS service provider on sending hosts generates this object. As it transits the network toward the receivers, network devices may modify the ADSPEC. As a result, the ADSPEC can be used to obtain cumulative information regarding the characteristics of the traffic path along which data is being transmitted. These characteristics include available bandwidth, maximum path latency, MTU size, and whether all routers in the path support RSVP.

Parameters advertised in the ADSPEC object must be considered as estimates only. These are subject to change as network conditions change and are accurate only to the degree that all interim devices affecting QoS modify the ADSPEC and do so correctly.

The "break-bit" in the ADSPEC warrants further discussion. This bit is set in case a router that does not support RSVP signaling is encountered in the path from sender to receiver. In the original vision of RSVP usage, in which every device along the path was expected to support RSVP, the break-bit might have been used to indicate an unusual failure to support QoS along a certain path. In the current model of RSVP deployment, in which only a small number of admission control agents are appointed to participate in RSVP signaling, it is likely that the break-bit will almost always be set. A set break-bit should not be taken as an indication that QoS will not be available.

The contents of a policy error object indicated by the QoS service provider may be more useful than the ADSPEC. Network devices along the path from sender to receiver insert policy error objects, usually under the control of a policy server. These can and should be used by the application to respond accordingly. The policy error object provides a communication mechanism between the policy management system and the application. The network manager determines (by authoring policies) which error objects are returned to applications under certain conditions. Policy error objects can be used, for example, to prevent an application from transmitting data in case admission was rejected.

For a list of standard policy error objects, see [RFC 2752]. Additional nonstandard objects may be defined by policy management systems (or applications).

12.4.7.3   Application Queries to the QoS Service Provider

Applications may query the QoS service provider for specific information by calling WSAIoctl(SIO_CHK_QOS) with any of these subcodes:

- **ALLOWED_TO_SEND_DATA**—This query requires the application to submit its flowspec. The QoS service provider responds by indicating whether the sender may send traffic in the absence of a RESV message. Note that this particular mechanism reflects a specific policy control associated with local area networks and the Subnet Bandwidth Manager (see Chapter 7, "The Subnet Bandwidth Manager and 802 Networks"). Applications are advised to issue this call before sending data and to comply with the response. Note that this mechanism is in addition to any higher-layer policy responses that may be returned from a policy management system and that may also advise an application to refrain from sending.

- **LINE_RATE**—This query returns the remaining capacity currently available on an interface. Note that this is the local capacity of the interface. As such, an application cannot use this to determine end-to-end capacity. At a minimum, it informs the application that the end-to-end capacity will be no higher than the indicated capacity.

- **LOCAL_TRAFFIC_CONTROL**—This query informs the application on whether traffic control functionality is enabled on a particular interface. If traffic control is not enabled, the application may choose to provide its own traffic scheduling.

- **LOCAL_QOSABILITY**—In certain cases, signaling may be disabled on a per-interface basis, under administrative control. This query informs the application on whether signaling is disabled on an interface.

- **END_TO_END_QOSABILITY**—This query indicates the break-bit status in the ADSPEC object. The utility of this information was discussed in the previous section.

12.4.8 Withholding Transmission

Two mechanisms exist by which applications may be advised by the network to refrain from sending. One of these is via the call to WSAIoctl(SIO_CHK_QOS) with the subcode ALLOWED_TO_SEND_DATA. The other is via a policy code obtained from a policy management system. The first mechanism is a standard mechanism that is available on shared networks that use a Subnet Bandwidth Manager (per the discussion of the SBM in Chapter 7). This mechanism can be used by the network manager to limit the amount of traffic transmitted by applications sending onto shared networks that are not capable of separating best-effort from higher-priority traffic. The network manager uses this mechanism to limit any signaled traffic transmitted onto the shared subnet, regardless of the application or sender generating the traffic. In most cases, this query will allow the application to send. In certain cases, it will not.

The second mechanism is not standardized. It allows for the definition of policy objects to be designated by the network manager or policy management system, which tell an application to refrain from sending. Any policy server along the path from sender to receiver may choose to append such a policy object to signaling messages for a specific flow.

12.4.8.1 Why Should an Application Refrain from Transmitting?

Application writers may ask why they should refrain from transmitting in response to indications from the network to do so. Conventional wisdom is to design the application to be as aggressive as possible with the network, to maximize the service that it gets from the network. This tendency is especially evident in the case of UDP streaming applications because UDP traffic is not rate-adaptive.

However, the ironic outcome of this approach is often outright refusal by the network manager to allow the application to be deployed in a managed network. Alternatively, network managers may agree to very limited deployments of a crippled version of the application—for example, one that is limited to very low bandwidth streaming. QoS mechanisms such as those discussed in this book make it possible for the network manager to control the impact of such applications on specific parts of a network. The network manager may initially use these mechanisms to prevent certain applications from overwhelming networks that have limited resources, allowing the application to be deployed, but reducing its priority relative to other traffic. As the network manager adds capacity to the network, the manager may switch to a strategy of actually prioritizing some limited volume of traffic from these applications.

By responding to policy-based indications from the network, the application developer may discover that the application becomes more deployable rather than less deployable.

12.4.9 The New Busy Signal

The network may reject application requests for QoS. Such rejections may appear at the sending host, the receiving host, or both. The QoS service provider indicates the rejection of a request to the application.

Two types of rejections exist. One rejection indicates that QoS is not available for the flow but does not preclude the sender from sending. The other rejection indicates that QoS is not available and that the sender must refrain from sending altogether. In the fully QoS-enabled Utopia in which each important application invokes QoS and the network is capable of traffic separation at all congested points, the outright prohibition on sending is not necessary. However, for the interim, the capability to suppress sending completely is extremely valuable.

The outright rejection maps to the classic telephony "busy signal." However, the other type of rejection represents a new type of busy signal that means: "The resources to provide you (the user) QoS are not available at present. You may hang up and try your call again later, or you may proceed with best-effort service." The application might offer the user various options, such as a retrying using a lower-bit rate CODEC. The network infrastructure might offer the best-effort service free of charge or at a lower charge than the QoS-enabled call. Applications should take note of the difference between the new busy signal and the outright prohibition on sending, and should use this feedback from the network creatively.

12.4.10 *Effecting Marking Under Application Control*

QoS components on Windows hosts provide both DiffServ marking and 802 `user_priority` marking of transmitted packets. Marking is based on the service type requested on the corresponding traffic flow, the admissibility of the request to the network, and the conformance status of the marked packet (as determined by the QoS packet scheduler). This mapping will be discussed further in the next chapter.

802 `user_priority` is marked in a packet's MAC header. As such, applications have no access to this mark. However, the DiffServ codepoint is marked in the IP header of each packet, in the fields formerly known as the IP TOS (type of service) field and the IP Precedence field. In legacy versions of Windows operating systems, applications can mark these fields by composing their own IP header or by calling `WSAIoctl(IP_TOS)`. However, in newer versions of the OS in which QoS is supported, applications are precluded from directly marking the DiffServ codepoint. The reasons for this are twofold:

- With the introduction of DiffServ, the meaning of the former TOS and IP Precedence fields has been redefined [RFC 2574] as the DSCP field. The interpretation of this field by network devices depends on the specific implementation of DiffServ in the network. Therefore, applications cannot be expected to understand the impact of any particular codepoint.

- Even if an application understands the impact of the various codepoints that it might mark, it cannot be trusted to do so. QoS mechanisms allow packets to be marked only subject to the approval of network policy. Applications cannot be allowed to bypass network policy.

Nonetheless, applications may effect the marking of DiffServ coedpoints and 802 `user_priority`. They do so indirectly by specifying a certain service type. Assuming that a request for the service type is admitted to the network, then the QoS service provider will mark packets with the corresponding DiffServ codepoint and `user_priority` value. Note that the mappings from service type to DiffServ codepoint can be modified either by modifying the static table in the sending host's registry (under administrative control) or by supplying a `DCLASS` and/or `TCLASS` object from the network to the sending host.

It is also possible to allow applications on certain interfaces to use the legacy mechanisms for marking DiffServ codepoints. To do so, it is necessary to configure a flag in the sender's registry (under administrative control). Hosts on which applications are capable of directly marking DiffServ codepoints may wreak havoc in a managed QoS network. As such, this functionality should be enabled with caution. In general, the network manager is advised not to enable direct application marking.

Note that there is no mechanism by which applications may directly mark 802 `user_priority`.

12.5   Enhancements Supporting Nonpersistent Applications

The QoS service provider in Windows 2000 is optimized to support persistent applications that use the Winsock 2 API. Enhancements are planned for subsequent releases and updates that will add support for applications that do not use the Winsock 2 API (such as Web-based and COM applications). For example, Web-based applications will be capable of requesting QoS on a URL basis. Support will also be added for nonpersistent applications, as described in the following section.

12.5.1   Support for Nonpersistent Applications

Two primary benefits result from host-based QoS mechanisms. One is the generation of signaling that tells the network what type of traffic and how much traffic will appear at specific points in the network. This signaling can then be used to coordinate resource allocation along the traffic path. The second benefit of host-based QoS mechanisms is the identification of traffic to the network management system (even when traffic is encrypted) at a granularity that otherwise might not be possible. Specifically, identification is at the granularity of user, application, and subapplication.

In the case of persistent applications, signaling serves both to coordinate resource allocation along the traffic path and, at the same time, to identify traffic to network management systems so that it can be appropriately handled. However, in the case of nonpersistent applications, there is no defined traffic path and end-to-end signaling cannot be used effectively. The classic DiffServ model (in which packets are marked for specific service levels without signaling) is well suited to nonpersistent applications. However, there is a problem with the classic DiffServ model. Packets should be marked and handled in cooperation with network policies. As discussed previously, it is often difficult or impossible to identify traffic in the network. The alternative is to identify and mark traffic on the transmitting host, where the user, application, and subapplication of the traffic is known. The problem with this approach is that the host is not typically integrated with the network policies.

In the signaling model, the host signals to the network using RSVP, and the net effect of network policy is reflected back to the host in the form of RSVP signaling). In the case of nonpersistent applications, an alternate mechanism is necessary to integrate the host with network policy. In the alternate mechanism, the network stack in the host operating system includes a classic policy enforcement point. (See Figure 9.19 and the related text in Chapter 9, "QoS Policy.") In this mechanism, policies can be pushed from the network management system to the host using standard policy protocols (such as COPS). These specify the marking to be applied to transmitted traffic based on user, application, and sub-application. The transmitting host can leverage the QoS APIs and inherent operating system knowledge to then classify and mark traffic appropriately. In this manner, marking for nonpersistent traffic can be integrated with network-wide policies.

12.6 Functionality Supported on Different Platforms

Differing levels of functionality are supported on different Windows platforms, as described in the following sections.

12.6.1 Windows 98

Windows 98 has limited QoS functionality. A Web update is available that can be used to update QoS functionality on Windows 98 Gold, Windows 98 Second Edition, and Windows 98 Millennium.

The basic Windows 98 operating system includes the QoS service provider and offers RSVP signaling. It does not support the following:

- Traffic control (marking, shaping, and other Layer 2 QoS functionality)
- Subnet Bandwidth Manager client or DSBM functionality (see Chapter 7 on the SBM)
- Generation of Kerberos-encrypted user IDs in signaling messages

Additionally, the GQoS API on Windows 98 offers a subset of the GQoS API on Windows 2000. There are slight differences between the two, so application programmers should use `WSAEnumProtocols` to determine the version of the GQoS API that is available on a particular host.

The Web update available for Windows 98 Gold, Second Edition, and Millennium adds the following functionality above and beyond the basic Windows 98 QoS functionality:

- DiffServ codepoint marking
- Subnet Bandwidth Manager client functionality
- An updated version of the GQoS API, compatible with Windows 2000

12.6.2   Windows 2000

Windows 2000 offers the full suite of QoS functionality described in this chapter. It includes the following:

- The full GQoS API

- RSVP signaling

- Generation of Kerberos-encrypted user IDs

- SBM client functionality

- Admission Control Service and DSBM functionality (except on Windows 2000 Professional)

- The full traffic control API

- A software packet scheduler that provides traffic control functionality over LAN media, including packet shaping and support for user_priority marking

- An IP/ATM traffic control provider, including support for cell shaping and per-conversation ATM signaling

12.7   Summary

This chapter described the GQoS API and the QoS service provider. The GQoS API is an extension to Winsock 2 that abstracts the complexities of QoS to the average application programmer, while allowing QoS-savvy applications to exert fine-grain control over QoS functionality. The QoS service provider responds to the GQoS API. It is the center of QoS functionality on the host, offering RSVP signaling, generation of Kerberos-encrypted user IDs, invocation of traffic control on behalf of QoS-aware applications, QoS status indications to applications, and other miscellaneous functions.

To invoke QoS, applications must first create a socket using either the UDP or the TCP QoS-enabled Winsock 2 service provider. The application may then proceed to invoke QoS using one of the standard Winsock 2 API calls, including WSAConnect, WSAAccept, or WSAJoinLeaf (for multicast). Alternatively, the application may call WSAIoctl(SIO_SET_QOS). This call may be used at any time to modify the QoS parameters in effect on a socket. Additional calls are available to help applications determine the appropriate QoS parameters and to learn the status of network QoS.

Applications include a sending and/or receiving flowspec in their call to the QoS service provider. These include service types and miscellaneous additional parameters, such as parameters that quantify the required QoS (quantitative applications). In addition to the sending and receiving `flowspec`, applications may use the provider-specific buffer to specify detailed QoS behavior, to override default behavior of the QoS service provider, and, most importantly, to supply application and subapplication IDs. To facilitate the use of the QoS APIs, the application is not required to specify all QoS parameters. The QoS service provider attempts to deduce the intent of the application and provides appropriate defaults for those parameters that are not specified.

The QoS service provider generates RSVP signaling in response to calls to the GQoS API. PATH messages are sent in response to a non-null sending `flowspec`. RESV messages are sent in response to a non-null receiving `flowspec`. The actual transmission of the messages begins when the QoS service provider understands that the application is interested in QoS in a certain direction and when it has the information necessary to compose the RSVP messages. Part of this information is conveyed explicitly in the application's call to the GQoS API. Other information is available implicitly via address and port parameters associated with each Winsock 2 socket. The QoS service provider includes a Kerberos-encrypted user ID in both RESV and PATH messages.

The QoS service provider invokes both greedy and nongreedy traffic control. Nongreedy traffic control (primarily traffic scheduling) is invoked on senders as soon as an application provides a sending `flowspec` (for quantitative traffic only). Greedy traffic control (marking packets for prioritization) is invoked by the QoS service provider only if and when the network approves admission of a traffic flow to a service level other than best-effort (as indicated by signaling responses from the network).

Applications are urged to heed responses from the network that are intended to prevent them from sending. In most cases, admission control failures will not prevent applications from sending. Instead, they simply limit the service provided to the application's traffic flow to the level of best-effort. However, by complying with those indications from the network that are intended to prevent transmission altogether, applications are more deployable.

The Traffic Control API and Traffic Control Components

Traffic control components comprise a significant part of the QoS-related functionality on hosts running the Windows 2000 operating system. Such functionality includes primarily traffic scheduling and packet marking, but also various media-specific functionality such as ATM UNI signaling and ISSLOW. Traffic control functionality is controlled primarily by the traffic control API (TC API). This chapter describes the details of traffic control components and the traffic control API.

13.1 Overview of Traffic Control Components and Their Functionality

Traffic control functionality has been discussed previously as one of the primary components of a QoS-enabled network. Routers and switches apply various forms of traffic control in the network. But traffic control is not limited to routers and switches. Recall that the network extends to the host operating systems. Because traffic control functionality tends to be quite processing-intensive, there is incentive to push this work to the periphery of the network whenever possible. By implementing traffic control in the network stack of each host, traffic can be shaped and marked at the periphery of the network, where it scales better than at the core. This section provides an overview of the traffic control components implemented in the Windows 2000 operating system, the traffic control API, and the corresponding traffic control functionality. Note that existing traffic control functionality is implemented only with respect to transmitted traffic.

13.1.1 Traffic Control Consumers and Traffic Control Providers

As discussed previously, traffic-handling mechanisms must be configured consistently across the network to provide useful services. The same applies to traffic control mechanisms on host operating systems. To be effective, transmitted traffic should be shaped and marked in a manner consistent with network-wide policies. To this end, the traffic control mechanisms on hosts should be invoked by agents that interact with the network's policy management system.

Because these agents invoke the services provided by traffic control components, they are referred to as *traffic control consumers*. The components in the operating system that actually shape and mark traffic are providing traffic control functionality as directed by the traffic control consumers. These components are therefore referred to as *traffic control providers*. Traffic control providers typically take the form of low-level drivers in the network stack of the operating system and include the hardware that these drivers control. Examples of traffic control providers are the QoS packet scheduler and ATM netcards, with their associated drivers. Traffic control consumers use the *traffic control API* (TC API) to invoke the services of traffic control providers. The concept of traffic control providers and traffic control consumers is illustrated in Figure 13.1.

Figure 13.1   Traffic Control Providers and Traffic Control Consumers

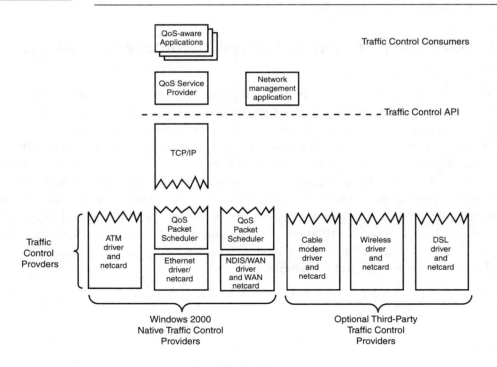

The QoS service provider that is part of Windows 2000 is a traffic control consumer. In addition, Windows 2000 includes three native traffic control providers (the QoS packet scheduler over Ethernet, the QoS packet scheduler over WAN, and the ATM traffic control provider) and an API by which traffic control consumers can invoke the services of traffic control providers. This modular structure enables independent software vendors to add value by writing specialized traffic control consumers or traffic control providers.

The following sections discuss traffic control consumers in further detail. Subsequent paragraphs describe the interface between traffic control consumers and traffic control providers, as well as the functionality that is expected from traffic control providers. This section concludes with a brief description of the Windows 2000 native traffic control providers.

13.1.1.1 First-Party Consumers

First-party traffic control consumers are consumers that invoke traffic control as agents of the applications that send or receive network traffic. The QoS service provider that is part of Windows 2000 is an example of a first-party traffic control consumer because it invokes traffic control at the request of QoS-enabled applications for the application's traffic. Note that in doing so, the QoS service provider is subject to the constraints imposed by the network policy system. It uses signaling to gain permission from the network policy system before invoking any greedy form of traffic control.

13.1.1.2 Third-Party Consumers

Third-party consumers invoke traffic control on behalf of a network management system. The traffic control invoked is applied to application traffic, but the application is passive in this process. An example of a third-party traffic control consumer is an application that resides on a network policy server (PDP) and remotely configures traffic control on hosts in a manner that shapes and marks traffic consistent with network-wide policies. The Windows 2000 Resource Kit includes a sample traffic control consumer in the form of the *TcMon* (traffic control monitor) application.

13.1.1.3 A Comparison of First- and Third-Party Traffic Control Consumers

There is not always a clear distinction between first-party traffic control providers and third-party traffic control providers, but the general concept is nonetheless useful. Because first-party traffic control consumers interact directly with the application, they are capable of invoking QoS based on information that would otherwise be available only to the application. This is particularly useful for quantifiable multimedia applications, but it is also useful for many qualitative applications.

Third-party traffic control consumers, on the other hand, generally operate with no direct knowledge of the application's requirements or the specific nature of the traffic generated by the application. As such, they often are incapable of supporting as high a QE product as first-party traffic control consumers. However, a significant advantage of third-party traffic control consumers is that they can provide QoS on behalf of applications that do not use the GQoS API.

Support for Nonpersistent Applications

In the initial release of Windows 2000, there is no support in the QoS service provider for nonpersistent applications. (For a description of persistent versus nonpersistent applications, see the section "Signaling for Qualitative Applications," in Chapter 5, "RSVP," and "Qualitative Services," in Chapter 6, "Differentiated Services"). These applications must instead rely on third-party traffic control consumers to provide host traffic control.

A hybrid of a first- and third-party traffic control consumer is planned for subsequent releases of the operating system. This traffic control consumer will invoke traffic control for nonpersistent applications on behalf of the network policy system. However, it will also provide APIs by which these applications can identify specific subsets of their traffic to the traffic control consumer. As such, this hybrid traffic control consumer will be capable of leveraging its unique position on the host operating system to increase the resulting QE product.

Adding Value via the Traffic Control API

The TC API makes it possible for independent software vendors to write traffic control consumers and traffic control providers. Third-party traffic control consumers represent a natural opportunity for adding value to the QoS functionality of the host operating system. A well-written third-party traffic control consumer can integrate host traffic control with a network-wide policy system to support those applications that are not supported via the QoS service provider.

The most likely opportunity for adding value to the host QoS capabilities is in writing traffic control providers for different media, such as cable modems, 1394 networks, and so forth.

Interaction Between Traffic Control Consumers and the Network Policy-Management System

As discussed previously, it is important that the traffic control consumer invoke traffic control in a manner consistent with the overall network policies. This requires that the traffic control consumer interact with the network's policy-management system. The QoS service provider interacts with the network by generating RSVP signaling. Signaling requests for resources are generated for individual application traffic flows. These are approved or rejected by policy servers that are part of the network policy-management system. The resulting decision is then returned to the QoS service provider so that it can invoke traffic control in accordance with the decision.

Third-party traffic control consumers typically operate differently. These tend to push policies to hosts affecting applications that do not invoke the GQoS API. Such policies often control aggregate traffic flows rather than the per-conversation traffic flows controlled by the QoS service provider. In addition, these tend to be pushed in a relatively static manner, as opposed to the dynamic nature of RSVP signaling. Third-party traffic control consumers must operate consistently with the network-wide policy-management system. The broader policy management system can invoke traffic control on hosts using one of two mechanisms, as illustrated in Figure 13.2. In Figure 13.2a, the policy management system uses DCOM to invoke the services of the traffic control providers via *TCCOM*. (TCCOM is available via the *Windows 2000 Resource Kit*. It is an agent that resides on Windows 2000 hosts and makes the TC API accessible to remote systems via DCOM.)

In Figure 13.2b, the policy management system vendor writes an agent that installs on the Windows 2000 host. This agent communicates with the policy-management system using the Common Open Policy Service (COPS) protocol (or any other protocol of the policy management system vendor's choosing) and invokes the services of the traffic control providers via the traffic control API.

The concepts discussed in this sidebar are also developed in Chapter 9, "QoS Policy." (See Figure 9.19.)

continues

Figure 13.2   Different Modes of Communication Between Traffic Control Consumers and Policy-Management Systems

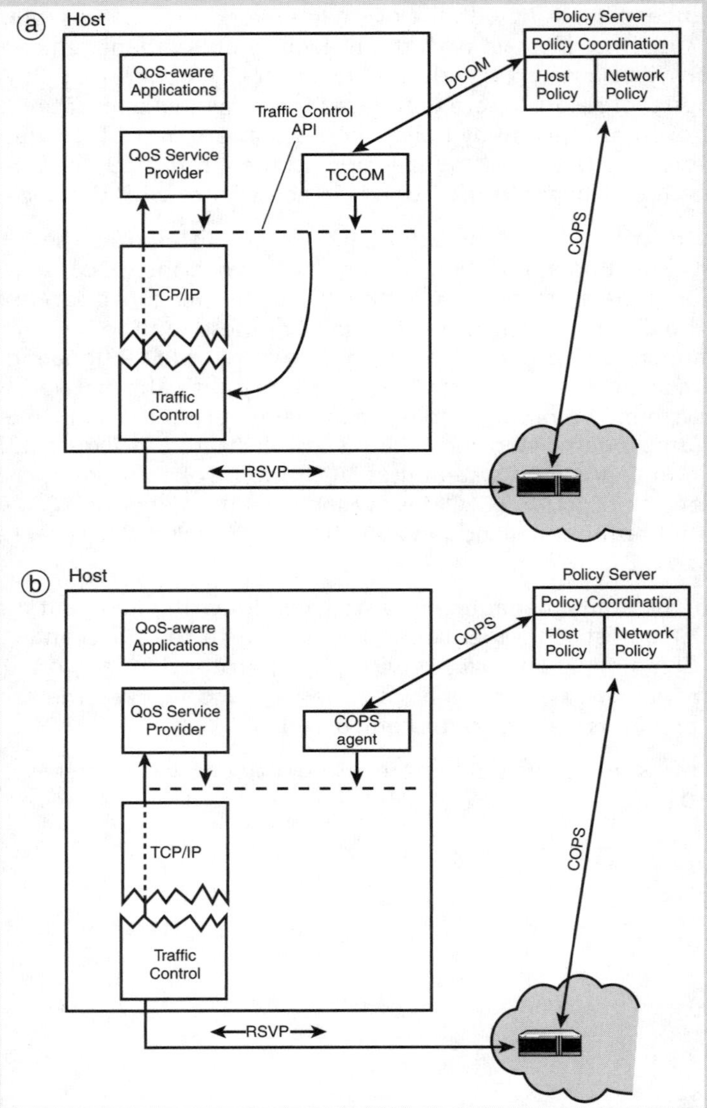

13.1.2 The Traffic Control API and traffic.dll

Traffic control consumers invoke the services of traffic control providers via the TC API. This API is mediated via a component of the operating system referred to as *traffic.dll* (*dll* stands for *dynamic link library*). This component resides in the user space of the operating system, as illustrated in Figure 13.3.

Figure 13.3   The Role of traffic.dll

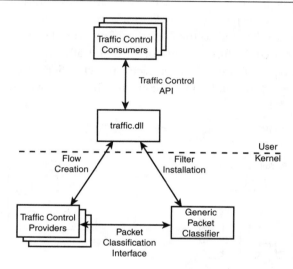

In response to calls to the TC API, traffic.dll configures the *generic packet classifier* (GPC) and the various drivers that provide traffic control functionality (the traffic control providers). In addition, traffic.dll provides information from the traffic control providers to the traffic control consumer. Configuration of the traffic control providers in coordination with the GPC can be quite complex; traffic.dll provides the important functionality of abstracting this complexity from the traffic control consumer.

13.1.3 Flows, Filters, and Classification

Fundamentally, the TC API enables the traffic control consumer to create *flows* and to determine the set of traffic that is directed to these flows. A flow is defined by certain behaviors, typically including a scheduling behavior and a marking behavior. A flow may include additional behavior such as fragmentation of packets (as in ISSLOW) or associated signaling (as in ATM UNI signaling). After the traffic control consumer has created a flow, it attaches one or more *filters* to the flow. The filters determine the set of packets that is directed to the flow and subjected to the defined behavior. (The term *filter* should be familiar from the discussion of classifiers and filters in Chapter 6.) Filters used for traffic control are based on the IP 5-tuple. They classify traffic based on the source and destination IP ports and addresses, as well as the IP protocol.

13.1.3.1 The Generic Packet Classifier

Filters are passed as parameters to the GPC. As traffic is submitted to the network stack for transmission, the GPC inspects each packet for a match to one or more of the filters. Matching packets are directed to the corresponding flow. The GPC is a generic classifier in the sense that it is used for functionality other than traffic control and can be configured to accept various types of filters. In its capacity as a classifier for traffic control functionality, it uses IP 5-tuple filters only. The role of the GPC in providing traffic control is illustrated in Figure 13.4.

Figure 13.4   The GPC and its Role in Providing Traffic Control

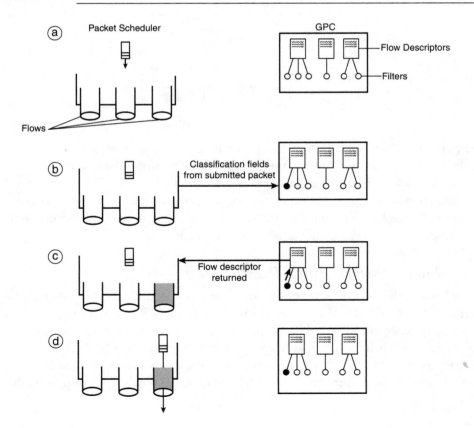

In Figure 13.4, the GPC is illustrated in cooperation with the QoS packet scheduler traffic control provider. It can cooperate in a similar manner with any other traffic control provider. The GPC contains a list of flow descriptors that describe traffic control flows that have been created in the traffic control provider. (These are opaque to the GPC, but not to the traffic control provider.) The GPC also maintains a list of filters, each of which is associated with a single flow descriptor. In Figure 13.4a, a packet arrives at the packet scheduler for transmission. The packet scheduler extracts classification information from the packet, which is submitted to the GPC (Figure 13.4b). The GPC matches the classification information against the list of filters. If a match is found, the GPC returns the corresponding flow descriptor to the packet scheduler (Figure 13.4c). The packet scheduler can now transmit the packet on the corresponding flow (Figure 13.4d). The interface between the traffic control provider and the GPC is optimized for performance.

13.1.4 Traffic Scheduling

Traffic scheduling functionality is one of the behaviors that can be implicitly invoked for a flow. Recall the queuing mechanisms that were described in Chapter 3, "Queuing Mechanisms." Traffic scheduling is the implementation of these queuing mechanisms on a transmitting host. The traffic control consumer does not directly specify a queuing mechanism. Each traffic control provider interprets the parameters provided by the traffic control consumer when a flow is created, providing the appropriate queuing behavior in response. The scheduling behavior of the native Windows 2000 traffic control providers will be discussed in further detail in the sections "The Structure and Behavior of the Packet Scheduler" and "The Structure and Behavior of ATMARP" later in this chapter.

13.1.5 Marking

Marking is another behavior that can be invoked via the TC API. DiffServ and user_ priority marking have been discussed previously. DiffServ marking is applied to any packets transmitted using the TCP/IP protocol, regardless of the underlying link layer. user_priority marking is applicable primarily to 802-style LANs. However, it may be applied to other link-layer technologies as well. The role of the native packet scheduler in effecting marking will be discussed in detail in the section "Marking Behavior" later in this chapter.

13.1.6 Signaling and Other Media-Specific Functionality

Traffic control providers may offer functionality in addition to scheduling and marking packets. Two specific examples of such functionality are link-layer signaling and link-layer fragmentation.

13.1.6.1 Link-Layer Signaling

Link-layer signaling applies to a number of media. The foremost example of link-layer signaling is ATM UNI signaling; another example is DOCSIS signaling, used to provide link-layer QoS on cable networks. Yet another example of link-layer signaling that is applicable to QoS is the emerging work on wireless QoS, based on signaling between transmitting nodes and base stations. Traffic control providers that use link-layer signaling may do so in response to requests via the TC API for the creation, modification, or deletion of a flow. Note that link-layer signaling does not replace network-layer RSVP signaling. Rather, link-layer signaling is a translation of the network-layer signaling to the protocol appropriate for the local medium. This is illustrated in Figure 13.5.

Figure 13.5	Link-Layer Signaling

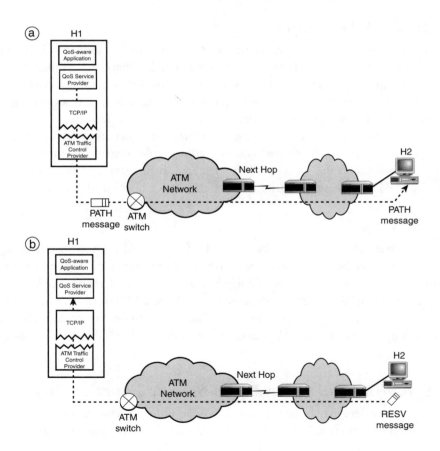

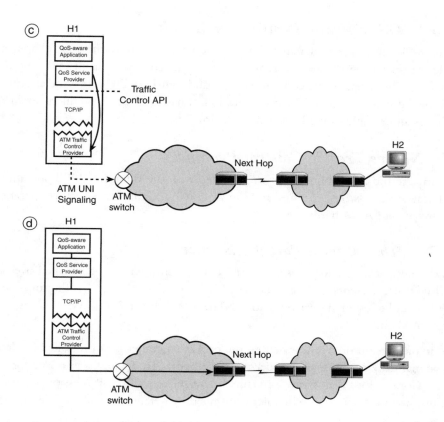

Figure 13.5 illustrates an ATM-attached sending host (H1) in the process of establishing an RSVP reservation to a remote host (H2). In Figure 13.5a, the QoS service provider on H1 generates an RSVP PATH message and transmits it to H2. In Figure 13.5b, H2 responds with an RSVP RESV message. Assuming that the RSVP request is admitted in the network, it eventually arrives back at H1's QoS service provider. The QoS service provider responds in Figure 13.5c by invoking greedy traffic control. To support the traffic control request from the QoS service provider, the ATM traffic control provider on H1 generates ATM UNI signaling to establish an ATM VC (Figure 13.5d) to the next-hop device on the route from H1 to H2.

13.1.6.2   Link-Layer Fragmentation

ISSLOW is an example of link-layer fragmentation. The packet scheduler and Windows 2000 native WAN drivers implement link-layer fragmentation under certain conditions to reduce the latency of interactive audio traffic. ISSLOW was described in Chapter 8, "QoS Over Layer 2 Media Other than 802."

13.1.6.3   Other Media-Specific Functionality

Specific traffic control providers may implement any means of traffic control appropriate to provide the traffic control services requested by traffic control consumers. The traffic control provider interprets traffic control requests and translates these into the appropriate action for the specific media. The configuration of hardware cell schedulers on an ATM interface is an example of media-specific functionality.

13.1.7   Native Traffic Control Providers

Two native traffic control providers are included with the Windows 2000 operating system. These are the *packet scheduler* and the *IP over ATM* component (in cooperation with ATM drivers and ATM hardware).

13.1.7.1   The Ethernet Packet Scheduler

The Ethernet packet scheduler is a software component that can be installed over any link-layer driver that presents itself as Ethernet, FDDI, or Token Ring. In addition, the packet scheduler can be installed over the native NDIS WAN driver. NDIS WAN is the driver that controls WAN interfaces.

In the initial version of Windows 2000, the packet scheduler is not installed by default. It must be manually configured on a per-interface basis. (To do so, use the Network and Dial-Up Connections dialog box.) In subsequent releases of the Professional version of the operating system, the packet scheduler is installed by default over all eligible interfaces.

The position of the packet scheduler in the network stack is illustrated in Figure 13.6.

Note

NDIS is the glue that interconnects network components in the network stack.

The subcomponents of the packet scheduler and their behavior will be discussed in depth in the section "The Structure and Behavior of the Packet Scheduler" later in this chapter. The following paragraphs offer a brief description of the traffic scheduling and marking functionality provided by the packet scheduler.

Figure 13.6   The Packet Scheduler

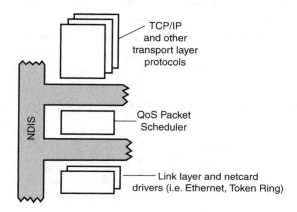

The Packet Scheduler

The Packet Scheduler and Traffic Scheduling

The packet scheduler provides packet-by-packet scheduling over LAN drivers and slow WAN drivers. It applies queuing mechanisms based on the parameters passed by traffic control consumers in the creation of a flow. The native packet scheduler is capable of the following queuing mechanisms:

- Strict priority queuing

- Deficit round-robin queuing

- Non-work-conserving traffic shaping

In the future, plug in modules for the packet scheduler may offer additional queuing functionality, such as class-based queuing (CBQ). (See the subsequent section titled "Scheduling Profiles.")

The Role of the Packet Scheduler in Marking

DiffServ marking in Windows 2000 is effected as a result of cooperation between the native packet scheduler and the TCP/IP protocol stack. Link-layer marking is effected by the packet scheduler in the case of 802-style LANs. In the case of other link-layer technologies, it is the responsibility of the relevant traffic control providers to do so as necessary. For certain link layers (such as ATM), marking may not be applicable.

Strictly speaking, DiffServ marking could be implemented without the cooperation of the packet scheduler. However, as will become clear later in this chapter, the native packet scheduler is in a unique position of being capable of determining the level of conformance of each transmitted packet to the parameters of the corresponding flow. This enables it to mark packets in accordance with their conformance level. In Windows 2000, DiffServ marking depends on the presence of the packet scheduler. In Windows 98, there is no packet scheduler. Certain versions of Windows 98 will provide DiffServ marking by the QoS service provider. However, because the QoS service provider cannot distinguish between conforming and nonconforming packets, these will not be marked differently.

13.1.7.2 Traffic Control over ATM and the IP over ATM Driver

Traffic control over ATM may be provided in various ways, depending on the configuration of the ATM network connection. Windows 2000 implements both *IP over ATM* (ATMARP) and *ATM LAN Emulation* (LANE). In the case of LANE, the ATM interface emulates an 802 LAN connection, making it possible to install the Ethernet packet scheduler over the ATM interface. Windows 2000 implements LANE version 1.0, which has no inherent support for QoS. Thus, in the case of ATM interfaces configured for LANE, traffic control functionality is provided exclusively by the packet scheduler.

In the case of IP over ATM, the native ATMARP driver is installed over the ATM adapter and its hardware driver. ATMARP acts as a traffic control provider in its own right, responding to calls from traffic control consumers by creating virtual circuits (VCs) of the appropriate service type and with the appropriate scheduling parameters. In this case, there is no packet scheduler. Instead, the inherent cell-scheduling capabilities of the ATM hardware are used.

13.2 The Traffic Control API

This section describes the TC API in detail and explains the general behavior of traffic control providers in response to TC API calls. The following section describes the specific behavior of the native packet scheduler. Note that this chapter should not be used as a specification of the TC API. For authoritative guidance on the TC API, refer to [TC_API]. Traffic control consumers must have administrative privileges to use the TC API.

Note

The TC API is discussed from the perspective of the traffic control consumer. Traffic control providers write to the complementary side of the API. From the consumer's perspective, the API is simplified by traffic.dll. From the provider's side, the API is somewhat more complicated. Traffic control providers must support NDIS (the standard network driver data and control plane interfaces), WMI (the Windows management interface), and the GPC interface.

13.2.1   Registering with Traffic Control

To invoke traffic control, traffic control consumers must first register as a client of traffic.dll by calling `TcRegisterClient`.

13.2.2   Selecting an Interface

After the traffic control consumer has registered with traffic.dll, it should call `TcEnumerateInterfaces`. Then traffic.dll responds by returning a list of those interfaces that are represented by a traffic control provider. Each interface is described by a friendly name and by the IP addresses associated with the interface.

After the traffic control consumer has identified an interface on which it is interested in invoking traffic control functionality, it opens the interface by calling the `TcOpenInterface` command. In return, traffic.dll returns a handle. This handle should be used for all subsequent traffic control calls on the interface.

13.2.3   Adding Flows and Filters

Most of the significant traffic control functionality is invoked by creating, modifying, and deleting flows and associated filters on open interfaces. These operations are described in the following sections.

13.2.3.1   Creating a Flow

To create a flow, the traffic control consumer calls the `TcAddFlow` API. This call is parameterized by the *generic flow* structure. The generic flow structure includes the same `SendingFlowspec` and `ReceivingFlowspec` structures that are used in calling the GQoS API. The `SendingFlowspec` structure specifies the service type to be applied to the flow and may include quantitative parameters in the form of a token bucket model. Most of the scheduling and marking behavior for the flow is derived from these parameters. The `ReceivingFlowspec` structure is not used at this time, but it enables traffic control for received traffic to be supported at a later date.

Traffic control providers interpret the information provided in the `SendingFlowspec` to deduce the appropriate traffic control functionality to provide in response. Providers make assumptions regarding the intent of the traffic control consumer in much the same way as the QoS service provider makes assumptions regarding the intent of QoS-enabled applications. As is the case with the GQoS API, traffic control consumers may include additional information in the generic flow structure to modify the default behavior of the traffic control provider. This information is included as a list of *TC objects* following the `SendingFlowspec` and the `ReceivingFlowspec`.

The effect of the service type, the token bucket parameters, and the various provider-specific parameters on scheduling and marking behavior will be described in depth in the section "The Structure and Behavior of the Packet Scheduler," later in this chapter.

13.2.3.2 Modifying and Deleting a Flow

After a flow has been created, its behavior can be modified at any time. Traffic control consumers modify flows by calling `TcModifyFlow` and supplying a modified parameter set.

Flows can also be deleted at any time (as long as no filters are attached). Traffic control consumers delete flows by calling `TcDeleteFlow` and specifying the handle of the flow to be deleted. No additional parameters are necessary.

13.2.3.3 Adding Filters to a Flow

The creation of a flow does not immediately result in any traffic control being applied. To apply traffic control, it is necessary to specify the set of traffic to which the behavior specified in the flow will be applied. This is achieved by adding one or more filters to the flow. Traffic control consumers add filters to flows by calling the `TcAddFilter` API. With this call, the traffic control consumer specifies a *pattern* and a *mask* using the *generic filter* structure. The pattern specifies values of fields in a packet's TCP/IP header, such as IP addresses and ports. The mask specifies which fields and which parts of each field must be matched for a transmitted packet to be directed to the corresponding flow. Thus, by including a mask, it is possible to specify filters that will match traffic aggregates.

Because the QoS service provider creates per-conversation flows, it always adds a single unmasked filter to each flow (all fields defining the conversation must match for a packet to be directed to the flow). However, third-party traffic control consumers will often create flows for aggregate traffic (such as all traffic to subnet 4.0.0.0). In this case, third-party traffic control consumers may add multiple filters to a single flow, any of which may be masked.

13.2.3.4 Deleting Filters

Traffic control consumers delete filters by calling `TcDeleteFilter`. As a result, the set of traffic that had been matched by the filter will no longer be directed to the flow.

13.2.4 Setting and Querying Traffic Control Parameters

Traffic control consumers may use the TC API to set and/or query traffic control parameters on a per-interface or per-flow basis, as described in the following paragraphs. These parameters will be discussed in further depth in the context of the packet scheduler behavior.

13.2.4.1 Per-Interface Traffic Control Parameters

Certain parameters are specific to certain traffic control providers. Others are generic and are available across traffic control providers. The following list exemplifies per-interface traffic control parameters:

- Maximum reservable bandwidth (generic)

- Maximum MTU supported (generic)

- Remaining uncommitted bandwidth (generic)

- Link speed (generic)

- Maximum outstanding sends (packet scheduler only)

- Flow count (generic)

- Detailed statistics, such as bytes/packets queued and sent (generic)

13.2.4.2 Per-Flow Traffic Control Parameters

Traffic control consumers may also use the TC API to query per-flow statistics. These statistics include information such as the following:

- Bytes transmitted on the flow

- Packets transmitted on the flow

- Number of nonconforming packets submitted on the flow

- Packets queued awaiting transmission

13.2.5 Remote Traffic Control

All traffic control functionality is also exposed via a COM interface. As a consequence, it is possible to invoke traffic control remotely. This feature enables traffic control functionality on hosts to be controlled from a centralized network management console (as illustrated previously). To invoke traffic control remotely, the calling program must have administrative privileges on the target host.

13.2.5.1 Lifetime of Flows and Filters

Flows and filters created via the TC API can be made to persist as long as the host operating system is running. They are cleared when the system is rebooted. When the TC API is used remotely, flows and filters persist after the remote agent is disconnected, until the target host is rebooted.

There is often a need for flows and filters to persist through reboots of the target host operating system. In this case, a service can be written to call the TC API following system reboots and recreate the required flows and filters.

13.3 The Structure and Behavior of the Packet Scheduler

The Ethernet packet scheduler is one of two native traffic control providers available in Windows 2000. This section describes the packet scheduler in detail.

13.3.1 Instances of the Packet Scheduler

As described previously, the packet scheduler can be installed over both LAN and WAN interfaces. A separate *instance* of the packet scheduler is invoked for each instance of either of the two types of interfaces. Each instance of the packet scheduler operates independently from other instances. Certain per-interface registry parameters may be used to control the corresponding instance of the packet scheduler. Instances of the packet scheduler are illustrated in Figure 13.7.

Figure 13.7   Multiple Instances of the Packet Scheduler

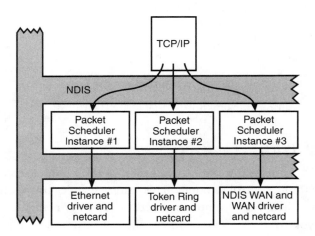

Figure 13.7 is similar to Figure 13.6, with the exception that, in Figure 13.6, the separate instances of the packet scheduler were not identified.

13.3.2 The Internal Structure of the Packet Scheduler

To discuss the behavior of the packet scheduler in detail, it is necessary to review the components of the packet scheduler. These are illustrated in Figure 13.8.

Figure 13.8   Internal Structure of the Packet Scheduler

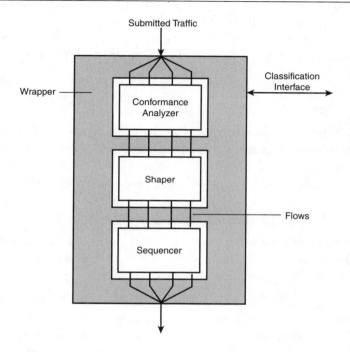

13.3.2.1 The Wrapper

The packet scheduler is represented to the operating system network stack by a wrapper. This wrapper handles the various operating system interfaces that are necessary to provide traffic control functionality. Within the wrapper, it is possible to construct a stack of scheduling modules. The default configuration of the packet scheduler includes the following modules:

- Conformance analyzer

- Shaper

- Sequencer

The wrapper intercepts packets submitted for transmission from network protocol modules. It uses the GPC to direct the submitted packets to the corresponding flows. The packets are then passed to the topmost scheduling module inside the packet scheduler. From here, they are passed down the stack, from module to module, until they are submitted to the netcard driver for transmission.

The wrapper also derives internal traffic control parameters from parameters supplied externally (primarily via the TC API). The primary internal parameters affecting the behavior of the packet scheduler are the ShapeDiscardMode of the flow, the token bucket parameters associated with the flow, and the *internal priority* of the flow. (These parameters are discussed in detail later in this chapter, in the section "Parameters Affecting Scheduling Behavior.")

13.3.2.2   Scheduling Profiles

A stack of scheduling modules is referred to as a *scheduling profile*. The default profile consists of the conformance analyzer, shaper, and sequencer, as described previously. It is possible to construct alternate scheduling profiles. Different instances of the packet scheduler may operate with different scheduling profiles, as appropriate for the particular underlying media.

13.3.2.3   The Conformance Analyzer

The conformance analyzer is the topmost module in the default scheduling stack. The role of this module is to determine the *conformance time* of packets that are submitted for transmission.

The conformance analyzer uses the token bucket parameters from the SendingFlowspec associated with a flow to determine the earliest time at which the next packet may be transmitted on the flow without violating the token bucket parameters. This is the *next conformance time*. When a packet is submitted for transmission, the conformance analyzer notes the current time and compares it against the next conformance time. If the packet is submitted too soon, the packet is deemed nonconforming, and the conformance analyzer stamps it with the next conformance time before passing it to the shaper. If the packet is not submitted too soon, it is deemed conforming, and the conformance analyzer stamps it with the current time and passes it to the shaper.

Note that the conformance analyzer does not delay or reorder packets. It simply stamps them with a conformance time and passes them on to the shaper. The conformance time is stamped in the packet wrapper, which is visible only to the operating system. The packet header and data areas are unaffected.

In the unlikely event that the ShapeDiscardMode of the flow is configured for discard behavior, the conformance analyzer will actually discard nonconforming packets. Discard mode is never invoked by default; the traffic control consumer must explicitly request it.

The conformance analyzer relies on token bucket parameters associated with a flow to determine the conformance time of each packet. (Flows that are created for the Guaranteed or Controlled Load Services are considered *quantitative* flows and have token bucket parameters associated with them by default.) On flows that do not have associated token bucket parameters, the conformance analyzer will be inactive, effectively deeming all packets to be conforming at the time they are submitted. Certain traffic control consumers may use the TC API to associate token bucket parameters with nonquantitative flows. In this case, the conformance analyzer will be active and will use the associated token bucket parameters to determine the conformance time of submitted packets.

13.3.2.4 *The Shaper*

The shaper is the next module in the packet scheduler's default stack. Its purpose is to provide the non-work-conserving queuing functionality of the packet scheduler. (Refer to Chapter 3 for a discussion of non-work-conserving queuing.) The shaper operates only on flows on which the `ShapeDiscardMode` is configured for shape behavior.

> **Note**
>
> There is an exception to this rule. When a flow is created with a finite *peak rate*, the shaper will shape the flow to the specified peak rate (but not to the token rate) regardless of the `ShapeDiscard` mode. The reason for this is as follows.
>
> Applications are expected to request shape mode when they require assistance in shaping traffic to conform to a certain token bucket profile. When they do not request shape mode, they are expected to shape their own traffic. In both cases, it is expected that the application wants its traffic to be shaped so that it is not penalized by policers in downstream network devices. Although applications may be capable of shaping transmitted traffic to an average rate, the peak rate is more problematic. Specifically, if an application submits to the network stack a buffer that is larger than the packet size, the network stack will create multiple packets and will transmit these back to back (violating any finite peak rate). Thus, by shaping to the peak rate, the packet scheduler allows the application to shape to the average rate and assists it to be sure that it is not penalized for its inevitable failure to shape to the peak rate.
>
> Note that even applications that do not specify a peak rate are automatically shaped to a peak rate that is equal to the media rate. This is the unavoidable result of sending on a media that has a finite rate.

The shaper compares the conformance time stamped in each packet against the current time. If the conformance time is earlier or equal to the current time, the packet is immediately passed to the sequencer. If the conformance time is later than the current time, the packet will be retained in the shaper until the current time is equal to its conformance time. In this manner, the shaper can be used to shape traffic on a flow so that it conforms to the associated token bucket parameters.

Packets submitted on flows that are not configured for shape mode will be passed immediately to the sequencer. Flows created for the Guaranteed Service type will, by default, be created in shape mode. Flows created for other service types will not. However, in certain cases, the traffic control consumer may use the TC API to explicitly configure flows of other service types for shape behavior.

13.3.2.5 The Sequencer

The sequencer is the lowermost module in the default packet scheduler configuration. The role of the sequencer is to determine the sequence in which packets are transmitted from different flows when the transmitting link is congested. Packets pass through the conformance analyzer and the shaper. From the shaper, they are passed to the sequencer. The sequencer then passes these packets to the netcard driver for transmission. If packets are submitted to the sequencer at a higher rate than the network can accommodate them, then packets must accumulate either in the netcard or in the sequencer. (The MaxOutstandingSends parameter, discussed later in this section, determines whether packets accumulate in the netcard or the sequencer when congestion occurs.)

If the network is not congested, packets do not accumulate in the netcard or the sequencer. In this case, the sequencer passes packets from the shaper to the netcard driver in a first-in, first-out sequence, and the netcard immediately passes the packets to the network. However, when congestion occurs and packets accumulate in the sequencer, the sequencer determines the next packet that should be passed to the netcard driver as soon as resources become available in the network. The operation of the sequencer is illustrated in Figure 13.9, under both noncongested (Figure 13.9a) and congested (Figure 13.9b) conditions.

Note

Note that in the scenarios illustrated in Figure 13.9, the MaxOutstandingSends parameter is chosen to prevent the accumulation of packets in the netcard. Thus, congestion in the network causes congestion in the sequencer. See the "Effect of the MaxOutstandingSends Parameter" section later in this chapter.

Figure 13.9   Operation of the Sequencer Under Noncongested and Congested Conditions

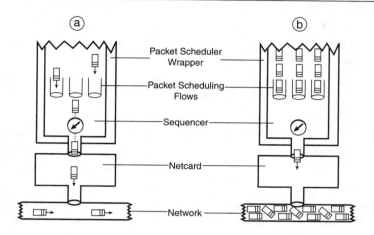

The sequencer applies the DRR+ work-conserving queuing algorithm to queued traffic. (The DRR+ scheme is described in Chapter 3.) DRR+ groups flows into priority classes. When a slot becomes available for transmission, the sequencer will always select a packet from a flow in the highest priority class. If there are no flows in this class, the sequencer selects a packet from a flow in the next-highest priority class. Whenever there are multiple flows in the same priority class, the sequencer uses a deficit round-robin method to determine the flow to be serviced next.

The service type for which a flow is created determines its priority class. (The mapping from service type to priority class will be discussed later in this section.) The lowest priority class is reserved for nonconforming flows. For flows in the same priority class, the DRR quantum is determined based on the token rate associated with the traffic flow (or a default value, in certain cases).

In addition to its role in sequencing packets, the sequencer applies a final conformance check to each packet. If the packet arrives at or after its conformance time, it is passed to the netcard driver. If the packet arrives before its conformance time, the sequencer causes the DSCP and 802 user_priority values marked in the packet to be re-marked to reflect the packet's conformance status. On shape-mode flows, packets are retained in the shaper until they become conforming. Thus, packets on these flows should never be re-marked in the sequencer. However, packets on nonshaped flows are passed directly through the shaper. Therefore, these packets may arrive at the sequencer before their conformance time. These packets will be re-marked. In addition, when a packet arrives before its conformance time, the entire flow is removed from its priority class and is placed in the lowest priority class until packets on the flow are again conforming.

Utility of the Sequencer

On high-speed interfaces, the rate at which the host network stack generates traffic rarely exceeds the capacity of the interface. Thus, the interface is not congested and the sequencer has no effect. On WAN interfaces, however, the interface is often congested, and the sequencer may have a significant effect.

13.3.2.6 The Timestamp Module

The *timestamp* module is a diagnostic tool used to characterize network performance. It can be installed in series with other packet-scheduling modules. When used in conjunction with the appropriate user-layer test programs, the timestamp module inserts both transmitted and received timestamps in test packets transiting the packet scheduler. By correlating and analyzing these timestamps on both a sending and a receiving host, it is possible to accurately characterize network performance to determine packet-by-packet latency. For further details on the timestamp module and related test tools, see Appendix A, "Troubleshooting and Demonstrating Windows 2000 QoS Functionality."

The timestamp module is used as illustrated in Figure 13.10.

Figure 13.10 Use of the Timestamp Module

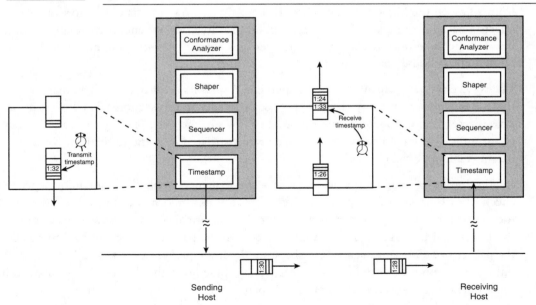

13.3.3   *Parameters Affecting Scheduling Behavior*

Packets are scheduled on each flow according to certain parameters associated with the flow. The parameters that most affect scheduling behavior are the `ShapeDiscardMode` of the flow, the token bucket parameters associated with the flow and the *internal priority* of the flow. These are discussed in the following paragraphs.

13.3.3.1   *The* `ShapeDiscardMode`

Four `ShapeDiscard` modes exist: *shape* mode, *borrow* mode, *discard* mode, and *borrow+* mode. The packet scheduler derives the `ShapeDiscardMode` directly from the service type associated with each flow, as follows:

- Network Control Service traffic—Borrow mode

- Guaranteed Service—Shape mode

- Controlled Load Service—Borrow mode

- Best-effort service—Borrow mode

- Null Service—Borrow mode

Traffic control consumers may override the default `ShapeDiscardMode` by explicitly specifying a `ShapeDiscard` mode object for the flow.

Shape Mode

Shape-mode flows are forced to conform to the token bucket parameters specified for the flow. Packets arriving in the shaper module before their conformance time are retained in the shaper until their conformance time arrives.

Borrow Mode

On borrow-mode flows, all packets are marked with a conformance time but are passed through the shaper directly to the sequencer, regardless of their conformance time. Packets arriving in the sequencer before their conformance time will be re-marked, and the corresponding flow will be demoted to the lowest internal priority. Because traffic on borrow-mode flows is not delayed in the shaper, it can *borrow* unused capacity from other flows—hence the name *borrow* mode.

Borrow+ Mode

Borrow+ mode is identical to borrow mode, except that packets on borrow+ mode flows are never deemed nonconforming. For further details on borrow+ mode, see the section "Emulating Simple Weighted-Queuing Schemes, later in this chapter."

Discard Mode

In discard mode, packets deemed nonconforming are simply discarded by the conformance analyzer.

13.3.3.2 Token Bucket Parameters

The conformance analyzer uses the token bucket parameters associated with a flow to determine the conformance time of each packet. The token rate parameter must be supplied via the TC API. The token bucket size and the peak bandwidth parameters can be defaulted by the packet scheduler if they are not explicitly supplied. The token bucket size defaults to the MTU size indicated by the underlying netcard driver. The peak bandwidth defaults to the link speed.

13.3.3.3 Internal Priority

The internal priority of a flow determines the priority class in which it is served by the sequencer. Internal priority is derived from the service type of a flow (as specified via the TC API). The service types recognized by the packet scheduler are listed here:

- Network Control Service traffic

- Guaranteed Service

- Controlled Load Service

- Best-effort service and Null Service

The service types are listed in descending order of internal priority. The internal priority of a flow always corresponds to the service type and cannot be modified except by the flow's conformance status. A flow that is deemed nonconforming is assigned the lowest priority (lower than best-effort traffic) until it becomes conforming once again.

13.3.4 Derivation of Parameters Affecting Scheduling Behavior

Figure 13.11 illustrates the derivation of the ShapeDiscardMode and internal priority as a function of service type.

Figure 13.11 Derivation of `ShapeDiscardMode` and Internal Priority

Service Type	ShapeDiscard Mode	Internal Priority
Network Control	Borrow	3
Guaranteed	Shape	2
Controlled Load	Borrow	1
Null Service Best-Effort	Borrow	0
Any non-conforming traffic	—	-1

Note

Priority 3 is highest priority, and priority –1 is the lowest. Packets deemed nonconforming are all handled together at lower priority than best-effort traffic, regardless of service type.

13.3.5 Overall Scheduling Behavior

Previous sections described the components of the packet scheduler and the various parameters that affect their behavior. This section describes the net scheduling behavior that results when flows of different types coexist in the packet scheduler.

Figure 13.12 is a simplistic illustration of the traffic control scheduling behavior under typical operating conditions.

The conformance analyzer monitors traffic on all flows. It marks the appropriate conformance time for all packets on Guaranteed Service (shape mode) flows and marks traffic on other flows as conforming or nonconforming. Traffic on Guaranteed Service flows is then passed to the shaper, where it is shaped to the corresponding token bucket parameters before being passed to the sequencer. Traffic on other flows passes through the shaper without delay. In the sequencer, traffic is classified into one of five priority levels based on service type and conformance status (as tabulated in Figure 13.11). Note that the network control priority level is not illustrated. Traffic is handled *between* priority levels using strict-priority queuing. Within each priority level, traffic is served using work-conserving DRR queuing. In addition, traffic in higher priorities is constrained to prevent it from starving lower-priority traffic.

Figure 13.12 Scheduling Behavior Under Typical Operating Conditions

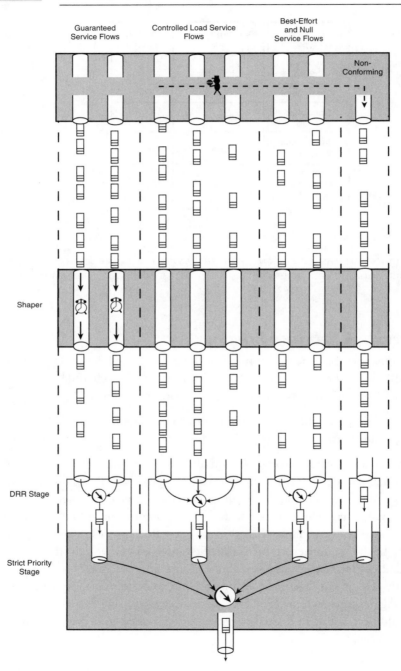

13.3.5.1 The Default Best-Effort Flow

By default, the packet scheduler always creates a default flow with the best-effort service type. This flow carries any traffic that is not classified to an explicitly created flow. No token bucket parameters are specified for the default best-effort flow. By default, all flows with the best-effort service type are created in borrow mode. As a result, traffic on these flows is never delayed in the shaper; it is passed directly to the sequencer.

If no other flows exist in the sequencer, then all packets on the default best-effort flow are passed to the network as soon as they are generated by the application, and the full network capacity is available to the flow.

On the other hand, if there are competing flows in the sequencer, packets on the default best-effort flow may be subjected to queuing delays. If the other flows are of a higher internal priority than the best-effort flow (as determined by the service type of the competing flow), then these will be serviced before the best-effort flow is serviced. As a result, the best-effort flow will be allotted only the network capacity remaining after the higher-priority flows have been serviced.

As traffic on higher priority flows diminishes, excess capacity is immediately available to traffic on the best-effort flow. Because this traffic is not shaped, it takes all available resources. In this manner, the best-effort flow *borrows* capacity from higher-priority flows.

13.3.5.2 Explicitly Created Best-Effort Flows

In certain cases, traffic control consumers may explicitly create a best-effort flow. For example, the QoS service provider temporarily forces application flows to the best-effort service level until the network admits them. When a best-effort flow is explicitly created, it competes in the sequencer with other explicitly created best-effort flows and with the default best-effort flow.

The sequencer shares available network capacity among multiple best-effort flows based on the token rate specified for the flow. The token rate is used both to determine the DRR quantum for the flow and to demote the flow's priority when it is nonconforming. Best-effort flows can be created without specifying a token rate. When best-effort flows are created without a token rate, they are never deemed nonconforming. However, the sequencer assigns a default quantum to these flows, equal to the MTU size of the corresponding interface.

13.3.5.3 Admission Control

Controlled Load Service flows and Guaranteed Service flows are explicitly created by a traffic control consumer. Based on their service types, these are assigned a higher internal priority than best-effort flows. As a result, traffic on these flows will pre-empt traffic in the sequencer on the default best-effort flow. Although this is the intended effect, it is necessary to limit the amount of traffic on high-priority flows so that it does not completely starve traffic on the best-effort flow. This is achieved by applying admission control and by using the conformance analyzer to police traffic on these flows.

When a flow created via the TC API maps to an internal priority higher than that associated with best-effort flows, the wrapper component of the packet scheduler applies admission control. It does so based on the token rate of the flow. (Requests to create high-priority flows that do not specify a token rate are failed with an error.) The packet scheduler tracks the total amount of bandwidth admitted and compares it against the NonBestEffortLimit. If the incremental bandwidth required for a flow would exceed the NonBestEffortLimit, then the packet scheduler rejects the creation of the flow. In this manner, admission control protects best-effort flows (and any flows with equivalent internal priority).

The NonBestEffortLimit is a per-netcard parameter. By default, it is equal to 20% of the media capacity. (The NonBestEffortLimit can be overridden under administrative control by creating a corresponding registry entry.)

> **Note**
>
> Note that, in the standard Windows 2000 product, admission control is not applied on WAN media.

Because best-effort flows are handled at the lowest priority (other than nonconforming traffic), they cannot starve other traffic and therefore are never subjected to admission control.

13.3.5.4 Controlled Load Service Flows

Although Controlled Load Service flows are not admitted beyond the NonBestEffortLimit, this in itself is not sufficient to protect resources for best-effort traffic. Recall that Controlled Load Service flows are, by default, scheduled in borrow mode. If an application violates its specified token bucket parameters, its traffic will be passed directly to the sequencer, where it will compete unfairly with best-effort traffic.

The conformance analyzer and sequencer work together to prevent this from occurring. Any traffic on Controlled Load Service flows that violates the token bucket parameters specified for the flow will be marked as nonconforming in the conformance analyzer. When this traffic reaches the sequencer, the entire flow will be demoted to a priority class lower than that of the best-effort flows. (Note that because the entire flow is demoted, rather than a single packet, there is no risk of reordering packets within a flow that is non-conforming.) When the flow becomes conforming, the entire flow will again be promoted to the priority level to which it is entitled.

Note

A nonconforming flow can become conforming if it has been delayed in the sequencer long enough that the current time is later than the conformance time of the packet at the head of the queue.

The net effect is that, as long as a Controlled Load Service flow remains conforming, its traffic will be prioritized above that of best-effort flows. Controlled Load Service traffic in excess of the token bucket parameters will be passed to the network as long as the network is not congested. However, in the case that congestion does occur, the excess traffic on the Controlled Load Service flow will not jeopardize traffic on best-effort flows. In a sense, this excess traffic borrows from the best-effort flows.

13.3.5.5 Guaranteed Service Flows

Guaranteed Service flows are subjected to the same admission control criteria as Controlled Load Service flows. Note, however, that Guaranteed Service flows are created, by default, in shape mode. This means that traffic on Guaranteed Service flows is retained in the shaper module of the packet scheduler until it becomes conforming. As a result, traffic on Guaranteed Service flows cannot borrow resources in excess of their token bucket parameters. However, all traffic submitted on Guaranteed Service flows is ensured to be conforming and is ensured to be transmitted at the corresponding priority.

13.3.5.6 Null Service Flows

Null Service flows are mapped to the same internal priority and ShapeDiscardMode as best-effort flows. Because the Null Service is used for nonquantifiable traffic, no token bucket parameters are associated with these flows. As a result, traffic on these flows is scheduled using the default DRR quantum (equal to the MTU size for the interface), but the flow is never deemed nonconforming (and therefore is never demoted in priority). Therefore, Null Service flows are scheduled equivalently to best-effort flows that do not have associated token bucket parameters.

13.3.5.7 Network Control Service Flows

Traffic on Network Control Service flows is allotted the highest priority in the sequencer. However, Network Control Service flows are not subject to the admission control and policing applied to other high-priority flows. As such, Network Control Service flows stand to starve traffic on lower-priority flows. Therefore, these flows must be created and used with caution.

Network Control Service is intended for low-volume, nonquantifiable traffic that is critical to the health of the network. Clearly, Network Control Service traffic should be allotted the highest priority because a failure to deliver Network Control Service traffic would result in failure of the network. Because this traffic is sporadic by nature, it is difficult to quantify it for the purpose of admission control. Fortunately, it tends to be low in volume.

Thus, lower-priority traffic must accept the necessity of Network Control Service traffic and must occasionally yield resources to it as a sort of network tax. The burden is on the traffic control consumer to use the Network Control Service carefully, for network critical traffic only and with restraint.

> **Note**
>
> Unlike the other service types, the Network Control Service type is not exposed directly to applications via the GQoS API. It is exposed only via the TC API. The QoS service provider invokes this service type for RSVP traffic.

13.3.5.8 Sharing Resources Among Flows of Equal Priority

The sequencer shares resources among flows of equal priority by using deficit round-robin scheduling (DRR). (See Chapter 3 for a discussion of DRR scheduling.) In DRR, flows are serviced at a rate proportional to their *quantum*. The packet scheduler assigns each flow within a priority class a quantum that is proportional to the flow's token bucket rate. Thus, as expected, within a priority class, more resources are allotted to flows with a higher token rate. Admission control should ensure that sufficient capacity is available to accommodate at least the requested token rate of all admitted flows.

13.3.5.9 Emulating Simple Weighted-Queuing Schemes

In borrow mode, the token rate parameter assigned to a flow is used both by the conformance analyzer (to determine the conformance of traffic on the flow) and by the sequencer (to assign an appropriate DRR quantum to the flow). In certain cases, the traffic control consumer may want to assign different weights to a number of flows that are not readily quantifiable and to simply divide the link capacity among the flows according to their relative weights. This is how weighted fair queuing works (see Chapter 3).

Different weights can be assigned by specifying different token rates for each flow. However, the token rates will have the side effect of causing the flows to be policed and excess traffic to be demoted as nonconforming.

Borrow+ mode makes it possible to use the token rate solely for the purpose of controlling the relative weights assigned to the flows, without causing traffic to be demoted for non-conformance. Thus, the conformance analyzer deems all packets on borrow+ mode flows to be conforming. As a result, the traffic control consumer can use the borrow+ mode to simulate simple weighted work-conserving queuing.

13.3.5.10 *Effects of Token Bucket Parameters on Scheduling Behavior*

Token bucket parameters are typically supplied by the traffic control consumer for both Guaranteed and Controlled Load Service flows. These should be selected carefully because they may have a profound impact on scheduling behavior.

Shape-Mode Flows

On shape-mode flows, the token bucket parameters are actually used to shape transmitted traffic. By selecting a token bucket size close to the packet size and a peak rate close to the token rate, traffic control consumers can shape traffic smoothly, emulating ATM constant bit rate profiles. Larger token bucket sizes and peak rates that are greater than the token rate will allow burstier traffic to be passed to the network. Note that a larger token bucket size will not cause traffic to be shaped to a bursty profile. If the application submits traffic smoothly, it will still be passed to the network smoothly. However, if the application generates bursty traffic, the larger token bucket size will allow bursts up to the token bucket size to be passed to the network unchanged.

Traffic control consumers must specify a token bucket size that is at least equal to or larger than the MTU size on the medium. This is to avoid the deadlock that would result if packets larger than the token bucket size were submitted to the shaper for transmission.

> **Note**
>
> Traffic control consumers should be careful to specify a token rate that is equal to or greater than the average rate at which traffic will be generated by the application. If the application consistently generates traffic at a rate that exceeds the token rate, traffic will back up in the shaper, consuming precious memory resources.
>
> Guaranteed Service flows are created in shape mode by default.

Borrow-Mode Flows

The choice of token bucket parameters does not directly affect the profile of transmitted traffic on borrow-mode flows. In fact, if the network is uncongested, the token bucket parameters will have no bearing on the transmitted traffic profile. However, if the network is congested, then traffic in excess of the token bucket profile will be demoted in priority and may cause traffic on the flow to be delayed, modifying the transmitted traffic profile.

> **Note**
>
> Controlled Load Service flows are created in borrow mode by default.

13.3.5.11   Effect of the MaxOutstandingSends Parameter

The MaxOutstandingSends parameter is a registry-configurable, per-interface parameter. It determines the effectiveness of the sequencer under congested conditions. The sequencer passes packets to the underlying netcard driver for transmission and receives notification from the netcard driver when each packet has been transmitted onto the network. Thus, the sequencer can track the number of packets outstanding in the netcard driver. The MaxOutstandingSends parameter determines the number of packets that the sequencer will allow to be outstanding in the netcard driver.

A large MaxOutstandingSends parameter enables the sequencer to pass packets to the underlying netcard driver without waiting for notification that the previous packet has been transmitted. This pipelines the transmission process, thereby improving performance on uncongested networks. However, if the network becomes congested, a large MaxOustandingSends value will cause packets to accumulate in the netcard driver rather than in the sequencer. As a result, the sequencer will have limited control over the sequencing of packets.

Conversely, if the MaxOutstandingSends parameter is small, the sequencer will be capable of more effectively controlling the sequencing of packets when the network is congested, but performance may be compromised when the network is not congested (because pipelining is not possible).

The two cases described are illustrated in Figure 13.13. In Figure 13.13a, MaxOutstandingSends is very small. As a result, packets awaiting network capacity cannot be passed to the netcard. Instead, they accumulate in the sequencer and are subjected to the sequencer's queuing behavior. In Figure 13.13b, MaxOutstandingSends is large. Packets awaiting network capacity are allowed to accumulate in the netcard. Consequently, packets do not accumulate in the sequencer, and the sequencer's queuing behavior has no impact on traffic scheduling.

Figure 13.13   The Effect of the `MaxOutstandingSends` Parameter

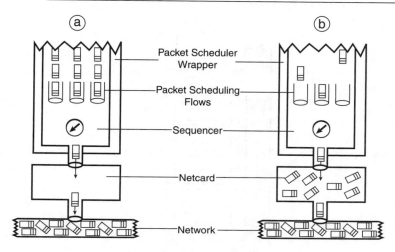

Note

Note that the discussion of the effect of the `MaxOutstandingSend` behavior assumes that the netcard has sufficient capacity to absorb packets awaiting transmission on the network. If the netcard driver's capacity is exceeded, then network congestion will be reflected at the sequencer, regardless of the value of `MaxOutstandingSends`. However, most netcards drivers have sufficient capacity to prevent this from occurring.

13.3.5.12 Scheduling Behavior on WAN Links

When the packet scheduler is used over WAN links, it does not reside directly over the netcard and its driver. Instead, NDIS WAN resides between the packet scheduler and the WAN netcard and driver, as illustrated in Figure 13.14. NDIS WAN is a native driver that operates over WAN netcard drivers. It provides various point-to-point protocol support, including multilink support.

When operating over NDIS WAN, the packet scheduler may operate in normal mode or in ISSLOW mode. The speed of the WAN link determines in which of these modes the scheduler operates. On high-speed links (above 128Kbps), the scheduler operates in normal mode. On low-speed links (128Kbps and below), it operates in ISSLOW mode.

Figure 13.14   Installation of the Packet Scheduler over NDIS WAN

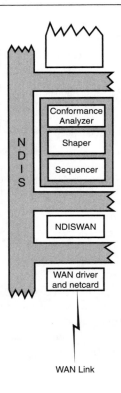

WAN Link

ISSLOW Mode

ISSLOW mode uses NDIS WAN's link-layer fragmentation capability to reduce latency for certain traffic on slow links. (For an explanation of ISSLOW, see Chapter 8, "QoS over Layer 2 Media Other Than 802.") When the packet scheduler operates in ISSLOW mode, it uses heuristics to determine when a certain flow requires ISSLOW latency reduction. Flows created for the Guaranteed or Controlled Load Service, to carry small packets at a slow rate, are considered to be carrying voice traffic in need of latency control. When these flows are detected, the packet scheduler causes NDIS WAN to apply ISSLOW fragmentation to other flows. The packet scheduler groups flows into nonfragmented (latency-sensitive) and fragmented (all other) flows. NDIS WAN fragments traffic on all fragmented flows to a specified link-layer fragment size. It services fragments from each of the two groups in round-robin fashion. As a result, traffic that is not latency-sensitive never delays latency-sensitive traffic by more than a single fragment's transmission time.

13.3.6 Marking Behavior

This section describes the marking behavior of the packet scheduler. Unlike scheduling, marking is considered greedy behavior because packets marked for a higher priority may displace other packets in the network. On the other hand, scheduling behavior is non-greedy. No matter what scheduling is applied, the packet scheduler will never send traffic at a rate higher than if it was not scheduled.

13.3.6.1 Parameters Affecting Marking Behavior

The primary parameters affecting the marking behavior of the packet scheduler are the service type and conformance status of a flow. A default mapping exists both for conforming and for nonconforming packets.

DSCP Marking

The default mapping from service type to DSCP for conforming packets is as follows:

- Network Control Service—0x30

- Guaranteed Service—0x28

- Controlled Load Service—0x18

- Null Service—0x00

- Best-effort—0x00

> **Note**
>
> These DSCPs select the class selector PHBs CS6, CS5, CS3, and CS0, which correspond to IP precedence values 6, 5, 3, and 0, respectively.

The default mapping from service type to DSCP for nonconforming packets marks all packets to 0x00.

It is possible to override the default markings. The first mechanism for doing so is by creating an alternate mapping table under the per-interface registry parameters `DiffServByteMappingConforming` and `DiffServByteMappingNonConforming` (corresponding to conforming and nonconforming packets, respectively). This is a static mechanism in the sense that it overrides markings for all flows of a given service type.

The second mechanism for overriding the DSCP marking behavior is by use of the `DCLASS` traffic control object. Traffic control consumers can supply this object via the TC API on a flow-by-flow basis. The `DCLASS` object takes precedence over both the default mapping table and the registry-based mapping table. It causes packets to be marked with the corresponding DSCP, regardless of the service type of the corresponding flow. The DCLASS object is more dynamic than the mapping tables in the sense that it can cause variations in marking from flow to flow, regardless of the flow's service type.

802 user_priority *Marking*

802 user_priority marks are derived in much the same way that DSCP marks are derived. The default mapping from service type to 802 user_priority for conforming packets is as follows:

- Network Control Service—0x07
- Guaranteed Service—0x05
- Controlled Load Service—0x04
- Null Service—0x00
- Best-effort—0x00
- Nonconforming—0x01

Note that there is no separate table specifying user_priority values for nonconforming packets. By default, all nonconforming packets are marked 0x01, regardless of service type.

It is possible to override the default 802 user_priority markings. The first mechanism for doing so is by creating an alternate mapping table under the per-interface registry parameter UserPriorityMapping.

The second mechanism for overriding the user_priority marking behavior is by use of the TCLASS traffic control object. Traffic control consumers can supply this object via the TC API on a flow-by-flow basis. The TCLASS object takes precedence over both the default mapping table and the registry-based mapping table. It causes packets to be marked with the corresponding user_priority value, regardless of the service type of the corresponding flow.

Marking for Non-802 Media

The packet scheduler does not directly mark the 802 user_priority in the MAC header of the transmitted packets. Instead, it inserts the user_priority value in the packet wrapper (used by the operating system). When the packet is passed to 802 media-specific drivers, the driver extracts the user_priority value from the packet wrapper and copies it to the appropriate field in the MAC header of the transmitted packet. In certain cases, various non-802 media may represent themselves as 802 media drivers. In these cases, the media-specific driver may still use the user_priority in the packet wrapper to generate the appropriate mark (or alternate prioritization mechanism) for the corresponding link layer.

13.3.7 Controlling the Behavior of the Packet Scheduler from the Active Directory

Certain registry parameters that control the behavior of the packet scheduler can be centrally managed across multiple hosts. The mechanism for doing so is Zero Admin Windows (ZAW). The following parameters can be modified using the ZAW mechanism.

- Marking tables for DSCP

- Marking tables for 802 `user_priority`

- `MaxOutstandingSends`

- `NonBestEffortLimit`

13.4 The Structure and Behavior of ATMARP

ATMARP is the IP-over-ATM driver in Windows 2000. It resides between the TCP/IP protocol module and an ATM netcard (and its associated driver). Together, ATMARP, the netcard driver, and netcard hardware provide traffic control functionality over ATM media to traffic control consumers. As such, the combination of these components behaves as an ATM traffic control provider. (Providing traffic control over ATM is complicated and is discussed in general in Chapter 8.) Among other things, the traffic control provider is required to generate ATM UNI signaling to establish and to tear down ATM VCs. The complexity of providing traffic control over ATM results in certain behavioral subtleties. To understand these subtleties, it is necessary to delve somewhat into the details of the ATM traffic control provider.

13.4.1 ATMARP Interfaces

Figure 13.15 illustrates the position of ATMARP in the protocol stack and its interfaces.

Two sets of interfaces exist: data plane interfaces and control plane interfaces. The data plane interfaces are standard NDIS interfaces. The TCP/IP protocol module passes packets to ATMARP for transmission through the ATM driver and the netcard. Received packets are passed up from the netcard, through its driver, to ATMARP, and then on to TCP/IP. At the level of ATMARP and below, packets are associated with a specific ATM VC. These are established via the control plane interfaces.

In the control plane, ATMARP interfaces primarily to NDIS and to the GPC. NDIS control plane interfaces provide standard NDIS binding functionality. In addition, ATMARP uses the NDIS interface and the associated *call manager* to create VCs as necessary. The GPC interface is used specifically for traffic control-related functionality. The GPC interface serves two purposes. First, through this interface, ATMARP is notified when a traffic control flow is created or deleted and is informed of the parameters of the flow. Second, when packets are submitted for transmission, ATMARP passes them to the GPC for classification and obtains a flow descriptor in return.

Figure 13.15   ATMARP and Interfaces

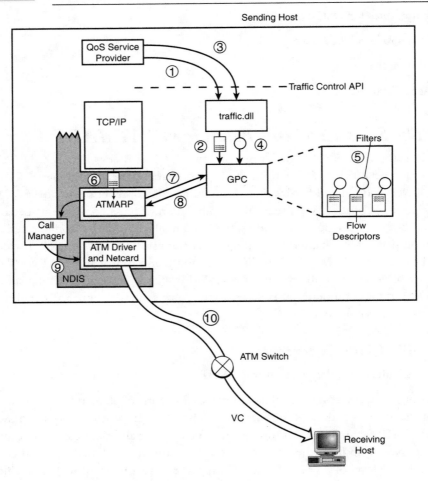

13.4.2 ATMARP Traffic Control Behavior

When a traffic control consumer creates a flow, traffic.dll installs the flow parameters in the GPC. The GPC, in turn, notifies ATMARP that a flow has been created. When the traffic control consumer adds filters to the flow, these are stored in the GPC and are associated with the corresponding flow descriptor. Subsequently, when ATMARP passes packets to the GPC for classification, the GPC finds the matching flow descriptor (via the associated filters) and passes it to ATMARP.

ATMARP uses the NDIS call manager to establish VCs of the appropriate type through the ATM network to the appropriate destinations. VCs are not established directly in response to the creation of a traffic control flow. Rather, VCs are established when one of the following two events occur:

- TCP/IP submits for transmission the first packet corresponding to a previously created traffic control flow.

- TCP/IP submits for transmission the first packet to a destination to which there is no existing VC and for which no traffic control flow has been created.

The resulting behavior is described in the following steps. Refer to Figure 13.15.

1. The QoS service provider (as the traffic control consumer) creates a flow for a specific service type and specific token bucket parameters.

2. traffic.dll installs a flow descriptor in the GPC.

3. The QoS service provider installs a filter on the flow. The filter describes the packets that should be sent on the flow based on the IP 5-tuple.

4. The filter is passed to the GPC.

5. The GPC internally associates filters with the corresponding flows.

6. A packet is passed to ATMARP for transmission.

7. ATMARP passes the packet to the GPC for classification.

8. The GPC classifies the packet and finds that it matches the filter associated with the previously created flow. It returns the corresponding flow descriptor to ATMARP.

9. ATMARP determines that there is no existing VC to carry the packet. Therefore, it calls the call manager to establish a VC to the destination to which the packet is addressed. It specifies the VC parameters taken from the flow descriptor.

10. The VC is established. Subsequently, packets classifying to the same traffic control flow *and to the same destination address* will be sent on the existing VC.

If a packet is submitted to ATMARP and the GPC does not return a matching flow descriptor, ATMARP must still deliver the packet to its destination. In this case, it creates a best-effort VC to the destination to which the packet is addressed. It is possible to have multiple VCs to the same destination, one for best-effort traffic and one corresponding to each traffic control flow associated with filters matching the same destination address.

Note the following subtlety with respect to the behavior of ATMARP: Because ATMARP establishes a VC in response to the transmission of certain packets, not in response to the creation of a traffic control flow, there is not necessarily a one-to-one correspondence between traffic control flows and VCs. In particular, the following anomaly may occur.

Assume that a traffic control flow is created and that a masked filter is attached to it. The destination address of the filter is masked so that it matches any destination address. The first packet submitted for transmission that matches the filter will result in the creation of a VC to the destination to which the packet is addressed. The VC parameters will be based on the traffic control flow parameters. Now assume that another packet is submitted for transmission to a different destination, but it still matches the filter in the GPC. The GPC will return a flow descriptor to ATMARP. Although ATMARP will note that there is an existing VC corresponding to the traffic control flow, the VC is not to the correct destination. In this case, ATMARP will create an additional VC, with the *same* parameters, to the new destination. The net effect is that when masked filters are installed on a flow, ATMARP creates a separate VC, each with the corresponding traffic control parameters to *each* destination.

The QoS service provider traffic control consumer never creates masked filters (because per-conversation RSVP does not require it to do so). Consequently, the anomaly described will not surface when the QoS service provider invokes traffic control. The anomaly may surface in response to third-party traffic control consumers that add filters with masked destination addresses. These traffic control consumers can avoid anomalous behavior by querying the TC API to determine the provider type and by refusing to install filters with masked destination addresses over ATM traffic control providers. Note that this anomaly is inevitable. There is no general notion in ATM of aggregating a number of unicast VCs to different destination addresses under a single set of VC parameters.

13.4.2.1 Mapping Traffic Control Flow Parameters to VC Parameters

When ATMARP establishes a VC for a packet that matches a traffic control flow, it selects the VC parameters based on the traffic control flow parameters. The type of ATM VC is determined as follows:

- Guaranteed Service traffic control flow—CBR VC

- Controlled Load Service traffic control flow—VBR VC (if supported by the netcard; otherwise, UBR VC)

- Best-effort traffic control flow—UBR VC

The token bucket parameters for the traffic control flow are used directly as the token bucket parameters for the ATM VC.

13.5 Behavior of Two Traffic Control Consumers

The QoS service provider is the default first-party traffic control consumer that is included with the Windows 2000 operating system. The Windows 2000 Resource Kit includes *traffic control monitor* (TcMon), which is a third-party traffic control application. These two traffic control consumers are discussed briefly in this section.

13.5.1 The Interaction of the QoS Service Provider and Traffic Control

The QoS service provider invokes traffic control services in a manner that ensures consistency with network-wide policy.

Invocation of traffic control by the QoS service provider was discussed briefly in the previous chapter "The GQoS API and the QoS Service Provider." It will be discussed again in this section from the perspective of traffic control functionality.

13.5.1.1 Initial Invocation of Traffic Control

As soon as applications invoke QoS from the QoS service provider, the QoS service provider invokes traffic control from the underlying traffic control provider. This is subject to certain caveats. First, the QoS service provider must have sufficient information to invoke traffic control. Second, traffic control must be invoked in a manner that is consistent with network-wide policy.

As discussed previously, the requirement for consistency with network-wide policies dictates that the QoS service provider may invoke *nongreedy* traffic control immediately, but must wait for network approval (in the form of an RSVP RESV message arriving either from the receiving host or from a proxy) before invoking *greedy* traffic control. As a result, there is a transient period following the application's initial request for QoS during which special traffic control constraints apply. This period is discussed in the following paragraphs. Note that if a RESV message is never received, the transient period may persist for the duration of the flow.

Nongreedy traffic control typically includes shaping (but precludes priority queuing). Greedy traffic control typically includes packet marking and priority queuing.

Recall that the service type of the flow determines the internal priority of the flow and the marking of packets on the flow (as illustrated in Figure 13.11). Thus, any invocation of traffic control prior to network approval must not specify a prioritized service type for the flow. As a consequence, when the QoS service provider first creates a flow using the TC API, it always specifies a service type of best-effort, regardless of the service type requested by the application. This ensures that the flow will initially be serviced based on a low internal priority and that packets on the flow will be marked for best-effort.

The QoS service provider is allowed to invoke the appropriate shaping behavior for the flow immediately because shaping is nongreedy behavior. By default, the shaping behavior is derived from the service type. Because the service type is initially forced to best-effort, the desired shaping behavior may not be applied. To obtain the shaping behavior appropriate for the flow, the QoS service provider may specify the appropriate ShapeDiscardMode object. As it happens, the default shape discard mode for all flows other than Guaranteed Service flows is borrow mode. Therefore, the QoS service provider must override the default ShapeDiscardMode only for Guaranteed Service flows. To do so, the QoS service provider initially invokes traffic control for Guaranteed Service flows by specifying the best-effort service type but setting the ShapeDiscardMode to shape.

Externally Observed Behavior During the Transient Period

During the transient period, traffic on Guaranteed Service flows will be shaped to their token bucket parameters but will compete with other traffic in the sequencer and in the network at the same priority as best-effort traffic. Traffic on Controlled Load Service flows will also compete as best-effort traffic during this period. Nonconforming traffic on Controlled Load Service flows will compete at less-than-best-effort priority.

Traffic on Null Service flows and best-effort flows will not be shaped, nor will it be demoted for nonconformance (no quantitative shaping parameters are associated with these flows). Instead, it will compete with best-effort traffic at whatever rate it is generated.

All traffic will be marked with the DSCP and 802 user_priority value corresponding to best-effort service during the transient period.

Enabling Greedy Behavior During the Transient Period

In certain cases, the network manager may want to operate the network without regard for network-wide policies, or using policy schemes other than signaling. In these cases, the network manager can eliminate the transient period by setting the EnablePriorityBoost registry variable for the interface of interest. This variable is read by the QoS service provider and causes it to invoke both nongreedy and greedy traffic control immediately upon the application's request for QoS. Use of this feature is generally not recommended.

13.5.1.2 Behavior Following Admission to the Network

When (and if) network policy admits a flow (as indicated by the receipt of a RESV message), the QoS service provider can begin to invoke greedy traffic control. It does so simply by modifying the service type of the flow via the TC API to the service type requested by the application via GQoS. At this time, it no longer needs to explicitly generate the ShapeDiscardMode object because the appropriate ShapeDiscardMode will be derived from the service type.

Following admission to the network, traffic will compete according to the internal priority derived from the corresponding flow's service type. Thus, traffic on Guaranteed and Controlled Load Service flows will fare better (assuming the netcard is congested).

Marking of Packets on Admitted Flows

Packets on admitted flows will be marked as described here:

- If a DCLASS and/or TCLASS object is returned from the network, traffic on the flow will be marked with the corresponding DSCP and/or 802 user_priority.

- If no DCLASS and/or TCLASS object is returned from the network, traffic on the flow will be marked based on the flow's service type and the DiffServByteMapping registry tables and/or 802 UserPriorityMapping registry tables for the interface of interest.

- If no DiffServByteMapping registry tables and/or 802 UserPriorityMapping registry tables exist for the interface of interest, packets will be marked based on the default mapping from service type to DSCP and to 802 user_priority, as specified earlier in this chapter.

Figure 3.16 illustrates the combined behavior of the QoS service provider and the QoS packet scheduler over Ethernet with respect to a Guaranteed Service flow, both during the transient period and after admission of the flow.

Figure 13.16 The QoS Service Provider and Traffic Control Behavior During the Transient Period and After Admission of a Flow

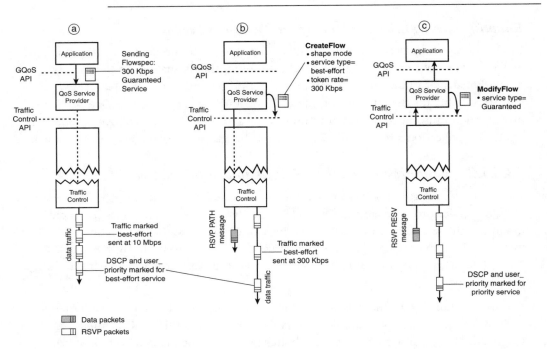

In Figure 13.16a, the application requests QoS via the GQoS API. It specifies a SendingFlowspec for the Guaranteed Service type for a token rate of 300Kbps. At this time, application traffic is not shaped. As a result, traffic is submitted to the network at the full 10Mbps media rate. In Figure 13.16b, the QoS service provider invokes nongreedy traffic control, specifying the best-effort service type (because the flow has not yet been admitted to the network), shaping mode (because it is a Guaranteed Service flow), and the requested token rate of 300Kbps. As a result, traffic transmitted on the flow is shaped to 300Kbps.

This is the transient period. During this time, traffic is not marked for prioritized treatment. It is marked best-effort and is treated as best-effort traffic both within the packet scheduler and in the network. In Figure 13.16c, a RESV message arrives from the network. In response, the QoS service provider notifies the application that its request was admitted and invokes greedy traffic control. To invoke greedy traffic control, the QoS service provider simply modifies the service type on the flow from best-effort to Guaranteed (the requested service type). At this time, traffic control will begin to mark traffic for prioritized service.

In the particular scenario illustrated, no DCLASS or TCLASS object is returned with the RESV message. Therefore, traffic on the admitted flow will be marked based on service type, conformance status, and a mapping table. If mapping tables have been created to override the default mappings, then marking will be based on these tables. If tables have not been created, then the default table will be used.

13.5.1.3 Network Control Service for Signaling Traffic

The QoS service provider always creates a Network Control Service flow to be used for RSVP signaling messages. Traffic on this flow is always allotted the highest internal priority and is always marked for the corresponding DSCP and 802 user_priority values, as specified by the default (or registry override) mapping tables. There is no signaling for the Network Control Service flow.

It is assumed that RSVP traffic is generated at a significantly lower volume than the associated data traffic. Therefore, the prioritization of RSVP signaling traffic without coordination with network policies will not unduly compromise service to other flows.

13.5.2 TcMon

TcMon is a third-party traffic control consumer. It is a utility that is included with the Resource Kit for Windows 2000. TcMon provides a GUI by which system administrators can discover interfaces that are traffic control providers, create flows, and attach filters on local and on remote hosts. It also enables the system administrator to monitor traffic control to observe created flows and statistics regarding the status of traffic on these flows. TcMon provides access to most of the traffic control parameters and objects, enabling the user to closely control the behavior of the traffic control provider, overriding default behavior as necessary.

TcMon makes use of the COM version of the TC API and can therefore be used remotely. Users of TcMon must have administrative rights on the target machine. Note that TcMon is not integrated with network policy; it is intended for demonstration purposes rather than for network-management purposes. TcMon is also useful for debugging purposes because it can be used to monitor the status of flows created by other traffic control consumers.

Figure 13.17 illustrates TcMon dialog boxes.

Figure 13.17   TcMon

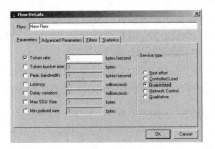

13.6   *Special Uses of Traffic Control*

In both the first- and third-party traffic control consumer model, the traffic control consumer configures certain flows and filters either on demand or, more statically, for traffic corresponding to individual conversations or for traffic aggregates that are identified by IP 5-tuples. Certain alternate modes of operation are described next.

13.6.1   *Limited Best-Effort Mode*

By default, the packet scheduler creates an internal best-effort flow in borrow mode, with no associated token rate. This flow carries all unclassified traffic, allowing it to make use of all resources remaining after higher-priority flows have been serviced. This mode of operation is called *unlimited best-effort mode* because there is no limit on best-effort traffic (other than the link speed). In the absence of explicitly created flows, this behavior is identical to the behavior that would be observed without the packet scheduler.

It is possible to configure the packet scheduler to operate in *limited best-effort* mode. In limited best-effort mode, the default best-effort flow is created in shape mode with a specified best-effort limit. As a result, best-effort traffic cannot consume resources beyond the specified best-effort limit. A network manager can use this mode when it is necessary to limit the overall amount of traffic generated by a transmitting host.

Limited best-effort mode is invoked on a per-interface basis by specifying the per-interface `BestEffortLimit` registry parameter.

13.6.2   *DiffServ Mode*

The packet scheduler can be operated in *DiffServ mode*. This mode is useful when the host is being used to route traffic from one interface to another. When operated in DiffServ mode, the traffic control consumer creates flows to emulate behavior aggregate PHBs (see Chapter 6, "Differentiated Services," for an explanation of PHBs and behavior aggregates).

When each flow is created, the traffic control consumer appends a DiffServ traffic control object. This object specifies one or more DSCPs and is used instead of attached filters to determine which packets should be directed to the flow. Note that conventional filters are ignored in DiffServ mode. In addition to specifying the DSCPs that are handled by the flow, the DiffServ object can also be used to specify both a conforming and a nonconforming codepoint to be used to re-mark traffic on the flow.

13.6.3 Automatic ISSLOW for RAS Dial-Up Servers

RAS dial-up servers operate much as a router does. The QoS service provider does not typically run on a router. As a result, ISSLOW is not typically invoked on RAS dial-up servers. This is unfortunate because ISSLOW mode is particularly useful for handling mixed audio and data traffic transmitted from RAS dial-up servers to modem users.

To address this scenario, it is possible to run the packet scheduler in a special dial-up mode. In this scenario, the packet scheduler uses heuristics to determine when an ISS-LOW-worthy traffic flow is traversing the scheduler. Specifically, the scheduler snoops RSVP messages for Guaranteed Service mode flows and the appropriate rate and packet size parameters. When it detects ISSLOW-worthy traffic flows, it switches to ISSLOW mode, causing packets on other flows to be fragmented.

> **Note**
>
> To operate in this mode on the standard Windows 2000 product, it is necessary to install a non-native utility. Subsequent releases of Windows 2000 include this utility natively.

13.7 Summary

In previous chapters, traffic control functionality was described primarily as functions in routers and switches. Recognizing that the network stack of the host operating system is both the first and the last hop in the network, it is important to provide traffic control functionality on hosts as well as on network equipment. Presently, traffic control functionality is implemented in Windows 2000 only and for transmitted traffic only.

The primary functions of traffic control are scheduling and marking of transmitted traffic. Hosts support traffic control consumers (that invoke traffic control functionality) and traffic control providers (that provide traffic control functionality). Traffic control consumers use the traffic control API to invoke the services of traffic control providers. This API enables third parties to develop traffic control consumers or providers to enhance the functionality of traffic control on the operating system.

Traffic control consumers fall into two categories. First-party traffic control consumers invoke traffic control directly, on behalf of applications. Third-party traffic control consumers invoke traffic control on behalf of network-management systems but apply it to application traffic flows. The application is passive in this process. Regardless of the type of traffic control consumer, it is important that it be integrated with the network-wide policy-management system.

The native traffic control consumer in Windows 2000 is the QoS service provider. This is a first-party traffic control consumer that is integrated with network-wide policy via RSVP signaling. TcMon is included in the resource kit for Windows 2000; it is not integrated with any network-management system and is intended for use only as a sample third-party traffic control consumer.

The native traffic control providers in Windows 2000 are the Ethernet packet scheduler and the ATM over IP driver (with its associated netcards). The Ethernet packet scheduler is comprised of a stack of scheduling modules that provide both scheduling and marking functionality. The scheduling modules include a conformance analyzer, a shaper, and a sequencer. Together, these modules enable a combination of work-conserving and non-work-conserving queuing algorithms to be applied to transmitted traffic. The packet scheduler also effects the marking of both DSCPs and 802 user_priority values in transmitted traffic.

Traffic control can also be configured to provide the following useful features:

- Overall rate limiting of a sender

- ISSLOW link-layer fragmentation for the protection of latency-sensitive audio traffic

- DiffServ router emulation mode

Traffic control functionality can be configured remotely from a central management console via the TC API. In addition, certain traffic control configurations can be downloaded at once to a broad set of hosts using the ZAW functionality available through the Microsoft Active Directory.

14

The Microsoft Admission Control Service

The Microsoft QoS components described in the previous two chapters are end-system components. They operate on hosts that are sending and/or receiving traffic that requires QoS. This chapter describes the Admission Control Service (ACS) that is available in the Windows 2000 Server, Advanced Server, and Data Center. The ACS is a network component rather than an end-system component. It operates on hosts that provide network management functionality. The network manager can use the ACS to control which subsets of network traffic gain access to specific resources at different points in the network. The ACS controls access to resources based on policies in Active Directory. It is intended to be used to manage network resources in an enterprise network.

Note

Note that the ACS does not provide policy control for nonsignaled traffic. It provides policy control for signaled traffic only.

This chapter begins with a discussion of the role of the ACS in Microsoft's QoS policy infrastructure. It follows with a discussion of the basic *Subnet Bandwidth Manager* (SBM), which is an important component of the ACS. The Windows SBM is based on the IETF proposed standard for the SBM [RFC 2814]. The Microsoft SBM subset of the ACS offers support for explicit admission control based exclusively on resource availability, regardless of the particular user or application requesting the resources.

Note

The IETF defined SBM is a protocol entity only. It intercepts RSVP messages for the purpose of participating in admission control, but it does not make admission control decisions itself. That said, most network devices that implement SBM functionality incorporate at least the basic capability to make an admission control decision based on resource availability per provisioned resource limits (resource-based admission control). (See the sidebar "Resource- versus Policy-Based Admission Control," later in this chapter.) Microsoft SBM functionality refers to both the SBM protocol entity and to the rudimentary resource-based admission control functionality.

The chapter continues with a description of the broader functionality of the ACS. The ACS contains the SBM functionality and builds on it by adding policy-based admission control. Microsoft's policy-based admission control makes it possible for the network manager to define policies governing availability of resources to specific users. These policies are stored in Active Directory.

Next, the chapter discusses the provisioning and configuration of the SBM and the ACS. A discussion of deployment scenarios follows. This section includes a discussion of an implementation of ACS on Remote Access Service (RAS) servers, as opposed to the SBM-based implementation. The chapter ends with a discussion of the extensibility of the ACS in support of third-party policy servers, along with a discussion of ACS security.

14.1   The SBM and the ACS—Microsoft's QoS Policy Infrastructure

Resource- versus Policy-Based Admission Control

Throughout this chapter, references are made to *resource-based* and to *policy-based* admission control. In resource-based admission control, decisions are made based on resource *availability* per provisioned limits. In policy-based admission control, decisions are made based on policies regarding the amount of resources that are allowable for *specific users* (or users that are members of specific groups).

The terms *resource-based* and *policy-based* may be slightly confusing. To clarify, note that the designation of *resource-based* admission control parameters is itself a matter of *policy*. Also, policies used for *policy-based* admission control specify the amount of *resources* to be available to users. The distinction between resource-based and user-based admission control can be summarized by stating that resource-based admission control decisions are made *regardless of* the requesting user, whereas policy-based admission control decisions are made *based on* the requesting user.

QoS policy was discussed at length in Chapter 9, "QoS Policy." In that discussion, the roles of *policy enforcement points* (PEPs), *policy decision points* (PDPs, or policy servers), and *policy data stores* were described. The functionality provided by the ACS is equivalent to the combined functionality of a PEP and a PDP (with respect to signaled QoS). The ACS uses the Microsoft Active Directory as a policy data store.

It is helpful to briefly review the role of the PEP and the PDP in signaled QoS. PEP functionality is typically supported on switches or routers that reside at strategic locations (usually congestion points) in the QoS-enabled network. Because switches and routers reside in the actual traffic paths, and because RSVP requests follow the traffic paths, these requests arrive at the PEPs. PEPs forward requests to their associated PDP. The PDP compares the information against policies in the policy data store and makes an admission control decision. The decision is passed back to the PEP, where the appropriate protocol action is taken. If the request is admitted, it is forwarded on its way. If the request is rejected, it is blocked and the appropriate policy-related error messages are sent in response. (Note that the PEP may participate in the admission control decision by checking for admissibility based on local resource availability.)

To fully realize the advantages of the Microsoft QoS policy infrastructure, it is necessary for Microsoft components to participate in the admission control process by intercepting signaled resource requests. However, Microsoft devices do not commonly reside in traffic paths.

Note

One exception is Microsoft's RAS dial-up server. See the section "ACS on RAS Servers," later in this chapter.

Consequently, to participate in the admission control process, Microsoft must be capable of intercepting signaling messages without residing in the traffic path. The obvious way to do so is to leverage the SBM protocol functionality described in Chapter 7, "The Subnet Bandwidth Manager and 802 Networks." This functionality requires that RSVP-aware senders residing on 802 networks listen for I_AM_DSBM messages on the network and direct RSVP signaling messages to the Designated SBM (DSBM) on the subnet. Thus, as long as a Microsoft device becomes the DSBM on a managed segment, it will be capable of intercepting signaling messages traversing the managed segment. (See Chapter 7 for an explanation of a *managed segment*.) With this in mind, Microsoft has built SBM functionality into Windows 2000 Server (and higher-functionality versions of the operating system) and has built standard SBM client functionality, which is enabled by default in all Windows 2000 hosts.

Note

Although the SBM is focused on 802 networks, the general concept can be utilized in other shared networks as well. For example, the SBM concept can be applied to cable modem networks and wireless networks. By building on the SBM, the ACS is poised to be useful in a variety of subnetwork types.

Microsoft's SBM implementation provides basic SBM functionality, which includes the SBM election protocol and the capability to intercept RSVP signaling messages. In addition, the Microsoft SBM is capable of applying resource-based admission control. The capability of the SBM to intercept signaling messages is leveraged further, to enable Microsoft to apply policy-based admission control based on user-oriented policies in Active Directory.

Note

See the section "Application-Based Policies," later in this chapter, for information regarding admission control based on application.

The standard SBM protocol functionality, coupled with the functionality to apply both resource-based and policy-based admission control, comprises the ACS.

Internal Structure of the Microsoft ACS

Figure 14.1 illustrates the internal structure of the Microsoft ACS.

Figure 14.1   Internal Structure of the Microsoft ACS

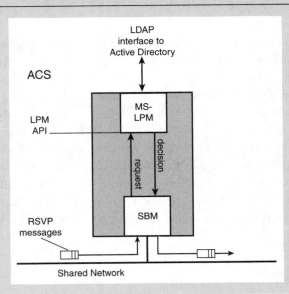

This figure illustrates the SBM component of the ACS, which intercepts RSVP requests from the network. These are passed up to the *Microsoft Local Policy Module* (MS-LPM), via the *LPM API*. The MS-LPM communicates with Active Directory using LDAP, to retrieve policy data. RSVP requests are compared against the policy data, and an admission control decision is returned to the SBM via the LPM API. The SBM reflects the results of the decision by generating the appropriate signaling messages on the network.

The MS-LPM and the LPM API will be discussed in further depth toward the end of this chapter, in the section "ACS Extensibility."

Figure 14.2 compares the Microsoft ACS with the equivalent PEP/PDP components.

Figure 14.2   Correspondence Between the ACS and PEP/PDP Functionality

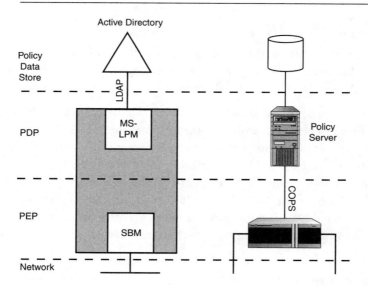

In Figure 14.2, the SBM component of the ACS offers functionality that is equivalent to that of a PEP in the sense that it intercepts RSVP control messages. In doing so, it provides the means to enforce *admission control* policies. Because it does not actually reside in the data path, it cannot enforce policy by directly impacting traffic handling. Instead, it can be considered to enforce policy only to the extent that explicit admission control enforces policy.

The LPM module of the ACS is analogous to a PDP because it is the component that reviews RSVP requests for admissibility based on policy. Finally, Active Directory is Microsoft's policy data store. A number of third-party PDPs use Active Directory as a data store. However, they may use other directories or data stores as well.

The reliance of Microsoft's ACS on the SBM protocol is limiting in the sense that it can be deployed only in 802 subnetworks. Nonetheless, creative applications of the ACS can be used to extend its reach to manage resources beyond the 802 subnetworks to which it is directly attached. In addition, ACS-related APIs enable third parties to build on the functionality provided by the ACS, further extending its utility. The ACS offers a way to integrate Active Directory-based policy into signaled QoS deployments. In the time since the ACS was delivered, a number of network equipment vendors have either delivered or announced similar functionality in the form of PEPs, PDPs, or both.

14.2 Microsoft's SBM

This section describes the SBM functionality that is the basis for Microsoft's ACS implementation. (This discussion does not apply to the implementation of the ACS on Microsoft's RAS server.) General SBM functionality was discussed in depth in Chapter 7.

Recall that the purpose of the SBM is to enable RSVP to operate in 802 networks with the same topology awareness with which it operates in routed networks. As a result, the SBM makes it possible to operate 802 networks at a higher quality/efficiency (QE) product than would otherwise be possible. Optimal improvement in the QE product is realized when the SBM is implemented in intelligent switches residing in the 802 network. Microsoft has implemented the SBM on a host platform. Although a host-based SBM does not offer the optimal QE product, it can raise the QE product of a network significantly. Microsoft's SBM provides the following useful functions:

- The SBM can be used to enhance the QoS provided to certain applications by controlling the volume of traffic competing for high-priority network resources.

- The SBM can be used to protect best-effort applications by controlling the impact of competing applications on network resources.

The following paragraphs explain how the SBM provides these functions.

14.2.1 Fundamentals of the SBM Resource-Based Admission Control

The SBM subcomponent of the ACS enables the control of resource consumption on a per-managed-segment basis, regardless of the application or user consuming the resources.

It cannot actually *enforce* resource consumption—instead, it relies on cooperating hosts and network devices to provide the enforcement. A simple example of this functionality is illustrated in Figure 14.3.

Figure 14.3   The SBM in a Simple 802 Network

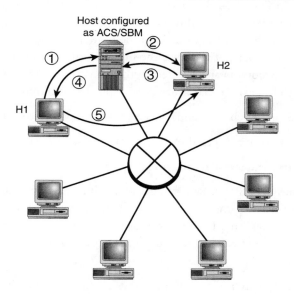

In this diagram, eight hosts are interconnected by a single IEEE 802.1D switch (hereafter referred to simply as an 802 switch). One of the hosts is configured as an ACS and provides the admission control functionality required. The other seven hosts source and sink traffic generated by several applications. Assume that these applications include an audio/video streaming media application and a variety of best-effort applications, including such applications as email and file sharing.

The switch illustrated offers simple aggregate traffic handling, using a single high-priority queue and a single standard-priority queue. Packets marked with a high 802 user_priority are directed to the high-priority queue. Packets marked with a low 802 user_priority are directed to the standard-priority queue. Packets from the high-priority queue are always transmitted ahead of packets from the standard-priority queue (this is strict priority queuing). The switch can offer high-quality service to traffic in the higher-priority queue only if the amount of traffic admitted to the queue is limited. The admission of excess traffic to the high-priority queue would compromise the quality provided by the high-priority queue, thereby rendering it useless to streaming media applications.

In addition, because the high-priority traffic is scheduled using strict priority queuing, excess high-priority traffic would starve best-effort traffic. Therefore, the SBM is provisioned with admission control limits to be applied in admitting requests for the high-priority queue. These limits take the form of a token bucket profile.

The hosts illustrated in Figure 14.3 support the Windows 2000 QoS functionality described in the previous two chapters. Briefly, this means that these hosts generate RSVP signaling messages on behalf of each streaming media traffic flow. These messages effectively request admission for a certain amount of traffic to the high-priority queue in the switch. In this example, the admission requests are directed to the SBM. Hosts mark traffic for the high-priority queue only to the extent that it has been explicitly admitted by the SBM.

Refer to Figure 14.3, in which H1 sends an RSVP PATH message toward H2:

1. The SBM client software in H1 directs the PATH message to the SBM.

2. The SBM forwards the message on to H2.

3. H2 responds with an RSVP RESV message, indicating the traffic rate and the service type desired. The SBM compares the requested rate against the provisioned limit (minus any resources granted in response to previously approved requests) and determines whether sufficient capacity remains in the high-priority queue to admit the request.

4. In this example, capacity remains, the request is admitted, and the SBM forwards the RESV message on to H1.

5. As a result, H1 begins to mark traffic that is transmitted on the admitted flow with a high user_priority value.

Note

The SBM signaling process is somewhat simplified in this example. Strictly speaking, the SBM protocol requires that PATH messages be multicast, as described in Chapter 7.

14.2.2   Issues Arising from the Switched Subnet Example

Although the example illustrated previously is simplistic, it serves as a useful basis for discussion. The following sections address issues arising from this example.

14.2.2.1 Mapping Service Types to user_priority Marks

In the network illustrated, traffic is handled based on 802 user_priority values in packet headers. The purpose of the SBM is to limit the amount of traffic marked with specific 802 user_priority values. It does so by refusing admission to host-generated resource requests when the configured admission control limits have been reached. But hosts request admission for a specified amount of resources at a certain *IntServ service level*, not for a certain *802 user_priority value*. The SBM controls the amount of traffic marked with a certain 802 user_priority value, as described in the following paragraphs.

Windows 2000 hosts mark traffic with certain user_priority values only on flows that have been explicitly admitted for a corresponding IntServ service type. (The default mappings from IntServ service type to user_priority value are documented in Chapter 13, "The Traffic Control API and Traffic Control Components," in the section "802 user_priority Marking"). With this knowledge of the mappings used by the host, a network manager can limit the amount of traffic in the subnetwork that is marked with a specific user_priority value by limiting the admission of requests for the corresponding service type.

In certain cases, the default mappings may not be appropriate. In these cases, the host mappings can be modified, either centrally or on a per-host basis. See the related discussion in Chapter 13, in the section "Parameters Affecting Marking Behavior," for more information."

14.2.2.2 Per-service and Aggregate Admission Control Limits

The Microsoft SBM functionality is accessed via the ACS user interface (UI). The ACS UI enables the network manager to provision separate resource-based admission control limits for Guaranteed Service requests and for Controlled Load Service requests. This makes it possible to support three service levels in the network (Guaranteed, Controlled Load, and best-effort), with explicit admission control limiting admission to the two higher-quality service levels.

The SBM also supports a simpler mode of operation, in which the manager can specify an *aggregate* limit on all explicit requests, whether for Guaranteed Service or Controlled Load Service. The per-service level limits are mutually exclusive with the aggregate limits. The network manager must choose one admission control strategy.

Note

The default behavior of the SBM is to impose no resource-based admission control limits.

14.2.2.3 *Trusting the Hosts*

As mentioned previously, the SBM cannot actually enforce the amount of traffic submitted for a certain user_priority level. It can only reject host requests for admission to a user_priority level. The SBM then relies upon the hosts to mark traffic for prioritized service only to the extent that it was admitted. Thus, hosts are trusted both to mark traffic only on the admitted flow and to submit marked traffic at a rate no higher than that specified in the admitted request.

14.2.2.4 *The* NonResvSendLimit

Even well-behaved hosts are not precluded from sending traffic in the absence of an admitted reservation. Instead, they are precluded from sending at a *prioritized service level*. This mode of operation is acceptable, provided that the network provides some means of traffic separation and that there is sufficient best-effort capacity to accommodate all best-effort senders. In the example illustrated in Figure 14.3, traffic separation is provided by isolating senders behind dedicated ports on a switch that handles traffic based on 802 user_priority. If multiple senders are sending onto a yellow-wire segment, for example, there is no means of traffic separation, and the mode of operation described is not particularly useful.

For such cases, the Microsoft SBM enables the network manager to specify a NonResvSendLimit. This parameter is broadcast to all hosts in the managed segment to which the ACS is attached. The NonResvSendLimit takes the form of a token bucket profile and specifies a per-flow limit that should be enforced by cooperating sending applications, as long as the corresponding flow has not been admitted. In addition to being supported in the SBM, the NonResvSendLimit must be supported in the attached hosts and by applications. The Windows QoS service provider (described in Chapter 12, "The GQoS API and Traffic Control Components") supports the NonResvSendLimit. A number of Microsoft applications respond accordingly. For further details on this functionality, refer to the section titled "NonResvSendLimit," in Chapter 7.

14.2.2.5 *Applying a Single Admission Control Limit to the Entire Subnetwork*

One of the compromises of a host-based SBM is that it is unaware of the topology of the 802 network. Thus, the admission control limits specified by the network manager are applied to any request originating at or terminating at hosts in the 802 network, regardless of the path taken by the corresponding traffic. In certain cases, all traffic may traverse a single shared-switch backplane. In such cases, it may be appropriate to subject all prioritized traffic to a single admission control limit, equivalent to some fraction of the capacity of the backplane.

However, in more complex 802 networks, this is often not the case. In networks consisting of a number of 802 switches, it might be appropriate to apply different admission control limits, depending on the path taken by admitted traffic. The compromise in QE product that results in the absence of topology awareness has been discussed previously (see the sidebar "Signaling and Topology Awareness" in Chapter 2, "The Quality/Efficiency Product," and the section "Signaling Density and QE Compromises" in Chapter 5, "RSVP"). When faced with this compromise, the network manager can choose to provision conservative limits or liberal limits, depending on expected usage patterns. Alternatively, if attaining the highest possible QE product is important, the network manager must use switches that offer integrated SBM functionality, thereby offering topology-aware admission control.

14.2.2.6 TCLASS *Handling*

The IETF specification of SBM functionality describes the role of the SBM in generating and handling the RSVP TCLASS object. (See Chapter 7 for details on the TCLASS object.) A standard SBM may generate a TCLASS object and append it to RSVP messages to specify the appropriate user_priority value to be used for a flow, overriding the host's default marking behavior. Microsoft's SBM does not generate TCLASS objects. However, it will *pass* TCLASS objects generated by third-party SBMs, unchanged. Microsoft sending hosts will respond to TCLASS objects generated by third-party SBMs.

14.3 *Policy-Based Admission Control*

The Microsoft SBM functionality described so far enables admission control based purely on resources requested and resources available. The additional policy-based functionality discussed in this section enables admission control based on the requesting user, the subnet from which the request originated, and corresponding policies in Active Directory.

14.3.1 *The Hierarchical Nature of Active Directory QoS Policy Information*

Windows 2000 hosts include NT user IDs in the RSVP messages that they generate (see the section "User Identification," in Chapter 12). In addition, each ACS is associated with a specific subnet (see the section "Correspondence Between Subnets and ACS Instances," later in this chapter). The ACS uses the NT user ID from an RSVP message and the subnet with which it is associated as indices into Active Directory to locate applicable QoS policy information. This information is hierarchically structured. When the ACS retrieves policy information from Active Directory, it locates the most specific applicable policy information in the hierarchy. The QoS policy information hierarchy is illustrated in Figure 14.4.

Figure 14.4   The QoS Policy Hierarchy

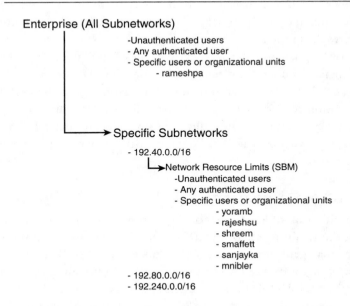

Two primary levels exist in the hierarchy: the *enterprise level* and the *subnet level*. The enterprise level is the highest level of the hierarchy. The subnet level is at the next-highest level. The ACS begins its search for applicable policy at the lowest and most specific level of the hierarchy: the subnet level.

14.3.1.1   Subnet-Level Policies

When an ACS receives an RSVP request, it first determines whether policies are defined *for the specific subnet with which the ACS is associated*. If they are, the ACS determines whether applicable user policies are defined in the associated subnet.

If the RSVP request contains an authenticated NT user ID (see the accompanying sidebar "Authenticated and Unauthenticated Users") *and* subnet policies are defined for that user, these policies will be applied. If the RSVP request contains an authenticated user ID, but no subnet policies are defined for that user, the ACS will determine whether an *Any Authenticated Users* policy is defined in the subnet. If such a policy is defined, it will be applied. If the RSVP request contains no authenticated user ID, then the ACS will determine whether an *Any Un-Authenticated User* policy is defined in the subnet. If such a policy is defined, it will be applied. If no applicable user policies are defined, then the ACS searches for applicable policies at the next level of the hierarchy: the enterprise level.

Authenticated and Unauthenticated Users

Authenticated users are users who are logged into an NT domain account. Unauthenticated users are users who are using the network but who are not logged into an NT domain. The ACS determines whether a user is authenticated based on the Kerberos ticket included in an RSVP message. Windows 2000 hosts automatically include this ticket on behalf of any user who is logged into the NT domain (see Chapter 12). Windows 98 hosts do not include Kerberos tickets in RSVP messages. Thus, Windows 98 users will be subjected to the policies defined for unauthenticated users. The same applies to users of other operating systems that do not participate in the NT domain security mechanisms.

Note

Note that the resource-based admission control limits described in the previous section can be specified for each subnet and override any per-user privileges. Thus, resource requests are approved based on the user only as long as the total current allocation of resources in the subnet does not exceed the total allowed resources per the provisioned resource-based limits.

14.3.1.2 Enterprise Policies

If no applicable policies are defined for the subnet with which the ACS is associated, it applies enterprise-wide policies. In a structure similar to subnet-specific policies, enterprise-wide policies may be defined for specific users, authenticated users, and unauthenticated users. If an enterprise-wide policy is defined for a specific user, it will be applied. If no policy is defined for the specific user, then either the Any Authenticated User policy will be applied, or the All Un-Authenticated Users policy will be applied, depending on the user's identity.

Note

The term *enterprise-wide* does not refer to the scope of policy *enforcement*, but rather to the *applicability* of policy. For example, an enterprise-wide policy does not limit the simultaneous consumption of resources across the entire enterprise. Instead, an enterprise-wide policy is a policy that is *applied* to an admission control request *regardless of the subnet* from which that request originates.

14.3.1.3 Policy Flowchart

Figure 14.5 illustrates the flowchart used to apply policy to a received admission control request.

Figure 14.5   Flowchart Illustrating the Application of Policy to a Received RSVP Request

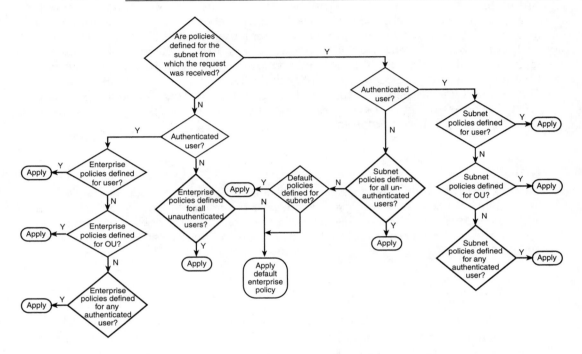

At the highest level, the first decision made is to determine whether or not there are policies authored for the specific subnet from which the request originated. If there are, these policies are traversed to determine whether the user is authenticated, and if so, whether there are policies applicable for the specific user in the subnet, or not. If there are no subnet specific policies, a similar traversal is made through enterprise policies (represented in the left half of the flowchart). Note that resource-based admission control is not accounted for in this flowchart.

14.3.1.4   Organizational Units

Just as policies may be defined for individual users, policies may be defined based on the *organizational unit* (OU) to which a user belongs. All users automatically inherit the policy defined for the OU to which they belong. If a policy is defined both for a specific user *and* for the OU to which that user belongs, the specific user policy takes precedence over the OU policy.

14.3.2   Application-Based Policies

The QoS service provider in Windows 2000 hosts passes application-provided identification information to the network in RSVP messages (see Chapter 12). This information is available for the purpose of applying admission control policies based on application and subapplication identity.

However, the version of the ACS that is included with the initial Windows 2000 release does not support policies based on application or subapplication identifiers. Subsequent releases will include comprehensive support for application-based policies in Active Directory and the ACS. In the absence of support for application-based policies in the ACS, network managers who want to implement application-based policies must look to alternate PDPs (compliant with [RFC 2752], [RFC 2872]) to do so. Alternatively, in certain cases, it may be possible to achieve the effect of application-based policies by running application instances on certain application servers in the context of a specific authenticated user ID, and defining the corresponding user-based policies in Active Directory.

14.4   Provisioning and Configuring ACS-Based QoS Policies in an Enterprise Network

This section describes the steps involved in provisioning and configuring SBM and ACS functionality and policies in an enterprise network. For the sake of brevity, this task will be referred to (for the remainder of this chapter) as *ACS management*. ACS management includes these tasks:

- Enabling ACS instances on certain Windows 2000 servers

- Configuring SBM operating parameters for each instance, including resource-based admission control limits

- Configuring policy-based admission control

The first of these tasks refers to enabling a specific server to act as ACS on a specific subnet. A multihomed server might host multiple *ACS instances*. Although enabling an ACS instance requires interaction with Active Directory, the focus of this task is the specific server on which the ACS instance is enabled.

The second task refers to the provisioning of SBM-related operating parameters and resource-based admission control limits on a subnet. These apply to all ACS instances enabled on the corresponding subnet. They are used only by the ACS instance currently operating as the DSBM for the subnet. The correspondence between ACS instances and subnets will be addressed in detail in the section "Correspondence Between Subnets and ACS Instances" later in this chapter.

The third task refers to the configuration of policies used for policy-based admission control.

14.4.1 The Role of Active Directory in ACS Management

Most ACS management is performed via Active Directory.

> **Note**
>
> In special cases, it is possible to configure an instance of the ACS to apply SBM resource-based admission control only without using Active Directory. This is referred to as *standalone* operation. For further details on standalone operation, visit Microsoft at www.microsoft/commmunications or email msqos@microsoft.com.

Refer to Figure 14.6 for some background on ACS management.

Figure 14.6   Active Directory, ACSs, and the Management Console

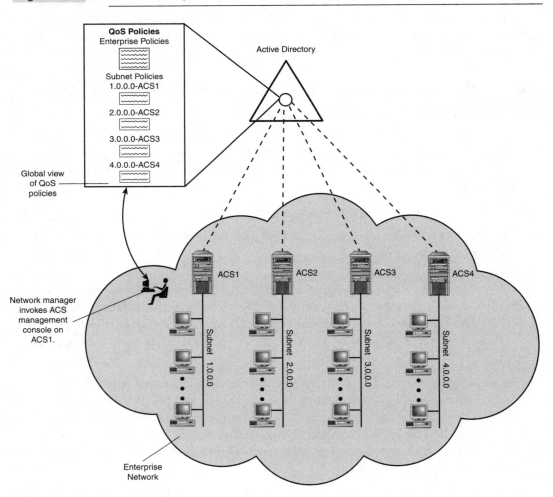

This figure illustrates an enterprise network with a number of physical subnets. A computer running Windows 2000 Server is physically attached to each subnet. An instance of the ACS service is enabled on each of these servers. Each ACS instance is attached to Active Directory (as indicated by the dashed lines). Active Directory contains enterprise-wide QoS policy information (as illustrated in the expanded view of the Active Directory contents). The QoS policy information in Active Directory controls the operation of all the ACS instances in the enterprise. A network manager is shown managing enterprise-wide QoS policy via an *ACS management console*.

14.4.1.1   *The ACS Management Console*

The network manager manages all specific ACS instances and QoS policy in general via the ACS management console. The management console offers a view into the QoS policies that are stored in Active Directory. It can be invoked from the Administrative Tools submenu on any Windows 2000 server that has been enabled as an ACS instance or from any server running Windows 2000 Administration Tools. (The particular host from which the console is invoked is immaterial.) The top-level dialog box of the ACS management console is illustrated in Figure 14.7.

| **Figure 14.7** | Top-Level View of the ACS Management Console |

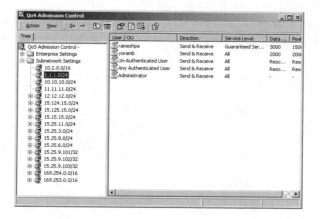

Note

The screen shots illustrated throughout this chapter are excerpted from the standard release of Windows 2000. Dialog boxes and specific UI details are subject to change.

The notation 1.1.1.0/24 is a standard way of indicating that this subnet is identified by a 24-bit subnet mask. Note that a number of subnets in Figure 14.7 indicate a 32-bit subnet mask, which implies a specific address (rather than an entire subnet). These entries correspond to ACS instances that are enabled on RAS servers. See the section "ACS on RAS Servers," later in this chapter for more information.

Note the Enterprise Settings and Subnetwork Settings entries, corresponding to the two levels of QoS policy hierarchy. In the example illustrated, a number of specific subnet policies have been defined under the Subnetwork Settings entry. The following paragraphs explain the correspondence between these subnets and ACS instances.

14.4.1.2   Correspondence Between Subnets and ACS Instances

When the ACS process initializes on a Windows 2000 server, it queries the host protocol stack to determine the IP subnets to which it is connected. The ACS process searches the Subnet Settings tree in the QoS policy section of Active Directory to determine whether its hosting server is listed as a server that is authorized to act as an ACS on the corresponding subnet. If it is, an ACS instance will be created. If there is no corresponding subnet entry—or if there is an entry, but the hosting server is not listed in the list of authorized servers—no ACS instance will be created. In this case, an error message will be logged to the system event log.

Thus, to enable an ACS instance, the name of the server hosting the ACS process must be added to the list of authorized servers under a subnet entry in Active Directory. Furthermore, the subnet entry under which it is designated must correspond to one of the subnets to which the server is physically attached. To authorize an ACS server on a particular subnet, the network manager uses the *Servers* tab of the Subnet Properties dialog box (illustrated in Figure 14.8). The network manager authorizes a server by adding the name of the server.

Figure 14.8   *Servers* Tab of the Subnet Properties Dialog Box

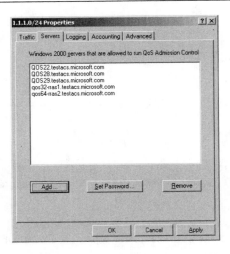

Multiple Servers per Subnet

In the interest of fault tolerance, it is possible to authorize multiple servers on a single subnet. Each of the authorized servers is eligible to act as the ACS on the subnet. However, only one server acts as the ACS at any point in time. ACS instances on each of the authorized servers run the DSBM election protocol to determine which instance will act as the ACS. If an instance fails, the election protocol is rerun, and an alternate ACS instance takes over. Figure 14.9 illustrates multiple servers per subnet.

Figure 14.9	Multiple Servers per Subnet

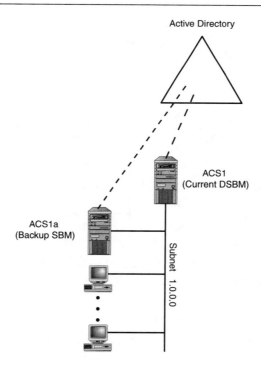

In this figure, ACS1 is the currently active DSBM on subnet 1.0.0.0. ACS1a, a server residing on the same subnet, serves as a backup SBM. If ACS1 stops operating, ACS1a will win the election and act as the DSBM.

Multiple Subnets per Server

It is allowable to designate the same server to host multiple ACS instances, each on a different subnet. This configuration allows a single, multihomed server to host ACS services on multiple subnets. To do so, the network manager attaches the hosting server to the appropriate subnets and authorizes that server under each of the subnet entries in Active Directory. Figure 14.10 illustrates a single server running ACS instances on multiple subnets.

Figure 14.10   Single ACS Server Serves Multiple Subnets

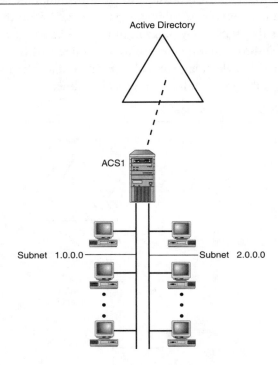

In Figure 14.10, ACS1 serves both subnet 1.0.0.0 and subnet 2.0.0.0. Separate instances of the ACS are enabled for each subnet.

14.4.2   Enabling an ACS Instance

To enable an ACS instance, it is necessary, but not sufficient, for the hosting server to be listed in Active Directory as an authorized ACS host on the corresponding subnet. The additional steps required to enable an ACS instance include these:

1. Verifying that the operating system version supports ACS

2. Installing the QoS Admission Control Service

3. Configuring the hosting server to be a member of a Windows 2000 domain

4. Starting the QoS Admission Control Service

These are described next.

14.4.2.1   Operating System Versions That Support ACS

The ACS is supported only on the following versions of the Windows 2000 operating system:

- Windows 2000 Server

- Windows 2000 Advanced Server

- Windows 2000 Data Center

- Higher-functionality versions of the operating system

Because the ACS is considered high-end functionality, the ACS is not supported on Windows 2000 Professional.

14.4.2.2   Installing the ACS Service

To run the ACS, it is necessary to install the QoS Admission Control Service. This is a subset of Networking Services. The ACS can be installed from the Windows 2000 Components Wizard.

14.4.2.3   Configuring the Server as a Member of a Windows NT Domain

The hosting server must be configured as a member of a Windows NT domain. Only users with administrative privileges and the appropriate domain credentials can join a server to a domain.

> **Note**
>
> For further information on Windows NT domains, refer to Windows 2000 documentation. Briefly, an NT domain is a group of computers that are part of a network and that share a common directory database. A domain is organized in levels and is administered as a unit with common rules and procedures. Each domain has a unique name.
>
> For proper operation, a domain user account for *AcsService* must exist. For further details on this account, see the section titled "Security" later in this chapter.

14.4.2.4   Starting the QoS Admission Control Service

When the ACS is installed and the hosting server is joined to a domain, it may be necessary to explicitly start the ACS.

As explained previously, when the ACS process initializes on a server, it searches Active Directory to determine whether it is authorized to instantiate an ACS instance on any of the subnets to which its host is connected. If it is not authorized, it shuts itself down.

Thus, if Active Directory is configured to authorize a particular instance of the ACS *after* the hosting server has initialized, it will be necessary to explicitly restart the service on the hosting server.

14.4.3 Configuring SBM Parameters on an ACS Instance

When an ACS instance is enabled in a specific subnet, it can be further provisioned and configured using the ACS management console. This section focuses mostly, but not exclusively, on the configuration and provisioning of the SBM functionality of the ACS. The following section describes the configuration of the policy-based admission control functionality provided by the ACS. The functionality discussed in this section includes a specific subset of the ACS behavior, as follows:

- Resource-based admission control limits to be applied to requests traversing the corresponding subnet

- Operating parameters of the SBM protocol

- The NonResvSendLimit value to be advertised on the corresponding subnet

- Policy-caching behavior of the ACS

- Logging behavior

> **Note**
>
> The first three of these are clearly SBM-specific functions. The last two are not actually SBM specific. Nonetheless, these are configured using the same mechanism that is used to configure SBM-specific functions. For this reason, they are discussed in this section.
>
> All the characteristics listed control the behavior of a specific ACS instance. Note, however, that these are not configured directly as characteristics of a specific ACS instance. Instead, they are configured indirectly, as *subnet* parameters. Whichever ACS instance is currently acting as the DSBM on the subnet inherits these operating parameters. (Servers acting as backup DSBMs also inherit certain parameters that are required to take over if the primary DSBM fails.)

To configure the SBM functionality, the network manager right-clicks on the subnet corresponding to the ACS instance to be configured (see Figure 14.7) and selects *Properties*. Figure 14.11 illustrates the top-level dialog box that appears.

Figure 14.11   SBM Configuration Dialog Box

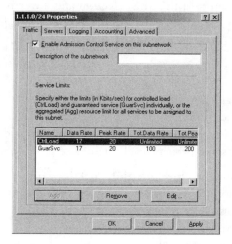

14.4.3.1 Resource-Based Admission Control Limits

The *Traffic* tab of the Subnet Properties dialog box can be used to configure the SBM resource-based admission control limits. The following limits can be configured:

- Per-flow average rate (*Data Rate*)

- Per-flow peak rate (*Peak Rate*)

- Total average rate admissible across all flows on the subnet (*Total Data Rate*)

- Total peak rate admissible across all flows on the subnet (*Total Peak Rate*)

These parameters can be configured separately for Guaranteed Service requests and for Controlled Load Service requests. Alternatively, a single set of limits can be configured, which are applied to all Guaranteed Service and Controlled Load Service flows in aggregate.

Note

Note that resource-based admission control limits are always applied by comparing the RSVP FLOWSPEC in RSVP RESV messages against the configured limits. This is in contrast to policy-based admission control limits, which can be applied to the contents of both RESV messages and PATH messages. See the section "General Policy Applicability," later in this chapter, for more information.

14.4.3.2 Operating Parameters of the SBM Protocol

Detailed operating parameters of the SBM election and advertisement protocol can be configured from the *Advanced* tab of the Subnet Properties dialog box. These include such parameters as the election priority and protocol-related timers.

Election Priority

The election priority parameter determines the priority at which the ACS participates in the election for DSBM on the subnet. A device participating at a particular priority level will always yield the election to a device participating at a higher priority level. When multiple devices participate at the same priority level, the device IP address is used as a tie-breaker.

The default priority assigned to the Microsoft ACS is priority level 4. This is in accordance with the SBM specification [RFC 2814], which states that host-based SBMs should be configured with the lowest priority level, router-based SBMs with the next-highest priority level, and switch-based SBMs with the highest priority level. These priorities are recommended based on the inherent topology awareness available to each type of device and the resulting capability of the device to optimize the QE product on the network.

Because it has a relatively low default priority, the Microsoft ACS will not become the DSBM on a subnet on which a switch or router participates in the election (unless it is explicitly configured for a higher election priority than the default). If the Microsoft ACS does not become the DSBM, Active Directory-based policies might not be applied. If the switch or router uses Active Directory as the policy data store, then Active Directory policies will still be applied. However, if the switch or router uses an alternate data store, Active Directory-based policies will not be applied. In this case, the network manager can force Active Directory-based policies to be applied by disabling the SBM functionality on the switch or router, or, alternatively, by raising the election priority of the Microsoft ACS on the subnet.

Note that because all eligible SBMs on a subnet inherit the election priority from the subnet parameters, all will inherit the same election priority. If multiple competing candidates have an equal priority, the protocol specifies that the tie will be broken based on IP address.

SBM Protocol Timers

The basic SBM protocol timers (*Keep Alive Interval* and *Dead Interval*) are set to the default values recommended in the SBM specification. These can be modified via the *Advanced* tab of the Subnet Properties dialog box. There should be no need for the network manager to modify these.

14.4.3.3 *Data Rate Before Reservation* (NonResvSendLimit)

This value can be configured in the *Advanced* tab of the Subnet Properties dialog box. It determines the value of the average flow rate parameter in the NonResvSendLimit object that the SBM transmits in its I_AM_DSBM message. This value can be used to control the behavior of cooperating hosts and applications on flows that are not admitted by the network. (For further details on the NonResvSendLimit, refer to the section "NonResvSendLimit," in Chapter 7, and to the discussion on the ALLOWED_TO_SEND_DATA query in Chapter 12, in the section "Application Queries to the QoS Service Provider.")

Note that the NonResvSendLimit object (in the I_AM_DSBM messages generated by the ACS) specified in the SBM specification includes not only the average rate, but also peak rate and burst size per-flow limits. The Microsoft SBM implementation inserts the value from the Data Rate Before Reservation field (from the *Advanced* tab of the Subnet Properties dialog box) into the average flow rate parameter of the NonResvSendLimit object. It inserts the media maximum transmission unit (MTU) size into the burst size and sets the peak rate to infinity.

14.4.3.4 *Policy-Caching Behavior*

The ACS caches policy information from Active Directory. As a result, it does not have to access Active Directory each time it receives an RSVP message. Each ACS instance caches information relevant to that instance. Specifically, it caches the enterprise-level policies and only those subnet-level policies that apply to the subnets to which it is attached.

From the *Advanced* tab of the Subnet Properties dialog box, it is possible to reconfigure the policy cache update interval. By default, the policy cache is updated every 30 minutes. Longer caching intervals mean that modifications to ACS policy made via Active Directory will take longer to be reflected in the decisions that the ACS makes. Shorter intervals increase the frequency at which the ACS retrieves its policy information, thereby increasing the overhead of this traffic on the network.

14.4.3.5 *Logging Behavior*

It is possible to configure the ACS to generate logs that can be used for accounting, billing, activity tracking, diagnostics, and so on. Two types of logs exist: accounting logs and RSVP message logs.

By default, both types of logs are written to files in a directory on the server hosting the ACS instance. Log files are limited in size. When a file has reached its maximum size, the ACS creates an additional file and writes to the new file until it is filled. This process continues until a maximum number of files has been written. At that time, the ACS overwrites the first file created. This mechanism facilitates programmatically moving data from the ACS into longer-term storage. The network manager can configure the following logging parameters from the Logging (RSVP message log) and Accounting (accounting log) tabs of the Subnet Properties dialog box:

- Location to which log files are written

- Maximum size of each log file

- Maximum number of log files generated

The network manager should be aware of disk usage and should limit file size and number of files accordingly.

The records generated by each ACS instance offer a local view of signaling activity only. To track network-wide resource usage, it may be necessary to consolidate information distributed across log files generated by multiple ACS instances. The log files generated are in clear-text format but do not conform to any specific accounting format. Microsoft does not provide specific tools to parse these.

Accounting Records

Accounting logs generate records that include the following information:

- Start and stop time of signaled sessions granted

- Rejections of signaled requests

- Identity and address of requestors

- Requested resource parameters

These can be used to track resource usage for the purpose of generating billing information, reprovisioning the network, and so forth. Accounting logs reveal nothing about actual resource usage. Instead, these track *requests* for network resources and whether or not these have been granted.

RSVP Records

RSVP logs record each RSVP message processed by the ACS instance. As a result, these tend to be quite large. They can be used to diagnose detailed signaling problems.

14.4.4   Configuring QoS Policies Based on User or Organizational Unit

The previous two sections focused on enabling individual ACS instances and on provisioning and configuring per-subnet operating parameters and resource-based admission control parameters. This section focuses on the configuration of per-subnet and enterprise-wide policy-based admission control parameters.

14.4.4.1   User Policy Dialog Box

The network manager can create user policies at the enterprise or subnet level by invoking the corresponding User Policy dialog box from the top level of the ACS management console (see Figure 14.7). The enterprise-level Policy dialog box can be invoked by right-clicking the Enterprise Settings entry and selecting Add Policy. The subnet-level Policy dialog box can be invoked by right-clicking the corresponding subnet entry and selecting Add Policy. The User Policy dialog box is illustrated in Figure 14.12.

Figure 14.12	The User Policy Dialog Box

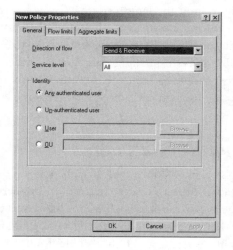

General Policy Applicability

From the *General* tab, the network manager controls how the newly created policy will be applied. The policy may be applied to the following:

- A specific user, all users of an OU, all unauthenticated users, or any authenticated user

- Requests for Guaranteed Service, requests for Controlled Load Service, or the sum of both (*All*)

- The send direction, the receive direction, or both

In contrast to resource-based admission control, in policy-based admission control, it *is* possible to create policies for individual service levels *and* for both service levels simultaneously. This limits resources granted at each level individually and the aggregate resources granted to the user. It is also possible, from the *General* tab, to disable a specific policy (by selecting Disabled from the Service Level menu). This has the same operational effect as deleting the policy from the directory.

The direction in which a policy is applied determines whether the policy will be applied to traffic *received* by the user or to traffic *sent* by the user. In the former case, it will be applied based on the credentials and RSVP FLOWSPEC in the user's RSVP RESV messages. In the latter case, it will be applied based on the credentials and RSVP SENDER_TSPEC in the user's RSVP PATH messages. The same policy may be applied in both directions.

Quantitative Limits

The *Flow Limits* and *Aggregate Limits* tabs can be used to specify the quantitative limits that are applied. Flow limits determine limits on each flow requested by the user. Aggregate limits determine the limits on the sum of resources requested across all the user's flows. It is possible to limit the length of time for which resources will be granted to the user on any flow by entering a time in the Duration field (available only on the *Flow Limits* tab). The ACS will time-limit flows persisting longer than the time specified by rejecting the corresponding refresh signaling messages after the specified time has elapsed. In the *Aggregate* tab, it is possible to limit the maximum number of independent flows that will be admitted for any user (in each direction). This is useful in preventing denial-of-service attacks.

14.4.4.2   Default Policy-Based Settings

Upon installation, the ACS is provisioned with default policy settings at the enterprise level. These allow any authenticated user to reserve up to 500Kbps across both service levels, in both the send and the receive directions. Each user is limited to two simultaneous flows (in each direction). Per-flow limits are equivalent to the aggregate limits. Unauthenticated users are restricted to 64Kbps in aggregate and only a single flow.

14.4.4.3   Recommended Policy Usage

Policy management is simplified by defining very general policies at high levels of the hierarchy and refraining from the specification of large numbers of fine-grain per-user policies. The default policies at the enterprise level will often be sufficient. If necessary, individual users with specific needs can be assigned policies on an exception basis. This can be done either at the enterprise-wide level or at the subnet level (if specific users should be entitled to more or less resources on a specific subnet). On resource-constrained subnetworks, it may be useful to define per-subnet resource limits.

14.5 Deployment Scenarios and Considerations

This section presents a number of deployment scenarios and discusses considerations related to these scenarios. As noted previously, the Microsoft ACS is limited in its deployment flexibility by its reliance on the SBM protocol. Some of the scenarios discussed are designed to specifically address this shortcoming. Consequently, they apply uniquely to the Microsoft ACS. Others may be more generally applicable.

14.5.1 802 Subnetwork Scenarios

In the scenario illustrated earlier in this chapter in Figure 14.3, audio/video traffic competes with best-effort traffic within a simple 802 subnetwork. QoS mechanisms may be used either to protect audio/video traffic from other traffic, to protect other traffic from audio/video traffic, or both. The network manager must select the appropriate strategy based on the different types of traffic offered to the network, the relative quantity of the different traffic types, and the relative importance of the different traffic. Several strategies are described in the following paragraphs, based on the network illustrated in Figure 14.3. Many of the considerations discussed apply equally to other types of networks.

14.5.1.1 IP Telephony

Assume that the network manager decides to introduce IP telephony on a LAN. The aggregate bandwidth required by the IP telephony traffic may be low enough that it does not starve best-effort traffic. However, telephony packets may get stuck behind queues of best-effort traffic, thereby compromising the telephony quality. Putting all telephony traffic in the high-priority queue fixes this problem, as long as the amount of traffic submitted to the high-priority queue is restricted. In this case, the network manager can provision the resource limits in the Subnet Properties dialog box to admit only a limited amount of traffic for high-priority service (and to the high-priority queue). Admitted traffic will enjoy high quality. Rejected traffic will compete on equal grounds with best-effort traffic.

14.5.1.2 Demoting the Priority of Streaming Video Traffic

In many cases, the aggregate bandwidth of the IP telephony traffic may be low enough that it can be admitted to the high-priority queue without adversely impacting the network. When this is true, explicit admission control may not be required for this traffic.

However, assume that the network manager now wants to deploy streaming video applications on the network. The resources consumed by streaming video are likely to be much higher. In the best case, streaming video must be prevented only from interfering with itself. In this case, the same strategy discussed in the context of IP telephony can be applied to limit the quantity of video traffic admitted for high-priority service.

However, in many cases, the introduction of nonadaptive streaming video traffic will threaten best-effort traffic. Simply downgrading video traffic above a certain limit might serve to protect the prioritized video traffic from the downgraded video traffic, but it will do nothing to protect the best-effort traffic. In certain cases, the network manager may prefer to actually *demote* the priority of aggressive traffic relative to that of best-effort traffic. In appropriately equipped 802 subnetworks, a user_priority value of 1 indicates that the corresponding traffic should be handled at a less-than-best-effort priority. The network manager can exploit this by modifying the mapping tables on the hosts to mark admitted traffic with a user_priority value of 1. As a result, admitted traffic will actually be demoted in priority, thus protecting the best-effort traffic on the same subnetwork.

Note that rejected resource requests for aggressive traffic will result in the corresponding traffic being marked best-effort and competing with other best-effort traffic. Thus, the network manager must be careful when defining the admission control limits for the aggressive traffic. One strategy would be to admit all resource requests for the aggressive traffic, so that it is always demoted in priority.

14.5.1.3 *Using the* NonResvSendLimit *Feature of the SBM*

If the video-streaming traffic originates only from hosts on the directly connected 802 subnetwork, the NonResvSendLimit feature of the SBM may be used to limit the impact of rejected video traffic on best-effort traffic. This parameter can be configured to some small limit based on the expected number of video flows and the capacity of the subnet. Assuming that the video-streaming application is well behaved, it will limit transmission on any flow that was not explicitly admitted, to the profile specified in the NonResvSendLimit. Use of the NonResvSendLimit is discussed in Chapter 7, in the section "NonResvSendLimit."

14.5.1.4 *Complex 802 Subnetworks*

The subnetwork illustrated in Figure 14.3 is very simple in the sense that there is only a single switch. In more complex topologies, subnet resource limits can be specified for the entire 802 subnet (see the section "Applying a Single Admission Control Limit to the Entire Subnetwork," earlier in this chapter).

14.5.2 Extending the SBM-Based ACS Beyond 802 Subnetworks

Previous examples illustrated how the Microsoft SBM-based ACS can be used effectively for managing resources on isolated 802 networks. However, these are rarely isolated. This section explores the use of the SBM-based ACS to manage resources when the 802 network is connected to other, routed networks.

14.5.2.1 Controlling Resource Usage on Remote Links by Limiting Admission Control to an 802 Network

Figure 14.13 illustrates an enterprise network that consists of three 802 LANs (LAN 1 through LAN 3), interconnected by routed WAN links.

Figure 14.13 Admission Control in an Enterprise Network Consisting of Multiple LANs Interconnected by WAN Links

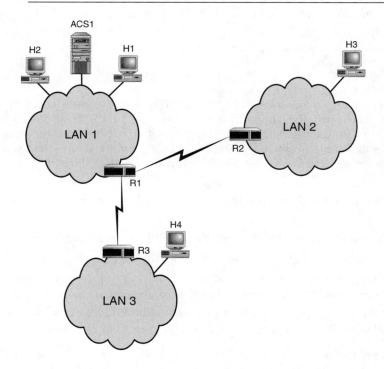

In this scenario, the WAN links are likely to be congested and require explicit admission control. The LANs are likely to offer much more capacity than the WAN links. The ideal admission control strategy for this scenario is to use router-based RSVP admission control

agents in R1 through R3 (at all WAN links). These routers should be configured, at a minimum, to apply resource-based admission control limits appropriate for the WAN links that they serve. They may also be connected to policy servers that apply policy-based admission control. Routers capable of acting as admission control agents are available from a number of vendors. The following sections discuss the use of Microsoft's SBM-based ACS to enable deployment scenarios such as the one illustrated.

In the absence of router-based admission control agents, the SBM-based ACS can be used to provide limited admission control functionality. For example, note that LAN 1 sports a shiny new ACS. This ACS can be configured with resource-based admission control limits for the subnet to which it is connected (LAN 1). Provided that R1 is a well-behaved SBM client, the limits configured on ACS1 for LAN 1 will be applied to *any* RSVP-signaled sessions terminating or originating at *any* host on LAN 1. These limits, therefore, will be applied not only to sessions that are local to LAN 1 (such as between H1 and H2), but also to sessions that traverse any of the WAN links connected to LAN 1 (such as between H1 and H3, or between H1 and H4). As such, ACS1 provides admission control for LAN 1 and for the WAN links connected to LAN 1.

> **Note**
>
> Hosts mark DiffServ codepoints (DSCPs) just as they mark 802 user_priority values. (See Chapter 6, "Differentiated Services," for a discussion of DSCPs.) Routers that support DiffServ use DSCPs to determine which traffic is entitled to high-priority handling. Thus, in the example illustrated, traffic on rejected flows will be marked with the best-effort DSCP, while traffic on admitted flows will be marked with a higher-priority DSCP.

However, there are problems with this approach, as described next.

Incapability to Differentiate Between Local and Remote Traffic

In the example illustrated, ACS1 is incapable of differentiating between sessions that traverse one of the two WAN links connected to LAN 1 and sessions that remain local to LAN 1. It may be possible to support 10Mbps of Guaranteed Service traffic (marked for user_priority value 5) in the LAN, but to support only 1Mbps of Guaranteed Service traffic (marked for DSCP equivalent to IP precedence 5) in each WAN link.

If ACS1 is provisioned to admit only 1Mbps of requests for Guaranteed Service on the LAN subnet, this will unnecessarily restrict sessions between H1 and H2. Similarly, it will unnecessarily restrict simultaneous sessions between H1 and H3 on the one hand, and between H2 and H4 on the other. If ACS1 is provisioned to admit more than 1Mbps of requests for Guaranteed Service, it might result in excess resource usage on either of the two WAN links. Thus, neither solution is ideal.

It would be nice to endow ACS1 with the capability to apply different admission control limits, depending on the path traversed by the admitted traffic. After all, this is the strength of RSVP signaling. Unfortunately, Microsoft's SBM-based ACS cannot do so.

Using User-Based Policies to Support Topology-Aware Admission Control

In certain cases, it may be possible to apply Microsoft's SBM in a manner that effectively applies different admission control limits, depending on the path traversed by the admitted traffic. Specifically, if users do not move between LANs, then different policies can be configured on ACS1 for users who reside on ACS1 than would be established for users who reside on remote networks. Maintaining large user lists can quickly become unwieldy, so it is necessary to be capable of creating policies based on user groups rather than individual users. In enterprises in which organizational units correspond to user locations, policies can be based on OUs instead of on individual users. Unfortunately, this is a fairly restrictive requirement.

Note that the links between LAN 1 and LAN 2 on the one hand, and between LAN 1 and LAN 3 on the other, can be controlled from ACS1. However, if there were a link between LAN 2 and LAN 3, this would require an ACS on either LAN 2 or LAN 3. The admission control policy applied to the link between LAN 1 and LAN 2 would then be the more restrictive of the policies provisioned on ACS1 and on the ACS on LAN 2. The suboptimal approach of using an SBM-based ACS can quickly become unwieldy when applied to any but the most trivial topologies. Nonetheless, in certain cases, it may serve as a useful, simple-to-deploy compromise.

14.5.2.2 Controlling Resource Usage on WAN Networks by Creating an Additional 802 Subnetwork

If router-based admission control agents are unavailable, the SBM-based ACS can be used to provide topology-aware admission control, albeit at some expense. Refer to Figure 14.14.

The network illustrated in Figure 14.14 is similar to the one illustrated in the previous example. R4 has been inserted in the path between LAN 1 and LAN 2, and R5 has been inserted in the path between LAN 1 and LAN 3. As a result, two new LANs have been created: LAN 4 and LAN 5. These are served by two shiny new ACSs, ACS2 and ACS3, respectively. Because the following is true, ACS2 can be used to apply admission control for traffic traversing the link between LAN 1 and LAN 2, without the undesirable side effects described in the previous example:

- All the traffic that traverses LAN 4 is traffic that also traverses the link between LAN 1 and LAN 2.

- All the traffic that traverses the link between LAN 1 and LAN 2 also traverses LAN 4.

Figure 14.14   Topology-Aware Admission Control Using the SBM-Based ACS

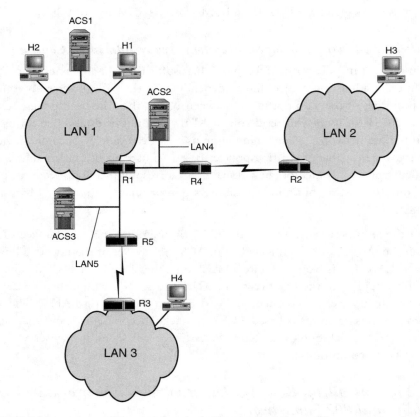

Similarly, ACS3 can be used to apply admission control for traffic traversing the link between LAN 1 and LAN 3. In this case, ACS2 and ACS3 would be provisioned to admit requests for up to 1Mbps of Guaranteed Service traffic. ACS1 would be configured to admit requests for up to 10Mbps of Guaranteed Service traffic. Sessions remaining local to LAN 1 would be restricted only by ACS1 and, therefore, would be limited to a total of 10Mbps of Guaranteed Service traffic. Sessions traversing either of the WAN links would be restricted both by ACS1 and by ACS2, and would be admitted accordingly.

Although this approach addresses the topology-awareness shortcomings of the previous approach, it requires deployment of additional routers, LAN interfaces, and Windows 2000 servers to do so.

14.5.3   ACS on RAS Servers

As illustrated in the deployment examples discussed previously, it would be really convenient if the routers serving the WAN links could themselves act as admission control agents. Such routers are available from a number of vendors. In addition, Microsoft offers a limited functionality solution in the form of the Microsoft RAS server product.

Consider again the network illustrated in Figure 14.13. It is possible to provide topology-aware admission control in this scenario (without the extra complexity illustrated in Figure 14.14) by replacing R1 with a Microsoft RAS server and operating an ACS on this server. The Microsoft RAS-based implementation of the ACS is subject to the following restrictions:

- It supports only point-to-point links (such as leased lines), not dial-up WAN connections.

- It provides admission control between point-to-point links and shared (LAN) networks to which it is connected. It does not provide admission control between two point-to-point links.

- It cannot provide admission control for the shared network to which it is attached. If it is necessary to provide admission control specifically for the shared network, a separate SBM-based ACS will be required.

- RSVP messages corresponding to multicast sessions will not be carried across the WAN links.

14.6   ACS Extensibility

In the interest of enabling multiple deployment options, Microsoft defines various interfaces by which the ACS functionality may be extended to integrate and interoperate with third-party products. These are described next.

14.6.1   The Local Policy Module API

The *Local Policy Module* (LPM) API enables third parties to integrate the Microsoft ACS into their policy platforms. Examples of the extensibility supported by the LPM API are illustrated in Figure 14.15.

Figure 14.15   Using the LPM API to Extend ACS Functionality

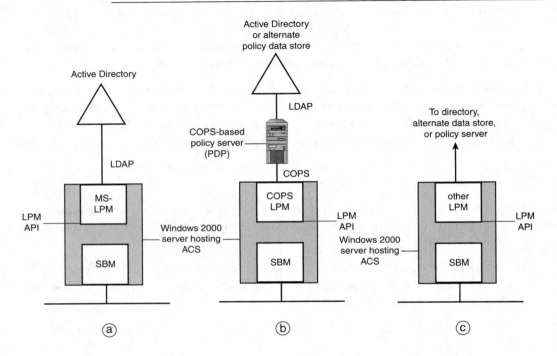

In Figure 14.15a, the standard ACS that is included in Windows 2000 is illustrated. The ACS includes the SBM module that is responsible for intercepting RSVP messages from the network. The RSVP messages are passed from the SBM module to the *Microsoft Local Policy Module* (MS-LPM) via the LPM API. The MS-LPM uses LDAP to retrieve and cache policies from Active Directory. When it receives RSVP requests from the SBM module, it evaluates the requests against the cached policies and returns an admit or reject decision to the SBM via the LPM API.

In Figure 14.15b, the MS-LPM has been replaced with a third-party COPS LPM. (See Chapter 9 for a discussion of the COPS policy protocol.) A COPS LPM is available from Intel and has been adopted or adapted for use by a number of policy system vendors. The COPS LPM receives the RSVP requests via the LPM API. It evaluates these requests using an industry-standard, COPS-based policy server (and the associated policy data store). It returns an admit or reject decision to the SBM via the LPM API.

In Figure 14.15c, an unspecified custom LPM replaces the MS-LPM. This LPM acts just as the MS-LPM and the COPS LPM, in the sense that it receives RSVP requests via the LPM API, evaluates them against policies, and returns an admission control decision to the LPM API. However, this LPM does not necessarily use COPS or LDAP to communicate with its policy server. It may use a separate policy server and policy data store, or may use a policy data store on a local disk for standalone operation.

14.6.1.1   Implementation of Third-Party LPMs

Third-party LPMs are written as dynamic link libraries (DLLs). The DLL executes on the ACS host. Further information on writing a third-party LPM is available from Microsoft.

14.6.2   Using the Microsoft LPM

An alternate extensibility option is illustrated in Figure 14.16.

Figure 14.16   Using the Microsoft LPM to Integrate Third-Party PDPs with Active Directory

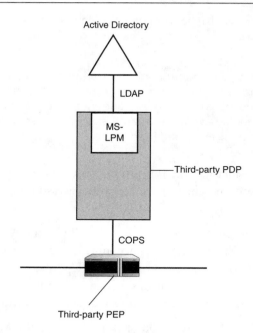

In this scenario, the MS-LPM, including its LDAP protocol and Active Directory policy-parsing logic, runs on a third-party PDP in conjunction with a third-party PEP. As a result, the third-party PDP can apply QoS policies from Active Directory. This is quite useful for the following reason: Recall that the Microsoft ACS is deployable only in shared networks (except for limited RAS server scenarios). Therefore, if the network manager is to deploy admission control agents in more general topologies *and* wants to leverage Active Directory-based policies, the manager requires a switch- or router-based PEP that uses a PDP that leverages Active Directory. The MS-LPM makes it easy to build such a PDP. Information on use of the MS-LPM for this purpose is available from Microsoft.

14.7 Security

Windows 2000 hosts typically include a Kerberos ticket and an encrypted user ID in the RSVP requests that they generate. The ACS is capable of verifying the authenticity of the request and extracting the clear-text user ID from the RSVP message. For this security mechanism to work, both the host and the ACS must be capable of authenticating themselves to a Kerberos *key distribution center* (KDC) and acquiring a Kerberos ticket for the *AcsService* account.

Note

The KDC is a Kerberos service that runs on a Windows NT domain controller. It issues ticket-granting tickets (TGTs) and service tickets for obtaining network authentication in a domain.

The ACS management console automatically attempts to create the *AcsService* account in a domain at the time a new ACS is authorized (unless the account already exists). If no account exists and the administrating user does not have the necessary privileges to create a domain account, it will have to be created explicitly by an authorized administrator via the Active Directory Users and Computers console.

The QoS service provider handles this process on the host, obtaining the credentials for the *AcsService* account on behalf of the user process (assuming that the user is logged into an NT domain).

Third-party PDPs can provide the same functionality as the ACS. To do so, they must acquire the password for the *AcsService* account. Using this password, the PDP can connect to the KDC and obtain a *credential handle*. Upon receiving host-generated RSVP messages, the PDP can then present this credential handle, with the Kerberos ticket from the RSVP message, to extract the authenticated identity information.

PDPs implemented on Windows 2000 platforms can use the Microsoft Security Support Interface (SSPI) APIs that are part of the Windows 2000 operating system to interact with the KDC. PDPs implemented on other operating systems must contact the KDC directly or may use alternate APIs designed to do so. For example, PDPs running on UNIX platforms may use the IETF's standard track Generic Security Service Application Program Interface [RFC 1509].

Note

Sample code for obtaining the *AcsService* credentials using either SSPI or GSSAPI is available from Microsoft [MS_KERB].

To simplify administration, it is recommended that participating hosts and the PDP belong to the same NT domain or Kerberos realm. ACS systems share the *AcsService* account. Any password changes for this account must be synchronized. Note that the mechanism described requires only that the hosts and the first-hop PDPs participate in the Kerberos security environment described. Third-party PDPs may use alternate security mechanisms beyond the first hop.

14.8 Summary

The Microsoft ACS offers the (signaled QoS-related) functionality of a combined PEP and PDP. As such, it can be used to manage network resources granted in response to RSVP-signaled requests, based on policies stored in Active Directory. Because Microsoft servers are typically not in the path of network traffic, the ACS must use alternate means to intercept RSVP messages. To this end, the ACS is implemented either on a host-based implementation of the SBM or, alternatively, on the Microsoft RAS server. This imposes certain restrictions on deployment scenarios. Nonetheless, the SBM-based ACS offers compelling functionality by unifying network resource management with Active Directory and leveraging existing security and administrative infrastructure. In the long term, Microsoft expects industry-standard PEP/PDP combinations based on switches and routers to proliferate. These will offer greater deployment flexibility while still leveraging the Active Directory infrastructure.

The ACS enables the network manager to provision admission control limits based both on resource availability (resource-based) and on user privileges (policy-based). ACSs in the path of signaled resource requests review each request and apply admission control by either admitting or rejecting the request. Windows 2000 hosts cooperate by marking traffic with 802 user_priority values and DiffServ codepoints based on the results of admission control.

ACS policies are hierarchically structured with enterprise-wide policies at the top of the hierarchy and per-subnet policies at the bottom. If the ACS finds an authenticated user identity in a resource request, it evaluates the request against provisioned policies in the following order of precedence:

- User policy for the subnet on which the ACS is active

- OU (to which the user belongs) policy for the subnet on which the ACS is active

- Policy for any authenticated user on the subnet

- User enterprise-wide policy

- OU (to which the user belongs) enterprise-wide policy

- Enterprise-wide policies for any authenticated user

If the ACS does not find an authenticated user identity in a resource request, it evaluates the request against provisioned policies in the following order of precedence:

- Policy for all unauthenticated users on the subnet on which the ACS is active

- Enterprise-wide policies for all unauthenticated users

In addition to the user-based policies, it is possible to provision aggregate resource limits on a per-subnet basis, independent of the requesting user.

All policies are managed via the ACS management console. This user interface serves as a window into Active Directory QoS policies. It can be invoked from any ACS or from any Windows 2000 server running the administrative tools utilities.

It is a simple matter to use the ACS to manage resources on an isolated 802 subnetwork. Typically, however, WAN links are more congested and benefit most from the type of explicit admission control provided by the ACS. When Microsoft RAS servers drive these WAN links, the ACS can be enabled on the RAS server. Otherwise, a number of industry-standard switch- and router-based PEP/PDP combinations are emerging. These are capable of providing explicit admission control on WAN links while still leveraging the Active Directory management infrastructure. Without switch- or router-based PEP/PDPs, it is possible to apply Microsoft's SBM-based ACS creatively to address a variety of deployment scenarios.

Microsoft supports the LPM API and makes the Microsoft LPM DLL available to third parties. These make it possible for third parties to leverage the SBM-based ACS for integration with third-party policy servers, or to use third-party PDPs to enforce policies based on Active Directory.

PART IV

Appendixes

Appendix A   Troubleshooting and Demonstrating Windows 2000
              QoS Functionality

Appendix B   References

Troubleshooting and Demonstrating Windows 2000 QoS Functionality

This appendix begins with a description of various tools that may be used to troubleshoot Windows 2000 QoS functionality. It continues with a brief review of the Windows 2000 QoS mechanisms and the types of network devices with which they interact. This review sets the stage for a discussion of the recommended methodology for troubleshooting Windows 2000 signaled QoS deployments. Finally, this appendix concludes with a section that describes a specific scenario for demonstrating Windows 2000 QoS functionality and shows how the troubleshooting methods described can be applied to this scenario.

Although Microsoft QoS mechanisms support both signaled and provisioned QoS for both unicast and multicast traffic flows, this appendix focuses on signaled QoS for unicast traffic flows.

A.1   QoS Troubleshooting Tools

This section discusses various Windows-based QoS troubleshooting tools and their use in troubleshooting QoS scenarios. Some of these tools are included with the standard Windows 2000 product. Others are available in the Windows 2000 Resource Kit. Yet others are available only by special request from Microsoft. The tools are described briefly in this appendix. For further details on each tool, see documentation associated with the specific tool.

tracert

This tool is included with the standard Windows 2000 product. It identifies all routers in the path, from sender to receiver. At the sender's command prompt, type the following command:

```
tracert  <receiver IP address>
```

After some time, the sending host will print the IP addresses of an interface on each router in the route from sender to receiver. This list will be helpful in identifying nodes that might be dropping or blocking RSVP messages or data.

wdsbm

This tool is available by request from Microsoft. It identifies the ACS/SBM (the DSBM) that manages the segment to which a specific host is attached. To invoke it, type the following command at the host:

```
wdsbm -i <local interface IP address>
```

wdsbm will respond by printing information regarding the DSBM that is handling RSVP messages transmitted from or destined to the interface specified. This information includes the IP address of the DSBM. Because the DSBM may block RSVP messages, it is helpful to know the address of the DSBM when attempting to isolate the location at which RSVP messages are blocked.

RSVP Tracing

RSVP tracing can be enabled in the standard Windows 2000 product. By enabling RSVP tracing on sender and receiver, the user can easily verify that the following is taking place:

- Applications are making the expected calls to the GQoS API (non-ACS hosts only).

- The QoS service provider is generating the expected RSVP messages for transmission to the network.

- The expected RSVP messages are arriving from the network.

Note

It is not possible for a single host to simultaneously host GQoS-enabled applications and the ACS service. On the ACS, the user can use RSVP trace files to inspect received and transmitted RSVP messages, but because there can be no GQoS-enabled application running on the ACS, there will be no GQoS API entries in the trace.

To enable RSVP tracing on a host, it is necessary to add the value `EnableTracing` under the following registry key: HKLM\System\CurrentControlSet\Services\RSVP\Parameters.

The value is of type `REG_DWORD` and should be set to `0x1`. Next, it is necessary to restart the RSVP service. To do so, type the following at the command prompt:

```
net stop RSVP <CR>
net start RSVP <CR>
```

Note

Applications that make use of the QoS service provider should also be stopped and restarted.

The QoS service provider will now generate a log file in the directory %windir%\system32\logfiles.

Log files are named RsvpTraceNN.TXT, where *NN* is a number from 00 to 09. Each log file is limited in size. As a log file is filled up, one is created with the next sequence number. When the last log file is filled, the first is overwritten. The user should inspect the list of log files and the created dates to determine which log file is currently being written. It is possible to monitor data being written to the log file in real time by typing the following command:

```
tail -f RsvpTraceMM.TXT
```

Here, *MM* is the trace file number.

Note

The `tail` command is available as part of Windows Services for UNIX. It is not part of the standard Windows 2000 product.

Further information on the RSVP message logs may be found in the Windows 2000 online help under "QoS" (only on machines running Windows 2000 Server or Windows 2000 Advanced Server).

netmon

The Microsoft Network Analyzer (netmon) can be used to monitor traffic on the network, to parse RSVP signaling messages, and to inspect DSCP and 802 `user_priority` markings in packet headers. netmon is included in the standard Windows 2000 product (and is available separately). It must be installed per the instructions in online help under "Network Monitor driver." Note that, depending on the version of netmon used, specific parsing functionality may or may not be available.

Note

It is possible to enable netmon on the sending or receiving host that is under test (the host generating or receiving RSVP messages or marked packets), or on an independent host that is attached to the network but that is not one of the hosts under test. The latter provides a more accurate indication of what is really happening on the network. For example, netmon running on a sending host may indicate that the host has generated a certain RSVP message or has marked a certain packet. However, network components below the netmon layer of the network stack (such as netcard drivers) may prevent the message from actually reaching the network or may alter packet markings before a packet is actually transmitted. This condition would be detected by running netmon on a separate host.

On the other hand, running netmon on the host that is being monitored provides a more accurate indication of what is actually happening on the host. The decision of whether netmon should be run on the host that is being monitored, a separate device, or both depends on the specific problem being investigated.

When running netmon on a separate host, it is important to ensure that the machine running netmon is not attached to the network via a dedicated port on a learning bridge type switch (most switches today are of this type). If it is, the switch may prevent it from seeing traffic that is not addressed specifically to the monitoring host. Generally, hubs and repeaters do not act as learning bridges and will flood traffic from each port to all other ports. Use such a hub or repeater to attach the monitoring machine to the same switch port as the machine that is being monitored.

Note that (consistent with Heisenberg) the addition of a monitoring machine in a manner that alters the network topology might impact the behavior of the system under test. For example, altering a point-to-point, switch-to-host connection by introducing a hub and a monitoring device may cause a different device to become the DSBM or may cause a change in the available bandwidth. The impact of any such changes in network topology must be considered.

Monitoring RSVP Messages

As a first step in verifying the transit of RSVP messages through the network, netmon can be installed on the sending and receiving hosts. Various capture filters may be configured. One filter might capture all traffic sent to or from the monitored host. An alternate filter might capture all traffic for the RSVP protocol (IP protocol 46). The capture should be started on each machine before the sending application is started. (RSVP messages are typically refreshed every 30 seconds. This should be taken into consideration when deciding how long to let the capture run.)

When the capture is complete, it is helpful to use the display filter to extract only RSVP messages from the captured data. Traces of RSVP messages should indicate a PATH message sent by the sender, arriving sometime later at the receiver. The receiver should respond with an RESV message, which arrives back at the sender. If the traces do not confirm this behavior, then one or both of the message types may have been dropped in transit or may not have been generated by the host. There should be no PATH-TEAR or RESV-TEAR messages in the trace, as long as the application is running an active QoS seesion. If there are PATH-TEAR or RESV-TEAR messages, this may be an indication that one of the application peers has terminated all QoS sessions or that an RSVP-aware network node in the path from sender to receiver has decided not to admit an RSVP request. Various RSVP error messages may indicate other problems.

Monitoring 802 user_priority *Marks*

Note that, counter intuitievely, netmon will reveal 802 user_priority marks only if it is run on a receiving host that does not have drivers capable of 802 user_priority (or on which 802 user_priority functionality has been disabled via the advanced configuration options). Drivers that are capable of 802 user_priority will generally strip off the 802 user_priority marks before handing the packets up to netmon so that they will not be observable. Because netmon can be used only to monitor user_priority marks on machines that are not enabled for 802 user_priority, it may be necessary to introduce a monitoring machine that is separate from the actual receiving host.

rsping

This tool can be used to quickly determine whether a certain network path is blocking RSVP signaling messages. It is available by request from Microsoft. Unlike RSVP tracing (which enables the user to *observe* RSVP messages arriving at or generated at a specific host), rsping actually enables the user to *generate* specific styles of RSVP messages for transmission to an RSVP peer. If it is suspected that certain RSVP messages are not arriving at their intended destination, rsping may be used to detect whether the network is at fault.

A number of options to rsping support the generation of differing types of RSVP messages. In all cases, both PATH and RESV messages are generated. However, it is possible to specify whether these should be generated for multicast or unicast sessions, the IntServ service type, and the flow rate. There are certain constraints—for example, multicast RESV messages will be of the wildcard filter (WF style), while unicast messages will be of the fixed filter (FF) style.

It is possible that the results of rsping indicate that the network is passing the RSVP messages being generated but that the network is dropping the specific messages generated by an application under test. In this case, the composition of the RSVP messages generated by the application likely differs from that generated by rsping. rsping should be invoked using the parameters that most closely emulate the RSVP messages generated by the application under test. These messages can be observed by inspecting the RSVP tracing file on the transmitting host.

Network Device Management Consoles

Various RSVP-aware network devices provide management consoles that may be used to monitor the presence of PATH state, RESV state, and installed reservations, or even to track individual RSVP messages arriving at the device. These tools are useful in case a device is suspected of dropping or rejecting RSVP messages in transit between sender and receiver.

Cisco routers provide a *CLI* interface. Useful commands are these:

- **sho ip rsvp int**—Shows the interfaces over which RSVP is enabled and the provisioned admission control limits (total and per-flow) available on the interface. Check that the capacity requested is less than the provisioned limits available. If RSVP is disabled on both interfaces in a path, the router should pass RSVP messages unhindered. However, if RSVP is disabled on one interface on a PATH, it may drop or reject all RSVP messages.

- **sho ip rsvp sender**—Shows PATH state. If a sender is transmitting PATH messages on a path including this router, then this command should show PATH state corresponding to the sender. If it does not, the PATH messages are being dropped or rejected upstream in the network.

- **sho ip rsvp res**—Shows RESV state. If a downstream receiver (a receiver on the other side of the router from the sender) is transmitting RESV messages upstream on a path through this router, then this command should show RESV state for the corresponding session. In the case of multicast, the presence of RESV state at a particular router does not confirm that RESV messages from a particular receiver are arriving at the router. Rather, it confirms that RESV messages from at least one receiver (that is, downstream from this router) are arriving at the router.

- **sho ip rsvp installed**—Shows installed reservations.

In addition, the command debug ip rsvp provides very detailed debugging information regarding message-by-message RSVP processing. Use this command with caution. Debug information will appear only on a console that is directly connected to the router's console port (not on Telnet consoles). In addition, debug mode may consume a significant fraction of the router's CPU bandwidth. Enabling debug from a Telnet port may leave the router so busy that it is incapable of supporting the remote Telnet, thereby disconnecting the user.

TcMon

This is the traffic control monitor, available in the Windows 2000 Resource Kit. It is described briefly in Chapter 13, "The Traffic Control API and Traffic Control Components." TcMon can be used to verify the creation of kernel traffic flows and to identify characteristics and statistics associated with interfaces (such as whether 802 user_priority is enabled) or with each flow (such as service type, tagging or marking in effect, bytes transmitted on the flow, and so on).

To install TcMon, run Setup from the TcMon install directory. When Setup completes, invoke TcMon by typing `TcMon <CR>` at the command line. The TcMon dialog box will appear. Be sure to select the appropriate interface on which to monitor traffic control. When looking for changes in flow parameters (such as changes in service type), it is helpful to enable auto refresh mode from the Refresh pull-down menu.

perfmon

This tool is included with the standard Windows 2000 product. It may be used to monitor traffic control, RSVP, and ACS parameters. To invoke perfmon, type `perfmon <CR>` at the command prompt. Use the + button to add counters. From the Add Counters dialog box, select Psched Pipe to monitor traffic control parameters such as the number of flows installed and the number of packets queued in various components of the packet scheduler. Select ACS/RSVP Service from the Add Counters menu to monitor parameters such as API calls, PATH messages, RESV messages, and so on.

qtcp

This tool can be used to measure end-to-end network integrity and service quality for the verification of QoS. It is available in the Windows 2000 Resource Kit. qtcp sends a sequence of test packets through a network and then reports on the relative queuing delay experienced by each packet. Packets that do not arrive at the destination are recorded as dropped packets. qtcp may be used either on a production network or on a controlled network that may be artificially congested. Online Appendix C (www.newriders.com) discusses qtcp in depth.

ACS Accounting Logs

The ACS generates accounting logs. These can be reviewed to determine such information as the following:

- Who is using network resources

- The date and time at which sessions begin and end

- Addressing information associated with sessions

Further information on the ACS accounting logs may be found in the Windows 2000 online help under "QoS" (only on machines running Windows 2000 Server or Windows 2000 Advanced Server).

readpol

This tool can be used to display the ACS policies in effect for the requesting user in a particular domain. It is available by request from Microsoft. This tool is the only way to identify the policies that apply to a specific user without using the ACS UI or having administrator privileges. readpol may be particularly useful in tracking the propagation of PATH or RESV messages when the ACS is suspected of blocking these because of restrictive policies.

Noise-Generation Tools

QoS mechanisms serve to grant certain traffic prioritized access to network resources. As such, the effects of QoS are measurable only when resources are scarce (when some part of the network is congested). To evaluate and characterize the benefits of various QoS mechanisms, it may be desirable to artificially congest a network in a controlled manner. The tools described next may be used to do so.

Note that to simulate noise as realistically as possible, it is desirable to generate multiple simultaneous sessions (on different source and destination IP addresses) and to generate traffic with a packet size distribution that mimics the pattern of traffic in a production network. This is because many of the QoS queuing mechanisms vary in effectiveness based on the number of simultaneous conversations and the distribution of packet sizes.

Note

Noise generation can tax the resources of a host. Ideally, test noise loads should be generated by independent dedicated hardware (such as the SmartBits traffic generator described later in this appendix). When host-based software traffic generators are used, these should be run on separate hosts (not on the device under test) to avoid interaction between the test software and the software under test.

- **ttcp**—This tool is available in the Windows 2000 Resource Kit. It can be used to generate udp or tcp traffic between two hosts. It is possible to control buffer size, number of buffers, ports used, and other miscellaneous parameters. It is not possible to control the rate at which the transmitter sends (other than by use of the packet scheduler and TcMon, to create a shaped flow for the ttcp traffic). Only one conversation is generated for each instance of ttcp. Multiple conversations may be established by invoking multiple instances of ttcp (these will all have the same source IP address). To cause ttcp to drive the network more aggressively, it is recommended that it be invoked with the -a and -c options.

- **loader**—This tool, which is similar to ttcp, is available from Microsoft, by request. It differs from UDP in that it reports data generation rate in real time via a GUI and that it uses multiple threads to send more aggressively.

- **smartbits**—SmartBits is a hardware-based traffic generator (manufactured by Netcom Systems). It can be configured to generate thousands of simultaneous sessions (across different IP addresses) of varying packet sizes at specific rates.

A.2 Review of Windows QoS and Host/Network Interaction

To set the stage for a discussion of a signaled QoS troubleshooting methodology, it is helpful to review the Windows QoS mechanisms and the types of network devices with which they interact. The following review is very brief and is not intended to replace the detailed discussions of Windows QoS mechanisms in Chapters 11 through 14. This discussion assumes familiarity with the contents of these chapters.

The use of signaled QoS is based on two sets of related functionality in Windows hosts:

- End-to-end RSVP signaling
- Traffic control

Sending hosts generate RSVP PATH messages for certain traffic flows. These messages flow toward receiving hosts. In response, receiving hosts generate RSVP RESV messages. The exchange of RSVP messages between senders and receivers does the following:

- Requests resources from the network for a specific flow, at a specific service level
- Informs the network and peer hosts regarding the traffic transmitted on the flow

Network devices may act as *admission control agents* by participating in RSVP signaling. Admission control agents approve or reject RSVP signaled requests for network resources either by passing the RSVP messages unhindered or by blocking certain messages and returning error messages in response. (One such admission control agent is the Microsoft ACS, which is discussed in Chapter 14, "The Microsoft Admission Control Service.")

Sending hosts apply traffic control to transmitted traffic based on the response of admission control agents to the host-generated signaling. Traffic control includes nongreedy and greedy components. Nongreedy traffic control refers to packet scheduling and is applied (for quantitative flows) regardless of the response of admission control agents. Greedy traffic control refers to the marking of packet headers for prioritized service with a DiffServ codepoint (DSCP) or 802 user_priority value. (See Chapter 6, "Differentiated Services," and Chapter 7, "The Subnet Bandwidth Manager and 802 Networks," for a discussion of DSCPs and 802 user_priority values.) Greedy traffic control is applied only when the corresponding flow is admitted by the network, as indicated by the unhindered arrival of RESV messages in response to PATH messages, at the sending host.

Thus, by blocking RSVP signaling for certain traffic flows, network devices acting as admission control agents may control access to prioritized service by preventing Windows hosts from marking traffic on the corresponding flow. The troubleshooting techniques described in this appendix focus on the cycle by which hosts signal for admission to a specific service level and then mark traffic (or not) in accordance with the results of the signaling request.

Types of Network Devices

From a QoS perspective, network devices can be roughly categorized by whether they participate in RSVP signaling (act as admission control agents) and by whether they handle traffic on an aggregate basis or a per-conversation basis. Thus, in deploying QoS, one can expect to encounter the types of device behaviors described in the following paragraphs. Note that the behavior of a specific device is not necessarily fixed. A device may exhibit a certain type of behavior depending on the manner in which it is provisioned. (See the section "Static Global Provisioning Policies," in Chapter 9, "QoS Policy.")

RSVP-Aware, Per-Conversation Traffic Handling

These devices implement conventional RSVP/IntServ functionality. They participate in RSVP signaling, and they extract and store classification information (in the form of an IP 5-tuple) from RSVP messages. This classification information is then used to identify traffic that is associated with specific conversations and to handle it on a per-conversation basis. These network elements ignore the DSCP and 802 user_priority markings in the packet headers.

These devices are typically RSVP routers. However, similar functionality may be implemented in certain high-end switches.

RSVP-Unaware, Aggregate Traffic Handling

Other devices are not RSVP-enabled. In contrast to the devices described previously, these do not participate in RSVP signaling and do not extract classification information from RSVP messages. These handle traffic in aggregate, typically based on DSCP (routers) or

802 user_priority values (switches) marked in packet headers. All traffic with the same DSCP (or 802. user_priority tag) is handled in aggregate. These are conventional DiffServ routers or mid- to high-range 802 switches.

RSVP-Aware, Aggregate Traffic Handling

A third category of devices participates in per-conversation RSVP signaling (to varying degrees) but handles traffic in aggregate, based on DSCP and/or 802.1p. Many of the RSVP-aware, per-conversation traffic-handling devices described previously can be provisioned to offer this type of behavior.

> **Note**
>
> For example, an RSVP-aware router may be provisioned to enable RSVP but to disable the associated per-conversation traffic handling. The RSVP signaling is used to offer explicit admission control per provisioned limits (and policy). However, instead of per-conversation traffic handling, these devices may be provisioned to handle traffic in aggregate, such as based on IP precedence markings (or DSCP).

The Admission Control Service (ACS) and the Subnet Bandwidth Manager (SBM)

Microsoft's *Admission Control Service* (ACS) is described in detail in Chapter 14. The ACS does not handle data traffic. Instead, it intercepts RSVP messages for the purpose of providing admission control based on resource availability and on *Active Directory*-based policies. Therefore, the ACS is in the *control* path, but not in the *data* path. As such, it represents yet another category of device. There are two implementations of the ACS, as described in the following paragraphs.

SBM-Based ACS

In one configuration, the ACS operates on a Windows server acting as the *Subnet Bandwidth Manager* (SBM). The SBM intercepts RSVP messages on shared networks (see Chapters 7 and 14 for an explanation of *shared* networks). As a result, the SBM is capable of admitting or rejecting RSVP requests traversing the shared network based on configured limits. If ACS functionality is enabled on the SBM platform, the SBM process hands the RSVP message to the ACS process for admission control based on policies in Active Directory. Note that the SBM and the ACS are only in the control path, not in the data path. Also, note that although there may be several SBMs on a shared network, only one of them is responsible for intercepting RSVP messages at any time. This one is known as the *Designated* SBM (DSBM).

RRAS-Based ACS

In an alternate implementation, the ACS is implemented on the RRAS routing platform. In this implementation, the ACS is inherently in the path of RSVP messages transiting the RRAS router's WAN interfaces. As a result, it is capable of admitting or rejecting the RSVP messages for the purposes of policy-based admission control. Again, the ACS component itself is not in the data path. However, the RRAS router is in the data path.

A.3 Troubleshooting Methodology

This section explains the general methodology that is recommended for troubleshooting signaled QoS deployments. At the highest level, the troubleshooting methodology is based on the following steps:

1. First, verify that RSVP signaling messages are traversing the network as expected and are not dropped or blocked for any reason. This consists of verifying that PATH messages are transiting the network all the way from sender to receiver, and that RESV messages are returning all the way from receiver to sender.

2. When it has been verified that the RESV messages are arriving at the sender, the next step is to verify that greedy traffic control is being correctly invoked and that it is effective.

This high-level approach is illustrated by the flowchart in Figure A.1.

Figure A.1	Top-Level Troubleshooting Flowchart

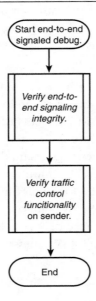

This approach is developed in the remainder of this section.

> ### Note
>
> In the remainder of this appendix, various tools are mentioned in **boldface**. These are
> described in detail in the first section of this appendix (titled "QoS Troubleshooting Tools").

Sketching the Network Topology

In troubleshooting signaled QoS deployments, a helpful first step is to sketch the network
topology. It is necessary to identify any network devices en route from sender to receiver.
These include the hosts themselves, any Microsoft ACSs, and switches and routers. It is
especially important to identify any devices that participate in RSVP signaling.

> ### Note
>
> Note that the ACS is not in the data path between sender and receiver, although its SBM
> component is in the RSVP control path. (This is explained in Chapters 7 and 14.) Therefore,
> it must be considered for the purpose of troubleshooting signaled QoS.

Both **tracert** and **wdsbm** are useful tools to be used in determining the network topology.
Briefly, **tracert** can be used to identify all routers in the path from sending host to receiving host. **wdsbm** should be used to identify SBM-based ACSs on any shared segments in
the path. It is important to identify these because they will intercept RSVP messages transiting shared segments.

Verification of End-to-End Signaling Integrity

Verification of end-to-end signaling integrity can be decomposed into two subprocesses.
The first subprocess is illustrated in the flowchart in Figure A.2. This subprocess uses the
RSVP tracing file on the sending and receiving hosts to track the generation, receipt, and
handling of RSVP messages at the hosts. (See the section "RSVP Tracing," earlier in this
appendix, for details on generating RSVP trace files.) The results of this subprocess will
determine whether the following are true:

- End-to-end signaling is completing

- End-to-end signaling is failing to complete because of handling of RSVP messages at
  the sending or receiving host

- End-to-end signaling is failing to complete because of handling of RSVP messages in
  the network

If it is determined that end-to-end signaling is failing because of the handling of RSVP messages in the network, then the second subprocess is invoked. This subprocess is illustrated in the flowchart in Figure A.3.

Tracking the Generation, Receipt, and Handling of RSVP Messages by the Sending and Receiving Host

The following paragraphs describe how the RSVP tracing file is used to track the generation, receipt, and handling of RSVP messages at the sending and receiving hosts. Refer to the flowchart illustrated in Figure A.2.

Note

In the descriptions of flowcharts in this appendix, numbers in parentheses correspond to numbers on the flowcharts.

In (1), the RSVP trace file on the sender is inspected to determine whether a RESV message for the session of interest has been returned to the sender. If it has, then end-to-end signaling is functional; the next step is to verify traffic control functionality, as illustrated in the flowchart in Figure A.4.

If no RESV message for the session of interest arrives at the sender, the RSVP trace file on the receiver is inspected to determine whether it has received the sender's PATH. If it has, the lower-left branch of the flowchart in Figure A.2 should be pursued. Otherwise, the lower-right branch should be pursued.

Note

Note that two different methods may be used to determine whether a RESV message has arrived at the sender. One method uses the RSVP trace file. To use this method, it is necessary to enable tracing via the Windows registry. The alternative method is somewhat less direct. It uses **TcMon** at the sender to detect a change of service type for the session of interest (from nongreedy to greedy) as an indication that the corresponding RESV message has arrived.

Figure A.2   Verifying End-to-end Signaling Integrity

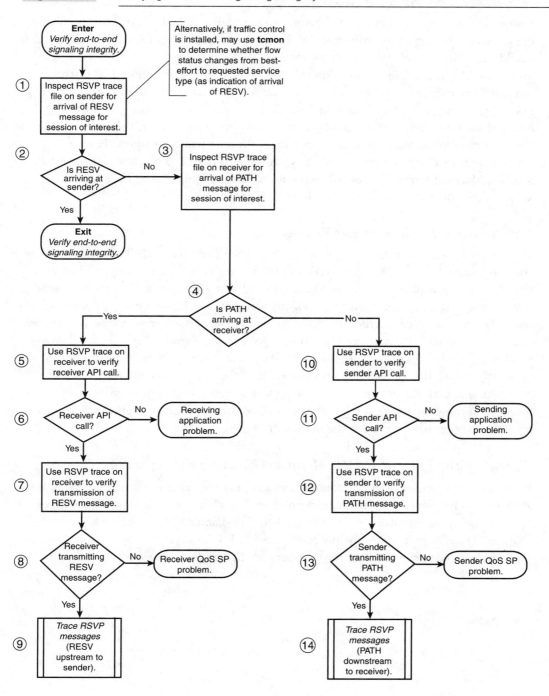

PATH *Message Is Arriving at Receiver*

Following the lower-left branch of the flowchart in Figure A.2, the RSVP tracing file on the receiver is inspected to verify that the receiving application has issued the API call that would cause the receiver to send a RESV message (5). If it has not, then there is likely a problem with the receiving application. If it has, then the trace file should be further inspected to verify that the QoS service provider on the receiver has sent the RESV message (7). (See Chapter 11, "The Microsoft QoS Components," for a discussion of the GQoS API and the QoS service provider.) If no RESV message has been sent, then there is a problem with the QoS service provider (or possibly with the manner in which the receiving application is invoking the services of the QoS service provider). If it has sent the RESV message, the next step is to proceed to the flowchart in Figure A.3 to trace the RESV message through the network on its route from receiver to sender (9).

PATH *Message Is Not Arriving at Receiver*

If the receiver has not received the RESV message, then the lower-right branch of the flowchart in Figure A.2 should be followed. In (10) the RSVP trace file is inspected to verify that the sending application has issued the API call that would cause the sender to send a PATH message. If it has not, then there is likely a problem with the sending application. If it has, then the trace file is further inspected to verify that the QoS service provider on the sender has sent the PATH message (12). If the QoS service provider has not sent the PATH message, then there is likely a problem with the manner in which the application is invoking QoS, or with the QoS service provider itself. If the QoS service provider has sent the PATH message, then the PATH message is being lost somewhere downstream, en route to the receiver. In this case, the next step is to proceed to the flowchart in Figure A.3 to further trace the PATH messages through the network (14).

Tracking the Flow of RSVP Messages Through the Network

If end-to-end signaling does not complete and neither the sending nor the receiving hosts are found to be preventing the completion of the signaling cycle, then RSVP messages likely are being intentionally blocked or are being mishandled in the network. The flowchart in Figure A.3 illustrates the process of tracing RSVP messages hop by hop through the network to determine where the messages are being blocked or mishandled.

Figure A.3 Tracing RSVP Messages Through the Network

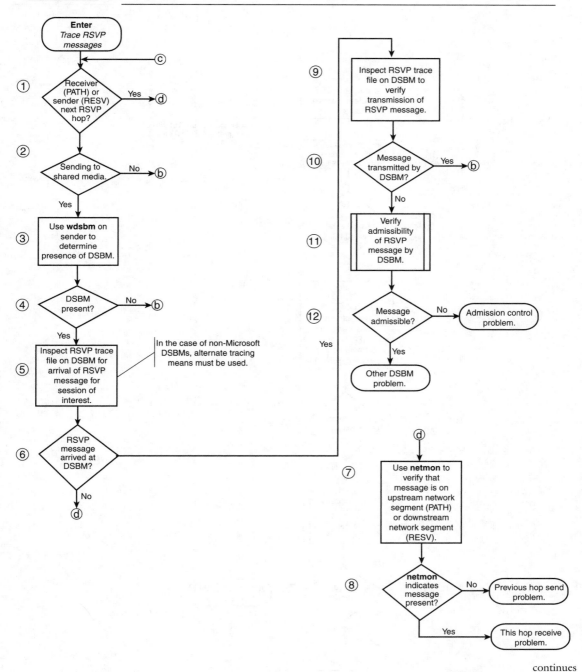

continues

Figure A.3 continued

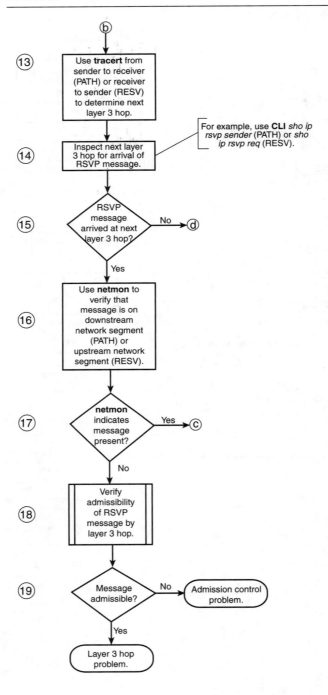

The flowchart in Figure A.3 should be used either to track PATH messages downstream from sender to receiver, or to track RESV messages upstream from receiver to sender. To aid in this process, it is helpful to identify each RSVP hop on the network path (see the previous section "Sketching the Network Topology"). In a purely routed network, RSVP-enabled routers are the only RSVP hops on the path. However, most networks include a shared or switched subnetwork. In this case, there may be a DSBM on the shared network that acts as an RSVP hop. The **wdsbm** utility can be used to identify DSBMs on the path.

The general process of tracing an RSVP message through the network is to use whatever means are available to inspect each RSVP hop for evidence of the receipt and the transmission of the message. When it appears that an RSVP hop has received but not sent the message, it can be concluded either that the message is intentionally deemed inadmissible at that hop or that the hop is malfunctioning. When an RSVP hop reports that it has sent the message, but the subsequent hop does not report receiving it, a network monitor (such as **netmon**) should be used to determine whether the message was successfully placed on the network by the previous hop.

Referring to the flowchart in Figure A.3, each RSVP hop is inspected on the path from sender to receiver (when tracing PATH messages) or from receiver to sender (when tracing RESV messages). When no RSVP hops remain, the trace is completed. Thus, in (1), the flowchart begins with a check to see whether the next hop is the receiver or the sender. If it is, then no RSVP hops remain. In this case, **netmon** is used (7, 8) to verify that the RSVP message was successfully transmitted by the previous hop. If there are RSVP hops remaining, it is necessary to determine whether the current hop is transmitting onto a shared segment (2). If it is not, then **tracert** can be used (13) to find the next RSVP hop. If the current hop is transmitting onto a shared segment, then the next hop may be a DSBM. In (3, 4) **wdsbm** is used to identify the next-hop DSBM. If there is no DSBM, then the next hop will be the next RSVP-enabled router in the path (13).

Tracing RSVP Messages Through a DSBM

If there is a DSBM (in the form of a Windows-based ACS), the RSVP trace file on the DSBM can be inspected to verify that the message has been received (5) by the DSBM. (If the DSBM is not in the form of a Windows-based ACS, then it will be necessary to use whatever logging or monitoring mechanisms are available for the specific DSBM device, to verify the arrival of the message.) If the message has not arrived at the DSBM, **netmon** (7, 8) can be used to verify that the message was successfully transmitted on to the shared segment on which the DSBM resides. If the message has arrived at the DSBM, the RSVP trace file on the ACS (or an alternate log file, if not a Windows ACS) should be inspected to verify that the DSBM transmitted the message onward (9).

If the message was received at the DSBM but has not been transmitted onward, the DSBM may have intentionally blocked it. This can be verified by checking the message for admissibility against the resource limits and policy used by the DSBM (11). If it is determined that the message should be admissible, there likely is a problem with the DSBM.

Note

Note that the ACS (and most DSBM implementations) will generate log entries for resource- or policy-based rejections. In addition, it should be possible to inspect these devices for resource limits that are in effect. RSVP messages can be inspected using network monitors to determine the resources that are being requested and the attached policy objects. Alternatively, on the ACS, RSVP trace logs list the contents of the RSVP message.

By comparing the request in an RSVP message with the resource limits and policies in effect at the admission control agent, it is possible to verify the admissibility of the request.

Tracing RSVP Messages Through Non-DSBM Hops

If the RSVP message is successfully forwarded by the DSBM, or if there is no DSBM between the current hop and the next hop, then **tracert** should be used to find the next RSVP hop (13).

Note

Note that **tracert** does not necessarily reveal the next RSVP hop, but rather it indicates the next IP router in the path. If the next router is RSVP-enabled, then it will also be the next RSVP hop.

Non-RSVP-enabled routers are not RSVP hops and are supposed to forward RSVP messages unhindered. However, certain routers may be configured (intentionally or unintentionally) to discard RSVP messages. If a non-RSVP-enabled router is suspected of dropping RSVP messages, **netmon** can be used to verify the presence of RSVP messages on both sides of the suspect router. Alternatively, **rsping** can be used to detect hops that are improperly dropping RSVP messages. If a router is found to be dropping RSVP messages, the network administrator should be asked to configure the router to pass them unhindered.

Also note that **tracert** lists hops in the direction from sender to receiver only. If RESV messages are being traced, the list must be traversed in reverse order.

When the next RSVP hop is identified, whichever management tools are available should be used to verify the arrival of the RSVP message at the hop (14). If the hop is a Cisco router, then Cisco's **CLI** may be used (as described earlier in this appendix). If the RSVP message has not arrived at the hop, **netmon** (7, 8) may be used to verify that the previous hop successfully transmitted the message to the network. If the RSVP message has arrived at the hop, **netmon** can be used to verify that this hop has successfully forwarded the RSVP message back to the network (16).

If the message has been forwarded onto the network, this hop is behaving properly and the trace is continued through the network (1). If the message has not been forwarded onto the network, this hop may have determined that it is not admissible. To determine whether this is the case, the message is inspected for admissibility (18). If it is not admissible, there is an admission control problem. (In this case, the policy system is functioning as it should.) If it is admissible, but the message has not been forwarded onto the network, then the hop is misbehaving.

Verifying Traffic Control Functionality on the Sending Host

When it is determined that end-to-end signaling is working correctly, the next step is to verify that traffic control functionality is being invoked in response. The QoS service provider on the sending host uses the TC API to invoke traffic control functionality. This appendix explains how to troubleshoot the traffic control functionality offered by the Windows 2000 Packet Scheduler. Note that this discussion does not address troubleshooting marking functionality beyond the sender, nor does it address troubleshooting actual traffic handling behavior in network devices in response to sender marking.

> **Note**
>
> The Windows 2000 QoS Packet Scheduler is the default traffic control provider on Windows 2000 hosts. (See Chapter 13 for a discussion of the QoS Packet Scheduler.) The Packet Scheduler provides 802 user_priority and DSCP marking (greedy) functionality as well as packet scheduling (nongreedy) functionality.
>
> The QoS Packet Scheduler can be installed on Windows 2000, but not on Windows 98. As a result, full marking and scheduling functionality is available only on Windows 2000.

Under normal operation, the QoS service provider creates a kernel traffic flow corresponding to each application traffic flow. The QoS service provider invokes nongreedy behavior as soon as the application calls the GQoS APIs. It invokes greedy traffic control later, after the network approves the corresponding signaling requests. Greedy traffic control should remain in effect as long as the application does not close (or otherwise terminate the QoS socket) and as long as the network does not reject the signaled request.

The flowchart illustrated in Figure A.4 describes the process of verifying traffic control functionality.

Figure A.4 Verifying Traffic Control Functionality

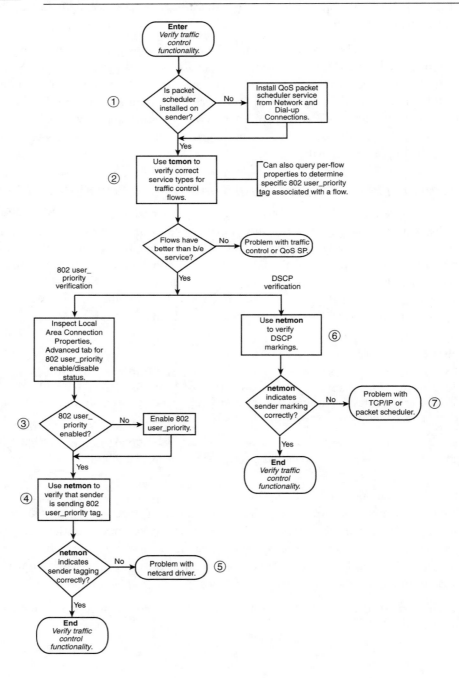

The first step in verifying traffic control functionality is to verify that the QoS Packet Scheduler service is installed on the sending host (1). After the QoS Packet Scheduler is installed, **TcMon** can be used to verify that the QoS service provider is properly creating kernel traffic flows and invoking the correct behavior (2).

Using TcMon to Verify the Creation of Traffic Flows and the Invocation of Greedy Traffic Control

Note

When invoking **TcMon**, be sure to select the appropriate transmit interface and to set it to auto refresh mode. **TcMon** will show all traffic flows that have been created in the kernel. In addition, it will show a flow for RSVP signaling traffic. This flow will be for the Network Control Service type and will remain active as long as RSVP is active.

Initially, **TcMon** will report traffic flows created on behalf of the application as being of the best-effort service type (recall that the service type of the flow determines the marking to be assigned to the flow's packets). The service type will remain the best-effort type until the network admits the corresponding RSVP requests (as indicated by the receipt of RESV messages for the session at the sending host). At that time, greedy traffic control will be invoked, and the service types indicated by **TcMon** will change to match the service types requested by the application. When this happens, packets on the flow should be marked in accordance with the service type indicated. If the indicated service types do not change from best effort, then either the QoS request has not been admitted by the network (see the previous section titled "Verification of End-to-End Signaling Integrity"), or there is a problem with the QoS service provider or with local traffic control.

Note

The procedure described relies on a change in service type as an indication that packets are being marked on a flow. The specific values marked can be deduced based on a knowledge of the mapping from service type to mark. However, the default mapping may be overridden by an alternate, registry-based mapping or by the inclusion of a DCLASS or TCLASS object with the returned RESV message. (See Chapter 13 for an explanation of marking behavior.)

In this case, **TcMon** can be used to determine the actual values used to mark packets on each flow. To determine the actual values used, inspect the per-flow parameters from the Parameters tab of the **TcMon** tool.

Verifying Packet Marking

The use of **TcMon**, described previously, indicates only that kernel traffic flows have been created for the appropriate service type and the 802 user_priority and DSCP values with which they *should* be marked. The next step is to verify that packets are *actually* being marked accordingly. Two branches are illustrated in the flowchart in Figure A.4. The left branch applies to 802 user_priority marking. The right branch applies to DSCP marking.

Verifying 802 user_priority *Marking*

802 user_priority marking relies on the cooperation of the native packet scheduler and a third-party netcard and netcard driver. The next step in verifying 802 user_priority marking is to check that the transmitting netcard is capable of marking 802 user_priority and that it is enabled to mark 802 user_priority (3).

To do so, select the appropriate netcard from the Network and Dial-Up Connections menu on the sending host. Then select the Advanced tab under the Configure button. There should be an option for enabling and disabling 802 user_priority (or 802.1p). If there is not, the netcard likely does not support 802 user_priority marking. If the option is available, be sure to enable it.

> **Note**
>
> Note that enabling 802 user_priority on the sender, but not on the receiver (or intervening switch), may result in a loss of connectivity. This can occur for a variety of reasons, primarily when the intervening switch or receiver is a legacy device. When an 802 user_priority tag is added to a maximum-length Ethernet packet, the total packet length exceeds the maximum length expected by legacy devices. As a result, the device may discard the packet. Most newer switches and receiving netcards can identify the 802 user_priority tag and respond accordingly.

After verifying that the netcard is capable of 802 user_priority marking and is enabled to do so, use **netmon** (or an alternate network monitoring tool) to verify that it is doing so (4). (See the accompanying sidebar, "Using Network Monitors to Verify Packet Marking.")

If the network monitor indicates that the netcard is not marking 802 user_priority, then either the netcard or the netcard driver is at fault (5).

Verifying DSCP Marking

DSCP values are marked by cooperation of the native packet scheduler and the native TCP/IP protocol stack. Use **netmon** (or an alternate network monitor) to verify that the sender is marking packets as expected (6). (See the accompanying sidebar, "Using Network Monitors to Verify Packet Marking.")

If the network monitor indicates that packets are not being marked with the expected DSCP, then either the packet scheduler or the TCP/IP stack may be at fault (7).

Using Network Monitors to Verify Packet Marking

To verify packet marking, it is necessary to use **netmon** (or an alternate network monitoring tool) to inspect the values marked in the 802 user_priority field or the DSCP field.

Network monitors predating the definition of the DSCP field (and many post-dating its definition, as well) will indicate the DSCP value in the IP Precedence or IP TOS fields of the IP packet header.

Network monitors predating the definition of the 802 user_priority field might not capture 802 user_priority marked Ethernet packets at all or may misrepresent them as having erred Ethernet headers. See the previous section, "QoS Troubleshooting Tools," for guidelines on the use of **netmon** to inspect packets for 802 user_priority values.

A.4   Demonstrating Windows 2000 Signaled QoS

This section describes a scenario that demonstrates aspects of Windows QoS functionality and the related troubleshooting process. The scenario described shows how the combination of QoS policy (via the ACS), 802 user_priority tagging on hosts, and network elements capable of 802 user_priority can protect the quality of a videoconference session in the face of a congested LAN link. A similar scenario can be demonstrated to simulate routed WAN links.

Note

The scenario described uses the NetMeeting application or the Phone Dialer application, both of which are included as part of the standard Windows 2000 product. In this example, the impact of QoS is most evident with respect to the video quality. Thus, a camera is required. By experimenting with parameters such as noise level and link bandwidths, it is also possible to use this demonstration to illustrate the impact of QoS on audio. In this case, a microphone is required.

continues

NetMeeting and Phone Dialer generally generate two RSVP sessions. One is for audio traffic and is for Guaranteed Service. The other is for video traffic and is for Controlled Load Service. The token bucket parameters for each may vary depending on the CODECS used. The typical range for the TokenRate parameter is 20–500Kbps.

Overview of the Demonstration Scenario

Figure A.5 illustrates the recommended configuration for this demonstration.

Figure A.5   Recommended Configuration

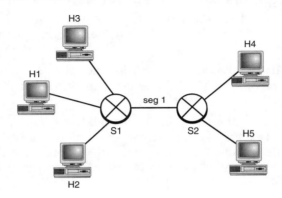

Table A.1 explains the role that each of the devices in Figure A.5 plays in the demonstration scenario.

Table A.1   Device Roles

Device	Role	Notes
H1	Signal sender	This device originates NetMeeting or Phone Dialer traffic to be protected.
H2	Noise source	This device acts as a source of noise to simulate network congestion.
H3	DSBM-based ACS and domain controller	Admission control server acts as a policy configuration point for the network administrator. It also serves as domain controller.
H4	Signal receiver	This device receives protected NetMeeting or Phone Dialer traffic.
H5	Noise sink	This device pulls noise through the network to simulate congestion.
S1	Congestion switch	The transmitting interface of S1 is the congestion point. This switch must be 802 user_priority capable.

continues

Device	Role	Notes
S2	Receiving switch	This device is not necessarily 802 user_priority capable.
seg 1	Congested link	This link must be limited to 10Mbps or another rate sufficient to cause congestion at outbound interface of S1.

> **Note**
>
> In Table A.1, "802 user_priority capable" means IEEE 802.1D-1998 compliant and implementing at least two traffic classes.
>
> All links illustrated are Ethernet links.
>
> S1 and S2 are not participating in RSVP signaling and are not acting as DSBMs.

Operating the Demonstration

The following steps describe the operation of the demonstration:

1. Configure ACS policy to restrict bandwidth for a specific user that has an account on H1 (for example, to limit the allowable data rate for the user to 10Kbps or less).

2. Start **loader** (or an alternate noise generator) on H2, with H5 as the noise receiver.

3. Log in to H1 using the user account specified in step 1.

4. Start NetMeeting or Phone Dialer on H1 and on H4.

5. Issue a call from H1 to H4.

6. Note the poor quality of the videoconference session on the receiver.

7. Remove the restriction for the specific user from the ACS.

8. Within 30 seconds, the quality should improve.

How It Works

When NetMeeting or Phone Dialer is started on the sender, it calls the GQoS API. This triggers the QoS service provider to send PATH messages on behalf of the sending application. Because the ACS is a DSBM on the local subnet to which the sender is attached, the sender will direct the PATH messages to the DSBM. Initially, policy in the ACS determines that the user is not entitled to the bandwidth requested. As a result, the ACS blocks the PATH message from progressing through the network and sends a PATH-TEAR message to the sender.

Because the sender's request for an RSVP reservation has been rejected, the sender will not invoke greedy traffic control, and the sender's traffic will compete with all other traffic in the network. Because of the noise generated by H2 and directed to H5, there will be congestion at the 10Mbps link, seg1. The NetMeeting or Phone Dialer packets will be starved of resources at this bottleneck, and only some small number of packets will actually arrive at the receiver, resulting in poor video quality.

When the sending user's restriction is removed from the ACS policy, the ACS will approve subsequent RSVP requests.

> **Note**
>
> Note that policy changes effected via the ACS user interface will be subject to two sources of delay. One source of delay results from the refresh interval at which the ACS updates its policies from the directory. The second source of delay results from the refresh rate of end-to-end RSVP messages. See the following discussion on the effects that delay the application of policy.

The next PATH message issued following removal of the restrictive policy will be approved and will be forwarded through the switches to the NetMeeting or Phone Dialer receiver. The receiver responds by issuing an RSVP RESV message back toward the sender. This message passes through both switches and arrives at the DSBM. At the DSBM, it will be approved and forwarded on to the sender.

At the sender, the reservation request will be considered to be admitted, and the sending QoS service provider will invoke greedy traffic control, changing the service type for the audio flow from best-effort to Guaranteed, and for the video flow from best-effort to Controlled Load. The sender's traffic control will begin tagging packets transmitted on the audio flow with user_priority 5 and packets transmitted on the video flow with user_priority 3. These subsequently get priority in S1 and bypass the queue that forms at the congested interface that transmits onto seg 1. All NetMeeting or Phone Dialer packets will arrive at the receiver, and the quality will improve.

Factors Delaying the Effects of Policy Changes

Note that the ACS policy UI actually changes policy in Active Directory. The ACS reads and caches policies from the directory at certain intervals. The default interval is 30 minutes. Thus, policy changes will be delayed by at least 30 minutes, unless this interval is changed. The interval can be specified in minutes from the Advanced tab of the ACS UI. Alternatively, for the purpose of expediting the effects of policy change in this demo, it is recommended the refresh interval be lowered to 15 seconds by creating the following registry value: HKLM\System\CurrentControlSet\Services\RSVP\MSIDLPM\DsCacheTimeOut.

This value is of type DWORD and represents the refresh interval in seconds. This overrides the value set via the Advanced tab of the ACS UI. Values below 15 seconds are not recommended because of the burden of frequent reads from the DS.

An additional source of delay results from the RSVP refresh interval itself. RSVP messages are refreshed every 30 seconds. These messages are the means by which policy changes are conveyed to hosts. Therefore, it is necessary to allow up to 30 seconds of delay before the effect of policy changes can be observed. Thus, with the cache interval in the registry set to 15 seconds and the RSVP refresh interval set to 30 seconds, a worst-case delay of up to 45 seconds can be expected before the effects of a UI policy change are observed at the receiving host.

Variations on the Demonstration Scenario

It is worth considering the following variations on the scenario described.

Varying Number of Sessions and Policy Configurations

If additional hosts are available, it is possible to configure two NetMeeting or Phone Dialer senders and two receivers. A different user account should be available on each of the two sending hosts. By configuring restrictions in the ACS for one of the users but not for the other, it is possible to show the relative quality of the two videoconference sessions side by side. This configuration avoids incurring the policy delays described previously when demonstrating the difference between QoS protected flows and non-QoS protected flows.

Examples so far have suggested creating a restrictive policy for a specific user. Alternate policy configurations would create a restrictive default policy for Any Authenticated User and a special nonrestricted policy for a specific user. Other variations are possible.

Demonstrating Other QoS Mechanisms

The scenario described illustrates the combination of per-conversation signaling with aggregate traffic handling. The ACS is the admission control agent. S1 provides aggregate traffic handling based on 802 user_priority. Alternate equipment can be used to illustrate other mechanisms. For example, routers can be used to replace the switches. The routers can be configured to enable RSVP/IntServ operation in which case, they are both acting as admission control agents and providing per-conversation traffic handling. Alternatively, the routers can be configured for aggregate traffic handling based on IP precedence (DSCP). In this case, they may also act as admission control agents (RSVP-enabled) or may rely on the ACS to offer policy-based admission control (RSVP-disabled).

Regardless of how the routers are configured, careful attention should be paid to the rate of the interrouter link. Typically, router-based demonstrations interconnect the routers via a simulated WAN link at a rate on the order of T-1 or fractional T-1. The noise and data rate should be chosen consistent with the interrouter link rate. For example, it makes little sense to expect QoS to carry a 1Mbps video stream over a 128Kbps link. When slower links are used, either a lower video rate should be used, or audio flows may be used instead.

Troubleshooting the Demonstration Scenario

This section describes the application of the troubleshooting techniques described earlier to the demonstration scenario.

Setup

First, verify that the equipment is configured correctly:

- A camera should be installed on H1. (To simplify the demo, protected traffic is sent in one direction only, obviating the need for a camera on H2.)

- Enable the QoS Packet Scheduler service, and install **TcMon** on H1.

- Configure the interswitch link for 10Mbps and 802 user_priority support.

- Configure switch-to-host links for 100Mbps and 802 user_priority support.

- Install a noise generator (**loader**) on H2. (Alternate noise generators may be used.)

- Configure ACS policy to deny reservations to the sending user on H1.

With the noise generator running, the videoconference session quality (as observed on H4) should be poor. If it is not, then either the noise generator is not running correctly (use **netmon** to verify), or the interswitch link is configured for 100Mbps rather than 10Mbps and is not acting as a bottleneck.

When poor quality has been verified, change the ACS policy to admit reservation requests from the NetMeeting sender. Quality should improve within 45 seconds. If it does not, proceed to troubleshoot this, as described in the following sections.

Sketching the Network Topology

Before proceeding, it's helpful to understand the network topology from an RSVP signaling perspective. In the configuration illustrated, PATH messages flow from H1 to the DSBM/ACS (H3) through S1, then S2, and to H4. RESV messages will flow back along the reverse path: H4 to S2 to S1 to the DSBM/ACS (H3) to H1. This topology can be discovered by inspection and does not require the use of **tracert** or **wdsbm**, as might be required in more complex topologies. In fact, because the network is completely switched and not routed, **tracert** will not provide any useful information. However, **wdsbm** can be used on H1 and on H4 to verify that the hosts see H3 as the DSBM/ACS.

Verifying End-to-End Signaling Integrity

The following sections discuss the process of tracking RSVP PATH and RESV messages as they move through the network. Be sure to qualify traces of RSVP messages with the sessions to which the messages correspond. NetMeeting and Phone Dialer use two QoS sessions: one for audio traffic and another for video traffic. These can be distinguished by the service type requested (Guaranteed for audio, Controlled Load for video) or by the specific QoS parameters (audio rate is lower than video rate).

Enable RSVP tracing on H1. Inspect the trace file for entries indicating the arrival of an RSVP RESV message. If no such entries are found, signaling is failing somewhere in the network. To isolate the part of the network in which signaling is failing, inspect the RSVP trace file on H4. Look for entries indicating the arrival of RSVP PATH messages from H1. If no entries are found, then PATH messages are being lost somewhere between the sender and the receiver. If such entries are found, then RESVs are not being properly generated or are being lost on their way back to the sender.

PATH *Messages Not Arriving at Receiver*

In the first case (PATH messages not arriving at receiver), determine whether PATH messages are being correctly generated by inspecting the RSVP trace file on H1. The file should contain PATH API entries, indicating that the sending application has requested QoS from the QoS service provider. If no such entries can be found, there is a problem with the sending application's invocation of QoS or with the QoS service provider. If PATH API entries are found, the next step is to look for PATH entries (immediately following the PATH API entries) indicating that the QoS service provider has sent a PATH message to the network. If PATH API entries are found, but there are no subsequent PATH entries, then there is likely a problem with the QoS service provider.

If PATH entries are found, the PATH messages are being generated by the QoS SP on H1 but are being lost in the network. The network includes the sending host's network stack, all network elements in the route from sender to receiver, and the network stack in the receiving host. In this case, it will be necessary to trace the transit of the PATH messages through the network.

As a first step in tracing the PATH messages through the network, invoke **wdsbm** on H1 to verify that the sender considers H3 to be the DSBM/ACS on the network. If it does not, there is a problem with the DSBM, and its configuration should be inspected to determine why it is not acting as the DSBM on the network. If H1 does report H3 as its DSBM, inspect the RSVP trace file on H3 to determine whether the PATH messages from H1 are reaching it. The RSVP trace file on H3 should show the arrival of PATH messages from H1 and their transmission on downstream.

If the RSVP trace file does not indicate that PATH messages are arriving at H3, then use **netmon** to verify that H1 is actually placing them on the network. **netmon** may be run on H3. If it indicates the arrival of PATH messages at H3, then there is a problem somewhere in the network stack of H3 above **netmon** or, more likely, in the receiving QoS service provider. However, if **netmon** does not indicate the arrival of PATH messages at H3, then H3's netcard is malfunctioning, or H1 is not placing the PATH messages on the network, or S1 is discarding the PATH messages. The best way to narrow down the problem is to run **netmon** on a separate machine to monitor the presence of PATH messages on the various segments between H1 and H3. This requires that the machine running **netmon** be connected to H1 or H3 via a dumb hub, not another port on S1. In addition, **rsping** can be used between H1 and H3 to verify that S1 is not discarding the messages.

If H3 does indicate the arrival of PATH messages, then the RSVP trace file should be inspected to determine whether the DSBM/ACS is forwarding them back onto the network towards H4. If entries are not found for the transmitted PATH messages, then the ACS likely is rejecting the PATH messages as a result of its policies. In this case, look for PATH-ERR messages sent toward H1. Verify that the policies configured in the ACS are correct.

If entries are found in H3's RSVP trace file indicating transmitted PATH messages, then the QoS SP on H3 considers itself to be forwarding the PATH messages from H1, and they are being lost somewhere in the network between H3 and H4. In this case, the problem may be in the network stack on H3 or H4, or in one of the intervening switches. Again, **netmon** may be used to trace the PATH messages through the network. A separate machine running **netmon** should be inserted at the three inspection points between H3 and H4. These include the segment connecting H3 to S1, seg 1 (between S1 and S2), and the segment connecting H4 to S2. Each of these segments will have to be broken and reconnected via a dumb hub attached to the host running **netmon**. In this manner, PATH messages can be tracked all the way to the network stack on H4.

If the PATH messages are determined to be lost in S1, then it is possible that they are being discarded because of the congestion at the interface to seg 1. In this case, they may not be marked with the appropriate *Network Control* priority 802 user_priority value. When using **netmon** to track PATH messages from H3, be sure to verify that they are marked with an 802 user_priority value of 7.

RESV *Messages Not Arriving at Sender*

If it is initially determined that PATH messages are arriving at the receiver, then either the receiver is not generating RESV messages in response, or the RESV messages are being lost in the network on the return route toward H1. The process of determining the point at which RESV messages are dropped is similar to that of determining the point at which PATH messages are dropped.

As a first step, inspect the RSVP trace file on the receiver, looking for RESV API entries. The presence of these entries indicates that the receiving application is correctly invoking receiving QoS. Their absence indicates that it is not.

If the receiver is generating RESV messages, these should be traced through the network. First inspect the RSVP trace file in the DSBM/ACS, and then, as necessary, use **netmon** to detect the specific point in the network at which the messages are being dropped.

Verification of Traffic Control Functionality

Verification of signaling integrity proves that RESV messages arriving at the sender. The next step is to verify traffic control functionality on the sender. To do so, install **TcMon** on the sender. From the **TcMon** dialog box, select the interface over which NetMeeting or Phone Dialer traffic will be sent. Configure **TcMon** for auto-refresh. **TcMon** should show three installed flows, one *Network Control Service* flow for RSVP traffic, one flow for audio traffic, and one for video traffic. The audio and video flows will be of the best-effort service type until reservations are approved for these flows. After reservations are approved, the service type for the audio flow will show as Guaranteed and, for the video flow, will show as Controlled Load.

Note that the transition of the flow service types (as reported by **TcMon**) upon receipt of the RESV messages for the corresponding sessions is a convenient mechanism for determining whether end-to-end signaling is functional without resorting to inspection of RSVP trace files. If service types remain best-effort, indicating a failure in end-to-end signaling, then it probably will be necessary to inspect RSVP trace files to narrow down the problem. However, if the service types do undergo the appropriate transition, then it is safe to assume that end-to-end signaling is working properly.

If **TcMon** indicates the expected transition in service types for the NetMeeting flows, then **TcMon** can be used to query the interface parameters to determine whether 802 user_priority marking is supported on the netcard. **TcMon** can also be used to inspect the actual marking in place for each flow. Alternatively, use the Advanced Configuration tab from the Local Area Connection Properties dialog box to verify that 802 user_priority functionality is enabled on the netcard. If there is no entry for 802 user_priority, the netcard does not support it.

If the sending host appears to be marking 802 user_priority, but audio and video traffic is still not being protected, there may be a problem with the netcard software or hardware. Use **netmon** (or an alternate network monitoring tool) to verify that the packets being transmitted by H1 are actually marked. If **netmon** is used, it is necessary to run it on a separate machine that is not equipped with a netcard driver that is capable of 802 user_priority (or on which the 802 user_priority functionality has been disabled). This machine should be spliced into the segment to which H1 is attached, using a dumb hub (as described previously in the section "QoS Troubleshooting Tools").

If **netmon** confirms that the sender is correctly tagging packets for high priority, yet flows are not protected, then it is possible that S1 is misconfigured. Verify that S1 is configured for 802 user_priority support on the port attached to seg 1.

References

The following list details the resources utilized in the writing of *Networking Quality of Service and Windows Operating Systems*. References are listed alphabetically according to the bracketed citations that appear throughout the text, or alphabetically by author.

Regarding Internet Drafts and RFCs

Internet Drafts are Internet Engineering Task Force (IETF) documents that must be considered works in progress and subject to change. These documents are updated or refreshed every six months (or more often). Each iteration is numbered incrementally. Updated versions will typically have the same title but a different index. The titles and dates for the Internet Drafts listed here are accurate as of the time of this writing. Internet drafts can be found at the corresponding IETF Web site: http://www.ietf.org/ID.html.

Requests for Comments (RFCs) are typically Internet standards or documents accepted for informational purposes. RFCs can be found at the corresponding IETF Web site: http://www.ietf.org/rfc.html.

[802.1D-1998] "Local and Metropolitan Area Networks—Common Specifications—Part 3: Media Access Control (MAC) Bridges (Incorporating IEEE P802.1p: Traffic Class Expediting and Dynamic Multicast Filtering)." 1998. Available at http://ieee.org.

[802.1Q-1998] "IEEE Standards for Local and Metropolitan Area Networks: Virtual Bridged Local Area Networks." 1998. Available at http://ieee.org.

[AGGREG] Baker, F., C. Iturralde, F. Le Faucheur, and B. Davie. "Aggregation of RSVP for IPv4 and IPv6 Reservations." Internet Draft, March 2000. Available at http://search.ietf.org/internet-drafts/draft-ietf-issll-rsvp-aggr-02.txt.

[CBQ] Floyd, S. and V. Jacobson. "Link-Sharing and Resource Management Models for Packet Networks." *IEEE/ACM Transactions on Networking* 3, no. 4 (1995).

[COMPRESS] Davie, B., S. Casner, C. Iturralde, D. Oran, and J. Wroclawski. "Integrated Services in the Presence of Compressible Flows." Internet Draft, February 2000. Available at http://search.ietf.org/internet-drafts/draft-ietf-intserv-compress-02.txt.

[CONCEPTUAL_MODEL] Bernet, Y., S. Blake, D. Grossman, and A. Smith. "An Informal Management Model for DiffServ Routers." Internet Draft, July 2000. Available at http://www.ietf.org/internet-drafts/draft-ietf-diffserv-model-04.txt.

[DCLASS] Bernet, Y. "Format of the RSVP DCLASS Object." Internet Draft, October 1999. Available at http://search.ietf.org/internet-drafts/draft-ietf-issll-dclass-01.txt.

[DKS] Demers A., S. Keshav, and S. Shenker "Analysis and Simulation of a Fair Queuing Algorithm." *SIGCOMM CCR* 19, no. 4 (1989): 1-12.

[DRR] Shreedhar, M. and G. Varghese. "Efficient Fair Queuing Using Deficit Round Robin." *SIGCOMM CCR* 25, no.4, (1995).

Feit, S. *Wide Area High Speed Networks.* Indianapolis: New Riders Publishing, 1999.

Ferguson, P. and G. Huston. *Quality of Service: Delivering QoS on the Internet and in Corporate Networks.* Wiley Computer Publishing, 1998.

Fortenberry, T. *Windows 2000 Virtual Private Networking.* Indianapolis: New Riders Publishing, 2001.

[GQOS_SPEC] MSDN at www.msdn.microsoft.com/library. Navigate via Table of Contents to: Platform SDK/Networking and Directory Services/Network Protocols/Quality of Service/QoS Reference.

[INTSERV_WEB] IETF Integrated Services Working Group. Available at http://www.ietf.org/html.charters/intserv-charter.html.

[IPSEC] Doraswamy, N. and D. Harkins. *IPSec: The New Security Standard for the Internet, Intranets, and Virtual Private Networks.* Prentice Hall, 1999.

[MCAST] Wittman, R. and M. Zitterbart. *Multicast Communication: Protocols, Programming and Applications.* Morgan Kaufmann, 2000.

[MCK91] McKenney, P. "Stochastic Fairness Queuing." *Internetworking: Research and Experience* 2 (1991): 113-131.

[MODEL] Bernet, Y., S. Blake, D. Grossman, and A. Smith. "An Informal Management Model for DiffServ Routers." Internet Draft, July 2000. Available at http://www.ietf.org/internet-drafts/draft-ietf-diffserv-model-04.txt.

[MPLS] Davie, B. and Y. Rekhter. *MPLS: Technology and Applications.* Morgan Kaufman, 2000.

[MS_KERB] "Windows 2000 RSVP Kerberos User Authentication Interoperability." Internet White Paper, January 2000. Available at `http://www.microsoft.com/windows2000/library/howitworks/communications/trafficmgmt/rsvp.asp`.

[Nag87] Nagle, J. "On Packet Switches with Infinite Storage." *IEEE Transactions on Communications* 35 (1987): 435-438.

[NULL_SERVICE] Bernet, Y., A. Smith, and B. Davie. "Specification of the Null Service Type." Internet Draft, September 1999. Available at `http://www.ietf.org/internet-drafts/draft-ietf-issll-nullservice-00.txt`.

[PG] Parekh, A. K. and R. G. Gallagher. "A Generalized Processor Sharing Approach to Flow Control in Integrated Service Networks." *IEEE /ACM Transactions on Networking 2 (1994): 137-150.*

[QUINN] Quinn, B. and D. Shute. *Windows Sockets Network Programming.* Addison Wesley, 1995.

[RED] Floyd, S., and V. Jacobson. "Random Early Detection Gateways for Congestion Avoidance" *IEE/ACM Transactions on Networking* 1, no.4 (1993): 397-413.

[REFRSH_REDUCT] Berger, L., D. Gan, G. Swallow, P. Pan, and F. Tommasi. "RSVP Refresh Overhead Reduction Extensions." Internet Draft, June 2000. Available at `http://www.ietf.org/internet-drafts/draft-ietf-rsvp-refresh-reduct-05.txt`.

[RFC 896] Nagle, J. "Congestion Control in IP/TCP Internetworks." January 1984.

[RFC 1157] Case, J., M. Fedor, M. Schoffstall, and J. Davin. "A Simple Network Management Protocol (SNMP)." May 1990.

[RFC 1349] Almquist, P. "Type of Service in the Internet Protocol Suite." July 1992.

[RFC 1509] Wray, J. "Generic Security Service API: C-bindings." September 1993.

[RFC 1633] Braden, R., D. Clark, and S. Shenker. "Integrated Services in the Internet Architecture: an Overview." June 1994.

[RFC 1779] Kille, S. "A String Representation of Distinguished Names." March 1995.

[RFC 1958] Carpenter, B. "Architectural Principles of the Internet." June 1996.

[RFC 2026] Baker, F., J. Krawczyk, and A. Sastry. "RSVP Management Information Base Using SMIv2." September 1997.

[RFC 2205] Braden, R., L. Zhang, S. Berson, S. Herzog, and S. Jamin. "Resource ReSerVation Protocol (RSVP)." September 1997.

[RFC 2207] Berger, L. and T. O'Malley. "RSVP Extensions for IPSEC Data Flows." September 1997.

[RFC 2208] Mankin, A., F. Baker, B. Braden, S. Bradner, M. O'Dell, A. Romanow, A. Weinrib, and L. Zhang. "Resource ReSerVation Protocol (RSVP) Version 1 Applicability Statement: Some Guidelines on Deployment." September 1997.

[RFC 2210] Wroclawski, J. "The Use of RSVP with IETF Integrated Services." September 1997.

[RFC 2211] Wroclawski, J. "Specification of the Controlled-Load Network Element Service." September 1997.

[RFC 2212] Shenker, S., C. Partridge, R. Guerin. "Specification of Guaranteed Quality of Service." September 1997.

[RFC 2213] Baker, F., J. Krawczyk, and A. Sastry. "Integrated Services Management Information Base using SMIv2." September 1997.

[RFC 2379] Berger, L. "RSVP over ATM Implementation Guidelines." August 1998.

[RFC 2380] Berger, L. "RSVP over ATM Implementation Requirements." August 1998.

[RFC 2381] Garrett, M. and M. Borden. "Interoperation of Controlled-Load Service and Guaranteed Service with ATM." August 1998.

[RFC 2382] Crawley, E., L. Berger, S. Berson, F. Baker, M. Borden, and J. Krawczyk. "A Framework for Integrated Services and RSVP over ATM." August 1998.

[RFC 2474] Nichols, K., S. Blake, F. Baker, and D. Black. "Definition of the Differentiated Services Field (DS Field) in the IPv4 and IPv6 Headers." December 1998.

[RFC 2475] Blake, S., D. Black, M. Carlson, E. Davies, Z. Wang, and W. Weiss. "An Architecture for Differentiated Services." December 1998.

[RFC 2481] Ramakrishnan, K. and S. Floyd. "A Proposal to add Explicit Congestion Notification (ECN) to IP." January 1999.

[RFC 2574] Blumenthal, U. and B. Wijnen. "User-based Security Model (USM) for version 3 of the Simple Network Management Protocol (SNMPv3)." April 1999.

[RFC 2597] Heinanen, J., F. Baker, W. Weiss, and J. Wroclawski. "Assured Forwarding PHB Group." June 1999.

[RFC 2598] Jacobson, V., K. Nichols, and K. Poduri." An Expedited Forwarding PHB." June 1999.

[RFC 2638] Nichols, K., V. Jacobson, and L. Zhang. "A Two-bit Differentiated Services Architecture for the Internet." July 1999.

[RFC 2686] Bormann, C. "The Multi-Class Extension to Multi-Link PPP." September 1999.

[RFC 2688] Jackowski, S., D. Putzolu, E. Crawley, and B. Davie. "Integrated Services Mappings for Low Speed Networks." September 1999.

[RFC 2697] Heinanen, J. and R. Guerin. "A Single Rate Three Color Marker." September 1999.

[RFC 2698] Heinanen, J. and R. Guerin. "A Two Rate Three Color Marker." September 1999.

[RFC 2746] Terzis, A., J. Krawczyk, J. Wroclawski, and L. Zhang. "RSVP Operation Over IP Tunnels." January 2000.

[RFC 2747] Talwar, M., F. Baker, and B. Lindell. "RSVP Cryptographic Authentication." January 2000.

[RFC 2748] Durham, D., J. Boyle, R. Cohen, S. Herzog, R. Rajan, and A. Sastry. "The COPS (Common Open Policy Service) Protocol." January 2000.

[RFC 2749] Herzog, S., J. Boyle, R. Cohen, D. Durham, R. Rajan, and A. Sastry. "COPS Usage for RSVP." January 2000.

[RFC 2750] Herzog, S. "RSVP Extensions for Policy Control." January 2000.

[RFC 2752] Yadav, S., R. Yavatkar, R. Pabbati, P. Ford, T. Moore, S. Herzog. "Identity Representation for RSVP." January 2000.

[RFC 2814] Yavatkar, R., D. Hoffman, Y. Bernet, F. Baker, and M. Speer. "SBM (Subnet Bandwidth Manager): A Protocol for RSVP-based Admission Control over IEEE 802-Style Networks." May 2000.

[RFC 2815] Seaman, M., A. Smith, E. Crawley, and J. Wroclawski. "Integrated Service Mappings on IEEE 802 Networks." May 2000.

[RFC 2816] Ghanwani, A., W. Pace, V. Srinivasan, A. Smith, and M. Seaman. "A Framework for Integrated Services Over Shared and Switched IEEE 802 LAN Technologies." May 2000.

[RFC 2872] Bernet, Y. and R. Pabbati. "Application and Sub Application Identity Policy Element for Use with RSVP." June 2000.

[RSVP_MPLS] Awduche, D., L. Berger, D. Gan, T. Li, V. Srinivasan, and G. Swallow. "RSVP-TE: Extensions to RSVP for LSP Tunnels." Internet Draft, August 2000. Available at `http://www.ietf.org/internet-drafts/draft-ietf-mpls-rsvp-lsp-tunnel-07.txt`.

[RSVP_WEB] IETF RSVP Working Group. Available at `http://www.ietf.org/html.charters/rsvp-charter.html`.

[SALTZER] Saltzer, J. H., D. P. Reed, and D. D. Clark. "End-To-End Arguments in System Design." *ACM TOCS* 2, no. 4 (1984): 277-288.

[SECURITY] Kaufman, C., R. Perlman, and M. Speciner. *Network Security—Private Communication in a Public World*. Prentice Hall, 1995.

[STD1] Reynolds, J. and R. Braden. "Internet Official Protocol Standards." March 2000. Available at `ftp://ftp.isi.edu/in-notes/std/std1.txt`.

[TC_API] MSDN at `www.msdn.microsoft.com/library`. Navigate via Table of Contents to Platform SDK/Networking and Directory Services/Network Protocols/Quality of Service/QoS Reference/Traffic Control Reference.

[TWO_TIER] Terzis, A., L. Wang, J. Ogawa, and L. Zhang. "A Two-Tier Resource Management Model for the Internet." *IEEE GLOBECOM 99*. December 1999.

[VW_DRAFT] Jacobson, V., K. Nichols, and K. Poduri. "The 'Virtual Wire' Per-Domain Behavior." Internet Draft, July 2000. Available at `http://www.ietf.org/internet-drafts/draft-ietf-diffserv-pdb-vw-00.txt`.

[YD] Yavatkar, R. and D. Durham. *Inside the Internet's Resource reSerVation Protocol: Foundations for Quality of Service*. Wiley Computer Publishing, 1999.

Index

Symbols

802 subnets
heterogeneous senders, support of, 286-287
legacy 802 subnets, 287-290
modern 802 subnets, 290-291

802 subnetwork scenarios, 623
complex 802 subnetworks, 624
IP telephony, 623
NonResvSendLimit, 624
streaming video traffic, 623-624

802 switch network
aggregate admission control limits, 603
hosts, trusting, 604
mapping service types to user_priority marks, 603
NonResvSendLimit, 604
per-service admission control limits, 603

subnetwork, applying single admission control limit to, 604-605
TCLASS objects, 605

802 user_priority marking, 582, 660

A

ABR (available bit rate), 300
accounting and billing, 402-403
accounting logs, 620, 643
ACS, 494-495
accounting logs, 643
described, 597
enterprise network consisting of multiple LANs interconnected by WAN links, 625-626
local and remote traffic, incapability to differentiate between, 626-627
topology-aware admission control, using user-based policies to support, 627

802 subnetwork scenarios, 623
complex 802 subnetworks, 624
IP telephony, 623
NonResvSendLimit, 624
streaming video traffic, 623-624
extensibility, 629
LPM API, 629, 631
Microsoft LPM, 631-632
third-party LPMs, 631
internal structure of, 599
LPM API, 629, 631
management of. *See* ACS management
Microsoft LPM, 631-632
overview, 600
RAS servers, 629
WAN networks, controlling resource usage on, 627-628
ACS instance, configuring SBM parameters on, 616
logging behavior, 619-620
NonResvSendLimit, 619
policy-caching behavior, 619

resource-based admission
control limits, 617
SBM protocol, operating
parameters of, 618
**ACS instance, enabling,
614-615**
ACS management
ACS instance, configuring
SBM parameters on, 616
logging behavior, 619-620
NonResvSendLimit, 619
*policy-caching
behavior, 619*
*resource-based admission
control limits, 617*
*SBM protocol, operating
parameters of, 618*
ACS instance, enabling, 614
installing ACS service, 615
*operating system versions
that support ACS, 615*
starting ACS, 615
*Windows NT domain,
configuring server as
member of, 615*
Active Directory, 610-611
*ACS management console,
611-612*
*multiple servers per
subnet, 613*
*multiple subnets per
server, 613*
*subnets, correspondence
between ACS instances
and, 612-613*
default policy-based
settings, 622
overview, 609
recommended policy
usage, 622
User Policy dialog box, 621
*general policy applicability,
621-622*
quantitative limits, 622

**ACS management console,
611-612**
**active configuration of
queuing schemes, 96, 99**
Active Directory
ACS management, 610-611
*ACS management console,
611-612*
*multiple servers per
subnet, 613*
*multiple subnets per
server, 613*
*subnets, correspondence
between ACS instances
and, 612-613*
packet scheduler, 583
administrative domains, 402
bandwidth brokers as
admission control agents,
403-404
RSVP, 404
*trade-offs resulting from,
405-407*
domain boundary issues, 402
*accounting and billing,
402-403*
*admission control
policies, 403*
**admission control, 19,
108-109, 147, 239-241,
574**
DSBMs, 284
multicast sessions, 285-286
*TCLASS object used to
negotiate user_priority
values, 284-285*
overview, 17
policing compared, 108
policy-based, 159-160
**admission control agent for
LANs, SBM as, 263-264**
DSBM, 265, 268-270
managed segments,
264-268
segments, 264

**admission control agents,
49, 323-324, 418, 428-429**
cable network, 477
density of distribution,
51, 53
**admission control
policies, 403**
**Admission Control Service.
See ACS**
**admission-control agents
(ACA), 180-182**
select congestion
points, 184
signaling density, 182, 184
**admitted flows, marking of
packets on, 589-591**
**AF PHB group, 17,
199-200**
TCBs, 223
schematic of, 226-227
SLS, 224-227
aggregate mechanisms, 20
**aggregate RSVP signaling,
165-166**
aggregate RSVP protocol,
166-167
establishing aggregate
reservations, 166
identifying aggregate
reservations, 166
**aggregate traffic handling,
43-45**
dynamic policies, 382-384
**application identifiers,
532-533**
**application-based
policies, 345**
**applications, GQoS service
provider information, 525**
API calls, responses to, 526
notifications, registering
for, 525
queries from applications to
QoS service provider, 525

**arbitrary network
conditions, 106**
assured forwarding PHB.
See **AF PHB group**
ATM
aggregation model, 312
cell tax, 295
circuit switching and
signaling, 295-296
benefits of, 296
compromises due to, 296
*RSVP/IntServ, mirroring
circuit orientation of, 297*
statistical multiplexing, 297
concepts of
*circuit switching and
signaling, 295-297*
*mapping IP to ATM,
298-300*
scheduling calls, 294-295
connection admission
control (CAC), 296
full heterogeneity
model, 308
homogeneous model, 310
IP over ATM and LAN
emulation, 314
LANE, 558
limited heterogeneity
model, 309
mapping IP to, 298-300
modified homogeneous
model, 311
multicast models, 307
overview, 19, 294
PVCs, 295-296
QoS support, 301
dedicated VCs, 305
*IP over ATM and LAN
emulation, 314*
*multiple point-to-point
PVCs, 302-303*
*point-to-point PVCs,
301-302*

RSVP mapping, 305
soft PVCs, 304
*VC management
supporting RSVP, 305-313*
RESV messages, 307
scheduling calls, 294-295
service types, 298
ABR, 300
CBR, 299
nrtVBR, 300
rtVBR, 299-300
UBR, 300
SVCs, 295-296
traffic control, 558
VC, 295-296
VCI, 295-296
ATM backbone, 425
admission control agents,
428-429
DSCP, nonsignaled traffic
translated to user_priority
from, 438
edge devices, 428-429
nonsignaled prioritized
traffic, 434
policy management system
used to configure edge
routers, 439
resources consumed in,
explicit admission control
for, 430
RESV admission control
for qualitative services,
432, 434
RESV admission control
for quantitative services,
430-432
traffic handling, 425-426
traffic transmitted onto
switched subnetworks,
policies regarding, 439-440
traffic transmitted onto,
policies regarding, 439
trust model, 434
UBR VCs, 429

ATM links, 128
**ATM traffic control
provider, 493**
ATMARP, 558
interfaces, 583
overview, 583
traffic control behavior,
585-587
VC parameters, 587
authenticated users, 607
authentication, 394
authored policies, 362-364

B
**backward-explicit
congestion notification
(BECN), 318**
bandwidth
defined, 10
queuing schemes
evaluation, 72
**bandwidth brokers as
admission control agents,
403-404**
RSVP, 404
tradeoffs resulting from,
405-407
**bandwidth constraints,
322-323**
admission control agents,
323-324
compression, 324
header compression, 325
hints, 325
**BBE (better-than-best-
effort) services, 34**
**behavior aggregate
classifiers, 213**
best-effort service, 206
**best-effort (BE) priority
traffic, 417**
bitwise round robin, 77
borrow mode, 569
borrow+ mode, 570

borrow-mode flows, 578

boundary provisioning

interior provisioning compared, 228-229

overview, 230

Braden, Bob, 103, 131

break bits, 144

buffer-management schemes.
See **dropping schemes**

building networks, 414

admission control agents, 418

down-level hosts, 422

hosts, 420

network-based application recognition, 423-424

policy management system, 424

simpler configurations of switched networks, 421-422

switched subnetwork requirements, 415

traffic-handling configuration in 802 switched subnetworks, 417

university campus network, 462

dormitory networks, 462-463

labs, classrooms, and administrative building networks, 463

C

cable network, 412

admission control agents, 477

cable plants, admission control in, 477

nonsignaled QoS within, 478

overview, 476

services, 476

traffic handling, 476

cable plants, admission control in, 477

cable-modem-connected end users, 475

CBR (constant bit rate), 299

cell tax, ATM, 295

central write, distributed read, 357-358

CIR, 318

circuit switching, packet switching compared, 110-111

Clark, Dave, 103, 131

class DRR, 82

class selector PHBs, 17, 200

class-based queuing

overview, 90-92

sharing hierarchy, 91-92

classification, 108

classifiers, 212

behavior aggregate classifiers, 213

filters, 213

ingress interface, based on, 214

multifield classifiers, 213

CLI, 28, 355

CODECS, 84

command-line interface, 28, 355

committed burst size (Bc), 319

committed information rate, 318

Common Open Policy Service Protocol. *See* **COPS**

compiled policies, 362-364

complex 802 subnetworks, 624

compression, 325

configuration mechanisms

overview, 21

provisioning mechanisms compared, 21-22

pushed mechanisms, 22

signaled mechanisms, 22

conformance analyzer, 564-565

congestion, 11, 64-65

congestion notification, 318-319

congestion-avoidance schemes. *See* **dropping schemes**

control plane, 499

Controlled Load Service, 117-118

applications, suitability to, 120

behavior of, 119-120

implementing, 120-121

parameters used to request, 118

Controlled Load Service flows, 574-575

COPS, 350

for provisioning, 354

for RSVP, 352-353

SNMP compared, 351-352

corporate campus network, 412

ATM backbone, 425

admission control agents, 428-429

DSCP, nonsignaled traffic translated to user_priority from, 438

edge devices, 428-429

nonsignaled prioritized traffic, 434

policy management system used to configure edge routers, 439

resources consumed in, explicit admission control for, 430

RESV admission control for qualitative services, 432, 434

RESV admission control
for quantitative services,
430-432
traffic handling, 425-426
traffic transmitted onto
switched subnetworks,
policies regarding,
439-440
traffic transmitted onto,
policies regarding, 439
trust model, 434
UBR VCs, 429
building networks, 414
admission control
agents, 418
down-level hosts, 422
hosts, 420
network-based application
recognition, 423-424
policy management
system, 424
simpler configurations of
switched networks,
421-422
switched subnetwork
requirements, 415
traffic-handling
configuration in 802
switched subnetworks, 417
overview, 413
**corporate campus
subnetwork, 411**
costs of signaling, 51
CS3 PHBs, 448
CS5 PHBs, 448

D

**data access interface
directory, 360**
data plane, 499
data storage model, 359
data stores, 27, 356-357
directory, 357
data access interface, 360
schemas, 360

user interface, 360-362
requirements of, 357
central write, distributed
read, 357-358
efficient data storage
model, 359
fault tolerance, 358
reusability of management
data, 359
security, 358
**DCLASS object, 178-179,
243, 445**
IntServ/DSCP mappings,
used to override, 385-387
dedicated VCs, 305
default best-effort flow, 573
**deficit round robin, 80,
82, 576**
density of distribution
admission control agents,
51, 53
defined, 42
designated SBMs. *See*
DSBMs
DiffServ, 16
architecture
DSCP, 194-195
overview, 193-194
per-hop behavior (PHB),
194-195
SLA, 196
SLS, 196
TC components, 196
customer traffic conditioning,
provider traffic conditioning
compared, 244-245
customers, adding, 374, 376
domains, 202
DSCP, 194-195
Frame Relay, 320
historical background,
191-192
DiffServ provider,
perspective of, 193

formation of DiffServ
working group and its
charter, 192
RSVP/IntServ and
DiffServ, 192-193
IP tunnels, 249
IPSec, 249
marking, shaping
compared, 247
multicast services, 248
PHBs, 16, 194
AF, 17
class selector, 17
and DSCPs, 195
EF, 17
services compared, 195
standard groups, 197-200
policy. *See* DiffServ policy
provider traffic conditioning,
customer traffic conditioning
compared, 244-245
provisioning
boundary provisioning,
228-230
dynamic, 235
interior provisioning,
228-229, 231-232
overview, 228
route-constrained services,
232-234
route-independent services,
234-235
simultaneous support
for route-constrained
and route independent
services, 232
static, 235
QoS mechanisms, mapping
to other, 247
regions, 202
RSVP, with, 135
admission control,
239-241
DCLASS object, 243

mapping RSVP signaled services to DiffServ services, 243-244
overview, 238
traffic classification, 241-243
RSVP/IntServ and, 192-193
services, 16, 201
  customers, 201
  dynamic, 210
  extent of, 209-210
  guarantees, levels of service, 203
  network boundaries, 201
  providers, 201
  quality of, 202-203
  scope of, 208-210
  static, 210
  traffic constraints, 202-203
  types of, 204-208
shaping, marking compared, 247
SLAs, 16, 196
SLS, 196
TC components, 196
TCBs, 217
  AF PHB group, 223-227
  gold service, 227
  schematic of, 219-220, 222-223
  silver service, 227
  VLL service, 221-223
  VLL service supported at DiffServ ingress, 217-218
  VLL service supported by SLS, 218-219
traffic conditioning
  blocks. See TCBs
  components, 212-216
  overview, 210, 212
trust boundaries, 245-247
trust domains, 245-247

DiffServ codepoint.
See DSCP
DiffServ mode, 592-593
DiffServ policy
components
  push provisioning model, 236-237
  real-time measurement, provisioning based on, 238
  signaling provisioning model, 237-238
push provisioning model, 236-237
real-time measurement, provisioning based on, 238
signaling provisioning model, 237-238
directories, 357
data access interface, 360
schemas, 360
user interface, 360-362
discard mode, 570
distortion-tolerant applications, 117
domain boundary issues, 402
accounting and billing, 402-403
admission control policies, 403
dormitory networks, 462-463
down-level hosts, 422
droppers, 216
dropping schemes, 70-71
random early detection, 93
tail dropping, 93
traffic types, suitability of drop schemes to various, 95
weighted random early detection, 94-95
DRR, 80, 82, 576
DRR+, 82

DSBMs, 265
admission control, 284
  multicast sessions, 285-286
  TCLASS object used to negotiate user_priority values, 284-285
density of distribution, 268
  dense distribution of, 269
  intermediate distribution of, 270
  sparse distribution of, 269
dynamic policies
  IP telephony, 418-419
  qualitative signaled traffic, 419-420
  video traffic, 418-419
forwarding PATH messages beyond, 280-281, 283
election priorities, 273
election protocol, 271, 273
fault tolerance, 273
intermediate distribution of, 270
managed segments, formation of, 271, 273
overview, 27
RSVP messages traced through, 655-656
sparse distribution of, 269
DSCP, 16, 194-195, 445
low bit rate links, 334
user_priority compared, 253-254
DSCP marking, 581-582
verifying, 661
DSL, 413
dynamic policies, 341-343
aggregate traffic handling, 382-384
contents, 392-393
DCLASS object used to override IntServ/DSCP mappings, 385-387
evaluation of, 392-393

identity objects, 388-389
translating, 396, 398
IP telephony, 418-419
operation of, 379-380
overview, 378
PATH messages, 387
PEP configuration
options, 387
policing and marking, 384
policy locators, 389-393
policy objects, 395-396
qualitative signaled traffic,
419-420
receiver proxying, 388
RESV messages, 388
RSVP objects, 388
RSVP/IntServ, 380-382
security
authentication, 393
integrity, 394
signaling, implementing
without, 398-399
video traffic, 418-419
**dynamic provisioning, static
provisioning compared, 235**
dynamic services, 468-469

E

edge devices, 428-429
EF PHB group, 197-198
efficiency
defined, 35
relationship with QoS
mechanisms, 38
RFC 1633, 107
egress interface, 62
egress policing, 435
elastic applications, 117-118
**election priority
parameters, 618**
end-to-end philosophy, 138
enterprise LAN
application-centric policy,
compiling and installing,
373-374

WAN links, interconnected
by, 625-626
*local and remote
traffic, incapabilitiy to
differentiate between,
626-627*
*topology-aware admission
control, using user-based
policies to support, 627*
enterprise-wide policies, 607
**Ethernet packet scheduler.
See packet scheduler**
event notification, 507
WSAAsyncSelect, 507
WSAEventSelect, 507
WSAGetQoSByName,
507-508
WSAIoctl (SIO GET
QOS), 507
excess burst size (Be), 319
**excess information rate
(EIR), 319**
**expedited forwarding PHB,
17, 197-198**

F

failed node detection, 177
fair queuing, 75, 77, 79
bitwise round robin, 77
deficit round robin, 80, 82
DRR+, 82
Nagle's fair queuing, 75-77
stochastic fair queuing, 79
weighted fair-queuing
schemes, 83
fault tolerance
data stores, 358
DSBMs, 273
FF reservations, 157
FIFO queuing, 66
**FIFO traffic handling
mechanism, 43**
filters, 213, 551, 559
flows, adding to, 560
flows, deleting from, 560

GPC, 552-553
remote traffic control, 561
FILTERSPEC object, 520
**first-party traffic control
consumers**
overview, 547
third-party consumers
compared, 547-548
flows, 551, 559
creating, 559
deleting, 560
filters, adding, 560
filters, deleting, 560
modifying, 560
remote traffic control, 561
FLOWSPEC object, 520
**forward-explicit congestion
notification (FECN), 318**
**fragmentable flows, non-
fragmentable flows
compared, 333**
frame delay ratio (FDR), 320
Frame Relay
DiffServ, 320
leased-line networks
compared, 316-317
overview, 314-315
QoS parameters
CIR, 318
*committed burst size
(Bc), 319*
*congestion notification,
318-319*
excess burst size (Be), 319
*excess information rate
(EIR), 319*
*frame delay ratio
(FDR), 320*
*frame transfer delay
(FTD), 320*
overview, 317
token bucket model, 320
QoS support, 320
DiffServ, 320
RSVP/IntServ, 321
VFRADs, 321

routed networks
  compared, 316
  RSVP/IntServ, 321
  VFRADs, 321
**frame transfer delay
  (FTD), 320**
free rider effect, 155-156
free riders, 310
full-duplex media, 62

G

**generic packet classifier,
  552-553**
generic QoS API. *See*
  GQoS API
gold service, 227
GPC, 552-553
GQoS API, 485-486
  application considerations
    *interpretation of
      information from Qos
      Service Provider, 534-537*
    marking, 539
    *persistent applications,
      nonpersistent applications
      compared, 533*
    *qualitative applications,
      532-533*
    *quantitative applications,
      531-532*
    *rejection of application
      requests, 538*
    *ServiceType parameter,
      530-531*
    *ShapeDiscard mode,
      533-534*
    *traffic control,
      disabling, 534*
    *transmission, withholding,
      537-538*
  interpretation of
    information from Qos
    Service Provider, 534
    *application queries,
      536-537*

*provider-specific buffer,
  535-536*
status codes, 535
overview, 497
persistent applications,
  nonpersistent applications
  compared, 533
qualitative applications,
  532-533
quantitative applications,
  531-532
RSVP signaling, 500
  PATH messages, 501
  RESV messages, 501
ServiceType parameter,
  530-531
ShapeDiscard mode,
  533-534
sockets, 502
  WSAAccept, 504-505
  WSAConnect, 505-506
  *WSAEnumProtocols,
    502-503*
  *WSAIoctl (SIO SET
    QOS), 504*
  WSAJoinLeaf, 506
  WSASocket, 503
traffic control, 501, 534
transmission, withholding,
  537-538
Windows 2000, 542
Windows 98, 541
Winsock 2, 497
  calls, 499
  control plane, 499
  data plane, 499
  notification events, 500
  parameters, 500
  service providers, 498
  sockets, 498-499
  WSAAccept, 499
  WSAConnect, 499
  WSAGetQosByName, 500
  WSAIoctl, 500

WSAJoinLeaf, 499
WSASocket, 499
GQoS service provider
  API calls, responses to, 526
  applications, information
    provided to, 525
    API calls, responses to, 526
    *notifications, registering
      for, 525*
    *queries from
      applications to QoS
      service provider, 525*
  event notification
    WSAAsyncSelect, 507
    WSAEventSelect, 507
    *WSAGetQoSByName,
      507-508*
    *WSAIoctl (SIO GET
      QOS), 507*
  notifications, registering
    for, 525
  PATH messages
    *SENDER_TEMPLATE
      object, 517*
    *SENDER_TSPEC
      object, 517*
    SESSION object, 516
    timing, 517, 519
  policy objects,
    generating, 524
  QoS parameters, 508
    FLOWSPECs, 508-513
    *provider-specific buffer,
      513-514*
  queries from applications to
    QoS service provider, 525
  RESV messages, 519
    defaults, overriding, 522
    FILTERSPEC object, 520
    FLOWSPEC object, 520
    *matching PATH and
      session state, 520-521*
    SESSION object, 519
    timing, 522-523

RSVP signaling, 514, 516
  PATH messages, 516-519
  policy objects,
    generating, 524
  receiver proxies, 523
  RESV messages, 519-523
traffic control
  invocation, 526
    greedy traffic control, 526
    interpreting traffic control
      parameters, 526-527
    mappings, 529-530
    marking, 527-530
    nongreedy traffic
      control, 526
    ShapeDiscardMode, 527
greedy traffic control,
  492, 526
Guaranteed Service, 121
  applications, suitability
    to, 123
  behavior of, 122
  implementing, 123-124
  latency, 123-124
  parameters used to request,
    121-122
Guaranteed Service
  flows, 575
guarantees, levels of
  service, 203

H

heterogeneous senders,
  support of, 286-287
  legacy 802 subnets, 287
    advanced host
      functionality, 288-289
    NonResvSendLimit,
      289-290
    TCP, use of, 287
  modern 802 subnets
    overview, 290
    per-conversation traffic
      handling, 291

heuristics, 334
high-priority traffic, 417
high-quality services,
  isolating from low-quality
  services, 54-55
highest-priority traffic, 417
home networks, 413
hosts, 7, 420
host operating system
  kernel-level components
    (traffic control
    providers), 491
    ATM traffic control
      provider, 493
    greedy traffic control, 492
    nongreedy traffic
      control, 492
    packet scheduler, 492
    traffic control
      functionality, 492
  Microsoft QoS
    components, 483
  user-level components
    GQoS API, 485-486
    QoS service provider,
      486-487
    Qos-enabled applications,
      484-485
    traffic control API,
      488-491
host resident PEPs, 400
  allocation of resources
    and, 400
  policy management
    system, 401

I

identity objects
  overview, 388-389
  translating, 396, 398
IETF applicability statement
  (RFC 2208), 135

implementation
  framework, 107
  admission control, 108-109
  classification, 108
  IntServ-capable network
    element, elements of,
    112, 114
  packet scheduler, 108
  RSVP, 109-112
individual application traffic
  flow, 104
ingress interface, 62
ingress policing, 435
Integrated Services. *See*
  IntServ services
Integrated Services Over
  Slow Links, 19, 593
integrity, 34, 394
inter-PDP communication,
  355
interior provisioning
  boundary provisioning com-
    pared, 228-229
  overview, 231-232
internal priority, 570
IntServ architecture
  implementation
    framework, 107
    admission control,
      108-109
    classification, 108
    IntServ-capable network
      element, elements of,
      112, 114
    packet scheduler, 108
    RSVP, 109-110, 112
  IntServ service model, 104
    aggregation of traffic
      flows, 104
    basis of, 105-106
    elastic applications,
      117-118

individual application
  traffic flow, 104
purpose of, 105
real-time applications,
  114,-117
reservations and admission
  control, 106-107
services of, 114
IntServ services, 118
  Controlled Load Service,
    118-121
  Guaranteed Service,
    121-124
  link-sharing service, 127
  Null Service, 125-127
overview, 102-103
requirements, 103
RFC 1633, 103
traffic handling, 108
IntServ service model, 104
aggregation of traffic
  flows, 104
application types, 114-118
basis of, 105-106
individual application traffic
  flow, 104
purpose of, 105
reservations and admission
  control, 106
RFC 1633
  arbitrary network
    conditions, 106
  efficiency, 107
  prioritization, 107
IntServ services, 118
admission control, 19
break bits, 144
Controlled Load Service,
  19, 118
  applications, suitability
    to, 120
  behavior of, 119-120
  implementing, 120-121
  parameters used to
    request, 118

Guaranteed Service, 19, 121
  applications, suitability
    to, 123
  behavior of, 122
  implementing, 123-124
  latency, 123-124
  parameters used to request,
    121-122
historical background, 101
ISSLL, 127-128
link-sharing service, 127
Null Service, 125
  implementing, 126-127
  interface, 125-126
RSVP, relationship with,
  132-133
IntServ-capable network
  element, 112, 114
IP mapping to ATM,
  298-300
IP multicast, 139, 150
IP telephony, 623
quality/efficiency product
  improvement, 45-48
signaling, 48, 50-54
IP tunnels, 249
IPSec, 179
DiffServ, 249
problems applying
  RSVP to, 179
protocol extensions sup-
  porting, 179-180
ISSLL, 127-128
ISSLOW
overview, 19
RAS dial-up servers, 593
ISSLOW mode, 580

J-K
Jamin, Sugih, 132
jitter, 10, 72, 114
jitter buffer, 115
Kerberos ticket, 632

kernel-level components
  (traffic control
  providers), 491
ATM traffic control
  provider, 493
greedy traffic control, 492
nongreedy traffic
  control, 492
packet scheduler, 492
traffic control
  functionality, 492
killer reservation
  problems, 155

L
label switching, 172
labs, classrooms, and
  administrative building
  networks, 463
LAN_LOOPBACK
  object, 283
LAN_NHOP object, 283
LANE, 558
LANs
higher-quality services, support for, 45-46
provisioning, 259
QE product, 254
traffic isolation, 256-257
user_priority. *See* user_priority
latency
defined, 10
Guaranteed Service, 123-124
low bit rate links, 325-326
  DSCP, 334
  fragmentable flows,
    nonfragmentable flows
    compared, 333
  heuristics, 334
  multilink fragmentation,
    327, 329-332
  RSVP, 333
  suspend/resume approach,
    332-333

queuing schemes
evaluation, 72
**latency-tolerant
applications, 117**
leaky bucket model, 85-90
**leased-line networks, Frame
Relay compared, 316-317**
legacy 802 subnets, 287
advanced host functionality,
288-289
NonResvSendLimit,
289-290
TCP, use of, 287
**less-than-best-effort (LBE)
service, 206-207**
**less-than-best-effort (LBE)
priority traffic, 417**
limited best-effort mode, 592
link-layer fragmentation, 555
link-layer signaling, 554-555
link-sharing service, 127
loader, 645
logging behavior, 619-620
accounting logs, 620
RSVP logs, 620
logical networks, 54-57
**logical provisioning,
364-366**
low bit rate links
DSCP, 334
fragmentable flows,
nonfragmentable flows
compared, 333
heuristics, 334
multilink fragmentation, 327
fragmenter, 330
*overhead, fragment size
compared, 329*
packet scheduling, 329-330
*preemption, levels of,
330-332*
prefix elision, 332

QoS, 321
*admission control agents,
323-324*
*bandwidth constraints,
322-325*
*latency issues, 325-327,
329-334*
*qualities of service, support
for different, 322*
RSVP, 333
suspend/resume
approach, 332
hardware suspension, 333
software suspension, 333
**low-quality services,
isolating from high-quality
services, 54-55**
LPM API, 629, 631
LSPs, 172-173

M

MAC service interface, 252
managed segments, 264-265
formation of, 271, 273
independent management
of each segment, 267-268
multiple managed segments
per subnet, 266
single managed segment,
entire 802 subnet as,
265-266
mapping, 529-530
qualitative services, 261-262
RSVP, 243-244, 305
traffic, 456-457
user_priority, 260
*mapping for qualitative
services, 261-262*
values, ordering of, 262
markers, 215

**marking, 527-530,
539, 553**
dynamic policies, 384
Ethernet packet scheduler,
557-558
shaping compared, 247
**MaxOutstandingSends para-
meter, 578-579**
medium priority traffic, 417
message bundles, 176
messages, 147-149
meters, 214
Microsoft LPM, 631-632
Microsoft QoS components
host operating system, 483
*kernel-level components
(traffic control providers),
491-493*
*user-level components,
484-489, 491*
overview, 483
policy enforcement
components, 493
ACS, 494-495
SBM, 494-495
**MinimumPolicedSize
parameter, 510-511**
**modern 802 subnets,
290-291**
MPLS, 171-175
multicast services, 248
multicast sessions, 285-286
multicast traffic
RSVP, 149
*fixed filter (FF)
reservations, 157*
free rider effect, 155-156
*killer reservation
problems, 155*
multilayer encoding, 154
*receiver heterogeneity,
153-154, 159*
reservation cycle, 152-153

reservation styles, 156-159
reservations, merging,
150-154
shared explicit (SE)
reservations, 157-158
wildcard filter (WF)
reservations, 158
multifield classifiers, 213
multilink fragmentation, 327
  fragmenter, 330
  overhead, fragment size
  compared, 329
  packet scheduling, 329-330
  preemption, levels of,
  330-332
  prefix elision, 332
multiple point-to-point
PVCs, 302-303
multiplexers, 216

N

Nagle's fair queuing, 75-77
native traffic control
providers, 556
  ATM, 558
  Ethernet packet
  scheduler, 556
    marking, 557-558
    traffic scheduling, 557
netmon, 639-640
  802 user_priority marks,
  monitoring, 641
  RSVP messages,
  monitoring, 640-641
Network Control Service
flows, 576, 591
network device management
consoles, 642
network devices, 12-13
network policy-management
system, 549
network QoS. *See* **QoS**
mechanisms

network resources
  allocating to certain
  traffic, 12
  application requirements, 10
  network devices, 12-13
  traffic-handling mecha-
  nisms, 10-11
network-based application
recognition, 423-424
node failure detection, 176
noise-generation tools,
644-645
non-802 media, marking
for, 582
non-work-conserving
queuing, 69
  overview, 83-84
  shaping parameters
    leaky bucket model, 85-90
    overview, 84
    token bucket model, 87-90
nonblocking backplane, 63
nongreedy traffic control,
492, 526
nonpersistent applications
  support for, 540-541
  traffic control
  consumers, 548
nonpersistent applications,
persistent applications
compared, 533
NonResvSendLimit,
289-290, 604, 619, 624
notification events, 500
nrtVBR (non-real-time
variable bit rate), 300
Null Service, 125, 185-186
  implementing, 126-127
  interface, 125-126
Null Service flows, 575

O-P

overhead
  defined, 39
  impact of QoS mechanisms
  on, 40
overprovisioned
networks, 32

packet classification, 12-13
packet marking, verifying
  802 user_priority
  marking, 660
  DSCP marking, 661
packet scheduler, 108, 492
  Active Directory, 583
  admission control, 574
  conformance analyzer,
  564-565
  Controlled Load Service
  flows, 574-575
  default best-effort flow, 573
  derivation of parameters
  affecting scheduling
  behavior, 570
  DRR, 576
  DSCP marking, 581-582
  802 user_priority marking,
  582
  explicitly created best-effort
  flow, 573
  Guaranteed Service
  flows, 575
  instances of, 562
  internal priority, 570
  internal structure of, 562
    conformance analyzer,
    564-565
    scheduling profiles, 564
    sequencer, 566-568
    shaper, 565-566
    timestamp module, 568
    wrapper, 563-564

marking, 557-558
  overview, 581
  parameters affecting,
    581-582
marking for non-802
  media, 582
MaxOutstandingSends
  parameter, 578
Network Control Service
  flows, 576
Null Service flows, 575
parameters affecting
  marking behavior
    802 user_priority
      marking, 582
    DSCP marking, 581-582
    marking for non-802
      media, 582
scheduling behavior
  admission control, 574
  Controlled Load Service
    flows, 574-575
  default best-effort
    flow, 573
  DRR, 576-577
  explicitly created best-
    effort flow, 573
  Guaranteed Service
    flows, 575
  MaxOutstandingSends
    parameter, 578
  Network Control Service
    flows, 576
  Null Service flows, 575
  overview, 571
  sharing resources
    among flows of equal
    priority, 576
  token bucket parameters,
    576-577
  WAN links, 579-580
  weighted-queuing
    schemes, 576-577

scheduling behavior,
  parameters affecting, 569
  internal priority, 570
  ShapeDiscard mode,
    569-570
  token bucket
    parameters, 570
scheduling profiles, 564
sequencer, 566-568
ShapeDiscard mode, 569
  borrow mode, 569
  borrow+ mode, 570
  discard mode, 570
  shape mode, 569
shaper, 565-566
sharing resources among
  flows of equal priority, 576
timestamp module, 568
token bucket parameters,
  570, 577
  borrow-mode flows, 578
  shape-mode flows, 577
traffic scheduling, 557
WAN links, scheduling
  behavior on, 579-580
weighted-queuing
  schemes, 576-577
wrapper, 563-564
ZAW mechanism, 583
packet switching, circuit
switching compared,
110-111
passive configuration of
queuing scheme
  examples of, 97, 99
  overview, 95-96
PATH messages 24-26,
140, 501
  802 subnet, routed
    through, 278-279
  data traffic, marking
    downstream path of, 142
  DSBM, forwarding beyond,
    280-281, 283

dynamic policies, 387
GQoS service provider, 516
  SENDER_TEMPLATE
    object, 517
  SENDER_TSPEC
    object, 517
  SESSION object, 516
  timing, 517, 519
network path,
  characterizing, 144
offered traffic,
  characterizing, 143-144
overview, 140-141
receiver, arrival at, 652
receiver, not arriving at, 652
reservation cycle, 147, 149
SBM clients, directed
  to, 280
PC RSVP, 487
PDPs, 27, 597
  distribution of, 349
  PEP and, 350
PeakBandwidth parameter,
509-510
peering agreement, 470-472
PEP, 27, 347-348
  dynamic policies, configura-
    tion options for, 387
  overview, 597
  PDP and, 350
per-conversation
mechanisms, 20
per-flow traffic control
parameters, 561
per-hop behavior. *See* PHBs
per-interface traffic control
parameters, 561
perfmon, 643
persistent applications,
nonpersistent applications
compared, 533
PHBs, 16, 194
  AF, 17
  class selector, 17

and DSCPs, 195
EF, 17
services compared, 195
standard groups, 197
   AF PHB group, 199-200
   class selector PHB
    group, 200
   EF PHB group, 197-198
physical provisioning, 364
point-to-point PVCs,
 301-302
policers, 417
policing, 442, 444
admission control
  compared, 108
dynamic policies, 384
isolating high-quality and
  low-quality services, 54-55
WANs, traffic originating in,
  456-457
policy decision point (PDP),
 27, 597
distribution of, 349
PEP and, 350
policy enforcement
 components, 493
ACS, 494-495
SBM, 494-495
policy enforcement point
 (PEP), 27, 347-348
dynamic policies, configuration options for, 387
overview, 597
PDP and, 350
policy errors, 162
policy flowchart, policy-based
 admission control, 607
Policy Framework
 (Policy), 136
policy installation, 362
policy locators, 161,
 389-393

policy management
 system, 424
CLI, 355
COPS, 350
  for provisioning, 354
  for RSVP, 352-353
  SNMP compared, 351-352
data stores, 356-357
  central write, distributed
   read, 357-358
  directories, 357, 360-362
  efficient data storage
   model, 359
  fault tolerance, 358
  requirements of, 357-359
  reusability of management
   data, 359
  security, 358
defined, 338
edge routers, configuration
  of, 439
features of, 338-339
host resident PEPs, 401
inter-PDP communication,
  355
layers of, 346
  CLI, 355
  COPS, 350-354
  inter-PDP communication,
   355
  policy decision point,
   349-350
  policy enforcement point,
   347-348, 350
  SNMP, 354
policy decision point,
  349-350
policy enforcement point,
  347-348, 350
SNMP, 354
value of, 345
policy mechanisms, 27-28

policy objects, 160, 395,
 454, 524
application identification, 524
multicast sessions, merging
  in, 395-396
user identification, 524
policy-based admission
 control, 605
enterprise-wide policies, 607
organizational units, 608
policy flowchart, 607
QoS policy hierarchy,
  605-606
resource-based admission
  control compared, 596
subnet-level policies, 606
policy-caching behavior, 619
POTS-connected end
 users, 474
prioritization policies, 344
priority queuing, 68, 72-74
processing cost, 72
provider networks, 412
admission control, 469-470
cable modem-connected
  end users, 475
overview, 465-466
peering agreement,
  470-472
policy servers, 473
POTS-connected end
  users, 474
Provider A's network, 473
Provider B's network, 472
provisioning, 472
push provisioning, 472
RSVP signaling, 473
signaling awareness, 470
SLAs, 467-468
  admission control,
   469-470
  dynamic services, 468-469

peering agreement,
   470-472
signaling aware,
   provider networks that
   are not, 470
static services, 468-469
traffic handling, 466-467
provider-specific buffer,
513-514, 535-536
provisioning
   boundary provisioning
      interior provisioning
      compared, 228-229
      overview, 230
   COPS for, 354
   dynamic provisioning, 235
   interior provisioning
      boundary provisioning
      compared, 228-229
      overview, 231-232
   LANs, 259
   overview, 228
   push provisioning, 472
   provider networks, 472
   route-constrained services,
      232-234
   route-independent services,
      234-235
   simultaneous support for
      route-constrained and
      route independent
      services, 232
   static provisioning, 235
provisioning and
configuration mechanisms
   combining with traffic-
      handling mechanisms, 41
   continuous nature of, 42
   impact on quality/efficiency
      product and overhead,
      40-41
   push provisioning, 43

provisioning mechanisms
   configuration mechanisms
      compared, 21-22
   overview, 21
push mechanisms, 28
push provisioning, 43,
236-237, 472
PVCs, 295-296
   dedicated VCs, 305
   multiple point-to-point
      PVCs, 302-303
   point-to-point PVCs,
      301-302
   soft PVCs, 304

Q

QE product. *See*
quality/efficiency product
QoS (Quality of Service)
   ATM support of, 301
      dedicated VCs, 305
      IP over ATM and LAN
      emulation, 314
      multiple point-to-point
      PVCs, 302-303
      point-to-point PVCs,
      301-302
      RSVP mapping, 305
      soft PVCs, 304
      VC management
      supporting RSVP, 305-313
   Frame Relay, 320
      CIR, 318
      committed burst size
      (Bc), 319
      congestion notification,
      318-319
      DiffServ, 320
      excess burst size (Be), 319
      excess information rate
      (EIR), 319

frame delay ratio
   (FDR), 320
frame transfer delay
   (FTD), 320
overview, 317
RSVP/IntServ, 321
token bucket model, 320
VFRADs, 321
low bit rate links, 321
   admission control agents,
   323-324
   bandwidth constraints,
   322-325
   latency issues, 325-334
   qualities of service, support
   for different, 322
QoS mechanisms
   aggregate traffic handling,
      43-45
   combination of traffic-
      handling mechanisms and
      provisioning and configura-
      tion mechanisms, 41
   continuous nature of, 42
   defined, 7-8, 32-33
   density of distribution, 42
   deploying applications not
      supported by, 416
   higher-quality services in
      LANs, 45-46
   higher-quality services in
      WANs, 46-48
   host/network interaction,
      review of, 645-646
   impact of, 38
   impact on quality/efficiency
      product and overhead, 40
   logical networks, 55-57
   network devices, 646
      ACS, 647
      RRAS-based ACS, 648
      RSVP-aware, aggregate
      traffic handling, 647

RSVP-aware, per-conversation traffic handling, 646
RSVP-unaware, aggregate traffic handling, 646
SBM-based ACS, 647
on Internet, 31-32
overhead, 39
provisioning and configuration mechanisms, 40-41
push provisioning and FIFO traffic handling, 43
quality/efficiency product, 31
defined, 35-36
raising, 36-39
relationship with bandwidth, 38
service needs, meeting, 9
signaling, 48, 50
aggregation of messages, 54
costs of, 51
density, 51, 53
importance of topology, 52-53
traffic-handling mechanisms, 40
QoS parameters, 508
FLOWSPECs, 508-509
MinimumPolicedSize parameter, 510-511
other quantitative parameter, 510
PeakBandwidth parameters, 509-510
ServiceType parameter, 512-513
TokenBucketSize parameter, 509-510
TokenRate parameter, 509-510
provider-specific buffer, 513-514

QoS policy
administrative domains, 402
bandwidth brokers as admission control agents, 403-407
domain boundary issues, 402-403
application-based policies, 345
applying, 362
authored policies, 362
compiled policies, 362
dynamic policies, 378-399
format of authored and complied policies, 363-364
policy installation, 362
signaling and traffic handling mode, 369-378
static global provisioning policies, 364-369
status reporting, 363
authored policies, 362
compiled policies, 362
defined, 337-338
dynamic policies, 341-343, 380-387
format of authored and complied policies, 363-364
hierarchical nature of information, 605-606
host resident PEPs, 400
allocation of resources and, 400
policy management system, 401
identity objects, translating, 396, 398
objectives, 338
policy installation, 362
policy management system, 338
data stores, 356-362
features of, 338-339
layers of, 346-355
value of, 345

policy objects, 395-396
prioritization policies, 344
relationship between policies, 343
reservation policies, 344
semi-static policies, 341, 343
applying, 370-371
authoring, 372
compiling and installing, 373-378
examples of, 372
signaling and traffic handling mode, 369
static global provisioning policies, 340, 343, 364
compiling and installing, 366-369
logical provisioning, 364-366
physical provisioning, 364
status reporting, 363
taxonomy, 339
application-based policies, 345
dynamic policies, 341-343
prioritization policies, 344
reservation policies, 344
semi-static policies, 341, 343
static global provisioning policies, 340, 343
time-of-day policies, 345
user-based policies, 344
time-of-day policies, 345
user-based policies, 344
QoS service provider, 486-487, 498, 587
admission to network, behavior following, 588
application queries, 536-537
application requests, rejections of, 538
initial invocation of traffic control, 587-588

interpretation of
information from, 534
application queries,
536-537
provider-specific buffer,
535-536
status codes, 535
Network Control Service
flow, 591
nonpersistent applications,
support for, 540-541
rejection of application
requests, 538
signaling traffic, network
control for, 591
QoS sockets
creating, 502-503
use of, 504-506
WSAAccept, 504-505
WSAConnect, 505-506
WSAEnumProtocols,
502-503
WSAIoctl (SIO SET
QOS), 504
WSAJoinLeaf, 506
WSASocket, 503
QoS-enabled applications,
484-485
qtcp, 643
qualitative applications,
532-533
qualitative services, 204-205
route-constrained qualitative
services, 205
route-independent
qualitative services, 206
quality/efficiency
product, 31
aggregate traffic handling,
43-45
defined, 35-36
high-quality services,
isolating from low-quality
services, 54-55

higher-quality services in
LANs, 45-46
higher-quality services in
WANs, 46-48
impact of QoS mechanisms
on, 40
logical networks, 54-57
overhead, 39
push provisioning and FIFO
traffic handling mecha-
nisms, 43
raising, 36-39
signaling, 48, 50
aggregation of
messages, 54
costs of, 51
density, 51, 53
importance of topology,
52-53
quantitative applications,
531-532
quantitative services, 204
queue-servicing
algorithms, 13
queues, formation of, 62
congestion, 64-65
queuing and forwarding,
63-64
queuing and forwarding,
63-64
queuing mechanisms
active configuration of
queuing schemes, 96, 99
application of, 95
active configuration of
queuing schemes, 96
examples of, 96-99
passive configuration of
queuing schemes, 95-96
bandwidth, 72
categories of, 66
dropping schemes, 70-71
FIFO queuing, 66

non-work-conserving
queuing, 69, 83-90
work-conserving queuing,
67-68, 72-83
class-based queuing
overview, 90-92
sharing hierarchy, 91-92
dropping schemes, 70-71
random early detection, 93
tail dropping, 93
traffic types, suitability
of drop schemes to
various, 95
weighted random early
detection, 94-95
evaluation of
bandwidth, 72
latency, 72
overview, 71
processing cost, 72
FIFO queuing, 66
formation of queues, 62
congestion, 64-65
queuing and forwarding,
63-64
latency, 72
non-work-conserving
queuing, 69
overview, 83-84
shaping parameters, 84-90
overview, 61
passive configuration of
queuing schemes, 95-99
processing cost, 72
work-conserving queuing,
67-68
fair queuing, 75-83
strict priority queuing, 68,
72-74

R
RAS servers
ACS, 629
automatic ISSLOW for, 593
readpol, 644

**real-time applications,
114, 116**
   distortion-tolerant
      applications, 117
   latency-tolerant
      applications, 117
   real-time intolerant
      applications, 116
   real-time tolerant
      applications, 116
**real-time measurement,
   provisioning based on, 238**
receiver heterogeneity, 159
**receiver orientation,
   138-139**
receiver proxies, 388, 523
receiver transitions, 312
refresh reduction, 175-176
   failed node detection, 177
   message bundles, 176
   slow refresh interval, 177
   SRefresh messages, 176
   trigger messages, 177
remote networks
   Remote Campus A
      through C, 460
      802 switch, 461
      *wide area links, QoS
      between remote campuses
      and, 461*
   Remote Campus D, 457
      *admission control,
      459-460*
      traffic handling, 458
remote traffic control, 561
reservation cycle, 147, 149
reservation policies, 344
reservations, 136-137
**reservations and admission
   control, 106**
**Resource Allocation
   Protocol (RAP), 136, 160**
resource pools, 55-57

**resource-based admission
   control, 596, 600, 602**
**RESV admission
   control, 147**
   qualitative services,
      432, 434
   quantitative services,
      430-432
**RESV messages, 24-26,
140, 142, 501**
   admission control, 147
   composition of, 145
   dynamic policies, 388
   GQoS service provider, 519
      defaults, overriding, 522
      FILTERSPEC object, 520
      FLOWSPEC object, 520
      *matching PATH and
      session state, 520-521*
      SESSION object, 519
      timing, 522-523
   overview, 145
   processing, 146
   reservation cycle, 147, 149
**reusability of management
   data, 359**
RFC 1633, 103, 106
   arbitrary network
      conditions, 106
   efficiency, 107
   prioritization, 107
RFC 2205, 135
RFC 2208, 135
**route-constrained
   qualitative services, 205**
**route-independent
   qualitative services, 206**
**routed networks, Frame
   Relay compared, 316**
rsping, 641-642
RSVP, 109-110, 112
   admission control based on
      policy, 159-160

admission-control agents
   (ACA), 180-182
   *select congestion
   points, 184*
   *signaling density,
   182, 184*
application of, 180
   *admission-control agents
   (ACA), 180-182, 184*
   *qualitative applications,
   signaling for, 185-186*
   RSVP proxies, 186-188
   snooping, 188
bandwidth brokers as
   admission control
   agents, 404
concepts and
   terminology, 136
   end-to-end philosophy, 138
   IP multicast, 139
   *receiver orientation,
   138-139*
   reservations, 136-137
   sessions, 139
   soft-state model, 137-138
COPS for, 352-353
DCLASS objects, 178-179
DiffServ with, 135
   *admission control,
   239-241*
   DCLASS object, 243
   *mapping RSVP signaled
   services to DiffServ
   services, 243-244*
   overview, 238
   *traffic classification,
   241-243*
end-to-end philosophy, 138
enhancements, 162
   *aggregate RSVP signaling,
   165-167*
   DCLASS objects, 178-179
   IP tunnels, 167-169
   IPSec, 179-180

MPLS, 171-175
node failure detection, 176
refresh reduction, 175-177
SBM protocol, 163-164
TCLASS objects, 178-179
tunnel reservations,
169-171
evolution of, 135-136
historical background, 131
DiffServ, 135
evolution of RSVP,
135-136
IETF applicability state-
ment (RFC 2208), 135
origin of RSVP, 131-133
RFC 2205, 135
RFC 2208, 135
support for RSVP,
133-134
IntServ, relationship with,
132-133
IP multicast, 139
IP tunnels, 167-169
IPSec, 179
problems applying RSVP
to, 179
protocol extensions
supporting, 179-180
label switching, 172
Layer 3 networks, operation
in, 274-275
low bit rate links, 333
LSPs, 172-173
mapping, 305
messages, 140
fundamental, 140-147
PATH, 140-144
reservation cycle, 147-149
RESV, 140, 142, 145-147
structure of, 140
mission-critical applications,
support for, 133
MPLS, 171-175

multicast traffic, 149
fixed filter (FF) reserva-
tions, 157
free rider effect, 155-156
killer reservation
problems, 155
multilayer encoding, 154
receiver heterogeneity,
153-154, 159
reservation cycle, 152-153
reservation styles, 156-159
reservations, merging,
150-154
shared explicit (SE)
reservations, 157-158
wildcard filter (WF)
reservations, 158
node failure detection, 176
Null Service, 185-186
origin of, 131-133
overview, 23-24
PATH messages, 24-26,
278-279
policy errors, 162
policy locator, 161
policy mechanisms, absence
of, 134
policy objects, 160
protocol, 140-149
qualitative applications,
signaling for, 185-186
receiver orientation,
138-139
refresh reduction, 175-176
failed node detection, 177
message bundles, 176
slow refresh interval, 177
SRefresh messages, 176
trigger messages, 177
reservations, 136-137
Resource Allocation
Protocol (RAP), 160
RESV messages, 24-26
scalability, 134

security, 161
sessions, 139
shared-segment 802 subnetwork, in, 275-276
signaling hosts, absence
of, 133
snooping, 188
soft-state model, 137-138
support for, 133
switched 802 subnetwork,
in, 276-277
TCLASS objects, 178-179
tunnel reservations
establishing, 170
identifying, 170
protocol for establishing, 171
Type 1 tunnels, 169
Type 2 tunnels, 169
Type 3 tunnels, 169
VC management supporting
RSVP, 305-312
changing QoS
requirements, 312
QoS translation, 313
receiver transitions, 312
signaling messages,
carrying RSVP, 312-313
RSVP_HOP_L2 object, 283
RSVP logs, 620
RSVP messages
PATH message, 652
tracking, 650
troubleshooting, 640-641
RSVP objects
dynamic policies, 388
LAN_NHOP object, 283
LAN_LOOPBACK
object, 283
RSVP_HOP_L2 object, 283
SBM protocol, required for,
283-284
TCLASS object, 283
RSVP proxies, 186
advantages of, 186-187
disadvantages of, 187-188

RSVP signaling
aggregate RSVP signaling.
See aggregate RSVP
signaling
GQoS API, 500
PATH messages, 501
RESV messages, 501
GQoS service provider,
514, 516
PATH messages, 516-519
policy objects,
generating, 524
receiver proxies, 523
RESV messages, 519-523
improving quality/efficiency
product on WANs, 48, 50
aggregation of messages, 54
costs of signaling, 51
density of signaling, 51, 53
importance of topology,
52-53
QE product, obtaining
higher, 258-259
RSVP tracing, 638-639
RSVP/IntServ
ATM circuit orientation
mirroring, 297
dynamic policies, 380-382
Frame Relay, 321
rtVBR (real-time variable
bit rate), 299-300

S

sample network
overview, 410
subnetworks
cable network, 412
corporate campus network,
411-434, 438
home networks, 413
overview, 411
provider networks, 412
university campus
network, 412

sample subnetworks
cable network, 412
corporate campus network,
411-413
ATM backbone, 425-434,
438-440
building networks,
414-424
home networks, 413
overview, 411
provider networks, 412
university campus
network, 412
SBM, 494-495
as admission control agent
for LANs, 263-264
DSBM, 265, 268-270
managed segments,
265-268
segments, 264
802 switch network,
601-602
aggregate admission
control limits, 603
hosts, trusting, 604
mapping service types to
user_priority marks, 603
NonResvSendLimit, 604
per-service admission
control limits, 603
subnetwork, applying
single admission control
limit to, 604-605
TCLASS objects, 605
election priority
parameters, 618
independent management
of each segment, 267-268
managed segments
independent management
of each segment, 267-268
multiple managed
segments per subnet, 266

single managed segment,
entire 802 subnet as,
265-266
multiple managed segments
per subnet, 266
overview, 26-27, 262,
597-600
protocol timers, 618
resource-based admission
control, 600, 602
single managed segment,
entire 802 subnet as,
265-266
traffic handling, 270-271
SBM clients, PATH
messages directed to, 280
SBM protocol, 163-164
directing PATH messages to
SBM clients, 280
forwarding PATH messages
beyond DSBM, 280-283
overview, 273-274
RSVP in shared segment
802 subnetwork, 275-276
RSVP in switched 802
subnetwork, 276-277
RSVP objects required for,
283-284
RSVP operation in Layer 3
networks, 274-275
RSVP PATH messages
routed through 802
subnet, 278-279
scheduling profiles, 564
schemas, 360
security
authentication, 394
data stores, 358
dynamic policies, 393-394
integrity, 394
Kerberos ticket, 632
overview, 632
RSVP, 161
segments, 264

semi-static policies, 341, 343
  applying, 370-371
  authoring, 372
  compiling and installing,
   373-378
  complex classification
   criteria, 376
  conflicting classification
   criteria, 376
  examples of, 372
  policing for, 377-378
  resource consumption, effect
   of classification
   criteria on, 377
SENDER_TEMPLATE
object, 517
SENDER_TSPEC object, 517
sequencer, 566-568
service level agreements.
  See **SLA**
service level specification, 196
ServiceType parameter,
530-531
services
  agreements governing
   received traffic, 209
  best-effort service, 206
  defined, 33
  dynamic, static services compared, 210
  extent of, 209-210
  integrity, 34
  less-than-best-effort service,
   206-207
  qualitative services, 204-205
   route-constrained
    qualitative services, 205
   route-independent
    qualitative services, 206
  quality
   efficiency, defined, 35
   examples of types of, 33-35
  quantitative services, 204
  scope of, 208-209

static, dynamic services
  compared, 210
  support for, 207-208
  traffic-handling mechanisms
   compared, 15
  types of, 204
   best-effort service, 206
   less-than-best-effort service,
    206-207
   qualitative services,
    204-206
   quantitative services, 204
   support for, 207-208
ServiceType parameter,
512-513
SESSION object, 516, 519
sessions, 139
shape mode, 569
shape-mode flows, 577
ShapeDiscard mode, 527,
533-534, 569
  borrow mode, 569
  borrow+ mode, 570
  discard mode, 570
  shape mode, 569
shapers, 215-216, 565-566
shaping, marking
compared, 247
shaping parameters
  leaky bucket model, 85-90
  overview, 84
  token bucket model, 87-90
shared explicit (SE)
reservations, 157-158
shared-segment 802
subnetwork, 275-276
sharing hierarchy, 91-92
Shenker, Scott, 103, 131
signaled QoS
demonstration, 661
  described, 663-664
  overview, 662-663
  policy changes, factors
   delaying effects of, 664

sessions and policy
  configurations, varying
  number of, 665
  steps for, 663
  troubleshooting, 666
   end-to-end signaling
    integrity, verifying,
    667-669
   network topology, 667
   setup, 666
   traffic control functionality,
    verifying, 670
  variations on, 665
signaling and traffic
handling mode, 369
  semi-static policies
   applying, 370-371
   authoring, 372
   compiling and installing,
    373-378
   examples of, 372
signaling density, 182, 184
signaling provisioning
model, 237-238
silver service, 227
SLA, 16, 196
  provider networks, 467-468
  services offered, 451-454
slow modem links, 128
slow refresh interval, 177
SLS, 196
SmartBits, 645
SNMP, 28
  COPS compared, 351-352
  overview, 354
sockets, 498-499
soft PVCs, 304
soft-state model, 137-138
SRefresh messages, 176
static global provisioning
policies, 340, 343, 364
  compiling and installing,
   366-369
  logical provisioning,
   364-366
  physical provisioning, 364

static provisioning, dynamic provisioning compared, 235
static services, 468-469
statistical multiplexing, 88, 297
status codes, 535
status reporting, 363
streaming video traffic, 623-624
strict priority queuing, 68, 72-74
subapplication identifiers, 532-533
Subnet Bandwidth Managers. *See* SBM
subnet-level policies, 606
subnets
    correspondence between ACS instances and, 612-613
    multiple servers per subnet, 613
    multiple subnets per server, 613
SVCs, 295-296, 427
switched 802 subnetwork, 276-277
switched networks, simpler configurations of, 421-422
switched subnetworks
    admission control, 435-438
    best-effort (BE) priority traffic, 417
    high-priority traffic, 417
    highest-priority traffic, 417
    less-than-best-effort (LBE) priority traffic, 417
    medium-priority traffic, 417
    policies regarding traffic transmitted onto, 439-440
    requirements, 415
    traffic-handling configuration in 802 switched subnetworks, 417

T
T-1 private leased lines, 444-445
tail dropping, 93
TC API, 488-489
    filters, 551, 559
        flows, adding to, 560
        GPC, 552-553
        flows, deleting from, 560
    flows, 551, 559
        creating, 559
        deleting, 560
        filters, adding, 560
        filters, deleting, 560
        modifying, 560
    interface selection, 559
    marking, 553
    overview, 558
    primitives, 489, 491
    registering with traffic control, 559
    remote traffic control, 561
    third-party traffic control consumers, 548-549
    traffic control parameters, 560
        per-flow traffic control parameters, 561
        per-interface traffic control parameters, 561
    traffic.dll, 551
TCBs
    AF PHB group, 223
        schematic of TCB, 226-227
        SLS, 224-227
    gold service, 227
    overview, 217
    schematic of, 219-223
    silver service, 227
    VLL service
        marking and shaping, 221
        supported at DiffServ ingress, 217-218
        supported by SLS, 218-219
        value-added SLS for, 221-223
TCLASS object, 178-179, 605
    SBM protocol, 283
    user_priority values, used to negotiate, 284-285
TcMon, 586, 643
    overview, 591
    traffic flows, verifying creation of, 659
telephony
    quality/efficiency product improvement, 45-48
    signaling, 48, 50-54
third-party traffic control consumers, 547
    first-party consumers compared, 547-548
    TCAPI, 548-549
    TcMon, 591
time-of-day policies, 345
timestamp module, 568
token bucket model, 87-90, 320
token bucket parameters, 570, 577
    borrow-mode flows, 578
    shape-mode flows, 577
TokenBucketSize parameter, 509-510
TokenRate parameter, 509-510
tracert, 638
traffic classification, 241-243
traffic conditioning
    blocks. *See* TCBs
    classifiers, 212
        behavior aggregate classifiers, 213
        filters, 213

ingress interface, based on, 214
multifield classifiers, 213
components, 212
classifiers, 212-214
droppers, 216
markers, 215
meters, 214
multiplexers, 216
shapers, 215-216
droppers, 216
markers, 215
meters, 214
multiplexers, 216
overview, 210, 212
shapers, 215-216
traffic conditioning components, 196
traffic control
ATMARP, 585-587
disabling, 534
GQoS API, 501
GQoS service provider
default traffic control parameters, selecting, 527
disabled traffic control, 527
greedy traffic control, 526
interpreting traffic control parameters, 526-527
mappings, 529-530
marking, 527-530
nongreedy traffic control, 526
ShapeDiscardMode, 527
shaping rate, modifying, 527
traffic control API. *See* TC API
traffic control consumers
automatic ISSLOW for RAS dial-up servers, 593
DiffServ mode, 593
first-party consumers, 547-548

limited best-effort mode, 592
network policy-management system, 549
nonpersistent applications, 548
overview, 546
QoS service provider, 587
admission to network, behavior following, 589-591
initial invocation of traffic control, 587-588
Network Control Service flow, 591
signaling traffic, network control for, 591
special uses, 592
automatic ISSLOW for RAS dial-up servers, 593
DiffServ mode, 592-593
limited best-effort mode, 592
TcMon, 587, 591
third-party consumers, 547-549
TCAPI, 548-549
TcMon, 591
traffic control functionality on sending host, verifying, 657, 659
traffic control parameters, 560
per-flow traffic control parameters, 561
per-interface traffic control parameters, 561
traffic control providers
link-layer fragmentation, 555
link-layer signaling, 554-555
marking, 553
media-specific functionality, 556

native traffic control providers, 556
ATM, 558
Ethernet packet scheduler, 556-558
overview, 546
traffic scheduling, 553
traffic handling
classification, 108
mechanisms for. *See* traffic-handling mechanisms
packet scheduler, 108
provider networks, 466-467
remote interfaces, 441-442
SBMs, 270-271
traffic isolation, 256-257
traffic scheduling, 553, 557
traffic-conditioning blocks. *See* TCBs
traffic-handling mechanisms, 10, 13
aggregate mechanisms, 20
aggregate traffic handling, 43-45
ATM, 19
combining with provisioning and configuration mechanisms, 41
congestion, 11
continuous nature of, 42
DiffServ, 16
PHBs, 16-17
services provided using, 16
SLAs, 16
802 user_priority, 15
FIFO traffic handling, 43
impact on quality/efficiency product and overhead, 40
interfaces, 11
IntServ
Controlled Load Service, 19
Guaranteed Service, 19
overview, 18

ISSLOW, 19
memory, 11
overview, 13-14
per-conversation
mechanisms, 20
services compared, 15
traffic.dll, 551
transmission media, 62
transmission, withholding, 537-538
trigger messages, 177
troubleshooting
ACS accounting logs, 643
loader, 645
methodology, 648-649
end-to-end signaling integrity, verification of, 649-652, 655-657
network topology, 649
packet marking, verifying, 660-661
traffic control functionality on sending host, verifying, 657, 659
netmon, 639-641
network device management consoles, 642
noise-generation tools, 644-645
packet marking, verifying, 660
DSCP marking, 661
802 user_priority marking, 660
perfmon, 643
qtcp, 643
readpol, 644
rsping, 641-642
RSVP messages, tracking, 650
DSBM, tracing through, 655-656
non-DSBM hops, tracing through, 656-657

PATH message, 652
through network, 652, 655
RSVP tracing, 638-639
SmartBits, 645
TcMon, 643
tools, 637
ACS accounting logs, 643
loader, 645
netmon, 639-641
network device management consoles, 642
noise-generation tools, 644-645
perfmon, 643
qtcp, 643
readpol, 644
rsping, 641-642
RSVP tracing, 638-639
SmartBits, 645
TcMon, 643
tracert, 638
ttcp, 644-645
wdsbm, 638
tracert, 638
traffic control functionality on sending host, verifying, 657, 659
ttcp, 644-645
wdsbm, 638
trust boundaries, 245-247
trust domains, 245-247
trust model, 434
ttcp, 644-645

U

UBR (unspecified bit rate), 300
UBR VCs, 429
unauthenticated users, 607
university backbone network, 463-464

university campus network, 412
building networks, 462
dormitory networks, 462-463
labs, classrooms, and administrative building networks, 463
overview, 461
university backbone network, 463-464
WANs, 464
prioritized qualitative service, 465
prioritized traffic to university campus, 465
user identification, 524
user interface directory, 360-362
User Policy dialog box, 621
general policy applicability, 621-622
quantitative limits, 622
user_priority
DSCPs compared, 253-254
mapping, 260
for qualitative services, 261-262
ordering of user_priority values, 262
overview, 252
provisioning 802 network, 259
services based on, providing, 254-255
mapping, 260-262
provisioning 802 network, 259
signaling used to obtain higher QE product, 258-259
simple use of 802 user_priority, 255-258

signaling used to obtain higher QE product, 258-259

simple use of 802 user_priority, 255-257

TCLASS object used to negotiate user_priority values, 284-285

value, determining appropriate, 257-258

values, ordering of, 262

user-based policies, 344

user-level components, 484

GQoS API, 485-486

QoS service provider, 486-487

QoS-enabled applications, 484-485

traffic control API, 488-491

V

VCI, 295-296

VCs, 295-296

ATMARP, 583-586

RSVP, management supporting, 305-312

changing QoS require-ments, 312

QoS translation, 313

receiver transitions, 312

signaling messages, carry-ing RSVP, 312-313

VFRADs, 321

VPNs, 411-412

W-Z

WANs

admission control, 444

aggregate traffic classes on private leased lines, 447-450

faster leased lines, 446-447

mapping traffic, 456-457

policing, 456-457

policy objects, 454

signaled requests, 455-456

SLA, 451-454

T-1 private leased lines, 444-445

aggregate traffic handling, 43-45

higher-quality services, support for, 46-48

interface, 440

links, scheduling behavior on, 579-580

policies, 444

aggregate traffic classes on private leased lines, 447-450

faster leased lines, 446-447

mapping traffic, 456-457

policing, 456-457

policy objects, 454

signaled requests, 455-456

SLA, 451-454

T-1 private leased lines, 444-445

signaling, 48, 50

aggregation of messages, 54

costs of, 51

density, 51, 53

importance of topology, 52-53

traffic handling on remote interfaces, 441

aggregate traffic handling on leased lines, 441-442

per-conversation traffic handling on slow leased line, 441

policing, 442, 444

university campus network, 464

prioritized qualitative service, 465

prioritized traffic to university campus, 465

wdsbm, 638

weighted random early detection, 94-95

weighted-queuing schemes, 576

wildcard filter (WF) reservations, 158

Windows 2000, QoS functionality and, 542

Windows 2000 Virtual Private Networking (Fortenberry), 412

Windows 98, QoS functionality and, 541

Winsock, 486

Winsock 2

calls, 499

control plane, 499

data plane, 499

notification events, 500

overview, 497

parameters, 500

service providers, 498

sockets, 498-499

WSAAccept, 499

WSAConnect, 499

WSAGetQosByName, 500

WSAIoctl, 500

WSAJoinLeaf, 499

WSASocket, 499

work-conserving queuing, 67-68

fair queuing, 75, 77, 79

bitwise round robin, 77

deficit round robin, 80, 82

DRR+, 82

Nagle's fair queuing, 75-77

stochastic fair queuing, 79

weighted fair-queuing schemes, 83

strict priority queuing, 68, 72-74

wrapper, 563-564

WSAAccept, 499, 504-505

WSAAsyncSelect, 507
WSAConnect, 499, 505-506
WSAEnumProtocols,
 502-503
WSAEventSelect, 507
WSAGetQosByName, 500,
 507-508
WSAIoctl, 500, 504, 507
WSAJoinLeaf, 499, 506
WSASocket, 499, 503

ZAW mechanism, 583
Zhang, Lixia, 132

Advanced Information on Networking Technologies

New Riders Books Offer Advice and Experience

LANDMARK
Rethinking Computer Books

We know how important it is to have access to detailed, solution-oriented information on core technologies. *Landmark* books contain the essential information you need to solve technical problems. Written by experts and subjected to rigorous peer and technical reviews, our *Landmark* books are hard-core resources for practitioners like you.

ESSENTIAL REFERENCE
Smart, Like You

The *Essential Reference* series from New Riders provides answers when you know what you want to do but need to know how to do it. Each title skips extraneous material and assumes a strong base of knowledge. These are indispensable books for the practitioner who wants to find specific features of a technology quickly and efficiently. Avoiding fluff and basic material, these books present solutions in an innovative, clean format—and at a great value.

MCSE CERTIFICATION
Engineered for Test Success

New Riders offers a complete line of test preparation materials to help you achieve your certification. With books like the *MCSE Training Guide*, and software like the acclaimed *MCSE Complete* and the revolutionary *ExamGear*, New Riders offers comprehensive products built by experienced professionals who have passed the exams and instructed hundreds of candidates.

New Riders Books for Networking Professionals

Cisco Router Configuration &Troubleshooting
By Mark Tripod
2nd Edition
330 pages, $39.99
ISBN: 0-7357-0999-8

A reference for the network and system administrator who finds himself having to configure and maintain existing Cisco routers, as well as get new hardware up and running. By providing advice and preferred practices, instead of just rehashing Cisco documentation, this book gives networking professionals information they can start using today.

Understanding Directory Services
By Beth Sheresh and Doug Sheresh
1st Edition
390 pages, $39.99
ISBN: 0-7357-0910-6

Understanding Directory Services provides the reader with a thorough knowledge of the fundamentals of directory services: what directory services are, how they are designed, and what functionality they can provide to an IT infrastructure. This book places the technology in context of the exploding market of directory services and helping people understand what directories can and cannot do for their networks.

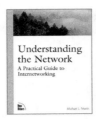

Understanding the Network: A Practical Guide to Internetworking
By Michael Martin
1st Edition
690 pages, $39.99
ISBN: 0-7357-0977-7

Understanding the Network addresses the audience in practical terminology, and describes the most essential information and tools required to build high-availability networks in a step-by-step implementation format. Each chapter could be read as a standalone, but the book builds progressively toward a summary of the essential concepts needed to put together a wide area network.

Understanding Data Communications
By Gilbert Held
6th Edition
620 pages, $39.99
ISBN: 0-7357-0036-2

Gil Held's book is ideal for those who want to get up to speed on technological advances as well as those who want a primer on networking concepts. This book is intended to explain how data communications actually work. It contains updated coverage on hot topics like thin client technology, x2 and 56Kbps modems, voice digitization, and wireless data transmission.

LDAP: Programming Directory Enabled Applications

By Tim Howes and Mark Smith
1st Edition
480 pages, $44.99
ISBN: 1-57870-000-0

This overview of the LDAP standard discusses its creation and history with the Internet Engineering Task Force, as well as the original RFC standard. *LDAP* also covers compliance trends, implementation, data packet handling in C++, client/server responsibilities, and more.

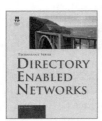

Directory Enabled Networks

By John Strassner
1st Edition
752 pages, $50.00
ISBN: 1-57870-140-6

Directory Enabled Networks is a comprehensive resource on the design and use of DEN. This book provides practical examples side-by-side with a detailed introduction to the theory of building a new class of network-enabled applications that will solve networking problems. DEN is a critical tool for network architects, administrators, and application developers.

Gigabit Ethernet Networking

By David Cunningham and William Lane
1st Edition
560 pages, $50.00
ISBN: 1-57870-062-0

Gigabit Ethernet is the next step for speed on the majority of installed networks. Explore how this technology will allow for high-bandwidth applications, such as the integration of telephone and data services, real-time applications, thin client applications, such as Windows NT Terminal Server, and corporate teleconferencing.

Supporting Service Level Agreements on IP Networks

By Dinesh Verma
1st Edition
270 pages, $50.00
ISBN: 1-57870-146-5

An essential resource for network engineers and architects, *Supporting Service Level Agreements on IP Networks* will help you build a core network capable of supporting a range of services. Learn how to create SLA solutions using off-the-shelf components in both best-effort and DiffServ/IntServ networks. Learn how to verify the performance of your SLA, as either a customer or network services provider, and how to use SLAs to support IPv6 networks.

Local Area High Speed Networks
By Dr. Sidnie Feit
1st Edition
655 pages, $50.00
ISBN: 1-57870-113-9

Local Area High Speed Networks gives you the technical background to plan, implement, support, and troubleshoot state-of-the-art LANs. This resource provides clear, detailed descriptions of LAN protocols and broad coverage of the features and capabilities implemented in real products.

Wide Area High Speed Networks
By Dr. Sidnie Feit
1st Edition
624 pages, $50.00
ISBN: 1-57870-114-7

Networking is in a transitional phase between long-standing conventional wide area services and new technologies and services. This book presents current and emerging wide area technologies and services, makes them understandable, and puts them into perspective so that their merits and disadvantages are clear.

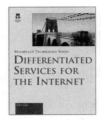

Differentiated Services for the Internet
By Kalevi Kilkki
1st Edition
400 pages, $50.00
ISBN: 1-57870-132-5

This book offers network architects, engineers, and managers of packet networks critical insight into the continuing development of Differentiated Services. It addresses the particular needs of a network environment as well as issues that must be considered in its implementation. Coverage allows networkers to implement DiffServ on a variety of networking technologies, including ATM, and to solve common problems related to TCP, UDP, and other networking protocols.

Quality of Service in IP Networks
By Grenville Armitage
1st Edition
310 pages, $50.00
ISBN: 1-57870-189-9

Quality of Service in IP Networks presents a clear understanding of the architectural issues surrounding delivering QoS in an IP network, and positions the emerging technologies within a framework of solutions. The motivation for QoS is explained with reference to emerging real-time applications, such as Voice/Video over IP, VPN services, and supporting Service Level Agreements.

Designing Addressing Architectures for Routing and Switching

By Howard Berkowitz
1st Edition
500 pages, $45.00
ISBN: 1-57870-059-0

One of the greatest challenges for a network design professional is making the users, servers, files, printers, and other resources visible on their network. This title equips the network engineer or architect with a systematic methodology for planning the wide area and local area network "streets" on which users and servers live.

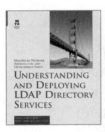

Understanding and Deploying LDAP Directory Services

By Tim Howes, Mark Smith, and Gordon Good
1st Edition
850 pages, $50.00
ISBN: 1-57870-070-1

This comprehensive tutorial provides the reader with a thorough treatment of LDAP directory services. Minimal knowledge of general networking and administration is assumed, making the material accessible to intermediate and advanced readers alike. The text is full of practical implementation advice and real-world deployment examples to help the reader choose the path that makes the most sense for his specific organization.

Switched, Fast, and Gigabit Ethernet

By Sean Riley and Robert Breyer
3rd Edition
615 pages, $50.00
ISBN: 1-57870-073-6

Switched, Fast, and Gigabit Ethernet, Third Edition is the one and only solution needed to understand and fully implement this entire range of Ethernet innovations. Acting both as an overview of current technologies and hardware requirements as well as a hands-on, comprehensive tutorial for deploying and managing switched, fast, and gigabit ethernet networks, this guide covers the most prominent present and future challenges network administrators face.

Wireless LANs: Implementing Interoperable Networks

By Jim Geier
1st Edition
432 pages, $40.00
ISBN: 1-57870-081-7

Wireless LANs covers how and why to migrate from propriety solutions to the 802.11 standard, and explains how to realize significant cost savings through wireless LAN implementation for data collection systems.

The DHCP Handbook

By Ralph Droms
and Ted Lemon
1st Edition
535 pages, $55.00
ISBN: 1-57870-137-6

The DHCP Handbook is an authoritative overview and expert guide to the setup and management of a DHCP server. This title discusses how DHCP was developed and its interaction with other protocols. Learn how DHCP operates, its use in different environments, and the interaction between DHCP servers and clients. Network hardware, inter-server communication, security, SNMP, and IP mobility are also discussed.

Network Performance Baselining

By Daniel Nassar
1st Edition
736 pages, $50.00
ISBN: 1-57870-240-2

Network Performance Baselining focuses on the real-world implementation of network baselining principles and shows not only how to measure and rate a network's performance, but also how to improve the network's performance. This book includes chapters that give a real "how-to" approach for standard baseline methodologies along with actual steps and processes to perform network baseline measurements. In addition, the proper way to document and build a baseline report will be provided.

Designing Routing and Switching Architectures for Enterprise Networks

By Howard Berkowitz
1st Edition
992 pages, $55.00
ISBN: 1-57870-060-4

This title provides a fundamental understanding of how switches and routers operate, enabling the reader to use them effectively to build networks. The book walks the network designer through all aspects of requirements, analysis, and deployment strategies, strengthens readers' professional abilities, and helps them develop skills necessary to advance in their profession.

Intrusion Detection

By Rebecca Gurley Bace
1st Edition
340 pages, $50.00
ISBN: 1-57870-185-6

Intrusion detection is a critical new area of technology within network security. This comprehensive guide to the field of intrusion detection covers the foundations of intrusion detection and system audit. *Intrusion Detection* provides a wealth of information, ranging from design considerations to how to evaluate and choose the optimal commercial intrusion detection products for a particular networking environment.

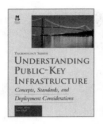

Understanding Public-Key Infrastructure

By Carlisle Adams and Steve Lloyd
1st Edition
300 pages, $50.00
ISBN: 1-57870-166-X

This book is a tutorial on, and a guide to the deployment of, public-key infrastructures. It covers such issues as certification, operational considerations and standardization efforts, and deployment issues and considerations. Emphasis is placed on explaining the interrelated fields within the topic area, to assist those who will be responsible for making deployment decisions and architecting a PKI within their organization.

The Economics of Electronic Commerce

By Soon-Yong Choi, Andrew Whinston, and Dale Stahl
1st Edition
656 pages, $49.99
ISBN: 1-57870-014-0

This is the first electronic commerce title to focus on traditional topics of economics applied to the electronic commerce arena. While all other electronic commerce titles take a "how-to" approach, this focuses on what it means from an economic perspective.

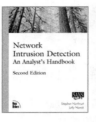

Network Intrusion Detection: An Analyst's Handbook

By Stephen Northcutt and Judy Novak
2nd Edition
480 pages, $45.00
ISBN: 0-7357-1008-2

Get answers and solutions from someone who has been in the trenches. Author Stephen Northcutt, original developer of the Shadow intrusion detection system and former director of the United States Navy's Information System Security Office, gives his expertise to intrusion detection specialists, security analysts, and consultants responsible for setting up and maintaining an effective defense against network security attacks.

Other Books By New Riders

MICROSOFT TECHNOLOGIES

ADMINISTRATION

Inside Windows 2000 Server
1-56205-929-7 • $49.99 US / $74.95 CAN
Windows 2000 Essential Reference
0-7357-0869-X • $35.00 US / $52.95 CAN
Windows 2000 Active Directory
0-7357-0870-3 • $29.99 US / $44.95 CAN
Windows 2000 Routing and Remote Access Service
0-7357-0951-3 • $34.99 US / $52.95 CAN
Windows 2000 Deployment & Desktop Management
0-7357-0975-0 • $34.99 US / $52.95 CAN
Windows 2000 DNS
0-7357-0973-4 • $39.99 US / $59.95 CAN
Windows 2000 User Management
1-56205-886-X • $34.99 US / $52.95 CAN
Windows 2000 Professional
0-7357-0950-5 • $34.99 US / $52.95 CAN
Planning for Windows 2000
0-7357-0048-6 • $29.99 US / $44.95 CAN
Windows 2000 Server Professional Reference
0-7357-0952-1 • $75.00 US / $111.95 CAN
Windows 2000 Security
0-7357-0991-2 • $39.99 US / $59.95 CAN
Windows 2000 TCP/IP
0-7357-0992-0 • $39.99 US / $59.95 CAN
Windows NT/2000 Network Security
1-57870-253-4 • $45.00 US / $67.95 CAN
Windows NT/2000 Thin Client Solutions
1-57870-239-9 • $45.00 US / $67.95 CAN
Windows 2000 Virtual Private Networking
1-57870-246-1 • $45.00 US / $67.95 CAN •
Available January 2001
Windows 2000 Active Directory Design & Deployment
1-57870-242-9 • $45.00 US / $67.95 CAN
Windows 2000 and Mainframe Integration
1-57870-200-3 • $40.00 US / $59.95 CAN
Windows 2000 Server: Planning and Migration
1-57870-023-X • $40.00 US / $59.95 CAN
Windows 2000 Quality of Service
1-57870-115-5 • $45.00 US / $67.95 CAN
Windows NT Power Toolkit
0-7357-0922-X • $49.99 US / $74.95 CAN
Windows NT Terminal Server and Citrix MetaFrame
1-56205-944-0 • $29.99 US / $44.95 CAN
Windows NT Performance: Monitoring, Benchmarking, and Tuning
1-56205-942-4 • $29.99 US / $44.95 CAN
Windows NT Registry: A Settings Reference
1-56205-941-6 • $29.99 US / $44.95 CAN
Windows NT Domain Architecture
1-57870-112-0 • $38.00 US / $56.95 CAN

SYSTEMS PROGRAMMING

Windows NDIS Miniport Development
1-57870-248-8 • $50.00 US / $74.95 CAN •
Available March 2001
Windows NT/2000 Native API Reference
1-57870-199-6 • $50.00 US / $74.95 CAN
Windows NT Device Driver Development
1-57870-058-2 • $50.00 US / $74.95 CAN
DCE/RPC over SMB: Samba and Windows NT Domain Internals
1-57870-150-3 • $45.00 US / $67.95 CAN

WEB PROGRAMMING

Real World Web Code: Techniques for Structured ASP Programming
0-7357-1033-3 • $39.99 US / $59.95 CAN •
Available March 2001
Exchange & Outlook: Constructing Collaborative Solutions
1-57870-252-6 • $40.00 US / $59.95 CAN

APPLICATION PROGRAMMING

Delphi COM Programming
1-57870-221-6 • $45.00 US / $67.95 CAN
Windows NT Applications: Measuring and Optimizing Performance
1-57870-176-7 • $40.00 US / $59.95 CAN
Applying COM+
0-7357-0978-5 • $49.99 US / $74.95 CAN

SCRIPTING

Windows Script Host
1-57870-139-2 • $35.00 US / $52.95 CAN
Windows NT Shell Scripting
1-57870-047-7 • $32.00 US / $45.95 CAN
Windows NT Win32 Perl Programming: The Standard Extensions
1-57870-067-1 • $40.00 US / $59.95 CAN
Windows NT/2000 ADSI Scripting for System Administration
1-57870-219-4 • $45.00 US / $67.95 CAN
Windows NT Automated Deployment and Customization
1-57870-045-0 • $32.00 US / $45.95 CAN
Win32 Perl Scripting: The Administrator's Handbook
1-57870-215-1 • $35.00 US / $52.95 CAN

BACK OFFICE

SMS 2 Administration
0-7357-0082-6 • $39.99 US / $59.95 CAN
Internet Information Services Administration
0-7357-0022-2 • $29.99 US / $44.95 CAN
SQL Server System Administration
1-56205-955-6 • $29.99 US / $44.95 CAN
SQL Server 7 Essential Reference
0-7357-0864-9 • $35.00 US / $52.95 CAN
Inside Exchange 2000 Server
0-7357-1027-9 • $49.99 US / $74.95 CAN •
Available February 2001

WEB DESIGN & DEVELOPMENT

OPEN SOURCE

MySQL
0-7357-0921-1 • $49.99 US / $74.95 CAN
Web Application Development with PHP 4.0
0-7357-0997-1 • $39.99 US / $59.95 CAN
PHP Functions Essential Reference
0-7357-0970-X • $35.00 US / $52.95 CAN •
Available February 2001
Python Essential Reference
0-7357-0901-7 • $34.95 US / $52.95 CAN
Qt: The Official Documentation
1-57870-209-7 • $50.00 US / $74.95 CAN
Berkeley DB
0-7357-1064-3 • $39.99 US / $59.95 CAN•
Available February 2001
GNU Autoconf, Automake, and Libtool
1-57870-190-2 • $40.00 US / $59.95 CAN

CREATIVE MEDIA

Designing Web Usability
1-56205-810-X • $45.00 US / $67.95 CAN
Designing Web Graphics.3
1-56205-949-1 • $55.00 US / $81.95 CAN
Flash Web Design
0-7357-0896-7 • $45.00 US / $67.95 CAN
<creative.html design>
1-56205-704-9 • $39.99 US / $59.95 CAN
Creating Killer Web Sites, Second Edition
1-56830-433-1 • $49.99 US / $74.95 CAN
Secrets of Successful Web Sites
1-56830-382-3 • $49.99 US / $74.95 CAN

XML

Inside XML
0-7357-1020-1 • $49.99 US / $74.95 CAN
XHTML
0-7357-1034-1 • $39.99 US / $59.95 CAN• Available January 2001

LINUX/UNIX

ADMINISTRATION

Networking Linux: A Practical Guide to TCP/IP
0-7357-1031-7 • $39.99 US / $59.95 CAN •
Available February 2001
Inside Linux
0-7357-0940-8 • $39.99 US / $59.95 CAN
Vi iMproved (VIM)
0-7357-1001-5 • $49.99 US / $74.95 CAN •
Available January 2001
Linux System Administration
1-56205-934-3 • $29.99 US / $44.95 CAN
Linux Firewalls
0-7357-0900-9 • $39.99 US / $59.95 CAN
Linux Essential Reference
0-7357-0852-5 • $24.95 US / $37.95 CAN
UnixWare 7 System Administration
1-57870-080-9 • $40.00 US / $59.99 CAN

DEVELOPMENT

Developing Linux Applications with GTK+ and GDK
0-7357-0021-4 • $34.99 US / $52.95 CAN
GTK+/Gnome Application Development
0-7357-0078-8 • $39.99 US / $59.95 CAN
KDE Application Development
1-57870-201-1 • $39.99 US / $59.95 CAN

GIMP

Grokking the GIMP
0-7357-0924-6 • $39.99 US / $59.95 CAN
GIMP Essential Reference
0-7357-0911-4 • $24.95 US / $37.95 CAN

SOLARIS

Solaris Advanced System Administrator's Guide, Second Edition
1-57870-039-6 • $39.99 US / $59.95 CAN
Solaris System Administrator's Guide, Second Edition
1-57870-040-X • $34.99 US / $52.95 CAN
Solaris Essential Reference
0-7357-0023-0 • $24.95 US / $37.95 CAN
Solaris System Management
0-7357-1018-X • $39.99 US / $59.95 CAN •
Available March 2001
Solaris 8 Essential Reference
0-7357-1007-4 • $34.99 US / $52.95 CAN •
Available January 2001

Other Books By New Riders

NETWORKING

STANDARDS & PROTOCOLS

Cisco Router Configuration &
Troubleshooting, Second Edition
0-7357-0999-8 • $34.99 US / $52.95 CAN
Understanding Directory Services
0-7357-0910-6 • $39.99 US / $59.95 CAN
Understanding the Network: A Practical
Guide to Internetworking
0-7357-0977-7 • $39.99 US / $59.95 CAN
Understanding Data Communications,
Sixth Edition
0-7357-0036-2 • $39.99 US / $59.95 CAN
LDAP: Programming Directory Enabled
Applications
1-57870-000-0 • $44.99 US / $67.95 CAN
Gigabit Ethernet Networking
1-57870-062-0 • $50.00 US / $74.95 CAN
Supporting Service Level Agreements on IP
Networks
1-57870-146-5 • $50.00 US / $74.95 CAN
Directory Enabled Networks
1-57870-140-6 • $50.00 US / $74.95 CAN
Differentiated Services for the Internet
1-57870-132-5 • $50.00 US / $74.95 CAN
Policy-Based Networking: Architecture and
Algorithms
1-57870-226-7 • $50.00 US / $74.95 CAN
Policy-Based Management
1-57870-225-9 • $55.00 US / $81.95 CAN •
Available March 2001
Quality of Service in IP Networks
1-57870-189-9 • $50.00 US / $74.95 CAN
Designing Addressing Architectures for
Routing and Switching
1-57870-059-0 • $45.00 US / $69.95 CAN
Understanding and Deploying LDAP
Directory Services
1-57870-070-1 • $50.00 US / $74.95 CAN
Switched, Fast and Gigabit Ethernet, Third
Edition
1-57870-073-6 • $50.00 US / $74.95 CAN
Wireless LANs: Implementing Interoperable
Networks
1-57870-081-7 • $40.00 US / $59.95 CAN
Wide Area High Speed Networks
1-57870-114-7 • $50.00 US / $74.95 CAN
The DHCP Handbook
1-57870-137-6 • $55.00 US / $81.95 CAN
Designing Routing and Switching
Architectures for Enterprise Networks
1-57870-060-4 • $55.00 US / $81.95 CAN
Local Area High Speed Networks
1-57870-113-9 • $50.00 US / $74.95 CAN
Network Performance Baselining
1-57870-240-2 • $50.00 US / $74.95 CAN
Economics of Electronic Commerce
1-57870-014-0 • $49.99 US / $74.95 CAN

SECURITY

Intrusion Detection
1-57870-185-6 • $50.00 US / $74.95 CAN
Understanding Public-Key Infrastructure
1-57870-166-X • $50.00 US / $74.95 CAN
Network Intrusion Detection: An Analyst's
Handbook, 2E
0-7357-1008-2 • $45.00 US / $67.95 CAN
Linux Firewalls
0-7357-0900-9 • $39.99 US / $59.95 CAN

Intrusion Signatures and Analysis
0-7357-1063-5 • $39.99 US / $59.95 CAN •
Available February 2001
Hackers Beware
0-7357-1009-0 • $45.00 US / $67.95 CAN •
Available March 2001

LOTUS NOTES/DOMINO

Domino System Administration
1-56205-948-3 • $49.99 US / $74.95 CAN
Lotus Notes & Domino Essential Reference
0-7357-0007-9 • $45.00 US / $67.95 CAN

PROFESSIONAL
CERTIFICATION

TRAINING GUIDES

MCSE Training Guide: Networking
Essentials, 2nd Ed.
1-56205-919-X • $49.99 US / $74.95 CAN
MCSE Training Guide: Windows NT Server
4, 2nd Ed.
1-56205-916-5 • $49.99 US / $74.95 CAN
MCSE Training Guide: Windows NT
Workstation 4, 2nd Ed.
1-56205-918-1 • $49.99 US / $74.95 CAN
MCSE Training Guide: Windows NT Server
4 Enterprise, 2nd Ed.
1-56205-917-3 • $49.99 US / $74.95 CAN
MCSE Training Guide: Core Exams Bundle,
2nd Ed.
1-56205-926-2 • $149.99 US / $223.95 CAN
MCSE Training Guide: TCP/IP, 2nd Ed.
1-56205-920-3 • $49.99 US / $74.95 CAN
MCSE Training Guide: IIS 4, 2nd Ed.
0-7357-0865-7 • $49.99 US / $74.95 CAN
MCSE Training Guide: SQL Server 7
Administration
0-7357-0003-6 • $49.99 US / $74.95 CAN
MCSE Training Guide: SQL Server 7
Database Design
0-7357-0004-4 • $49.99 US / $74.95 CAN
MCSD Training Guide: Visual Basic 6 Exams
0-7357-0002-8 • $69.99 US / $104.95 CAN
MCSD Training Guide: Solution
Architectures
0-7357-0026-5 • $49.99 US / $74.95 CAN
MCSD Training Guide: 4-in-1 Bundle
0-7357-0912-2 • $149.99 US / $223.95 CAN
A+ Certification Training Guide, Second
Edition
0-7357-0907-6 • $49.99 US / $74.95 CAN
Network+ Certification Guide
0-7357-0077-X • $49.99 US / $74.95 CAN
Solaris 2.6 Administrator Certification
Training Guide, Part I
1-57870-085-X • $40.00 US / $59.95 CAN
Solaris 2.6 Administrator Certification
Training Guide, Part II
1-57870-086-8 • $40.00 US / $59.95 CAN
Solaris 7 Administrator Certification
Training Guide, Part I and II
1-57870-249-6 • $49.99 US / $74.95 CAN
MCSE Training Guide: Windows 2000
Professional
0-7357-0965-3 • $49.99 US / $74.95 CAN
MCSE Training Guide: Windows 2000 Server
0-7357-0968-8 • $49.99 US / $74.95 CAN

MCSE Training Guide: Windows 2000
Network Infrastructure
0-7357-0966-1 • $49.99 US / $74.95 CAN
MCSE Training Guide: Windows 2000
Network Security Design
0-73570-984X • $49.99 US / $74.95 CAN
MCSE Training Guide: Windows 2000
Network Infrastructure Design
0-73570-982-3 • $49.99 US / $74.95 CAN
MCSE Training Guide: Windows 2000
Directory Svcs. Infrastructure
0-7357-0976-9 • $49.99 US / $74.95 CAN
MCSE Training Guide: Windows 2000
Directory Services Design
0-7357-0983-1 • $49.99 US / $74.95 CAN
MCSE Training Guide: Windows 2000
Accelerated Exam
0-7357-0979-3 • $69.99 US / $104.95 CAN
MCSE Training Guide: Windows 2000 Core
Exams Bundle
0-7357-0988-2 • $149.99 US / $223.95 CAN

FAST TRACKS

CLP Fast Track: Lotus Notes/Domino 5
Application Development
0-73570-877-0 • $39.99 US / $59.95 CAN
CLP Fast Track: Lotus Notes/Domino 5
System Administration
0-7357-0878-9 • $39.99 US / $59.95 CAN
Network+ Fast Track
0-7357-0904-1 • $29.99 US / $44.95 CAN
A+ Fast Track
0-7357-0028-1 • $34.99 US / $52.95 CAN
MCSD Fast Track: Visual Basic 6,
Exam #70-175
0-7357-0019-2 • $19.99 US / $29.95 CAN
MCSD FastTrack: Visual Basic 6,
Exam #70-175
0-7357-0018-4 • $19.99 US / $29.95 CAN

SOFTWARE
ARCHITECTURE &
ENGINEERING

Designing for the User with OVID
1-57870-101-5 • $40.00 US / $59.95 CAN
Designing Flexible Object-Oriented Systems
with UML
1-57870-098-1 • $40.00 US / $59.95 CAN
Constructing Superior Software
1-57870-147-3 • $40.00 US / $59.95 CAN
A UML Pattern Language
1-57870-118-X • $45.00 US / $67.95 CAN

We Want to Know What You Think

To better serve you, we would like your opinion on the content and quality of this book. Please complete this card and mail it to us or fax it to 317-581-4663.

Name _____

Address _____

City_____State_____Zip _____

Phone _____

Email Address _____

Occupation _____

Operating System(s) that you use _____

What influenced your purchase of this book?
- ❏ Recommendation
- ❏ Cover Design
- ❏ Table of Contents
- ❏ Index
- ❏ Magazine Review
- ❏ Advertisement
- ❏ New Rider's Reputation
- ❏ Author Name

How would you rate the contents of this book?
- ❏ Excellent
- ❏ Very Good
- ❏ Good
- ❏ Fair
- ❏ Below Average
- ❏ Poor

How do you plan to use this book?
- ❏ Quick reference
- ❏ Self-training
- ❏ Classroom
- ❏ Other

What do you like most about this book?
Check all that apply.
- ❏ Content
- ❏ Writing Style
- ❏ Accuracy
- ❏ Examples
- ❏ Listings
- ❏ Design
- ❏ Index
- ❏ Page Count
- ❏ Price
- ❏ Illustrations

What do you like least about this book?
Check all that apply.
- ❏ Content
- ❏ Writing Style
- ❏ Accuracy
- ❏ Examples
- ❏ Listings
- ❏ Design
- ❏ Index
- ❏ Page Count
- ❏ Price
- ❏ Illustrations

What would be a useful follow-up book to this one for you?_____

Where did you purchase this book? _____
_____

Can you name a similar book that you like better than this one, or one that is as good? Why?

_____
_____

How many New Riders books do you own? _____

What are your favorite computer books?_____
_____

What other titles would you like to see us develop? _____
_____

Any comments for us? _____
_____
_____
_____

Networking Quality of Service and
Windows Operating Systems, 1-57870-206-2

www.newriders.com   •   Fax   317-581-4663

Fold here and tape to mail

New Riders Publishing
201 W. 103rd St.
Indianapolis, IN 46290

How to Contact Us

Visit Our Web Site

www.newriders.com

On our Web site you'll find information about our other books, authors, tables of contents, indexes, and book errata.

Email Us

Contact us at this address:

nrfeedback@newriders.com

- If you have comments or questions about this book
- To report errors that you have found in this book
- If you have a book proposal to submit or are interested in writing for New Riders
- If you would like to have an author kit sent to you
- If you are an expert in a computer topic or technology and are interested in being a technical editor who reviews manuscripts for technical accuracy
- To find a distributor in your area, please contact our international department at this address.

nrmedia@newriders.com

- For instructors from educational institutions who want to preview New Riders books for classroom use. Email should include your name, title, school, department, address, phone number, office days/hours, text in use, and enrollment, along with your request for desk/examination copies and/or additional information.
- For members of the media who are interested in reviewing copies of New Riders books. Send your name, mailing address, and email address, along with the name of the publication or Web site you work for.

Bulk Purchases/Corporate Sales

If you are interested in buying 10 or more copies of a title or want to set up an account for your company to purchase directly from the publisher at a substantial discount, contact us at 800-382-3419 or email your contact information to corpsales@pearsontechgroup.com. A sales representative will contact you with more information.

Write to Us

New Riders Publishing

201 W. 103rd St.

Indianapolis, IN 46290-1097

Call Us

Toll-free (800) 571-5840 + 9 + 7477

If outside U.S. (317) 581-3500. Ask for New Riders.

Fax Us

(317) 581-4663